RADIO PRO:
The Making of an On-Air Personality and What It Takes

by Joe Martelle

BearManor Media
2012

Radio Pro: The Making of an On-Air Personality and What It Takes

© 2012 Joe Martelle

All rights reserved.

For information, address:

BearManor Media
P. O. Box 71426
Albany, GA 31708

bearmanormedia.com

Published in the USA by BearManor Media

ISBN—1-59393-256-1

Here's what America's Professional Broadcasters are saying about Joe Martelle & his insightful, one of a kind book, Radio Pro, on how to be a successful air-personality!

"Before I became a colleague of Joe's, I was an unabashed fan. I can't think of a better mentor than one of the best on-air performers in the business."

– Jordan Rich, WBZ Boston air personality

"Joe Martelle is the Radio Pro's radio pro! Joe and his many contributors to his book have much to share within these pages about the radio industry. If, you're considering a career in the exciting world of radio, *Radio Pro* is must read!"

– Les Howard Jacoby, Florida air personality and programmer

"If one were to look up Radio Pro in the dictionary, a picture of Joe Martelle would be smiling at you! I've known Joe for over 30 years, as a co-worker and I'm proud to say as a friend. And, in my 40 years in broadcasting, you will not find a more comprehensive account of what radio is all about than in Joe's book. Carefully written and researched by one who has lived it, Joe Martelle. If, you have always been fascinated by the "world of radio broadcasting" this book is the true consummate journal to entertain, inform, and enlighten you about what you hear and the people who bring it to you."

– Steve Feldman, Broadcast/cable Sales Executive, Comcast Spotlight, Miami FL.

"Radio Pro is a must read for all would be and current air-personalities. Find out just what being a real radio pro is all about with Joe Martelle, a top-rated morning show personality, who has fought the ratings battles in markets from Boston to Houston! Joe learned how it's done in the trenches and knows what it takes to be a Radio Pro!"

– Joe Ford, legendary Houston TX air personality and voice-over talent.

"In the many years I worked with Joe in Florida, he has been an example of what a true broadcaster should be. Bright, intelligent, witty and he has a keen understanding of the audience he is targeting. Radio pros and listeners are lucky to have Joe in the industry. I highly recommend his book."

– Mark McCray, Operations Mgr/Program Director, Radio One, Dallas, TX

"Joe Martelle will guide you through the inside world of radio few have seen. Nobody can uncover this aspect of broadcasting like Joe. His book, *Radio Pro* is insightful and entertaining."

– Cary Pahigian, Marketing Manager, Saga Communications, Portland, ME.

"A career as an 'on-air' radio pro is a road that is constantly under construction… paved with potholes, deep depressions and many hills to climb."

Table of Contents

Dedications vii

Acknowledgements xv

About the Author xxix

The Beginning 1

Chapter 1. Learn From the Masters – Radio's Pioneer and First Air Personalities 7

Chapter 2. How To Develop Your Own Air-Style 39

Chapter 3. How to Break Into Radio 73

Chapter 4. How To Be Successful Air Personality 93

Chapter 5. The Seven Powerful "P's" to Perfection as an On-Air Radio Pro 117

Chapter 6. How To Communicate Effectively 145

Chapter 7. The Importance of Show Prep 165

Chapter 8. The Art of Interviewing 185

Chapter 9. Attitudes and Actions 211

Chapter 10. Program Directors, Friend of Foe? 233

Chapter 11. Inside the World of General Managers 279

Chapter 12. The Role of Consultants 299

Chapter 13. A Woman's Perspective on Working in Radio and On the Air 323

Chapter 14. How To Win in Morning Drive 349

Chapter 15. Radio Promotion: Marketing & Publicity 415

Chapter 16.	Radio Formats: News, Talk and Sports	453
Chapter 17.	Radio Formats – Music	537
Chapter 18.	Attorneys, Agents, Ratings and Contracts	565
Chapter 19.	Some Things To Know About a Career as an On-Air Pro	581
Chapter 20.	Who Inspired the Radio Pros Who Contributed to This Book	611
Chapter 21.	Radio's Future	637
	Afterword	661
	Index	667

Dedications

Bob MacNeil
Fred Foy
Cousin Brucie Morrow

BOB MACNEIL
"When I was training to become a broadcaster the simple rule was never say anything on the radio you wouldn't want your mother to hear. Of course that was in the late 60s and times have certainly changed since then. In 1984, I achieved a professional goal of becoming a news director in Boston radio. It was at 98.5-WROR. That's where I met Joe Martelle. Not only did I anchor the news on the popular "Joe and Andy" show, Joe and I became close friends. Our friendship has endured in part because we share the same philosophy and values about radio: Just be yourself. Our respective careers have taken us to a number of stations, and for Joe to several states and cities. "Radio Pro" is the book we should all read, especially those just starting out, because it sends a positive and important message about the medium. Joe's 40-year career is a testament not only to his endurance but also to his style and class. He's nearly done it all and he's been on top because he's never compromised his personal or professional character. I've learned a lot from my friend over the years. And to his credit, I've never heard him say anything he wouldn't want his mother to hear."

– Bob MacNeil

Many thanks to my friend Bob MacNeil, whose professional broadcast career began in 1968. He was the News Bureau Chief for *Metro Networks* in Boston and responsible for writing and editing news summaries for Metro's wire service. Bob also wrote and anchored the news on four New England radio stations every morning. He is also a Senior Lecturer at Curry College in the Boston suburb of Milton. A resident of Reading, Massachusetts, he spends much of his time at his cottage in York Beach, Maine.

FRED FOY

"You, the reader, are about to join a young dreamer on his quest for a career in radio. The path he traveled had many obstacles, but his determination and strong faith in his creator surmounted them all. He is my valued friend, who refers to me as his saddle pal, to which I respond with, "Thank you, Kemosabe." This exchange of greetings will be made clear later in his journey. Now, it's time to turn the page and begin his quest."

– Fred Foy

Fred Foy (Frederick William Foy) is one of America's most famous announcers/narrators. His distinctive voice is best remembered for doing the introduction on the popular *Lone Ranger* radio and television series. Fred joined the radio series in 1948 and most broadcast historians would agree that his stentorian delivery of the program opening, *"Return with us now to those thrilling days of yesteryear, the Lone Ranger rides again!"* is perhaps the most recognized opening in all of American radio. In 1960, Fred joined the announcing staff of the ABC Network in New York, and with his other duties spent five years as announcer on the *Dick Cavett* television show. After more than 20 years with the network, the Detroit, Michigan, native retired. Until his passing at Christmastime 2010, Fred Foy lived with Fran, his wife of 60 years, in Massachusetts. Fred and the author were friends for over 20 years. I am indebted to him for his kind words and will always remember him with great fondness.

COUSIN BRUCE MORROW

"First of all, we all know what **Radio** means - an efficient (if not the most efficient) means of human (and at times not so human) communication. Of all mass communication devices Radio has become the most intimate, direct, non-invasive and certainly the most economically reliable. Now what about that partial word **Pro**? The definition, according to the dictionary (remember them?) - a **Pro** is a shortened form for the word 'professional' - a professional is a person who is engaged in an activity for livelihood or gain and has become an expert in the practice. Okay, I will accept the above definition; however, when it comes to our profession they shortchanged us. Here is my addition: a person who has developed a skill to communicate with honesty, directly, energetically and is able to transmit true emotion.

"The audience today has become extremely sophisticated and can spot a phony quicker than they can turn off that radio. Today's Radio Pro must reach the audience directly - one-on-one. We never talk at our listeners, we must talk to them. The audience must receive the honest emotion of the Radio

Pro. Genuine, sincere warmth and always remember that energy. When you are having a good time at that mike, so is the listener. If you do not feel good before a broadcast and you cannot cover it - **Cousin, GO HOME**! Never cheat that listener. This talking to people has been developed over several decades. This was not a natural early radio learning curve. If you listen to some of our radio ancestors, you will hear what I mean. They sounded stiff, disinterested and certainly disconnected (pardon the pun). Today, nobody can do that and get away with it. My friend and cousin, Joe Martelle, and a few others have practiced this for years and have developed this sought-after communication skill. Read his words, study his pages and you just might become a Radio Pro."

– Bruce Morrow

In the early 1960s, under the direction and ever-present ear of radio genius Rick Sklar, *WABC -77* on the AM dial in New York City, was one of the strongest forces of Rock Radio in America. Bruce Morrow, known to his millions of loyal listeners as "Cousin Brucie," was a member of the station's incredible air-staff. Bruce became one of America's most popular and recognizable radio personalities. Listening to Cousin Brucie's warm, friendly on-air style was like joining in on one big party hosted by everyone's friend, Bruce Morrow.

Thanks to *WABC's* 50,000-watt signal, it was possible for folks to listen to his nighttime show up and down the Eastern seaboard and that's where I come in. While starting out on the radio in Maine, I enjoyed listening to Cousin Brucie, because WABC banged up the coast and came in loud and clear like a local Portland station. Later, in the mid-'80s, during my on-air years in Boston, it was my privilege to meet and share my mic with this legendary broadcaster. On occasion, Bruce would join me to co-host my all-request oldies show, *Saturday Night "Live" at the Oldies* on the original *Golden-Great-98.5-WROR*. We have remained friends to this day. Today, Cousin Brucie is still doing what he loves to do, playing those great oldies and talking with his friends every week on Sirius X-M Satellite Radio. He sounds as great as ever!

Radio Pro is dedicated to two legendary Boston broadcasters, **Roger Allan Bump** and **Jess Cain,** who both passed away in 2008. Bob MacNeil remembers Roger:

"Webster's Dictionary defines mentor as "A trusted counselor or guide." It defines friend as "One attached to another by affection or esteem." To me, Roger Allan Bump, or simply Roger Allan, as he was known to his many devoted radio listeners, was all of the above.

When I transferred to Curry College from Grahm Jr. College, Roger was the first person in the Communications Department I met. I needed him to okay some courses I'd taken at Grahm. If approved, I would be a full junior. Needless to say, I was a very nervous 20-year-old kid, not sure how to approach this Boston radio news icon. He'd been News Director at the Yankee Network based in Boston, and was heard on radio stations all over New England. At the time, he was News Director of WRKO, "The Boston Rocker," the city's #1 rock radio station.

As it turned out, "Roger," as he insisted that his students call him, quickly approved the courses, and then wanted to know all about me! Not only did he quickly become my mentor, but he was my friend for the next 40 years. When he died in June 2008, I lost not only a close personal friend, but a confidant who I still turned to for advice. Just a week before his passing, we spent a day together. He gave me a number of precious books about radio and broadcasting. They range from biographies of William Paley, former head at CBS, and Edward R. Murrow to William F. Buckley's take on the media, and a work about the communication industry. Roger told me about each one as though he'd just finished reading it.

Roger was always reading and keeping up with friends and former colleagues, as well as industry trends. He'd often call me with news I wasn't aware of. A former national executive board member of the Radio, Television News Directors Association (RTNDA), he traveled the country pushing for news standards. Roger believed that the only way someone could learn broadcasting, especially news, was to start in the "tall grass." He saw the demise of small-market radio, and private ownership, as a great loss to communities, and as a teaching tool for aspiring broadcasters. One of my first jobs was at WKOX in Framingham, MA. Roger lived in the next town and listened to my newscasts each day! I could always expect a weekly call, with a friendly critique that only a trusted mentor and friend could give. Roger's life was very full and he is missed by so many, including his incredible wife Carolyn, their five children and many grandchildren. It goes without saying that those of us who were touched by him are better people."

– Bob MacNeil

"Success in any medium depends on the strength of a personality to be a perfect fit for that medium. Many actors today are the voices in TV and radio commercials, because it's the trained actor's voice that stands out. Jess Cain was an actor on Broadway and TV in the 1950s and applied those talents in his daily Boston radio program on WHDH for decades. Jess Cain adapted to the radio medium because that's what professionals do. He created a radio community every day that let thousands of New Englanders wake up to his humor and characters; his conversation and warmth; and his big tent approach told listeners that everyone was welcome! Comedy, Jess would say, doesn't have to hurt unless you're busting a gut laughing. Jess' comedy would caress and not kill. He worked during a time when the radio audience was a broad section of the population. It was true broadcasting for the day and not the narrowcasting of today. Walk down the streets of Boston with the man and you would not reach your destination without a double take from A passersby, an outstretched hand, or even a friendly shout from across the street. He'd never stop reading or jotting down notes for a bit to be used the next morning because he knew being a broadcaster was a lifestyle that never ended. Every event or chance meeting became fodder for the show. The job was never complete, never done. His show was a speeding train that departed every morning at full speed and did not slow down for anything, because he knew his listeners had lives that would not stop for his schedule. He had to keep the train moving on their schedule. The show was about them...not him. Jess Cain just happened to be the man in the role of a lifetime, as the conductor."

– Peter Casey

Harry Harrison

Harry Harrison, one of the all-time great morning-show hosts on New York City Radio, was inducted to the New York State Broadcasters Hall of Fame on November 12, 2009. No one is more deserving of the honor. For many years I knew Harry from afar because of his reputation as a real radio pro. I have only known Harry for a few years, but our friendship is not measured in years, but in the values we both share; family, friends, love of God and the strong belief that good guys do win in the end. Since I first reached out to him for his input regarding this book, and our initial conversation, something clicked and I felt we would become "fast friends" and we did!

During the past few years, Harry has sent me much reading material on many radio personalities. He has also forwarded many pearls of wisdom, including the attached humility prayer. I believe it is important to include it in our book as a reminder to each of us, whether on the radio or not that humility and a humble heart is the key in every way to being a winner on the radio and in life. Thanks, Harry!

HUMILITY PRAYER

Dear Lord,

Please deliver me from the compulsive habit of thinking I must always have something to say on every occasion.

Release me from the craving of trying to straighten out everyone's affairs.

Restrain my mind from the recital of boring, endless and pointless details… give me the wings to get to the point. And though I dare not ask for grace enough to enjoy the tales of others, help me to endure them with patience and tolerance.

Give me reasonable doubt---and less cocksureness when my memory and viewpoint seem to clash with those of an opposing opinion.

Teach me the glorious lesson that sometimes I may be wrong.

Lord, give me the ability to see good things in unexpected places—and unexpected talents in people.

*Give me the grace to tell them so. Help me be reasonably good, honest, cheerful… but not a saint (because we all know some of **them** are hard to live with).*

Teach me to be thoughtful but not moody…helpful but not bossy, observing but not critical.

And though with my vast store of self-proclaimed wisdom---it seems a pity not to use it all up, please remember, Lord, I want a few friends left at the end.

So—teach me to be ever grateful—and to let me never forget Your grace—and the help of Others.

Amen.

Dedications • xiii

Roger Allan Bump

Jess Cain

WBZ Ops Mgr. Peter Casey (wrote dedication to Jess Cain).

Bob MacNeil (wrote dedication to Roger Allan) toasts author at author's 50th birthday party, Glen Magna House 1991.

Fred Foy — pioneer radio broadcaster and the Lone Ranger's radio announcer.

Cousin Brucie Morrow in Sirius Studio.

Acknowledgements

RADIO PRO IS DEDICATED first and foremost to my mom and dad, Jenny and Marty, who put up with me blasting music at all hours of the night while playing radio in my basement studio with high-school pals Johnny Ward, Eddie McDonough and Bob Willett. Thanks to my sister, JoAn, for being the star of our radio-TV productions, and older sister, Rosie, who encouraged me at age 16 to enter a *"So you wanna be a DJ"* contest at WCSH, Portland, Maine, which by a stroke of luck I won. I'm most thankful to the show host, Bob Arnold, who sensed my passion to be on the air and gave me my first shot in front of a live mic by being a high-school reporter on his afternoon show.

My heartfelt thanks to the Jesuits and teachers at Cheverus High in Portland Maine, especially, Rev. Fr Bernard Murphy, who saw something worth saving in me, when I almost flunked out my freshman year. All my fellow Cheverians, class of 1959, particularly, Joe Coffey, Freddy Metcalf, Dave Levasseur and my longtime friend Vinnie Bruni.

I am also grateful to those who opened the broadcasting door for me and who reached out with a helping hand. There were many during my 41-year career, including, the late radio pro Tom Shovan, who shuttled me around to different stations, so I could get a feel for what *real radio* was all about.

Thanks to Bob Joyce and John Ricker, for hiring me without experience at Ch.-8-WMTW as a cameraman early on in my broadcasting career, while pursuing my dream of one day being on the radio. My deepest appreciation to the late J. Alan Jasper, then-owner of WIDE-Biddeford, ME, for taking time to teach a green kid all about radio. My thanks to Linwood Pitman and Jack Atwood for hiring an even greener kid as a weekend announcer at Ch.-6 Portland, while I attended Emerson College-Boston to learn more about broadcasting.

Thanks to the staff at WFAU-Augusta, Maine, my first on-air job. I was fired and quickly learned a valuable lesson from owner Norm Gallant. Management does not appreciate having their station's format changed without permission. Something you future radio wannabes need to keep in mind. My thanks to my co-workers at Maine radio stations, WIDE, Biddeford, and Portland stations, WGAN, WLOB and WCSH. Also, to the staff at WLW Cincinnati, WROR, Boston, KLDE, Houston and WEAT "Sunny 104.3" West Palm Beach. A word or two about the folks behind the scenes who gave life to my book. First and most importantly, publisher, Ben Ohmart, who has shown extraordinary patience in the face of numerous delays involving my book. Thanks, Ben for believing in me that I had a special story to share. To fellow writer, Dave Menefee, who offered his expertise on the art of writing . A debt of gratitude to my editor, Michael Schemaille who put forth many long hours on this project. My deepest appreciation to my friend, production manager, Sandy Grabman, who willingly jumped in at the eleventh hour to pass along her insightful expertise and who kindly took time to answer my many questions. Thanks also to John Teehan, who brilliantly set my text and photos to print, and to Jill Wilson for taking time to transfer the photos to CD for John. You have all helped to make

Radio Pro a reality and I am so appreciative of your efforts on my behalf. Many thanks to my USMC boot buddies at Parris Island, S.C. Plt 248, I Co. 2nd Battalion, Jimmy Lorrain, (we still exchange e-mails on a weekly basis to this day), Bobby Connolly, Dickie DiBiase, Bill Roberge and Clif McKenney. It doesn't seem possible it was over fifty years ago that we stood at attention in front of our Senior Drill Instructor, S.Sgt. Frank Holiwski. Also Semper Fi to my fellow Marines with the 10th Engr Co. USMCR, Portland, Maine, especially my long-time friend, Gunny Frank Leavitt. Thanks, guys, for your words of support and encouragement to keep at it when things got tough. All my love to our daughter, Karen and granddaughter, Lissa, my mom-in-law, Ruth and all our family members. As mentioned there were hundreds of contributors to this book, but one person is very special. She contributed in so many ways, as an advisor, supporter and crisis manager. She willingly sacrificed many of our precious hours, days, months and years together, which enabled me to spend countless hours required for researching and writing this book. She not only graciously gave me the space needed to accomplish this work, but stood by me through good and bad times. She supported me during my on-air years in Boston, Houston and West Palm Beach and has always been an integral part of my radio career. Her unselfish ways, unending words of encouragement and invaluable input helped me see this book through to the end. Without her caring and loving support, I never would have written Radio Pro, let alone completed such a difficult task. Therefore this book is as much hers as it is mine. She was mentioned quite often on my radio show, but seldom received the credit she so rightfully deserves. As for titles, she never really had one, so let's give her one right now. From here on out, let's refer to her as the Executive Producer of my life! This special person is my loving wife, Kimmie. Our book,

Acknowledgements • xvii

Radio Pro, is also dedicated to you sweetie. Thank you from the bottom of my heart. I love you! If, I've omitted anyone, please forgive me. I assure you it was not intentional, it's just that sometimes my memory cells up and leave without my permission.

This is the complete list of Radio Pros and others who contributed to this book. A debt of gratitude to the following individuals, who graciously gave of their time and input to make this book possible. My sincerest thanks to each of them.

Mike Addams – longtime AM Drive talent-Magic 106.7-Boston
Malcolm Alter – longtime radio traffic reporter-Boston
Jo-anne Ansbro, and her late husband, George, who was an announcer at ABC for an incredible 59 years!
Jeanne Ashley – air-talent-Kansas City & Miami
Tom Baker – radio mgr – Boston/ San Diego
Matt "The Cat" Baldassarri-oldies air-talent, formerly with X-M satellite
Dick Bartley – syndicated oldies show air-talent
Tom Bergeron – former AM-Drive talent-Boston, today popular network television personality
Gary Berkowitz – former air-talent PD & Mgr. Today, radio consultant specializing in the AC format
Dick Biondi – legendary WLS Chicago air-talent
Mary Blake – radio news journalist-formerly RKO, Boston, today WBZ
Don Bleu – AM-Drive talent -Star 101.3-San Francisco
Bruce Bradley – former air-talent-WBZ Boston, also NY/St. Louis
Barbara Bridges – PD/air-talent-Nashville MIX-92.9
Scotty Brink – former air-talent, now VO expert, Oklahoma
Ross Brittain – AM-Drive talent -WOGL-Philadelphia
Fred Bronson – writer-Burbank, CA, author Billboard #1 Hits series
Roger Allan Bump – one-time Boston radio news journalist. Radio Pro is dedicated to him, and also Jess Cain
Alan Burns – radio consultant
Jack Casey – former air-talent, today GM, WERS-Boston-Emerson College station
Peter Casey – Director News Ops – WBZ-Boston
Sean Casey – air-talent-Philly & Boston
Joe Castiglione – longtime radio voice of the Boston Red Sox
Ron Chapman – legendary AM-Drive talent-Dallas-for 32 years the voice KVIL-AM
Kevin Charles – air-talent-Houston

Joe Chille – AM-Drive talent -30-year voice of WJYE-Buffalo
Gregg Clifton – Attorney/agent – Phoenix
Lissa Coffey – air-talent-writer-Los Angeles
Stacey Cohen – Los Angeles air-talent-creative agency-Redondo Beach, CA
Joe Cortese – air-talent/production CBS Boston
"Ryan" Rick Cote – air-talent-Boston, today -pm-drive talent & Acc't Dev. Mgr-WABK-Augusta, Me.
Linda Cruze – air-talent – Houston
Tom Cuddy – radio mgr/programming NYC
Mrs. Howard Culver – late husband was well-known radio actor, star of children's 1950s radio show *Straight Arrow*
Capt'n Dan (Paul Zmuda) – AM Drive talent-KKLI, Colorado Springs, Co.
Jeff Davis – air-talent/VO expert-Chicago & Hollywood
Steven Dee – former air-talent, today, owner radio show prep service-Morning Skoop.com GJ, CO
Joel Denver – former air-talent/writer-today Pres. Pub. AllAccess.com
Joe Desimone – former air-talent New Orleans/Portland, ME. Today agency owner, Portland, ME.
Laurie DeYoung – AM-Drive talent-25 years WPOC-Baltimore
Rose Diehl – PD/air-talent – Topeka, Kansas
Shawn Dion – air-talent – 94.5 – Shreveport, LA
Dale Dorman – legendary air-talent Boston
Amy Doyle – former radio programmer-today VP-MTV
Shelly Dunn – AM-Drive talent – San Diego, CA
Pete Falconi – air-talent-PD-Boston, today station owner, Newburyport, MA
Steve Feldman – radio sales Boston & West Palm Beach; today, sales with Comcast in Fl.
Bill Figenshu – former air-talent & Mgr. Today, head of own agency
Joe Ford – well-known air-talent-Houston, today VO expert in Texas
John Forsythe – longtime AM-Drive talent 93.3-KOB-FM – Albuquerque, NM, now on-air (2010) in Orlando, Fl.
Brian DeGeus Foxx – Music Dir/Mornings KSFI-FM Salt Lake City
Fred Foy – retired ABC Network announcer, famous as one-time narrator on radio's Lone Ranger
Rod Fritz – longtime Boston news voice, today with WBZ-Boston
Bob Fuller – one-time popular Portland, ME, air-talent, today radio station owner with JJ Jeffrey

Acknowledgements • xix

Dr. Joe Galati – liver specialist Houston, talk show host "Your Health First" Houston, TX

Bill Gardner – AM-drive talent, Phoenix and Los Angeles

John Gehron, radio management – Boston & Chicago with CBS and today working with internet radio

Steve Jay Gilinsky – air-talent-station owner-Magic-101.7FM-Binghamton, NY

Larry "Commander" Glick – legendary all-night radio personality WBZ-Boston

Mike Haile – AM Drive talent/GM WHMS-WDWS-AM, Champaign, Illinois

Donna Halper – former air-talent, today radio consultant

Bob Hamilton – morning show service, newradiostar.com, Carmel, CA

Mark Hannon – radio management-CBS Boston

Harry Harrison – the morning-mayor of New York City airwaves for over 44 years at WABC & WCBS-FM

Hugh Hewitt – nationally syndicated talk show host

Chuck Igo – former Boston-air-talent, today AM-Drive Oldies 100.9-WYNZ, Portland, ME.

Les Howard Jacoby – well-known programmer-air-talent – Florida

JJ Jeffrey – popular Boston & Chicago top-40 jock. Today, on-air & station owner with Bob Fuller Portland, ME.

Tim Johnson – Intranet Director-Clear Channel Univ.-Houston

Lou Josephs – former air-talent, programmer, today radio consultant

Dan Justin – PM Drive air-talent – MAGIC-106.7 – Boston

Barry Kaye – well-known singer-entertainer/air-talent Houston, TX

M.G. Kelly – legendary syndicated air-talent Oklahoma City and Los Angeles

Skip Kelly – air-talent-West Palm Beach, Fl and West VA

Steve King – popular air-talent in Chicago, today, all-night host with wife Johnnie Putman on WGN

David Kruh – former RKO-Boston radio engineer

Jim Labarbara – popular Greater Cincinnati air-talent

Bob Lacey – syndicated morning drive show host – Bob & Sheri Show

Gary LaPierre – former longtime morning drive news voice on WBZ-Boston, today VO expert

Don Latulippe – longtime air-talent – Boston area, recent inductee, Massachusetts Broadcasters Assoc.

Doug LaVallee – former air-talent -WCSH-AM-970-Portland, Me and also Honolulu air-talent & PD

Scott MacKay – air-talent Boston and Chicago area

Bob MacNeil – radio news journalist/New Dir. ROR-Boston, also teacher at Curry College-Milton, MA
Cindy Maguire – air-talent-Washington, DC-Virginia area
Sam Malone – AM-Drive talent – MIX 96.5-Houston, TX
Julee Mara – air-talent -morning show producer – Boston
Wink Martindale – popular air-personality & host of 19 game shows, including the favorite *Tic-Tac-Dough*
Dan Mason – former air-talent and PD, today, Pres.-CEO CBS Radio
CC McCartney – former air-talent-Nashville, now recognized VO talent
Mark McCray – former morning drive talent/PD -X-102.3 – West Palm Beach, FL, today Dallas, PD
Chris "Mack" McGorrill – Ops Mgr. Saga Comm. Portland, ME
Joe McMillan – air-talent, Boston-Portland, ME; today, VO talent
Kelly Monson – AM-Drive talent at KBZN – 97.9 "The Breeze" on Salt Lake City
Melanie Morgan – San Francisco-based and nationally-known talk talent
Bruce Morrow-New York City-based and nationally-known radio personality, currently on Sirius Satellite
Harry Nelson – PD and former air-talent San Fran., Boston & Portland ME, Today, partners in record label
Norm N. Nite – Oldies show host, currently on Sirius satellite "live" from R& R Hall of Fame-Cleveland
Richie Norris – weekend air-talent – Albany, New York, on Magic 100.9
Paula O'Connor – radio manager-programmer Boston
Jack Oliver – longtime radio personality and PD KEYN Wichita, Kansas
Lorna Ozmon – former air-talent, PD, Mgr. Today, radio consultant
Cary Pahigian – Group Mgr. Saga Comm. Portland, ME
Judi Paparelli – air-talent-Boston and So. Florida, nationally synd. talk show host
Alice Pearce – former radio producer/promotions. Today, with Ski NH
Jerry J.D. Pelletier – popular AM-Drive talent, West Palm Beach; presently, on-air in Lexington, KY
Paul Perry – air-talent, afternoon-drive-WROR -105.7 – Boston
Dick Purtan – Detroit's most popular & recognized radio voice. Dick retired in 2010 from WOMC-104.3
Johnnie Putman – Chicago's all-night radio voice as co-host with her hubby Steve King on WGN

Nancy Quill – the midday favorite on MAGIC-106.7 for the past 28 years (she began in '82)

Ted Quillin – one of LA's first Top-40 jocks on KFWB in 1958. Ted is an original and true radio legend

Sunny Quinn – veteran West Palm Beach midday radio personality

Sally Jesse Raphael – one of America's most popular radio and television talk show personalities.

Phil Redo – former Boston-air-talent at the original WROR-98.5, now in radio management

Jack Riccardi – midday host News/Talk 550AM KTSA San Antonio

Jordan Rich – a favorite Boston-air personality, presently weekends on WBZ

Anna-Marie Ritter – AM Drive talent on Nashville's Mix-92.9.

Bob Rivers-he gave us those fun, twisted Christmas tunes; AM-Drive personality on KZOK-102.5 in Seattle

Dave Robbins – VP-GM CBS Radio-Chicago, recently (2010) moved to Orlando, FL and the CBS Group

Dean Rogers – one of Portland, Maine, radio's favorite air – talents for over 30 years

Lindy Rome – former Florida air-talent, now self-employed

Dave Ryan – the personable Minneapolis AM-Drive talent is on KDWB-101.3

Walter Sabo – internationally recognized broadcast consultant

Bob Scherago – one-time radio engineer WTIC Hartford, later worked for and retired from Voice of America

Tom Shannon – legendary Buffalo radio voice of the Niagara Frontier on rockers WKBW and CKLW.

Surfer Joe Shevenell – former air-talent-WLOB Portland, Maine

Bob Schuman – on-air personality, Detroit, Indianapolis, Boston, Tampa, and Jacksonville, FL

Matt Siegel – top-rated Boston morning drive talent at KISS-108 for almost 30 years.

Mollie Simpkins – Mgr. Metro – Baltimore

Frank Kingston Smith – former air-talent Boston, NYC, today, he & his wife own their own business

Ken Smith – air-talent and oldies programmer, formerly with X-M Sat. in DC

Linda Smith – one-time radio producer WROR-98.5, today with Comcast

Peter Smyth – Pres.-CEO Greater Media

Rick Snyder – one-time Albany, NY & Portland, ME, air-talent, segued to radio sales and never looked back!

April Sommers – air-talent working alongside Don Bleu in San Francisco at Star 101.3

Bob Spicer – radio production whiz for years in Boston at RKO General and later Greater Media stations

Kevin Straley – radio manager, most recently with X-M Satellite since its inception, presently, VP Programming TuneIn

Greg Strassell – VP-programming CBS Radio Boston

Lee Strasser – former GM, West Palm Beach CBS Group, now heads own talent rep firm

Paula Street – popular midday voice on OLDIES-103-Boston for the past 22 years

Dick Summer – Boston /NYC air-talent, today, VO and podcast keep Dick busy, www.dicksummer.com

Mark Summers – Florida-based air-talent

Melissa Sweeton – rocked Nashville for 30 years at WSM-FM, Magic 96 and WGFX-104.5. Today VO expert

Alan Tolz – producer for Jerry Williams. He & Steve Elman wrote a book about Williams, "Burning up the Air"

Pam Triolo – air-talent WPB, Fl. Now owns a creative agency in So. Florida

Alpha Trivette – former Morning drive talent in Atlanta on B-98.5

Dick Tufeld – former network announcer in '40s & '50s on *Space Patrol*. Voice of robot on TV's *Lost in Space*

Willy Tyler – PD-AM Drive talent at Classic Hits, My 92.5 – Billings, Montana

Brad Wallace – Dir. Of Marketing & Promotions-WLS-Chicago

Mark Wallengren – Longtime Los Angeles morning drive voice on KOST 103.5 FM

Ed Walsh – Morning drive news co-anchor on WBZ Boston

Nancy Widmann – first woman Pres., at CBS, Mgr WCBS-FM NYC, today heads own agency

Mark Williams – syndicated talk show host based in California

Debbie Enblom Wolvos – still photographer and former radio-TV news journalist in Minneapolis and Boston

Guy Zapoleon – radio consultant

ABOUT THE BOOK

Author's disclaimer: *The text in this book is written from the author's perspective, and therefore, when the narration refers to "I" or "We" it is meant to imply it is the "voice" of the author, unless otherwise stated.*

Acknowledgements • xxiii

Radio Pro is written from the viewpoint of a broadcast professional, Joe Martelle. It is the author's primary intention to give both the casual reader and student—tomorrow's radio star—the best information and advice possible, while bringing to those interested in an on-air career a better understanding of what it takes to be a "real" radio personality and on-air performer. Therefore, *Radio Pro* not only reflects the author's opinion, but also the generous support and input of hundreds of fellow broadcasters. Their unselfish willingness to share their invaluable expertise on what it takes to be an air personality makes this a very special one-of-a-kind book.

In addition to being a How To book, *Radio Pro* is also a historical reference source on the history of broadcasting and pioneer radio personalities, and how it affects those desiring a career as an air personality in today's market. For example, Chapter One showcases many of radio's first air personalities from Arthur Godfrey to Jack Webb.

Chapter eight involves the Art of Interviewing. How to conduct an interview and what to avoid, with in-depth pieces on Mike Douglas, Sally Jesse Raphael, Bill O'Reilly, Art Linkletter and others. Chapter 13 gives you an inside look from a Woman's Perspective on Working in Radio and on the air. There is a brief history of pioneer radio women with profiles on women who have played a significant role on the air, including Vaughn DeLeath, Judith Waller, Bertha Brainard, Ruth Lyons, Kate Smith, Mary Margaret McBride, Arlene Francis, Jean King and over 35 additional women who paved the way for today's women in broadcasting. The chapter also presents in-depth stories about Martha Jean 'the Queen' Steinberg, Alison Steele, Yvonne Daniels and others. And, for you radio wannabees, broadcast consultant, Donna Halper and others share their knowledge on what it takes particularly for women to be stars on the radio today.

Chapter 16 is a 3 part chapter. Part 1 covers a brief history of radio news and pioneer journalists, audio advancements in radio news coverage, the deregulation by the FCC and its impact on radio news. Part 2 features the history of talk radio and radio's earliest talk personalities right up to the present crop of talkers with comprehensive stories on several radio pros, including Fr. Edward Coughlin, Howard Stern, Herb Jepko, Long John Nebel, Larry King and others. Part 3 of this chapter covers the history of sports on radio with advice from pioneer broadcasters to you, future radio sportscasters, on how to be a great air personality covering sports. Sound input from Bob Prince, Harry Caray, Ned Martin, Ken Coleman, Curt Gowdy, Lindsey Nelson, Joe Castiglione and others. So, you see, *Radio Pro* not only tells you how to be a great air personality, but gives you outstanding advice from the "real" radio pros of yesterday and today!

Radio Pro also showcases many of todays radio formats and personalities. It also covers changes in broadcasting over the years and how it affects the radio industry today and your future as an air personality.

Hopefully, in reading this book, you will discover it is like having your own personal classroom with one huge difference. Instead of just one great lecturer, you have the benefit of the views and opinions of over one-hundred and fifty of broadcastings best conveniently found at your fingertips. As you read their personal career experiences, you will notice that I primarily reached out to air personalities, management and support staff, from specific radio formats. They include AC (Adult Contemporary), Oldies, Rock, and News, Talk and Sports. This was done for one very specific reason. They are the radio formats that I worked closely with during my 41 year on-air career and which I am most familiar with.

As a future radio star, you can make the most of this How To book on the making of an on-air personality and what it takes by putting into practice the many helpful suggestions from the radio pros who have contributed their insightful comments. If, you can glean just a few examples from these knowledgeable professionals, who have survived the daily battles of working in radio, then the our mission will have been served.

You can give *Radio Pro* further significance by using it as a road map to help navigate your own journey around the many obstacles, and set-backs you may encounter in search of your own on-air career. It is my fervent wish that you will find this book informative, insightful, entertaining, helpful and maybe even a little inspiring. May the Good Lord bless and guide you as you pursue your dream of being on the air and a real Radio Pro!

I'd love to hear from you. You can reach me at RadioProJoe@aol.com. Until then, I'll hear you on the radio!

Most Sincerely

Joe Martelle
Author: *Radio Pro*
June 2012

AUTHOR'S NOTE: During my forty-one years on radio, it was my pleasure to meet and interview many stars from radio's Golden Age and celebrities from the entertainment field, movies, television, sports and music. Some of the information contained in this book is taken directly from interviews and informal chats with these wonderful people. They include, but are not limited to, the following:

Danny Ainge
Mrs. Jo-anne Ansbro (wife of announcer George Ansbro)
Gene Autry (Mrs. Jackie Autry)
Marty Barrett

Mrs. Leta Beemer (wife of radio's Lone Ranger, Brace Beemer)
Dick Benjamin
Mrs. Grace Boyd (wife of actor Bill Boyd, who played Hopalong Cassidy)
Pres. George Bush
Laura Bush
M.L. Carr
Pres. Jimmy Carter
Joe Castiglione
The Conigliaro Brothers
Dick Clark
Larry "Buster" Crabbe
Mrs. Howard Culver (wife of actor Howard Culver, who starred as radio's Straight Arrow)
Rosemary DeCamp
Andy Devine
Mike Douglas
Ron Ely
Chad Everett
George Fenneman
Eddie Fisher
Carlton Fisk
Susan Flannery
Doug Flutie
Fred Foy
Kirby Grant
Curt Gowdy
Reed Hadley
John Hannah
Bob Hastings
Charlton Heston
Tim Holt
Bob Hope
Bruce Hurst
Bob Keeshan
Ben E. King
Jay Leno
Mark Lindsay
Phillips H. Lord
Susan Lucci
Don MacLaughlin
Jock Mahoney
Marjorie Main

Harry Marble
Gary Marshall
Paul McCartney
Darren McGavin
Don McLaughlin
Ed McMahon
Gary Merrill
Al Michaels
Clay Moore
Bob Murphy
Ty Murray
Chuck Negron
Peter Noone
Chuck Norris
Yoko Ono
Johnny Pesky
Rico Petrocelli
Gene Pitney
Dick Radatz
Duncan Renaldo
Mary-Lou Retton
Debbie Reynolds
Marjorie Reynolds
Derek Sanderson
Charlie Simmer
Dick Simmons
Buffalo Bob Smith
Charles Starrett
Bill Stern
Dick Stockton
Gale Storm
Mary Stuart
Marion Sweet
Roy Thinnes
Dick Tufeld
Bobby Vee
Bobby Vinton
Dawn Wells
Mary K. Wells
Mary Wilson
Rick Wise

Acknowledgements • xxvii

MY THANKS TO THESE WONDERFUL FOLKS for sharing their personal insight into the world of broadcasting and show business. I am most grateful for having had the opportunity to be friends with many of them.

Much of the material gathered for this book came from the author's personal collection of notes, articles, photographs, and interviews conducted and collected during his broadcasting career. The author pored over hundreds of magazine and newspaper articles and other documents pertaining to radio and personalities. Information was also obtained from hundreds of celebrity and personality interviews conducted by the author or from informal conversations with selected individuals. Thanks to Jill Wilson, who kindly gave her time to set-up the photos for this book and provided a plethora of computer info.

In addition to the list of books below, suggested reading includes any of the following magazines from radio's Golden Age (the 1920s to '50s) *including Colliers, Popular Electronics, Radio Guide, Radio Mirror, Radio-TV Mirror, Life, Look, Pageant Quick, Reader's Digest, Saturday Evening Post, Sunday Parade, Time,* and *TV Guide.* For further reading, the author suggests the following books which are directly related to broadcasting:

Abbot, Waldo – *Handbook of Broadcasting* – McGraw-Hill – NY & London 1941

Ansbro, George – *I Have a Lady in the Balcony* – McFarland & Co., NC 2000

Autry, Gene with Mickey Herskowitz – *Back in the Saddle Again* – Doubleday 1978

Bannon, Jim – *The Son that Rose in the West*-Devil's Hole Printery-Plano, Texas 1975

Billboard Book of Top 40 Hits 7th Edition by Joel Whitburn, Billboard Books, NY 2000

Buxton, Frank and Bill Owen – *The Big Broadcast (1920-1950)* -The Viking Press, NY 1972

Buxton, Frank and Bill Owen – *Radio's Golden Age*-Easton Valley Press 1968

Bronson, Fred – *Billboard Book of #1 Hits Series*-5th Edition – Billboard Books, NY 2003

Clark, Dick with Fred Bronson – *Dick Clark's American Bandstand* – Collins Pub. June 1997

Doolittle, John – *Don McNeill and His Breakfast Club* – Univ. of Notre Dame 2001

Douglas, Mike with Thomas Kelly & Michael Heaton – *I'll be Right Back* – Simon & Schuster 2000

Downey, Morton, Jr. with William Hoffer – *Mort! Mort! Mort!* -Delacote Press NY 1988

Dunning, John – *Tune in Yesterday* – Prentice-Hall 1976

Forrest, Richard E. Pub. *Yearbook of Radio-TV-1964-27th Annual Edition* – NY 1964

Franklin, Joe with R.J. Marx – Up *Late with Joe Franklin* – Scribner, NY 1995

Freeth, Nick – *Remembering the 40s* – Barnes and Noble 2002

Glenn, Norman R. Ex VP, Sponsor – *A 40 Year Album of Pioneer Radio Stations*-Sponsor Inc. 1962

Goldsmith, Alfred &Austin C. Lescarboura – *This Thing Called Broadcasting*-Henry Holt & Co. NY 1930

Gowdy, Curt – *Cowboy at the Mike* – Doubleday, NY 1966

Gowdy, Curt with John Powers-*Seasons to Remember* – Harper-Collins 1993

Harmon, Jim – *The Great Radio Comedians* – Doubleday 1970

Harmon, Jim – *The Great Radio Heroes* – Ace Books (Doubleday) 1967

Hollis, Tim – *Hi There Boys and Girls* (America's local children's TV progs.) Univ. of Miss-Jackson 2001

Keeshan, Bob – *Growing Up Happy* – Doubleday (Bantam) Dell Pub. Group 1989

Lackmann, Ron – *Same Time, Same Station*-Guide to Radio – Facts on File- NY 1996

Lamparski, Richard – *Whatever Became Of* series – Crown Pub. NY 1967+

Morrow, Bruce with Laura Baudo – *My Life in Rock 'n' Roll Radio*-Beech Tree Books, NY Oct. 1987

Nachman, Gerald – *Raised on Radio*-Pantheon Books, NY 1998

Osgood, Dick – *WYXIE Wonderland* (History of WXYZ-Detroit) Bowling Green, Univ. 1981

Perry, Dick – *Not Just a Sound-The Story of WLW*-Prentice-Hall, Inc. NJ 1971

Phillips, Wally – *The Wally Phillips People Book*-Caroline House, Sept. 1979

Settle, Irving A. – *A Pictorial History of Radio*-Grosset & Dunlap 1967

Stern, Bill with Oscar Fraley – *The Taste of Ashes*-Henry Holt & Co. NY 1959

Storm, Gale with Bill Libby – *I Ain't Down Yet*-Bobbs-Merrill Co. 1981

Swartz, Jon D. & Robert C. Reinehr – *Handbook of Old Time Radio*-Scarecrow Press, MD 1993

Tolz, Alan & Steve Elman – *Burning Up the Air*-Jerry Williams-Talk Radio-Commonwealth Eds. 2008

Woolf, Bob – *Behind Closed Doors*-Atheneum, NY 1976

Photographs: unless otherwise noted, all photos are from the author's personal collection or were supplied by the individuals who commented for this book.

Thanks to Dale Patterson and his wonderful tribute to radio website: Rock Radio Scrapbook for some of the personality quotes used in this book.

About the Author

JOE MARTELLE, when just eight years old, listened to two of his all-time favorite radio adventure programs, *The Lone Ranger* and *Sgt. Preston of the Yukon* for the first time. From then on, he was hooked and being on-the-radio is all he wanted to do.

In his teens, Joe built a small radio station in the basement of his family's home and although, he could only broadcast to his mom's kitchen radio, upstairs, he was on the air.

Joe's dream of being on a real radio station became a reality, when at age 16, he won a "so you wanna be a dee-jay" contest on his hometown radio Station, WCSH-Portland. The host of the show, Bob Arnold, must have sensed Joe's deep passion for radio, because his mic debut led to a weekly spot on the station broadcasting news of his high school, Cheverus. Ironically, as fate would have it, twenty years later, Joe would manage the same station.

After graduating from high school, Joe took a few side-steps in his quest to be on the radio, including a semester at St. Francis Xavier University in Canada, where he was more interested in listening to the local Antigonish radio station, CJFX, then tending to his studies. After dropping out of school, he returned to Portland and worked at Brighton Avenue pharmacy. Not wishing to be a soda jerk for the rest of his life, even though the perks were quite good, including getting to know all the young ladies who stopped by for a sundae. He felt life was becoming a dead end, so he enlisted in the Marines. His radio career seemed light years away, but Joe never stopped dreaming of one day being on the radio even while marching in the hot, humid heat of Parris Island, So. Carolina.

After active duty, once again, Joe returned to family and familiar surroundings in Portland. Hoping somehow, in someway, to finally get his radio career on track, he never relinquished his desire to be a radio personality.

Working all nights at Cushman bakery loading trucks, he saved his money with an eye on taking a broadcasting course at Emerson College in Boston, which he finally did. At long last, his dream of being on the air became a reality, when he obtained his first full-time on-air job in Augusta, Maine. His joy was short-lived. It was a disaster. Joe was promptly fired. You can read all about the misfortune he experienced, which he readily admits was his own fault, in chapter 9, Attitudes and Actions.

Although, faced with many terrible lows and terrific highs in his forty-one year radio career, Joe Martelle preserved through it all, willing to weather any storm and to accept each new challenge with a positive goal of moving forward to new heights. Never losing his passion for playing in the game of radio, he believes his firings, and other challenges, including several serious health issues made him a better person and helped him become one of the most popular radio personalities and a listener favorite in Maine, Boston, Cincinnati, Houston and his final radio home, West Palm Beach, Florida.

If, you too have a dream of being an air-personality, read on! You will learn from Joe and over 150 other radio pros on how to survive the downside of an ego-driven business, and how to become a successful air personality and real, RADIO PRO!

Martelle family (left to right) standing: sister Rosemarie, dad-Marty, Mom-Joan sitting holding baby sister JoAn, author in soft hat.

Our dad, Marty, passed away in October 1978. Mom, remarried in 1990. (L-R, author, sister Rosie, step-dad Larry Garwitz, mom and sister JoAn)

Author's high school graduation photo, 1959.

Rev. Fr. Bernard Murphy, Cheverus High School, 1956.

Halloween today- author's daughter Karen with her daughter (our granddaughter) Lissa.

Author and wife, Kimmie with long-time friend, Rev. Fr. Jerry Hogan, 1990.

Author on-air (standing) in studio at WIDE Biddeford, ME. 1963.

Author running camera for "Teddy Bear Playhouse" WMTW-TV, Ch. 8, Poland Spring, ME. (Photo credit: Joe Novick, 1963)

The Beginning

GROWING UP IN THE LATE 1940S, the fun thing to do was play cowboys with my pal Richie Lawlor and other neighborhood kids from nearby Sagamore Village. Something else we all enjoyed doing was listening to the radio. After school, the radio was loaded with exciting action-adventure programs for kids: *Jack Armstrong-The All-American Boy; Tom Mix and His Wonder Horse, Tony; The Flying Rancher, Sky King; The Adventures of a Comanche Indian Chief, Straight Arrow* and one of my favorites, *Sgt. Preston of the Northwest Mounted Police with His Great Lead Dog, Yukon King*.

I was lucky to have been born at a special time in broadcast history to enjoy the best of two radio worlds. The 1940s, right on the cusp of radio-changing formats from what is affectionately referred to as Radio's Golden Age, complete with its line-up of superb dramatic and comedic programs, and the fifties and radio's transition to a more music format with those first great Rock n' Roll DJs, led by Alan Freed. But, before we get too far down the road in my life and radio career, please allow me to take you back in time … *to those thrilling days of yesteryear* and explain how and where my love and passion for radio all began.

The year was 1949. I was just eight years old!

The small G.E. wall clock hung precariously by a single nail on the wallboard above my dad's workbench in the basement of our Brighton Avenue home in Portland, Maine. It was almost 5pm!

"Wow, better hurry," I thought to myself. "It's almost time!" Gingerly, stepping up on an empty wooden tomato box—to give my growing eight-year-old frame a much-needed boost in height, I reached up and turned on Dad's Philco radio. The warm, orange glow illuminating from its dial always seemed to say, "Welcome." It was a special table model radio, in its place of honor high above the workbench on the first shelf and just a tad to the right of our cellar window. As I turned the radio on, it crackled, hummed and whistled. I always felt like I was tuning in some far-reaching planet from a distant galaxy. Slowly turning the dial and trying to tune in one of our local Portland radio stations, I faintly heard the barking of a familiar friend. Turning up the radio volume, I listened carefully. There was no mistaking that dog! It was **Yukon King**! The bravest and strongest lead dog in the world and faithful companion to my radio friend, **Sgt. Preston**.

Jumping down off the box before it collapsed from my enthusiastic jumping for joy (let's just say, my forty-eight inches in height was almost equivalent to my waist size. Okay, so I was a pudgy kid! I certainly didn't want to break my dad's favorite tomato box), I plunked myself down, nice and comfy in one of his over-sized soft chairs, which he just happened to position directly beside our big ole warm furnace. It was late November in New England, the time of year when it begins to get dark around 4:30 in the afternoon. A light snow had just begun to fall and watching the snowflakes gently tap dance against the basement window helped set the scene for one of my favorite radio adventure programs, *The Challenge of the Yukon*, or as we kids liked to call it, *Sgt. Preston and King*! Later on, the show's creator, George W. Trendle, and others must have picked up the hint from us kids, because they also began referring to the program as *Sgt. Preston*.

Closing my eyes, while listening to the latest chapter unfold, I imagined that I was riding alongside the famous Mountie, with Yukon King running freely by our sled. Together we were mushing our team of huskies forward across the frozen tundra of the Yukon, to apprehend and arrest another lawbreaker in the name of the crown! *On, King, on you huskies!*

The year was 1949 and, to my way of thinking, this was radio broadcasting the way it was meant to be heard and enjoyed! At the tender age of eight, I was hooked …on radio! Yes, as far back as I can remember, even at such a young age, I always wanted to be on the radio. Listening to all those incredible radio programs really got me excited about my future career as a radio personality. My first lethal injection of the broadcasting bug hit me while listening to Sgt. Preston, but some credit has to go to the greatest radio announcer-narrator of them all, **Fred Foy**.

Fred implanted his indelible mark on me when I was just a little guy listening to him on the radio. Every Monday, Wednesday and Friday night precisely at 7:30, we would sit and stare at the orange glow from my dad's Philco radio. It's amazing we didn't suffer from a case of agent orange of the eyeballs! Like millions of other youngsters, we anxiously awaited the first stirring strains of "The William Tell Overture," a theme which magically signaled to boys and girls across America that The Lone Ranger and great white horse, Silver, were about to ride straight into our living rooms! As soon as the theme began and the opening gunshots sounded, on came the unmistakable booming voice of our announcer, Fred Foy! Mister perfect diction, with his warm, pure, and resonant delivery captured our imagination with his vivid description of another thrilling Lone Ranger adventure. That's the way I wanted to sound on the radio when I grew up.

I LOVE radio, still do! It's all I ever really wanted to do. Ask anyone who knows me, including my sweet wife, Kimmie, and she'll agree; radio has always been my first love! This is one kid who actually enjoyed being home sick. It gave me a chance to discover all those great daytime radio shows that I could never listen to while in school. Nothing escaped my prepubescent ears, either, from morning variety-talk shows like *Don McNeill's Breakfast Club* and *Arthur Godfrey Time* to daytime radio's dramatic fare, the daily soap operas! Although I must admit, my mom would throw a suspicious glance my way when I'd insist on listening to *The Road of Life* or *Oxydol's Own, Pa Perkins*.

One of my favorite radio personalities was Don McNeill, the congenial host of ABC-Radio's long-running *The Breakfast Club*. I learned so much about personality radio by listening to his broadcasts. The program came on the air at nine, weekday mornings, which was about an hour late for a future radio wannabe to catch if he wanted to make it to school on time.

One of the first things that struck me about the show is how much fun they all seemed to be having. Don and his breakfast gang *made radio real*. He and his cast could be serious one moment, as he read a heartwarming letter from a loyal breakfast club member, and a minute later, make you laugh with the corniest joke ever to come out of a Midwestern hay field. *The Breakfast Club* was unrehearsed and without a script, which was totally unheard of during Radio's Golden Age.

McNeill's [1] easy-going style was a pleasure to listen to and his interviewing technique was outstanding. Before going on the air, Don would have his studio audience fill out cards and then he would answer various questions. During the show, if a comment struck him in a special way, he would call on that audience member. The rapport usually was instantaneous and most times, the "bit" would be a home run, primarily because McNeill would listen to what the person was saying and would play off it. Listening is just as important as speaking and is a great tip for future radio stars. I was always moved when the program would take time out for a silent moment of prayer. Even after all these years, I can still hear his words to this day ..."*each in his own way, each in his own words, for a world united in peace, let us bow our heads and pray.*"

One day I was home from school with the flu, and naturally, we were tuned in to the *Breakfast Club*. Sitting in the kitchen with Mom, I was feeling quite ill, and rested my hot feverish face on our red and white table top. The metal surface felt cool against my warm face. During prayer time, I managed a weak smile as McNeill spoke those righteous words. They touched me then and still do to this day. They serve as a shining example of *how* what you say on the radio can deeply affect and touch others.

I make no secret about modeling much of my own on-air style after legendary radio pro Don McNeill. I learned about personality radio by listening to him and other radio pioneers like Arthur Godfrey and Art Linkletter.[2] They were absolutely the best in the business when it came to projecting their own personalities on the air. They were experts in the art of interviewing. Any minor success I may have had in interviewing is because of what I learned and borrowed from them.

Your homework assignment:

You can learn so much by listening and watching these radio masters at work. I strongly suggest you pick up their DVDs, CDs or cassettes and study their style. Pay particular attention to the way they conduct interviews.

Here is a partial list of pioneer radio personalities to learn from: Mel Allen, Jack Bailey, Martin Block, Galen Drake, Ralph Edwards, Arlene Francis, Arthur Godfrey, Curt Gowdy, Dennis James, Larry King, Robert Q. Lewis, Art Linkletter, Mary Margaret McBride, Don McNeill, Garry Moore, Edward R. Murrow, Bert Parks, Joe Pyne, Gene Rayburn, Vin Scully, Jean Shepherd, and Bill Stern.

Pioneer television personalities to study include Steve Allen, Bob Barker, Jack Barry, Sandy Becker, Johnny Carson, Dick Cavett, Dick Clark, Bud Collyer, Bill Cullen, John Charles Daly, Phil Donahue, Mike Douglas, Hugh Downs, Winn Elliot, Bob Eubanks, Sonny Fox, Arlene Francis, Dave Garroway, Sheila Graham, Merv Griffin, Monte Hall, David Hartman, Warren Hull, Tom Kennedy, Jim Lange, Joan London, Ted Mack, Hal March, Randy Merriman, Ed Murrow, Jack Narz, Jack Paar, Jane Pauley, Sally Jesse Raphael, Charlie Rose, Tim Russert, Diane Sawyer, Dinah Shore, Tom Snyder, David Suskind, Mike Wallace and the entire team on CBS-TV's *60 Minutes*, also, Barbara Walters and Betty White.[3]

These personalities were and are some of the best when it came to the art of interviewing.[4]

There are several ways to obtain radio and television programs from the personalities mentioned.

You can go online and Google to search for an individual performer. For the Golden Age of Radio, *Radio Spirits* is an excellent source for programs, especially those of Jean Shepherd and other radio performers. Also check out *The Old Time Radio Digest* website and ask for information about a specific radio personality. Regular contributors to the OTR site are always most helpful in replying to such requests. Many radio and television performers have donated much of their material, their shows, interviews, etc. to various colleges and universities. This information can also be obtained by searching the web under an individual's name. If you live in or near Chicago, Los Angeles or New York City, or if you plan to visit one of those cities, be sure and check out the Museum of Radio-TV Broadcasting. They are located in each of those locales and have recordings and file information on many radio and television personalities. It's always wise to call in advance of your planned visit, to learn days and times when each facility is open to the public.

Two of my all-time favorite network radio announcers are Fred Foy, who is previously mentioned, and George Ansbro. Both gentlemen transcended radio's Golden Age to have lengthy careers in television. Fred moved from radio's *Lone Ranger* to ABC-Television with many assignments, including acting as Dick Cavett's announcer. George Ansbro, after 18 years as the voice of radio's *Young Widder Brown,* also announced numerous programs at ABC-TV. When he retired in 1989 after 59 years on the air, all for the ABC Network, George Ansbro held the world's record for length of service to network radio and television.

There have always been radio personalities, dating back to broadcasting's earliest days. In 1920, Dr. Frank Conrad, an assistant chief engineer at Westinghouse Electric in Pittsburgh, played recorded music on his experimental radio station 8XK from a studio and transmitter he built in his garage in Wilkinsburg, PA. In doing so, he probably became the world's first disc jockey. When he exhausted his own record collection, and to satisfy the requests from his regular listeners for different music, he approached the Hamilton Music store. They gave him an unlimited supply of records in exchange for on-air mentions that all records heard had been provided by the Hamilton Music store in Wilkinsburg. Dr. Conrad agreed and thereby gave the world its first radio advertiser way back in 1920.

"If I listened to everyone, who had an opinion on how I should sound, I wouldn't be me on the radio!" (author)

Over the years, how often did I try and convey that message to my numerous program directors and managers. I DO listen to what my heart and mind tells me. If I didn't, I couldn't live with myself. You'll find it mentioned again and again in this book, you need to be *you* on the air. As a real on-air Radio Pro, the more you stick to who you really are, the more opportunity you will have to win and be successful! As soon as you begin to change your natural style on the air, you will begin to lose that comfortable *you* sound. Lose it and you'll ultimately be heading down the path to failure.

Where do you begin to find your own personality?

A good place to start is by studying and learning from the masters. Respected film director Orson Welles learned directing by watching John Ford. Comedian Eddie Murphy honed his comedic timing by watching Richard Pryor. It's okay to imitate others, as long as the *real you* stays intact.

Before they became famous, the Beatles began by imitating Chuck Berry. They'd listen to his American records, lift words and phrases, and decide how they wanted to do it. A lot of things John and Paul did, says Beatles producer George Martin, were dead copies of things they had heard. Paul McCartney's singing style, according to Martin, was a take-off on 1950s rock 'n' roll legend Little Richard. So, you see, it is permissible to borrow a little piece of your favorite personality, and adapt it to yourself.

Learning from the masters also applies to radio wannabes. Learning from radio's first pros is the key in developing *who you are* as a radio personality.

Life lessons from a Radio Pro by Joe Martelle

From my mom, I was told to stand-up straight, act like a gentleman, and to keep my mouth shut. From the Jesuits at Cheverus High School, I was told to sit up straight, act like a Christian gentleman, and to keep my mouth shut. From the Marine Corps, I was told to stand up straight, act like a Marine and to keep my mouth shut! Can you imagine the relief I felt, when I finally landed on-the radio, and was paid to keep my mouth open, and no one seemed to mind if I didn't sit or stand up straight! Speaking of one's mouth, this is good advice, whether you're on the radio or not: God gave us two ears and only one mouth, so He must have meant for us to do twice as much listening as talking.

Notes
1. Read more about Don McNeill in Chapter 1
2. Read more about Don McNeill , Arthur Godfrey, Art Linkletter and other pioneer radio personalities in Chapter 1
3. TV's Golden Girl Betty White had her own weekday afternoon variety show in the 1950s on NBC-TV
4. Learn more about The Art of Interviewing in Chapter 8. If you are already on the air and doing your thing, why not dig out some tapes of these long ago and mostly forgotten radio-TV masters and take a refresher course in how to handle a great interview.

CHAPTER 1

Learn From the Masters – Radio's Pioneer and First Air Personalities

"The magic word is imagination"

– Pioneer broadcaster, Himan Brown

RADIO RULE TO REMEMBER: Learn from radio's pioneer personalities, but **keep your own unique style.** The key to developing and molding your own air personality is never losing the whole part that is *you*. Find someone you enjoy listening to on the radio. Legendary radio pro Cousin Bruce Morrow[1] grew up in Brooklyn listening to the venerable **Martin Block**, host of WNEW's *Make Believe Ballroom*. Ask yourself, who do you enjoy listening to on the radio? Study that personality, and what they say and do on their show. What makes them so appealing to *you*? Do they make you laugh? Perhaps it's how they interact with their listeners in a warm, friendly way. Is their behavior on-air outrageous? Take a little piece of your favorite radio personality and see if any of their style can mesh with who you are! If the answer is yes, you're on your way to developing your own special air style.[2]

Incidentally, don't feel radio is a shrinking profession. Today, the number of AM & FM radio stations in the US. exceeds 14,000. Even with downsizing and cutbacks within the broadcast industry, if you're sincerely interested in an on-air radio career, with so many radio stations available there is plenty of room for you. All you need is lots of passion and desire, coupled with a little talent.

Radio's First on-air pros

Unfortunately, space does not allow a list of every personality who contributed to the birth and advancement of radio as a viable source of entertainment and information. It would take several volumes to give proper credit to those who paved the way for today and tomorrow's radio stars. We have endeavored to highlight some of radio's first great personalities, along with a brief sketch of how and why they became so popular. As a future radio star, you can learn a lot from these legends of the kilocycles. You may not be able to fill their shoes, but you can certainly follow in their footsteps.

> *"On May 10, 1927, Boston's Hotel Statler became the first hotel to install radio headsets in each of its 1300 rooms."*

Radio's Pioneer and First air personalities

During radio's formative years, broadcasters scooped up any performer who happened to come a' calling. There is a certain amount of success that automatically goes along with being first. Two of the very *first* to bring their act to radio were vaudevillians **Joe Weber** and **Lew Fields**. They were followed by **Billy Jones** and **Ernie Hare**, a vaudeville singing team who first went on the air as early as 1921. In August 1926, **Billy & Ernie** were handed their own show on NBC, when the Happiness Candy Company sponsored them as one of radio's first two-man teams. Known as *The Happiness Boys*, they became two of radio's first real stars and were among broadcasting's first personalities to gain a huge audience. The Happiness Boys were a pleasant mix of fun and music. The popular funny guys told a few jokes and sang a couple of songs during their half-hour time slot on Friday nights at 8:00 pm. **Billy & Ernie** paved the way for today's morning drive radio teams, even though they were light years apart from today's shock jocks.

The Happiness Boys were followed by **Gene and Glenn.** Gene Carroll and Glenn Rowell were also two of radio's earliest and popular teams. Their morning show, *The Quaker Early Birds Program,* not surprisingly named after their sponsor Quaker Oats, first began on NBC in 1930. Their fifteen-minute show, heard six days a week, had Gene & Glenn playing music, talking, and doing "bits" which featured Gene doing character voices. Another duo, **Vic and Sade,** debuted on NBC's Blue Network on June 29, 1932. **Will Rogers** was another notable radio pioneer who became one of America's most popular radio entertainers during the 1920s and early 1930s, with his political comments and his basic common sense. His relaxed "aw shucks," down-home monologues, delivered in an easy to take, one-on-one style was tailor-made for radio. Oklahoma-born Rogers was a storyteller and had the type of personality that his listeners could identify with. On the air, Will talked about things that everyone had in common, including their dislike of power-hungry corrupt politicians. He was warmly welcomed during the dark days of America's Great Depression and his voice became America's conscience.

Rogers gave the impression he was just a simple, common, everyday kind of man, which was far from the truth. His "aw shucks" country style was his public persona. No way was Will Rogers common, but he had the gift of the common touch which appealed to America's listening audience. His down-home monologues were often delivered in a natural style, while he was twirling a lariat!

In his book, *Back in the Saddle Again*[3], *celebrated* cowboy star **Gene Autry** describes Rogers on-radio this way: "His wit struck sparks. It focused on the foibles of all of us, but especially politicians and the rich and famous. Whatever material Will needed came out of his own fertile mind." Listening to Rogers on radio was like eavesdropping on someone's private conversation. He felt Americans were skeptical of intellectuals, especially show-business types and truly believed the public likes to think great stars evolve from everyday people just like themselves: nice folks, who just happened to get lucky. Being on radio in the mid-1920s brought Rogers before an entire nation and made him a national celebrity and star. Will personified all that was good about America. He was the quintessential American and his loyalty to Uncle Sam came shining through every time he spoke before a mic. He took pride in his Cherokee heritage and seldom let his audience forget it.

Will Rogers, along with his pilot, Wiley Post, was killed in a plane crash in Alaska on Aug. 15, 1935. At the time of his death, at age fifty-six, Rogers was one of America's most beloved personalities. An entire nation mourned his passing.

Radio Pro Lesson learned: Will Rogers was well liked on-radio because *he was himself* on the air.

One phrase you will read again and again throughout this book is *be yourself on the radio*. Will Rogers spoke in simple language and talked about things his listeners could identify with, from politics to family squabbles; important things for future radio personalities to keep in mind.

Radio's First On-Air Pros

Roxy Rothafel and his gang began on radio in 1923. It was radio's first program broadcast live from a theater, originating first from the Capitol Theater, later the Roxy, and finally Radio City Music Hall. Roxy led the orchestra even though he couldn't read a lick of music. Evidently he had a feel for the beat, because he did fine leading his gang of musicians. Roxy's Gang continued on radio until 1935.

Helen Hahn was one of radio's first female announcer/hosts on WBAY in New York. Helen has competition as far as being radio's first female announcer from **Bertha Brainard**[4], who made regular appearances on WJZ's *Broadcasting Broadway* in 1921.

Graham McNamee, a native of Washington, DC, made his radio debut in 1923 and became one of radio's first and most popular personalities.

Long before George W. Trendle's masked *Lone Ranger* first rode his magnificent stallion, Silver, on radio's airwaves in January 1933, there was another masked man on radio! In 1923, ten years prior to the Ranger's radio debut, singer **Joseph M. White** wore a mask on WEAF Radio in New York. Interestingly, his mask was made from silver, *sterling silver*. Another thing both masked radio performers had in common: their contracts stated that whenever they appeared in public they had to wear a mask. Now, I don't know about you but wearing a sterling silver mask had to be a little uncomfortable, let alone cold, during those frigid Northeast winters!

Ed Wynn began on WJZ Radio in Newark, New Jersey[5], in 1922. He was the first entertainer to present a complete comedy program on radio. Wynn played the "perfect fool" in one of radio's first comedy efforts. Ten years later, for a reported salary of $5,000 a week, his *Fire Chief Show for Texaco* began on NBC. Interestingly, Wynn was terrified by the thought of being heard by millions of radio listeners and suffered from acute "mic fright." So, don't think you're the lone stranger when it comes to being shy around a mic; even some radio legends had to deal with the same malady. During one of his first broadcasts, Ed Wynn's voice trembled so much in fear that the word *soooo* came over the air as a high-pitched nervous cackle. Unaware of his nervousness, listeners loved it and thought it was part of his act. It was so well-received that Ed kept it in his act and the word "*soooo*" became one of radio's earliest catch-phrases.

Eddie Cantor, the little comic with the big bulging eyes, was one of the biggest stars of early radio. Eddie could do it all: sing, act, tell jokes and even dance on the air. In 1931, the great vaudeville entertainer moved to radio as star of NBC's *Chase and Sanborn Hour* on Sunday nights. Cantor is credited with introducing the live studio audience to radio. This major radio pro serves as a prime example to future radio stars of not being afraid of change. In 1949, with the coming of television and the face of network radio changing, Eddie became a DJ. A year later, he left radio for television. In 1952, Cantor suffered a heart attack. He never bounced back and passed away on October 10, 1964.

Kathryn Elizabeth Smith was a lovable lady with a big singing voice from Greenville, VA. She debuted on radio in 1929, and was heard continuously until the late '50s. She is best remembered for introducing the song "God Bless America" on her program on November 12, 1938. Read more about Kate Smith, one of America's greatest radio personalities, in Chapter 13.

Rudy Vallee was America's first pop singing star. He began making guest appearances on radio in 1928 and a year later starred on *The Fleischmann Yeast Hour*. It was one of network radio's first hour-long variety shows. It gave a number of future stars their first network exposure, including Fred Allen, Gene Autry, Jack Benny, Edgar Bergen, Milton Berle, Eddie Cantor, Alice

Faye, Red Skelton, Kate Smith, and many others. Rudy Vallee remained on radio until 1947. He was 84 when he passed away in 1986.

Vic and Sade were the Gooks, a family who lived on Virginia Avenue. They debuted on NBC's Blue Network on June 29, 1932, and occupied "the little house halfway up the next block" five times a week, first on NBC and later simulcast on both NBC and CBS until September 1944.

Singer **Vaughn de Leath**[6] was known as the original radio girl and is credited with being the first woman to sing on the air. As the legend goes, in January 1920, at age nineteen, she was invited to sing "The Old Folks at Home" in front of a phonograph horn in the original Lee De Forest lab. Dr. De Forest, no doubt intrigued that both their last names included the word *De*, said Ms De Leath's bluesy-sounding contralto voice was perfect for a radio mic. He knew what he was talking about, because a year later in 1921 she was present for the opening of WJZ. In 1931 she was crooning on CBS and in 1934, Vaughn De Leath hosted a popular morning show on WMCA in New York City.

Comedian **Al Pearce** and his gang joined the NBC Blue Network in 1933 and was a radio favorite for a decade.

Lum n' Abner, Chester Lauck and Norris Goff, opened their 'Jot 'em Down Store in Pine Ridge, Arkansas, in 1931 and had a long, successful run on radio (NBC, CBS & ABC) until May 1953.

In 1926, the Chicago-based vaudevillian team of Freeman Gosden and Charles Correll were doing a black face[7] act as Sam 'n' Henry on WGN radio. In March of 1928, they moved to competing station WMAQ, but were unable to obtain the rights to the names Sam and Henry. It was then that they gave birth to **Amos n' Andy.** Under their new names, the team lit up the faces and lives of millions of listeners during the difficult days of the Great Depression. Americans were left with little to be happy about and, for a little while every week, folks could escape the day-to-day realties of having little food and money by laughing along with the antics of Amos n' Andy. During the early 1930s, they were so popular that movie theater marquees stated the movie would promptly stop at 7pm, which was show-time for the boys. The theater would pipe in the broadcast, so the audience wouldn't miss the popular twosome. It was the only way movie houses could maintain an audience.

The main characters on the half-hour comedy program were centered around two African-American men, Amos Jones played by Freeman Gosden and Andy (Andrew H. Brown) voiced by Charles Correll, although Gosden and Correll were white. Their tremendous popularity wasn't based on whether the characters were black or white, red, green, brown or purple, but because radio listeners could identify and relate to their true-to-life adventures. Amos n' Andy was a classic example of real warmth and wit on the air. At the peak of their popularity, their listening audience was estimated to be more than

40 million, a record at the time. Amos n' Andy remained two of radio's most successful and popular personalities for over thirty years.

In the late '50s, when radio changed,[8] Amos n' Andy changed right along with it. They became two of the country's most famous and popular disc jockeys. Their nightly program on the CBS radio network, *The Amos n' Andy Music Hall*, featured the duo playing popular records of the day. In between songs they did short Amos n' Andy vignettes and sometimes guest stars like Frank Sinatra would stop by to chat. It was America's loss when Amos n' Andy called it quits and turned off their radio mics for the final time on November 25, 1960.

Future radio talent can take a lesson from two of radio's all-time most popular personalities, Amos n' Andy: Don't be afraid of change, and don't let your ego keep you from changing with the times. To change doesn't mean changing who you are on the air.

When admiring a radio personality's sound, whether it's talent from yesterday or today, don't be an exact copy! But, *borrowing* a little piece of their style and adapting it to your own air presentation is not only encouraged but strongly suggested. Quite often, the dreams of future radio personalities begin when inspired by a major talent.[9] In the case of this author, my inspiration at the tender age of eight, came from the *Lone Ranger's* radio announcer, Fred Foy.

Fred Foy[10] was one of the few announcers to step out of radio's past and successfully make the transition to television. For many years he was on staff at ABC in New York. From December 1969 through 1972, Fred was Dick Cavett's announcer on the talk master's late night show on ABC-TV. However, he is best remembered for his long association with radio's *Lone Ranger*. There was so much narration on the program that his voice was as familiar to millions of devoted listeners as the man who actually played the masked man, Brace Beemer. Folks who ran into Fred would often ask him to do the famous Lone Ranger opening. "As soon as they find out who I am, they ask, can you do it? I don't mind," replied the always affable Fred, "it's wonderful to be remembered!"

"*Return with us now to those thrilling days of yesteryear…from out of the past come the thundering hoof beats of the great horse Silver! The Lone Ranger rides again!!!*" (The Lone Ranger character is owned by Classic Media, Inc.)

There were other outstanding personalities from Radio's Golden Age who made their indelible imprint on me when I was growing up. **Arthur Godfrey and Don McNeill** were two! Since Don was on at nine and Arthur at ten (EST) while I was in school, I only caught their programs during vacation days or when I was home ill. Godfrey and McNeill were two of the best one-on-one communicators on the radio, which also made them superb on-air salesmen. As an air personality, you need to be a good sales person and *move* the client's product. Listening to them, I took in every word they said and hoped to be half as good as them one day on the radio. Later, in preparation for my own radio career, I readily borrowed some of their style.

From his first weekday show on the CBS radio network, April 30, 1945, until his final on-air farewell in 1972, Arthur Godfrey had an infallible effectiveness on the air. America's radio listeners accepted the Old Redhead, as he was affectionately called, as part of their own family. Partly it was his droll way with a song, as he often accompanied himself on the banjo, but it was his complete and total genuineness on the radio which people enjoyed. He was breezy and believable. What you heard is what you got with Godfrey, "the quintessential composite American," the kind of guy it's fun to share a few minutes of your time with over a cold beer. What made Arthur Godfrey one of radio's all-time great personalities can be traced to his decision to *be himself on the air*. Super advice for future radio stars.

Godfrey began on radio in 1929 on WFBR Baltimore. He was billed as Red Godfrey, the warbling banjoist. He even picked up his own sponsor, The Triangle Birdseed and Pet Shop, and was paid five dollars per show for playing his banjo and singing a few songs. In 1930 he became a staff announcer at WRC, the NBC Washington affiliate, but his transformation in radio took place in 1931, following his near-fatal car crash. The car he was driving hit a truck head-on, which broke numerous bones and placed him in a full body cast. Godfrey was immobilized for five months.[11] During his long months of rehabilitation and while lying in his hospital bed, he spent much of the time listening to the radio. It was the first time he realized how really intimate radio was. Radio became Arthur's friend and companion. He also came to the conclusion that much of the radio programming, especially the way commercials were presented, was garbage. He thought announcers and moderators sounded affected and drooled into the mic. Not that they were poor speakers, in fact, he thought many were actually pretty good, but instead of *talking* they were *reading*, and therefore convincing no one on what they were trying to sell. Their delivery, Godfrey believed, was ineffective because they tried to appeal to groups of people. Right then and there in his hospital bed, he made himself a promise, that when he returned to the air, he would do things differently. His air delivery would be directed to just one guy in the imaginary radio audience.[12] It would be like sitting down with an old friend, and shooting the bull.

After his release from the hospital, Arthur Godfrey returned to the air at WRC in the nation's capitol. He promptly put into play what he had thought about while recuperating from his accident; *one-on-one radio communication*. However, this personal on-air style[13] met with the strong disapproval of station management. Arthur's ad-libbed comments, particularly the negative ones that were usually directed at his sponsors, were strongly discouraged by his bosses, as you might imagine. He was his own person and kept doing radio his way. It eventually led to his split with NBC in 1933. Godfrey walked out in a huff, and later apologized, but was refused reinstatement.[14] He wasn't out of work very long. Another DC station, WJSV, later WTOP, the CBS affiliate, hired him. It was the beginning of a long, successful, and productive relationship with CBS that lasted for almost four decades.

Arthur Godfrey was extremely popular with his listeners because he was spontaneous on the air and projected an "I don't give a damn" attitude. Often times, he'd throw away a commercial script and begin ad-libbing and poking fun at his advertisers. Sponsors cringed, but his listeners loved it! He could get away with poking fun at his sponsors, because his listeners *bought* their products. His unique air style attracted tons of advertisers. He screened his prospective clients with a fine-toothed comb and was ever vigilant of his reputation for telling it like it is. No sponsor made it on his show without his approval. Godfrey could afford to be choosy: his daily network radio show was sold out with a long waiting list of sponsors. The man moved merchandise! With a lazy-voiced warmth and easygoing approach that immediately put you at ease, he sold boatloads of Lipton tea and soup. It was like listening to a life-long friend. Radio listeners across America believed and trusted in what Arthur Godfrey was *saying* and *selling*.

At one point, his weekly family of listeners was estimated to be over 40 million. Godfrey had his finger on the pulse of what was happening in the world and when asked was never shy about offering his opinion. In a January 1957 interview, five years before the Vietnam War, and forty-five years before the death and destruction of 9/11, Arthur Godfrey was asked what kind of world he hoped the future would bring for America's children. "The kind of world where we have eliminated the constant threat of war. I think we can do it by being so powerful that no one will attack us. You know," Godfrey continued, "it's going to take only one plane and one bomb to blow up a whole city. And the enemy can get through despite radar and fighter planes." Godfrey, a one-time pilot, added, "During WWII, no American bombing mission was ever stopped short of its target by enemy action. So, let's face it, if we can do it, so can the enemy. The answer is to be ready to knock out any enemy the moment war is declared. We must sit back here like a cocked pistol and scare anyone from fighting us."

During a 1950s interview with *Radio/TV Mirror Magazine*, Godfrey was asked what advice he had for those interested in an on-air career. "You've got to have character, above and beyond talent," he repeated, "you've got to have character. Radio brings people just as close as your next door neighbor. You need to think about talking to them. Not to a mass, but just one or two. Your listeners will get to know you intimately, and you'd better grow on them! Your personality develops by improving your character." When asked how a future radio personality develops their character, Godfrey replied, "You've got to do things like study, travel, play sports, but stay away from *joints*." Since the pioneer radio pro's comments were made in the 1950s, it's a safe bet that when referring to "joints," he was describing a word that identified unsavory barrooms, and liquid libation, and not today's accepted meaning of the word. Although, both types of joints are probably well worth staying away from!

Arthur Godfrey was the best salesman on radio. At the peak of his popularity, he was the single most valuable commodity at CBS Radio. He brought home the bacon to the tune of 12% of the network's total advertising revenue. Arthur Godfrey's salary soared and he was fond of saying he made $400,000 before the average man started his workday. He worked hard, and his weekly radio duties alone, not including his TV shows, placed him directly in front of a CBS mic for 17½ hours! Arthur Godfrey was one of the few stars of radio's Golden Age to successfully make the transition to television. He hosted several top-rated TV shows, including *Arthur Godfrey's Talent Scouts* from 1946 until 1954. During this time, he continued his daily network radio show until he pulled the plug on himself on April 30, 1972. It was an emotional farewell—twenty-seven years to the day after his program began on CBS Radio. Later in his life, Godfrey contracted lung cancer and devoted most of his time to that fight, along with a new cause as an ecologist and conservationist. He made a comeback of sorts in the early '70s doing info commercials for Axiom, a Procter & Gamble laundry product. Still conscious of his reputation for being a tell-it-like-it-is guy, when he learned from congressional hearings that Axiom had as much polluting power as washing power, he publicly rebuked it and stopped pitching the product, saying, "How can I preach ecology and sell this stuff?" His broadcasting career over, Arthur Godfrey retired to his Virginia farm. The king of all on-air salesmen and one of broadcasting's first personalities passed away in 1983.

Radio's good neighbor and the power of a true radio personality

Don McNeill exemplified what Arthur Godfrey had developed to perfection; the art of speaking to *just one person* when on the radio. McNeill's on-air style was as smooth as butter, especially when it came to delivering a word or two from his many commercial sponsors. McNeill's popularity with America's radio listeners took off when he became host of ABC's *The Breakfast Club* on June 23, 1933.

The show became one of network radio's longest running and most successful programs and took pride in being corny and folksy. His greatest appeal and charm was the fact he made no bones about being just a country boy at heart. In 1952, and at the height of his popularity, in an interview with *Radio/TV Mirror* magazine, McNeill described how he approached his early morning radio show. His words spoken over fifty years ago still serve as good advice for today's radio personalities and future radio stars: "Our show, The Breakfast Club, belongs to the listener as well as to us, and I want you to know what I'm thinking about when we go on the air. I visualize one person getting up in the morning and he's got problems. Maybe the mortgage is due, his wife is sick, or his kid is flunking Latin. This guy, listening to our show doesn't feel so good and if we can coax him into his first smile of the day, then we've done a good show. We try to touch his emotions."

Radio Pro lesson: Radio is emotional. Reach out and touch your listeners and they'll respond.

Growing up in Portland, Maine, in the 1950s meant plenty of snowy no-school days. It was during those snow-bound days that I got to listen to Don McNeill. I learned many things about how to become a radio personality by listening to him. Years later, when pursuing my own radio career, I applied what I heard him say and do to my own style and it seemed to work for me. They may well work for you, too! Here they are!

- I learned that it's OK to have fun on the air, but not in a mean way, and to have a little class
- I learned that to have a successful radio show, you need others to contribute
- I learned not to be self-righteous and that being humble and a little self-effacing can be a good thing
- I learned to interview well, you have to really listen and respond to what your guest is saying
- I learned how to play off a live studio audience by studying his ability to get folks to open up to him
- I learned the importance of being warm and fuzzy on the radio and of being one's self
- I learned to be honest and respectful of the listener to be sensitive to them, to treat them as family and never take them for granted
- I learned it's okay to be a little corny and silly, but also when to be serious and sensitive
- I learned how to effectively sell a commercial and the importance of making a sponsor smile
- I learned the importance of one-on-one communication

A radio wannabe like me learned so many things from listening to Don McNeill,[15] including the innate goodness of people. I enjoyed the letters and poems sent in from his listening family, which he shared on-air. Many were funny, while others sad, some uplifting, but each was based on true-life incidents. I mention elsewhere in this book that a particularly moving moment for me as a boy, home from school and sick with the flu, was when Don would reverently ask members of his live studio audience and those listening at home or at work to take time out for a moment of silent prayer. His words are forever etched in my mind: *"Each in his own words, each in his own way, for a free world united in peace, let us bow our heads and pray. Amen."*

Wouldn't it be nice to hear those poignant words spoken on radio today? It's sad to think that a country founded on Judeo-Christian principals has all but lost its way when it comes to moral and religious values. Evidently, many of today's air personalities don't believe it's fashionable to mention God on their shows, or, heaven forbid, asking for a helping hand from one's creator.

It seems light years ago that another popular radio and television personality, **Red Skelton**, would close his television program, by saying, "God Bless." Can you even imagine a radio or TV personality in today's culture closing their show by praising the Lord! Wait! Hold on! Come to think of it, there is one television personality who signs off his weekend program on Fox with "God Bless." Kudos to Mike Huckabee. Now, if only a few radio personalities would follow suit, I'm sure our creator would be most appreciative. Apparently, many of today's broadcasters believe any reference to the Lord was something done on the air way back when and just wouldn't be hip or cool in today's modern world. Isn't it funny how it seemed to work so well for Don McNeill on radio and for thirty-five years! I guess more than a few listeners apparently found it appropriate and enjoyed it.

Don McNeill's moment of silent prayer and memory time segment were some of the finest moments on his long-running program. It was also fun when he would speak with a member of his studio audience, live on the air and totally unrehearsed. After leaving radio, McNeill explained why he loved the live mic so much. "Some folks in radio point out to me that by inviting unknown and uncoached guests to our ABC microphone was taking an awful chance. These other broadcasters," he added, "preferred recording and editing their stuff before the broadcast, but I liked risking it live."

Following his final broadcast, December 27, 1968, and after 35 years on network radio, McNeill taught a broadcast news workshop at Marquette University.[16] One day in class, he was asked by a student for his opinion on program censorship and what was *in* good taste on the air. "Good taste," he responded, "should be the ruling factor. I was my own censor on the *Breakfast Club*. I'd cut things if I thought they were in bad taste." As to radio's future, McNeill replied, "Broadcasting is one business where you can defeat the computer. You can't computerize personality, warmth or charisma."

Don McNeill, or "Papa" as he was affectionately known to his grandkids and great grandchildren, passed away in 1996. One of pioneer radio's first real on-air radio pros was 89.

Arthur Godfrey and **Don McNeill** were true radio legends and real radio personalities. Listening to them was not only a lesson in how to do personality radio, but how to do it the right way! Both Godfrey and McNeill had a few things in common. Each had his own morning show on network radio that enjoyed a long, successful run. Godfrey was on CBS for twenty-seven years and McNeill was on ABC for an incredible thirty-five years. On radio, they both displayed their own special brand of sincerity and down home folksiness. Godfrey, born in New York City on Amsterdam Avenue and 112th Street and raised in Hasbrouck Heights, New Jersey, was a bit on the brash side on the air, with an almost biting humor. Arthur loved poking fun at his sponsors. Don was a Midwesterner from Galena, Illinois, and displayed a more laidback but mischievous style, which I like to refer to as "frisky friendly down-home style." Both McNeill and Godfrey each had a spontaneous wit and irascible side to their personalities which made them unpredictable and fun to listen to.

Godfrey and McNeill also had another important quality which made them invaluable commodities and contributed much to their long and successful careers as real radio pros. They were gifted with a warm, natural way of selling their sponsors' products. Whether Arthur was endorsing the rich, full-body taste of Lipton tea, or Don was enthusiastically chatting about the juicy, goodness of Swift's premium bacon, which you could almost hear and see sizzlin' away in your frying pan, both radio personalities were superb on-air salesmen.

Radio Pro lesson learned: A good way to insure your own radio longevity and marketability as an air-talent is to first and foremost *learn how to sell a commercial*!

John F. Sullivan was another of broadcasting's first real radio pros. His name must have sounded more fitting for a pro boxer than a radio pro, so he changed it to **Fred Allen**. The future radio star was born in Cambridge, right across the majestic Charles River from Boston, MA, on May 31, 1894. As a youngster, Allen worked in the Boston Public Library, earning twenty cents an hour as a librarian's aide. It's where he developed his love of literature. He read everything he could get his hands on!

At thirty-eight, Fred Allen eventually entered radio through vaudeville's door, as an outrageous social commentator. He came equipped with a flat, nasal-sounding twang uniquely his own, along with an intelligent wit which made him one of radio's biggest and brightest stars. He wasn't a town clown, but his whining voice seemed tailor-made for radio and earned him a thousand dollars a week, which included salaries for his supporting cast. His topical wit was second to none. He could be flip, witty and caustic all at the same time. He was anti-establishment and strongly disliked show business and everyone associated with it.

Interestingly, even though Fred Allen became one of radio's most popular comedians, there was a time when he almost didn't make the grade. After auditioning Allen in 1929, a CBS executive said, "He'll never make it on radio." At the time, some radio suits felt Fred Allen came across as too bizarre and too savvy for the down-home, all-American radio listener. He proved them all wrong in 1934, when he landed his own radio show. Originally called *The Hour of Smiles*, it was later retitled *Town Hall Tonight*, and finally, *The Fred Allen Show*.

Take note, future shock jocks and Howard Stern wannabes: During radio's formative years, nobody on the air battled the censors and powers-that-be more than Fred Allen. In today's anything-goes air presentation, Allen's comedic lines seem tame and mild, but in the '30s and '40s, network censors held a tight leash on him. They knew his reputation for pointed satire and watched him closely; any sexual innuendo was fatal! Allen often complained that each week fifty percent of his material wound up in the toilet. He felt the censors looked at everything as taboo! Even though he was watch-dogged by censors, Fred Allen managed to get away with more than most other radio personalities of the day. He also pushed the envelope more than the others did, too. Fred took pride in his reputation for being a rebel and enjoyed making the network censors squirm. On his broadcast of April 20, 1947, he was cut off the air for about 30 seconds for saying something derogatory about NBC. Later, as a guest on Jack Benny's show, and in typical Fred Allen candor, he referred to the incident by saying, "NBC that big-hearted organization gave me those 25 seconds as a vacation."

Fred Allen came from the same school as many popular comedians of the day, Ed Wynn, Joe Penner, Jack Pearl, Bob Burns and others, but Allen's comedic routine was the most literate on radio. Allen's bits on radio were filled with wild metaphors and similes, which he often applied to the latest news headlines. A regular feature of Fred Allen's program was Allen's Alley. Half the fun of Allen's Alley was his weekly stroll down his imaginary street and knocking at doors, usually finding one of his cast of characters at home. The feature was really just another opportunity for Fred to bounce news-of-the-day topics off members of his cast.

Pay attention, radio talent, especially morning show hosts, who whine they need help with someone to write their material. Even though Allen had three writers, he wrote 90% of what was heard on his weekly radio program. No one knows you better, or can write better material for you than *you*! The comedian vacationed every summer at Old Orchard Beach, Maine, where he wrote jokes and prepared future radio scripts. He once said, "The town was so dull, the tide went out and never came back." Because Fred Allen worked so hard, burnout was inevitable. It was only a matter of time before the wear and tear began to show on him. As sometimes is the case with the biggest of the big, his show became predictable.

In the late forties, the one constant about radio, change, which is mentioned so often in this book, was taking hold again. A new kid on the radio block, *Stop the Music* on ABC, became the final nail in Fred's coffin. The new program offered listeners a chance at winning big money, and by comparison Allen's show seemed old. Even though he offered a $5,000 bond to anyone who was called by *Stop the Music* while listening to his program, his ratings continued to drop. The ratings plummeted, dropping from a high of a 28-share of the listening audience to less than half that, while *Stop the Music* zoomed from zero to a 20-share in a matter of months. Allen's sagging ratings began to toll the death knell for his show. His last radio show aired on June 26, 1949, on NBC, almost eighteen years after cracking the mic with his first comedic line.

Fred Allen [17] passed away on St. Patrick's Eve 1956, while taking one of his nightly strolls - no, not down Allen's Alley, but up 57th Street in New York City. Radio's one-time comedic genius was 62.

Jack Benny was another of radio's *first* real on-air pros and a friend and contemporary of Fred Allen. Born on Valentine's Day, 1894, in Chicago and raised in nearby Waukegan, Benjamin Kubelsky would shorten his first name to Benny, combine it with Jack, and with his stage name, Jack Benny found plenty of radio fame! The Jack Benny radio program premiered on NBC's Blue Network [18] on May 2, 1932, and was a smash hit. In 1934, his show was sponsored by Jell-O and moved to 7pm on Sunday nights, a time slot he would own for the remainder of his program's long run, first on NBC and later on CBS. [19]

For more than twenty years, Jack Benny was one of radio's most successful and popular comedians. By his own admonition, he wasn't the wittiest person to step in front of a mic and his dependence on his writers was well known, but Jack understood something special about radio comedy, and that was timing. It proved to be one of his strongest attributes. Benny also had a real sense for what was funny and he could deliver a funny line better than anyone else in the business.

Jack Benny was tremendously popular on radio because he accurately perceived radio as an informal setting where America's families gathered together to listen to his radio family. Jack made it a point to play directly to those folks. In this way, the listener got to know and relate to Jack's radio family, and could identify with the same situations in their lives that he faced every week on radio.

Benny's longtime friend and fellow comedian George Burns described how Jack changed radio. "He did something no other comedian had ever done before," said Burns, "he eliminated most of the jokes." Jack depended on everyday situations that came up in life, perhaps, exaggerated a little bit, but nevertheless incidents that could happen to anyone and his listeners could identify with.

Radio Pro lesson: know your audience and key demographics and play to them!

Comedian **Fred Allen** was another of Jack Benny's friends and a pretend on-air archenemy. Fred loved Jack and credited Benny with leading the way for future radio and television situation comedies. "Practically all comedy shows on radio and later television owe their structure to Jack's conceptions," said Allen, "he was the first radio personality to realize that the listener is not in a theater with a thousand other people. When they tune in to Jack Benny, it's like tuning in to somebody else's house." Benny was also the first comedian on radio to realize you could get huge laughs by ridiculing yourself instead of your cast mates. Jack Benny became a leader and master at utilizing self-deprecating humor.

Another early radio star**, Steve Allen**, also attributed Jack Benny's success to timing. In the entertaining and informative book *Raised on the Radio* author Gerald Nachman[20] quotes Allen on Benny's success: "A split second delay here, a word there, can cause a joke to misfire. Jack Benny never missed! Sure footed as a cat, he walked confidently through a monologue or a sketch, feeling his way with the delicate sensibility of the true craftsman that he was! He instinctively sensed the right moment to speak, and when was the most advantageous time to remain silent, and allow his audience the all important needed time to react."

Future radio wannabes can learn so much from one of radio's first on-air pros, Jack Benny. He was generous in every way to members of his show. He paid them well and let them contribute their ideas and welcomed their input. If on rare occasion he would lose his cool, he was quick to apologize - a rarity amongst major stars in any form of the entertainment field.

After twenty-three straight years on radio, **Jack Benny** left the air on May 22, 1955, but his show continued on the air in re-runs until 1958. Jack's longtime writer Milt Josefberg is quoted as saying, "For years, the Jack Benny Show was one of the few constants a listener could depend on in the ever-changing world of radio." Benny was one of the few radio stars to make the transition to television, but it wasn't easy. He never appeared to be completely comfortable on the tube. When asked to compare radio to television, Benny replied, "There was a time when Americans were emotionally involved with their radio personalities. I came at them gently, quietly through their ears. Television never made that kind of direct emotional impact." These insightful words from one of America's first radio pros, Jack Benny, who passed away from cancer on December 26, 1974.

Canadian-born Arthur Kelly, aka **Art Linkletter** moved to California and first broke into radio in 1933 as a staff announcer on KGB San Diego. Linkletter's big network radio break came when he made an audition recording for producer John Guedel and his show, *People Are Funny*. Art got the gig and his network radio, and later television, career was underway! He was quick on his feet with an off-the-cuff remark, which made him a perfect emcee. By the time he was handed the reins on April 3, 1942, as host of *People Are Funny* [21] on NBC, the smooth-talking radio pro was ready to go! His easygoing on-air style made him a natural to calm down nervous contestants on the popular show, which he hosted for seventeen years until its final broadcast in 1959. It was top-rated for more than eleven of those years. The TV version debuted in 1954 and ran until 1961.

Linkletter's other popular show, *House Party,* began airing weekday afternoons on CBS Radio in 1945, and moved to television in 1952. The two-time Emmy-winning program aired on CBS radio and TV for 25 years giving claim to being one of the longest-running daytime variety shows, all while staying with the same sponsor, General Electric. Art Linkletter was not only one of radio's first on-air pros, but one of the best ad-lib people in the business! A favorite feature of *House Party* was a kids corner segment, *Kids Say the Darndest Things.* Art interviewed five children between the ages of five and ten, and he possessed an amazing talent when it came to chatting with kids. You can read more about Linkletter's gift of talking with kids in interviews in Chapter Eight, which is dedicated to him, the "Art" of interviewing. Art Linkletter's show-business career lasted for over 60 years! And, by the way, for you future radio people and seasoned pros alike, who wonder and worry about contracts and such things, take note from one of radio's pioneer broadcasters. For twenty-six years on CBS radio and television, over a half-century's partnership, Art Linkletter never had a contract! Year after year, he and the network would agree to just keep on going.

George Burns (Nathan Birnbaum) and Gracie Allen, who were married in real life, were among the many vaudevillians who attained great success on the radio. They also helped lead the way for today's radio teams. In 1942, they appeared on the radio as a married couple and their program moved from being filled with stand-up comedy and bits to a full-fledged situation comedy. If you want a great lesson in how to interact as the straight man on your radio show with your off-the-wall partner, pick up a few of George & Gracie's old radio shows, along with a DVD from their TV shows. Their routines may be dated, but listen and observe their natural wit and timing. George was the straight man for funny girl Gracie, who was gifted with a natural sense of humor. On the air, when his patience was exhausted by Gracie's ditsy, scatterbrained-but-innocent double talk, illogical statements, and malapropisms, an exasperated George would always end with, "*Say goodnight, Gracie,*" which she would obligingly do complete with a cute, warm smile.

Burns and Allen first aired on CBS in 1932, but over the years they jumped back and forth between NBC and CBS. In October 1950, George and Gracie made the move to television where they remained on the air until 1958. Gracie passed away in 1964 at age 60. George, at 78, found success as a film star in hits such as *Oh, God!* In 1976, he won an Academy Award for his performance in *The Sunshine Boys.* On March 9, 1996, two months following his 100th birthday on January 20, and just when we believed he had found the fountain of youth and would be with us forever, George Burns, who played God so well in the movies, left us to meet the real God … face to face.

Another of network radio's earliest husband and wife teams were **Jim and Marian Jordan,** who for 21 years as **Fibber McGee & Molly** lived at their mythical radio address 79 Wistful Vista. A mainstay of their program, which used sound effects to the fullest, was the running bit of McGee's cluttered front hall closet. Radio listeners knew instinctively by the mere mention of McGee opening the front door to the closet that what was about to happen next was the sound of a mighty crash! In reality the sound effects men simply dropped pots and pans on the floor, but to the listener it was Fibber opening his closet door and a ton of items falling out around him. He usually would comment in a low voice, "One of these days, I've got to get around to cleaning out that closet!" The predictable "routine" was masterful in its use of sound effects on the air and it became one of radio's most recognizable bits. Their popular weekly half-hour comedy series began on NBC in 1935 and ended as a fifteen-minute feature in 1956 on NBC's weekend program service, *Monitor*.

Jim and Marian knew their roles[22] and played them well. Jim as Fibber McGee was a stumbling, bumbling boob of a lovable hubby, a teller of tall tales who was always dreaming up ridiculous "get rich quick" schemes. Molly was his sweet, devoted wife, who loved McGee even with all his human frailties. However, when totally exasperated with his antics, Molly would cry out one of the show's more familiar catchphrases, "Heavenly days, dearie" or "'T'ain't funny, McGee." The McGee's home-style humor had the charm of believability, because their on-air roles reflected who they were in everyday life; unassuming nice folks that you wished were your neighbors. Marian passed away in 1961, at age 63. Jim lived until age 91 and died in 1988.

Growing up, **Gene Autry** was my favorite cowboy star. I was no doubt influenced by my dad, Marty, who loved listening to Gene on radio. When it was *Melody Ranch* time, Dad would grab his harmonica and accompany Gene on a few tunes. Dad's favorite was "Red River Valley." No one played back up for Mr. Autry with more enthusiasm than my dad!

Gene Autry's *Melody Ranch* show enjoyed one of the longest runs on radio. It debuted on January 7, 1940, and ran for sixteen years, [23] with its final broadcast on May 13, 1956. Gene was always on the same network, CBS, and always on for the same sponsor, Wrigley's Doublemint gum.

Gene Autry also holds the distinction of being the only performer to have *five stars* on the Hollywood Walk of Fame, for live performance, motion pictures, radio, recording, and television. Gene's rags-to-riches story is enough to inspire anyone to keep reaching for the stars, although his rise to stardom was not without its share of disappointments. His desire to escape the poverty he knew as a child drove him on. His tenacity and determination to make it as an entertainer should serve as a shining example to those of you who desire to be air-talent, for Gene first made his mark as an entertainer on radio. When his motion picture and television career was over, and Gene rode off into the sunset for the final time on his horse, Champion, the cowboy star moved back to broadcasting. As the head of Golden West Broadcasters, Gene owned numerous radio and television stations. On October 2, 1998, Gene's wife, Jackie, turned 57, the same day her loving husband passed away in his sleep at their home in Studio City, California. The cowboy boss man was 91.

Martin Block was the first big-time disc spinner, or disc jockey, [24] on American radio. He will always be remembered as the King of all DJs. Martin began hosting his imaginary, make-believe music ballroom show in 1934 on WNEW-1130 AM in New York City. The program continued well into the 1950s, when Block retired and was replaced by future Gotham radio legend, Joe Franklin.[25]

In the 1930s, when Block moved from California to New York City, there were plenty of radio personalities, but he was the first to pretend big bands were live in his crystal studio in his make-believe ballroom. Listeners could actually envision people gathered around the bandstand, as Martin painted an incredible mental picture of the sights and sounds of the bands and their music. He also possessed incredible power on the air. He could make or break a record, and the giants of the music industry would do almost anything to appear on his show or to have their records played on it.

During the 1940s and '50s, and probably even before, it was not uncommon for record label promoters to give DJs lots of goodies in exchange for having their records played on the radio. The practice was known as "plugola." In many major cities, like Chicago and Detroit, popular disc jockeys were often sought out to receive gifts for playing certain records on their shows. This is not meant to point an accusatory finger at Martin Block or any other radio personalities from that era that played records on their shows. It is intended *only* to show that plugging a song on the radio for the right price was a commonplace and accepted practice. Whether it was cash or other exotic forms of payment, freebies were readily offered and accepted by DJs in exchange for having a record aired. Some popular DJs were often made part-owners in record companies, in hopes of receiving continuous on-air plugging of the company's product. One record company admitted it had twenty-five local disc jockeys on a regular monthly payroll, ranging from $25 to $200 each. In 1960, the U.S. Government's Congressional hearings into the practice and subsequent payola scandals supposedly put an end to plugola.

Martin Block was on the radio twice a day, mornings and nights. He was the only air-personality in New York City to be on two shows on two different stations at the same time. He would pre-record [26] his *Make-Believe Ballroom* show on WNEW and then zip across town to announce the WNBC's *Chesterfield Supper Club* starring Perry Como and Jo Stafford. As host of *Make Believe Ballroom* [27] Martin Block will always be remembered as one of America's first DJs and radio pros, but his road to success was not an easy ride. In his early on-air days with his Ballroom show, recording companies and performers were dead-set against the airing of what they called "unfair competition." They were upset that radio personalities like Block were playing records on the radio instead of featuring live talent. Eventually, as time passed and the record companies showed huge profits from having their artists' records played on the radio, record company execs became convinced that recorded music programs such as Martin Block's actually gave the troubled record companies a much-needed shot in the arm. Instead of hurting music talent, disc jockeys like Martin Block helped increase the popularity of the performers by playing their records on the air.

Martin Block and other radio personalities and announcers from Radio's Golden Age were gifted masters at ad-libbing. By listening to them, we radio wannabes learned the correct way to "sell" a commercial with warmth and sincerity, how to conduct interviews, and most importantly, how to ad-lib and shoot the breeze on the radio with the greatest of ease. Listening to the work of these radio pioneers is an education unto itself.

Authors note: I highly suggest locating their work in the Museum of Broadcasting or elsewhere and listening to these broadcast pioneers. It is truly an education unto itself.

Popular bandleader **Paul Whiteman** first began on radio in 1927 and over the course of a twenty-five-year career hosted a variety of music shows. Among his many radio programs, he played DJ! In 1947, Paul Whiteman became a radio disc jockey for the ABC Radio network. As previously stated, Martin Block was one of the first DJs to play records on the radio, [28] but his show was local while Paul Whiteman became the first radio personality to play records on a national radio network. Up until that time, no air personality had played recorded music on a radio network, as everything was done live, including the orchestra. Whiteman's record show was broadcast coast-to-coast every weekday afternoon from 3:30 to 4:30pm and was a huge success, making millions for the ABC Radio network.

Morning drive radio teams are nothing new! Breakfast chatter on the radio, especially with hubby-and-wife teams, goes back to pre-World War II days.

Frank Crumit and Julia Sanderson may lay claim to having been radio's first husband-and-wife team to find success and stardom. The couple first appeared on CBS Radio in 1929, sponsored by Blackstone cigars. They remained a popular radio twosome for more than ten years. And, a special note for today's radio talent who play the popular game "Battle of the Sexes" with their listeners: the next time you play the game, you may want to pause for a moment and give thanks to Frank and Julia Crumit; they launched radio's first version of "Battle of the Sexes" back in the 1940s. ***Breakfast with Binnie & Mike*** was a half-hour daily morning talk show in the late 40s. Their show, hosted by film star Binnie Barnes and her husband, movie producer and sports announcer Mike Frankovitch, was broadcast from their Beverly Hills home. Their children, two birds, family dog, maid and whoever else stopped by for a cup of Joe joined in the conversation about anything and everything.

Ed and Pegeen Fitzgerald began their morning gab-fest in 1940 on New York City's WOR. One cool thing about their morning show is that it was broadcast from their apartment on East 36th Street. The Fitzgeralds did not use a script. They let their talk flow naturally, which is solid advice for all radio talk masters. Whatever was on their mind was fair game: news stories from the morning headlines, listener mail, whatever. Like most husbands, Ed was on the cranky side and quite often acerbic, while Pegeen was blessed with loving patience. The format was not unlike many of today's morning shows, only with one major difference: Ed liked to review books. Pegeen loved to chat about beauty and gave fashion tips, which only proves that some things women enjoy hearing and talking about never change. Don't misunderstand; Pegeen was by no means a fluff-type personality. She was bright and hip. It was her idea to do an intimate conversational show with her hubby from their home. By 1945, Ed and Pegeen were big business on the radio and in high demand. They left WOR in 1945 and moved across town to WJZ, then the ABC outlet.

Dorothy Kilgallen and her husband, actor **Richard Kollmar,** [29] replaced the Fitzgeralds and Dorothy and Dick became rivals and competitors for Ed and Pegeen. WOR's *Breakfast with Dorothy and Dick* was broadcast live from their own New York apartment. Talk about a big difference in on-air styles! The Fitzgeralds were down-to-earth, pleasant folks who often got into heated debates on their show. They were a far cry from the prim and proper Dorothy and Dick.

The popularity of both hubby and wife teams on New York City's airwaves led to a third morning team, **Tex McCrary** and his wife, **Jinx Falkenburg.** [30] Jinx was born in Spain and moved to California with her family while in her teens. She later became a Powers model and actress. Tex, a columnist, had an easy Southern drawl and gentlemanly manners. When coupled with wife Jinx's beauty and intelligence, they made an appealing combination on radio for years. Their good looks certainly didn't hurt when they made a successful transition to television in the mid-1950s, where they remained huge favorites until the early 1960s.

If you were to select a radio pioneer to serve as the model for today's radio shock jocks it would have to be **Bob** (color his middle name blue, as in humor) **Hope!** Born in England on May 29, 1903, Leslie Townes Hope was known as a dirty jokester, probably because with just the right inflection and insinuation, he could completely change the meaning of even a few proper words. Hope, known as America's most infamously nasty radio comic, was repeatedly censored by NBC for punch lines deemed "unacceptable" for the air, even though in listening to some of his broadcasts from the 1940s and '50s, his risqué content seems tame by today's so-called standards. It was Hope's delivery and wisecracking set-ups that established his naughty persona. Bob was an expert at double meanings and went for the line with a vengeance! The audience always seem to sense when "naughty Bobby" was about to unload one of his "nasty" lines.

On one of Bob Hope's radio shows, the exchange between Hope and his guest Dorothy Lamour, the original sarong girl, really heated up the airwaves… and the NBC switchboard! In the script, Lamour said, "I'll meet you in front of the pawnshop." After slowly answering, "Okay," Bob paused just long enough to prepare the audience and then added with his boyish grin, "and you can kiss me under the balls." The audience roared with laughter while NBC censors reached for both the mic kill switch and the Alka-Seltzer. On another show, while cozying up to a leggy blonde, Hope suggested with a devilish and salacious tone, "Why don't we go over to my place and play television?" "How do you do that," she coyly asked. "Well," Bob said, grinning broadly, "I'll turn your knobs while you watch my antenna rise!" With lines like that and on live radio, Hope constantly risked being cut off the air, and he often was!

Sixty years ago this type of humor was not only deemed to be in "bad taste," but also unacceptable for broadcast. Today, these Bob Hope one-liners and jokes seem almost innocent and mild given today's permissive society. It's just another example of how our lower standards have completely changed America's view of what is perceived to be in "good" taste and acceptable on radio and television. Bob Hope had one of the longest-running programs on radio, beginning in 1938 and continuing for 18 years until 1955, all on NBC. Hope also had a successful run on television for many years.

Bob Hope's buddy **Bing Crosby** loved radio! No one sounded more at home in front of a mic than Bing. Whether chatting informally in his folksy, neighborly manner or by singing in his laidback Crosby style, Bing had the gift of knowing how to communicate on a one-on-one [31] basis with the listener. In the words of another radio legend and pro, Eddie Cantor, "Bing treated radio as if it were an instrument of introduction to your living room."

On the air, Bing did what he did best, *he was himself.* You will read these words over and over again in this book: to be successful on the radio, *be yourself.* Bing loved radio because he didn't have to worry about how he looked, dressed or camera angles. It's one reason why he stayed away from television for so long. He loved the anonymity that radio provided.

Bing Crosby was first heard on CBS radio on September 2, 1931, on his own fifteen-minute program. Thanks to his nationwide radio hook-up, he rose to instant stardom. Crosby's big move in radio took place in 1935, when he left CBS to join rival network NBC as host of the hour-long variety program *The Kraft Music Hall*. The program was tailor-made for Bing's easygoing, casual style. His listeners [32] liked what they heard and his weekly Thursday night radio show was always at the top of the Hooper audience ratings. Bing stayed with Kraft for ten years.

In 1946, Bing, wanting more "free time" for golf and other aspects of life and not being tied down to a fixed weekly time on radio, wanted to tape his show. His sponsor, Kraft, the advertising agency and the network, NBC, feared the program would sound "canned." When Bing insisted, they said no, and he quit. Kraft brought back the original host of the *Music Hall*, Al Jolson. Bing never missed a beat, and moved over to the ABC radio network with his new sponsor, Philco. Switching from live to discs, [33] and later tape, wasn't strictly to free El Bingo up from being at the studio at a "fixed" time for a "live" broadcast. Hardly. You see, Crosby had a vested interest in a new invention called audio tape and a little company called the Ampex Corporation. Ampex developed tape technology from German magnetic recordings found after World War II. Before tape, transcription discs or wire recorders were the only thing available for recording programming. It was virtually impossible to edit either, but with tape you could easily edit out mistakes or flubs or cut a program's content if it ran over-time.

Philco Radio Time with Bing Crosby became the first major network radio show in the history of broadcasting to be transcribed. As strange as it may sound in today's hi-tech world, back in the fall of 1946 many were apprehensive about whether or not it would work. Skeptics in the industry felt that the radio audience wouldn't buy a pre-recorded show. Crosby believed the public couldn't care less either way. By pre-recording his program, Bing, under the direction of Bill Morrow and Murdo MacKenzie, could edit out flubs and portions that didn't feel right and produce a smooth half-hour show the listener would enjoy. Another big advantage of taping a show was that rehearsals and recording sessions could be scheduled around the convenience of everyone involved. To calm down the nervous radio types, a clause was inserted in Bing's contract that stated if his Hooper rating fell below a 12-share of the audience for any four consecutive weeks, he would immediately revert back to live shows.

On October 16, 1946, *Philco Radio Time*, no doubt helped by Bing's opening-night guest, Bob Hope, placed in the ratings' top ten. However, following a number of lesser-known guests, Bing's ratings began to drop and by the end of his first month on the air for Philco, his Hooper rating had dropped to 12.2. Radio rumors began rumbling that Bing would be back live, and soon. But, as radio luck would have it, his ratings stayed steady at around a 12-share as more attention was given to scheduling guests. Bing Crosby's program wrapped up the year with a decent 16 share of the audience. Bing and audio tape proved to be big winners and set the standard for radio's future with the use of audio tape.

The Bing Crosby show aired on ABC every Wednesday until June 1, 1949, then moved to CBS for Chesterfield's, also on Wednesday nights, from 1949 through 1952. GE climbed on board in 1952 as Bing's sponsor and his program moved to Thursday nights. In 1953, Bing sang on the radio on Sundays, and in 1954, his show went into a daily fifteen-minute format, airing until 1956. A syndicated version of the Crosby show aired on radio from the late 1950s until the early 1960s.

It has been said by some industry insiders that off the air Bing was shy, aloof and hard to get to know. Whether that's true or not is left to conjecture by others, but one thing is known to be fact: On the radio, Bing Crosby was the consummate perfectionist and a real radio pro. The crooner from Tacoma, Washington, will always be remembered as one of America's outstanding entertainers. Broadcasting, and specifically radio, which he loved, would serve his memory well not only by saluting him as a great air personality, but also for his contribution to the technical side of the industry. Bing Crosby became the first major radio star to record his program and, by doing so, advanced the industry light years by using audio tape.

As a native Mainer who spent 15 years of his broadcasting career in Maine and another 20 in Boston, I would probably be drawn and quartered, or at least placed in the stocks at Quincy Marketplace, if I didn't mention two of Boston's all-time favorite radio pros, **Bob and Ray.** The zany and talented duo spent their pre-network radio days on the air in Boston and were pathfinders for today's radio teams. Robert "Bob" Brackett Elliott, born in Boston, and Raymond "Ray" Walter Goulding, born north of the city in Lowell, first teamed-up in 1946 on Boston's WHDH AM-850. [34] Bob played the music and Ray read news on the station's AM-drive show. Their ad-libbing and goofing around after the news soon had proper Bostonians giggling over their coffee. Their timing with each other was a gift. Each knew the other so well that a simple word or phrase would have them taking off in a new direction.

If you love doing funny stuff on the radio, do yourself a favor and listen to some of Bob & Ray's outstanding work. We'll tell you where to obtain a sampling of their work later in this chapter. They were masters of satire and lent their voices to a cast of characters they created. Bob played many, including inept news reporter Wally Ballou, snappy sportscaster Biff Burns, and Kent Lisle Birdley, a wheezing, stammering, old-time announcer. Ray did all the female voices, along with mush-mouthed book reviewer Webley Webster and soap star Calvin Hoogavin.

Spoofs of popular radio shows of the day was another feature of Bob & Ray's show, including the continuing soap opera *Mary Backstage, Noble Wife*, which was an amusing take-off on radio's popular soap at the time, *Backstage*

Wife. Another favorite daytime radio drama in the 1950s, *One Man's Family,* became *One Fella's Family. The Gathering Dusk was* a heartwarming soap story of a girl who found unhappiness by leaving no stone unturned in her efforts to locate it. Other continuing Bob & Ray parodies included the children's shows *Mr. Science* and *Tippy the Wonder Dog.* Their commercial spoofs included *Gerstmeyer's Puppy Kibbles,* the dog food guaranteed to turn any household pet into a man-killer, and fictitious sponsors like *Einbinder Flypaper,* the brand you've actually grown to trust over the course of three generations, and *Grime,* the magic shortening that spreads like lard.

On July 2, 1951, Bob & Ray [35] made the big jump to New York City and NBC. Later in their career, Ray Goulding was asked to describe their success. "We've spent all these years trying to entertain each other," he laughed, "and that's a good way to make a living." For two years, Bob & Ray played Bert & Harry, the Piel Brothers, in a hilarious series of commercials for Piels Beer. The duo made a full circle of network radio, leaving NBC in 1953 and doing a TV show on ABC. In 1954, they returned to local radio in New York, and the following year they began five-minute comedy bits on NBC's weekend programming service, Monitor. In 1956, Bob & Ray took a spin at being disc jockeys on the Mutual Radio Network. In June 1959, their unique style of comedy could be heard on CBS. They hosted a 15-minute, five-times-a-week show which ran for about a year before they dropped out of radio until 1962, when WHN-New York offered them a four-hour afternoon drive show.

In 1965, they took a few years off from radio. Five years later in 1970, their Broadway show, *The Two and Only,* opened. In 1973, Bob & Ray began broadcasting for WOR, the flagship station of the Mutual Network in New York. They stayed with the station for three years until 1976, when they said so long to their radio audience forever with their familiar sign-off, "This is Ray Goulding, reminding you to write if you get work, and Bob Elliott, reminding you to hang by your thumbs." Their radio partnership prospered for half a century until Ray's passing from a heart attack in 1990. Their final radio series aired on NPR in 1990. Bob & Ray were inducted into the Radio Hall of Fame in 1995.

Whoever heard of a ventriloquist on radio?" Those were the words Edgar Bergen said to Rudy Vallee in December 1936, when asked to appear on Vallee's show. Bergen and his dummy, Charlie McCarthy, did appear on Rudy's show and people loved them! In May 1937, Chase & Sanborn decided to sponsor **Edgar Bergen & Charlie McCarthy**, along with the rest of their wooden-headed friends, Mortimer Snerd and Effie Klinker.

Charlie was a bad little playboy who wore a tuxedo, top hat and a monocle. He smoked cigarettes, was a big-time flirt, and could match wits with the best of them. When regular guest W.C. Fields would appear on the show, he and Charlie would really get into it. In one exchange, Fields threatened to carve Charlie into a venetian blind, but the dummy got a bigger laugh with,

"That makes me shudder." In time, Charlie became even more popular on the program than the real person, Edgar Bergen, but Bergen wasn't complaining. In 1945 he was making $10,000 a week from the radio show alone, along with another $100,000 yearly in royalties for Charlie McCarthy merchandise. Bergen & McCarthy left NBC in 1948, but returned to the air a year later on CBS. Coca-Cola was their new sponsor and carried the show until 1952. In 1956, after almost 20 years as one of radio's most popular programs, Edgar Bergen placed Charlie in his suitcase for the final time and they both left the world of radio for good. Edgar Bergen died in his sleep on September 30, 1978 in Las Vegas. He was there performing at Caesar's Palace as part of his farewell to show business after a 56-year career. As fate would have it, he had willed his wooden friends Charlie McCarthy, Mortimer Snerd and Effie Klinger to the Smithsonian Institution one week before his passing.

A ventriloquist on radio!! Who would have thought it possible? There were many, including radio management, who believed Bergen's act wouldn't work simply because they reasoned an audience had to actually see the ventriloquist and his dummy doing their thing. What these doubting Thomases overlooked is the beauty of radio is the use of one's imagination. As listeners, we actually believed that bad boy Charlie McCarthy was a real person, and not just a dummy cut from a block of pine. Edgar Bergen's success on radio proves once again that if you have a dream and want it badly enough, whether it's a career on the radio, a ventriloquist or whatever, hold on to it and don't let anyone stop you from turning your dreams into reality!

Jack Webb, star of radio and TV's long-running *Dragnet*, was told he didn't have a voice for radio! Long before *Dragnet* creator and star Webb [36] found success on radio, television and in the movies, his *on-air* career almost came to a screeching halt before it even began! While a student at Belmont High School in Los Angeles, Jack, because of his resonant voice, was asked to emcee and introduce his friends' pick-up band. It went over pretty well, and later the band decided to cut a series of records. Once again, young Jack was asked to do the intros and add a little banter and background info about the group. He waded through a wave of fear and stepped up to the mic to introduce the band's first number. His script shook and some of his words trembled, but overall, he felt he did okay with his performance. The recording engineers and people in the control room felt a little differently. As kindly as he could put it, the engineer said, "See here, son, your voice is too deep, it's too granular, too fuzzy to record well." Jack Webb didn't say a word, as the studio tech continued, "In case you're hoping for an announcer's job, you might as well know now as later, your voice rules you out!"

Segue ahead a few years to 1953. After finding much success on both radio and television, a letter is delivered to Jack Webb's Hollywood office, the setting of the popular *Dragnet* radio and TV series. It reads, "Dear Mr.

Webb: our speech class wants you to know that you have been voted the radio personality with the most compelling voice on the air."

Radio lesson learned: Don't let anyone tell you that because of the sound of your voice or for any other reason, you'll never make it as an air personality. If you have the desire and passion, you'll make it!

Author's Note: There were so many talented personalities during radio's formative years that it is virtually impossible to list them all here. The author has endeavored to give you a look at some who impacted greatly on his decision to pursue an on-air radio career. Many of the early radio pros mentioned and others as well are available on audio tape, CD, and other formats. There is a wealth of knowledge to be gained by listening to and learning from these early masters of personality radio. Don't be intimidated by how good they sound on the radio. With a little practice and seasoning, you can sound just as good!

Notes:
1. Bruce Morrow has kindly written one of the introductions for this book
2. Chapter 2 deals exclusively with how to develop your style for radio
3. Gene Autry's personal memoir, *Back in the Saddle Again,* written with Mickey Herskowitz, published in 1978 by Doubleday & Co.
4. Bertha Brainard is profiled in Chapter 13 – pioneer radio women
5. WJZ later moved to New York City
6. Read more about Vaughn de Leath in the chapter Pioneer Radio Women
7. Unconscionable today following the civil rights movement of the 1960s and how Americans feel about stereotyping and racial profiling
8. The inevitable *change* in radio is covered in Chapter 9, Attitudes and Actions, and also in Chapter 21
9. Read more about "who inspired the radio pros" in Chapter 20
10. Following WWII, Foy was the announcer/narrator on radio's *Lone Ranger*. He remained with the program until its last live broadcast on Sept. 3, 1954. Fred graciously provided one of the introductions for this book.
11. Later in his career, Arthur Godfrey mentioned in several interviews how his near-death car accident was the turning point of his life and his future as a radio personality.
12. Over 75 years ago, Godfrey knew the key to effective on-air communication, which is still practiced by today's real radio pros, *"when you're on the radio, talk to one person"*
13. How to develop your on-air style is covered extensively in Chapter 2
14. How to effectively communicate with your boss is covered in Chapter 11, Inside the World of Radio GMs
15. Don McNeill's Breakfast Club aired on ABC Radio weekdays from 9-10AM ET. The show broadcast from various Chicago hotels, during its 35 years on the air, but in August 1963 it began its daily fun fest from the Allerton

Hotel, on Michigan Ave., which renamed its meeting room "The Clouds Room." which could seat an audience of two hundred. Another feature of the show was that it broadcast from various cities across America, a tradition which began in the '40s and continued until the program's final broadcast in the '60s. Don McNeill's Breakfast Club aired on the ABC radio network for 35 years. Its final broadcast was on December 27, 1968. For additional information on the life and career of Don McNeill, suggested reading is *Don McNeill and his Breakfast Club* by John Doolittle, University of Notre Dame Press, Notre Dame, Indiana.

16 Marquette Univ. in Milwaukee's Memorial Library Archives houses an extensive collection of print and electronic material which documents the development of Don McNeill's career as host of the *Breakfast Club*. **Please note:** to gain access to the materials requires advance arrangements with the staff. For those interested in listening to some of McNeill's broadcasts to learn first-hand what made this man one of radio's all time great personalities, Chicago's Museum of Radio-TV has several audio tapes available.

17. For further reading, Fred Allen published his own memoirs, *Treadmill to Oblivion,* in which, among other revealing things about radio, he wrote, "Radio smelled of yesterday's levity."

18. NBC Radio operated two radio networks, the Blue and the Red. The FCC did not regulate or license networks directly. However, it could influence them by means of its hold over individual stations. Consequently, the FCC issued a ruling that "no license shall be issued to a standard broadcast station affiliated with a network which maintains more than one network." NBC argued this indirect style of regulation was illegal and appealed to the courts, but the FCC won on appeal, and NBC was forced to sell one of its networks. It chose to sell "the Blue" on Oct. 14 for $8 million to Edward J. Noble, owner of Life Savers candy and the Rexall drugstore chain. In mid-1944, Noble renamed the Blue Network, (ABC) the American Broadcasting Company.

19. In 1949, CBS scored a great coup in radio history by luring Jack Benny away from NBC with a contract involving $2 million and tax breaks.

20. Recommended reading: *Raised on the Radio* by Gerald Nachman, published by Pantheon Books, NY, a div of Random House, 1998

21. Art Baker was the first host of NBC's *People Are Funny*

22. Knowing your role on the radio is so important. Read more in Ch. 14, How to Win in Morning Drive

23. Gene Autry's *Melody Ranch* radio show was interrupted for two years during WWII when he enlisted in the Army Air Corps.

24. In his book *Up Late with Joe Franklin,* Franklin credits one-time popular N.Y. Daily News columnist and radio personality Walter Winchell with coining the phrase "disc or disk jockey." Winchell is profiled in Chapter 16

25. Joe Franklin began working for Martin Block in 1945. His primary job was to select records that were played on Block's show, *Make Believe Ballroom*. The program aired Saturday mornings and counted down America's Top-30 hit songs of the past week. Following Block's retirement, Joe took over hosting the show. There is also evidence (stated elsewhere in this book) that Jerry Marshall, another WNEW-AM radio personality, also hosted *Ballroom* following Block's retirement.
26. Long before tape recorders, programs were recorded on transcriptions, which were round 16" glass-based records
27. *Make Believe Ballroom* was the first commercially successful record program on radio. The title of the program had been used earlier in Los Angeles by Al Jarvis.
28. There were many radio personalities who played records on the air, going back to radio's earliest days in the 1920s with people like Dr. Frank Conrad and many others who were true pioneers in playing recorded music on America's airwaves.
29. Actor Richard Kollmar was best known to radio listeners as the star of *Boston Blackie*, a prime-time syndicated mystery show on radio in 1945.
30. Their first radio show was *Hi, Jinx*, which debuted on WEAF, NYC April 22, 1945. Jinx's real name was Eugenia Lincoln Falkenburg
31. How to communicate effectively on the radio is covered in Chapter 6
32. The C.E. Hooper Company measured radio audiences. In March 1950, it was purchased by A.C. Nielsen Co., another ratings company.
33. Three aluminum discs that recorded ten minutes on each side at 33 1/3 rpm would produce one half-hour program
34. After Bob & Ray left WHDH, Ray Dorey was in AM-Drive, followed by one of Boston's most popular personalities, Jess Cain, who is one of two radio pros this book is dedicated to, the other is Roger Allan.
35. **Author's note:** I strongly urge anyone who aspires to do comedy on the radio, to listen to the talented team of *Bob & Ray*. Many of their shows are available for listening at the Museum of Television & Radio, New York and Los Angeles. You may purchase CDs of their shows from Radio Spirits in Wallingford, Connecticut. Information is available at www.radiospirits.com Another super source for Old-Time Radio programs and many personalities mentioned is from Jon Foulk, who provides excellent service at www.OTRCAT.com.
36. Prior to starring in *Dragnet*, Jack Webb was featured on several other radio programs, including acting as the star of *Pat Novak for Hire* on ABC, as *Jeff Regan, Investigator*, on CBS and as the star of *Pete Kelly's Blues*, a 1951 summer replacement crime-drama series on NBC.

Learn From the Masters • 35

Pioneer Radio Pros- Montage #1. Top left: Dr. Frank Conrad, Helen Hahn (one of radio's first woman announcers. Middle from left: Ed Wynn (on right of photo) with Graham McNamee (early 1930s), "Happiness Boys-Billy Jones & Ernie Hare, Eddie Cantor. Bottom left: Will Rogers, Kate Smith, and Rudy Vallee.

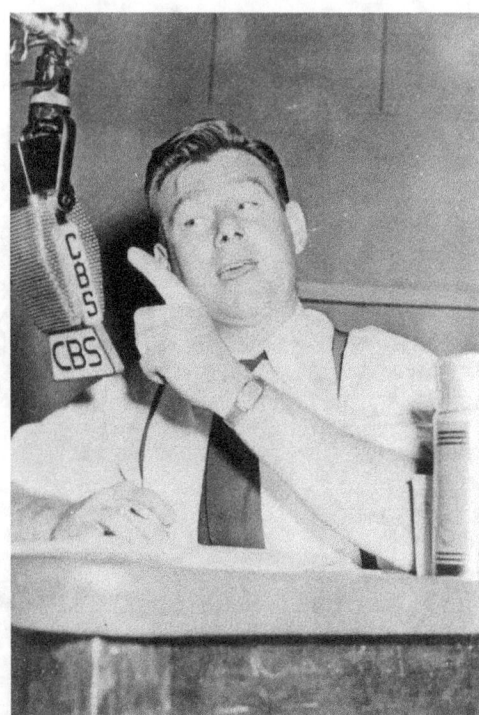

Arthur Godfrey

Don McNeill

Learn From the Masters • 37

Montage - top from left: Fred Allen, Jack Benny, Art Linkletter. Middle-from left: Fibber McGee & Molly (Jim and Marian Jordan), Edgar Bergen & Charlie McCarthy, George Burns (with cigar) and Gracie Allen. Bottom L to R, Martin Block on WNEW, Arlene Francis, Richard Kollmar and Dorothy Kilgallen on WOR mic, bottom center insert photo is of Tex and Jinx (Falkenburg) McCrary and NYC Mayor Robert Wagner, circa 40's/50's.

Montage- top from left: Bob Hope, Bing Crosby and Al Jolson, Bob and Ray (Bob Elliott & Ray Goulding. Middle row from left: Gene Autry (photo used with permission by Autry Qualified Trust and the Autry Foundation), Amos n' Andy (Freeman "Amos" Gosden and Charles "Andy" Correll [photo from Radio- TV Magazine -May 1957], Bottom from left: Jack Webb (on NBC mic), Ed McKenzie, aka Jack the Bellboy.

CHAPTER 2
How To Develop Your Own Air-Style

"Let people you admire show you the way, then use your own creativity to build on that base"

– Radio Pro Don Berns on how to develop your own radio personna

ONE OF THE FIRST QUESTIONS radio wannabes often ask, after "How do I break into the business," which is covered in the next chapter, is **"How do I develop my own style for the air?"** The answer is both easy and complex. The easy part is to *be yourself*, but what goes into that is an entirely different issue. Let me explain. Before going on the air for the very first time (and it may be a good idea to do it every time thereafter), ask yourself this question; what do I wish to accomplish with this special opportunity that is my own radio show? Think about it, keeping in mind that being on the radio is a privilege.

One of the most important points to remember as you develop your own air style is to **be yourself!** More than 150 best-in-the-business broadcasters took time to contribute to this book, and nearly all made reference to one significant point on how to be a successful air-talent...you need to be yourself on the radio! Always approach your show with passion. Relax, stay loose, have fun and enjoy every moment of being on the air. Let go of any inhibitions. Dare to be different! Take a look at some of today's successful air personalities; Don Imus, Laura Ingraham, Tom Joyner, Ryan Seacrest, Scott Shannon, and others. Each personality is totally different, and whether you enjoy listening to them or not, each has a presence and style uniquely their own. You are unique, too. The Good Lord only made one of you, so be yourself!

In the mid 1960s, as the program director at WIDE in Biddeford, Maine, I'm happy to say I gave "Ryan" Rick Cote his first on-air shot as a high-school reporter. It worked out great! Later in our radio careers, we worked together on the air at WROR Boston. For the past twenty years, he has been an air-talent and in management at WABK in Augusta, Maine. When it comes to finding your own air style, Ryan says, "Don't imitate heroes; even a perfect imitation makes you just a second best to Opie or Imus. Their success came by being original. No one is going to be a better "you." You'll go through a lot of booze, therapy or relationships trying to be anything else." More from Ryan later in this chapter.

Use your own abilities and uniqueness on the air. There is only one Howard Stern, some say, thanks be to God, while others truly believe the man walks on water. The point is, don't be a poor copy of an original. There is nothing etched in stone hidden away in a secret radio mausoleum that says to be a successful air-talent you have to follow the same path as everyone else. On the contrary! Always strive to be yourself, but be willing to try new things, *without changing who you are*. And, always keep in mind that if you allow yourself to be dependent on the approval of others, you'll be setting yourself up to be disappointed. Be great in your own unique way and let others think and say what they will.

You are encouraged to follow the examples and suggestions outlined in this book by some of America's top radio pros, but that doesn't mean changing your style and in the process losing your own unique sound and personality. You are a one-of-a-kind radio personality with your own special brand. Don't ever forget it! You need to travel your own road.

By identifying and acknowledging your own imperfections as an on-air-talent, and don't worry, we all have them, you will begin to find your comfort zone and what your own style is all about as an on-air radio performer. By being open and honest with yourself about what you need to work on is when you will find yourself on the right road to a successful on-air career.

Firstly and most importantly, you need to identify the area that best fits your personality. The *who* and *what* you are all about. Where is your personality the weakest? For example, if you are not the world's wittiest person, admit it. There's nothing more uncomfortable than trying to listen to someone on the radio who thinks he or she is funny and they're not! How many times have you glanced down at your car radio and winced when an air-talent tries to pull off an unfunny joke? Painful, isn't it! In my own case, there was a time I fancied myself a pretty clever and funny guy on the air. You'd think I would have learned from the caption under my Cheverus High School Class picture: "Seems to amuse himself with his own jokes." Not exactly a super endorsement of my comedic ability. As soon as I realized where my strengths were on the radio, and with a little helpful advice from knowledgeable programming people, I was on the right track.

If you're one of the lucky ones like I was, to have proficient programming minds like Walter Sabo and Gary Berkowitz nudging you in the right direction, all the better. The key is to listen to their input and advice. You don't always have to accept what they offer as gospel, but at least extend them the courtesy of listening to their suggestions to see if it applies to you and your air style. You may be surprised at how right-on they are.

Accepting advice wasn't always an easy thing for me to do. It's hard to admit that I've always been from the school of "I know what's best for me and my show." Putting it another way, Marvin Gaye's 1960s hit "A Stubborn Kind of Fellow" could have been my theme song. Don't make the same mistake I did and assume that a helpful suggestion means trying to change who you are on the radio. A good programmer who knows talent would never do that, and most often that's not the intent of their message. Listening to advice from my PD, GM,[1] or others in charge on how to perform on my show wasn't always easy for me to accept, let alone carry out. Case in point: when PD, and later consultant, Gary Berkowitz, tried to tell me, "Joe, you have a natural, God-given ability. All you have to do is open the mic and say, 'Good Morning,' and your warm, friendly smile comes shining through and makes your listeners feel welcome. That's ALL you have to do to be a hit!" My own ego wouldn't allow me to hear his message. For the longest time, I believed he was simply placating my ego. I thought, "Thanks, man, but what about the funny line I got off right after the 7:10 morning news break?" I was completely missing his point that my special on-air strength was being warm, fuzzy and friendly. Today it seems so obvious to me. Of course, it's now over thirty years later. In the interim, I've been blessed with a little success, along with a few slaps upside the head just to drive home the point!

It's important to remember, helpful suggestions from your program director, manager or consultant are just that, *suggestions*! Try not to throw a hissy fit or go bananas when they offer their advice. Refusing to accept input from supervisory personnel gives the impression that you suffer from a case of out-of-control ego. Based on my own experience, rest assured this is not *always* the case. It's more like we're protecting that which is near and dear to us, our own creations. Radio personalities are not unlike any other creative artist. Emotions run high and feelings get hurt especially when we believe we are giving our best performance every time we go on the air. Consequently, whenever advice is forthcoming, quite often many radio pros look at it as a personal attack on their integrity as an artist. Whether their thinking is totally off-the-wall is not the issue. When management tells talent "their performance" needs to be corrected or how it may be improved, stand by! No matter how well-intentioned the message, it is like waving a red flag in front of a bull. Constructive criticism (don't you just love the sound of that?), as it is so often called, is one of the most difficult tasks for any supervisor to handle. It is also one of the most difficult things for air-talent to accept.

Here are a few thoughts which may make the process a little more tolerable for both parties. Air-talent needs to keep in mind that management has the right to express their views and to pass along what they believe is solid input. On the flip-side of the coin, talent has the right to either accept or reject their input, based on whether or not they feel it will improve or damage their performance. Keep in mind, we're specifically referring to a talent's on-air style and not station formatics, which is an entirely different subject and covered elsewhere. In most instances, criticism from those in a position of power is not intended to find fault with a talent's personality. It is meant to *enhance* their delivery. Air-talent is smack-dab in the middle of the playing field, while the station programming team is coaching from the sidelines, away from the heat of the action. Management hears things talent may be totally unaware of because the talent is so caught up in the moment and doing their thing on the radio. As a talent, you need to confront your own strengths and weaknesses. Learn what you as a personality can bring to your show every day. Play to your positives while trying your best to eliminate most of your negatives and you, too, will be a radio winner!

Personality can denote so many different things. Eddie Murphy, Jay Leno, Will Ferrell, and Tina Fey are talented comics and personalities, but there is a world of difference between them. There is also a huge contrast between a Johnny Carson-type [2] air personality and a Howard Stern. Johnny was warm and genuine, the master of ad-libs and off-the-cuff remarks. Howard Stern, on the other hand, can be crude and lewd with a more in-your-face style. Both are personalities, but very different and with a uniqueness all their own. I was never a wise guy - well, not intentionally, anyway. That's just not me, either on or off the radio! Humility aside for a moment, I can get a funny line off with the best of them, but always being the funny guy on the radio wasn't me. Oh, I had my comedic moments, but being Mister Funny Man was not my forte. Did I ever wish I could dump my straight role and be the funny guy? You betchum! But my personality was better suited as the "set-up" guy; Mister Warm and Friendly.

Today, in listening to many morning radio teams, it seems to me everyone wants to get the last funny line in before going to a song or a commercial break. It's like listening to the old radio and TV show *Can You Top This*.[3] Personally, I find it annoying and juvenile to hear everyone fighting to steal the spotlight. Morning shows are supposed to be a team effort with defined roles. Trying to out-funny each other is a big problem with morning drive radio teams. I believe the reason many morning radio shows have declining ratings is because of acute listener fatigue! It's so important to establish roles on your show. Know yours and stick to it! Listeners get accustomed to hearing certain voices on their favorite radio station, and hearing those voices react in a certain way is reassuring to them. Air-talent may look at "defined" roles as typecasting, but I prefer to call it familiarity and a comfort zone for the listener. Don't forget the listener can't see the people on the air and can only hear them. So, when the straight man delivers the funny line and the funny person doesn't, it's confusing to the ear. The listener's attention span, with background noises, voices and interruptions, is limited, so it's more critical than ever to stick to your role on the radio. Another point: too much superfluous chit-chat and too many voices leaves the listener wondering who said what!

From Christmas, 1983, until the spring of 1992, being Joe on Boston radio's *Joe and Andy Family* was one of the high points of my forty-one years on radio. It was one of the most enjoyable times in my broadcasting career and also one of the most lucrative. My radio partner Andy Moes took me places I never would have achieved on my own. It was a righteous ride! We laughed a lot, both on and off the air. We had fun and really entertained ourselves. Thankfully, our loyal listeners went along for the ride and made us one of Boston's top-rated and most popular morning radio teams!

In the early 1990s, after a successful run of almost ten years on Boston radio, Andy and I went our separate ways. He moved over to WEEI-AM to host his own morning show. I stayed at WROR, then known as MIX-98.5. It was not a successful move for Andy. I truly believe one reason he missed the mark in his first attempt as quarterback on his own morning show was not entirely his fault. I feel it was due to a lack of defined roles. The few times I had a chance to listen to Andy, usually from air-checks since we were on the radio opposite each other, it sounded to me like he wasn't allowed to just be funny Andy. In his new role as the morning-show quarterback, he was responsible for driving the bus and handling all the formatic stuff, which I know he loathed. No longer could Andy just be the funny guy on the show. He was the ringmaster, too. It glaringly stood out when Andy would try to deliver a funny line and another member of his team would jump in and try to out-funny him! It was a classic example of the old radio and TV show *Can You Top This*. When this happens, a case of who gets the last funny line in, the person usually left out of the entire scenario is the all-important listener!

Being the straight guy or set-up person on the radio isn't always fun

Much to his credit, my Boston radio partner Andy would often remind folks that I had the more difficult role on our show. He knew he got most of the laughs and more adulation as the funny guy on

Joe and Andy,[4] but he was also sensitive about my feelings. When accolades were tossed his way, and deservedly so, he would kindly say, "All I have to do is to stand over to Joey's left and tell a few funny jokes. He does all the really hard stuff!" I guess if you call running the equipment, playing the songs, inserting commercials, and making sure we were on time as hard stuff, then I qualify. I did control all of that, but if my role was defined as the meat and potatoes on our show, Andy certainly provided all the necessary sweet and spicy condiments and a whole lot more! We each had respective roles to do our show and we did them!

Even though Andy was the designated funny guy on our show and would deliver the punch line, there was always ample room for me to weave my own special brand of humor into our show. What was natural for me was my storytelling ability, which is another style, and if you have it, develop it and let it flow on your show. God blessed Andy with the gift to be naturally witty, where I had to work at it! If you find yourself playing straight man to the funny guy on your show, here's a piece of friendly advice: thank your lucky stars, smile, and make sure accounting spells your name correctly on your paycheck! In other words, as my one-time co-worker and longtime Boston radio personality Larry Justice would say, "Take the loot and scoot." You're in a great job and doing what you always dreamed of doing being on the radio, don't ever take it for granted!

Remember, I said you must stick with your role on the radio. Well, I'm going to break that rule for just a moment. As the set-up person, you shouldn't allow the show to become too predictable. Occasionally, it's okay to stray from your role, just don't do it very often. Once in a great while, being human, the little radio devil would come out in me. To satisfy my own comedic side and unbeknownst to Andy in advance, I would divert from our usual modus operandi and drop in a funny line. Whenever it happened, a look of total surprise would cross his dimpled cheeks, but he always took it good naturedly and would laugh his raucous, delightfully unique Andy laugh. When I'd stray over to his role, he never got upset, which sadly, is so often the case with many of today's air-talent.

Radio Pro lesson: Don't let your ego get so far out of control that you don't allow others to bask in the spotlight once in awhile.

Andrew Moes was too big a man to ever let things like that bother him. When I would unexpectedly drop a funny line on him just to make sure the show wasn't becoming too predictable, inevitably during the next commercial break he'd look over at me, wink, and say, *"Good one, Joey."* If it ever bothered him, he never let on. Andy was very much a "do whatever pleases you" kind of guy! He would often say with a chuckle, "As long as the show does well and I get paid, I couldn't care less about the other stuff, Joey. I'm an overweight man with a heart condition and don't need any stress."[5]

Like most partners, in or out of radio, Andy and I had our differences. Keep in mind, our contrasting personalities which worked so well on our show would sometimes clash off-the-air. You can't place two creative talents in a room no bigger than a broom closet for four hours every day without having an occasional problem. However, in the ten years we worked together, I can honestly say we only had one major blow-up which quickly blew over.

The Good Lord must have needed a few chuckles, because He called Andy home in February 2001. A massive stroke silenced his witty mind and wonderful laugh. He was just fifty-one. I am proud to have worked with him and to have called him my friend. I miss him and there isn't a day that goes by that I don't think of him and smile.

As the set-up person on your show, always be prepared!
Being the straight man on the radio usually means you will be responsible for most of the set up work on your show. It's not an attempt to load more work on one team member than the other, that's not the case. It's because, as the lead person, you run the controls and know where the show elements fit best around commercials, news, traffic, and other features. So don't look at this important element of show prep as being extra work. [6] Instead, look at it as part of your job description. Every night I'd block out our show, leaving room for our ad-libs and Andy's prepared show bits. I would also jot down funny comeback lines for myself, just in case our ad-libbing required a snappy one-liner. It's a definite safety net which you may want to consider doing, so that you as the straight man are not left standing there with your mouth open, going "Duh." Don Powers, my GM at WCSH Radio in Portland, Maine, in the late 1970s once told me, "Sometimes, nothing works better than a prepared ad-lib." I couldn't agree more. It's not a sign of weakness to write down some of your ad-libs. Being prepared is being smart and the only way to find lasting success on the radio! Even though Andy was the designated funny guy on our show and would deliver the punch line, there was always ample room for me to weave my own special brand of humor into our show.
File this under "Always be yourself on the radio, no matter what!"
One Friday morning in November 2002, while in morning drive at Sunny-104.3 in West Palm Beach, Florida, I showed up on the air with a case of…maestro, please cue the *Dragnet* theme, *dum, da dum dum*, the dreaded HICCUPS! Not one every 10 or 15 seconds, but two and sometimes three at a time. You should have heard me trying to say, "Sunny - 104 (hiccup) point three!"

One thing I've learned in radio is that when you get lemons, you try and make lemonade! So, we did what every good morning show does, we decided to open the lines and let our family of listeners call in with a cure! No one ever said morning drive radio was rocket science. I mean, hey, what else could we do? It was quite obvious that your ole pal Joey was having some kind of gastric problem of the throat variety, so why not have a little fun with a tough situation!

The bit took off, and BIG! Our listeners called with all sorts of home remedies, like swallowing two spoonfuls of sugar! Did anyone notify Mary Poppins of my dilemma? All the sugar did was send my sugar level through the roof and made me more hyper than I already was. Callers offered various ways of drinking water while holding one's breath! For example, how about this one: bend over and drink a cup of water from the opposite side of the cup, all while holding your breath! Oh, yeah, that was loads of fun. The only thing that happened was the front of my shirt got soaked and, of course, I still had the hiccups! We not only had our regular listeners calling, but doctors, chiropractors, and even witch doctors and psychics! Most thought it was pretty hilarious to listen to a guy on the radio hiccupping every few seconds while trying to talk. I'm happy they got a kick out of it, but, believe me, having the hiccups for almost 24 straight hours was anything less than funny.

Since I had a personal appearance that night at an area mall to officially welcome Santa, something had to be done to relieve my hiccups! Either that or moms and dads bringing their tots to see Santa would think the jolly ole gent had a serious battle with the spirits going on and we're not talking about the holiday kind! I called my own doctor - at least ten times! Talk about driving the office staff nutso, but all they said was "hiccups will run their course and some patients have had them for days!" Wonderful, just what I wanted to hear! But wait! Another doctor who was a regular listener called, and said..."try FLEX-ALL!" "Flex-all," I thought, "what the hell is that?" Come to find out, Flex-all is a muscle relaxant. The doc had been listening to me on the radio and diagnosed that I had trapped gas below my diaphragm which was causing me not one, not two, **but three hiccups about every 15 seconds!**

There's only one problem with Flex-all: it makes you very, very sleepy. Not a good idea to take it in the middle of your wake-up show. I did pop one when I got home from the station and almost slept through Santa's big arrival at the mall, one of our largest advertisers! Like I said, almost! Our doctor friend and listener even showed up to make sure his radio patient was relieved of his dreaded hiccups! For the sake of Santa's reputation, I was hiccup free!

Post note: The doc strongly suggested that every radio guy and gal who has experienced a case of the dreaded...*dum, da dum dum*...**HICCUPS** to have a bottle of Phazyme on hand. He said you can get it at any pharmacy without a prescription. On the box it's advertised this way, "Phazyme, serious medicine for serious gas!" Don't think we didn't have fun with that line on our show!

My reason for sharing this story is simple! ***Basic Radio-101****-be yourself on your show!* If you have a simple problem like hiccups, who in your audience can't identify with it? Run with it! What makes it funny listening is that you are their friend on the radio who has hiccups. You'll have your listeners talking to themselves, saying, "How is he going to deal with this and be able to finish his show? We need to help this poor guy out!!!" All the one-liners, jokes, prepared bits, etc. will never, ever take the place of REAL SITUATIONS with REAL PEOPLE ON THE RADIO!

Note: this true slice of author Joe Martelle's radio life actually occurred on November 15, 2002.

As mentioned previously in this chapter, one of my better moves as PD at WIDE in Biddeford, Maine, in the 1960s was hiring **"Ryan" Rick Cote**. At the time, he was a local seventeen-year-old kid who attended St. Louis High School. Rick was hungry to be in radio and his passion was quite obvious. After classes, he would do what so many radio wannabes do: hang out at their favorite local radio station. He was willing to do almost anything, including running across the street to either the Puritan or Nutshell restaurants, our only two choices, to grab us a cup of coffee or a sandwich. His friendliness and desire to be on the air paid off. It didn't take long for me to decide to give the future radio star a chance to host his own hour-long show every Saturday morning. *High School Billboard* was a "teens, topics and tunes" show with Rick as the host and supported by other teens from area high schools. They discussed news stories and current events of interest to teens. I always looked at that show as a teen edition of NBC's *Meet the Press*. The show became extremely popular and so did Rick. His popularity on the *Billboard* show soon led to a regular shift at the station. Rick Cote's radio career was off and running.

Some forty years later, following his start in radio at WIDE, I'm happy to say we are still in touch. I asked Ryan how a person develops their own air style. Before I share his comments, please know I did not pay him nor did I place a choke hold on him to say these kind things. "Growing up, I listened and studied the styles of Bruce Bradley [7] on WBZ (Boston), Joey Reynolds on WKBW (Buffalo), but most of all to a local favorite, Joe Martelle," says Ryan. "The three made radio relevant. If you didn't listen to them you missed what was really going on. The first two were deadly humorous, but Joe Martelle had a mastery of producing a cohesive show that drew you in and involved you."

Ryan Cote makes a strong point about *being yourself* on the air. "Oh, somewhere, some PD will tell you you're the worst announcer or personality they've ever heard. They are WRONG! Don't work for them or anyone else who doesn't believe in your talent and what you bring to your show. Get a brain trust of people who will enable your courage when yours falters. We all need a support system. Be patient," he continues, "you can't do things differently until you see things differently. One final point about being on the radio and you. Those kids you see playing outside without a care in the world, you've got one inside you. Let him or her loose on the air!" Today, Ryan is in afternoon-drive and creative marketing director at one of Central Maine's most listened to radio stations, WABK in the Capitol of Augusta.

Southbound down the Maine Turnpike from Augusta and Ryan Cote is my hometown, the port city of Portland. Any morning, you punch up 100.9 and more than likely, you'll catch another of my radio pals, **Chuck Igo**.

In 1998, Chuck and I worked together at the second incarnation of WROR Boston. Today, he is the morning drive personality at Oldies 100.9-WYNZ in Portland. Growing up in the Boston radio market and thanks to his mom and dad's radio, Chuck had the opportunity to listen to many personalities, Carl DeSeuse, Dave Maynard, Bruce Bradley, and Jess Cain. As the younger brother of four sisters, Chuck says, "The radio was usually tuned to the Wimmex Good Guys (WMEX-1510AM), including Arnie 'WooWoo for YouYou' Ginsburg, Melvin X. Melvin, and others." Chuck was an ear-witness, as he proudly proclaims, to the birth of Top-40 radio in Boston when 680-AM-WRKO, today a talk radio station, brought a rock-contemporary alternative to the airwaves! "In the morning, it was Dale Dorman playing the hits and John Masters with RKO's 20/20 News."[8] Of the many who had an impact on his desire to enter radio, Chuck Igo credits Harvey Warfield. "He was the one individual who was perhaps blessed with a few extra minutes during his air-shift to offer encouragement over the phone to me, a young teenager with a desire to get into radio. He was the one who told me that if radio was truly my passion then not to let the fear of rejection stop me from trying."

As far as how future radio stars can develop their own style, Chuck Igo believes that imitation is the sincerest form of flattery. "Early on," says Chuck, "my first full-time program director, Cary Pahigian at WGAN in 1981, used to give me homework: listen to other personalities, Jess Cain and Tom Kennedy on WHDH [both of whom Igo would eventually work with] and Dave Maynard and Bruce Bradley on WBZ. My assignment was not to duplicate what they did," emphasizes Chuck, "but to try and learn from their delivery and incorporate it to that which I might do. It was more like learning the 'how, when and why.' How did they manage to get to the point in under fifteen seconds, complete with call letters and still hit the post."[9]

When is the appropriate time to use humor or a great piece of prep? Igo believes the best rule for humor is *funny happens*. "Pre-planning jokes do not always flow as well as desired, and forced humor stands out like a 45rpm, starting out at 33 and 1/3. The best bits I've heard on the air," he says, "usually leave both the listener and the air personality laughing."

As far as talking up a song on the air, Chuck Igo believes, "Most times, a musical or topical tie-in could make a most memorable impression. Pacing one's delivery with the overall tone of the music helps keep the message over the vamp [the very beginning] of the song." In wrapping up his comments, Igo quotes one of his radio mentors, Cary Pahigian: "Every time you turn on the mic, you should sound like you just won the lottery!"[10]

Author's note: Even though some of Chuck Igo's comments pertain more to technique on the air, rather than how to develop an on-air style or persona, his points are well taken and they will enhance your overall delivery, especially if you are in a music-driven format.

Laurie DeYoung has been a permanent fixture in morning drive at WPOC-93.1 Baltimore for over thirty years. She has this advice for tomorrow's radio stars on how to develop their own style for the air: "Be real, be unique, develop your own style. And most importantly," she adds, "figure out what you're good at and spend 95% of your time doing it on your show."

Growing up in Maine in the late 1950s meant AM radio was still the big dog on the dial in town! One of the more popular out-of-town Top-40 radio stations we could pick up at night was WKBW Buffalo. Its powerful 50,000-watt signal boomed into Portland like a local station. One of my favorite air personalities on the station was **Tommy Shannon**.[11] I liked his style and the way he sounded. He joined the air staff at KBW in late 1957 at age 19, and spent a year and a half doing weekends, another prime example of taking whatever job is offered to get your foot in the door. Tommy next moved into the 6 to 9 pm slot vacated by **Dick Biondi**, who left to join another super radio station, WLS Chicago.[12] Some fifty years later and now in his 70s, the "Wild I-tralian," as he is known and loved by his legions of loyal listeners, is still on WLS-FM-Chicago's True Oldies station every weeknight. Dick still enjoys doing what he has been doing for the last half-a-century; playing great oldies, talking to the folks and, most importantly, being himself on the radio! Today, Tom Shannon lives most of the year in California with a lady he dated in college forty-two years ago. True to his roots, he still maintains a home in Buffalo, which he claims as his real hometown.

In the summer of 2007, I caught up with Tommy and asked what advice he has for tomorrow's radio stars on how to develop their own air-style. "Listen to everybody who is currently doing a show," Shannon began. "Try to judge the best in your opinion and let their good points influence you and the style that you're trying to develop." The one-time Buffalo radio pro added, "As with everything else in life … practice, practice and more practice." He also thinks it's important for a future radio pro to get a well-rounded education, no doubt alluding to the unstable business of being in radio. "If you are in college or a university, stay in school and learn your craft, whatever it might be. It's always good to be able to fall back on, because you just never know, when you may need it. In my case," he continues, "I graduated from a teachers college with a BS in Education, Art and English and for a while I did teach. If you're in a college that has a communications course, even better. And, keep in mind, no matter what you may think at the time that some courses may not be the most interesting things in life, they do add to your personal make-up and what goes into making you a well-rounded and knowledgeable person, which can only help you develop into becoming a real radio pro."

The man should know. He is one of Buffalo's living radio legends, who spent over 50 years on the air. Tommy Shannon retired from full-time radio at WHTT-FM Buffalo in 2005. Looking back on his radio life, he believes, like many other air personalities, that *being yourself* on the air is most important.

Popular radio and TV personality **Wink Martindale** believes the best advice he was given on how to develop your own air style was passed along by his Sunday school teacher, Charles "Chick" Wingate. "He was not only my Sunday school teacher," says Wink with a grin, "but he also managed a local radio station, WPLI in Jackson, Tennessee. Chick gave me my first radio job at age 17, upon my graduation from Jackson High School. I made $25 a week, but for a kid who practiced ad-libbing commercials around the full-page advertisements in *Life* magazine, in the back bedroom, pretending I was on the air, I would've paid them to work at the station. Chick Wingate always told me, 'Be yourself.' Don't try to emulate others and their styles. Just be yourself and you'll be fine. I've always remembered those words and I've always tried to live up to them. I can truly say, his advice 'worked' for me."

Winston Martindale, who picked up the name "Wink" from a childhood friend, thinks it's important not to copy others you've seen or heard. "Build your radio show and your own personality around subjects that you personally like and enjoy, subject matter that you are familiar with." The legendary radio pro and the warm, personable host of nineteen television game shows, including the popular favorite *Tic-Tac Dough*, suggests watching TV pro Regis Philbin to pick up on his style. "Watch Regis at the top of his show, *Live*, and how he talks about things that happen to him. He shares his life in story form with you. Take away from that things you've done and experienced during the past 24 hours and incorporate those happenings in your life on your show. Those things don't have to be funny and overly interesting, but over the long haul you will find that your listeners will be able to relate. You will become just one of them and chances are what you do with your spare time they do as well." Wink and his wife Sandy are the proud parents of four. The Southern gentleman is still doing what he loves best, hosting a weekday radio show. His syndicated *Music of Your Life* radio program is heard from noon until 3pm on over 250 radio stations. **Note:** Regis stepped down as co-host on "Live" in 2011.

C.C. McCartney, no relation to Paul, is another real radio pro. His ratings have always been amazing and usually at the top of the ratings report card. C.C. is well known for his work on legendary CHR radio stations around the country, including KILT and KRBE, both in Houston, KIMN Denver, and his long-term stint at WSIX in Nashville. As far as which style to use on the air, CC agrees with Wink Martindale; "Just be yourself. The Lord only made one of you, so why try to sound like anyone else?" Today, CC is in the voice imaging business and I'm sure you've heard his one-of-a-kind voice on countless country radio specials.

Nancy Quill has been the top-rated midday personality on Magic 106.7 Boston for the past twenty-five years, an amazing feat considering the topsy-turvy, ever-changing world of radio. Nancy says she literally grew up in the radio business. Her dad Joe Quill was the epitome of the radio guy that could do it all. "Our dad was co-owner and general manager of WRLM-FM in Taunton, MA. He was also an air personality, roving reporter, copywriter, program director, and salesman extraordinaire. My sister Barbara and I not only learned from the best," she proudly boasts, "but we learned all about radio by watching my dad. He taught me to be myself, don't be a yukker, to be personable and when you're reading copy, for goodness sake, know what you're saying, don't just read words!" [13]

Brian (deGeus) Foxx is music director and the morning drive guy at KSFI in Salt Lake City. Brian grew up in Northern California in the Bay Area. Brian deGeus, who goes by Brian Foxx on KSFI, believes that radio today is not so much about voice as it is style and personality. "Even if a station's format is liner driven, there is a personality that shines through. I always thought it was a good idea to listen closely to someone you admire on-air," says Brian, "try to emulate the qualities they may have into your own style." Brian also urges radio newbies to get to know people within the industry to get your foot in the door.

A suggestion for radio wannabes: Find an on-air personality you admire, then plead, cajole, or even offer to wash their car and babysit their precocious kids if they'll let you shadow them around for a day or two. You will learn so much from observing a real radio pro at work.

Matt "The Cat" Baldassarri was music director and air-personality of *50s on 5* on Sirius-XM Satellite Radio until 2008. Matt grew up on Boston's North Shore and says he was bitten by the radio bug by listening to legendary radio personalities Joe Martelle, Larry Glick, Charles Laquidara, Peter Wolf, and Little Walter. Matt says he began his radio career at age thirteen hosting a weekly oldies show on his high school's FM station WBMT in Boxford, Massachusetts.

Baldassarri believes a future radio star must learn about style from the past. "Now that doesn't mean that you should imitate the past," he quickly adds, "but there is a really good reason why successful jocks of the past were successful. They had a way of connecting to their audience. A good air personality is a friend, a companion. A radio personality who talks down to his or her audience or mocks their listeners will never last past the 'shock' factor. Human beings don't like to be treated that way for long." Matt says, "A DJ needs to be 'cool' but not 'too cool' for the room. This is a person you want to be friends with and be cool enough to 'hang' with. 'Too cool' means they are above their audience and that all important personal connection will never be made. So learn from the past," insists Matt the Cat, "just put your own spin on it and basically add your own passion and interest to the basic formula and you'll succeed." Matt and his popular *The Night Prowl* can now be heard on the Internet.

Jack Casey is General Manager of the Emerson College Radio station WERS 88.9 FM, which was voted the #1 college radio station by both the Princeton Review and The Associated Press. Before entering the world of academia, he enjoyed a distinguished radio career, including successful collaborations with broadcaster Bob Henabery at WZZP in Cleveland and later at WMJX in Boston.

Bob was the consultant and Jack was the program director. Long before his lucrative radio years, I managed to snag him for weekend air work while he was a student at Emerson College. I was a young PD at WIDE in Biddeford, Maine. [14] "The owner of the station was J. Alan Jasper, who taught us all a few things about how to act on the radio," says Jack. "He taught me never to talk about underwear on the air. Keep in mind that was back in the early 1960s." As far as style is concerned, Casey feels in today's radio world being real is essential.

Jack Casey believes the days of the super-jive jocks on radio is over. *"Today's listeners want to* connect with a real person. However, they don't want to hear about your problems.[15] They want you to be the best 'you' can be. The 'you' who you bring to a party, who has everyone laughing and wanting your number. The 'you' who doesn't want to get out of bed in the morning unless you find a way to make that amusing or otherwise compelling. I don't know who said it first, but legendary New York programmer Steve Kingston always defined style on the air as 'brief, bright, real and relevant.' I couldn't agree more," says Casey. "Crafting one's communication into a work of art is what separates the pros from the hacks. Economy of words is essential. If you can say it in 60 seconds, can you say it in 30, 15 or 10 seconds? Proper word selection can make you an audio artist. Style aside, creative content is essential as long as it touches people, as long as you make a connection."

Bob Lacey is one half of the popular morning drive radio team of *Bob & Sheri*. His radio partner is **Sheri Lynch** and they've been a team since 1991. Their spontaneous wit and cutting-edge humor is heard on more than 60 affiliates across the country. Bob took his first radio job in Providence, Rhode Island, at the tender age of eighteen, after realizing that his career fronting a New England rock band would never get him on the airwaves. At twenty-two, he launched the first-ever nighttime phone-in show on the powerful Charlotte, North Carolina, AM station, WBT.

Bob Lacey has strong feelings about developing your own style for radio. "If you really have the desire to make the grade as a real on-air radio pro, realize who you are, and what your strengths are," says Lacey. "The great Steve Allen once said, 'If you aren't funny by the age of 12, you never will be funny.' If that's the case, then find out what makes you special. Ask yourself why people should listen to you. If the answer is 'I am funny,' or 'I am interesting,' then great! Hone your skills and dedicate yourself to serving your masters."

The syndicated morning radio pro goes on to say, "If the answer to your own question is 'I don't know what is special about me, I just want this cool job and not have to learn math,' then, please, for your sake, for your kid's sake, and for the rest of who are trying to make some kind of creative job out of this, the lowest rung on the show-business ladder, do something else. Only you know the truth. If after reading my thoughts you still want to be on the radio, then you might just do great. But I doubt it. Good luck."

Legendary air-talent **M.G. "Machine Gun" Kelly** began his radio career in Ada, Oklahoma, on KTEN. At the time he was a junior in high school. Later, M.G. moved to KOMA in Oklahoma City, WCGL-Cleveland, KSTP Minneapolis and at age 21 was shooting straight on KHJ Los Angeles. M.G.'s advice on developing your air style is to be unique. "Set your sights," says the broadcast pro, "Find your own style and stay focused. You have to learn to be a team player and a 'rebel' at the same time. Politics can get in the way in many cases. Don't sell yourself short. Focus is everything to being a success."

Kelly, who was inducted into the Rock and Roll Hall of Fame in 1998, shares this slice of his own radio life: "When a door was slammed in my face, I either kicked it down or found another entrance. It is much harder today than it was in 1970, but where there is a will…" [16]

Donna Halper attended Northeastern University Boston, where she was the first woman announcer in the school's history. She began hosting a nightly show on the campus radio station in October 1968. Donna completed two master's degrees from Northeastern and went on to a successful career in broadcasting, including more than twenty-three years as a radio programmer and management consultant in markets of all sizes. Ms. Halper is the author of three books and is working on a fourth, a history of talk shows.

Because of her extensive radio background, I turned to Donna to get her input from a woman's perspective on what style works for women on the air: "Women need to be themselves. That sounds like a cliché, 'to be yourself,' but it's the best advice. When you try to be somebody you aren't, you'll sound fake. I was told by a consultant," she continues, "to sound more sexy when I was first on the air, but that wasn't my natural style. I thought my voice was warm and friendly. When I tried to be sexy, it sounded really artificial. Female disc jockeys need to find a style that is natural for them so they can concentrate on relating to the audience, rather than on some phony act."

Radio pioneer **Galen Drake** was a mainstay on the radio in the 1940s and '50s. "To be successful on the radio," he offered, "you may want to think about adapting your style as a *story-teller*," which proved to be the key for him. In a March 1959 article in Radio-TV Mirror, Drake said, "Telling stories goes back to ancient times. That's when the village story-teller was the popular man of the community. He was the one who went off to visit neighboring tribes and came back with tales of strange and wonderful places and events, bits of gossip about the people he had seen and met, myth and fact, truth and fantasy. The villagers could never get enough of his stories. I tried to expand this idea," pioneer personality Drake continued, "mainly because I like to talk with those who can tell me things that I never knew before. When I can pick up some really odd bit of information and pass it along to my listeners, or explore some myth, I get the same kick out of it that they do!" Sounds like Drake was not only a story-teller on radio, but was also a myth-buster!

Developing your style of being a story-teller for talk radio
Nationally heard talk show host **Mark Williams** has strong words for future radio talk show hosts on how to develop their on-air style. Mark holds nothing back, so saddle up and hold on tight: "Learn how to tell a story. Entertain me with a story, make me laugh, make me gasp, make me feel a range of emotions, bring me into your story and do it without any calls for three straight hours! When you get to that point, you have the beginnings of being a talk personality. Know what YOU think about something. We already know what Rush thinks and what Howard thinks and by the way," Williams asserts, "boobs and butts or sex in St. Patrick's Cathedral is NOT talk radio. It is just plain sick and low-rent."

Williams continues to lay it squarely in your face on how to make it as a talk show host and what he believes are the steps to develop your air style to get to that point: "Be able to build your point, respond to challenges, or you are not convincing anybody about anything. You are an appliance, like the toaster or the TV, assigned the job of cutting through the massive noise and clutter to attract as many ears as possible for the sales force to hit the streets and charge confiscatory advertising rates."

"Think Vince McMahon," adds Williams. "The greatest talk shows are those where *Meet the Press* meets *WWE*. You are a journalist, but like all journalists, you produce a product called Entertainment. You also have to survive a gauntlet of hacks, freaks and morons who in another life would be coming out of the back of a wolf. These are the Peter Principled parasitic corporate survivors who populate front offices in most industries, we are no different. As a talk show host, whether you have been in radio since breakfast or have supped on the radio cup for a very long time you need to STAND OUT! Find the take on a front of mind, gut issue that nobody else has got. Take immigration for example. When I talk about illegal immigration, I don't rant the predictable. I grab my recorder and go down to the protest or the day labor camp and I talk to the illegals! Then I air what they say and let the listeners on either side get inflamed and respond. Sometimes, if you let the story tell itself, you get a far better show."

Some may think Mark Williams' next piece of advice for radio wannabes who think they want to talk it up on the public airwaves is rather radical! "SKIP SCHOOL," he says, "move to a distant city or a foreign country. When I talk about Iraq on the air, I can say I've been there, under fire, up close and personal. When I do a national talk show and I get a call from Nebraska," says Mark, " I can make a local reference to the Wild Bill Cody Memorial not far away, or the postcards of giant ears of corn at the Super 8 Motel off Interstate 80, been there. All of a sudden, I'm not a disembodied voice coming out of an appliance. I'm real! I know your town; I'm a friend, even if we disagree. I've still heard about where you come from or someplace just like it and you're not used to hearing that from an appliance."

"Everybody's story is different," continues Williams. "I was a disc jockey on WSAR in Fall River, Massachusetts, when a change in management brought a change in format from music to talk. They fired most of the staff and made me the overnight guy on the radio. I used the next three years to get a college education on the air. If a book came out, I interviewed the author, read the book and then interviewed the author again! Books ranged from *Cosmic Dawn*, a book on quantum physics, to *The Three Stooges* and a guest who was Moe Howard's daughter. Scientists from the Jet Propulsion Laboratory and science writer Ben Bova were regular guests. We had the Viking probes en route to Mars and Pioneer destined to leave the solar system. I once called Australia live on the air," smiles Williams, "just to see if toilets really do flush in the opposite direction down there. I even had the local cops suit me up and sic a dog on me on the air. Are you taking notes or better yet, getting my drift. Taking phone calls forced me to learn and learn and then learn some more, because I encountered an entire universe of new ideas different from mine and I had to defend mine."

The universe Mark Williams encountered when he made the move to WRKO in Boston as a morning news-talk producer was immensely huge and even more different. [17] "That has been the case with each move up and down or laterally ever since," he says. "I'm still learning. Not a show ends where I don't learn something new, sometimes even a completely new take on something that I thought that I had decided on and set in stone. I hope you get to experience the same things."

Another talk radio host, **Jack Riccardi**, urges all radio wannabes to "Be yourself. Not a character, not a copy. I wasted years in music radio," the midday talk show host on KTSA San Antonio says, "copying other jocks who I admired, and doing it poorly, only to discover it didn't sound right and didn't work. When I relaxed and played it for 'real,' it was easier for everyone listening and for me."

In August 1957, I was getting ready to enter my junior year of high school, the same month **Dick Clark** first took to his TV podium as host of *American Bandstand*. Like so many other teens, I quickly became a regular viewer of his weekday afternoon show. Watching the kids from South Philly dance to the latest pop/rock hit songs of the day became the in thing to do.

I learned so much from listening to my many radio mentors, but watching Dick Clark's smooth, sincere and casual on-air style made me wish that I could be just like him. There's no question that some of my own air style and persona was borrowed from Clark by watching his mannerisms as host and star of *American Bandstand*. Now is a good time to again remind future radio stars that it's okay to emulate someone's air style, as long as you don't lose yourself in the process.

Fast forward two years, to October 1959. Dick is on board a commuter train between New York and his home outside Philadelphia. He is in the middle of an interview with a Herbert Kamm, a writer for *TV-Radio Mirror*. "What is it that makes Dick Clark so popular?" asked the interviewer. "Let me try to answer it generally," Clark replied, gazing out the train window as the countryside zipped on by. "The most long-lasting people, especially in television [but it also applies to radio] are those who are able to be themselves. This is a talent in itself. There are people who are able to be only what the lines written for them require them to be, and you get to know them as friends, as well as performers, because they do this so well. But, those who are truly themselves, I think are the most durable."

Clark also made reference to his critics. "There are people, especially the caustic critics who say, 'What do you do up there on the *Bandstand*? You stand there and talk!' Well, there happens to be a need in this medium, whether it be television or radio for people who stand there and talk, who tie all the ends together and do it pleasantly."

For thirty years that's exactly what Dick Clark did! He tied all the loose ends together in a personable and professional manner and made American Bandstand one of network television's most popular programs. [18] He did the same thing on his syndicated radio show, *Rock, Roll n' Remember*.

Dick Clark is truly one of America's broadcast legends. I will always be indebted to him for his kindness and inspiration. In December 1985, thanks to input from one of his writers, my friend Fred Bronson, Dick selected me to participate as a judge on his ABC-TV special, *America Votes the #1 Songs*. The program aired March 17, 1986, and was #1 in its time slot. I was honored to play a small role alongside someone I admire so much. Thanks, Dick, for some great golden memories. **Note:** Dick Clark passed away in April 2012.

Tom Bergeron is one personality, like Dick Clark, who stands there, talks and ties the ends together quite pleasantly. Most folks watching Tom Bergeron's comedic wit, which always guarantees his audience a fun time, probably think his entertainment roots were planted in television. *Nay, nay!* to borrow a few choice words made famous by Boston radio legend Commander Larry Glick. No way!

Tom Bergeron cut his comedic teeth on TV without pictures – *radio* - and in Boston. The truth be known, Tom and I were friendly radio competitors in morning drive. Tom was on WBZ on Soldiers Field Road, while I was a short drive away by Fenway Park on the original WROR-98.5.

After an absence of too many years, I caught up with Tom and asked him if he would participate in this book. Not only did he agree to do so, but he returned his comments to my entire list of several hundred questions within hours. OK, so I fibbed about the number of questions - it was more like four. My point is, with his busy television production schedule and commuting between coasts, to take time to respond in such a timely fashion to a guy he hadn't heard from in years speaks volumes about the man. In a "take care of yourself and screw the rest" society, it's reassuring to know there are still nice folks out there like Tom Bergeron.

The Emmy Award-winning Bergeron began his broadcasting career in his hometown of Haverhill, Massachusetts, and when he was growing up, his only career goal was to work in radio. "A television career wasn't even a consideration," says Tom, who today splits his time living in Connecticut and California with his wife Lois and their two daughters. "When I was young, I only wanted to be a radio guy. Well, that's not completely accurate," he adds with his now trademark mischievous twinkle. "Around eight years old, for a few months, I desperately wanted to be a superhero. However, unable to find any radioactive spiders or gamma ray experiments in the neighborhood, I went back to my dreams of broadcasting."

Growing up north of Boston, the powerful 50,000-watt voice of WBZ was a major influence in Bergeron's career. "Among the BZ roster of great radio pros, my absolute favorite was Larry Glick," boasts Tom, proudly. [19] "I found him first on the overnight shift, where the true characters of the world were his telephone regulars, and later on late at night, where enough of the show's wee hour flavor still remained. Larry was funny, always curious and an exceptional entertainer. Listening to him crystallized my career goal. I wanted THAT kind of show." Years later, when Tom landed the morning drive slot at WBZ, the station he grew up with, they became friends, a friendship which continued until Larry's passing in 2009. Tom credits Larry with helping him develop his own air style. "As I grew up, the mischievous and disembodied voice of Larry Glick was the gold standard to me."

One of my questions for the host of ABC's # 1 hit show *Dancing with the Stars* was "How does a future radio star develop their air style?" "That's easy," Tom replied, "**be yourself.** Or, more accurately, a somewhat exaggerated version of yourself. For Rush Limbaugh, it means being a larger pompous ass than he probably is in private. Howard Stern admits the part of himself he gives free reign to on the radio, the perpetually horny emotional twelve-year-old, wouldn't work in real life. But it still is a part of who he is." Tom Bergeron admits it took him years to stop acting like a radio announcer and start allowing his own sensibilities to come through. "What emerged was not too different from my off-air personality; a basically nice guy," he humbly says, "with a hair-trigger sarcastic streak."

Bergeron acknowledges that not all radio formats lend themselves to individuality, and the freedom to develop your own personality, especially when first starting out. "The key is not to allow yourself to become generic on the air. This will inevitably lead to disagreements with management or, at worst, occasional firings. So be it," says Tom. "It's possible to find ways to infuse any format with your own personality. I know. I've done it. The horrible alternative is ending up an interchangeable voice introducing another 50 minutes of soft rock."

When I asked Tom, a member of the first class of inductees to the Massachusetts Broadcasters Hall of Fame, what he attributes his radio success to, he answered in a philosophical manner. "**One,** I always treated every gig as an opportunity, never allowing myself NOT to bring my 'A game,' and **two,** sheer dumb luck. That said, I believe luck only presents itself when you're striving for excellence. I don't want to get too mystical here, but I'm a major proponent of the theory that when you put out positive energy, you're more likely to find it coming back to you. For me, that's been a guiding principle and I've seen it work with remarkable consistency."

For four fun-filled years, my next door neighbor along CBS radio row in West Palm Beach, Florida, was my pal, **Jerry Pelletier.** Jerry is a winner in every sense of the word! He's a great guy and a super air personality. He works extremely hard to put on the best show possible *every day*. I know, I competed against him. Jerry, known as J.D. to his loyal listeners on country-based WIRK in West Palm Beach, had been waking up South Floridians for 13 years until April 2009, when management decided to head off in a new direction, only without their popular morning guy. It seems to happen so often in radio. Decent air-talent and good people get cut loose every day, victims of the bottom line. JD believes the best advice he can pass along to a future radio wannabe about style is "Don't let anyone tell you who you are! You need to know it, or find out for yourself. Once you do," the popular wake-up personality now on-the-air in Lexington, Kentucky, adds, "keep your integrity and be you! No one can be better than you."

Jeff Davis was at WLS Chicago from April 17, 1974, until November 1, 1988, but adds, "That's just as an on-air personality. I've probably never been without a presence at WLS since '74, since I'm still the 'voice' of the station and will continue in that role for some time to come." When Jeff was asked what the best way for tomorrow's radio stars to develop their own special style for the air, he replied the same way so many other successful radio pros have done throughout this book: "Just *be yourself*. Talk to just one person. Radio listeners crave that connection that you as an air-talent have the capability to make." Jeff Davis believes strongly that a good voice helps, but it's not what makes a personality good. "It's what you do with your voice that matters, and how you make people feel with what you say. The gritty edge of people who push their voices unnaturally is called 'puking' and people who do it are called 'pukers.' Use your natural voice."

In the '80s and '90s, when I was in morning drive at WROR Boston, **Sean Casey** was my counterpart in afternoons.[20] He was extremely popular with the driving home crowd. Born and raised in South Philly, Sean spent hours hanging on street corners, singing doo-wop. It was during the era when TV's popular *American Bandstand* originated its afternoon national dance party from the studios of WFIL-TV-Channel 6. When asked if he ever danced on *Bandstand*, Casey emphatically answered, "Yes! I was a semi-regular and, as a matter of fact, Dick Clark still owes me a sports coat for demonstrating the first spotlight dance with a young lady named Joanne."

In the early '60s, Sean headed his own group, The Spokesmen, which also included Dave White and Johnny Madera.[21] Earlier, in the late '50s, Dave White found fame as first lead tenor with Danny and the Juniors. Dave White and John Madera also wrote two rock n' roll classics, "At the Hop" and "Rock & Roll is Here to Stay." The Spokesmen also hit the *Billboard* charts in October 1965 peaking at #36 with "The Dawn of Correction," which was an answer song to Barry McGuire's hit "Eve of Destruction."[22]

Like so many other future radio pros who grew up in the fifties, Sean Casey was raised on rock radio and in Philadelphia, the premiere Top-40 radio station to listen then was WIBG, known to its faithful followers as "Wibbage." Philly has always had great radio pros, but back during rock's formative years, the City of Brotherly Love had some of the best on-air-talent in the business: Joe Niagara, Bill Wright, Sr., Jerry Stevens, Bob Mitchell and "Humble" Harvey Miller. Sean listened to all of them and studied each style, but says he really wasn't inspired to go into radio by anyone. "I really didn't know what the hell I wanted to do when I graduated from Bishop Neumann High in South Philly," says Casey. "I was accepted at LaSalle College, but never showed up. One of my singing buddies, Bob Cullen, decided to attend Bessie V. Hicks School of Broadcasting-Video Arts and Drama, so I decided to join him." Sean laughs and says, "Later, Bob bought the school. I became one of the school's successful graduates, broadcasting full-time classical and R&B on WDAS AM & FM."

Sean Casey's other on-air stops included Dover, Delaware; Trenton, New Jersey; and for awhile at the Philly station he grew up with, WIBG. His resonant pipes were also heard in America's #1 radio market, New York City, on WOR-FM, WPLJ and WCBS-FM. Sean arrived on the Boston radio scene in 1976 at WHDH and then moved over to WROR-FM. Casey attributes his own air success to attention to detail, persistence, networking and, most importantly, a thick skin! As far as developing one's air style, he says, "Study all deliveries from every audio format. Remember, all those great jocks I listened to at Wibbage in Philly. Work on what is most comfortable for you," he adds, "and appreciate and learn from others, but be yourself. And keep one important thing in mind," he adds with a smile, "the radio business doesn't need another someone else."

Frank Kingston Smith [23] is another radio icon who has been on the air in some of America's largest cities, including Philly, New York, and Boston. It was my pleasure to work with "Big Frank," as his friends call him, in 1979 at the Original Golden Great 98-WROR Boston. Frank believes that no matter what your style on the radio and whatever you do, "Don't be humble. Don't tell everyone how good you are, but be good so everyone else talks about you. Keep thinking that you are the best thing on the air and like the cult movie, *The Promise*, you will be the best thing on the air!" Frank urges all future radio stars to "Be an original. I can remember guys in northern New Jersey thirty years ago," he says, "who were touting themselves as the 'Second Most Outrageous' in New York and New Jersey, not naming Don Imus as Number One! If you are naturally that way, do it, if your PD will let you. If not, don't force it. Like when Wolfman Jack was hot. Bob (Wolfman) Smith originated that act, and as far as I'm concerned, it died with him! The Greaseman brought back the style but not the personality. The Boogieman followed. Don't DO that. DO YOUR OWN ACT! If you don't have one, that's okay too," grins Big Frank, "try to make out with the radio, yuh know? Be something that some ONE will remember fondly."

Mike Haile has been in mornings at WHMS in Champaign, Illinois, for thirty years. In addition to his wake-up duties, he is the Assistant General Manager of WHMS and WDWS, and you think you have a busy day! The man loves radio and knew early on in his young life that it was the path for him. "I was one of the lucky people, who at age five knew what career path I wanted to take. My father had a friend who was a salesman at WHB in Kansas City. In 1957, my father took me down to see his friend and get a tour of the station. Over the next four years we lived in Kansas City and I got to make a couple of trips a year to the station. Each time I was mesmerized by what I saw. I was hooked. In 1965, at age 13, I got my third-class radio license and I began making tapes in my basement on a reel-to-reel tape machine I borrowed from my neighbor and with one record player I was Mike Haile the DJ." [24]

Mike Haile has worked full-time in radio since 1970, when he was hired at KWOW-AM in Pomona, California. At the time, he was also a full-time student at Cal State Long Beach and graduated in 1974. During his on-air career, Mike worked at Los Angeles-area radio stations KFI, KOST and KRLA Pasadena. When the opportunity presented itself to program a new station, WKIO-K-104 in Champaign, Illinois, he jumped at it! With an air career of almost forty years, Mike Haile is another radio pro worth listening to on how to develop your own air-style. Simply stated, he says, "I am Mike Haile every day. I don't have a different on-air personality and an off-air personality. Being yourself on the air is the most important thing about being a successful radio pro; however, listening to top air-talent can be a great help in improving one's on-air performance. While Harry Harrison, Nick Charles (at KXOK in St. Louis) and others helped influence my craft, at the end of the day, I am just plain Mike Haile who is lucky enough to be on the radio." [25]

Dan Justin and I were co-workers at the New WROR in the late '90s. "Danny Boy," as he's known to his loyal listeners, has been a fixture on Boston radio for over twenty-five years, the major portion of it in afternoon drive. He is currently in his ninth year riding home with folks, every weekday afternoon from 3 until 8pm on Boston's Magic 106.7. Dan landed on this planet in 1956, and really didn't pay much attention to radio until the mid-'60s, when he listened to 68AM-WRKO and their Top-40 format. When FM burst upon the scene, he was hooked! "I listened to RKO and WMEX right into the '70s," Dan admits, but then along came FM. "WOW! It was so cool. I listened faithfully to WVBF 105.7, known as F-105, and remember two great jocks in particular, Bud Balou and Magic Christian." Dan agrees with other radio pros that the best advice for developing your own air-style is to be yourself, but adds, "Be an individual. Don't try to copy anyone else. It's okay to admire a jock's style and delivery, but make sure you incorporate your own fantastic personality, because I know you have one!"

Joe McMillan is a popular radio talent and voiceover expert. Joe's dulcet tones have rocked the airwaves at WJBQ & WGAN-Portland, Maine, and at Boston radio stations WHDH, WVBF, WROR and OLDIES-103. He was also on in afternoon-drive at KABL in San Francisco. When it comes to finding your own air-style, Joe agrees with other radio pros to "Be yourself," but emphasizes, "it's not easy being yourself! I sound better today because I'm more me on the air. Nobody can do you better, NO-BODY! Sometimes, being you on the radio can be a lifelong search in learning to like yourself!" Joe McMillan also urges all radio talent to do their best everyday! "The results will vary from day to day, but the EFFORT should NOT!! And whatever you do, don't burn bridges. God knows, I've blown some up, but I have a firm belief in God. He's looked out for me. I've been doing radio for 38 years!"

When Joe and I exchanged e-mail in the spring of 2007, he mentioned how happy he was. He had moved to Bucksport, Maine, and was happy in morning drive at WNSX-Ellsworth-Bangor, Maine, working for old friends!

Things were great, he wrote, he had been at the station for two years, had bought a house, and was recently remarried. A totally happy man, still doing what he loved, being on the radio! A short time later, he wrote that he had been fired. Radio can sometimes be a cruel and heartless lover.

Jeanne Ashley has been on the radio since she first hosted a two-hour Saturday morning show while in high school in Okinawa, Japan, on the Far East Network. She readily admits, "I was awful," but adds, "It was great fun and a learning experience." Her first paid radio job was at AM-1490 (then WPEX) in Hampton, Virginia, as a sales person. "I failed miserably, but the owner and morning guy, Joe Moore, thought I might do well as a sidekick. Of course," she gleefully adds, "that was my goal all along. I did everything at the station, morning show, billing, janitorial, you name it, all for $100 a week, but I was in radio!" Jeanne's next radio move was to Upstate New York, where she spent ten years at WLZW Utica and WYYY Syracuse, before the snow chased her out Kansas City way. She joined the Star 102 line-up in 1999 and handled their top-rated midday show, until 2010, when she left to be on the air in Miami. Jeanne has received many accolades from radio pros, including Jon Zellner, VP at XM Satellite Radio, who says, "Jeanne is the consummate professional and easily the best adult contemporary air-talent in the country."

Jeanne offers this advice on developing your own air-style. "The best jocks, in my opinion, have always been the most human-sounding. I think that quality is even more important today. People can get their music anywhere. If someone is turning on the radio, it's our responsibility to give them something they can't get from their iPods. Radio people tend to forget how intimate our medium can be. My advice is to approach your air work from the most human place you possibly can." She also empathizes, for those just starting out, "Forget what you think you know about radio, come in with a clean slate. Find someone in the industry you admire and ask them to mentor you. Don't ever be afraid to ask questions. Learn everything you can about every department in the station; sales, promotions,[26] programming, even engineering. The most valuable people in radio today are those utility people who can do it all."

Paula Street has been heard exclusively on Oldies-103.3 Boston for over 20 years. She has a fun personality and smooth delivery. In the '80s and '90s, when I was on the air in AM-drive in Boston, I felt blessed that I didn't have to compete against her. She's that good! In fact, I took it as a great compliment when people would compare my warmth and friendliness on the radio to her on-air style. Paula's air shift is middays, 9:00 a.m.-2:00p.m., which makes her a perfect companion to listen to while working during those hours. A native of Wheaton, Illinois, Street grew up outside Philly, then moved to Dallas and College at the University of Texas at Arlington, but says some of the best summers of her life were spent in Colorado, where she learned to trout fish with her dad and granddad, a sport she still enjoys to this day.

Paula Street admits she fell into radio. "My first radio job was answering the phones for a talk show, while doing weekends at 98-KZEW, a Dallas-Fort Worth rock station. Later, I did nights at KRQX-AM, a classic rock station." She left to join KLUV Dallas, remaining with the station for five years before moving to Boston in February 1988. Street has been on middays at Oldies-103.3 ever since and recently celebrated her twenty-third year on the station, in the same time slot! An amazing feat for anyone in radio.

With her long and successful track record as a popular radio personality, Paula was asked specifically to direct her comments to future *female* radio stars and how women may develop a particular air-style. "The advice I would give females going into radio is simple: YOU CAN'T FAKE IT! If you have a PD, usually a man, who wants you to be a little more sexy or sultry sounding, or whatever it is that you are NOT, you might have a problem. I believe," she continues, "people are smart enough to know if you are being genuine and real. I think they know if you care about what you are saying on the radio and sense if you are talking to them or at them." Paula Street, one of Boston's top-rated radio talents, says she has worked with some great program directors and some horrible ones. [27] "The great ones," says Paula, "are always the ones who helped me become more ME on the air."

In 1999, radio pro **Joe Ford** and I worked back to back at KLDE, the Oldies station in Houston. I was the morning drive guy and Joe followed me in middays. Joe's advice to tomorrow's radio stars on how to develop an individual style is to *do your homework*. "Study the guys that built the foundations of radio, and see what made them special. Then, take some of those proven ideas and mold them to fit yourself. Remember," adds the member of the Texas Radio Hall of Fame, "you don't have to be vulgar to score ratings, because the folks that use filth as their crutch will soon be crippled as talent."

Ford recalls what renowned radio talent **Robert W. Morgan** once told him: "The guys who are consistently good, sound the same everyday, and never get so controversial that they piss people off, will ALWAYS find work in radio. Unfortunately," adds Joe, "it ain't easy to be real creative and different in today's radio climate when you have consultants and GMs, sales reps and PDs breathing down your throat with restrictions on content and short talk intervals, coupled with ultra-tight music playlists. However, and to put a positive spin on being on the radio today, there are ways to overcome a few of these regulations and the talent who discovers them will find their niche in broadcasting."

Jack Oliver started in radio in 1968 and is still doing his thing today on KEYN Wichita, Kansas. The veteran air-talent and program director feels the best way for a radio wannabe to develop their own air-style is to find a mentor. "E-mail the best in the business, they will e-mail you back," insists Jack. "Listen to jocks on-air and off-air. Model yourself after someone that is successful and find out why they are." The Wichita Radio Hall of Fame member says, "The choice is yours. Stay with it and NEVER give up, always go for it." Oliver also urges those interested in a career on the radio to read and educate themselves about radio. "Learn all you can about the entertainment and the psychology of the listener, but most importantly, have the best attitude of anyone you have ever met or known!"

Pete Falconi spent the last twenty-five years in radio management as a programming and operations executive in the Boston area. Today, he and his partner Carl Strube, a former music executive and radio station owner, own and operate radio station WNBP in Newburyport, Mass. Like so many other radio pros, Pete believes the key to finding your own individual style on the air is to *be yourself*. "Don't try to emulate someone else. Be the real you on the air. Secondly, be a good listener. You can learn from so many people than just your PD." The final piece of advice Pete Falconi offers is to be patient. "There are very few overnight sensations. Listen, learn and patiently work your way up the ladder, be it market size or an internal position."

Here are some basic points to remember in developing your own air-style:

- **ALWAYS BE YOURSELF** on the radio. You are real…you are special, you are unique and you are of great value.
- **Stay focused on the things you can do** and don't over think the things you can't do! **"CAN DO"** should be two words you keep repeating to yourself over and over.
- **Be willing to learn** and a teacher will appear.
- **ALWAYS bring a positive, passionate attitude** to the air.
- **DON'T ALWAYS** expect to get the results you want right away… **keep working at it!**
- **Be careful what you say,** because your words become actions and your actions become habits.
- **Be disciplined.** Discipline is doing what you know you must do, as often as it takes and as difficult as it may be to complete the task at hand.
- **Always speak to your listene**r, not down to them.
- **If you're not the world's greatest ad-libber,** don't beat yourself up, write down prepared ad-libs!
- **Have confidence in what you do,** whatever style you use.
- **Have courage to make mistakes**—-it'll make you sound human and not a pre-recorded voice track.
- **You can't miss the mark by using self-deprecating humor.**
- **Keep a proper balance on your show of** excitement, happiness, sadness, joy. Keep balance on your show and you'll always keep your show full.

- **Be steady and consistent.** Have the patience to let your style unfold at a reasonable pace.
- **Don't ever forget the basics.** You may have the coolest style and be the greatest radio personality on the planet, but if you get away from the formatics and what you know, that's when you'll begin to falter and eventually fail as an air personality!

Advice from Radio Pros on How to develop your own air-style:

- **Harry Harrison**-Morning Mayor of New York City radio for 44 years at CBS-FM, WABC and one of the original WMCA Good Guys: "No matter what you do or what your style is on the radio, always have a winning attitude and have confidence in yourself and your ability."
- **Paula Street**- Oldies-103, Boston: "Your style depends on what type of format you're doing, but be comfortable with who you are"
- **Sean Casey**- Former Boston radio personality- WHDH, WROR and WPLM: "Appreciate and learn from others, but be yourself."
- **Paul Perry**- afternoon drive, WROR Boston: "Find someone to role model. If you're interested in radio then you must have one or two people you've heard that you enjoy and admire. Listen to what it is they do that you like, and try to incorporate that 'special something' into who you are."

Author's note:
My second full-time job in radio was at a small Southern Maine radio station, WIDE Biddeford. It's where I received my baptism in the business and learned much about radio. One of my co-workers with whom I developed a close friendship was **Mike Matoin.** His air-name was Mike Gray and he was a natural-born communicator. He was one of the most personable-sounding air personalities I ever heard. Mike gets credit for giving me advice on how to develop my own air-style which I pay forward to you. He suggested, "Take a little piece of someone you like listening to on the radio, borrow a slice of another, add them to what you're all about and, voila!, slowly you'll find the 'real you' on the radio."

A parting tip for tomorrow's radio stars on developing your own air-style: "Dare to be different."
The woods would be awfully quiet if only the birds who sang the best were allowed to sing. Use your God-given talent to the best of your ability. Your day-to-day positive action, both on and off the radio, will make an enormous difference in your life and career as a radio pro. The trivial aggravations we all face, though virtually insignificant, can totally overwhelm you if you allow

them to do so. Don't let them! Pay attention to the things that matter and ignore the ones that don't.

Author **Richard Bach,** who penned the best-selling *Jonathan Livingston Seagull,* said it best: "Your only obligation in any lifetime is to be true to yourself." Never have these words been more prophetic than when applied to radio air-talent. No matter what anyone says to you, especially when given as input regarding your own unique air style, *always be true to yourself!* Do the best you can with your own God-given talent. As far as your own unique air-style is concerned, look at it this way: You were born an original, don't die a copy. To make a serious impact and lasting impression on the radio, and in life, whatever reflects you and your personality best is what will be your recipe for success. Whether it's humorous, outrageous, warm n' fuzzy, informational, whatever ... stick with what you do best. For example, take well-known radio personality Howard Stern. He was one of radio's first potty-mouthed naughty boys. Others have followed him and whether you love his style or loathe it, you have to admit, he was first and is an original.

> *"Nothing great was ever achieved without enthusiasm."*
> Ralph Waldo Emerson

Notes:
1. Learn more on how to work with program directors and managers in Chapters 10 and 11.
2. Johnny Carson will always be remembered best for his 30 years as the popular host of NBC-TV's *Tonight Show,* but he started in radio. While attending the Univ. of Nebraska, Johnny worked part-time at KFAB in Lincoln. After graduation in 1949, he hosted an afternoon talk show on WOW Radio in Omaha called *The Squirrels Nest.*
3. *Can You Top This* was first heard on radio in 1940 on WOR NYC. The premise was simple: listeners would mail in jokes on any subject and a panel of funny folks led by Peter Donald would try to top them with jokes of their own on the same subject. By 1940 the show was so popular it was picked up by NBC and aired every Saturday night. It remained on radio until 1953. It went on ABC-TV in 1950 with Wink Martindale as the original host. In 1970 *Can You Top This* was revised for syndication.
4. Read more about the unique style of *Joe n' Andy* in Chapter 14, How to Win in Morning Drive Radio
5. Eventually Andy lost a lot of weight, but damage had been done to his loving heart.
6. The importance of show prep is covered in detail in Chapter 7
7. Renowned radio pro Bruce Bradley candidly comments on how to be successful radio personality in Chapter 4.

8. Longtime popular Boston radio pro Dale Dorman comments in Chapter 14, How to Win in Morning Drive
9. "Post" is a radio term referring to the point where the vocal begins in a song
10. Additional comments from Cary Pahigian can be found in Chapter 11, Inside the World of General Managers
11. Tommy was also on the air at CKLW, the Windsor, Ontario-Detroit radio station on three separate occasions, totaling 18 years. Shannon was also on television almost as long as he was on radio. In 1972, he moved from radio to the TV side at Ch.-7 Detroit as host of the morning show, a post he held for about a year. Tommy also did specialty shows, the weather and hosted the Michigan Lottery for two years. He also hosted a *Bandstand* type TV show. Later, in Denver, Tom Shannon hosted *Afternoon at the Movies*.
12. Dick Biondi comments on getting fired in radio in Chapter 9, Attitudes & Actions
13. Barbara Quill is another radio pro I had the pleasure of working with at WGAN-AM 560 Portland, ME. We also worked together at the original WROR-98.5 Boston. Barbara was a dedicated, hard-working news pro on both radio and television. It was broadcasting's loss when she left radio to teach English and Journalism at Coyle-Cassidy High School in Taunton, MA. I'm hoping she will find a way, even on a sometime basis, to get back on the radio. Broadcasting needs more classy and talented people like Barbara Quill.
14. My early years in Maine radio at WIDE-1400AM Radio are covered extensively in Chapter 6
15. **Author's note:** I respectfully take issue with my longtime friend on this point. During my many years on the air, including almost 20 in AM-Drive in Boston, my listeners knew when I had a tough night and consequently, a difficult time getting up the next morning. If I had a headache or a hang nail, our listeners heard all about it on our show. Of course, we did our best to make it humorous. Jack is right about making your story compelling, so that your listeners will stay with you and not button push and wind up somewhere else on the dial. Our listening family at the original ROR-FM (later MIX-98.5) apparently didn't mind our "storytelling," since we were always blessed with high ratings. Keep in mind, always endeavor to leave your listeners on a high note, with a humorous twist to any story or bit you share on the air. The old saying, "leave 'em laughing" still holds true today. One additional point: a minimum of words has always been the rule on a Top-40 station or any music-intensive format. However, time spent talking and the length of your break obviously depends on the type of format you are working. For example, talk radio or a personality-driven morning drive show would not necessarily apply to an "economy of words" scenario.

16. For more on M.G.'s career, visit his website at www.mgkelly.com
17. Boston is where Mark Williams and I first worked together. I was in morning drive on ROR-FM and Mark was a producer, down the hall, on our sister station RKO-AM
18. In the fall of 1987, after 30 years, Dick Clark and ABC parted company. ABC wanted to cut the program to a half-hour and Dick preferred to keep it an hour. Bandstand went into syndication for a year and a half, later moved to the USA Cable Network with a new host, 26-year-old David Hirsch, who just happened to be the same age as Clark when the show began its long, successful run on ABC-TV in 1957. American Bandstand was television's longest-running musical series. The program was also the first network series devoted exclusively to rock n' roll music.
19. Larry Glick, who passed away in February 2009, is remembered in Chapter 16.
20. Before Sean Casey's arrival at WROR, afternoon drive was handle by another Boston radio legend, Larry Justice. His familiar salutation, "Welcome to the Halls of Justice" was heard for many years over Boston-airwaves, first on WBZ and later ROR-FM.
21. As a member of the Philadelphia-based pop singing group The Spokesmen, Sean Casey sang under his real name, Roy Gilmore.
22. "Eve of Destruction" got as high as #1 on Billboard's music charts in August 1965.
23. Today, Frank and his wife Linda operate Showtime Promotional Products in Scottsdale, AZ
24. The FCC required all radio station board operators to hold a 3rd-class radio-telephone license to take transmitter readings
25. Note to future radio stars, do what Mike Haile did. Pick the best on the radio, in your estimation, listen closely to them, study their delivery and what makes them so popular and then apply it to your own personality.
26. The importance of radio promotion is covered in Chapter 15
27. The role of radio station program directors is covered in Chapter 10

How To Develop Your Own Air-Style • 69

Ryan "Rick" Cote today - (2009) former Boston and now Augusta, ME radio pro on WABK.

Joe (author) and Andy waving hello- remote broadcast from Boston Harbor Hotel (late 1980's) WROR 98.5FM- Boston. Person in BG wearing headphones is our producer Linda Smith.

Ryan "Rick" Cote, host of High School Billboard, WIDE Radio Biddeford, ME. early 1960's.

Chuck Igo, Boston and Portland ME air personality

Tom Shannon, legendary WKBW Buffalo air pro (also CKLW-Detroit-Windsor Ontario, Canada)

Wink Martindale, nationally know Radio/TV personality.

Jack Casey, former air personality, now GM, Emerson College station WERS-FM-Boston.

Bob Lacey, nationally syndicated morning-drive radio personality.

Dick Clark, broadcast icon and nationally known radio-TV personality, producer.

M.G. Kelly, Los Angeles and national air talent.

How To Develop Your Own Air-Style • 71

Frank Kingston Smith, Philly, NYC and Boston air pro.

Tom Bergeron, former air pro and now popular network TV star.

Sean Casey, Boston and Philadelphia air personality.

Mike Haile, radio GM and air talent-WHMS-Champaign, Illinois.

Joe McMillan, former Maine and Boston air personality, now voice-over talent.

Paula Street, (photo -Naomi Stock) long-time Boston mid-day personality WODS.

Joe Ford, legendary Houston radio pro.

CHAPTER 3
How to Break Into Radio

"The audience must accept you as a human being, before it can accept you as a comedian, announcer or newscaster."

– Legendary pioneer radio personality Durwood Kirby

BEFORE WE GET INTO THE NITTY-GRITTY of this chapter, here are some excellent words of advice from **Joel Denver,** the president & publisher of AllAccess.com, on the real reason you should want to be an air personality. The former air-talent and radio PD feels that anyone wanting to get into radio should be doing it for the love of the art of it—not the money. "Anytime you focus on money, it becomes a bad goal," says Joel. "If you focus on the product and your skill set, and you can exploit and expand your own talent, the money will come. Maybe not at your present job, but somewhere down the line."

Breaking into radio, especially on the air, is not easy! With today's multiple market ownerships and downsizing, getting your foot in the door is tough. However, if you persevere and don't mind getting a few facial burns from doors being slammed in your face, with a little bit o' luck, you will eventually land a position on the radio. There is one necessary quality required to be a successful on-air-talent and that's *passion*![1] If you're not passionate about being on the radio, then forget it! Having God's gift of talent is an important part of the total package, but passion is the key to having a successful career on the radio. More than one hundred broadcasters have generously given of their time and shared their expertise to make this book the best possible resource available to help guide you to a successful on-air radio career. Nearly all listed passion as the key ingredient in reaching that goal!

The first question a radio wannabe usually asks is *"How do you get that first break?"*

To obtain the answer to this all-important question, *Radio Pro* reached out to some of America's top broadcasters. We begin with **Gary Berkowitz**, to whom I am indebted for helping launch my major market radio career in Boston. He is one of the nation's most respected broadcast consultants. In 1979, he hired me for fill-in air work at the original Golden Great 98.5-WROR-Boston. Without his encouragement and support, I never would have reached the level of success I enjoyed on the radio. Gary says syndication is one of the big problems for those looking to get that first break in radio. "There is so much syndication, especially on AM, with radio talk shows like Rush Limbaugh, Laura Ingraham, Glenn Beck, Sean Hannity, and others that precious little air time is left for live local shows. Syndicated programs are fed to radio stations in all size markets across America which makes it more difficult than ever for future radio stars to break into local radio. There are fewer stations, especially AMs, to start at," says Berkowitz. "Fewer stations need or have live bodies around the clock, much of which is voice-tracked. With that being said, there are still plenty of places to start."

Gary Berkowitz began his own air career, while attending Emerson College in Boston. He worked at WEIM in Fitchburg and WSAR in Fall River, both Knight Quality stations in Massachusetts. "If you really want it, you will find a place to break in and most importantly to learn. The big difference in today's radio world is many young broadcasters are bypassing the Fitchburg, MAs of the world and are starting in the Baltimores! That's both good and bad." Berkowitz believes small market radio trains you well for the big time. He also has an ominous warning to future radio stars: "Be prepared to work long, hard hours and make very little money in the beginning. Take any job you can to get in the station you want to work for. Be the 'go-to' guy. Always have a can-do attitude. Be the one who always says 'YES!' Attitude is 99% of getting in the door in radio."

Berkowitz, a radio consultant who specializes in AC (Adult Contemporary) radio stations, is well acquainted with a can-do positive attitude. As a 13-year-old kid growing up in Oceanside, New York, he was hooked on great New York City radio stations like WMCA and 77-WABC. One of his earliest radio influences was Rick Sklar, who was the genius PD behind music-radio WABC during its hey-day in the '60s and '70s. "I must have applied to him 100 times at WABC," Berkowitz laughs, "but I never got the gig. Years later, we met when I was PD at PRO-FM in Providence. He needed a summer place to store his daughter's stuff, who was a student at Brown University. Rick called me and she ended up storing her stuff at our place and he and I became fast friends. Only in radio!" Moral of the story: if you want to get in good with a major market PD, let their college kid store their stuff at your house!

Ted Quillin was one of America's first Top-40 radio personalities! While on the air at legendary KFWB in Hollywood from 1958 until 1961, he was rated the number-one personality in the nation by C.E. Hooper.[2] Ted was also a personality with other great stations, including KRLA-Pasadena, KORK-Las Vegas, KFI in LA and KFOX. In 2005, he was inducted into the Nevada Broadcasters Hall of Fame. Until his passing in early 2011, Ted continued doing what he loved, being on the air. Still blessed with a great radio voice, he kept his hand in broadcasting with a classic country show on KDSS in Ely, Nevada, and a show on the Internet on Rockit Radio, heard on your friendly computer at http://www.rockitradio.net/programs.html.

Born in Oklahoma City, Ted and his family moved to El Paso, Texas, and that's where he was first bitten by the radio bug. "I listened to morning personalities on several stations," says Ted, "and one day I finally got the nerve up to call two morning personalities on KEPO. I went to the station and told them flat out that I wanted to be an announcer. They agreed, so I became a gopher go for this, go for that, got their coffee, learned to rip the news from the wire service, and just picked up everything I could." Talk about truly wanting to be in radio! Ted would hitchhike, walk or get a ride each morning to be at the studio by 6am. "I worked from 6 to 7, then went to school. I was 17. The two morning men were Ollie Remand and Saul Peredez. I learned by osmosis by watching them and hanging around each morning and learning everything I could about radio." In the summers Ted worked part-time as a board operator and announcer and learned how to cut commercials. He remembers the moment he really got hooked on being on the air: "It was the day they let me read the hog reports on the farm and ranch portion of their show," he laughs, "That did it for me. If you want to be on the air badly enough, you'll do it, too!"

While working as a teenager at El Paso's KEPO, Quillin received a call from Chuck Blore.[3] "Chuck was the PD at the Top-40 station in town, KELP. We became acquainted and he asked me to cut some commercials with him. We worked for several days and nights on them and in doing so became friends and he offered me a time slot as disc jockey on KELP. It was a Gordon McLendon station and the ratings were TERRIFIC.[4] We had 50s and 60s in the Hooper Ratings Service. As a matter of fact, the national reps said the numbers were too big and they had to tone them down so people would believe them!"[5]

At KELP, Ted was production manager and Chuck Blore was the program director. As a blossoming young radio star, Ted's career was about to soar even higher. When Chuck accepted an offer from KFWB Hollywood, Ted Quillin was the only personality he took with him. Ted went on to become one of the original "Seven Swingin' Gentlemen," who took Rock and Roll radio into Los Angeles at the legendary station.

So you see, it could happen to you! If you really want to get your first on-air break in radio, do as Ted Quillin did. Read the hog report and do it willingly and enthusiastically. It may just bring home the bacon for you!

Mark Williams is a familiar talk-radio voice across America. He has worked in radio from border to border and as another popular talk show host, Rush Limbaugh, says, "From sea to shining sea." I got to know Mark when we both worked for the General, RKO-Radio Boston, back in the 1980s. His advice for nailing down your first radio job is "Find the smallest, most wretched radio market that you can find, in a place as different from home as you can find and work there for a year. Do every job in the station, become part of the community, build a record of accomplishment. When I was PD at WWDB in Philadelphia," adds Williams, "I would not even talk to somebody who presented me with a resume filled with education but no long-term small market work. Call me when you can do the job! Move to a distant city, learn the names of streets, drive a cab for a year, pick grapes just do it for a year or two, things so drastically out of your comfort zone and alien to you that your mind and world view will have to expand just to survive."

Mark Williams has come a long way since his first radio job, selling commercial time at $4.00 a minute, when he could get that much, at 1000-watt daytime station WPEP in Taunton, MA. Today, Fox News Channel sends a town car once a week to take him to a TV studio where he does his thing for them. He writes a regional newspaper column in California and appears as a freelance host on a dozen or so radio and TV stations in major markets and for a couple of networks, all while working to launch his New Media venture. Mark has come a long way since he was a four-year-old and his dad took him on a tour of the factory where he worked. "While I'm sure it was his idea to show me just how hard it was to come by money," says Williams, "what he did demonstrate was that working for it was not the way to get money. I decided to get a really cool job like being on the radio or on television. I did and I'm still learning"

Jack Oliver has been in AM-Drive along with PD duties at KEYN in Wichita, Kansas, for the past five years. Before that, he was PD at KKRD for an incredible 24 years. Jack feels that radio stations still need people, so if you want to be on the radio bad enough start hanging around your favorite station. "Be helpful. Be a problem solver for the PD. It's just like the old days," the Wichita Hall of Fame radio veteran says. "To start out, you may have to work the bad hours or shifts or run tapes on the weekends, but do it! Learn computer skills, web page design and how to do production. This is a great way to work your way into an air shift. Some college courses can teach these things, too, which is invaluable in helping you get a foot in the door at a station. Start out by hanging around your favorite radio station and offer to help solve problems for the PD."

My friend, **Les Howard Jacoby** was my program director at **Sunny 104.3** in West Palm Beach in 2001. Les had a spectacular run at Sunny. During his ten years as PD, the station was consistently #1 with double-digit figures in the ratings. Les feels that today's "Baby DJs," as he calls them, have a very difficult task ahead of themselves trying to break into the industry. "Once upon a time fresh talent was developed in small markets, where young jocks were allowed to experiment and learn their skills. With the advent of satellite-delivered syndicated programming, as well as voice-tracking, 'live' all-night positions and even the 7pm-midnight shows have for the most part dried up, in both large and small markets." That said, the longtime Florida air personality and programmer adds, "There are still a few radio companies who believe in developing and maintaining their own talent. Much like Major League baseball teams have a talent development program called the Minor Leagues, these companies use their smaller markets as training grounds, often moving developing talent to a larger market within the company, when there is an opening and the talent's skills have improved to a level that earns a promotion." Jacoby urges all radio wannabes to search AllAccess and other radio websites.[6] Look for job openings which often will state, "Willing to train radio newcomers."

Celebrated Dallas radio pro **Ron Chapman** says it's tougher today for new kids to cut their teeth in radio. Ron joined KVIL-AM-Dallas in 1960 and was a popular personality on the station for 32 years! From 2000 until June 24, 2005, he did mornings on Dallas Oldies station 98.7-KLUV-FM. Chapman, probably the most listened to morning radio personality in the history of the Southwest, says, "It's tougher in today's homogenized radio environment to break into radio. I believe, when a radio company becomes large enough that they're listed on the New York Stock Exchange, they begin making decisions for the wrong reasons. They think less about community and audience, and more about their stock price. If the price goes down, the quickest way to kick it back up again is to fire hundreds of people and close three divisions. Wall Street loves that kind of thinking and the stock goes back up! The station staff and the listener lose. Now, to really answer your question on how to break into radio," laughs Chapman, "it's tough! When most stations are influenced by consultants who only want to repeat tested phrases from their latest focus group, it's particularly difficult to let a personality break through. So if you're lucky to nail down the 7pm to Midnight slot, do it like it's morning drive, which is the prime shift on any station, and try to squeeze your personality into whatever confines the 'one-liners' allow. Do it better tomorrow than you did today and still better the next. Prepare, deliver, shine at whatever shift they throw at you! If your own station doesn't notice, the competition will."

Paul Perry is WROR-Boston's PM-Drive personality. He has been entertaining New England radio listeners for almost thirty years. For those planning to attend college and study communications, he says, "Get involved with the college radio station. With fewer small stations around with live talent, there is less opportunity to grow your air personality. Now, more than ever, finding a place to develop your skills has become a challenge." In addition to his on-air career, Paul has been a teacher in the communications field and has taught Radio and TV courses at Emerson College in Boston and Deane Jr. College in Franklin, MA, but the majority of his time has been spent at New England Tech, a college that offers Associate and Bachelor degrees in Telecommunications. Paul Perry developed the radio curriculum for the college in 1990.

Paul was 25 when he and a friend bought a small station in Woonsocket, Rhode Island. "During the five years we owned it, one of our biggest problems, next to not having enough money, was finding entry-level DJs. This was the focus of the curriculum I developed for New England Tech. The key to success at the college level is hands-on training. Theory is important," says Perry, "but radio is a 'show me,' performance-based industry. The ability to do it and do it well is what it's all about. College radio can give you the all-important opportunity to learn by doing."

Steve Gilinsky is co-owner/VP and GM at Magic101.7 in Binghamton, New York. His first full-time job in radio was at WINR in Binghamton in December, 1979. Steve's advice on how to get your foot in radio's door is direct. "I tell people not to get into the business! Seriously, I'd say college, and more college. I did not go to college and I really don't regret it, because I made it, but many do not make it, so they need something to fall back on. If you really want to get into radio you must go after your dreams. Don't get discouraged. Put 2000 percent into it and you never know. Besides," he adds, "if it doesn't work out as an air-talent, there's radio sales which really did it for me." 7

Pete Falconi, a former Boston radio programmer and today a station owner, got his break in radio by writing a column for a free weekly paper published by radio station WSRO in Marlboro, MA. "I was a junior in high school and didn't have a driver's license, so my mom would drive me to the station to deliver the column. She did grocery shopping while I hung around the station." After doing a few coffee runs and clearing the AP wire, Pete was offered a job running the control board during coverage of local Little League baseball games. "Less than a year later, I got the 'big call' when someone was out sick. I was needed to go on the air from 6pm until sign-off. A whopping two hours and 15 minutes. I even wore a tie," says Pete. His advice: "Hang out at your local radio station and be a gopher."

Scott Mackay began his radio life in Keene, New Hampshire, in 1979. Mackay's long career has taken him "From Boston to Denver and every town in between," lyrics borrowed from Barry Manilow's "It's a Miracle." Scott and I worked together at MIX-98.5 Boston before he headed off to the Windy City and AM-Drive on Chicago's *True Oldies station*, WLS-FM. Scott tells anyone looking to break into radio, "Work hard. Take whatever job is offered and work hard at it. Be involved in as many areas as you can be, but always be honest going in. Tell the station what your goals are and make sure it is possible to achieve them. You never start at the top," says Scott, "so plan on working your way up the ladder no matter what you have done before. Get under one of the talents' wings and work hard for that person. Kids are always being called sponges because of what they pick up, like bad words, from their parents and peers…so learn to be a sponge again as an adult. Minus the bad words, it'll help."

Matt "The Cat" Baldassarri was music director for the '50s XM5 music channel.[8] Little is known about Matt the Cat, but rumor has it that he disappeared right around the same time the Russians sent up Sputnik in 1957. He left his Boston home with nothing but a stack of rhythm and blues records and a bag of 100-proof catnip. He still orbits the earth, rockin' away via the Internet every Friday night with his weekly "cat fight."

What advice does Matt the Cat, the former host of the Night Prowl Show and Harlem on Sirius-XM Satellite Radio, have for radio wannabes still in high school or college on how to prepare for a career as a future air personality? "It's kind of funny, but my advice in this department is advice I never took myself. You see, I was so busy performing on both my high school and college radio stations that I never took any internships. I just didn't have time." Baldassarri, who grew up just north of Boston, didn't participate in an internship program because he felt it would be of little benefit, since he was already on the air in a major market. "Well, after college I found it very difficult to break into the saturated Boston commercial radio market. I received one rejection letter after another. The nice part was that at the bottom of most of the standard rejection letters, the PDs had written a personal message telling me how much they liked my air-check." The bitter pill for Matt to swallow was the words that followed. "They said they just couldn't hire someone with my style right now, since all their decisions came from corporate in New York." He believes an internship may have helped. "Perhaps if I had some internship connections, I may have been better prepared for the career dry spell I experienced. I've seen how friends of mine have benefited from internships and I've also seen how interns at XM Radio have gone on to full-time positions."

So, here's Matt's advice: "Take advantage of every opportunity to learn and experience radio, even if it's not a glorious on-air position. Overnight board-oping won't kill you," he laughs.

Matt the Cat believes if you are serious about getting into radio then go to a college that specializes in radio.[9] "I highly recommend going to a college that has a major radio station and takes their radio department seriously. Emerson College is that kind of school and that's the only reason why I went there.[10] College radio may not be pro commercial radio, but it's a great way to get experience. You'll also be able to put together a killer air-check and make industry connections." Matt believes it was the connection that he made at Emerson and WERS that later helped him get a job at XM Satellite radio.

Matt continues, speaking about some of his early influences: "I had the opportunity to listen to your shows, Joe [referring to this book's author], on the original oldies authority-98.5-WROR. My nightly call-in show is greatly based on your Saturday Night 'Live' at the oldies show," says Matt. "I never missed a week. As you know, the play lists were a lot looser back in the '80s. I heard so many records on your show that I never would have heard on WODS or any other local outlet. Your interaction with your audience, Joe, on both of your shows, Saturday Night 'Live' at the Oldies and your morning show, Joe and Andy, was something that has always stuck in my head. You always treated your listeners like family and that's a feeling I have strived to achieve." [11, 12]

Alice Pearce was one of my first producers on Saturday Night "Live" at the Oldies at the original WROR 98.5 back in the early 1980s. At the time, Alice was a full-time student at Boston College. "The excitement of being a twenty-year-old college student and having a chance to work at a major market radio station," she says, "and getting to be such an active and involved part of Saturday Night 'Live' at the Oldies while making a whole round of new friends was unbelievable. The friendships that I established at WROR provided me with such a great support system following my graduation and during my first several years as a young, single professional living in Boston."

Alice has some solid advice for those of you still in high school who want to make radio a career, whether as an on-air personality or in some off-air capacity. "The best advice is to get *experience, experience, experience.* As soon as I made my mind up that a career in radio is what I wanted I began knocking on radio station doors. During my senior year in high school, I interned at a small, local radio station in a nearby community; my job at the station included helping the afternoon DJ prepare his newscast, select music and by helping the traffic department by putting commercials on carts. [13, 14] Remember those things? This was back in 1977. When I got to Boston College," Pearce recalls, "the first thing I did was get involved with the college radio station. I volunteered for on-air slots on both the carrier current AM station which was only heard on campus and the non-commercial FM station." Alice says getting involved with your college radio stations is a must. "If you go to college and radio is your dream, check out the campus station. I did and it helped me to learn first-hand how radio works. I got involved in music, news programming and quite often ended up in director positions. By the time my junior year rolled around, I got an internship at WROR and worked with Joe Martelle every Saturday night on his oldies show, which was an invaluable learning experience. I worked hard, learning everything I could and doing everything I could."

Alice Pearce spent seven years in radio, seven years in public relations and the past sixteen in marketing with Ski New Hampshire. When I first contacted Alice about providing some insight for future radio wannabes on how to obtain their first job, her initial reaction was, "Wow, I haven't had to think about radio for so long. I've been out of the business for so long, Joe, I'm not even sure how relevant my input is, but I'm happy to tell you what seemed to work for me. Newbies in radio need to network," she says. "Radio is a small business in which everyone knows each other. At least that's the way it was for me when I worked in the business from 1977-1984 and I'm not sure it's changed since then. [Author's note: It hasn't.] The more people you have a chance to meet, the more people you can contact when you are looking for new opportunities," adds Pearce.

Pearce continues, emphasizing the importance of getting your teeth into working in real radio while you're a student: "Working in real radio situations through internships or part-time jobs is probably more important than any course work you can take in college. By all means, take those communication classes if they are available," she urges, "but real on-the-job work experience is more important than the courses themselves." Alice also says it's important to have a good base in writing and marketing. "The communications industry is evolving so rapidly to the point where radio station websites and streaming is probably even more important than live listening on traditional radio, so it's probably a good idea to have a strong foundation in some new media applications as well. Most importantly," she concludes, "be yourself and stick to your values as a guide to your decision-making in your job and in your career."

Amy Doyle was another super-talented person I enjoyed working with during my years on the radio in Boston at WBMX-MIX-98.5, formerly WROR and today in 2011, sports radio. Amy was a friendly, upbeat radio newbie and recent Boston University grad when she joined our radio station's promotions department in the early 1990s. Her warm, happy personality is what prompted me to recruit her for our MIX morning show. She proved to be an invaluable asset. Every morning Amy would dish out juicy entertainment news stories as our own resident Dirt Devil. She possessed a winning combination of charisma and talent. There was an easy-to-take way about her air-style and everyone connected with our show, both on and off the air, including my wife Kimmie, knew Amy Doyle was destined for bigger things! We were right! After a few years in radio programming, Amy moved on to MTV. Today, she is Senior Vice-President for Music and Talent at MTV, MTV2 and mtvU.

Amy believes the most important thing for future radio stars to keep in mind is that the entertainment business is a lot smaller than one might think. "My best advice is to always treat people with respect, no matter what their position is. I can almost guarantee that you will continue to cross paths with people you worked with on your first radio job, and along the way, somewhere down the line, so treat everyone with respect." Amy Doyle agrees with her predecessor at WROR, Alice Pearce, about the importance of networking: " It's really important. I transitioned from radio to television because I continued to network with people I respected and learned from and that ultimately led to a great position at MTV."

This book is all about how to become an on-air radio personality. However, not to disillusion any future radio wannabes, but being on the air probably will not be your first job in radio! In fact, I strongly suggest you take advantage of any and every opportunity that comes your way to get your foot in the radio door! That means *any* job, whether it's running the board for a local game or syndicated show, or answering the phones! Don't be choosy and picky, or you may find yourself flipping burgers for a very long time and wondering why your radio ship hasn't come in to port yet!

Sometimes, lady luck will open a small window for you. It happened that way for former Mix-107.3 Washington, DC, nighttime personality, **Cindy Maguire**.[15] Her radio career began in a most unusual way. In 1992, Cindy was attending a community college taking accounting courses. A local radio station, WFQX in Strasburg, Virginia, ran a contest where you would have to identify an elevator version of a classic rock song. "One particular day, the DJ wasn't having much luck with getting a winner," recalls Cindy. "None of his callers seemed to know the proper name of the song. Even though I had NEVER called a radio station before, I decided I would help out and call in to properly identify the song. It was 'Saturday Night's Alright for Fighting' by Elton John. The DJ actually answered my call, after taking five or six wrong guesses. I was the first person to get the correct answer!" About a week later, Cindy says she was out running errands and decided to stop by the station and claim her prize. "I wasn't employed at the time and while I was at the station asked if they were hiring."

Radio Rule Reminder: *don't ever be shy when it comes to asking about a job.*

Much to Cindy's surprise, and according to her own admonition, the way she was dressed, cut-off sweatpants as shorts, a T-shirt and hair in a pony-tail with no make-up, the answer to her question regarding a job was a resounding yes! The Traffic Director's receptionist, office-assistant, and morning-show sidekick had just given her notice. Cindy Maguire had never been on the air in her life, so they really weren't interested in putting her in as the morning-show sidekick, but she was definitely qualified for the other parts of the job, so she said, "Why not!" and went for it!

Radio Point to Remember: To get your foot in the door, take whatever radio job is available!

Since WFQX was a small-market radio station, Cindy had the opportunity to learn all aspects of the radio business, from the office procedures, including traffic, to sales and production to promotions. [16] After working at the station for about six months and soaking up everything in sight about radio, her big break to get on the air finally happened. The Program Director asked Cindy if she ever thought about going on the air. "He wanted to train me," she explains, "just in case they needed an emergency fill-in air personality. Well, wouldn't you just know it, two weeks later that opportunity came totally out of the blue and I found myself on the radio!" Cindy decided, and rather unselfishly, that just because she was now on the radio it was no reason for her not to stop working in the office, so she did both. She worked in the office during the week while working part-time on-the-air on weekends. "I did that for about a year and a half, until I was offered a full-time on-air position doing middays at another station, WKMZ in Martinsburg, Virginia." Cindy took the on-air position and stayed with the station for 6 ½ years before moving on up to the Washington, DC, radio market.

Cindy Maguire's story should serve as an inspiration for anyone interested in *how to break into radio*. Her story serves as a prime example of a person who was ready and willing to do anything necessary to get into radio! It paid off big time, when she eventually got her shot at being on the air.

Bottom Line: Be willing to do anything in the radio station to get your foot and *mouth* in the door!

In the early 1970s, I worked with Cincinnati's "Music Professor," **Jim LaBarbara,** at the Nation's Station, WLW. Jim first began on the Queen City airwaves in 1969. He is one of the best air-talents on radio when it comes to sharing stories about the artist and music he plays with his listeners. Jimmy is another radio legend who has great passion for what he does. "For more than forty-seven years, I've had the best job in the world," the Hall of Fame radio pro boasts. "Radio, you've really got to want it. During the summer before my senior year in college, I got my foot in the door at a little station in Titusville, Pennsylvania. I wanted advice on whether I could make it in radio and on the air. Specs Howard, the morning man at giant WKYC in Cleveland, agreed to listen to my air-check. I remember how nice he was. His partner Harry Martin listened for a few seconds and told me I had to project my voice and went on to tell me that he had been in the Harry Simeone Chorale and started singing. Harry suggested I take singing lessons as well. So, I did, my senior year in college."

Three and a half years later, Jim LaBarbara got his dream job, working all night at 50,000-watt WKYC, the very same station where Specs and Harry did the morning drive show. "I was so excited to see them again after my show," recalls Jim. "When they both walked in to do their show, I said, 'Hey, guys, do you remember me' and I added, 'Harry, thanks for the advice, I took singing lessons!' He burst out laughing and yelled, 'Hey, Specs, they hired the dummy! They hired that dumb kid! I was putting you on, kid! It was a joke!'

Of course, I laughed right along with them. I didn't care, singing lessons or not. Like I said, I had made it to my dream job at WKYC. If you love radio, you'll do whatever it takes to get your foot in the door."

Skip Kelly is a familiar radio voice to listeners in South Florida and in West Virginia. He is on the air middays at Classy 92.1-WRLX in West Palm Beach and voice-tracks afternoon drive on Star 94.7 in Ft. Pierce Florida, and weeknights from 7-Midnight at 98.7-Country WOVK in Wheeling, West Virginia. As if that's not enough air-time, hard-working Kelly also manages to handle weekend mornings at KOOL 105.5-WOLL also in West Palm Beach. He credits *Duncan Dewar* as his inspiration to pursue an on-air radio career. "The first DJ I can remember hearing was Duncan. He had a great radio voice and was witty and seemed to say all the right things at the right times." Skip liked the way Duncan Dewar talked up the ramps of songs and hit the post flawlessly each and every time.[17] "How cool, I thought. That sounded like fun and I knew I could do that, too. I began practicing in my bedroom with my records and a fake microphone. In fact, later, when I was looking for my first paying gig," he recalls, "I taped an entire show of his, transcribed everything and recorded it word for word, the same songs he used, everything, except, of course, it was my voice. I got my first paying on-air gig from that tape and I am forever grateful to Duncan for inspiring me. I am still in touch with him today."

Skip Kelly believes the best way to break in to radio is to be well rounded and be willing to pick up a fumble and run with it. He also feels that being a radio newbie means being a sponge and learning everything about every facet of the radio station, from programming and management to promotion and sales! "Learn all you can. Once you get hired, you need to become a versatile and valuable member of the station team," he advises. "That means volunteering willingly for the non-paid station events and lowly assignments nobody else wants. It means showing up early to work to 'see and be seen.' Above all," he stresses, "be a team player and a go-to guy that everyone knows they can count on. The days of four and out the door are gone![18] The buzzword for the 2000s is multi-tasking."

For many radio pros, the passion and desire to be on the radio seems to be in one's genes. You are born with it. Take my longtime friend, **Rick Snyder**. In the early 1970s, he and I worked together at WLOB -AM 1310 in Portland, Maine. I was his successor on the coveted morning drive slot that he and his former wife Mary-Jo handled so well for almost five years. Notice I used the word "successor." I did not replace them, for I truly believe they were irreplaceable. Portland listeners loved the hubby and wife team of *Snyder & Snyder*. But, as so often is the case in radio and quite often without rhyme or reason, management decided to make a change. I was available and in need of a job and was hired by my pal, Bob Anderson.[19] Ricky moved into sales at the station and we became friends. Some thirty-five years later, we're still friends and remain in touch.

Rick grew up in Syracuse, New York, in the 1950s and was able to listen to out-of-town stations on his family's old Zenith console radio. It was quite the adventure for the youngster to be able to dial around and hear voices from New York City, Buffalo, Boston, Detroit, Chicago and other cities. "I was a teen in the '50s, and Rock 'n' Roll was in its infancy and every day was a music adventure as new artists and new sounds hit the airwaves." Rick's big radio break happened when Tommy Saunders allowed him to sit in on his Saturday Night WOLF pack party, answering phones and helping with the music. "Tommy hired me for the all=night show at WOLF in the summer of 1961. I was twenty. After four months on overnights, I went to afternoon-drive. It was a great time for me on a great station in a great time of my life. Every day when I'd wake up I'd say, 'Hey, I'm going to work at the radio station today!' And I was never late!" Rick Snyder's advice to aspiring radio stars, looking to break in: "Go for it! If you love it and you want it, don't give up. Make it happen. It's up to you!"

Nancy Quill has been a permanent fixture middays on Magic-106.7 in Boston for almost thirty years! Her program is the longest-running and most listened to in Boston radio. Her advice to future radio stars on how to break into the business: "Take any shift available to get experience: weekends, overnights, holidays! Nothing is better," says Nancy, "than actually being on the air to improve."

Mark McCray is a PD in Dallas. I asked my longtime friend, as an African-American, how difficult it is today for "people of color" to break into radio. "It's difficult for ANYONE to get into the business these days. There are fewer jobs and many people fighting for the ones available," was his reply, "so there is competition for everyone. Where it can be difficult for African-Americans specifically is when it comes to breaking into formats that are not urban-based." McCray also has this solid advice for future radio stars: "Be persistent but not annoying. If there is a job you REALLY want, go for it hard! Don't just send your resume and CD, follow-up with a phone call or e-mail. Send your potential boss something that will make him or her go 'WOW!'"

Matt Siegel has dominated Boston radio's morning drive-time ratings for the past thirty years. Matty has hosted his show continuously on Kiss-108 since 1981. I asked my former competitor where he sees future radio wannabes finding a place to break into radio to develop their personality. "This is, of course, the question guys my age hate the most! The truth is it is much harder than ever to learn the craft, because the overnight jobs are mostly gone to voice-tracking. But, then again, not as many guys try. There are lots of online shows and you could probably start your own. One thing that has not changed," adds Matty, "if you are smart and funny and won't let rejection stop you, you'll make it."

Jack Casey is the GM of the Emerson College station in Boston, WERS 88.9. Jack has an extensive background in broadcasting as an air-talent and programmer. He and I go way back to our earliest days in broadcasting as fledgling radio wannabes. He agrees with other radio pros that there are fewer entry-level jobs for air people now. "However," Casey adds, "once you get that foot in the door, the corporate culture in radio is actually more stable than in decades past. An air-talent who aligns their personal brand with that of the station, for example," he says, "Matty in the Morning at Kiss 108 Boston can spend most of their career at just one station. Having said that, learn to voice track," he urges future radio stars. "Weekend air-talents are always in demand and radio can be a rewarding part-time occupation."

Malcolm Alter has been the Boston commuters' familiar traffic voice for over thirty years. He advises those wanting to be on the radio to keep their eyes and ears wide open. "Be flexible and ready and willing to jump into something which you may qualify. If you think you don't qualify, make it your business to do just that," urges Malcolm. "Read the trade magazines and keep abreast of what's going on in radio. If you see something that's available, learn everything you possibly can about it until you're some sort of expert. If you don't get the job the first time, you may get it eventually." Lastly, the popular radio traffic reporter says, "Be aggressive, but not cutthroat. I've seen a lot of that around and unfortunately that's something you will have to deal with. Network! Mix with and meet people and keep in touch with them. Make a good impression. Remember, you may not always land your radio job the first time around, but there's always the next time!"

Never give up on your dreams of being on the radio!

My forever friend, **Doug LaVallee**, was blessed with one of the most resonant set of pipes the good Lord ever placed between a set of tonsils. I'd often tease him that his deep voice came from the cold we both caught back in 1954, as members of the Lincoln Jr. High School band and marching in the rain at the Western Maine Music Festival in Auburn, Maine. Doug's voice became even deeper while mine still sounded like a kid going through puberty. As a native Northern New Englander like me, one of the Boston stations Doug LaVallee grew up listening to was WBZ. "I was around thirteen, and my fascination was with radio and one personality in particular, 'Juicy Brucie' Bradley on BZ. [20] I was always fascinated by his wonderful deep voice and his ability to talk up the beginning of a song without EVER stepping on the beginning of the lyrics. I would practice doing it at home by playing records on my old 45 record player. It was not an easy task but after weeks of practice, I was getting the hang of it and did it quite well.

"At age sixteen," Doug recalls, " I decided I wanted to be on the radio just like Juicy Brucie, so I made what I thought were the best audition tapes ever on my home tape recorder and sent them to all the radio stations in my hometown of Portland, Maine. I felt confident," he laughs, "that I would hear back from at least one of the stations, but it never happened. I was totally crushed but never gave up the drive or desire to be in broadcasting."

One year later on his seventeenth birthday, Doug got his first big break in broadcasting. "I was hired as a weekend booth announcer at WCSH-TV, Channel 6 in Portland. After graduating from Portland's Deering High at age nineteen, I landed the afternoon drive spot at WCSH Radio and remained with the station for nineteen years." In the sometimes strange circle of life, Doug and I actually got to work together at CSH Radio in the late 1970s. He says, and I concur, "If you want something bad enough, like being on the radio, which we both did, don't give up!" We didn't! My pal of over fifty years, Doug LaVallee also programmed KGU in Honolulu and was on the air at KGNR and KCTC Sacramento before retiring from radio in 1989.

Consultant **Guy Zapoleon** started his radio consultancy business in 1992. Guy has these words of advice for future radio wannabes on how to break into the business: "If you have these qualities: God-given talent, an engaging personality, and an instinct about what people want to hear, find a programmer or manager or even talent at a radio station that is interested in nurturing new talent and mentoring future radio stars. When you find that person, express your interest in working with them in any entry level job that could lead to an on-air position, even part time. Go to the radio station and DO THIS IN PERSON!! Stay in contact with that person via phone or e-mail, and if you don't get in the door the first or second time, continue to stay in touch with them and meet them in person. Develop at least a couple of people that could possibly help you. In other words," emphasizes Zapoleon, "don't put all your eggs in one basket, although that one person might be the one that lets you break in."

Author's note: These stories based on true-life radio experiences from real radio pros all have one central theme: to break into radio, you need to be passionate about the business and do whatever it takes to get your foot in the door! Don't ever give up!

"Success doesn't come from discovering some hidden formula. It comes from consistently working hard and taking advantage of opportunities which present themselves."

Ralph Waldo Emerson left us his thoughts on the true meaning of success.
    "to laugh often and much
    to win the respect of intelligent people and the affection of children
    to earn the appreciation of honest critics and endure the betrayal
        of false friends
    to appreciate beauty
    to find the best in others

> *to leave the world a bit better place, whether by a healthy child,*
> > *a garden patch or redeemed*
> *social condition*
> > *to know even one life has breathed easier because you have lived; this is to have succeeded."*

There is no mysterious outside force holding you back from becoming a real radio pro! It's no big secret that one's actions always speaker louder than one's words, even those of a radio personality.

Your success as an on-air-talent isn't a matter of chance. It's a matter of *choice*—the choices you make.

Success isn't something you can sit back and wait for it to happen. It's something you can make happen with consistently hard work—there is NO substitute!

A real radio pro knows that "success" is gained by working through challenges." Just like life itself, there will always be challenges and temporary road blocks in radio! The secret to success is not to let them become permanent obstructions in reaching your goal. Each new challenge provides a "gateway" to even greater success as an on-air radio pro. Accept challenges that will inevitably come your way. Let's face it, if there isn't a challenge every now and again in your career, then you wouldn't have the opportunity to achieve and succeed as an on-air radio pro. When the challenges are the greatest is when you have the opportunity to excel at what you do and to be your best!

Self-discipline is one of the keys to success as an on-air radio pro! Discipline is controlling your own behavior! You have the ability to make your own choices and to follow them, so always do your best to insure that you will make the right choices. Every day use your discipline to take advantage of new opportunities.

Don't ever chase after success!

It will be easier to catch the elusive butterfly of love than to try and catch success. Instead, allow success to happen by savoring and enjoying all the opportunities that come your way. Acclaimed broadcaster David Frost said it well. "Don't aim for success. If you want it, just do what you love and believe in and it will come naturally." As the saying goes, try and take things one day at a time. Don't get too far ahead of yourself and where you are. Things happen in their own time and for a reason, even though they may be difficult to understand at the time. Radio pioneer and comedian **Eddie Cantor** said it best: "It takes twenty years to make an overnight success."

There is one certain way to reach your goal and that's to keep plugging away at it! All you have to do is make the commitment to do great radio, day in and day out! Take the necessary actions required and keep doing them over and over again. If you're not advancing as fast as you like, it's because YOU and you alone are the reason! Blaming someone or something else is absolutely wrong. If you keep looking at yourself as a "victim" you will never get ahead. Once you stop acting in such a way, you will easily move forward, so stop playing the "blame game" and watch the limitations to your own success begin fading away!

Notes:
1. Passion on the radio is fully described as one of the 7 Powerful P's in Chapter 5.
2. C.E. Hooper was a ratings service.
3. Chuck Blore is a radio programmer who was hired by legendary broadcaster Gordon McLendon at KTSA in San Antonio, Texas.
4. Gordon McLendon started KLIF-AM Dallas in 1947 in the basement of the Cliff Towers Hotel which was located across the Trinity River from downtown Dallas in the suburb of Oak Cliff, hence the station call letters, KLIF. As far as the origin of radio's Top-40 format, you can read the story behind the legend in Chapter 17- Music Formats.
5. "Reps" is short for "representative" in advertising. A radio station usually has a local "rep" to handle local and regional commercial business and a national rep for national sponsors and advertisers.
6. Former radio personality Joel Denver is President, Publisher and co-founder of AllAccess.
7. Steve Gilinsky and my longtime friend Steve Feldman discuss radio sales in Chapter 19, Some Things to Know About a Career in Radio.
8. In 1999, Matt was one of the first on-air hosts at XM Satellite and had a dedicated, loyal listening base. In October 2008, he along with 100 other employees, were laid-off following XM's merger with Sirius Satellite.
9. Matt had an air-shift on Emerson College station WERS-FM 88.9 Boston. For four years, he hosted a '60s soul show, *Soul Bucket*.
10. Author's note: the importance of attending a well-respected college or university with a solid broadcast department, like Emerson, can't be stressed enough. In the early 1960s, I attended Emerson as a night student in their broadcast communications course. Seventeen years later, during one of my out-of-work and on-the-beach periods in radio, another Emersonian, Gary Berkowitz, was working late one night in his office at ROR-FM, Boston. He was the PD and had been listening to my air-check. While perusing my resume, he noticed the word "Emerson." He called me at my home, we chatted, and later, he hired me. Ego aside, I'd like to think Gary liked what he heard, but I also believe it was that all-important college connection which opened the door for me to major market success in Boston.
11. Author's note: I was allowed to play whichever songs I determined fit the oldies format for our request show, as long as it charted on Billboard's

Top-100. The oldies we played on SNLATO were not restricted to number one or even top-ten status. We played ALL the hits, something I wish more radio stations would do today instead of only playing from a small list of a few hundred titles. How short play lists have hurt radio today is covered by consultant Guy Zapoleon in Chapter 12.

12. WODS is the popular Boston Oldies station. Several of their air staff members comment in this book.
13. The definition of traffic in a radio station refers to the commercial log and the placement of programs and spots by a person, called the traffic manager.
14. Carts, or cartridges, were approx. 3 x 5" in size and about 3/4" in thickness. The length of time of the tape in each cart could vary in length from 30 or 60 seconds up to several minutes. They were first used for recording commercials and station jingles, but later many stations recorded songs on individual carts.
15. In March 2008, Cindy Maguire suddenly left MIX-107.3 in DC. Several attempts to contact her for additional comments were unsuccessful. We heard she was on the air in Northern VA, but can't confirm. We thank her for her comments on how to break into radio.
16. The beauty of working in a small market radio station and being able to learn all aspects of the radio business.
17. "Hitting the post" is a term that refers to a DJ talking over the very beginning of the instrumental bridge of a song (record/CD) and stopping just before the vocal begins.
18. "Four and out the door" refers to an air-talent who only does their air shift (usually 4 hrs long) and nothing more and can't wait to vacate the station, hence the expression.
19. Bob Anderson was a popular personality on Portland, Maine, radio for 40 years. He was also a good friend and a great guy. Bob suffered a fatal heart attack while doing what he loved to do and did so well, being on the radio and hosting his morning show on WYNZ, Saturday, March 29, 2003. He was 59.
20. Outspoken radio pro Bruce Bradley tells it like it is in Chapter 4, On How to be a Successful Air Personality.

How to Break Into Radio • 91

Joel Denver, former air-talent, now Pres. AllAccess.com.

Gary Berkowitz, consultant AC (Adult Contemporary) Radio stations.

Jack Oliver, long-time Wichita, KS radio personality on KEYN.

Ted Quillin, legendary radio pro, one of LA's first Top-40 jocks.

Ron Chapman, legendary Dallas morning air pro.

Matt "the cat" Baldassarri, oldies talent, formerly host on X-M satellite.

Alice Pearce and author, one time producer of author's oldies show on WROR-98.5-Boston. Early 1980s.

Doug LaVallee on mic in foreground Bob Shaw in background at WCSH-970AM, Portland, ME, 1960s.

Chapter 4
How To Be a Successful Air Personality

"A real radio pro knows success is not the result of spontaneous combustion. You have to set yourself on fire"

– author

Success or failure as a radio pro depends entirely on your own attitude!

Success does not necessarily happen when and where you begin your radio career. If it did, not many would ever be successful. Success comes from what you decide to do with what you have and is achieved through a consistent plan and not by a single action.

The first steps to success are desire and passion. You must want it badly! Your passion and desire for success must be so strong that you breathe it and feel it in every fiber of your body! You can be whatever you want to be, all you need to do is set your mind to *just do it*! All that matters is what is in your mind and heart. You also need to make your own breaks and opportunities. Every time you go on the air is a brand-new opportunity for success. The way you think, feel, act and respond every day you're on the radio are the keys to success as an on-air radio personality.

You will never succeed on the radio or off until you truly believe you can succeed.

Legendary air personality **Bruce Bradley** doesn't pull any punches in telling it like it is on how you can be successful on the radio. "My thoughts on how to be successful on the radio today are about as relevant as that old fart who does the E-harmony.com commercials on how to hook up! Nevertheless, says Bruce, "It takes balls, talent and focus! These are the only words anybody needs to know for success in radio or anywhere else," adds Bradley with gusto, who throughout the '60s was a major player in afternoon-drive on WBZ-Boston. "You've got to have balls to think you can hold the attention of thousands of people for hours at a time and make them come back tomorrow. Now, if you have talent, somebody will hire you and you'll find out together. How do you know it's worth a try? Listen to the best people on the best station around and, if you can say, 'Hell, I could do that!' then you're on your way, but bear in mind," he warns, "Don Imus and Howard Stern never had anybody to compare themselves with. They are originals and better than the best."

Focus is the third ingredient that Juicy Brucie, as he was known to his faithful followers, believes is important to achieve success on the radio. "Focus is so important and overlooked," emphasizes Bradley. "Try to think of what you're going to say or do next on the air, Duh! Hardly anybody does it. And back to balls again. When the ratings come out and ANYBODY is listening to ANY OTHER station during your time period, you should be pissed. No, MORE than pissed, you should be outraged! When politicians say that 51% is a mandate, they're lying. Every pol wants every vote and if they don't, they're not worthy of even trying for office. In this one instance," adds Bruce, "you need to think like a politician. When I was fourteen, I listened to the best that New York City had to offer then, WNEW-AM, but I didn't say, 'I could do that.' I said, 'I'm better than they are already!' And, that's what I mean about balls!" Bruce Bradley concludes his to-the-point comments with a warning shot fired directly across the bow of all future radio stars. "During the birthing days of your career, more than one person in the business will tell you that you're no good and to get out of it. Ignore them all, because they are assholes from Hell."

Successful radio talents like Bruce Bradley say and do what unsuccessful people wouldn't do!

The radio road to success is no secret expressway; it's right there before your eyes and in plain sight. Anything worth having, including success, does not happen in a hurry. Be patient and keep plugging away. *Keep trying* is a good rule to follow. There will be times when you will mess up and make mistakes, but don't ever quit! Never quit on yourself! Former NBA Superstar **Michael Jordan** said, "I have missed more than 9,000 shots in my career. I have lost almost 300 games. On twenty-six occasions I have been entrusted to take the game's winning shot and missed. And, I have failed over and over again in my life and yet, that's why I succeed." To echo Michael Jordan's words, to be a success you need to take risks. Always keep in mind, *"To lose is to learn."* Don't go looking to make mistakes, but don't avoid them either. We all need to be in circumstances that challenge us, if we are to grow and improve. When there is the possibility of failing, there is also the possibility of winning, to make that great game-winning shot! Like Michael Jordan, you need to run the risk and take a chance.

Success comes from being able to make mistakes and accept the risk of failure.

Mistakes may serve as a great reminder that none of us have all the answers! Our mistakes give us a golden opportunity to learn from them. Therefore, you should NOT BE AFRAID of making a mistake! During the 2009 deciding NBA play-off game between Los Angeles and Orlando, it became quite apparent midway through the game that Orlando's shooting became cold. They missed so many shots the players were getting gun shy about throwing the ball up towards the hoop. It was almost as if they were saying, "Not me, I don't want to fail" and would quickly pass the ball off to another team-mate, who would in turn pass the ball! Always make the second effort and you'll find yourself succeeding more often than not. If you're willing to make a third, fourth, and even fifth effort, you'll reach a much higher level of achievement. If you don't put forth the effort, how will you ever know if you will contribute to the overall success of the team? Making a mistake in a game or on your show is no reason to pull back or to suppress your creative output. Making a mistake is a lesson in how to avoid making the same mistake in the future. Whether in sports, on the radio, or in life, don't be afraid of failing. You need to run the risk if you wish to succeed.

When your desire to succeed is more intense than staying within your comfort zone, you will succeed.

Your success as an on-air radio personality does NOT come from entirely avoiding mistakes. It comes from minimizing their negative effect on you and finding a positive way to move ahead and getting on with the business at hand. Failure does not keep you from succeeding. In fact, failure quite often leads to success. There is NO failure that can keep you from moving ahead in a positive manner as an on-air-talent, or for that matter anything in life. It makes no difference how many times you have come up short of your goal, success is always out there, right around the next corner. Champions are made but you still have to put forth the effort. The process isn't always easy. We all have liabilities and many times it's easier to focus on them rather than on our assets. To become a radio pro is to maximize your assets and minimize your liabilities, but also to realize that BOTH exist within you.

I had one boss tell me, "Joey, you show up every day and give 110% but it's unrealistic for you to expect everyone to do that." I looked her right in the eye and said, "Then I don't want them on my team!" If you show up and TRY hard and come up short with, say, 85%, that's OK, but I want you to suit up to play hard and at least TRY and give the show 100% effort. I don't think that's too much to ask. I have a hard time with radio folks who mail in a show! Every time you crack the mic, it should be your best break EVER, or at least make the effort to try and make it sound that way!

Work at being a champion on the radio every day! You'll feel your assets growing and you'll feel good about it. You'll also feel your liabilities diminishing and feel good about that. You can strengthen your assets every day by getting to know them and by playing them up to the best of your ability! Each time you get it wrong in radio, and believe me, you will, I promise you this, you will learn more about how to do it right! Every move you make, whether it worked in a positive manner or not, will bring you that much closer to success. Don't hesitate. Go ahead and make your move, take the next step and another, until you reach your goal as a successful air personality and radio pro.

Contrary to common belief, failure is NOT the opposite of success. At least not in my book! Failure can often lead *to* success. The greatest success stories are usually found in failure. Chicago radio pro **Dick Biondi** got fired more times than he cares to recall, but today, now in his late 70s, the 'Wild I-Tralian' is still goin' strong and doin' his thing weeknights on Chicago's True Oldies Channel, WLS-FM.[1] If you fail your first time out of the box, don't give up! Just think if Christopher Columbus had given up and turned back. No one would have blamed him, but no one would remember him either.

Another familiar voice on Chicago's WLS is **Jeff Davis**. He has an interesting take on how to be successful on the air and in life. "In order to become successful in any endeavor, you must be an observer first, brave enough to ask questions, and secondly, you have to be patient enough to be silent until you have learned enough to be an asset to the next generation. The fact," Davis asserts, "is that any personality-driven business has ego as its prime element. It doesn't become a problem unless you have decided you know more than anyone else. An out-of-control ego[2] not only can make you look stupid, but can cause people to walk on the other side of the street when they see you in public."

Davis, one of radio's premier voice-over experts whose "voice" has been heard on WLS-Chicago for the past 35 years, believes one of the keys to a being successful both on the radio and in life is to possess a good attitude, "which means to have a sense of cooperation, a sense of humor and the knowledge that this is a journey and not a destination. In order to remain viable one must never stop learning." Jeff Davis believes much of the reason he currently has a raging, successful career is based on the following: "A passion to continue to learn, staying relevant to the business, maintaining a good attitude and never taking oneself too seriously. One more thing, *noli nothis permittere te terere*, which roughly translates to 'don't let the bastards wear you down.' Davis adds, "There are a lot of them in broadcasting. Many of them couldn't find their butt with a GPS receiver. There are also truly great people in the business. If you have to wade through some bad times you'll eventually find a normal situation, unless your name is Moses and you're in a desert somewhere. In that case, finding it could take forty years. In all these years," says Davis, "I've never been unemployed so that either means I know something other people don't know or I've been kissing lots of butts. Just remember, if you get them to do what you want them to do it's not butt-kissing. It's called manipulation! Or maybe it's man-lip-ulation. I suppose that would depend on your point of view."

The difference between being successful and failing is the ability to keep on trying. Jeff Davis' mention of Moses brings to mind that many examples of this are found in the Holy Bible.

Moses could have just as easily given up. He had a tough childhood, lived with a foster family, possessed a fiery temper, a stuttering tongue, and even a crime record, but when God called him, he said, "Yes!"

Joshua had seen the "promised land" and then been forced to wander in the wilderness for 40 years with cowards who didn't believe as he did that they could possess the land. Because he was so discouraged and beaten down, he could have easily thrown in the towel and given up, but he was willing to go when the Lord said, "Go!"

Peter had a hard time making the transition from fisherman to "fisher of men." He sank while trying to walk on water, was strongly rebuked by Jesus for trying to tell him what to do, and denied knowing Jesus in the very hour Jesus needed him most. He could have seen himself as a hopeless loser, but when the opportunity came to preach before thousands on the Day of Pentecost, he responded.

Moses, Joshua and Peter, a bunch of losers? I think not! No matter what you've done, you're not a failure or a loser until you give up on yourself and quit trying.

To be a successful air personality, you must continually strive to be better not just against the competition but against yourself. Your goal must be to do better than your last show. Being competitive not only puts you on the right track to success but also helps you to become a better person. How so? By learning from your failures and capitalizing on your wins, you will develop as a human being.

I'm lucky! I was blessed with many positive influences during my "growing up" years. Caring folks who took time to show by example that to make it in life, you need to "hang in" against adversity and never give up. My Italian grandparents, Nonna ma and Nonna pa Pio, straight off the boat from the old country, and my mom and dad, first-generation Italian-Americans, worked hard and never quit. They overcame tremendous prejudices and obstacles to forge a life for themselves and for my sisters and me. The Boy Scout Troop leaders of Troop 95 and my time serving as an altar boy at St. Peters Catholic Church in Portland, Maine, under the watchful eye of Father Romani, taught me so many values I can't even begin to list them all. Those stalwart men in black at Cheverus High school didn't give up on me during my freshman year when I flunked Latin and almost every other subject. A Jesuit teacher, Father Bernard Murphy, wouldn't let me give up on myself! It took two sessions of summer school in the August heat, but I graduated with my class.

Senior Drill instructor Staff Sgt. Frank Holiwski of Plt 248- I Company, 2nd Battalion, USMC Recruit Training Command, Parris Island, South Carolina, wouldn't tolerate my quitting. In our 9th week of boot camp, I was hospitalized at the Beauford Naval Hospital with an infection in my right forearm. I missed three training days. Upon being discharged, I was weak but had to complete two PT tests to resume training, or risk being set-back to another platoon. Through gut determination, coupled with fear of being recycled, I forged ahead and graduated with my platoon and the guys I enlisted with 13 weeks earlier. It wasn't because I was some kind of macho guy. Far from it! The point is, I simply did not want to fail! If you want it badly enough and are willing to give it your all, you will not fail either.

A real radio pro keeps doing great radio over and over again, day in and day out on a consistent basis. It is the only way to obtain success and to avoid failure. Funny thing, I have always had a deep respect for failure, almost to the point of being afraid of it and that's okay. If you have fear of failure than you'll do everything in your power to avoid it and not fail! It seems throughout history successful persons have failed at some point in their lives.

The key to winning is never to give up!

Sir Winston Churchill took three years to get through the eighth grade because he had difficulty learning English. Years later, Oxford University asked him to speak at commencement exercises. Winnie arrived at the ceremony with his usual attire of cane, top hat and cigar. As he approached the podium, the crowd rose to its feet and applauded. Sir Winston removed the cigar from his teeth and placed his top hat on the lectern. Looking directly at the eager audience and with much authority resonating from his voice, he cried, *"Never Give Up!"* Several seconds went by in total silence. He rose up on his toes and shouted again, *"Never Give Up!"* His words thundered across the audience. A profound silence engulfed the crowd as Sir Winston Churchill reached for his hat and cigar, steadied himself with his cane and descended the platform. His oration was over! Churchill's six-word commencement speech was no doubt the shortest, yet most eloquent, address ever given at Oxford. His message was one every person present remembered for the rest of their lives. No matter what obstacles or setbacks you may face in life or in your radio career, always remember, Sir Winston Churchill's admonition, *"NEVER GIVE UP!"*

My petite Italian mom Joan, or Jenny as she was known to her family, was a fighter. She never quit anything she set out to do. She instilled in my sisters and me the importance of *stick-to-it-ness,* even when times are tough. We didn't just listen to Mom's words, we watched her in action. I knew how to make it through life and my radio career because she led the way. She showed my sisters Rosie and JoAn, and me, that if you put your mind to it, you can accomplish anything.

"Your actions affect your attitude and your attitude drives your actions."
Like so many others in this game of life, every now and then, a few curveballs have come my way. Believe me; I have had more than my share of curveballs, fastballs and even a couple of bean balls thrown at me. A couple of times during my forty-one years on the air, I've dealt with a few serious health issues. Thanks to the grace of God, I manage to dodge those bullets and feel fine. Here are a couple of slices of my personal life. In November 1995, my contract was not renewed at WROR-98.5 Boston. Why? Here's the deal. In November, I was rushed to Newton-Wellesley Hospital for emergency lung surgery, which resulted in the removal of the middle lobe of my right lung. Not fun. During my recovery, the station I called home for over sixteen years, and in spite of my solid ratings in morning drive, usually rated number one or two, decided to *go in a different direction.* Yes, *go in a different direction.* Words, I'm afraid, you will become all too familiar with as an air-talent. My contract was not renewed. Guess they thought I was ready to expire, but I fooled them! Seriously, I was devastated, confused, angry, and hurt. After busting my butt for the station for many years, they discarded me like yesterday's garbage. No goodbyes, not even a thanks and good luck phone call. As a matter of fact, I didn't receive any phone calls from management. They swept me out like I never existed.

Radio wannabes, take note of one of the down sides to being in the talent pool. As tough as it sounds, a radio personality is nothing more than a commodity. If management decides they can live without you, for whatever reason…you're gone!

As upset as I was and, believe me, I was, it never occurred to me to quit! My one goal was to get back to what I loved doing, being on the radio and chatting with my family of listeners. I tried afternoon drive at the New ROR-FM, but it didn't work out and I opted out of my contract. Suffice to say it was a tough lesson, but I'm a morning radio guy!

In 1998, my wife Kimmie and I, along with our critters, moved to the Lone Star State. I was back in morning drive where I belonged, on Houston's oldies station, KLDE. For two years, I had a ball, y'all! My comeback was successful and the ratings were top-shelf. However, destiny struck again. I again found myself hospitalized, this time with open heart surgery and a triple bypass. Once again, during my recovery period, about six weeks, the station found it convenient to change directions. During my absence, KLDE was sold to Cox Broadcasting, underwent a frequency change and guess what? Yup, you got it, even though I had decent ratings, they decided to *go off in a new direction,* only without me. Of course, I'm sure the fact I was about to enter the option year of my three-year deal and due for a fat raise had nothing to do with their decision to release me. Right! The first two years of my contract, I accepted less money as a show of good faith. I was promised a big bump up the third and last year. But, of course, my salary had nothing to do with the station's decision to let me go. Nah. They just wanted to go off in a new direction, which is entirely their prerogative, but it still hurts.

Finding myself on-the-beach again, and out of work, it didn't enter my mind to quit! All I wanted to do was get back on the radio! I did return to the air and not too far from a real beach in West Palm Beach, Florida, at Sunny-104.3. For four years, I enjoyed top ratings and loved living in the land of orange blossoms, gators and lizards. Well, maybe living with gators and lizards is stretching it a wee bit. In April 2004, another curveball was tossed my way. I was rushed to Jupiter Hospital in Florida with pneumonia. Doctors discovered three nodules on my vocal chords. I couldn't speak for thirty-one straight days, and yes, I still wanted to return to the air! But with no voice, no radio show. My forty-one-year career was over! Thankfully, due to a great speech therapist, Anne Davis, the grateful prayers of many and the healing hand of the Lord, my voice returned. I truly am blessed. I truly am blessed to be able to speak again.

These examples of my own down periods in radio are not mentioned to gather sympathy. They are merely meant to show you that totally unexpected things happen in life. A career can be derailed in the blinking of an eye when the unexpected happens, which sometimes are totally out of our control.

No one purposely sets out to fail, but when negative things happen that set you up for a fall, get back up! Look at it as a new challenge. The Japanese have a saying: fall seven times, get back up eight!

Disappointments and setbacks in your radio career can have a way of becoming a positive turning point. When something doesn't work out, as in the case of my voice loss, I wasn't exactly jumping for joy saying, "Something good will happen from this, I just know it!" On the contrary, I was terrified. My long career was suddenly over and I could feel my livelihood slipping away with it. I was worried and wondered how we would survive! Both Kimmie and I have a strong faith in God and deep down, we believed that once again, He would see us through another dark chapter in our lives.

I'm not going to kid you, as strong as our faith is, it can be extremely difficult to, "Let go, let God," when the mortgage is due. I'm also a big believer that the good Lord helps those who help themselves.

During my voice loss and what I refer to as my long, silent spiritual journey, I began formulating a plan. It was during those thirty-one straight days without a voice that I became serious about writing a book about my forty-one years in broadcasting. Let's be real, talking for a living had been an important part of my life for a very long time. It's a good thing I'm Italian and can talk fairly well with my hands! While I was totally bummed about not having a voice, my wife Kimmie was thrilled for one reason. It was the first time in our married life she could begin and end a sentence without my constant interruptions! I'm teasing. She was as concerned about my voice loss as I.

To remain busy and not drive my lovely wife totally out of her squash, I decided to move forward and write this book, *Radio Pro*. I'm hoping it will help educate future radio stars on exactly what it's like and what it takes to be an air personality. Life is funny, from a negative comes a positive. If I hadn't experienced the loss of my radio career, I probably never would have gotten around to writing *Radio Pro*. That's how life is! One minute it slaps you across the face to get your attention, the next minute it hands you a beautiful bouquet of roses. You can always adjust and persist in the direction of your career goals no matter what road blocks you may encounter. It's just that sometimes you may have to drive around the mountain rather than over it. You are always in control of your life and your dreams. Your actions and attitudes will determine which direction you will take.[3]

As strange as this may sound, I truly believe that if you don't experience the pain of failure, you can never fully appreciate all the good things that can happen. Each failure you experience can be a positive and valuable lesson. When misfortune strikes, the worst thing you can allow to happen is to be overcome with a feeling of despair. Don't become overwhelmed by your circumstances. Sure, there are frustrations, disappointments, pain and challenges, but you have the power within you to overcome every one of them. Stop worrying and wondering and waiting for someone else to make things better. Begin taking your own steps to improve your situation. To reach a new port, you have to set sail, not lie at anchor. You need to sail off in the direction of your dreams, not drift aimlessly in a sea of despair.

Donny Osmond was a guest a few times on my morning shows in Houston and in Florida. He gets credit for saying this: "As you climb the ladder of life, you go up one rung at a time. Sometimes, you don't think you're progressing very much until you step back and see how high you've really gone."

Don't let anyone steal your dreams of being on the radio.

In 1962, while attending night classes at Emerson College Boston, I was summarily told by our speech professor Gerry Kroeger that I "would never make it as an announcer" and he recommended that I transfer to television production. Needless to say, I was devastated, but was unwilling to let go of my dream of being on the radio. Somehow I managed to convince him to let me stay in his class. Years later, after almost twenty years on the air in Boston as one of the city's most successful radio personalities, I would occasionally stop and reflect on who got the last laugh. To this day, I'm not sure if Professor Kroeger was serious, or if he was just giving me a motivational kick in the posterior! In retrospect, perhaps, it was a little bit of both. [4]

Many well-known radio personalities far more successful and popular than I also ran into those in positions of power who made disparaging comments about their ability to make it on the radio! Take radio pioneer **Fred Allen**.[5] After auditioning for a CBS executive in 1929, the "suit" was quoted as saying, "Allen will never do. He's too bizarre and savvy for so homey a medium as radio!" Fred Allen proved the man wrong and not only went on to host one of radio's most successful programs, but also became one of radio's biggest stars during broadcasting's formative years. Allen was first and foremost a writer who worked tremendously hard on every script for every show. He was also a master ad-libber and rebel who pushed the NBC censors to the edge of insanity with his off-the-cuff, on-air comments. One popular feature of his show was a stroll down "Allen's Alley" with a stop and chat with his assorted cast of characters who inhabited Allen's Alley. For Fred Allen (take note Don Imus and others), ethnic humor was a handy comedic tool. After WWII, certain Jewish groups were not pleased with one of his regular characters, Mrs. Nussbaum, played so believably by Minerva Pious. Allen had to fight to keep her on his show. Many listeners were shocked when Allen first used the word "schmuck" on his show, which is Yiddish for penis. Tough talk on radio today, let alone in 1945.

Successful radio personalities must be willing to take responsibility for their own actions.

Your actions affect your attitude and your attitude is the motivation that drives your actions. Whether it's through your actions or through your attitude, there is always a way to introduce a more affirmative perspective into your career as a radio pro. Even if you can't bring yourself to take action, at least you can project a more positive attitude. It is so important in your career and in life. Although many circumstances will be totally out of your control in radio, you always have the ability to control yourself and your own actions. Diversions and distractions will always be present in your radio career, the same as they will be in life, but you are always in control of how you choose to let them affect you. The key is to get your attitude and your actions working consistently in the same direction.

In 1999, I was in morning drive at KLDE-Houston. **Tim Johnson** was our promotions and marketing guy. Today, he is Internet director for Clear Channel University in Houston. Tim believes the steps to success for a radio personality are three-fold. "You have three clients that need your love and attention," he begins. "The first is your audience. Every time you open the mic is your opportunity to build a better relationship. It's like dating. Make them feel admired and inspired. Strive always to get the next date. The second clients you need to focus on are the station clients. Build a closer relationship with the biggest clients on the AE's list.[6] You can survive down ratings if the clients love you and want to advertise with you no matter what. The third clients you need to cater to in your quest for radio success are other station employees. Make sure the receptionist and the General Manager or Market Manager's assistant loves you. They have more influence than you know. Candy and treats go along way with the support staff. Flowers on Valentine's Day for the female employees will win you big stars, but do it secretly. Everyone loves a surprise, and you will be found out in time and receive many accolades. Oh, by the way," Tim smiles, "that's how I met my wife!"

Former Seattle morning drive pro **Bob Rivers** urges future radio stars to identify very successful people who are leaders that you admire. "Make it a game. Since there are so many successful people to choose from you can be fussy. Watch what they do and see if it helps you. They don't all have to know they are your influences, but it is helpful if one or two take you under their wing. The best way to get that happening," adds Rivers, "is to get an internship at a radio station and give it everything you've got. The host of the show or even some managers will happily accept an invitation to lunch and all love being asked their opinion."

America's top radio pros offer their insight in how to be a successful radio personality.

To be a successful radio personality, like anything else worth having in life, means working at it! There is no substitute for hard work. One of the hardest working guys we know in radio is **Tom Joyner**! His daily morning show is syndicated across the USA and heard by over ten million listeners.

Born in Tuskegee, Alabama, he began his broadcasting career in Montgomery, Alabama, immediately following his graduation and worked at a number of stations before moving to Chicago and joining WJPC-AM. In the mid 1980s, Joyner was simultaneously offered two positions: one in morning drive at KKDA (K-104) in Dallas, and the other in afternoon drive at WGCI in Chicago. Instead of choosing one over the other, Tom decided to take both jobs. For years, he commuted daily by plane between the two cities earning the nickname "The Fly Jock"! Tom Joyner is the perfect example of hard work in motion. His passion for radio and willingness to work hard at two air shifts at different radio stations in two different cities is living testimony that if you have the desire, and stamina, you too can be a successful radio pro. Tom Joyner's determination to make it as a radio pro would not allow him to fail.

Two of my radio pals and former co-workers, **Sean Casey** in Boston and **Joe Ford** in Houston, both agree that to be a success in radio, you need to have thick skin!! Sean says, "Being successful means being persistent, giving attention to detail, networking and 'thick skin.'" Joe Ford agrees about the thick skin. "Thick skin, definitely, and being prepared for anything! I'm not saying to be paranoid and always on the lookout for doom and gloom, but be aware of the fragile nature of the radio business. It's a good idea to keep yourself involved in other ventures so when the boom is lowered you won't be 'destroyed' or depressed and will be able to keep food on the table."

Bob Lacey is co-host with Sheri Lynch on their popular syndicated morning-show, "Bob & Sheri." The team has been nominated four times for Billboard's Air Personality of the Year. Lacey says, "The avenue to a successful on-air radio career is to make friends with the best sales people at your company and become as important as you can to their success. The closer you are to bringing a buck through the door, the more value you have to a company. Never depend on a format, program director or consultant for your success. **It is up to you!** Formats change, PDs get fired. The only thing you have to sell is what is unique about you and if there is not that much that is unique get out of radio because it will break your heart! You must ask yourself, can I do this at fifty? Stay ahead of the curve and you will succeed!"

Laurie DeYoung has been in radio for over 30 years, twenty-four of those at WPOC Baltimore. The best advice she has to someone interested in a radio career and hoping to succeed is "Be real, be unique and develop your own style. Be flexible," adds Laurie. "Radio is asking more of people all the time. Most importantly, figure out what you're good at and spend 95% of your time doing it on your show. Don't ever get to a place where you think you've figured it all out. Be open to new ideas. Stay fresh, keep learning and whenever you can, get around people who are smarter than you. Remember, when the fun is gone, you should be, too."

Joe Cortese and I worked together at the original WROR-98.5 Boston from the mid-1980s to the early '90s. Joe, a successful air personality for over thirty years, offers these words of advice to would-be radio stars: "Listen and learn, the good and the bad. Radio is a lot like sports. You're going to be on some great teams and some not so great. Take the right path when it comes to your discipline. Work hard," says Cortese, "and you'll always make it!"

Barry Kaye and I worked together in the late '90s at KLDE, Houston's Oldies station. He says, "To be successful on the radio it takes luck, luck, luck and luck! Period! I was at the right place at the right time. And, I was blessed by the Lord. How else could a DJ from Beeville, Texas, go to Los Angeles-Hollywood in six years," he asks with a king-sized Texas grin. "With that said, I do know within my soul I had this incredible energy, extreme want and desire to be the best radio DJ, which kept me working 21 hours a day. I was constantly wanting to better myself," the Texas Radio Hall of Fame member relates. "I would listen to my tapes and try and make it sound better—for years I did this. It does take a lot of luck, extreme hard work and if you're lucky enough to be born with charisma and talent, and one final thing, you've got to REALLY want it, you'll make it. My hard work," Barry proudly boasts, "led me to being voted the #1 Disc Jockey in America." It's an honor my friend Barry Kaye should be proud of receiving. The year he won in 1974, his competition included some of the BEST radio personalities in the business, Charlie Van Dyke, Robert W. Morgan and Wolfman Jack!

Judi Paparelli and I have been friends for years. Judi was one of Boston's popular air personalities. Today, she produces and co-hosts Hollywood Plus Radio and is writing a book on the American workplace. What words of wisdom does Judi have for future radio wannabes to forge a successful career? "Feel lucky and work hard," she says. "Since my first day on-air, I have always felt lucky to have a job in radio. As simple as it sounds, my love of the industry and enthusiasm for hard work have given me an 'edge' and have afforded me many great opportunities. Learn the basic skills, and prepare each and every time before turning on the mic, then, once the mic is on… HAVE FUN!"

Dean Rogers has been a mainstay on the Northern New England radio scene for over forty years. Dino and I are graduates of Cheverus High School in our hometown of Portland, Maine. In the late 1970s, we worked together at WCSH-AM-970 in the city. Dino shares his own expertise for radio wannabes on how to make it. "First of all, don't believe what you see on TV. Radio stations are not like WKRP. Radio is a job just like any other job. However, if you're on the air and make a mistake, more people know about it than if you were sitting behind a desk. Being on the air is a blast. Be yourself and don't be a phony. No one likes a phony. When you're on the air, you can influence a lot of people, remember that and you'll go a long way to reach your goal as a successful radio personality."

Dave Ryan is the successful morning drive guy on KDWB-(101.3FM)-Minneapolis. Dave gives future radio stars three rules to follow to be a successful on the radio: "Show up on time, don't steal anything and do a little more than you're expected to do. It's an amazing formula for success," says the Colorado native. "It's funny; most people will live their entire lives without learning it."

Ken Smith, with whom I worked in Houston at KLDE, has been in radio since 1969. In recent years, Kenny was PD of the '50s channel on Sirius XM radio, a position he held for eight years. As far as words of wisdom for future radio wannabes, he laughs and says, "I wished I had some because I would have used them to propel my own career. However, and in all seriousness, this is what I have learned along the way. You must learn your craft in all aspects. You must have the 'chops' or forget it. This takes brutal self-honesty. Never stop developing or making the mistake of thinking you've arrived. To understand the future, you must first know and understand the past. Do your homework on the successful jocks and what made them successful. How were they different, how did they manage to touch the souls of their listeners and command such loyalty. What made them stand out, legendary radio personalities like, the real Don Steele, Imus, Wolfman Jack and Robert W. Morgan. Learn about PDs who were secure enough to pick the most talented air personalities and allowed them the necessary freedom to be creative and entertain. Read their bios and books about the biz and learn!"

Paul Perry is another longtime popular radio personality in Boston. He says, "There are three things an aspiring radio personality must possess to be successful." He has heard them referred to as the triangle of success. "You may have more of one than another, but all three must be present to succeed."

Number one is talent: "All the desire and discipline in the world won't make you a great quarterback if you don't have the talent for the job. If you don't, then maybe there is another job for you in the industry that you love, other than being on the air. Oh, and by the way," insists Perry, "not having the talent isn't something a Program Director, Manager or Consultant should tell you. It's something that you will know on your own once you've made the attempt."

Number two is desire: "If you really want something, as Sinatra said in his hit song, 'My Way,' then 'take the blows,' but you get up and fight on another day. I've often said, that I love what I do, but I don't always love where I do it. The desire to win and succeed has to outweigh the negatives."

Number three is discipline: "Of the three this is the only one you can control and maybe that's why I think it's the toughest," explains Paul Perry. "Unlike talent, while it can be developed to the best of what you have, ultimately, you either have what you need or you don't. Unlike desire, which you can't manufacture, it's there or it isn't. Discipline, on the other hand, is different because it's under your control. It's doing your homework, keeping your head in the game, doing all the things that you know winners do, even if you don't feel like it! Being unprepared and forgetting the fundamentals shows lack of discipline and one-third of the triangle of success is missing."

When you make sacrifices and put out extra effort you will succeed as a Radio Pro.

During my earliest days in radio if anyone ever told me that to be a success I'd have to sell my home, survive a divorce after almost twenty years of marriage and work my way back through firings and several major health issues, I would have laughed in their face, looked 'em straight in the eye and without hesitation said, "Pass!" No one this side of being sane would be willing to endure that kind of gargantuan sacrifice. It's almost like selling your soul to Lucifer! Unfortunately, it did happen to me. No, not all at once, but slowly, and over time, it happened to me. Sadly, including a failed first marriage. Who was at fault? Who knows, things happen in life. I do know this: my passion and desire to be number one in my profession along with an insatiable appetite to be on the radio was a lot stronger than staying put in my hometown and working a cushy 9-to-5 job with so-called security. Right or wrong, I opted for the volatile, high-profile world of radio, where security is practically non-existent. I am not suggesting or recommending in the least that in order for you to be a successful radio personality you need to follow my path. Just be aware that being a top-rated radio pro comes complete with a price. Sometimes, you or those you love may have to pay dearly.

To be a success on the radio, you must learn to be flexible. To survive, like the willow in the wind, you need to be flexible or you will surely break. During my own forty-one-year radio career, many times I was reluctant to bend in the wind and go with the flow. As a result, I nearly wound up breaking. It takes strength of character to continue when faced with difficult situations. It also takes a strong will to stay focused when it would be easier to "pack it in" and walk away. It takes strength and determination to carry on against seemingly difficult odds. We have a tradition in the Marine Corps. of never retreating. We may advance in a different direction, but retreat? Hell, no! To be a success, you need to have confidence in yourself. Confidence is another "must have" in the make-up of a real radio pro! If you feel you don't have it, then you'd better get busy in a hurry finding it!

In my own life, surviving thirteen grueling weeks of Marine Corps. boot camp in sand flea-infested Parris Island in the August heat helped me develop confidence really fast! For those of you who do not desire such a drastic course in confidence building, I strongly suggest you begin with something a little easier, like a leap of faith in yourself. Once you accomplish one small task, move forward to another. Each time you take on a new challenge, make it a little more difficult than the previous one. *Keep pushing yourself*, without stretching yourself to the breaking point.

Sometimes, sacrifices need to be made for goals reached and rewards to be gained.

Sacrifices need to be made on your way to becoming a radio pro. Whether married or single, you will find there will never be enough time to do all the things you want to do in life. Your family will suffer because instead of attending that Little League play-off game or annual school concert, you'll be summoned to emcee a charitable event or pull an extra weekend air-shift, because someone banged in sick. Yes, you too can be successful on the radio if you are willing to sacrifice anything and everything to achieve it.

Your dream of an on-air radio career is of your own choosing. You can ask your wife, hubby, girlfriend, boyfriend, mom, dad, brother, best friend to share it, but your dream is yours and yours alone. What are you willing to give up, and if need be, sacrifice, willingly or unknowingly to obtain it? At the same time, it's neither fair nor right to ask someone else in your life to endure the hardships that may occur along the way so that you can fulfill your dream! I am neither a psychologist, psychiatrist or relationship counselor, but have seen a few of them in my time to know one thing: You need to be involved with the right person while you're trying to "make it" on the radio; a partner who is willing to unselfishly sacrifice their dreams to see you live out yours. A spouse, partner and friend who is willing to accept the cold-hard facts that sometimes and more often than I care to admit, they will have to take a backseat and make many personal sacrifices so you can "follow your dream" of being a star on the radio. I tasted both the sweet and bitter fruits of life on my own journey as a radio pro. My wish for you is that your trip to success will be easier with a minimal of personal sacrifices that will not involve hurting others. There's no question, being successful on the radio or in anything is a series of life lessons, some of which can be painful and difficult.

What are you willing to sacrifice and give up to be a successful on-air radio personality?

Here are the personal thoughts from some of America's radio pros on what personal sacrifices they or those in their lives made in order for them to follow their dream of being on the radio.

Nationally known talk personality **Melanie Morgan** sacrificed more than a couple of things to pursue a successful radio career, and she tells it like it is. "I gave up my formal education in college, relationships, money, postponed marriage, delayed child-bearing and the aspirations by my disappointed parents for a real job. Other than that," she laughs, "I sacrificed nothing in my grasping, ambition-fueled ascension down the career ladder."

Malcolm Alter, my friend and former co-worker at ROR-Boston, is a familiar radio traffic voice to Boston commuters. He says the key word to success is "survival." "I befriended Boston radio legend Norm Nathan long before I ever sat in front of a mic, and got lots of advice. One thing he told me," says Malcolm, "was to know when to make changes, as far as jobs are concerned. One of the most important is to take any job and keep working to keep momentum going. That was the advice I got from Ken Carter, another Boston Radio Pro who owned WRYT (now WROL). The station I was at changed formats and fired the entire staff except for two people. They offered me a part-time job at a reduced salary. Ken, in his fatherly way, told me as distasteful as it was in a hostile environment, it would be wise to stay. In this way, he said, you can always be heard by somebody looking to hire. You also have the facility to prepare an audition tape. In spite of what may be going on at the station, you can still smile and go on the air and sell yourself. Even after all these years in radio, I'm still learning survival skills."

Jeanne Ashley was the midday star for ten years on Kansas City radio's Star 102 before heading for South Beach and Miami radio in 2010. Jeanne says, "I will always be grateful to my ex-husband for his support during my early radio years. The long hours and the low pay must not have been easy on him. He also was willing to give up his teaching job and move to Kansas City when I was offered the job at Star 102."

Stacey Cohen has been involved in the radio biz for over twenty-five years. She began her career as an on-air-talent at KNIX in Phoenix and was one of the first women in the country to co-host a morning-show with another female while at KOMP in Las Vegas. Today, in addition to her on-air duties with Metro in LA, Stacey runs her own talent agency, Cohen Creative. She lives with her three sons in Redondo Beach. Reach out to her at go4it@adelphia.net. As far as personal sacrifices to follow her own dream of being on the radio, Stacey says, "My kids got to see a great deal of the country as a result of my career. My oldest, who is 19 now, at 10 years old, had not been to the same school two years in a row. It got to a point," she laughs, "where I looked at my dog one day and said, 'What is our area code? I can't remember!' So, I started to name my dogs after the city we were in so I could remember where I was! At that point, I decided to get off the air and get into sales. Oh, by the way, I now have three dogs and one is named Hollywood, just in case I have one of those forgetful moments. So the real sacrifice was that my dogs got goofy names! I actually think my kids benefited in ways from our traveling adventures in radio."

Jim Labarbara, Cincinnati's music professor of the air! Jim's sacrifices? For openers, how about starting all over again by reinventing yourself on the air and taking a pay cut? He did! "Be ready to change and adapt in radio," says Jim. "I was a Cinti radio vet of more than 25 years when I got the call from the FM Oldies PD asking if I'd be interested in doing afternoon drive. I was working morning drive on the AM Sports Talk station. My boss was a good friend and let me go. I took a pay cut to make the move! I knew I could cut it. I didn't want any preconceived ideas about me to stand in the way. Every day we would go over my air-check, five days, three days and then once a week. I wanted to fit my personality into the station's format. It worked!" Jim believed in his own ability and took a *leap of faith* even though it meant leaving a comfortable position and taking a pay cut! He remained with the station for more than a dozen years! Today, he is still doing his thing on a country station which serves Northern Kentucky.

Chicago radio pros **Steve King** and his wife **Johnnie Putman** host the all-night show on WGN-Chicago. Steve says, "My first reaction to this question [about sacrifices made to pursue radio dreams] is to think of my dad. When I made the decision to try a career in radio after ten years on the road and in recording studios as a rock singer/musician, he was incredibly supportive. I know it must have been hard for him. Living in the house I'd grown up in while I attended Midwest Broadcasting School and waiting for that first radio job, I never had the feeling he couldn't wait for me to leave. He was always more than patient and, as I said, supportive. When I finally got my first radio job at WJOB in Hammond, Indiana, he gave me some great advice: 'Remember, you're the new kid on the block, so whatever happens, do your best to stay at that first station for at least a year and learn everything you possibly can and set yourself a goal and stick to it.' There were times during that first year when I REALLY wanted to quit that station, but I forced myself to stay for a year and learned everything I could about production, and anything else I could find an excuse to be a part of.

"During the record Chicago snowfall of 1967," Steve recalls, "I was one of four people who made it to the station. What was normally a 25-minute drive took me eight hours. When I got to the station, I was on the air for over 24 hours straight. We had NO network programming and because of the emergency, we were talking all the time providing the needed information and didn't play any music. A few days later when the roads were finally cleared and management arrived at the station, they took us all out to a local clothing store to purchase some things that had a little less fragrance to them!"

Steve always kept his dad's advice in mind about setting a goal in radio. "When I started in radio, I set myself a goal of five years to be working for a major station in a major market, hopefully my hometown of Chicago. I began in radio in May 1966 and, in May 1971, I was hired to do afternoon drive at Chicago's WBBM-FM. Through some luck, persistence, and hopefully a bit of talent, the five-year plan worked out to the month. At that time in Chicago radio, the top music stations were WLS and WCFL, so my next goal was to work at one of them! After a few years at BBM-FM, I was contacted by both stations. After meeting with Tommy Edwards, who was interim PD at WLS, we came to an agreement and I wound up working for the winner of the last major-market AM radio Top-40 battle, WLS! By the way, I've always felt that Tommy never got the credit he deserved for turning WLS around. When I was hired, WCFL had jumped ahead of WLS in the ratings. In the summer of 1973, Tommy hired me, Bob Sirott and Jim Smith (Music Director) from WBBM-FM, along with Yvonne Daniels from WSDM-FM.[7] The very next book the ratings turned and WLS was again on top. I'm not taking anything away from John Gehron who came in as permanent PD and did and incredible job.[8] John is the best and certainly deserves the credit for ultimately winning the battle, but it was Tommy Edwards who initially put the players in place.

"I know I've gone a little off course in answering your question," says Steve King, "so let me return to the 'personal sacrifices' theme. The sacrifice that has been a constant over the twenty years Johnnie and I have been at WGN is the hours. We're almost always functioning with sleep deficit. Do we love doing our show? Absolutely! Overnight radio," adds King, "allows you to develop a relationship and an intimacy with your audience that no other time slot does. Do we hate having to be awake during the day when we should be getting sleep but have to be up working on the breaking news story that's going to be the focus of tonight's show or because that's when the doctor, lawyer or management schedules the meetings? Absolutely," King says emphatically. "As we've often said, if we didn't do this together, it's very doubtful we could have stayed on the all-night shift at WGN this long." You can reach out to Steve King and his wife Johnnie Putnam at http://www.steveandjohnnie.com. **Note:** On December 9, 2011, Steve & Johnnie did their 6200 show on WGN. It was their final broadcast, after 26 years as the warm, entertaining hosts of Chicago's popular all-night show.

Joe McMillan has been a successful Boston, Portland, and New England radio pro for many years. When it came to personal sacrifices from following his dream of being on the radio, Joe had more than a few. As he points out, "How about supporting two daughters, April and Heather, and never having enough MONEY, but I remember at the start of my radio career money never mattered. I LOVED what I did. The other sacrifice made was never being able to hang on to a house long enough to build any real equity. I always had to move on to the next radio job."

Being competitive does not mean winning at all costs.

Author's note: I honestly believe there is a misconception about being competitive! Competitiveness, for my money, does not mean winning at all costs. Being competitive means *always doing your best.* Trying harder than the next guy and never giving up on yourself or your goal to succeed. To me, that's the stuff winners and champions are made of, and the sign of being a true competitor. To constantly try and improve your performance and to do today's show a little bit better than yesterday's. You will be a success and reach your goal as a real radio pro by taking it step by step and not by leaps and bounds. The old saying "Take life one day at a time" was tailor-made for radio talent with one slight addition; take it "one show at a time."

"Don't aim for success. If you want it, just do what you love and it will come naturally." David Frost.

Excellence is probably the single most important ingredient to success!

Excellence on the radio is more than a skill. Excellence is an attitude, the right attitude! Excellence is within your reach. All that is necessary is for you to commit and reach out and grab it! If you approach your show and air-work on a consistent basis with passion, commitment, and attention to detail with focus and persistence, the end result will be excellence. Excellence should be your goal!

Achievers, both in and out of radio, concern themselves with excellence but do not obsess over perfection. Trying to achieve excellence in your daily work is not easy and can be extremely difficult, but you will be richly rewarded for your hard work and dedication by achieving great success. No matter what type of work you do, always strive for excellence.

Dr. Robert Schuller composed this list of "secrets to success."

- Know that every problem has a limited lifespan
- Know that every problem holds positive possibilities
- Know that every problem will change you
- You can choose what your problem will do to you

Dr. Schuller gives excellent examples of his own reasons for success, but I honestly believe the biggest secret to success is *there is no secret!* I'll say it again; you and you alone are responsible for the direction of your radio career and whether or not you will be successful. As you reach out and find new opportunities in radio and in life, no one can stop you but yourself. Keep in mind, anything of value, including a career as a radio personality, requires a lot of hard work. Remember the saying, no pain, no gain! Or, how about, when the going gets tough, the tough get going. Yeah, all of those motivational quotes you've heard over and over again. Well, here's another one you can add to your list. Hopefully, you'll remember this one. Credit Oakland A's owner Charlie Finley for saying it first: "Sweat and sacrifice equals success."

I have always believed there are many similarities between a Major League athlete and a major radio talent. The great Dodgers coach **Tommy Lasorda** said it best when describing a real Major League pro, but he also could have been talking about a real radio pro! "In the face of adversity," Tommy said, "you must maintain the self-confidence and determination that made you a success. You have to believe in yourself before others can believe in you! Success is being truly happy at what you do! The difference between the 'possible and the impossible' lies in a person's determination!"

Dave Robbins was for many years the VP, General Manager with CBS Radio, Chicago. He has an interesting philosophy on how managers and air-talent can get along and be successful. "One overriding premise," he begins, "you become what you think about. You are the President and CEO of 'You, Inc.,' a personal service company. Therefore, deliver the best service and your business will flourish, like any successful business. Offer poor service, whether as a manager or air-talent, like a bad attitude, or creating problems and issues that others must clean up, and your business You, Inc., will surely fail. Your success or failure in life is 100% up to you. You are where you are in your career today because that is where you are choosing to be at this moment. If you like where you are, keep doing what you are doing," says the Chicago radio vet. "It's not the fault of your boss, co-workers, parents, a bad format, a budget cut, your brother, or anything else outside of 'you'! 'If it is to be, it is up to me' is the call to action for success. Successful people take what is handed them, regardless of how bad it is and find a way to succeed with it. There is no such thing as a problem," adds Dave Robbins. "There are only opportunities. If you look at your life in this fashion, success will be heaped upon you."

Legendary Dallas radio personality **Ron Chapman** began his career at KLIF in 1959. From there, he joined KVIL in 1960, where he was on the air for thirty-two years. "Whenever someone approaches me and says, 'I'm told I have a good voice, should I try radio?' I always agree that YES, they have an excellent voice," says Ron. "Now, the question is, do they have anything to SAY? The day of the great voices went out with the Red & Blue Networks.[9] Today's air person should be the best informed human in the city," adds Chapman. "Not to show off what they know, but to be ready to react if a subject comes up.

"Young people ask me if they should subscribe to *Billboard* to keep up with what's happening in music and radio. I always suggest they forget the trade papers and concentrate on what the listener finds interesting: your local paper, *USA Today*, *People*, *US*, even *The Enquirer*. The average listeners doesn't care who played lead guitar on that song, but they might want to know which *American Idol* contestant got cut last night. If the Lakers folded, it would be worth a mention. So be what the 'folks' are into, not what the industry is."

Success as a real on-air radio pro is built upon effort and commitment. It is also built upon patience, persistence and perseverance.[10] To work so hard at becoming a success only to walk away because one more obstacle stood in the way is a tragedy. Rest a while if need be, but *never* give up! If you feel passionate enough about being on the radio to begin your journey, then it's important enough to finish it! Always be willing to take just one more step towards success! It may be the one that finally gets you there!

The real key to a successful on-air career is to take what talent you have and do something useful with it. Keep working hard! Put time in on what goes into your show and your effort will pay off. You will reap the benefits. Make your show a unique radio experience for your listeners. Every time they hear your voice on their favorite radio station, you want them to smile and say, "Hey, I really like this guy or gal!" The key to your success and longevity on the air is to create a need for your presence on the radio. You need to put out such a good product that your listeners will feel compelled to listen to you every day, lest they miss something! One of the ways to accomplish this is to use your imagination. Radio's special gift to the human mind and ear is the ability to use one's imagination.

The use of imagination on the radio is explained further in the next chapter.

As a talent, always do your best to keep an open mind and listen to what management has to say about your show content and your performance.[11] It does not mean you have to become a "yes" person to their input and opinions. Your ability to succeed as an on-air radio personality depends greatly in keeping yourself focused on what you know and feel in your gut is best for you! Defend it tenaciously, and hold on to your own unique style of who you are and what you bring to your show every day. Always keep in mind who you are and the real value of what you have to offer, while trying to keep an open dialog with your bosses. Saga Communications GM/VP Cary Pahigian says it best: "Build a relationship from day one and work at it, even if you have to do the heavy lifting."

You may not be familiar with Zoe Koplowitz, but she is an amazing woman. She is quoted as saying, "Either you have your dreams or you live your dreams. I'm not all that remarkable. I just keep putting one foot in front of the other until I get to where I have to go. Everybody's got their finish line in life. This is mine. People need to know that success isn't always all about winning." Zoe Koplowitz, a woman suffering from multiple sclerosis, made those comments after she walked the New York City Marathon in twenty-eight hours, with the aid of two custom-made canes. Always do your best, no matter what the circumstances and what is happening around you! Believe in yourself! If you think you can, you can and you will!

Notes:
1. Chicago's True Oldies channel 94.7 began using the call letters of its sister station WLS-FM in 2011
2. How an out of control ego can damage your career is covered in chapter 14
3. Your Actions and Attitudes is covered in detail in chapter 9
4. The Professor and the author's story is covered in detail in chapter 9
5. Pioneer radio pro, Fred Allen is profiled in chapter 1
6. A& E is the abbreviation for Account Executive
7. Read more about Chicago air talent, the late Yvonne Daniels in chapter 13
8. how to handle adversity and survive difficult times in radio is covered in chapter 9
9. The Red & Blue Networks were both originally owned by NBC. Later, NBC sold the Blue Network, which became ABC.
10. The Seven Powerful "P's" to Perfection are discussed in chapter 5.
11. How talent can live and work with management is covered in chapter 11.

How To Be a Successful Air Personality • 115

Bruce Bradley, Boston, NYC, St. Louis air pro.

Jeff Davis, Chicago, Hollywood voice over pro.

Author's graduation photo, USMC boot camp, Parris Island, So. Carolina, 1960.

KLDE-94.4 Houston morning-drive team, along with promotion assistant Earl Forbes (left) and author, the late Marty Ambrose, Linda Cruze and Kevin Charles.

Lindy Rome and author on-air at Sunny-104.3 WPB, FL, circa 2003

Stacey Cohen, Los Angeles morning news/traffic anchor.

Radio Pros, Barry Kaye and C.C. McCartney

Steve King and Johnnie Putman, all night personalities on WGN-Chicago.

CHAPTER 5
The Seven Powerful "P's" to Perfection as an On-Air Radio Pro

"The dimensions of the radio are truly to be treasured"

– Charles Osgood, CBS commentator

THERE ARE MANY DIFFERENT QUALITIES that go in to the make-up of radio personality. I have highlighted seven which I believe are the most important! Here are the *"7 POWERFUL Ps"* to perfection as an on-air radio pro.

The first and most important Powerful "P" is PASSION.

Do you feel passionate about being on the radio? If not, and you want to be successful, then you better get your internal fires burning right now! If you do feel passionately about being on the radio, then you need to build on that feeling every day on your show. The more you display your deep-down passion to your listeners and yourself, the more fulfilling your time will be on the air. Former KGB San Diego morning talent Shelly Dunn says, "If radio is something you want, do it *passionately*." The very best actors, athletes, musicians and on-air-talent are not consumed with being the best! They are consumed with **a passion** for what they do!

Greater Cincinnati radio's Music Professor, Jim LaBarbara, believes "words like *passion, love* and *dedication* may sound hokey, but if you don't have all of that then find another career. You'll probably make more money and be happier."

Joel Denver is the president/publisher and co-founder of the AllAccess Music Group which since 1995 has offered the largest daily updated collection of free information to radio and record businesses on the Internet.¹ Today AllAccess is the #1 Internet destination for all the major industries. Joel says, "Passion is necessary to be successful in radio or any profession. You must have real passion for your skills and have a burning desire to excel, and in the case of radio, to entertain and inform. If you feel that doing your four and hitting the door is all that it takes in radio, well, step aside for someone who wants to do all they can to be a part of the community and make a difference in the lives of their listeners."

Every time, you throw that mic switch on, do so passionately!

Talented musician and record executive Quincy Jones is credited with this solid piece of advice: "Do what you love to do, feel passionate about it, and the fame and money will follow. That's the way it always happened for me." To be a successful on-air radio pro you must feel passionate about what you do and be totally committed.² You can't do a great show one day and mail it in the next. That's not how to accomplish your goal of becoming a radio pro! Remember, *what you passionately pursue, you will have!*

Tom Cuddy was VP of Programming at WPLJ-New York City and the ABC-FM radio stations, now Citadel Broadcasting, for eighteen years. Tom believes passion is the number-one priority in being a successful on-air radio pro. "Make sure you have incredible passion for radio," Cuddy says, "that you are willing to make radio the priority in your life as you start your career, and that you want it bad enough that you're willing to make many sacrifices to get ahead." As a youngster, growing up in the Boston suburb of Newton, Cuddy credits popular WBZ radio personality Dave Maynard as the guy who got him hooked on radio. "I was in fifth grade and remember seeing Dave in action, and that was it! I was hooked! I said to myself, 'That's what I want to do' and I never changed my mind." When it comes to having a deep-down passion for radio, Tom Cuddy puts his money where his mouth is. "I remember around the time I was graduating from high school, I wanted to get my foot in the door at area radio stations. To pay my dues," he says, "I was offered holiday shifts. One Christmas, I worked from 6pm Christmas Eve until 6am Christmas Day running a holiday special on WSAR Fall River, Mass. Then I drove about 20 miles to Attleboro, Mass, and went on the air at WARA from 10am until 6pm, Christmas Day. 20 hours in radio stations when I could have been home with my family, but that's how passionately I felt about radio."

Before going on the air, try to get yourself in a frame of mind where you approach each new show with a healthy attitude and a feeling of gratitude for being able to be on the radio. Legendary WBZ-Boston all-night radio personality **Larry Glick** would give himself a pep talk before going on the air.³ According to the late popular talk personality, his nightly ritual went something like this. "Lorenzo," as he often referred to himself, "You will have a great show tonight. The people love you and you love them. It will be a great time." Larry passes on these words of positive thinking to tomorrow's radio stars: "If you think you can, you can and you will, but first you must think it in your own mind that you will have a great show!" Radio legend Larry Glick is right. You can achieve anything in life, including a successful air career, as long as you first believe it in your own head that you can do it and pursue it passionately!

John Forsythe, no, not the famous television and movie actor but nevertheless a famous radio pro who has dabbled in movies and for nearly two decades, woke-up New Mexicans on KOB-FM and believes passion is not only lacking in many of today's new talent but throughout the radio industry. "The struggle I see new talent having is the same one I'm dealing with - a lack of passion in the business. With big corporate radio, we get bare-bones budgets and a lack of passion for competition. Oh, they want you to win," Forsythe says, "just without any tools and, oh yeah, don't win too big. Two of the stations we used to celebrate crushing in the ratings are now owned by us and in our cluster! We're supposed to do our best to try to protect them." Forsythe, a native of New Mexico, also handled morning shows in Miami, Dallas and San Diego, and offers this advice to today's air-talent and future radio wannabes: "Forget where your check comes from and work for your own show. Take all that creative passion and put it to work for yourself."[4]

Barbara Bridges is PD and handles a two-hour midday shift on the number one station in Nashville, Mix-92.9-WJXA. Barbara believes strongly in passionate talent. "I look for people who have passion. They either love what they do or I can see the potential in them for something great."

Longtime Boston radio program director **Paula O'Connor** agrees, "If you are passionate and lucky enough to work at something you love make yourself available. No task is too big or too small. You will overcome any setbacks because you are passionate about what you do." Paula believes that as an air-talent, "You also have to be willing at times to take a step back in order to get two steps ahead."

Dave Robbins, formerly Director, CBS Radio Digital Programming Chicago, brilliantly describes passion. "'Passion' is made up of two words," he begins, "'pass' and 'ion.' You are passing ions, literally passing electricity. If you have passion for something, you have an electrical charge for it and will pass it to and attract others with the means to advance you to the next level. You will stand head and shoulders above the pack. All highly successful people in any field have this same quality, so simply be the one who has it in your field of radio. By having that burning fire inside you, you will be unstoppable. Find your passion and follow it!"

Keep in mind, your desire for success must be so strong that it is almost constantly on your mind. Talent and ability definitely play an important role in your level of achievement as an on-air-talent, but there is another important factor that plays an even greater role and that is your *passion to succeed.* You can possess every God-given ability in the world and have all the resources behind you to help get the job done, but if you don't possess passion and desire you will never achieve greatness!

Number 2 on the list of 7 Powerful "P's" is being POSITIVE.

Author's note: My own professional on-air career carried me far simply by my trying to remain positive! I took on many different positions in radio for which, I'm sure at the time, I was not the best or most qualified candidate. However, I always did my best and gave it my best shot. I showed up determined to prove to the world that I was the best person for the job! *Projecting a positive attitude* and showing confidence in your ability to accomplish the task at hand, even when you're ready to die inside and sweating profusely on the outside, is the mark of a real radio pro. I always tried to remain confident. When presented with an opportunity, I gave it my all to do the job to the best of my ability, even if I was sometimes naïve as to what the job entailed and what was expected of me at the position. My philosophy, right or wrong, has always been that it is better to have tried and failed then later to feel the pain of regret and wondering 'What if.' Always try to be more positive than negative. Your quest to be a success on the radio and in life will go a lot further!

Many talented air people I worked with had a practice of always expecting the worst in radio. I can't really say that I blame them. At times, radio can be both troubling and turbulent. Sometimes, I would find myself subscribing to the same negative philosophy. After you're in the radio game for awhile, you begin to develop a sixth, or sick, sense about what's coming down the line. Often times, it would border on the negative. Some radio people do this as a self-defense mechanism to avoid being disappointed down the road. Try not to get in the habit of expecting the worst or assuming bad things are about to happen! Many of us prepare for the worst in a situation to avoid being hurt. However, when you focus on the worst, you actually push yourself in a negative direction without even realizing it. A more effective position is to *always expect the best!* As the song goes, you've got to 'accentuate the positive and eliminate the negative and latch on to the affirmative!'[5] Support your thoughts with action by being prepared. If you expect the best, you'll be sending out positive vibes and you will actually be able to better handle whatever comes your way, good or bad.

Even though you may be totally committed to being positive in your life and career, often times unexpected negative incidents will occur, like getting fired! [6] Let's face it, during such tough times, it's hard to wear a happy face, let alone be positive. When it happens, don't beat yourself up over it! Accept it, try and learn from the experience and move forward. If you blow an opportunity or find yourself on the short end of the stick because of a program or management change, it's normal to be upset, but it's not the end of the world. Allow yourself a few minutes to gripe and moan and then let go and move on!

Is it realistic during these down times to remain positive?

The answer is yes! Being positive is all about what you create in your own mind, no matter how many negative things may come your way. Staying positive is just as important in bad times as in good, and probably more so. When the entire world seems to be against you, staying positive is a powerful ally. I'm afraid your career as an on-air radio pro will not always live up to your highest expectations. There will be times when it will be filled with low points and disappointments. But, for every negative, you will experience thousands of positives. For every setback, there will be countless ways for you to move forward. The radio world may sometimes be cold and cruel, but there will always be a bright new tomorrow! At times, the life of an air-talent can be unfair, but it can also be fun and loaded with excitement and adventure. No two days in a row are exactly the same in the life of a radio pro. As disappointing as the low points can be, the high spots are incredibly high!

In the late 1980s and early '90s, **Linda Smith** was our producer for two of Boston's most popular radio shows, *The Joe and Andy Family* and *Saturday Night "Live" at the Oldies* for the original Golden Great 98.5- WROR. Linda urges all air-talent to remain positive and be enjoyable to work with. "I'll put this as politely as I can," says Smith. "I've seen very talented, well-known candidates interview for positions and not land them. Why? The anus factor and you know what it's really called. As talented as they are, they're just not worth the trouble they'll cause. These types can't be managed, can't work as a team or with the rest of the air-staff, think they're above the station format, the rules, etc., etc. You get the picture. Always put your best foot forward and project a **positive** you!"

How to remain positive.

An excellent way to remain positive when something negative is happening around you is to focus on someone or something in your life you can genuinely appreciate. It may be your wife, girlfriend, boyfriend, hubby, brother, sister, great aunt, neighbor's dog, your cat or even a mini-horse, whatever makes you smile and feel good about life and yourself! Whether it's something spiritual, like your faith, or even material, like your car, apartment, computer or your house, look for something you appreciate and value. It will take your mind off what's going wrong and help to override the negative and bad experience of the moment. Your positive thoughts will increase ten-fold. It's impossible to keep negative thoughts from occurring. It's to be expected when life hands you a bad hand, especially those daily dilemmas and anxious anxieties that seem to cry out for your attention. The secret is not to hold on to them. When bad stuff comes down, try to put some time and distance between you and the problem. Drop back a couple of yards and rest. Enjoy the quiet beauty of being alive. It will fill you with a powerful energy that will rejuvenate you and help you to think more clearly.

When and if troubling times find their way to your doorstep, you will be better prepared to accept and handle them if you project a positive attitude! If you continue to accentuate the positive, you'll find the negative will be greatly reduced and often times completely eliminated. Grab the many opportunities that will come your way and always project a positive attitude and you will always wind up a winner! In writing this book and reaching out to legendary radio talent, I became fast friends with one of the best, Harry Harrison. For forty-four years he was the "Morning Mayor" and top-rated in the number one radio market, New York City. Harry says, "Be positive, upbeat and happy. If the voices on your radio don't sound like they are enjoying themselves, the listener won't either!"

Number three on the list of 7 Powerful "P's" is PREPARATION.

"If you prepare yourself and still come up short in the radio ratings race that doesn't mean you're a loser. You're only a loser when you don't prepare to go on the air." – Author

Kevin Charles is a familiar voice to Houston radio listeners. In 1999, Kevin was my producer on KLDE. I asked him to pick what he thinks is the most important **"P"** from our list of seven: passion, positive, preparation, practice, perseverance, performance and patience, which is the most important to possess in order to be a successful radio personality.

"This one is almost a trick question," was his immediate response, "because all of the 'P's' are intertwined, each feeds off the other. But, if I had to pick one, I would say **PREPARATION** is at the top of the list. I believe preparation is the key to success in radio and life in general. Preparation comes from passion. It inspires a positive attitude because you know you are ready for anything. Practice is part of my preparation, just like a good actor rehearses his part, I must constantly work to improve my performance, oops, there's another one of your **'P's** popping up, Joey."

Ross Brittain currently heads up the morning show at WOGL-FM-Philadelphia and is editor of The Ross Brittain Report, a syndicated morning show prep sheet. Ross says he's astounded at the lack of preparation put into shows. "The best shows and the ones which sustain themselves put in an amazing amount of prep time." Brittain, one of the original members of Z100's Morning Zoo in NYC from 1983 until '95, also did mornings at WABC-NYC in both music and talk formats, says, "Content will always be king. With podcasting and downloads to cell phones, the content of your broadcast needs to be better than ever, but those short two- and three-minute bits will have to stand alone, just as they always have. [7] Right now, as broadcasters, we're placing the bits around the stop sets [commercials], but the bits are nothing more than the content which will eventually be delivered by other forms—if radio owners and operators have their way."

Ross Brittain's point is well taken. Your show content better be top shelf and the only way to insure that it is through **preparation**, done well in advance of going on the air.

Dave Robbins of CBS Radio believes a real radio pro must *set goals*. "You can only achieve that which you set as a goal to achieve. Success is not by accident, it is the intersection of **preparation and opportunity.** If you are prepared when opportunity happens, you will be rewarded with success. Set your goals and make them very specific: the type of job you want, the place you will be working at, etc. You can achieve anything you want to achieve. Any success I have is due to my parents telling me all of these lessons at an early age. Where you are today, or your past," emphasizes Dave Robbins, "has nothing to do with where you can be in the future. Start today to build a better you."

You must be prepared before you go on the radio. That's why show prep is so important.[8] You need to stay focused on the big picture, but you also need to take care of the smallest details, for they combine to make big things come together as you head towards your goal as a real on-air radio pro. If you don't take time to handle the smallest detail, whether it be writing one more piece of show prep material or recording one more bit to make it sound perfect, than you'll never hit your heights as a real radio pro. Being prepared is *your key* to having a popular and successful show.

In 1950, **Gene Baker** was emcee on KHJ Los Angeles' top-rated *Weekday Club 930*. The program aired weekday afternoons from 2 until 4pm. Commenting in *Radio-TV Mirror* in May 1950, Gene stressed the importance of air-talent doing their homework before going on the air. Long before his show ever went on the air, Gene did his homework on what listeners liked or didn't want to hear on the radio. To his credit, Baker did a nationwide survey of all radio stations in the United States that had outstanding success with record shows. He discovered that, without exception, they all agreed on two important points. One, the host of the show should keep talk to a minimum—remember, this was over 58 years ago. Secondly, only the tops in pops, the biggest hits of the day, should be played on the show.

This proves once again that being on the radio really isn't brain surgery. It also points out that things haven't changed much during the last fifty years as to what listeners want to hear on the radio - more music and less talk! As a former air personality, it's not something I'm thrilled about hearing. I would fight tooth and nail about the importance and relevance of talk or personality even on a more music-oriented station, but for the sake of keeping peace in the radio family, let's agree on this: For music-intense radio stations, more music and less talk still appears to be the winning formula. How much of a win has been debated by both air-talent and programmers for years.

Take a page from the playbook of former LA Radio's Gene Baker - when you're prepared, you'll always find yourself at the right place at the right time. Remember, luck is what happens when preparation meets opportunity.

Number four on the list of 7 Powerful "P's" is PRACTICE.

"Building one's confidence about going on the radio doesn't just happen and come out of the blue. It's the result of consistently hard work, PRACTICE, dedication and preparation."

I'm sure you've heard the expression, *practice, practice, practice* until you get it right! That is so true of being on the radio. Reading commercial copy, introducing songs with little gems of relevant and interesting info about the artist, telling stories on the air in a relaxed, natural flow, all this and so much more is what goes into being a real on-air radio pro. All of this is only accomplished after it is done repeatedly over and over. **Practice,** as is the case with so many endeavors in life, is the key to success. Make it a habit. Practice will make your on-air delivery almost perfect. The beginning of a habit is like a piece of invisible thread. Every time you repeat the action, you actually strengthen the strand of thread. You keep adding another thread and another and with each repetition it becomes a strong length of rope! Practice is the same way.

Bob Rivers was the top-rated morning guy at KZOK 102.5 Seattle.[9] He has an interesting take on practice. "In the beginning of my career," he says, "I was a time and temp liner card reader. I wasn't quick on my feet and I was nervous in interviews. The main asset I had was a great radio voice. I also wrote lyrics for song parodies that were successful, but took hours to put together.[10] I didn't really know if I could ever be funny or interesting on the spot. I read a book by Jay Leno where he said that getting good at joke telling was like lifting weights; if you did it every day you would get stronger. Today, I'm happy to say that I can bench press a 200-pound joke!"

Throughout my entire life and radio career, I've always equated sports and team play with radio talent. The mission statement is the same: *put numbers up on the board and win!* To accomplish this you must have great talent who are willing to play together as a team! Just like a winning sports team, a great radio station is made up of great individual air personalities who brilliantly execute the basics and the format in special ways, day in and day out! Practice may not make you perfect, but it sure cuts down on the margin of error. There is absolutely no substitute for hard work, and practice is part of it.

The Seven Powerful "P's" to Perfection as an On-Air Radio Pro • 125

Hall of Famer and Celtics superstar **Larry Bird** knew all about the value of practice: "My coach once told me, 'Larry, no matter how much you work at it, there's always going to be someone out there who's working just a little harder. If you take 150 practice shots, he's taking 200.' And that drove me!"

Speaking of sports, for those of you interested in being a sportscaster or play-by-play person, longtime Red Sox broadcaster **Joe Castiglione** suggests you "Read all about the rules and the history of the game and learn as much as you can." [11] Castiglione, who has been the voice of the Red Sox since 1983, says it's important to talk about the sport with people in the game - coaches, scouts, and ex-ballplayers. As far as becoming proficient at play-by-play, Joe says, "Take in a ballgame, sit in the stands and practice calling the balls and strikes of the game into a tape recorder. You can always turn the volume down on the TV set and do the same thing." My longtime pal Joe Castiglione brought back a few memories for me and maybe you, by mentioning the use of the tape recorder to do play-by-play.

During my early days in radio, I had fun covering the Red Sox for a few stations in Maine. In the late 1970s, at Sox spring training camp, then located in Winter Haven, Florida, I became friendly with sportscaster **Dick Stockton**, who today is with FOX-TV Sports. At the time, Dick was the TV voice of the Sox. I was eager to receive a few play-by-play pointers from the pro and just as Joe Castiglione suggested, Dick offered the same advice: practice doing play-by-play of any game by talking into a recorder. As a youngster, Stockton would sit in the back of Yankee Stadium and speak into a tape recorder doing play-by-play as if he was actually on the air. If it's good enough for seasoned play-by-play men like Joe Castiglione and Dick Stockton, it was good enough for me and may work for you!

Number five on the list of 7 Powerful "P's" is PERSERVERANCE (*honorable mention Persistence)

Perseverance is the quality of being persistent. Being persistent is the difference between not achieving and great achievement. New England Patriots owner **Bob Kraft**, who I'm proud to say is a friend who listened to our Boston morning show *The Joe and Andy Family*, has the perfect explanation for perseverance. Bob says, "Perseverance is how things get done, because eventually most of the world will just give up."

April Sommers was a member of Don Bleu's morning show on Star-101.3 in San Francisco. She got her radio start at Ohlone College in Fremont. "They have a great little station, 89.3 KOHL," she says with pride. "I was lucky to be a part of it." But the longtime Bay Area air-talent emphasizes that radio is a hard business. "You have to be flexible. Be willing to do anything, any job, any time of day and be able to roll with changes." As far as surviving in the radio game, Sommers advises, "The more versatile you are, the longer your career will be."

Being a success on radio often times is closely associated with a personality's courage and ability to recover, to pick up the pieces and carry on from his or her most recent failure, like having a bad ratings book.[12] **Don't give up!** Carry on and move forward towards your goal of being a real on-air radio pro! Don't get caught up in believing and living the expression, *woulda, shoulda, coulda.* Instead, think, I *can and I will!"*

In 1928, a thirty-three-year-old man named **Paul Galvin** was faced again in his life with failure! He failed twice before in business and now his competitors had forced him to fold his latest venture in the storage battery business. Paul was convinced, however, that he still had a marketable and viable idea. With the $750 he was able to raise, he actually bought back the battery eliminator portion of the inventory and then took his invention and built a new company, one which succeeded. Eventually, Paul Galvin retired from his company but not before it became a household name: *Motorola.* When he retired, Paul advised others not to fear their mistakes. "You will know failure, but continue to move on." A failure isn't really a failure until you quit trying. So, the next time you have a down ratings book or a bad day on the air and you feel like a failure and want to pack it in and walk away, remember the words of Motorola founder, Paul Galvin, *"You will know failure, but continue to move on!"*

Author's note: My own personal dream was always to be on the radio and no one and nothing could stop me from fulfilling my dream. No obstacle was too large to stand in my way or to stop me. There were a few times when it seemed insurmountable forces were at work to undermine me and keep me from reaching my goal as a successful on-air radio pro, but I never quit. Many times, I wondered aloud, what was going on and why I was faced with so many road blocks, and believe me, there were many. But, through it all, I persevered. I never felt like throwing in the towel and quitting. Well, maybe a face cloth or two, but never the whole towel.

Legendary radio pro **Joe Ford,** who I was fortunate to work with during my time on the air in Houston in the late '90s, says he persevered as an air-talent by developing a thick skin. "I was always prepared for whatever came my way," says the Texas Radio Hall of fame member. "I was always aware of the fragile nature of the radio business." Ford says, "I kept myself involved in so many other radio-related ventures that I was never destroyed or depressed when bad news came my way." Joe Ford offers this solid advice to radio newbies: "Develop a sideline, like voiceover work. That way, if you find yourself out of work, you won't starve and lose your home while waiting for your next on-air gig."

Arthur Godfrey was one of America's most popular radio pros, and is covered in depth in Chapter One. In a May 1957 interview with *TV-Radio Mirror,* Godfrey made an important point for all air-talent to heed. In referring to being on the air, he said, "You can't take yourself for granted in this business. You must constantly keep working and improving." That's exactly what the radio/TV legend did, over and over again during his long career. He was always ready and willing to persevere and try something new.

Persistence is the difference between making it or not making it! The enemy of persistence is that little voice deep down inside that keeps saying, "Give up!" So, tune that little voice out and keep on going. Persistence isn't really all that complicated; all you have to do is keep working at it until you complete the mission. I remember, quite vividly, the break-up of my on-air partnership in morning drive with the late Andy Moes. Our partnership had been top-rated on Boston radio for almost ten years. I had to reinvent myself as a solo act. It was tough going. More on how persistence worked for me in the lines ahead.

There will be days when you may think you don't have what it takes to persist in your attempts to make it as a radio personality. Radio is a tough business! I had more than my share of troubling times, which brought on some serious doubts about whether I could and would succeed! When this happens, the key is to hang on just a little bit longer. We've all heard the expression, "If he had only hung in just a few more minutes!" How sad it would be if your ship finally pulled in to port and you had just left the dock!

Radio's special gift to the human mind and ear is the ability to use one's imagination. Using one's imagination on the radio doesn't have to be just a memory and throwback to radio's Golden Days in the 1930s, '40s and '50s, when the airwaves were filled with dramatic and comedy shows of every type and description. Radio today is pitifully lacking of what it does best, *the use of imagination!* As an air-talent don't be afraid to use yours. Be an image builder on your show. Create *word pictures* for your listeners to visualize.

Here's an example of how to do it.

Instead of saying on your show, "Our dog acted really goofy last night," paint a word picture. Example: "Last night, our silly but lovable lab, Tucker, kept tossing his toy hedgehog up in the air and catching it in his mouth. Wouldn't you just know it, eventually he tossed it high enough to hit our brand-new, expensive chandelier, which not only smashed to the floor in a zillion pieces but caused a short circuit and we lost power. No lights. No flashlight handy to find the phone. Ever try to reach an electrician at ten o'clock at night? We were lucky! He eventually showed up around midnight! Friends, my first alarm clock rattles my sleeping brain at 3:15am. So if I sound a little grumpy this morning, blame my dog, Tucker, not me!"

Get the picture? Now it's your turn. Here's a simple little exercise for you. Take a slice of your own life and paint a word picture for your listeners. And forget about brevity, which many PDs have been preaching for years.

You know what they say, "Be tight and brief." Say it in two minutes or less or off with your head! Don't worry about that here. We'll discuss tight, brief and bright elsewhere in this book.

> *"Don't be afraid of change, to change is to mature and to mature is to go on recreating yourself over and over again. Let's face it, without change life would be boring. The same is true about changes in radio."*

The one constant in radio is change! How to survive the ever-evolving, changing world of radio.

One thing you can bank on in radio is change! As a radio personality, you will find conditions change in radio on an almost moment-by-moment basis. What you found to be true yesterday about you and your show could be gone today. What worked well once on your show may now fail to bring home the desired results for both you and the radio station. When conditions change, you have an opportunity to change with them. Stations change hands, management and programming change, formats change, and along with these changes your circumstances change. When changes are taking place around you, instead of making a judgment call seize the opportunity to take a closer look at what is happening so you can take advantage of the opportunities you may find in them.

During my nearly 17 years on the air at the original WROR Boston, I experienced three big changes involving physical moves. First, the station moved from the Channel-7 building at Government Center to 3 Fenway Plaza in the Harvard Medical Building and finally to studios and offices on Huntington Avenue in the shadow of the Prudential Tower. At ROR-FM, I also saw no less than nine general managers and eight program directors come and go! The format was tweaked a dozen times or more. One day we were playing the Supremes and Elvis, the next day Adam Ant and Blondie. There was even a change in call letters from ROR to BMX! Take it from one who has lived through all these changes at the same radio station: the one thing you can count on in radio is change. You need to persevere and be patient. Rather than be upset and afraid of change, look for the little hidden messages in them. You have the ability to choose which direction to take and to make those changes fit your needs. If you don't change with radio, you will soon find yourself on the outside looking in. When and if you are presented with an opportunity to change and start anew, grab it!

Legendary radio pioneer **Will Rogers** said it best, "Even if you're on the right track, you'll get run over if you just sit there."[13] Don't be afraid to change your act. In the early '90s, when ROR changed formats from an oldies-based radio station to a more contemporary sound, it meant the end of a ten-year air partnership I had with Andy Moes on our AM-Drive show, *The Joe n' Andy*

Family. Andy left and I had to reinvent my act in morning drive. Management informed me that I was in fact auditioning for my own job! It made little difference to the new powers to be that we had been top-rated for years. I was beginning from square one with the new format. They made no bones about it. Either I went along with the new program and fit their new format, or I'd be out and someone new would be in. Sure, it hurt and it was scary! No longer did I have a partner to play off. For all intents and purposes, my security net was gone! I was faced with two choices: sink or swim. When faced with this new challenge, I remember thinking back to my recruit training days as a Marine at Parris Island. One test you had to pass to graduate was swimming the length of the Olympic size pool. Sound easy? Sure, if you're a swimmer! I wasn't. It was swim or you were washed out and set back, which meant starting your training cycle all over again with a new platoon. I wasn't particularly fond of the idea, so I learned really fast how to do the backstroke and qualified. Thankfully, my competitive nature took over. I wanted to show the new suits that I had been a successful solo act before and could do it again. More importantly, I needed to prove to myself that I could handle the new format on my own, and to make the necessary adjustments in my own on-air delivery without changing who I was. I'm not suggesting to change means changing the essential essence of who you are on the radio, not at all! But, sometimes, we can hold the past so tightly to our chest that it leaves our arms too full to embrace the present.

I knew I could handle the new format, which meant less talk and more music. It took lots of hard work but I managed to rework myself on the air and luckily the ratings reflected it. I passed the test and kept my job. Once again, persistence paid off! Change can be fun and rejuvenating! It also can be necessary for survival as a radio personality. Let me add an important point about less talk on a more music format. "Less talk" isn't easy. In fact, the opposite is true. It means you have to be more succinct and clever in less time. Personally, I found it easier to handle talk. Being afforded the luxury to converse about a topic with few time restraints is a joy. On the other hand, trying to say something relevant, funny, interesting or entertaining in 10 or 20 seconds every time you open the mic can really tax your creativity. If you don't believe me, put it to the test and try it some time! Always keep in mind, when you're through changing in radio, you're through!

Change can be a challenge. A big challenge! Not many of us enjoy change. It's been said about the only thing that enjoys change is a baby! Change is important and should be perceived as an opportunity and not as a threat. However, change is not always easy, even if you hope and pray for it. As the old saying goes, be careful what you wish for, it just may come true! When change happens, it can leave us melancholy, for what we leave behind is a part of ourselves. Radio didn't die when television came on the scene in the late

'40s, because it changed and took the necessary steps required to survive. It wasn't easy saying goodbye to old friends like comedies and dramas, but those type of programs abandoned radio for television. So, radio was left to reinvent itself and did so with music and DJ-personality-based shows.

As previously mentioned in Chapter One, radio's legendary team of **Amos n' Andy** had to change formats with the times. Their popular situation comedy which began in 1925 was one of America's all-time favorite radio shows. At the peak of their career their nightly listening audience was estimated to have exceeded 40 million and by 1939, their weekly salary had soared to more than $7000.[14] Their program ran for thirty years on NBC and CBS. Even though they were top-rated and embraced by millions of loyal listeners, their radio careers may have ended if they hadn't been willing to change. In 1954, when network radio changed directions, because of the impact from the television, Freeman Gosden as Amos and his partner Charles Correll, Andy moved to a new music-intense format. Sound familiar? *The Amos and Andy Music Hall* aired Monday through Friday night at 7:05 and on Saturdays from Noon -12:30. Nobody heard them complaining about being on the air six days a week!

Their new CBS radio network show was music-based and featured the popular comedians as disc jockeys. They played hit songs of the day and sprinkled their tried-and-true Amos n' Andy bits between records. Guest stars were also a feature of their show. Some critics say the popular comedians lowered themselves after being two of America's biggest radio stars, and were nothing more than glorified DJs. As if DJ is a dirty word! Many others were brutally critical saying they should have packed it in and stepped away from the mic, rather than humiliate themselves in their new format. I say, give 'em a break. *Amos n' Andy* should be complimented for their willingness to change when radio did. I'm sure they were well-compensated for their weekly music shows and it must have been part of their decision to stay on the air. But, being consummate radio pros, I choose to believe Amos n' Andy wanted to continue entertaining their loyal listeners for as long as they could. The popular team serves as a shining example for every radio personality today. There will be times when you may have to swallow your pride, make adjustments and change your act to survive in radio. Freeman Gosden and Charlie Correll were true radio survivors. Because of their ability to change when radio changed, they continued entertaining millions while still drawing their huge paychecks. After thirty-five years, the radio legends finally stepped away from the mic on November 25, 1960.

Many air personalities think, "Hey, why change?" They believe things have been working well for themselves for a long time on the radio, so they play it safe and think "Why mess it up?" They continue along their ole merry-way with the same old tired bits. They refuse to adjust to changes going on from the competition and what's happening in the marketplace. All of a sudden, the new act across town knocks the stuffing out of them in the ratings war and "Mister & Mrs. No Change" are left scratching their heads, wondering, "What happened?" Always keep looking in the mirror to see how you can change. It's important to continually make adjustments to your own act if you are to improve and succeed. This does not mean changing your award-winning personal style. That's not what we're talking about, but always be willing to fine-tune and *improve* on what you do best!

Always be ready and willing to change with radio

Even the most popular and famous radio pros are not afraid to make necessary adjustments. Take another legendary comedian and entertainer, **Eddie Cantor**, who first began on radio in 1931. Twenty years later, he was still on the air, hosting a disc jockey program on NBC, which ran from 1951 until 1954 when he morphed again and moved to television. I use radio's legends like Eddie Cantor and Amos n' Andy as shining examples of how important it is to accept change. If these stars of radio's Golden Age are willing to accept change, you can too!

In the late 1940s, when television came on the scene, some folks decided to prematurely put radio on a respirator, thinking it was taking its final breath, but radio fooled everyone by changing. Today, facing competition from multiple outlets for music, including iPods and the Internet, there are those doubting Thomases who are again sounding the death knell of radio's demise. There is no doubt radio is faced with having to change again to survive, a task the medium is all too familiar with. I feel radio will rally as it has done so in the past and will survive.[15]

Not every change and move will be the correct one, but sometimes it is necessary to take a chance. If you do make a mistake, don't become unglued. As soon as possible, get back in the groove!

Sometimes, taking the wrong road is part of the journey and finding your way back is your challenge.

Accept challenges that will inevitably come your way. A challenge is meant to do one very important thing, and that's to build strength of character. Challenges, like change, can be difficult and can be extremely difficult to handle. They can be stressful and demanding, but they can also be a real blessing. A challenge is like holding up a mirror of your life, putting it right out there in front of you to decide what's important and what isn't.

Always carefully consider your choices, whether it's taking a new shift at the radio station or moving to another spot on the radio dial in town. Weigh the pros and cons of the move carefully, but don't over think your choices and get caught up in them. If you get so concerned about making the perfect choice, you may come up short and fail to make any choice at all. Instead of waiting for the perfect choice, which may never come your way, make the BEST choice from the options presented.

When deciding to move to a new radio station, check your prospective new radio home out as much as possible. It's better to do lots of homework before you make a move and be safe, than it is to be miserable later on. Check out your prospective new employer as much as they're checking you out! Don't ever be seduced by the allure and seemingly sweet smell of success when it comes packaged in a major market opportunity. A move to a larger radio market often means more problems and stress on a larger scale.

Here is a to-do list for you, before making the decision on whether to take that new on-air position.

1. Check the image and reputation of the station in the marketplace. Is it received favorably?
2. Try to speak with present or past employees to get their take on what management is like to work for. [16]
3. Has the station been a consistent ratings winner in the marketplace?

Don't be afraid of change!

The rewards from your radio career can be great if you choose to follow your gut and act on new opportunities that present themselves. I'm not saying to be a risk taker and take off in any old direction and grab anything that comes along; quite the contrary! You know in your heart what feels right and what doesn't. Act on the opportunity that feels like it could be the right fit for you. Radio is full of new and exciting challenges. Keep your options open to take advantage of them. Your best barometer on what is right for you is your gut. If it feels right, do it! On the other hand, if you have any doubts, don't! Remember to think positive once your decision is made!

Number Six on the list of 7 Powerful "P's" is PERFORMANCE.

Nancy Quill on Magic 106.7 Boston has been a consistent performer on the station since 1982. Her midday show is the longest-running and most listened to program in Boston radio. Nancy attributes her long success record on the radio to a number of elements coming together. "Consistency and longevity have been my friends in this business," she says, "but I couldn't have that without working for a company [Greater Media] that is committed to the format and supportive of my work. The most important aspect of being consistent with your on-air performance is this: every time you push a button and open your mic to speak, it's got to feel like you're performing it for the first time."

Nancy has been on the same station and in the same time slot, middays, for over twenty-six years. She equates performance on the radio to a Broadway play. "You're an actor performing the same thing night after night. Every night needs to be as fresh and new as it was on opening night or else the play gets pretty stale. It's the same thing with radio," she says. "The spark has to be there every single day no matter what's going on in your life. That's what makes a pro. Sure, you stumble from time to time because we're human. Your listeners will connect with you," Nancy adds, "if you sound real, personable, and that you enjoy what you're doing."

Radio is filled with loads of stress-filled situations, both on and off the air. Radio can and will wind you up in a tight little ball, if you let it…so don't! The more uptight you become, the more mistakes you'll begin to make. Do the best job possible on your show. If you screw up a break, forget it. Don't over think it and let it mess up your next one! Try not to worry about things that will probably never happen. For example, *"I wonder what the PD thought about that last bit. Did I keep my guest on too long? That last phone call went nowhere."* Worrying about what others think, especially while you're on the air, will deep-six your performance faster than the speed of sound. You'll drive yourself nuts worrying about what others think about the content on your show.

In the final analysis, the only person who matters as to whether or not you're doing a good show is *you!* Of course, it helps if your PD & GM think you're doing a good job, too! Keep in mind, everyone fancies themselves a program director! Each has an opinion, both good and bad, about how your show should sound. Sure, some of it can be hurtful, but you can't let it affect the way you hit the air every day. You can't worry what others say and think. You can't control their actions. Some people will love what you do, while others will dislike you and loathe what you say. It's simply the nature of the animal. As difficult and as tough as it may be at times, you *can't* and *must not* let their negative opinions impact your performance. Instead, let your presentation speak for itself. If you trust yourself and your God-given talent, you'll be pleasantly surprised how much you can accomplish, probably more than you ever imagined.

Note to Air-Talent:

You need to continue to push the envelope with your content right up to the edge! Notice, I said, up to the line and not over it. You must be creative, innovative and, yes, even on occasion, take a chance and try something that may get you in hot water. In presenting an interesting daily show and we're not necessarily talking shock jock radio, but in any show with relevant, topical content, you will undoubtedly and occasionally say or do something totally stupid, simply because of the free-flowing nature of live radio. When you do, take a deep breath, step back and if it necessary and it feels right, apologize for the error of your ways…then move on!

Fair warning to those in charge of programming content on radio:

If you *continually* remove content that is even remotely considered to be controversial, edgy or daring, you'll wind up with boring and dull radio. If you *continue* to edit your air-talent and keep them under a fine microscope and micro-manage them, you'll not only drive them away, but also your all-important listeners. Encourage and support your air-talent to constantly be better entertainers - don't discourage them!

Advice for both air-talent and management to heed.

Listen up, air-talent. Your Program Director and Manager have a right to their opinions on what goes out over their airwaves. Funny, it's something I always had a problem grasping, too. To me, it was always my show and my responsibility. To some extent that's true, but the overall sound of the radio station falls squarely in the lap of your management and program people. Listen to their suggestions and always try to keep an open mind when it comes to their input on what they believe is good for you and your show. This may come as a total shock to talent, but management has more to be concerned about than just you and your show. You are a piece of the pie, another spoke in the wheel. They are responsible for the entire staff and the total sound of the radio station. I'm afraid it was one radio lesson which took me a very long time to learn, and more importantly, to accept. Don't be a slow learner like me. Instead of getting in management's way, do your best to make life a little easier for them and yourself.

As is the case with most things in life, and radio is no exception, compromise is the key to success. Try to keep it in mind, but also remember that during the course of the actual show, you as the quarterback and you alone should get to call the shots with no outside interference. When the show is over and when you're off the air *is* the only time programming and management should offer their input on how your show sounded and what went right or wrong with it. [17]

To prove a point, there was an ugly incident one afternoon involving the dean of Boston talk radio, **Jerry Williams,** and WRKO Program Director, **Mel Miller**. At the time, the early 1990s, I was in AM-Drive on WROR and Jerry was in afternoon-drive on our sister station, WRKO. I happened to be at the station for a rare afternoon meeting and heard the confrontation. Jerry was on from 2-6pm. At some point during the first hour of his show, all hell broke loose. Apparently, Mel Miller was in his office listening and became agitated and quite upset when he thought the dean had gone a little long with one of his callers. During a commercial break, Mel Miller raced down the hall, burst into Jerry Williams' on-air studio and began berating him about the lengthy call. That's all the senior radio pro needed to hear. Jerry jumped up and in a loud and heated voice, which is probably still reverberating through the hallowed halls of RKO to this day, lashed back at Mel. "Would you walk out on stage while Sinatra was performing?" he screamed. Dumbfounded, Mel stood there staring at Jerry as

Williams continued his verbal attack. "Well, don't ever come in here when I'm on stage, because I'm Sinatra!" We all had a good laugh over that line.

Jerry Williams' analogy of comparing himself to Ol' Blue Eyes may have been a bit over the top, but his message spoke the truth and was loud and clear. Don't ever bug talent when they're on the air. Nothing is so important that it can't wait until the show is over and talent is off the air, period! Talent also should never be hot-lined (telephoned) over content while on the air, unless of course they have totally flipped out and put the station's license in jeopardy. In that case, you'll probably get yanked off the radio right in the middle of one of your creative bits. Don't say you weren't warned. The best way to avoid any unpleasant situations from popping up right in the middle of your show is to always think about what you're going to say and do on the radio before you open the mic!

My former PD, now consultant, **Gary Berkowitz** once told me, "Joe, you can't be held responsible for what you don't say on the air!" It's sound advice and may prevent polyps from developing in your tummy! Speaking of Berko, Gary was very creative in ways to get his point across. One morning, while I was on the air at ROR-Boston, and in the middle of a taking a five-minute break for the news, he walked in the studio handed me a Polaroid camera and said, "Here, take my picture." My initial reaction was skeptical. "Just take the photo," he repeated, as he held up a 5x7 card. On it, he had written just one word, "*THINK*." After the photo developed, he handed it to me, smiled and said, "Now, put this on the control board in front of you and think about me listening before opening the mic." You know what? It worked!

For the past twenty-five years, **Joe Cortese** has showcased his talents on Boston's WBMX.[18]

Joe joined the station in 1983 when it was the original WROR, handling the night shift. He moved to middays in 1991, when the station became Mix-98.5. As a solid performer and one of Boston's longest-running air personalities, Joe jokes, "On the frequency 98.5, I've played everything from Patsy Cline to Pearl Jam." I asked my former co-worker and friend his thoughts on how to be consistent on the air. "Joe," he began, "you once told me you never know who is listening so always do your best. What you do is an art and you have to accept the critics. Be tough but flexible." Flexibility is the key word to success for Boston radio's Joe Cortese. In 2001, Joe moved over to sister station WODS-Boston as the APD and Imaging Director.

Speaking of always doing your best on the radio, this next story drives that point home in a nice way. It truly emphasizes the importance of always being on your game. One Christmas season, we were gathering items to auction on our morning show on WROR -Boston to raise monies for the station's Children's Christmas Fund. We discovered quite by accident **John Travolta** listened to our morning show while on his way to location filming sites in the Boston area.

We theorized he must have been scanning the dial one morning and landed on us by mistake. Unable to believe what he was hearing, he probably felt sorry for us and decided to try and figure out what we were all about! Of course, I'm teasing! We were absolutely thrilled to learn he dug what we did!

At the time, Travolta was filming the movie *A Civil Action*. Many mornings when the actor would arrive on location, instead of staying inside his RV, far away from his adoring fans who were gathered outside, he would mingle with them and sign countless autographs. They loved the approachable star and he seemed to get a kick out of the entire commotion they caused.

It was during one of these impromptu morning meet-and-greet sessions that John Travolta graciously autographed three copies of his book, *Propeller One-Way Night Coach*, for our charity auction. His autographed books brought in many dollars to help buy warm clothes and toys for Boston's needy kids. I had the good fortune to bid on one of his books and was ecstatic to learn I had won! His book is proudly displayed on our library bookshelf. After his kindly gesture towards the people of Boston, I have always had a fondness in my heart for the man. It's so refreshing to know that John Travolta, a true mega-star, is also a kind-hearted and generous person. It also proves a valuable point: when you're on the radio it's important to always do your best because you never know who might be listening. Every listener is important and deserves to hear you at your very best, but there may be one person listening who can truly make your performance special and memorable. Actor and good guy John Travolta did that for me at Christmastime in 1997.

You must consistently do your best air work, regardless of your circumstances. In the late 1980s, when I was on the air in AM-Drive at WROR in Boston, our parent company RKO General was forced to put WROR and WRKO up for sale. As the story goes, the tire and rubber division of the company ran afoul of the Justice Department and good ol' Uncle Sam said they had to divest themselves of their radio properties. For my money, it was a political football that was totally ridiculous and unnecessary. If fines were in order for improprieties that's one thing, but to punish a company so severely and make them divest of their broadcast properties is still difficult for me to fathom to this day. I honestly believe that with all the multiple ownership stuff going on today, if something similar happened now the government would probably slap them with a fine and look the other way! RKO was one of the best radio companies I ever worked for, and it was terrible to lose them as an owner and employer, let alone as a viable broadcast commodity.

RKO recognized the importance of air-talent and were extremely generous with excellent salaries and state-of-the-art equipment. It seemed as if their Boston radio stations were up for sale for years. It had to be at least four or five years, and perhaps even longer. Delays by lawyers and the FCC along with changes in the administration in Washington created even more of a circus atmosphere. It was a prime scenario of what a political football is all about. During these turbulent and unsettling times, it was extremely difficult to stay focused with the stations in such a state of flux. No manager worth his salt wanted anything to do with the place. Most of them logically reasoned that since there was no future with the ownership, there was no reason to get involved. The stations became one big revolving door. We had so many sales people in and out; I couldn't begin to tell you their names. During this time we had half a dozen GMs and at least as many program directors. The sale of the stations dragged on and on, and it was far from a pleasant atmosphere. On the air, it was a different story! It was showtime as usual! Listeners loved ROR & RKO. They were their radio stations. They didn't know or give a damn about what was taking place behind the scenes.

The on-air programming quality at WROR and WRKO never wavered and it's a huge credit to staff members, both on and off the air, who hung in and took pride in what they did. They continued to turn out a quality on-air product on a daily basis. It was virtually impossible for the average listener to detect that off the air the stations were in turmoil. Amazingly, both stations continued to do fairly well in the ratings considering all the changes taking place behind the scenes. I mention all of this for one very important reason! No matter what is taking place around you, the only thing that is important when you're on the radio is what is coming out of the speaker and it better be good! It's your job as an on-air radio pro to make sure your performance is always top-shelf, no matter what personal problems or circumstances you may find yourself in.

Do your own thing on the radio and always do it to the best of your ability!

This is directed to both radio wannabes and seasoned pros alike: try really hard to not get involved in what's going on outside your own space. Do your thing and keep doing it to the best of your ability, with what you have right now. Believe me, it will pay off! If you always do your best, you will never find yourself off the air and away from radio for very long! You may have periods when you're on-the-beach and between jobs, but you'll always bounce back. During my own down periods my friend, the late actor Robert Urich, would pump me up, saying, *"Don't worry, Joe. The good guys get more turns at bat, and you're a good guy!"* I'm passing these important words on to you! You know in your heart you're a good person and have what it takes to make it on the air, so when the going gets tough, hang in there. You'll be back up at bat before you know it!

Number 7 on the list of 7 Powerful "P's" is PATIENCE.

Many think of great artists as suddenly being overwhelmed with genius. More often than not they have shown a great deal of patience in their work. Their greatest efforts have been the result of working day and night over long periods of time to accomplish their goal. Leonardo da Vinci worked on *The Last Supper* for ten long years, being so attentive to his work that quite often he would forget to eat. It has been said that Beethoven rewrote each bar of his music at least a dozen times. It took the Beatles seventeen takes to record one of their earliest hits, "Love Me Do." It also took the song two years to reach the American Billboard Music Charts in May 1964, after first being released in Great Britain in 1962.[19]

Try to hold onto your patience today and the next day and the next.
    Former KGB San Diego morning talent **Shelly Dunn** says that when you're looking to break into radio, you really need to mark your time and **be patient.** "I knew that I loved broadcasting, but the biggest problem for me was the pay cut from being a waitress/bartender in college. I certainly didn't mind the tip money that I walked away with every night from the college restaurant/bar that I worked at for years, so when I took my first radio job making ends meet was tough. But, I was able to get the overnight shift at the college radio station.[20] My first night on the air started at 3am! I was to play songs off vinyl albums. I was on the air until the morning guy and my boss came in at 6am. I was so scared; I brought my brother with me. He loved adventure and I needed the emotional support."
    With her brother Darren's help, Shelly Dunn was able to cue up songs and even followed the format, almost. "The place was a mess by the time the morning guy came in, but we made it happen. Each night got a little better until I was allowed to fill in for afternoon broadcasters or middays. After some time, Jeff Freund, the program director at KATT in Oklahoma City, heard me and called my PD, Michael Baily, and asked if I would be interested in a news position at KATT. Of course I was interested, but again money and surviving was a problem! Jeff gave me 30 hours a week to start at six dollars an hour. Once again, I could have made more money in a bar but I WAS IN REAL RADIO!! After a few months, here's where patience comes in to play again, I was able to talk Jeff into giving me a salary with benefits," boasts Shelly. "I think he started me at around eighteen a year. I was so glad to have it!! So, there was some patience required to hang on until the money got better and I'm so glad I did. Radio has been the greatest ride of my life and well worth the wait."

One of the definite keys to being a success on the radio or in any career is patience. You get the chicken by hatching the egg, not by smashing it! Patience is definitely a virtue for a real radio pro.
    I must admit, patience is one virtue whose practice personally gives me the greatest challenge. I'm not sure it's my hot Italian blood or what, but I've always been impetuous and quick to pull the trigger. I wouldn't exactly describe my personality as "ready, shoot, aim," but that's fairly close to being

on target, or at least the way it used to be. Losing one's temper and flying into a rage just isn't cool, and thankfully, the aging process has a way of keeping one's personal fire from raging into an inferno. By practicing patience, you will go a lot further in life and also in your career as a radio pro!

When others give you headaches and present you with problems, try and look at them as giving you a chance to practice patience. Sound silly? The next time it happens give it a shot and see what happens.

Patience is a powerful tool that can help you handle almost every imaginable situation, especially those big ol' fat negative bombs which are dropped unexpectedly right in the middle of our laps. Practice being patient. It will help you avoid making careless calls and costly mistakes.

In 1961, while majoring in Communications at Boston's Emerson College, my speech professor, the late **Gerry Kroeger**, apparently grew increasingly weary of hearing my New England accent when I read aloud in his class. Words and phrases like, "Pahk the cah in the Hahvahd yahd," seemed to sound all right, but there was one important letter missing: the "R's." Like most Mainers, my accent of dropping "R's" was fairly evident.

One night after class, Professor Kroeger called me over. His words hit hard, directly to my heart and totally knocked the wind out of my sails. "Mr. Martelle," he began in his deep, overpowering and resonant voice, "I'm recommending that you switch to TV production. You simply don't have what it takes to be a radio announcer. I think you'll do well as a director or cameraman." I stood there for what seemed an eternity, dumbfounded, practically shaking in his presence. Whether intentional on his part or not, Professor Kroeger seemed to talk down to his students in an almost arrogant manner and with his tall stature, it gave him the ability to make one feel infinitesimally small. At that point, I felt like the lowest form of insect on the planet. My initial reaction was to tell him off! My sensitive side was hurting. Who was he to smash to smithereens my dream of being on the air! I finally found my tongue and searched for the proper words. "Mr. Kroeger," I began, with a grapefruit-sized lump in my throat, "it's my dream to be on the radio. I'll do anything to improve, I promise to work hard. Give me extra homework, anything, but all I want to do is be on the radio." I practically got down on bended knee and begged the big man to allow me to stay in his class.

I'm not sure it was the desperate pleading look in my eyes, or my obvious sincerity, but something clicked with him. I must have hit a soft spot. Looking up from his papers, he issued me an ultimatum. "Very well, young man, here's what I want you to do," he dictated. "You must read aloud at every opportunity. Read from newspapers, magazines, news copy, the Holy Bible; whatever you can get your hands on. Read, read, read and make sure you pronounce each and every word properly! You need to rid yourself of that dreadful New England accent." He concluded his verbal barrage with one parting shot. "You have a tendency to drop your R's, which makes you sound like a hick from the sticks." Now, to fully understand how the man sounded, you need to picture this towering person with perfect diction slowly. enunciating. each. and. every. word. in his deep resonant voice. Charlton Heston's delivery as Moses in *The Ten Commandments* had nothing on Professor Gerry Kroeger!

I followed the big man's advice to the letter. Every time, I picked up a newspaper, magazine or even the back of a cereal box I would begin reading aloud, no matter where I happened to be at the time. When I began reading the *Herald* or *Globe* out loud on the "T," nervous riders would eye me up and down and slowly move to another part of the car. It didn't bother me and actually worked out quite well. I was improving my speech and never had to worry about grabbing a seat even when trains were filled to the max. After a while, Professor Kroeger began calling on me more often to read aloud in his classroom. As my accent faded away, I became less self-conscious about reading in public. I completed his class with a C+; far from exemplary but good enough to give me six credits towards my Communications degree from Emerson. More importantly, my dream of one day being on the radio was still very much intact.

To this day, following a successful forty-one-year career as a top-rated radio personality in several major markets, including almost twenty in Boston, I'm still not sure if Mr. Kroeger truly believed I would never make it as a radio announcer, or if he was just giving me a much-needed boot in the butt to work harder on my speech and diction. Whichever it was, it worked. A word of friendly advice to you radio wannabes: when someone is in a position to critique your performance, try not to take offense and get upset. Their advice may be just a gentle boot in the derrière to motivate you to work a little harder.

When and if you find yourself faced with a difficult situation and the possibility of your own dreams disintegrating before your very eyes, take time out and practice being patient. There is no sudden leap to success as a real radio pro. The way to achieve greatness is by taking one piece of the pie at a time…step by step…drop by drop (in some cases of your own blood). You must do great radio, day in and day out. Patience also gives you a much-needed "time out" to stop and think, and to avoid making a costly mistake. Patience is a powerful tool that can help you handle almost any situation.

Practice being patient. Success doesn't happen overnight, unless you happen to find yourself a finalist on *American Idol*. Be patient. Bide your time! Learn as much as you can about radio and then you'll be ready when a move up comes your way. If you can learn to balance your personal ambition with patience, I think you will be blown away by the positive results.

There you have them; what I believe are the most powerful 7 P's to succeed as an on-air radio pro! **PASSION, POSITIVITY, PREPARATION,**

PRACTICE, PERSEVERANCE, PERFORMANCE and **PATIENCE**, with honorable mentions to Persistence, Pride, Promotion and Perfection. Of course, the bottom line is NEVER GIVE UP. In the words of tennis pro, Billie Jean King, "Champions keep playing until they get it right." So do Radio Pros.

Honorable mention:
    We've already covered persistence. PRIDE as in always "take pride" in your performance, your station, your show, and most importantly in yourself and what you bring to the airwaves. PROMOTION: always look for ways to promote your station, your show, and yourself. And…always strive for PERFECTION in ALL that you do!

Notes:
1. You can reach out to Joel Denver at www.allaccess.com.
2. How to Become a Successful On-Air Pro is covered more in Chapter 4
3. Larry Glick passed away in February 2009 and is remembered in Chapter 16.
4. John Forsythe left KOB-FM in Sept. 2010 and in 2011 is on the air in Orlando, Florida.
5. "Accentuate the Positive" was written by Johnny Mercer. He recorded it for Capitol Records with the Pied Pipers and Paul Weston's Orchestra on Oct. 4, 1944. The song got as high as #2 on the Billboard charts. It was also recorded by other artists including Bing Crosby and Perry Como.
6. How to handle getting fired is covered in depth in Chapter 9, "Attitudes & Actions."
7. Podcasting means your broadcast show bits will need to be able to stand alone.
8. Chapter 7 covers the importance of show prep material
9. Bob Rivers left the station in the fall of 2010
10. Bob Rivers' song parodies were first syndicated by the ABC Radio Network. His *Twisted Christmas* CD is a classic!
11. Learn more about the world of radio sports in Chapter 16 – "Formats"
12. Read more about ratings and how they affect your career as an air-talent in chapter 18.
13. Pioneer radio pro Will Rogers is profiled in Chapter 1
14. Source: John Dunning's *Tune in Yesterday* -Prentice-Hall 1976
15. Read more on radio's future in Chapter 21
16. Keep in mind, a fired and disgruntled former employee is not always the best person to ask for advice on whether or not you should seek employment at the same place.
17. The role station program directors and managers play is covered extensively in Chapters 10 and 11

18. WBMX is no more. In 2009, the call letters changed to WBZ-FM and the music died. In its place is Boston's first FM sports talk station.
19. Beatles story credit to my friend of over 35 years, Fred Bronson, who has written a series of books on Billboard's Hot 100 Hits.
20. Shelly Dunn attended Oklahoma Univ. in Norman, OK which was about a 20-minute drive to the big city.

The Seven Powerful "P's" to Perfection as an On-Air Radio Pro • 143

Tom Cuddy, NYC radio management.

John Forsythe, Albuquerque, NM and Orlando, FL morning-drive talent.

Ross Brittain, Philly morning-drive talent.

April Sommers, air talent, Don Bleu Morning show, San Francisco.

Nancy Quill, Boston mid-day air personality.

Gary Berkowitz holding up "think Joey" card.

Joe Cortese, Boston air personality.

Chapter 6
How To Communicate Effectively

"I'm not talking too fast, you're listening too slow"
– the legendary radio pro, B. Mitchell Reed

AS STRANGE AS IT MAY SOUND, you will find most problems in a radio station revolve around a total breakdown in communication! I know it sounds ridiculous. After all, radio is a business built on communication, but as absurd as it may sound, I'm afraid it's true. It's one of the idiosyncrasies of the industry; people who are capable of communicating so well on the radio have such a difficult time doing so off the air. It was my experience that the biggest breakdowns in communication were among air-talent, programming and management. However, a lack of communication in the radio workplace is a serious problem and is not just restricted to the air staff and programming personnel. On the contrary, sales, the front office and other station staff members also seem to find it difficult to communicate their thoughts effectively to one another, but for the purposes of this book let's deal strictly with the breakdown in communication between talent and management. One word always seems to rear its ugly head in many radio stations, and that one word is **ego**! When a battle of the egos develops, rational thinking and speaking to each other in a civil manner usually take a backseat to struggles for power and control.

It's no big secret that air-talent can often display huge egos, especially when in heated discussions and put on the defensive by management. When this happens, the original issue of discussion is soon forgotten. Tempers get dangerously close to the boiling point and logical thinking is cast aside. It becomes even uglier when a light bulb goes off in a GM's head that he or she is the boss and doesn't have to put up with this out-of-control, moronic attitude from an underling member of his or her staff! Guess what? They're right and a red flag should immediately go up in the face of the disgruntled talent, but usually doesn't! In a fraction of a second, a simple difference of opinion can mushroom into a serious problem of *who controls the turf*. All rationale goes flying out the window as the now-heated debate becomes a power struggle between two highly opinionated and super-charged personalities!

Longtime friend **Jack Casey**, who today is GM of Emerson College radio station WERS-Boston, believes talent should treat managers and PDs as coaches, not as adversaries. "In the long run, if your relationship is adversarial," he says, "you probably won't last long and if you do, your stay will be a stressful one."

When a conversation becomes a conflict, is it a point of no return?

Well, no doubt cooler heads should prevail, but radio is a game built on emotions. Sometimes those same emotions that make an air-talent a great personality can be their worst enemy when tempers flare and strong feelings spiral out of control.

In West Palm Beach, when I was in morning drive at Sunny-104.3, my GM was **Lee Strasser**. He was tough but a fair manager. There was nothing shy about the two of us when we got together to "discuss" an issue. Whenever I was really "fired-up" about something I thought important and would begin to raise my voice to make a point, Lee had a unique way of defusing me. As I ranted away and dangled precariously over the edge of common sense in dealing with my boss, Lee would always rise to the occasion and earn his stripes as the GM. Did he raise his voice and shout back at me? Not at all. Instead, he would lean back in his chair, or stand up (depending on how agitated he was) take a deep breath, and I mean a **deep** breath, and say, "Joey, relax, do as I do, take a deep breath." The first time he pulled this on me, I wanted to grab him by his stacking swivel and say, "Hey, I'm serious about this problem. Don't be condescending and tell me to breathe slowly."[1] I soon realized it was his way of calmly cooling my overcharged emotions. In doing so, he completely defused what could have been a serious situation for me, like getting canned for insubordination! Occasionally, when I was so pumped-up about something on my show or the station and on the brink of losing it, Lee's deep breathing technique would do the trick. Quite often, watching him do his deep-breathing exercises and insisting I follow suit would make me laugh and ease the tension even more. I'm not saying this will work for every talent and manager who find themselves in a heated argument, it is a suggestion that worked for us.

"People who can only tear down and destroy others with their venomous verbal attacks only grow weaker with every word that they spew forth."

Hopefully, the following suggestions may help to alleviate the problem of miscommunication between air-talent and management. Sometimes "communication" means projecting yourself and your image with fewer words. As my longtime friend and former PD and consultant Gary Berkowitz once told me, "Less is more!"

Reasonable people can agree to disagree. You don't have to be disagreeable in doing so. How to communicate effectively with management:[2]

Do you want to spend your time at work creating enemies of your PD, GM and others or would you rather build meaningful working relationships? The answer should be quite obvious! However, trying to achieve that goal in a business loaded to the gills with fragile egos is not that easy! Nothing is gained by those in a management or in supervisory positions who insist on being control freaks and turn a deaf ear to the thoughts and suggestions of those who work for them. Compromise is one of the keys to successful communication. If you insist on being argumentative and this is directed to everyone - not just those in charge - you will never win, let alone be a winner!

Dick Purtan is regarded as Michigan's most respected and recognized air personality.[3] For many years he handled morning drive in Detroit at Oldies 104.3-WOMC, until his retirement in 2010. He was inducted into the National Radio Hall of Fame in November 2004 and the Michigan Association of Broadcasters Hall of Fame in 2003. Purtan offers these little pearls of wisdom on how air-talent can get along with the suits. "The best way to get along with management is to understand management's goals and to help them attain those goals in cooperation with them. This is not to say that you have to do everything their way, but indeed to do it your way, using your unique talent and personality as vehicles to attain the common goal. Management has the tools and you have yours," he emphasizes, "and if you, as a personality, command a large and desirable audience the station management will value your distinctly unique approach towards everyone's success."

It is much easier from a talent's perspective to deal with those in authority or a position of power through "cooperation" rather than "conflict." As an air personality, you will be much happier if you try and go along with the program rather than fight management tooth and nail at every turn. Pick your battles carefully and constantly ask yourself, "Is this one worth fighting for?" Management, on the other hand, must be open to the suggestions and input from talent and listen closely to their concerns. Cooperation is the key to effective communication! Conflict is a no-win situation for both sides.

Remember that everything you say and do has a consequence, and every consequence has a lesson to be learned! Consequences can be excellent teachers. Through consequences, you will quickly learn what works and what will come back to bite you in the butt! It is important to know that communicating can be done more effectively when you add one simple word to the equation: kindness.

Ross Brittain currently heads up the morning show at WOGL 98.1 Philadelphia and is editor of *The Ross Brittain Report,* a syndicated morning show prep sheet.[4] When it comes to dealing with management and pushing the limits on your show, Ross, like many other radio personalities, feels this way: "It's always easier to ask for forgiveness than to get approval to do something edgy, so if you're going to do a stunt, don't ask for permission before hand, which gives the 'suits' complete deniability."

One simple technique to help you communicate more effectively with others.

There is one technique that you can use to help improve your effectiveness in communicating with others. This simple procedure will help you become a better leader and more importantly, a better person. First of all, listen to what the other person is saying. Next, imagine yourself in the other person's shoes. That's it! If you take a moment to really listen and picture yourself in the other person's place it may help you understand the reason for their actions and what they are feeling. It also may give you a little more insight into their motives for taking your head off! Maybe not entirely, but in some small way it may improve the dialog between the two of you. Try looking at things from their perspective! If nothing more, you will improve your understanding of their situation while increasing your own ability to be understood. Let's face it; everyone wants to be heard and to be understood. Be tender of heart. To defuse your adversaries' aggressive behavior towards you, try smiling! Laugh a little instead of being somber and heavy. It may help lighten your load and those of others around you. It may even brighten your day.

Empathy is probably one of the most important emotional qualities a radio personality can be blessed with. I truly believe being empathetic will make you become a better communicator. Try being empathetic to the demands placed on your co-workers, your boss, and your listeners. Being empathetic is not necessarily a quality you need to be born with, and like anything, it can be acquired if you're willing to work at it.

Each of us is blessed with an original one-of-a-kind perspective. If you take time to reach out and seek new perspectives, you will accomplish many rewarding things in your life and career. I firmly believe that being empathetic will increase your chances of success as a real on-air radio personality.

Another important point in effective communication is not to be overly sensitive to the comments of others. Throughout my life and radio career, quite often I'd hear the words, "You are way too sensitive. Stop being so sensitive!" It drove me crazy. Personally, I believe sensitivity is a great quality in an air personality. It gives you insight into how people are feeling. However, being overly sensitive can also be detrimental to your own well-being, particularly if you constantly misconstrue or take to heart everything someone says. Try to take things lightly and not quite so serious.

A chip on your shoulder can become a lead weight to your own success.
If you find yourself in an argument with someone, try and understand why the other person is upset and in disagreement with you before making a judgment .Words spoken in haste and spur of the moment decisions can often lead to further problems and needless hostility between individuals. Always step back, take a deep breath, and think before you jump down someone's throat! You will avoid stress and anxiety if you pause for just a few moments. There are times when you will find yourself in a situation which requires immediate action, but most often, your best response in a hotly debated discussion is to take no action at all. It's better "To let go and let be." If you think you can do something to ease tensions and help the situation in a positive way, then by all means do so. But, if you believe your reaction will create more discord and add fuel to the flames then cut your losses and move on! Don't waste time and energy on a lost cause and react in a negative fashion. It will only satisfy your ego for the moment! It may be necessary to follow through to get matters resolved, but save those actions for later. It's best to try and resolve matters after both parties have had time to cool down and to think things over.

The Apaches have a great saying, "*We'll talk after the blood has dried on the rocks.*" Take time to think about the entire scenario and perhaps how you could have better communicated your thoughts.

Do this before any further discussion with the person you had a disagreement with. Take a good, long look at what happened and see how you would like things to improve in future discussions with this person. When you have a falling out with someone, it is important to remember to not keep score! Let go of the need to keep track of how many times you feel you've been misused and abused. Just remember, there are some things you can change, like your own actions, and some things you can't, like the actions of others.

My second full-time job in radio was at the small station, WIDE in Biddeford. Maine. It's where I received my baptism in the business and learned much about radio. I am indebted to that 1000-watt radio station and Mike Matoin, Howie Martin and Alan Jasper, the three men who in 1963 took me under their wings and taught me to so much about the business of radio. I will always be grateful to them for helping to forge the foundation for my radio career. Small mom-and-pop radio stations are just as important today as they were back then for those wanting to be on the radio. They were, and are today, a place where tomorrow's radio stars can learn by doing and gain invaluable on hands experience. Just like Major League Baseball has a farm system where players can develop and work on the fundamentals of the game, small market stations work in the same way for radio personalities, allowing future broadcasters to hone their communication skills.

My friend **Craig Worthing** was also a member of the air staff at WIDE Radio. Craig didn't cotton much to being a DJ, but had an amazing gift for talk radio and interviewing. It must have been that Craig's hero Jack Paar rubbed off on him, because he was just as opinionated as Paar, which made him so good on the air.[5] In my opinion, Craig was a natural talk show host. Everyone who knows and loves Craig, and I mean this affectionately, will tell you he has a big mouth; a mouth which served him well on the air but often betrayed him as well. He was great at ad-libbing and could easily fill an hour of time talking about anything and everything, including the sex life of the tsetse fly (which he did!). Craig didn't need callers. His personality could easily carry him through a three- or four-hour show without breaking a sweat. Simply said, Craig Worthing was one of the best talk show hosts in the business. Off the air was an entirely different story, for that big friendly mouth of his always seemed to get him in trouble.

Craig was a people person who loved championing other people's causes, even if it was none of his business. The late Frank Fixaris, a respected Portland sportscaster who Craig and I both worked with at WGAN in the late 1960s, described him this way: "Craig should have been born back during the days of the Knights of the Round Table. He's always trying to rescue folks, whether they want to be or not!"

Craig had a strong dislike for running his own control board and was far from being technically inclined. Quite often he would mess up while on the air - records played at the wrong speed, dead air, and things like that, but his biggest problem was *NEVER* remembering to turn off his mic! He also had trouble keeping his mouth shut when the mic was supposed to be off and wasn't! More than once he found himself in deep doo-doo because of his error, and quite often it led to his dismissal. For some strange reason, Craig's mouth usually got him in trouble when I was away and out of town and couldn't be reached. This was 1964 and there were no cell phones, so when you were away, you were really away and totally out of touch! Craig's firings happened with such regularity that I actually hated going on vacation, because every time I did, the owner would fire him. It became such a regular occurrence that when I would arrive back at the station, instinctively the first thing I did was check to see if Craig's name was still listed with the others on our mailbox. If his name was gone, I knew something had come out of his giant trap and he had been fired![6] Of course, Craig would call me, contrite as always, and I'd go to the owner, plead his case and get him re-hired. It was my first real experience at being a chief-enabler.

However, there were some pretty good reasons why I always managed to get him reinstated. One, he was a good soul. Yes, he did have a big mouth and would be the first to admit it, but Craig was a kind-hearted person. Secondly, he was extremely talented and, from a budgetary consideration, like the rest of us at WIDE Radio, he worked really cheap!

Radio lesson 101: Always make sure your mic is in the off position, when not in use!

Let me give you just two examples of Craig Worthing's close encounter with a hot mic. The first involved a live remote program we aired every weeknight on WIDE Radio. Yes, I said a live program every night. In the early sixties, block programming was still in vogue, especially in small single station radio markets like Biddeford, Maine.[7] The program was the nightly recitation of the Holy Rosary live from St. Joseph's Church in Biddeford. Biddeford Maine had a large French-Canadian population, many of whom were Catholic, so usually there was a full congregation gathered in the church to accompany the priest as he led them in the Rosary. All Craig had to do was read the introduction from a cue card that was in the control room and Father Franc would do the rest. Sound easy? Sure, but not when you factor in Craig "anything can happen" Worthing at the controls.

The introduction to the "live" remote broadcast went like this: "Now as a public service, WIDE Radio takes you live to St. Joseph's Church in Biddeford for the nightly recitation of the Rosary … and now, here's Father Franc." That's all Craig had to read and do: introduce Father Franc and the good priest would take it away for the next 15 or 20 minutes, depending on how fast his delivery would be on any given night. Father Franc would take his air-cue from a radio he kept by his pulpit, and he wasn't always quick about turning down the radio's volume.

As Craig prepared to read the intro and throw the cue to Fr. Franc, he was in a jocular mood. He also had a studio filled with local high-school kids who he loved playing up to. It was against station policy to have anyone in the station after hours, let alone in the control room, so our friend Craig had already broken rule #1. He read the intro as written and tossed the priest his cue, along with a few added words of his own, "… and now here's Father Franc and Mother Goose." Always good for a funny line, Craig forgot to turn his mic off after cueing Father Franc. Craig's added words blasted out of the radio, because Father Franc didn't turn the volume down quickly enough at his end, so the words, "'Father Franc and Mother Goose" reverberated throughout the high walls of the Gothic church, resulting in hysterical laughter from the assembled congregation. But, that's not all! Because Craig's mic was left open, the kids in the studio also howled with laugher. For you non-Catholics, the recitation of the Rosary is done in a solemn and highly respectful manner and is not meant to be accompanied by laughter, let alone of the hysterical variety. There are some old-timers in town who actually believe even to this day, when the wind blows just right through the open stained-glass windows of St. Joseph's Church in Biddeford, that same hysterical laughter can still be heard.

I can't remember if Craig was fired and later re-hired, or if the entire incident was forgotten thanks to good-natured Father Franc, who actually seemed to get a kick out of it. As innocent as it may sound by today's radio standards, believe me, it was a big deal back in the early '60s and required lots of explaining to the boss man! Craig Worthing was a unique piece of work and one-of-a-kind talent. Let's just say, the "Father Franc, Mother Goose" line pales in comparison with Craig's next close encounter with an "open mic" and his wide-open mouth! The next time he was really in big time trouble. The incident involved the boss's wife and another lesson in how NOT to communicate while on the air.

To prepare you for the next part of our story of "the mic and the mouth," let me draw you a mental picture of the station's layout. WIDE was located on the second floor of an office building, downtown on Main Street. The studios and offices were directly across the hall from Yvette's Beauty Salon. The owner, Yvette, was a wonderful, jovial, and rather rotund older lady with a beehive hairdo, who loved everyone. There was only one problem with Yvette's! Whenever she gave a client a permanent wave (and most often she had several going at a time), the pungent, rotten-egg smell would waft across the hall like a deadly mist and slowly drift into our studios. To give you an idea how bad the smell was, quite often it was worse than what emanated from Saco Tannery directly across the Saco River, where they tanned horse hides. That odor was pretty nauseating, and the beauty parlor odor was almost as bad.

As you walked in the door to the station's office area (it was one of those doors with frosted glass with the call letters stenciled on it), there was a very small seating area in an alcove with two large leather green chairs and an old Philco console radio. You know, the type your grandfather would listen to complete with a bright orange glow illuminating the dial. We were an AM station and that big, beautiful radio was always tuned to our dial position, 1400. The sound was incredible and it was always turned on and up. The alcove opened to an open office area which had two or three desks. It looked into our main studio which came complete with a large window. This served two purposes: staff and guests could see the person on the radio and watch in total amazement as they performed on the air, sort of like watching a monkey in a cage at the zoo, and the window also served as a security measure. The air person could see the outer office, the alcove area and watch for anyone coming and going from the station.

And now to continue with our next thrilling chapter of a "hot mic and a big mouth":

On this particular night, Craig was on board preparing his 6pm local newscast. As is the case in most smaller stations, an announcer/DJ usually does more than just his or her regular air-shift. Craig's situation was no different than thousands of others who work in small and medium radio markets across America. His shift involved doing the 5:05 and 6:05pm local news followed by special programming until 8pm, a three-hour pop music request show called *Teen Time* until 11pm, and then soft romantic instrumental music on *Cozy Corner* until the station signed-off at Midnight. As previously mentioned, in the early 1960s block programming was the rule in most single station small markets. The 1960s and earlier is when radio, in accordance with FCC rules and regulations, required stations to broadcast a certain amount of special interest programming. WIDE tried to program something for every member of the family.

On the infamous night of the big episode of the "mic and the mouth," I just so happened to be working late at the station adding new music. I was seated off to Craig's right in a corner of the control room. It's not unusual for the PD of a small station, or any size station for that matter, to practically live at the station. In addition to handling the morning show from 6 'til 10am, I had administrative duties, music playlists to go over, copy to write, tons of production, recording commercials and so on, and being at the station at six at night was not out of the ordinary. You radio wannabes, think long and hard before accepting the role of a PD.[8] The title sounds good and it may supplement your meager earnings as an air personality, but you have to love and live the job! No salary will ever be commensurate with the amount of time and hours you will put in. In 1964, when I took the PD post at WIDE, my salary increased by ten dollars a week from $85 to $95, and I was most grateful! I didn't do it for the cash, though. I loved radio, was having a ball and probably would have taken the job without any increase in pay.

There was no secret that the boss's wife, Barbie, was not a huge fan of Craig's. Honestly, I think the feeling was mutual. For one thing, she thought Craig made too many flubs in his newscasts and he knew how she felt about his air work. She was always nice to me; perhaps a little distant, but always polite and kind.

Just as Craig was set to do his five-minute local newscast at 6:05, following Yankee Network News on the hour, in came Barbie, and planked herself down in one of the green leather chairs on the left-hand side of the tiny alcove.[9] From the control room window it was difficult to see the chair because it was partially hidden by a small wall. About the only thing you could see were her shoes, but make no mistake, Craig knew the rest of her was there, too. In his mind, she was ready to listen and take note of every flub he made on the radio. She was a spy ready to report back to the BIG GUY, her hubby, on how he was screwing up again on the airwaves! Directly across from where Barbie was seated was that big ol' Philco Radio turned up nice and loud to WIDE. Before going on the air, I heard Craig mutter something under his breath about her. I couldn't make it out but I'm positive they weren't sweet sentiments about Barbie. I thought her presence in the tiny reception area listening to him would affect his reading of the news, and I was right. Craig made numerous mistakes. It was almost like watching a hanging man twisting and turning on the gallows, gasping for air.

Finally and mercifully, what seemed to be the longest five-minute newscast in the history of radio was over and I breathed a heavy sigh of relief for him. He played a commercial cartridge and pushed his headphones back from his ears. I stood up and took a few steps closer to where he was seated behind the control board, trying to get a better look through the control room window to see if Barbie was still there. Now, it's important to know that it's common practice to turn the mic pot (control) down before turning it on, in order to avoid feedback from the studio speakers which every radio person cranks up to maximum volume. Turn the mic pot down, turn the toggle switch on, and when you're ready to speak, roll open the pot and begin yakking. Every talent does it.

As the commercial played, I noticed Craig was peering menacingly through the control room window in the general direction of the boss's wife, or at least at her shoes, because from our vantage point that's about all we could see of her. All of a sudden, in a loud voice Craig blurts out, "Look at her out there! I can hear her now. 'There he is flub-dubbing about on the airwaves again.' **SHE PISSES ME OFF!**" Yup, you guessed it! The mic pot was turned up, not down, and loud and clear as a bell right over the commercial that was playing and directly out of the front speaker of that lovely Philco console radio came Craig's salvo at Barbie! Barbie's head shot around the corner of that wall faster than greased lightning or any kind of lightning, for that matter! Now we had no problem seeing all of her! She glared at us! The look on his face was priceless. In a millisecond, he turned ashen. I think I did too, and I was an innocent bystander who just happened to be in the wrong place at the wrong time! We both quickly glanced down at the mic pot; it was wide open! I mean *wide open*, with the switch in the on position. I quickly motioned with my hand for him to pot it down. Just then, I saw Barbie immediately jump up and walk briskly down the hall past our studio with the kind of walk with an attitude that only a woman scorned can give off. She was a lady on a mission and was headed straight for the corner office and her hubby, the owner and General Manager.

If I recall correctly, it was shortly after that incident that Craig left the hallowed halls of WIDE Radio for the final time. I'm afraid neither I nor help from the United States Supreme Court would be able to hear his appeal on this one. He was a goner.[10]

Radio lesson 101: It's always a good idea to make sure your mic switch is off when you're finished doing your thing on the radio!

Communicating effectively on the radio is a God-given gift.

The gift of communication is just that, a gift! The gift of communicating on the radio on a one-on-one basis is truly special. Many radio folks would die to be able to do so. If you have this ability as a personality consider yourself to be extremely blessed, for it is a gift.

Don't be a communication hog on the radio!

Make sure you give others an opportunity to speak. Communication, especially on the air, is talking in an effective, emotional way to reach others. Two-way talk radio is just that - two people conversing, and not one person shouting and over-riding the other, whether it be show host, guest, or caller. Effective communication is saying your piece then keeping your mouth shut, allowing the other person to respond without interrupting them! [11]

During radio's Golden Age, the 1920s through the early '50s, network radio announcers were celebrities who were treated as well as the top radio stars of the day. Radio announcers were cordially welcomed at top restaurants and nightclubs and were invited guests to special events. NBC news personality David Brinkley[12] once remarked, "NBC believed it was only fitting that after 6pm, all their announcers on its network were required to wear tuxedoes. Network executives felt announcers would take their positions more seriously if they dressed for the part."

As strange as it may sound, even during my own forty-plus years on radio, whenever I "dressed up" to go on the air, whether we were expecting a special guest or just because I felt like wearing something a little nicer than a t-shirt and jeans, I noticed my approach to the show was different. I'm not so sure I took more pride in being on the air because of my attire, but there's no question my attitude was somewhat different, perhaps even a little more positive.

One of radio's first great announcers was Boston native Ed Herlihy. Talk about a talented communicator! For sixty-three years, he "caressed commercials" and introduced many programs on both NBC radio and television. Herlihy was an announcer's announcer. His authoritative, warm, and friendly delivery was the voice of Kraft Foods and the *Kraft Music Hall* for many years. Interestingly, like so many announcers from radio's golden age, Herlihy never took a lesson.[13] These announcers were all individuals with their own gifted styles, but one thing they had in common was their ability to communicate.

Unlike many of today's air personalities, announcers during radio's formative years had to have perfect diction and pronunciation. The goal of every network radio announcer was absolute perfection on the air, a far cry from today's loosey-goosey air style. During radio's golden era a fluff or mispronunciation would strike terror in the heart and mind of any announcer who perpetrated the goof. It would also be discussed for days on end by network executives and listeners alike. I'm sure yesteryear's outstanding radio announcers and personalities would be perplexed if not appalled by what goes out over our nation's airwaves today.

Your Voice and You.

In 1964, the late **J. Alan Jasper** was my boss at WIDE in Biddeford, Maine. He gave me the best advice I ever received on how to use my voice on the air. He urged me to "smile" when I spoke. When you smile as you speak, your voice sounds warm and friendly. You also sound more convincing, confident and enthusiastic when reading the all-important commercials.

Peter Casey, WBZ Boston's Director of News and Programming, advises all future radio talent to work on that voice! "I hear too many people on the air in major markets," says Casey, "that have not developed their voices yet. This is especially painful to hear for news anchors and reporters. Learn the range of your voice and go take some acting lessons. Not just voice lessons," suggests the veteran radio programmer. "It is important to have some voice coaching, but what some voice coaching leaves out is that acting lessons can give your voice range and style."

In October 1968, **Donna Halper** became the first female announcer in Northeastern University's history.[14] After graduating, she went on to a successful career in broadcasting, including more than twenty-three years as a radio programming and management consultant. Donna says women have to learn how to modulate their voice so that it comes from their mid-range. "When women get excited, upset or angry, their voice tends to go up into the upper register and they sound shrill or even squeaky, whether they want to or not. It is perfectly fine to express any emotion you want, but do it by projecting the voice, rather than by letting it drift into those upper registers. This is difficult to explain on paper," she continues, "of course, I'd be happy to demonstrate the technique to any female announcer, or a good vocal coach can do the same thing." Donna also points out that there are college courses in voice and articulation or public speaking that can help. "It's just a matter of learning to control the voice and using it like the finely tuned instrument that it is." For the past eighteen years, Ms. Halper has been an adjunct instructor at

Emerson College in Boston, where she teaches in the Journalism department and in the Institute for Liberal Arts.

Author's personal note:

Your voice is a delicate instrument, don't abuse it! Of course, if your radio format of choice is "screaming" Top-40 then forget what I just said. Just hope and pray you don't burn your pipes out! In May of 2004, I lost my voice because of three nodules on my vocal chords, requiring speech therapy along with voice rest. I learned a valuable lesson from my speech pathologist, **Anne Davis**. She informed me that we can damage our voices in everyday speaking, let alone pushing it to the max while on the air. Don't push your voice too hard when you are on the radio. Another sobering fact Ann passed on, which makes perfect sense, is that in time all parts of our bodies wear out, including our voices. As air-talent you need to treat your voice gently and with care!

A suggestion from one who has lost his voice, take out insurance, even if it means paying more each month on your health coverage. You never know when you may lose the ability to speak. I never expected it to happen to me, but it did. As fate would have it, I lost my voice. It has returned, thanks be to God, but it was a frightening time. I not only faced the end of my career, but the unexpected loss of income. A few years before losing my voice, my wife Kimmie had the presence of mind to insist we take out extra insurance coverage on my voice. Not wanting to think negatively, I resisted! She insisted, saying it would be a safety measure in the unlikely event something happened and I couldn't speak. Thankfully, I listened to her. It was an option benefit on our insurance coverage, and we paid extra for the premium. It is identified as short- and long-term illness disability insurance. If you're on the air, I strongly suggest you look into it and take out extra insurance on the most valuable asset you have, *your voice.*

Some worthwhile tips on how to use your voice effectively on the radio:

- Experiment with your voice but never abuse it. It is a delicate instrument that needs tender loving care
- Try different voices. Work on that celebrity impersonation if that's your shtick.
- Don't ever push your voice so much that you strain your pipes.
- Don't ever be a monotone, unless you're doing an opera broadcast and even then, you don't need to sound monotonic. Be expressive.
- *Always paint pictures with your voice*—especially when sharing a story with your listeners.

- *Be emotional with your voice.* Remember: no tears in the voice, no tears in the hearts of your listeners.

Communicating via the written word.

Another form of communication is *the written word.* Communicating via the written word is never an easy thing to do, especially with today's hi-tech, speedy way of communication called e-mail!

In many ways, it is an invaluable tool for businesses and families and friends to stay in touch. As a matter of fact, because of my own voice issues, 99% of the contacts made for this book, at last count over 150 broadcasters, never would have been possible if not for e-mail. I am most grateful for its technology because without it, this book never would have enjoyed the input from so many participants. My editor, Mike and typesetter, John both live in Rhode Island. Sandy, the production Manager resides in Oklahoma, while our publisher and boss man lives out of the country. Without the services of e-mail, regular contact with them would have been virtually impossible. So, I for one am most thankful for electronic mail.

However, this marvelous discovery does not come without an inherent downside. Quite often messages sent at the speed of light become misinterpreted. The brevity of words from the "sender" can easily be misconstrued and the intention of the message be completely lost by the "receiver." One reason for miscommunication is the person on the receiving end of the message can not see or read the person's face who is sending the message, i.e., is the person laughing, angry, in a teasing playful mode or whatever? More often than not, e-mail can be left wide open to misinterpretation. It is difficult without seeing or hearing the other person to fully comprehend their intentions via written words in an e-mail.

A good rule of thumb to follow is: if you must be brief, choose your words very carefully to avoid as little chance for error in communicating as possible. Personally, even after I have thought long and hard about my content before sending, a few of my own e-mails have been misconstrued, testing the strength of a few friendships. Thankfully, I haven't lost any friends yet because of a poorly written or misconstrued e-mail. Well, at least none that I know about.

The bottom line is, whether written or spoken *always* choose your words carefully. Your words do not magically disappear after you speak or write them. They go out and connect in a good or bad way with others. Of course, you can easily delete the printed text from your computer and try to erase them from your mind. The point is, words you write or say can come back to you one way or another, either in a positive or negative way.

New York City's legendary morning mayor of radio, my friend Harry Harrison, has great words to live by: "Don't say or do anything today you'll regret tomorrow." It speaks volumes, especially about words spoken or written hastily via e-mail. Think twice before hitting that send button!

Written memos are another way of communicating. As with e-mail, they too can often be left open to misinterpretation. Some are written poorly and in a threatening manner with little hope of receiving much, if any, cooperation from the staff members they are intending to reach. Here is an example of two actual memos from management to air-talent. You decide which one will get more cooperation from the air-staff:

Example #1

Actual notes taken from a memo written by a radio station manager to members of the air-staff:

LISTEN UP, PEOPLE! THERE IS NO FOOD…AND NO DRINKS OF ANY KIND, INCLUDING WATER OF ANY KIND, ALLOWED IN ANY OF OUR STUDIOS. AN ACCIDENT INVOLVING LIQUID COULD CAUSE DAMAGE TO THE CONTROL BOARD AND TAKE US OFF THE AIR. THE LUNCH ROOM IS A SHORT WALK FROM THE STUDIOS. THIS POLICY WILL BE ENFORCED. ANY VIOLATION OF SAME WILL BE VIEWED AS A SERIOUS BREACH OF YOUR CONTRACT AND WILL BE DEALT WITH ACCORDINGLY. **The Management!**

(Note: In reality the air studio is a long jog to the lunchroom, let alone a brisk walk. *No water!?* Tough to do during a high-profile intense-busy personality radio show, and *impossible* during a talk format.)

Example #2.

IN CASE ANYONE HAS FORGOTTEN, I WANT TO REMIND YOU OF A POLICY THAT IS MANDATORY AT OUR RADIO STATION. NO ONE IS ALLOWED TO HAVE ANY FOOD OR DRINK, WITH THE EXCEPTION OF WATER, IN ANY STUDIO AT ANY TIME.

HOWEVER, THERE IS AN EXCEPTION. BECAUSE OF THE LENGTH OF WEEKEND SHIFTS, A TABLE HAS BEEN SET UP IN THE BACK OF THE STUDIO FOR ANY FOOD OR DRINK YOU WISH TO BRING IN WITH YOU. OBVIOUSLY, IT IS NOT THE WISH OF MANAGEMENT TO SEE YOU, AS VALUABLE MEMBERS OF OUR AIR STAFF, PERISH FROM LACK OF NOURISHMENT, ESPECIALLY WHILE YOU ARE ON THE AIR ENTERTAINING OUR LISTENERS. PLEASE REMEMBER TO KEEP FOOD AND WATER AWAY FROM THE CONTROL BOARD AT ALL TIMES. THANK YOU FOR YOUR CONTINUED COOPERATION!

Which memo, #1 or #2, do you find to be written in a friendlier, more cooperative tone and makes you more likely to follow the request set down by management? Which memo makes your blood pressure rise to dangerously high levels that you immediately want to deep-six it, and makes the little devil in you want to push the "cooperation and follow the rules level" to the limit? You make the call, but I think the decision is easy.

Here is another example of a poorly written memo to air-staff members:
ATTENTION RADIO AIR STAFF MEMBERS WHO ARE OBVIOUSLY DEAF TO THE SOUND OF A TELEPHONE RING! WHEN YOU HEAR A TELEPHONE RINGING WITHOUT BEING ANSWERED, WHETHER OR NOT IT IS YOUR RESPONSIBILITY, AND EVEN IF IT IS ON SOMEONE ELSE'S DESK, PICK IT UP AND ANSWER IT! TAKE A MESSAGE. DON'T BE A COMPLETE DUMMY AND IDLY SIT AT YOUR OWN DESK CHATTING AWAY ON YOUR PHONE EXTENSION WHILE THE NEARBY PHONE IS RINGING OFF THE HOOK!

The memo speaks for itself. No further explanation is needed as to how poorly the message is written. Is it any wonder that staff members react in negative fashion and the spirit of cooperation is lost? Think twice before sending a written memo. Write the first draft and put it aside. Read it later and if need be, rewrite it before sending! Always keep in mind it's "the spirit of cooperation" you are trying to achieve, and a hastily written or mean-spirited memo is not the best way to accomplish that goal.

Freedom of Speech and how far to take it on the radio! Just one man's opinion.
How often have you heard someone say, "Hey, it's my right to say what I feel!" There's no doubt freedom of speech is one of the greatest rights we have as Americans. I'm a big supporter of the First Amendment, but being on the air, contrary to what you may have heard, is not the proper place for profanity. Doing a radio show is a huge responsibility. My philosophy has always been to keep it clean. Don't be a potty mouth! In recent years, it seems air-talent has been given a license to kill - the English language, that is! What is deemed to be in good taste and acceptable content by most civilized Americans has all but disappeared from many programs. It's my belief the FCC has been way too lax in interpreting what is offensive to the listener on our public airwaves. For quite some time, the FCC has allowed the so-called shock jock to get away with more and more of what was commonly referred to as blue humor.

In the 1950s, '60s and '70s, albums with sexual connotations from comedians like Redd Foxx, if even aired on radio, were relegated to after Midnight hours with many words bleeped out. By today's so-called standards that type of material pales in comparison to some of the vile content and vulgar language that is readily used on radio today. What has happened to standards and good taste on radio? For one thing, the FCC has turned a deaf ear to the situation, but it also can be attributed to one over-ruling factor, *the American public*. The programming people listen to and watch are based on one thing - popularity. Programmers subscribe to one basic philosophy: "Give them what they want!" It would appear from the permissiveness of our nation's airwaves this is what the public wants or at least doesn't care enough to voice their displeasure. Status quo seems to be the byword today. Obviously, if you listen and approve of what's being broadcast than you can expect more of the same.

Many listeners are afraid to open their mouths and speak out against anything found to be offensive, because there is a watchdog organization standing by ready to defend someone's right to say what they want regardless of how raunchy and lewd it may be. You also have rights governed by the First Amendment. You can and should speak out against what you believe is indecent language. The FCC does have stringent guidelines against using foul language on the air but how strictly it's being enforced is another matter. I agree with our founding fathers that every American has the right to say what they feel, but I also believe it is wrong to use our public airwaves in a manner that is deemed by the majority to be vulgar and in bad taste. Now, this is where it really gets interesting. Who is to say what is vile, vulgar, and in bad taste with what's said on the air? I guess you could begin with George Carlin's well-scripted seven words you can't say on the air! I think we are all quite familiar with them, so there is no need to give them additional ink. When it comes to greater permissiveness with profanity on radio, the medium's younger sister, television, certainly hasn't helped the deplorable situation! They not only say it on TV, they show it!

My feeling is bad language has no place on radio or TV. But then again, the days of Opie and Andy have long since departed the airwaves, and in their place is a quite different-sounding Opie with his radio partner Anthony. If you haven't heard the boys, their act is light years away from the homespun, family fare that was *Mayberry RFD*. The RFD with **Opie & Anthony** stands for something a far cry from Rural Farm Delivery. It's more like Radio Freaking Distasteful. But, hey, who am I to be critical of the lads. The last time I checked they were doing just fine in the ratings, so someone is listening. See what I mean about taste and America's listening habits?

The question is, when did we lose all sense of what's good and decent? The language used on many radio shows today is atrocious. As adults, we have all used words that we'd never dream of repeating in front of our moms, so why use them on the radio? Honestly, I'm not so sure there is ever an appropriate time or place to use foul language. Well, I take that back just a little. Maybe a sharp expletive has magical healing powers when you accidentally jam your finger in a car door, but for the most part, using profanity is uncool and a sign of not being very classy. It's a bad habit and like any bad habit, it needs to be dropped, especially while on the air!

Notes:
1. "Stacking swivel" is a military term and refers to a hook on an M-1 rifle used with others to stack arms.
2. Read more about management and talent "working amicably" in Chapter 11-Inside the World of General Managers
3. Dick Purtan comments in Chapter 14-How to Win in Morning Drive Radio
4. Ross Brittain comments in Chapter-20-Who inspired the Radio Pros
5. Jack Paar was a high-school dropout who did stand-up and entertained servicemen during WWII. He hosted several TV shows during the early '50s before hosting NBC's *Tonight Show* from July 1957 until March 1962. Jack was a conversationalist who could also deliver a joke. Viewers came to expect the unexpected as highly charged emotions flew between Paar and his guests. What made Jack Paar a super talent was his mercurial personality.
6. How to deal with getting fired is discussed in Chapter 9, "Attitudes and Actions."
7.- Block programming meant a variety of different programs. For example, in the early 1960s at 6pm WIDE carried world and national news from the Yankee Network, followed by local news, sports and weather. At 6:15 it was either Paul Harvey or Fulton Lewis, Jr. 6:30 was the Rosary, followed by a full hour of French music and hosted by a French-speaking host. At 8pm, *Teen Time* was a three-hour program geared to teens, with top-40 hit songs and requests. At 11pm, following a news wrap up, was *Cozy Corner*, an hour of lush, romantic instrumentals until sign-off at Midnight.
8. The role of PDs in radio is covered in detail in Chapter 10
9. Yankee Network was a regional network that was based in Boston at WNAC (later WRKO). Yankee fed newscasts to affiliated stations in New England.
10. Craig Worthing moved on to the nearby medium market of Portland, where he found greater fame as host of WGAN-AM 560s Maineline. Later, he was on the air in Utica, New York, and for many years was a popular talk show host in South Florida.
11. The art of interviewing is covered in Chapter 8
12. David Brinkley is profiled in Chapter 16-Radio Formats-News
13. Read more about radio's first on-air pros and learning from the Masters in Chapter 1, Radio's First On-Air Personalities
14. You can reach Donna Halper via e-mail at dlh@donnahalper.com.

How To Communicate Effectively • 163

Air staff, WIDE – 1400 AM Biddeford, ME. Community Chest parade, left to right: Mike Matoin, author, and Craig Worthing, 1963.

Dick Purtan, legendary Detroit morning-drive radio pro.

Donna Halper, radio consultant.

Chapter 7
The Importance of Show Prep

"He had all this preparation. He made us look bad, but we loved him dearly."

– Bob Eubanks speaking about Casey Kasem's when both were on-air at KRLA

The value of show prep to you and your show.
"IF YOU DON'T DO WHAT YOU NEED TO DO TO PREPARE, YOU WON'T WIN." Adopt the Boy Scouts' motto, when it comes to show prep, **BE PREPARED!**

Kiss-108's Matt Siegel is one of Boston's top-rated morning show radio personalities. During my twenty years on radio in the hub we were friendly competitors. We ran into each other one day at a mall, when both our wives were shopping. His wife picked up some cutlery and jokingly pointed one of the knives at him. Matt, glanced over at me, grinned and said, "Joe, do you ever get the feeling life is one big bit and we're always doing show prep?!" Matty's comment says it all regarding show prep. It's omnipresent! Show prep is everywhere, all around you in everything you say and do!

As an air-talent you need to be a SHOW PREP junkie!
Whenever you watch television, see a movie, read a newspaper, pick up a magazine, go online, or shoot the bull with your wife, do so with show prep in mind.

The late Boston air personality **Jess Cain**, to whom *Radio Pro* is dedicated, made this comment when asked how much time should be spent on gathering show prep material: "A good rule of thumb to follow in actually writing and preparing show prep is *one hour off the air for every hour on the* *air."* Cain always carried a small notebook and pen with him to write down those fleeting moments in life and everyday funny lines which can and do pop up unexpectedly, anywhere and everywhere, even in a darkened movie theater. You'll know you are the quintessential show prepper and a little loony when you're at the movies with your honey in a darkened theater and you try writing a funny line from the flick on your popcorn box. Remember, show prep material is found everywhere. I would often carry a few index cards in my pocket to jot down a few facts from a magazine article which may have caught my attention while sitting in a doctor's office. Later, when more convenient, I'd transfer the info from the card to a computer file with the name of the article or personality, and the date and publication.

Today, of course, you can send yourself a text message a funny line or piece of info to retrieve later. Just keep in mind, computers crash and valuable show prep material can be lost. Keep those handwritten cards and the file box as a backup.

Show prep is everywhere. Clip it and save it!

At home, in your office, by your computer, keep a pair of scissors handy just in case you come across a newspaper or magazine article that grabs your attention and piques your interest. I had so many pairs of scissors floating around at one point that our house looked like a shrine to *Edward Scissorhands!* You may not have time to read the story at that moment, or necessarily need it for the next day's show, but clip it and keep it in a "future file" folder for a future show. You never know when you may need to refer to a particular article to verify or support your point of view on a subject. When you have time, convert it to a computer file if you like, but always keep the hard copy in a box somewhere, just in case your computer crashes and valuable show prep material is lost.

Your on-air credibility and you!

Do your homework! Your own credibility and believability is on the line with your listeners. Take the extra time and steps necessary to research and check out the smallest details. The simplest trivia question should always be researched through at least two and preferably three different sources. You never want to give out erroneous information and wrong facts. It's the fastest way to lose credibility with your listeners. If you continually make mistakes, ultimately your listeners will go away and take your ratings with them. Online sites like Google and Yahoo!, along with newspaper files and the libraries of colleges and universities, are excellent sources of information for your show; just make sure you check and recheck all your facts before hitting the air with it. As the late ABC News journalist Frank Reynolds said, "Let's get it right." Being "accurate" in what you put out on your show and over the air doesn't just apply to news stories and journalism.

There was a time early in my career when I considered myself pretty decent at ad-libbing. "Who needs to prepare and write things down?" Not I, said the cat! "Show prep is for those who aren't with it and don't know what's going on in the world," was my attitude. Man, talk about a first-class idiot - that was me! Even the most gifted, funniest talent in the world needs to do show prep. Why do you think Jay Leno meets with his writing staff every night following his *Tonight Show*? It's not just to share a few snappy jokes and a couple of slices of pizza! It's to do show prep.

No talent wants to be predictable.
One of the dangers of NOT preparing is going to the well once too often, when a funny retort or comeback line is needed. Do that once too often and your listener will say the line before you get it out of your mouth! Very few air personalities are blessed with the ability to carry around thousands of one-liners in their heads. This is just another reason why show prep is so important.

We went to the radio experts for their input on the importance of show prep on your show:
Walter Sabo is a leader in media programming and management. He has the distinction of being the youngest Vice President in the history of ABC and NBC, landing both posts before the age of thirty. Since 1984, Walter has been President of Sabo Media, a New York-based programming and management company. It was the year when our paths first crossed. I was in morning drive at the original WROR 98.5-Boston with my partner, Andy Moes. One morning following our show, *The Joe and Andy Family*, Walter approached me in the hallway, complete with a cigar in one hand and a warm handshake from the other. "Come on," he said, "we're going for a short walk." Our casual short walk lasted over two hours and traversed almost the entire length of fashionable Newbury Street in downtown Boston.

What Walter accomplished borders on brilliance in promotion and marketing and it didn't cost the station a dime![1] Sabo walked me through the front doors of nearly every shop on Newbury Street, introducing me to sales clerks, managers, owners, anyone he could find! His intro went something like this, "This is Joe Martelle, he does a fine radio program mornings on 98.5-WROR right here in Boston. Have you ever listened to him?" Practically hiding behind the man, and blushing brightly his intro would be my cue to say "Hi," and jot down a name to say hello to the person the next morning on my show. We'd chat for awhile like you would in meeting any new friend.

Walter always left them with a gentle reminder to be sure and listen the next morning to 98.5-WROR, with the reassurance that I would say hello to them and their place of business. Before walking out the door, he would turn to the closest female employee (the station was targeting female listeners)

"May we have your vote to listen to Joe?" he would ask in an almost pleading way. How could the lady respond with anything but, "Yes, of course." It was almost as if I were running for election and in a way, I was. He was sking for their vote to listen to me and our station. It was a brilliant move by Walter Sabo and something I have always remembered. It was also the closest I ever came to being involved with my own "get out and vote for me campaign. It may work for you."

Walter Sabo says every radio mega star he has worked with and observed close up truly believes in the value of show prep! "There are two common traits to every radio mega-star I've had the privilege to work with, and those stars include Casey Kasem, Howard Stern, Neil Rogers, Bruce Morrow, Bubba the Love Sponge, Bill Carroll, Craig Carton, the late Paul Harvey and many more. They spend all day preparing their next show. They do nothing else. They prepare, prepare and prepare. They are obsessed with their show. They do nothing else. They are never happy with the results of today's show. They know every show could be improved and the next show will be improved. It drives them," says Sabo.

Show Prep is about your life. Bring those relatable experiences to your show to share with your listeners!

America's top radio pros share their expertise on how they use show prep and why!

Dave Ryan is the morning super-star personality on KDWB 101.3 in Minneapolis. Dave admits show prep is an obsession of his. "I can't do enough. Even after I have a great show planned, I still feel I want to do more!" Dave, who calls himself a dork because he doesn't try to be anything that he is not, says he does at least a few hours of show prep every single day. "I write, organize and research every day. And remember," the radio pro emphasizes, "having an interesting life is about the best show prep there is. Too many hours in front of the computer can keep you from actually going out and experiencing things you could be talking about on your show tomorrow. So, in the end, it's important to strike a balance between sitting at your computer writing bits and actually going out and having a life and making yourself an interesting person."

Boston radio pro **Paul Perry** agrees with Dave Ryan that having life experiences is probably the best type of show prep that you can do. "Some of the most engaging and real discussions on the air," says Perry, who is currently in afternoon drive at WROR-Boston, "are about things you experience, or witness, that most all people can relate to. Being relatable to the listeners is the golden link between you and them. So, when it comes to show prep, always have your eyes and ears open. Your life is part of show prep, as long as it passes the relatable test."

Anna Marie Ritter is responsible for the morning news on Nashville's #1 radio station, MIX-92.9. She feels this way about show prep. "You have to

MAKE SURE you bring good material to the table; ideas, life experiences, stories that are well-targeted to your station demo, in our case, females. The stories must be compelling and relatable to your audience."

Bring your life to your show - Talk about what you experience and know.
By talking about what you know on your show, your family, your pets, your car, golf game, whatever you're living through, share it with your listeners. You have the inside track on telling the story on your show better than anyone else. Everyday happenings are also great fodder as show prep: things like the checkout lady at the grocery store who actually smiled and said, "Have a nice day," running ten minutes late for the movie because your wife was feeling "fat" and felt the need to change her outfit three different times, running over your son's brand-new skateboard while backing out of the driveway because you were in a hurry to meet your buds for a round of golf. Better the board than your boy! How about cutting a guy off in traffic and flipping him the bird before speeding away because you're running late for your appointment with your new dentist, only to learn upon arriving at his office that he just arrived moments before you and is totally upset because some guy cut him off in traffic and flipped him the bird. Uh-oh! These are all situations that your listeners can identify with. Whatever you see, do and experience is all preparation for your show!

Make a story about a *slice of your life* compelling and interesting.
Here is another important point about relating a story on your show and sharing a slice of your life with your listeners. Unless you are a reporter on CBS's *60 Minutes*, or ABC's *20/20* where factual reporting is a necessity, don't worry about being 100% accurate in retelling your story for the air. It's your job as a radio storyteller to make it interesting, compelling and even humorous, so go ahead and exercise your right to creative poetic license. Take the actual event and embellish it a little. It's okay, really it is. The important thing is that your story interests and entertains your listeners. Leaving them smiling and feeling good should be your mission. Always try to end your story with a laugh, or at least leave 'em with a chuckle.

SAVE EVERTHING FOR YOUR SHOW!
Remember, when it comes to show prep, **save everything!** Start today training to be a pack rat. The neatnik in your life, like my wife, may get upset with additional clutter, but saving material is vital to your future success on the radio. Your show will chew up and spit out as much information as you wish to put into it. You never can have too much info for your show. If you don't need a piece of material on today's show, save it for another day! But, *save, save, save*! Of course, it's easier said than done, but with today's technology, mp3 files and more, your show stuff takes up less space.

MAKE IT A POINT TO SAVE YOUR IMPORTANT INTERVIEWS.
You know the portion of the interview that is a killer and a home-run! Even if you just save a couple of minutes of the celebrity interview, you know which stuff to keep and what to dump. Saving the important stuff gives you a leg up on your competition when it comes time to air it again on your show, because news warrants it.

Show Prep means saving EVERYTHING! Here's a quickie story to prove my point.

When legendary entertainer **Bob Hope** passed away in 2003, I said a Hail Mary for the repose of his kind soul and quickly ducked into my archives, which consists of boxes and boxes of tapes in the basement of our home. It took me a while to find what I was looking for, but eventually I dug out an interview with Mr. Hope that was recorded in 1977(!). The interview was taped over the phone. I was on the air in Portland, Maine, at WLOB, Mr. Hope was at his home in Toluca Lake, California, and was preparing to visit Portland for a performance at the Cumberland County Civic Center. My Bob Hope interview from almost thirty years earlier proves how important it is to save, save, save! We chatted about everything from Andy Gibb, a guest on his recent TV special, to Red Skelton and Dionne Warwick. We even chatted about ice on the golf course in LA, which he experienced that morning. I hadn't heard our taped conversation in almost thirty years. It was on a cartridge and ran about three minutes. At first I was hesitant to play it, you know, ego and all! "What did I sound like back then?" raced through my demented mind. Would I sound stupid, etc. etc. My fears were put at ease when we played it. First, I sounded the same and there was no mistaking the friendly voice of Bob Hope. The first call we took after airing the interview was from a Sunny-104.3 listener. I was on the air at the time in West Palm Beach. The listener's name was Linda, and she raved about hearing Bob Hope's voice. "It's the best thing I've heard either on radio or TV since Mr. Hope passed on!" she exclaimed. She then gave me the ultimate compliment. "While listening to you and he talk, Joe, I could just imagine Bob Hope sitting in his big over-sized comfy chair at his home in California. It was such a pleasant conversation to be allowed to listen in!" It pleased me to hear her words and I knew we had done our job.

To complement our tribute to Bob Hope and our taped chat from the past, we took calls from listeners who had a close-up, funny, or warm encounter with Mr. Hope. We even had an out-of-town caller from North Carolina.[2] He had served on a sub during WWII and had seen Bob's USO Show at Pearl Harbor in 1944. His story was warm and entertaining. His call was followed by another Sunny-104.3 listener who was a former LA Defense Attorney. His memory of Bob Hope involved his staff and the great entertainer. One morning his office staff was missing for quite some time. He went outside to a coffee van that frequented the building, only to see a long white stretch limo and noticed a crowd of people including his office staff sitting and chatting with Bob Hope. Bob bought them all coffee and a pastry and said, "I just like chatting with folks…unannounced!" It was a great salute to Bob Hope, all made possible because an interview had been saved from thirty years earlier. Part of your show prep should be to SAVE everything! You never know when you may want to recycle it on your show.

Show prep material should always be directed at your primary target audience.

To begin with, make sure you have a complete understanding of who your target demo is and which audience your station is trying to reach. This is of the utmost importance. You wouldn't necessarily be talking about having a few beers with your buds at Hooters if you were trying to reach female demographics any more than you would be talking about your wife's scrapbooking class if you were trying to hit men 18-plus. I'm not saying these topics should be taboo, but most of your show prep material should be geared to your specific "target" audience. If you don't know what your primary target audience is, ask! You should always try to present your material to reach as vast a listening audience as possible. It always blew my mind and drove me crazy when management would look first at the total 12+ numbers when the station, along with my ratings bonus structure, was geared to how well we did with females 25 to 54 years old.[3] Keep in mind, no matter what your station target demo is station managers and programmers can be greedy little souls who want and desire as much of the ratings pie as possible. This can be a difficult and frustrating situation for air-talent. I've been there more than a few times during my own radio career!

Sometimes the station's "primary" target audience can be confusing.

This example of what the "powers to be" want you to do on the air can be most confusing, not just for a radio newbie but for a senior radio pro, too. Your beloved program director will keep telling you to direct your show prep and content to a young "hockey mom," around thirty years old, who has two kids and works outside the home. So, being a good radio do-bee that's what you do, but when the ratings come in, the first number management turns to are the total 12+ audience numbers. They also look at you with a straight face and say, "Yeah, you did okay with females but overall, your male numbers are down! Get 'em up!" So, as a hard-working radio talent, you follow orders! To get your male numbers up, you begin directing more of your content towards, you got it, the hockey mom's hubby! Next thing you know, you're called in on the carpet for presenting content that is not directed to the station's primary listener…a hockey mom with two kids who works outside the home! A few wacky radio merry-go-rounds like this one had me talking to myself on more than one occasion. Do your best to learn exactly who the station is going after as far as demographics are concerned. It won't always be easy. Do your best to find out, but be prepared for the unexpected!

Begin with a Day Sheet.
Before you even think about working on show prep, set up a **day sheet**. This is a simple process of taking a sheet of paper and blocking out each hour of your show that you are on the air. At the top left hand side of the page leave an underlined space for the day, date and hour (see example on next page). Next, type on each page regular fixed elements on your show for that hour, for example, News, Traffic, Weather, etc. Leave a blank space (at least 2" to 3" in depth) between these regular elements on your show, so you can write or type specific things for that day, such as current interesting news events, celebrity gossip, music history, special birthday greetings for listeners, one-liners, and so on. At specific times, write in your "show bit" for that hour. Perhaps it's movie trivia on Mondays at 7:20am, just before a traffic update. Write it in. Not the question; you can add that later, just the title of the "fixed" regular bit for that day and hour. It is also a good idea to write in specific station promotion reminders at the top of the page. This is particularly important for jam-packed, info-tainment type morning shows where talent has a tendency to be so wrapped up with guests and doing bits that station promos are lost in the shuffle or even completely left out.

The world of morning drive radio is chaotic and fast-paced. Do yourself a favor and write down important station promotions. Don't trust your memory! You have too many other things on your mind. A one-line reminder written at the top of each page should do the trick quite nicely and serve as a tease for you to mention it. For example, the upcoming "free" station concert is this Saturday! Your mention should make your PD smile and serve as a shining example that you are a team player and care about the station and not just your own show!

Following a day sheet is a good habit to get into regardless of the air-shift you are working: middays, PM-Drive, nights, whatever! It is not just a tool for morning drive. If you envision yourself landing the plum AM-Drive slot one day, developing "good habits" early in your air career is a must. A daily day sheet is a good beginning.

When prepping your show, divide it into **four separate segments:**
Set-up each hour of your show as a complete package that is made up of four 15-minute shows within each hour. For example:

First Segment: The top of the hour, which may include a newscast, until quarter past the hour.
Second Segment: 15 past the hour until the bottom of the hour at 30 past.
Third Segment: Half-past the hour until 45 minutes past the hour
Fourth Segment: From 45 to the top of the hour.
In other words, you want to break each hour of your 3- or 4-hour morning

drive show into four quarter-hour segments. Make sure each segment includes all the basic elements that you would have in any hour of your morning show - traffic, weather, entertainment news, music and other services. **Note:** time checks, temp & brief weather condition should be given in every break and as often as possible. A basic radio rule to remember whether you're in or out of morning drive is to give the station call letters or station slogan first! For example: MIX or SUNNY 104.3 should always be the FIRST thing out of your mouth when you turn on your mic! They should also be the last thing out of your mouth before going into music or a commercial stop-set.

Sample Day Sheet

This day sheet is a sample that was used at one time on one of my Boston morning drive time shows. It was set up to reflect a "full-service" AM-Drive radio show, with news/weather and traffic at the top and bottom of every hour. There were five breaks or stop sets (commercials) within each hour. Bits/features and phone calls were aired around and into each stop set.

SAMPLE DAY SHEET FOR YOUR SHOW 6-7AM hour

_____   _____
(DATE - DAY)   (HOUR)

6:00am- News/weather/traffic
6:10am- 1st break after 1st song_____
6:20am- 2nd break in hour Regular "bit" or feature (ex: Movie Monday -trivia_____ before going into commercial stop-set

*winning trivia caller can be aired between songs or before info update on half-hour
6:30am- 3rd break in hour/before news/traffic update on the half-hour-
6:40am- 4th break in hour/before commercial stop set
6:48am- 5th and final break in hour Regular "bit" or feature_____

**7:00am—News/weather/traffic

Note: do a separate sheet for each hour that you are on the air!

Where do you find show prep?

When I first began doing show prep for my radio show back in the dark ages of the '60s, yes, that's the *1960s*, books were a great source of material. *Chase's Calendar of Events*, which has been around for more than fifty years, was and still is a biggie for air-talent looking for show prep material. *Chase's Calendar* allows you to find out what's going on any day of the year, anywhere across the globe! This comprehensive and authoritative reference source covers special events, worldwide holidays, festivals and historical data. I also gathered show prep material from many other books on news events, sports, movie and TV trivia, and even books about silly stuff. A few that come to mind: *Wanted: Dumb or Alive, Real Duct Tape Stories* and *Loony Laws & Silly Statutes*. There are many fun books available that can add so much to your show. Have fun browsing and searching them out at your favorite bookstore or online. One music reference book that is an invaluable source of information about pop music facts is *Billboard's Book of #1 Hits*. It is well-written and researched by my friend, Fred Bronson. I would have been lost without it. Check it out!

Show prep is found everywhere and in everything!

You can get great show prep from watching TV, both news and entertainment programs. Another great source is from daily conversations and people you come in contact with – everywhere! If you hear a funny line or something that gives you an idea for a show bit, immediately make a note of it before you forget it! There are too many different things that you will experience during the course of a seemingly "normal" day, so don't trust your memory in recalling it later. You need a "tickler" file to bring it all back later on. Carry a small notebook with you wherever you go! With today's cell phone capabilities, you can text message yourself and pick it up later.

Show prep material can also come from the mouths of kids, both little and big! *When you hear it, make a note of it!* Great show prep material can even be found in a darkened movie theater while holding your honey's hand. If a funny line pops up in the movie write it down with your free hand. Do it on the back of her box of popcorn if need be, *but do it!*

The Internet is a valuable research tool to gather show prep material.

Many books that I used as reference sources on my show are invaluable for today's air-talent in gathering show prep material. Today, however, you have one super tool many of us didn't have: **the Internet!** The books mentioned here and others, along with newspapers and magazines, can be found online. Today, great show prep info is virtually at your fingertips through the magic of the Internet.

Why you should subscribe to a prep service.

As a morning show talent, my life was made so much easier by two veteran guys who provide two superb show prep services. Bob Hamilton's *Morning Star* and Steven Dee's *Morning Skoop* were invaluable references. For many years, from my radio time in Boston to Houston and South Florida, I contributed on a weekly basis to "Ham's" service. Talk about a great source for creative ideas! Morning drive people exchanged their successful show bits every week.[4] Later in this chapter, Ham spells out in detail how instant information is readily available for today's air-talent thanks to technology and the Internet.

In the early 2000s, during my on-air days in West Palm Beach, I also subscribed to Steven Dee's show prep service. In my humble opinion, Steve's service, like Bob Hamilton's, is one of the best! Just for the record, I have no vested interest in either of their services. I only speak from first-hand knowledge of knowing both men and having used their services. Their show prep services are different, but both provide top-shelf info-tainment news and bits for radio shows while making life easier for the personalities in their daily search for relevant content.

Steven Dee, President and founder of *The Morning Skoop*, spent eighteen years as an air personality. He has a strong intuition of what works best in morning drive. His *Morning Skoop* has been around since 2002 and he takes pride in providing high-profile personality prep for radio's top morning personalities. Steve believes that one of the biggest challenges for air personalities is finding time to sit down to prep a show. "How do I know this? Because when I started in radio," Dee readily admits, "I was young and dumb. I knew nothing about the business. I quickly realized how much work it was going to take to achieve success as a personality. I tried to learn as much as possible."

Dee knows how hectic the life of a radio personality can be, especially in morning drive. "When I landed my first morning show position, my life got really hectic. Everybody wanted a chunk of my time. Of course, I said 'yes' to everyone. I hosted parades, beauty pageants, county fairs, telethons, you name it and I was there! On top of that, I had remote broadcasts on weekends. I found myself working non-stop." His point is that being a dedicated morning personality is time-consuming. "If you want attention, you have to be in the public's eye," Steve emphasizes. "It means you don't have a lot of time to prep your show. It's imperative that you have a great prep service at your disposal."

Dee, the creative force behind *The Morning Skoop*, strongly believes one of the biggest mistakes a morning show can make is thinking they're great, no matter what they say or do. "Because the ratings are good," he continues, "they think they're doing everything right. WRONG! While the ratings may be good at that moment, things can change in an instant. A morning show down the dial can subscribe to a great prep service and knock you off your pedestal in the blink of an eye. There's no room for complacency in radio, especially in morning drive radio. If you become complacent, someone's going to eat your lunch."

Steven Dee candidly talks about Show Prep services and some of the most asked questions.

What if your station won't invest in a great prep service for you?
"This is the one thing I hear most from morning show personalities," says Steve. "Their radio station won't pay for a prep service. If that's the case," he urges, "pay for it yourself. If the prep service adds a lot of value to your show, pay for it! After all, you're investing in your own career and in your future! Besides, you can write it off as an expense on your taxes."

What if the prep service is barter or trade and your station won't air commercials?[5]
Steven Dee suggests talking to management. "Let them know the value of the prep service, and why your radio station will benefit from the service." He also suggests strongly in including a show prep service in the terms of your contract.

Here are just a few reasons why **Steven Dee,** publisher of *The Morning Skoop,* believes every morning show should subscribe to a great prep service:

- **Your life as a radio talent is hectic. You don't have time to prep your show fully.**
- **A great prep service is going to be working for you** while you're on the air, or doing remotes, hosting events, spending time with your family, and having a life.
- **A great prep service knows what's interesting;** they have a lock on what listeners really want to hear in the morning.
- **A great prep service is creative.** Creativity is extremely important to success in morning radio. A great prep service should be able to come up with ideas you haven't thought of. The service should provide celebrity contact information. If you aren't doing celebrity interviews, you should be. A great prep service will provide celebrity contact information.
- **A great show prep service provides high-quality audio clips.** Take advantage of prep services that provide audio. It will add a lot to your show. It provides entertaining contests and hot phone topics. Phone topics are a big part of morning radio. Get interactive. A great prep service should provide topics that will get your phone ringing.

Steven Dee says, "It's time to take your morning show to a new level. Get on the Internet and search for 'radio show prep.' Sample the different services available, then get together with your morning show team members and discuss which services would most benefit your show and your listeners."

For more info on *The Morning Skoop,* visit www.themorningskoop.com or call 1-800-614-4892.

Show prep provider Bob Hamilton believes show prep has entered a new era.

Another proven radio pro in providing information to morning radio shows in America and around the world is my longtime friend, **Bob Hamilton**. For a good portion of my 41 years on the radio, I was a proud subscriber and contributor to "Ham's" daily morning-show service, Radio Star.

"I did my own on-air morning radio show in the '60s. Top-40 radio was the era of the one-liner. If you weren't doing weather or music intros, you were setting up a joke so you could deliver a punch line. My show prep material," says the veteran radio pro, "consisted of every joke book I could afford to buy and what was in the morning paper. I neither communicated with nor knew any other morning radio people. And, the idea that I would hear another show, which I could only do if I was on vacation, and to borrow something from them sort of constituted stealing and testimony to failure of my own creativity. I was never ready for the next show. It seemed like I was on the air all the time, sort of a dog chasing a car that I would never catch. And all the people," Hamilton continues, "I had to learn from were all working in the same market I was trying to move up from."

Through a quirk of fate, "Ham" wound up in New York City and was named head of promotion for a record company. His job was to travel the US and visit with radio station program directors. "It was throwing Br'er Rabbit into the briar patch," he recalls. "I took the third, fourth and fifth airplane flights of my life all in one day and met Ken Dowe and Michael O'Shea at KLIF in Dallas, then Bill Young at KILT in Houston and ended with a late night supper with Buzz Bennett at WTIX in New Orleans." Ham says he learned more radio in that one day than he had in his previous ten years of being on the air. "I know this is hard to believe," he continues, "but in those days there were no radio programming magazines. Radio jocks and program directors were rarely seen in the pages of leading publications like *Billboard* and *Broadcasting Magazine*. You had to be a GM to get in the pages of *Broadcasting* and *Billboard* only wrote about you when you moved to another station."

Bob Hamilton says radio guys didn't go into the record promotion business in those days (the late '60s and early '70s), so when he hit town and wanted to talk about radio with the PD and the jocks he was a rarity. "I was a radio guy through and through. I knew my stay in the record business would only be temporary, so I wrote down every idea, every philosophy, every piece of instruction I got from the top radio pros, from WLS in Chicago to KHJ in Los Angeles to WABC in New York City, and cataloged it into my notebook. I also got up early and listened to the morning show in every market I visited and wrote down every new idea I heard on the air. I also made a note of every one-liner, every funny feature, every unique way of coming out of a record. While other record promotion people had trouble getting in to see the PD," laughs

Bob, "the doors were soon swung wide open for me as I was delivering radio news and ideas from the most recent markets and stations I had visited."

Those radio station visits inspired Bob Hamilton to widen his visits on a larger scale. He took his copious notes and began the radio industry's first newsletter dedicated to radio programming, sending it out weekly to thousands of program directors. "That little newsletter," says Ham, "developed into the radio industry's leading magazine in the early '70s. *The Radio Report* was simply the sharing of ideas from PDs and air-talent with each other. We were simply the conduit."

Bob Hamilton always dreamed of having a radio station for radio that could be heard all over the country. In 1982, thanks to the development of the desktop computer, his dream was about to become reality. He learned a new technology would allow you to put information on a mainframe computer that could be accessed via phone line from any kind of computer from any place in the world.[6] "It was what I had dreamed about; instant information and almost unlimited space for all the stories we wanted to write," he smiles. Bob found a company in Newport Beach California that was willing to help set it up on a big VAX computer. *Radio Star* was born.

With *Radio Star* up and running Bob Hamilton hit the road again to preach the word to PDs about his service. There was only one problem. Bob soon learned that few PDs had computers and quite often he heard, "What's a mo-dem?" "When I tried to explain it, I sounded like 'Cosmic Bob,' which became my nickname. But there were some, like Dave Van Dyke and Dave Robbins, who got it and after four years I had enough supporters in radio to at least keep the lights on."[7] Ham still got up early to listen to different morning shows in towns he visited and wrote down the ideas he heard. One morning listening to a show in Nashville, he realized there was never a time that he listened to a show that he didn't find at least one thing to write down. With radio guys getting computers, he envisioned the new technology would allow them to send their ideas to him instantly. He thought that if he could get 100 shows to send him at least one idea a week that would be 100 great ideas! It worked! "We called it *Radio Superstar* rather than *Morning Star* or something like that, because I wanted it to be a service for personalities in all day parts. There were certainly afternoon drive people who could use it as well." *Radio Superstar* began in 1987 and continues to this day.

The basic concept, according to Ham, is based around Captain John Smith's rule of Jamestown, Virginia, in 1607: "No work, no eat." Each member of *Radio Superstar* has to send in three ideas each week. If they don't, they lose access until they contribute. It's the only way it will work," he insists.[8]

In 2003, Bob Hamilton hit the road again to visit morning radio shows across North America. He says it was gratifying to follow them in at 4am to the computer room and watch their printers spout out huge mountains of prep material from the Internet from *Superstar* and other information sources. However, he was somewhat dismayed that despite the fact the radio industry has been able to get instant and unlimited amounts of information for over twenty years from computers, radio still subconsciously hung onto the weekly magazine idea or the daily newspaper concept of news and info. "Stations had the computer in one room, the printer in another, and kept the Internet out of the control room. Air-talent brought stacks and stacks of paper into the studio, but the computer had only been used for the program log and music playlists. It was only until recently, "adds Hamilton, "that the net has become part of the show."

Now with the Internet as part of the show, thanks to Bob Hamilton's ingenuity, air-talent can use Google, Wikipedia, Yahoo! and YouTube during their shows, with sound clips at their fingertips to instantly take on new directions. "Today's radio talent is never, ever far away from the net. Laptops and desktops at home or in the office, PDAs and broadband everywhere means they can e-mail or IM another member of the show about an idea, research a concept on Google, grab a sound clip, watch a video or get a phone number, instantly. Now, that's some kinda way to gather show prep!" proudly exclaims Bob Hamilton.

Hamilton is a broadcast leader in bringing radio talent together to exchange information and show bit ideas. "Today," he suggests, "the word 'prep' has changed from a noun to a verb."(He hates the word "prep" and has never used it.) "In fact," Bob adds emphatically, "it's time we buried it forever and replaced it with the word 'live.' With RSS feeds, soundboards, live webcams, instant video clips and so on, you can have an idea for tomorrow's show at 2pm and by 2:05pm have it researched and complete with pertinent audio, then inform everybody on the show at 2:10pm that it's going to be on. In the old days," Bob says, "you waited until you got home to look it up in the encyclopedia. Five years ago, you would wait until you got home to look it up on the computer, then print it out when you got to the station. Today," he proudly states, "you flash the idea and insert it into the show's schedule in just a few minutes."

Author's note:

All of what my longtime friend Bob Hamilton says about having instant access to the net in the radio station control room is true and so important. His passion and enthusiasm for the use of instantaneous info via computers is obvious and inspiring. His super service provides all of it and a whole lot more! But, I still believe you need some sort of a road map to determine where your show is headed, and that's where a printed day sheet becomes important. On any radio show, especially in morning drive, there can only be ONE quarterback calling the plays and putting the ball in play. Even with instantaneous info and sound, SOMEONE still has to have a game plan in hand when all the "players" meet at 5:30 or 6am to go on the air! There are way too many elements involved in a morning show just to "wing it" or willy-nilly pull things up at random from the Internet. It goes without saying the net is an invaluable tool to obtain instantaneous sound on almost anything, from a news event to a celebrity sound bite. It adds luster to a special show bit, but you still need a day sheet, and that is printed out on good ol' paper. I think there's room for both in today's ever-evolving radio world.

Please keep in mind that part of show preparation is bringing your own inter-personal relationships and slices of your own life to your show. In my opinion, these elements can only be done "outside the studio" and well in advance of the hectic, fast-paced atmosphere that is morning-drive radio. You need notes, handwritten or typed in advance, to be able to tell a story in a coherent way about something that occurred in your daily life.

As much as it can be a royal pain in the butt and quite often can get in the way of having a life, show prep is a must! It's a lot like working out and getting in shape to play in a big game. But, unlike the NFL, where a team usually only plays one big game a week, in radio it's game day, every day! You need to prepare to be ready! It always amazes me that many talented air personalities don't feel show prep is necessary. They feel it's fine to wing it, and to a certain extent that's cool. No radio show should be entirely scripted. Keep in mind some of the best shows are when talent lets go, ad-libs and lets it flow! Sometimes, you can over-prepare your show. Don't let prepared bits or written words get in the way of what radio is all about, *immediacy*, and what's happening on your show "in-the-moment!" It's the fun and excitement of being on "live" radio. Therefore, there should be plenty of room for ad-lib situations.

On most shows, being "in the moment" usually takes care of itself with random listener calls. How can you possibly script one of those? Well, wait just a minute! If your show takes lots of listener calls based on a specific theme of the day or question, even that can be scripted. Write down in advance possible comebacks and one-liners to interact with the caller. Of course, timing and the placement of these lines is most important. You may find yourself sitting there with a dozen different comebacks, but none may fit the conversation. It happens even on the best prepared shows, and that's when your ad-libbing and spontaneity come in to play. It is important to have prepared bits or lines ready to use around *fixed* elements in your show, like in and out of news, traffic, and weather. Another place is "in and out" of commercial stop sets. Remember, being prepared makes for a smoother sounding you!

By its very nature, live radio can produce some wild and unpredictable situations, many of which are totally out of your control as an air-talent. The bottom line is that it's your show and you are responsible for what goes out over the air. You need to be prepared for any possible situation.

When I did mornings in Boston, squirreled away in my briefcase were special folders packed with notes, jokes and written material all geared to and around the weather. Needless to say, the files changed with the seasons. Winter can be particularly unpredictable in New England. There's nothing worse than trying to drive through a foot of freshly fallen snow at 4am on your way in to the station, and receive word on your cell that school has been canceled! Great! There goes three hours of last night's show prep, right out the window! It doesn't have to be a problem *IF* you're prepared! This is where the stormy weather show prep material comes in mighty handy. If you don't have a "storm" emergency file on hand, you'll find yourself scrambling around the news room looking for every bit of fill material you or your producer can scrounge up. It can be particularly unnerving when your PD calls just before you hit the air and tells you to dump the format and go into all-information mode because of the storm! There goes the format and your calm demeanor with it right out the front door of the station!

You have material, all right, just not the right material to complement the storm-related events of the day. Your format has just gone from music-intense to news and talk! It can cause a heck of a lot of stress, or you can come off as "Mr. Cool and in-the-know Joe," if you just take time to prepare in advance for the unexpected! Remember, you need to have relevant content to add to the mix during those unexpected happenings in radio when your station goes from a music-intense morning show to talk and information to keep your family of listeners apprised of the latest storm-related news, closings, no-school announcements, cancellations, weather and traffic updates and so on. You are the quarterback and the person designated to tie it all together. You need appropriate information along with humorous and interesting bits. So, as the Scouts say and do, "BE PREPARED!"

Always be prepared to go on the air!

For morning drive talent, where more personality is usually the rule, even on music-intense stations, talent knows instinctively by the end of their first break what kind of a show they will have! If you feel you're on a roll and at the top of your game with both sides of your brain smokin,' it may be a great day to save your prepared material for a rainy day. On the other hand, you're feeling a little punky and not on your best game, that's when show prep is a necessity! By preparing certain aspects of your show in advance, you also eliminate the possible "up and down" cycle of some good and some bad shows depending on how you feel. Show prep gives you and your show the consistency required to be a radio winner!

Grade your performance and your daily show.

I took a great deal of pride in always going on the air prepared. Later, after we were off the air, I would grade my performance, as well as other talent and elements of our show. The grading system was the old-fashioned way with A-B-Cs. I didn't bother grading below a "C." I figured if we averaged around a "C" once too often there would be no "Joe show" to grade anyway. Most mornings, we did a great show and I awarded us an "A" or a "B." Very seldom, if ever, did we do a *bad* show and earn a "C." Show prep can keep you from getting low grades on your show and your performance. If you are totally prepared to the best of your ability and for any possibility before you go on the air, then it's virtually impossible to fail and do a bad show.

John Forsythe woke up Albuquerque listeners for more than two decades on KOB-FM.

He does two types of show prep: "One is 'vertical' preparation of tomorrow's show," as he explains. "We plot out what we'll do throughout the run of the show. We often don't stick with it. If something more timely pops up, that is the beauty of radio. We also work on 'horizontal' prep, since the real challenge is often getting people to return to the radio and show every day. If we can create bits, features, soap opera-type adventures that revolve around the show's characters that can last days or even weeks, we can increase our 'days spent listening' for our TSL.(Time Spent Listening)."

Forsythe says they use several prep services, but often declare "prep-free" days which forces him and the others on his show to use their creativity to land upon what their listeners are needing and feeling in their lives.[9]

Bob Rivers: "Be in the moment."

Seattle morning radio personality Bob Rivers says part of show prep is being in the moment!

"Especially with interviews," adds the twenty-year radio pro, "you must be in the moment, listening, being curious and empathetic. If I'm not, then I'm not ready to do great radio. Every aspect of show prep is like that. You can't possibly watch every award show, read every tabloid, stay up on every political event and know the answers to every question out there, but you can follow your curiosity, thinking all day long about the experiences you are having, shows you are watching, and the people you interact with." Rivers believes you need to cultivate your curiosity and empathy. "You will find the moral dilemmas that make great entertaining radio in everyday life. For example, yesterday a cashier handed me change for a hundred after I gave him a twenty," says Bob. "What do you think I did about it? What would you do? An experience as simple as this and the curiosity to examine it with your audience is one example. Watch the phones 'explode,' as they say. Lots of people would keep the money. Would you, and if yes, why?"

Here's another example of how Bob Rivers brings his own life experiences to his listeners by simply watching television. "I caught an episode of *King of Queens* where Doug had a dream in which he was cheating on Carrie.

That has happened to me, too," he adds. "So, on our show, I asked, 'Has it happened to you?' If I am literally cheating in my dream, knowing I have a wife and kids, when I wake up, what should I do? Did I cheat? On the other end of the spectrum, is it so perfectly okay that I should just enjoy it and try and roll over and pick up where I left off? Is it a sign of trouble or some sort of healthy release? Notice how I am playing with my own fantasies and curiosity," laughs Rivers, "while asking the listener to come along for the ride."

This is all part of show prep. Take a sequence from a popular TV series, place your own brand on it, and get your listeners involved. You need to train your audience to use their imagination. In time, they will be very entertaining and entertained because you've let them in on how to do it.

Show prep, it's all around you!

Whether it's collecting just one additional piece of topical material, reading the bio or book on the next morning's guest, or forcing yourself to sit in front of the tube watching one more potential *American Idol* while your eyelids are so heavy they're drooping down to your navel, show prep must take precedence over **everything** else! Yes, even that!

Here are some additional places to search on the internet for "Show Prep" information:

Show Prep services:

- **Bits & Pieces-Bitman-** David
- **Mega Prep-** Johnny Vega-edgy topical show prep
- **MorningMouth**@tds.net "The Morning Show "Boot Camp" people
- **Morning Probe-** Mike Marino
- **Morning Skoop-** Steven Dee
- **On the Wire-** Pat Reeder & Laura Ainsworth
- **Radio Star-** Bob Hamilton
- **Ross Brittain Report-** Ross Brittain
- **Talent Tool Kit-** Perry Simon
- **The Complete Sheet** (affiliated with Mega-Prep)

Other sources for information:
- **AllAccess-** Joel Denver-one of the best on the Internet
- **California Air-checks-** George, the man knows how to do it. Quality video air-checks
- **insideradio**.com-Kelli Grisez
- **Northeast Air-checks**-Rick Kelly. My friend Rick has a vast

assortment of air-checks
- **ReelRadio**.com
- **rockradioscrapbook.ca** (great source for quotes from radio pros)

More websites to gather information for show prep:
- **440 International Those Were The Days**-Today in History
- **Chase's Calendar of Events**-Lists special days, weeks, months, celebrity birthdays, holidays, events
- **Daily Celebration**— Today in history and more. Motivational quotes, bios, profiles. Updated daily
- **Hippy Calendar**-Important dates in hippy history, famous birthdays and upcoming events
- **Name Day Calendar**-It's time to celebrate your Name Day
- **On-This-Day.com**-A daily history resource
- **Ron Smith Oldies Calendar**-The birth, deaths and events this week in Rock N' Roll History
- **The 366 Days of the Year**-Lists famous events and celebrity birthdays/deaths each day of the year
- **Today's Movie History**-Internet Movie Database

Notes:
1. The importance of promotion for your station, your show and you is covered in Chapter 15
2. His wife was listening and called him from South Florida to tell him what we were doing and to call our show
3. 12+ demographics in ratings refer to all listeners from age 12 to 65+, both male and female
4. Bits are usually prepared features of various lengths, depending on content which can range from humorous sketches, telephone calls, or even serious content and contests.
5. Barter is the airing of commercials in exchange for a service, like a show prep service or jingles to the radio station
6. There were many types of computer systems in those days (1982). The industry hadn't yet settled on PCs and Macs.
7. Dave Robbins contributes elsewhere in this book.
8. Author's note: I agreed. It sounded like a good deal to me when I was on the air and contributing to *Super*Star*. You send in three new ideas once a week and you get hundreds back. Now that's the kind of trade I like to make!
9. As of 2011, John Forsythe had left New Mexico and was on the air in Orlando, Florida

CHAPTER 8
The Art of Interviewing

"I wanted to be in radio. It was my passion."
— veteran Baltimore Radio Pro, Buzz Bennett

The art of interviewing is being interested and attentive to what the other person is saying.

Interviewing is a special skill all its own. Conducting a good interview takes practice, practice and more practice! For more specifics on the art of interviewing, we reached out to numerous radio pros with one question, "How do you conduct a successful interview?"[1] Their answer was always the same: *Listen to what the person is saying* and do your homework before the interview begins.

Radio pro **Bob Rivers** moved to Seattle in 1989 and until 2010 was hosting the morning show on KZOK.[2] He says, "A radio show host deals with multiple guests, topics, personalities, news items, and all kinds of issues that are ever changing." Early in his career, one of Rivers' mentors was **Larry King**, and he actually got to spend some time on King's show while living in Maryland. "I remember asking Larry," he recalls, "'How do you interview everyone from presidents to astronauts to rock stars without being nervous? After all, it must be impossible to know enough about these people to ask the right questions!' Larry replied, 'Never be afraid of what you don't know! That's where all the great questions come from. I was born naturally curious and that's my gift.' This was very empowering to me," continues Rivers. "By placing myself in the role of being curious, I had a point of view from which to explore all sorts of things. For example, I don't know anything about being an astronaut. But I did wonder what it must have been like to know you were only one of a few men to circles the earth? Did it make you more or less spiritual? Did you find yourself more or less connected with mankind? Are spacesuits uncomfortable? How long does it take to get used to zero gravity? What part of the training was the hardest? It's all about being curious."

Rivers feels it doesn't take much time to train yourself to be curious, either. "You don't have to know everything. You just need to know enough to have the questions pop into your head. In my case, I typically read a bio and brief for ten minutes or so on each interview and my mind is racing with so many questions I can never get to all of them."

Be a good listener and *be in-the-moment* during your interview.

Larry King also told Rivers that most bad interviewers are simply not listening. "Larry once had a news gal interview him with a list of questions. She was looking at her list and asked him a question he had already worked into a previous answer. To be really good, you can have notes and guidelines, but you'd better be in the moment, reacting in an instant, changing course, getting ideas from what is actually happening rather than how you wanted it to go." Rivers was a guest on *Larry King Live* during the 1988 Baltimore Orioles losing streak. "I had been doing an on-air marathon for team spirit that would eventually last 258 ½ hours," he recalls. "I was nervous to be on a big national radio show. With Larry that night were sports media stars like Bob Costas and Joe Garagiola. Yikes! Larry introduced me something like this: 'Our next guest may be one of the greatest sports fans of all time. The Baltimore Orioles have lost their first 12 games in a row. Radio host Bob Rivers of 98 Rock has taken this worst start in baseball history and turned it into a rallying cry for fan support and through thick and thin has vowed to stay on the air until they win a game!' At this point, Joe and Bob chimed in and were having fun with it, too. As I'm listening to this introduction, I'm thinking these guys are going to be a blast to talk to and are very supportive. Suddenly, all my fears melted away."

Later, Rivers realized, Larry King had taken a fairly ordinary guest, not a world leader, and made it sound very interesting. "Larry was raising the audience's expectations and raising my confidence by how he presented me. To this day, I never forget that moment and I always try to realize the effect of my words on everyone in the room as well as those listening." Bob Rivers leaves you with this tip on prepping for an interview: "Write an introduction for each guest ahead of time, usually Joe [Downtown Joe on his show] writes it the night before. By the time we are done building the guest up, they are ready to be intimate with us right out of the gate, even if this is their 13th interview in a row."

It's important to prep for the interview but also important to listen to what is being said.

Gary LaPierre was the voice of New England on WBZ Boston for forty-two years! His rich, comforting voice was always there to let people know the news stories of the day. Gary's ability to communicate is legendary throughout the broadcast industry. On numerous occasions he anchored the nationally syndicated network radio program, *Paul Harvey News and Comment*.[3] "Doing Paul Harvey was huge, Joe…I mean freakin' huge. If you're in radio, you know there is no bigger radio show in the entire world that you could do." LaPierre readily admits the first time he subbed for the legendary Harvey he was nervous. "I was shakin' so bad, Joe, the first time I went to New York City to do the show that it was almost like my first radio job, and at that point," says Gary, laughing, "I had been in the business for twenty-five years."

LaPierre is a gifted interviewer who lists some of his favorite one-on-one interviews as the Beatles, Muhammad Ali, and Ronald Reagan. I asked Gary his thoughts on what he believes goes into a good interview. "Number one, listen. Listen to the answers," replied the winner of several Edward R. Murrow Awards.[4] "Too many interviewers have their list of questions and they stick to that list no matter what the previous answer is. If you can't break away from your list of questions within the first two answers, chances are you're not listening. I don't think I've ever asked a question that I didn't already know the answer to. I remember watching an old pro in Boston once," says LaPierre. "He asked his first question and the celebrity answered, 'That's a really stupid question.' The old pro went on to question number two. Sad, sad, sad. Remember that you are just as important in your field as your subject is in theirs. Don't ever be intimidated. Do your homework. God knows, now more than ever, there's info on just about everybody out there, I was going to say do your research," adds LaPierre, "but in 2011, let us say, Google 'em."

Lifestyle designer and relationship expert **Lissa Coffey** has found herself on both sides of the celebrity interview; as an interviewer and as the interviewee.[5] "Do your homework before the interview," says the former Radio/TV print journalist. "Too often interviewers think they can just wing it without reading the book or having any background information. The interviewee can tell right away what's going on, and the audience can, too." The award-winning author believes it's good to have some prepared questions, but during the interview keep yourself open for spontaneity.

Like other radio pros, Lissa urges interviewers to listen to what the person is saying. "If questions come up from those remarks, ask them. You don't necessarily have to stick to the script." Coffey is in total agreement with well-known talk-show host Sally Jesse Raphael, in that you need to give your guest the opportunity to promote their book or website.[6] Absolutely, she says. "You may be a great guy or gal and fun to spend time with on your show, but this is the real reason they are spending their time doing the interview. They won't be happy if you say goodbye and sign-off before they have a chance to give the audience their info."

Coffey says it's important to mention your guest's name throughout the interview, to reinforce their identity to your listeners who may be tuning in midstream. The author of several lifestyle books, including the widely read *What's Your Dosha Baby? Discover the Vedic Way for Compatibility in Life and Love*, offers this important tip to insure your guest will make a return visit to your show: "After the interview is over, get online to personally thank the guest off-the-air. This kindly gesture will help you maintain a relationship with them, so that you can call on them again when you need them."

For my money, one of the best broadcast journalists in the business today is **Bill O'Reilly.** His nightly news and commentary program, *The O'Reilly Factor*, is both interesting and informative. It is one program that is must viewing in our home and we always try and watch it. I enjoy Bill's thoroughness in reporting a story and admire his attempt at accuracy in presenting all sides of an issue. However, there is one aspect of his on-air presentation that drives me up a wall, and that's when he interrupts his guests! After watching him for years, I feel confident saying that I'm sure he is unaware how frequently he interrupts his guests. It does happen, and all too often. Bill appears to be a type-A personality which plays in to his overzealous and anxious behavior. Quite often in his enthusiastic attempt to get to the nuts and bolts of a story, and to make his point heard, he rushes in with an almost reckless abandon.

O'Reilly, to his credit, has admitted on his own program that it's his job to keep the guest and the interview on-track. I agree! It is one of the duties as the host or moderator of a program to make sure the guest is gently nudged in the right direction to insure they are adhering to the line of issues and questions raised by the host. However, it is also the job of the host to insure that a guest feels relaxed and comfortable. It's the old adage, "You get more flies with honey than vinegar." It's really no different in interviewing. If you want good repartee with your guest, it's better to gently hold their hand rather than put a chokehold on them.

Interview rule #1: a guest should always be given the time to *express themselves fully*. Of course, in today's hurry-up broadcast style of short, sound-bite interviews, it's almost impossible to have a meaningful dialogue with a guest!

Guests should be allowed the courtesy of responding to a question without being interrupted. I am afraid **Bill O'Reilly** and others in the media, both on radio and television, suffer from a broadcasting disease known as *interviewer interuptus!* When Bill interrupts guests before they finish making their point, I often try to help him out! Sometimes, I find myself trying to get his attention by talking to the tube, urging him to *be still and know*. Sometimes, I will yell at my TV friend Bill, telling him to shut up!

Apparently, he doesn't hear my sideline coaching, or pretends he doesn't hear me, because he continues right on interrupting his guest, which is very annoying. In all seriousness, interrupting a guest is not one of the finer points of interviewing. I find O'Reilly's interruptions of his guests to be troubling and annoying. Troubling, because when it occurs Bill comes off as the big bad bully on the block. He sounds like he's beating up on his guest and couldn't care less about their opinion. Personally, I feel O'Reilly is too competent a journalist and professional broadcaster to intentionally conduct himself in such a tactless manner. His interviewing technique is usually a no-nonsense, in-your-face, go-for-the-jugular approach. This is quintessential Bill O'Reilly, which can be compelling viewing and listening. What becomes annoying is when he asks a great, "out of the park home run" question and doesn't allow his guest to finish their thought! Bill gets so worked up and anxious to make *his* point that he often steps on the guest's reply. It seems to happen more often when the guest disagrees with his point of view. Coincidence? I'm not sure. Just like on Fox News, we'll let you decide the next time he does it.

It is my opinion that when Bill O'Reilly interrupts his guest it is not intentional. He may not even be aware he's doing it. Many times when your adrenaline is pumping, it's tough to control your feelings, let alone your tongue. Yes, I know, a pro should always be in control, but air-talent are human, too. It's also difficult for talent to see, let alone acknowledge, their own shortcomings. It seems to me that simply watching one of his own interviews would be enough to break the man of his own irritating habit. One problem involving air-talent is that too many managers are afraid to offer suggestions or, heaven forbid, point out shortcomings to the cash cow at the network or station. They often feel, "Big deal, so he interrupts, he or she is still number one so don't screw with it," and talent gets a pass. Of course, down the road when numbers begin to slip, these same "suits" sit around, scratching their heads wondering where the ratings went. Sometimes, an honest evaluation of a talent's performance can fix a small annoying air habit before it develops in to a major problem for all concerned.

You may find this hard to believe after I knocked him for interrupting his guests, but I am a big Bill O'Reilly fan. Truth be known, I knew Bill O'Reilly way back when. I first met him in the late 1980s, when we were both on the air in Boston. Bill was a reporter for Channel 7, while I was on the radio in morning drive, co-hosting **The Joe and Andy Family** on the original WROR-98.5. At the time, the station was running a contest trying to find Boston's most eligible bachelor and guess who was in the running? You got it! He wound up as a guest on our show and was everything you would hope to have in a great guest. He was witty, funny and very entertaining! Funny thing, I can't recall if he won the contest or not, but I don't think we interrupted him. After all, he *was* a guest on our show. I remember there was a certain swagger about the man. You couldn't help but notice it when he walked in our studio. Even today, you can see, sense, and feel it in his demeanor. Bill gives off self-assuredness in a ten-block radius. It's a cockiness, a confidence that one gains from being the product of a Catholic education. I feel qualified saying that, because I graduated from a Catholic school, myself. So, I am quite acquainted with Bill's "don't tread on me" attitude. Christian gentlemen have it ingrained in them, which is probably part of the reason he is so good at what he does.

After Bill left Boston, we kept tabs on his career, including his eventual rise to the top at Fox News! Bill O'Reilly is one of the best broadcast news journalists in the business today, and a much-needed voice in a liberal-dominated medium, but please, Bill, don't interrupt. Let your voice be still when your guest has the floor.

To recap, show hosts, remember it's your guest who is in the spotlight, not you!

One of the things that really bugs me when listening to an interview is when the show host asks the guest a question and then doesn't allow the person time to respond before stepping all over them! It's rude and totally unsettling for the listener or viewer. And, we're not just talking about personalities in East Podunk doing this; we're talking about BIG BOY Broadcasters! In fact, some of the biggest names in the game are guilty of this less-than-professional behavior. It must be that their egos are so inflated they don't even realize they're doing it! Heed the message, both radio newbies and you seasoned vets! It's annoying, so cool it! Park that overactive brain of yours in neutral and hold your over-aggressive tongue for a few minutes until your guest completes their thought. Interrupting a guest's conscious flow of thoughts is not only rude but is not conducive in your attempt to conduct a good interview.

It's important to have a spirited and meaningful discussion initiated by the host, but not to the point of upstaging a guest. Your guest is center stage, not you! You need to take a backseat for a few minutes. Everyone knows it's your show. We like you or wouldn't be listening or watching in the first place. We have plenty of time to hear your views and opinions, so please extend us the courtesy of hearing the opinions of your guests for a few minutes. Park your ego back in the Green Room and give your guest time to shine in the spotlight. It goes without saying that the opinions of the host are important, but so are those of the guest. If you're not interested in what they have to say, do yourself and your listeners and viewers a favor and don't have them on! Hearing both sides of an issue is vital to reach a rational decision on any subject. As the interviewer, you want the listener or viewer to walk away with something learned from the exchange of ideas, not with a feeling of "What the heck was that all about?"

Don't ask a question and then answer for your guest.

Another pitfall to avoid when interviewing is asking your guest a question and then answering for them. How many times have you heard this happen? Annoying, isn't it! It was covered in detail earlier in this chapter, but here is another example just to reinforce the point:

The day following the 2008 Republican convention in St. Paul, Minnesota, one of America's leading talk show hosts, **Sean Hannity**, had Minnesota's Governor on his show. He wanted the Governor's opinion on Republican John McCain's newly selected running mate, Sarah Palin. This is how the exchange went, to paraphrase: "So, Governor, what did you think of her performance last night?" Before his guest could answer, Sean jumped in and added, "Personally, I think she did a great job and hit it out of the ballpark, blah, blah, blah." Don't fall into the trap of asking your guest a question followed immediately with *your* opinion. Don't answer for them. This is dangerous ground for three very important reasons. First and most importantly, it's rude. Secondly, your thoughts and opinions may differ from those of your guest, but because you feel so strongly about your point of view, you may dissuade them from giving you their honest take on the subject. After all, it is *your* show and they don't necessarily want to be at odds with you. Let's be real here, they want to be invited back. And, thirdly, your listeners really want to hear how they respond to your question.

As the host, it's your show, and your listeners/viewers have the opportunity every single day to hear your opinion on everything. Conversely, in most instances we usually only have a few minutes at the most to hear the views and opinions of a guest. Therefore, please give your listeners the opportunity to hear what they have to say.

The aforementioned is by no means a personal attack against Sean Hannity. He is an excellent communicator. It is merely one example of how not to interact with a guest during an interview. Sean is not the lone show host when it comes to air-talent asking a question and then immediately answering for the guest. It appears to be a more common *modus operandi* these days for both local and national talk show hosts. Don't fall into this annoying habit. Ask the question, then sit back, hold your tongue and give your guest the opportunity to reply.

Interviews should be conducted in an air of comfort for the guest.

David Letterman may be a late night TV star on CBS, but he got his start in radio as a talk show host on WNTS Indianapolis. In a magazine interview, Letterman said he feels a host needs to create a comfort zone for a guest during an interview and adds, "If I can't make my guest feel comfortable for two minutes while they're on the air then I'm not doing my job."

An interview should be more than a question-and-answer session. It should be a conversation. The greatest interviewers never begin by saying

"My first question is," they begin by saying, "How are you," or "Welcome," and then go on from there. Many well-known broadcasters, especially talk show hosts, hide behind the brevity excuse. They claim they don't have time for a small talk or a friendly hello with all the commercials and stuff they need to get in, and need to get right to the meat of the matter! To me that's total BS! It takes a second to say, "Hi, how are you!" If you need to save time within the context of your interview, cut out the superfluous suck-up chit-chat and trying to impress your guest with how really intelligent you are. This may come as a rude awakening for many personalities, but it's your guest who is being interviewed, not you! We know how good you are and for the most part what your take is on life and everything that surrounds it. That's why we listen or watch you in the first place, because one, we like you, or two, find you interesting. But, when you have a guest on your show we want to know how they feel about the subject at hand! Let them shine in the spotlight!

The great **Johnny Carson** knew this better than anyone. He was the host and his name was on the show. He was the star, yet he let his guests take center stage under the spotlight. Johnny knew that if you're going to be there night after night, there's no reason to hog the spotlight—sooner or later you'll get more air-time than you know what to do with. Be gracious and generous with the spotlight. Give your guest time to shine.

One of the absolute best at the art of interviewing was the late **Mike Douglas**. For two decades, Mike's name was synonymous with daytime television in America, but his broadcasting roots were firmly planted in radio. First in the 1940s, as a singer on *Kay Kyser's Kollege of Musical Knowledge* and then in the '50s as host of the Chicago radio show *Hi, Ladies* which, as the name implies, was directed at women, particularly housewives. Mike Douglas's easygoing style and polite on-air mannerisms immediately put his guests at ease, resulting in spontaneous conversation. Mike was conversant on almost any subject and during his twenty years on television he interviewed thousands of celebrity guests. They ranged from Presidents to heads of state, prominent political figures, show-business types, and others, always chatting away in an informal way which was the hallmark of Douglas's ability to bring out the very best in his guests. He had a special talent to put his guests at ease and made them feel comfortable enough to relax and be themselves. It was a special gift that few have, and Mike Douglas was one of the chosen few. I learned so much about the technique of how to conduct a meaningful interview by watching him perform his magic on the air.

I always wanted to meet and interview Mike, and the radio gods must have been tuned in, for they granted my wish in 2003. I was on the air in morning drive at Sunny-104.3 in West Palm Beach. Mike and his wife Gen lived in the area. It was another special radio moment for me. To say I had butterflies in the pit of my tummy upon meeting Mike Douglas is no exaggeration. I remember telling myself, "You've been doing this for a lot of years, Joe. Now act like a pro, and not like some crazed fan."

My friend and fellow broadcaster **Judi Paparelli** has her own take on why even seasoned radio pros get a little nervous before interviewing someone special. During her twenty-five-year broadcast career, Judi has shared a mic with thousands of celebrities. She believes there is a true fan lurking inside every radio pro, however long they have been on the air. I agree with her! "No matter how many big names you'll interview in your career, and no matter how immune you become to the effects of dealing with the famous," she says, "when you come across a certain celebrity that you've idolized and always wanted to meet, it's tough to avoid gushing a bit. When it's honest and not overdone, I don't think there's anything wrong with being upfront about your admiration, as long as the hero-worshiping doesn't get in the way of a great interview. Every now and then, I think listeners enjoy an un-jaded radio moment when a host meets a hero and becomes a kid again."

My anxiety in meeting Mike Douglas was immediately put at ease by his warmth and kindness. On the air, we talked comfortably about a variety of things, including his book, *I'll Be Right Back* and his 1966 hit song, "The Men in My Little Girl's Life", about which he fondly reminisced. The one special thing I recall most vividly during our time together is how he lovingly he talked about his wife Gen and their three daughters. When he spoke of them, it was with a special pride and almost reverence. You could actually feel his love for them coming through the radio.

During my radio interview with Mike Douglas, I asked about the many guests he interviewed and his own special technique. In his typical fashion, the modest man immediately took the spotlight off himself and talked about the ability of other talented interviewers. "When it comes to interviewing, Joe," he smiled, "Johnny Carson is the gold standard. Johnny had a wide range of talents, like no one else before or after. If the talk show and interview format was a national sport, Johnny's mantel would be filled with MVP awards. Johnny knew that a good host and interviewer, whether it be on radio or TV, is gracious. A good host also doesn't interrupt, doesn't top his guest's story with one of his own, doesn't jump all over a punch line and most importantly doesn't get in the way of his own show. That's the number one rule, Joe, and Johnny Carson wrote the book on it."

The time I spent chatting informally on the radio with Mike passed all too quickly. He thanked me warmly for having him on our show. That's right; this broadcast legend thanked *me* for having him on! Here I was bursting with pride for finally meeting a broadcast icon I looked up to, and he's thanking me. It proves once again, the bigger they are, the nicer they are! Mike wrapped up our interview beautifully, with these parting words: "Gen and I spend our days with family and friends, people we love dearly. We both haven't forgotten the simple lessons of Mother Teresa. In our own small way, we try and do something good every day that will benefit someone else in some special way." Having Mike Douglas on my show was a special gift on the grandest scale that I will always treasure. We had planned to get together again and have a "cup of Joe" as he put it, to chat further about the mysteries of life and radio, and maybe even get in a round of golf, which was his passion. For one reason or another it never came to pass, perhaps primarily because I didn't want to intrude on his private time with his family. Now, looking back, I wish I had. Mike Douglas, a touch of class, passed away on his eighty-first birthday, August 11, 2006.

How to interview kids, by the master, Art Linkletter.

Pioneer broadcaster, **Art Linkletter**, to whom this chapter is dedicated, was another master interviewer, especially with children.[7] According to Art, "The best interviews are under ten and over seventy-five. Kids, don't know what they're saying and older people don't care." In 1934, his last year at San Diego State Teachers College (now San Diego State University), Art was hired to do commercials on local station KGB. The job led to radio work at the California Pacific International Expo as an emcee, which led to similar work at fair venues in San Francisco and Dallas. He later said he did more than 9,000 fair broadcasts. Hey, radio wannabes, take note: you gotta start somewhere!

Linkletter's big network radio break came when he made an audition recording for producer John Guedel and his show *People Are Funny*. Art got the gig and his network radio and later television career was underway, a show-business career that would last for over 60 years!

Two of his shows, *People Are Funny* and *House Party*, seemed like they were on the air forever. The highlight of his weekday afternoon program *House Party* was a kids' segment, *Kids Say the Darnedest Things*. Art interviewed five children between the ages of five and ten. The kids sat down to be interviewed in a casual, friendly way by Art, who sat "eye to eye" with his little subjects. It was a fun segment with kids answering Art's questions in total honesty and whatever came from their little minds. Time and again, it made their parents wish radio and TV had never been invented.

The kids corner on Linkletter's *House Party* on CBS Radio and Television, grew in popularity because of cute, revealing exchanges like this: One little boy mentioned his dad was a policeman who arrested lots of burglars. Art asked him if his mother ever worried about the risks involved with his dad's job. "Naw, she thinks it's great," he answered. "He brings home rings and bracelets and jewelry almost every week!" Linkletter put together kids' hilarious comments like that in his book *Kids Say the Darnedest Things*. The book became one of the Top-14 bestsellers in American publishing history and was #1 for two consecutive years.

Art Linkletter says he always wanted to be on the radio, but readily admitted he didn't have an angle until he discovered kids were a great interview! In a *Radio/TV Mirror* magazine article, Art, the master of them all, said, "Kids know when they're being set up and they don't appreciate it. The trick is never to let on what one of them said is funny, because in reality, they're not trying to be funny. They're just kids saying anything and everything that comes out of their mouths, usually in an honest and innocent way." The congenial Linkletter emphasized, "You also need to take your time when doing an interview, don't rush it." Of course, in today's radio and TV world of ten-second sound bites it's almost impossible to have a meaningful, leisurely-paced interview.

As an honored alumnus of San Diego State University, Linkletter donated documents and papers which are now part of a major exhibit of his work. The collection documents his spectacular career in broadcasting and as the writer of twenty-three books. The pioneer broadcaster remained in excellent physical health well into his 90s. When asked his secret to longevity. He smiled and said, "You live between your ears. You can't turn back the clock, but you can rewind it." Pioneer radio pro and master broadcast interviewer Art Linkletter passed away at age 97 on May 26, 2010.

Ken Smith was Program Director of the '50s Channel on Sirius XM satellite radio for eight years. He and I worked together in the late 1990s at KLDE Houston (Today, Cox-owned "K-Hits"). The longtime radio pro has been on the air since 1969 and during that time has conducted countless interviews. Ken believes the best advice for radio newbies to keep in mind is to **be prepared.** "Do your homework on the interviewee and write out intelligent questions that you intuitively know that he/she will be interested in answering. Think about what your listener might ask if given the chance, maybe something they always wanted to know! Set up the question by giving a little background and then shut up until your interviewee finishes. He or she will appreciate this and the fact that you took the time to investigate your subject." Ken Smith goes on to say that it's your job as the show host to keep the interview moving and in the direction you want to take it. "If your guest needs a little prodding then at least let them finish their sentence before speaking. If you don't exactly get the answer you were looking for, try rephrasing the question in a manner that might be a little easier to answer. Try to create an air of friendly comfort if you can."

Dr. Joe Galati hosts the radio talk show *Your Health First* every Sunday night on KPRC 950AM-Talk Radio in Houston, Texas. He agrees with Ken Smith that the most important thing about handling an interview is to *be prepared.* "Lack of preparation is insulting to the guest and will make you as a newcomer to radio and interviewing feel all the more insecure while speaking with them." Doctor Joe, a well-respected liver specialist who is also

Medical Director at Methodist Hospital in Houston, says it's important to convey to your listeners that you are familiar with the topic and guest. You need to lend credibility to the entire discussion by being familiar with the topic. It's impossible to fake it. You need to have all the facts available to do, so do your homework. Guests are impressed and honored when you take time to research their past, including some of the minor contributions they have made to their area of expertise. Doctor Galati also points out that Dale Carnegie stated years ago that people are more interested in hearing about themselves than others. "Help bring out the best in your guests by letting them talk about what they know best, their field of expertise and themselves." You can check out Dr. Joe Galati's website at www.yourhealthfirst.com.

My last celebrity interview before losing my voice,[8] which ended my 41-year on-air career, was with **Paul McCartney**. The music legend was scheduled to be in concert at the National Car Rental Center in Sunrise, Florida, which is right outside Ft. Lauderdale. I was invited to have an exclusive, one-on-one interview with the one-time Beatle and, like a fool, I almost passed on it! Why? Because the interview was scheduled for 6pm on a Friday, which meant I had to drive over an hour in rush hour traffic to get there! I know, poor me. Sounds silly, right! But, to a radio guy doing morning drive at Sunny-104.3 in West Palm Beach, the thought of doing anything at the opposite end of your work day ain't exactly cool, even if the interview is with a music genius like Paul McCartney.

No morning drive person is overly excited about doing anything extra after signing off on his or her show on a Friday morning. We smell the weekend and can't get to the exit door fast enough! Hold that elevator; just let me grab my headphones and coffee cup! To show you how fried I was, my scheduled interview also happened to fall at the end of one long and stressful week in radio-world. About the only thing I was anxious to do was settle down with my wife, Kimmie, and chill out!

Thankfully, dawn broke over my thick skull! "*Hey, mister fool,* this isn't just another interview, it's with Paul McCartney!" Here I was lucky enough to be given an exclusive once-in-a-lifetime opportunity to have a sit-down in-person one-on-one interview with pop music legend Paul McCartney, and I had the audacity to want to mull it over! More than a few of my brain cells must have been out to lunch that day! I quickly grabbed hold of my senses! Take a nap, Joey boy, and run don't walk to keep your interview with Sir Paul!

Was I uptight and nervous? Who wouldn't be! But, during my many years on the air, and having handled thousands of interviews, I never found myself so distraught that I'd be shaking all over before meeting a celebrity. I'd describe it more like a queasy feeling in the pit of my gut, almost like you experience before a big game. I think that's good. An adrenaline rush helps to keep you on your toes and focused to do the best job possible. If you find yourself with a queasy feeling before an interview, don't be overly concerned; just make sure you don't barf all over your guest. Quickly excuse yourself and make a beeline for the restroom. We've all experienced those nasty little bugs in the tummy at one time or another. It's natural and if a broadcaster tells you they haven't don't trust them with your checkbook.

Make sure you're prepared to handle the interview by doing your homework. I've found that being prepared helps you relax, knowing you've done all you can to ready yourself for the interview. I took great personal pride in always being prepared for my interviews. Like so many other guests before him, I did my homework and was ready to meet and greet Mr. McCartney. I read everything I could find on the man, studied his long list of music credentials from his days as a member of the Beatles to his solo career with Wings. I wrote, rewrote and reworked my list of possible questions at least several times. If anything, I was always over-prepared for an interview. It made perfect sense to me to have more than enough info about a guest than not enough. Magic-106-Boston morning personality Mike Addams, who at one time was my PD at the original WROR Boston, thought I over-prepared.[9] During one of his critique sessions, Mike told me, "Joey, you give me ten pounds in a five-pound bag." Of course, I took it as a compliment, but I'm sure my pal Mike meant it in a totally different way! Too much info, Joe!

The big day arrived, May, 20, 2002, and butterflies were doing somersaults in my stomach. As my pal and PD Les Jacoby and I drove to the venue, I thought about how to begin my interview session with Sir Paul McCartney. A superstar of McCartney's magnitude had been interviewed a zillion times by the best in the business. I didn't want to open with the same old stock in trade questions. His birthday was about a month away on June 18, just two days after mine, so I decided right then and there that would be my introduction. I'd wish Sir Paul an early birthday greeting!

After exchanging personal greetings, I mentioned we had something in common. He looked dumbfounded, like I was going to say that we both had illegitimate children by the same woman or something totally off the wall! When I said we shared the same birthday month and I wanted to be the first to wish him a happy birthday, I could feel him relax. He smiled broadly, laughed and seemed to love it! I could tell my birthday greeting took him totally by surprise and set the stage for an enjoyable time. Keep the birthday greeting in mind for your next celebrity guest if you find yourself stuck and don't know exactly how to open the conversation. It works wonders to put your guest at ease. It's a safe bet to mention something meaningful to a guest, as long as it's not too personal and embarrassing. If possible, run your idea past their personal assistant first to see if he or she thinks it appropriate. Some people may be super-sensitive about their age or some other aspect of their personal life and you don't want to go there. Play it safe; be sure and ask the assistant out of earshot of your guest, in order to maintain an element of surprise. There's nothing worse than opening your interview on a downer.

My actual interview time with Paul McCartney was scheduled for about ten minutes, but we both went on and on like lost buds for about twenty minutes. I was having a great time and Paul seemed to be enjoying himself, too. His publicist Geoff was sitting off to one side, keeping an eye on things including the time. He must have sensed the feeling of camaraderie between us. He smiled broadly and gave me a thumbs-up to continue and to go longer than scheduled. I focused primarily on how much fun Paul was having on tour and then gently segued to the tribute portion of his show which is dedicated to the memory of his late wife Linda and deceased Beatle-mates John and George. That's when the sensitive side of Paul McCartney came shining through. "Sometimes it's very difficult, Joe," he said somberly, "I'll catch someone's eye out in the audience and they're beginning to lose it and I'll look away, so I won't lose it, too. I've told the band, one night I may lose it but think the audience will understand. These are different times."

My interview with Paul McCartney was far from simply a question-and-answer session. In fact, my list of questions went out the window right after I wished him a happy birthday![10] Our time together was more like an easy, "go with the flow" conversation between two old friends who hadn't seen each other in ages. Paul seemed to really enjoy radio and reversed the order of things. At one point, he took my mic, holding it in front of me, when I'd ask a question and then speak into it when he would reply. It really amused him and he seemed to get a big kick out of being the man in control of mic placement. I have photos to prove it!

Paul McCartney and I even had a similar radio upbringing. We were both raised on the radio. As a young boy Paul's father set up a radio receiver and headphones for him and his brother so they could listen as they went to sleep. Paul said, "Listening to radio plays and music did incredible things for our imagination." He blew me away by revealing that some of the sounds on the opening of the *Sgt. Pepper's Lonely Hearts Club Band* album were taken from his memories of listening to the radio. He came up with the idea of opening the album with the sound of a crowd laughing after he recalled hearing laughter from an unseen studio audience of a radio show. "You didn't know what made them laugh. Did someone's pants fall down? What was it," he laughed. "That's what we were trying to create on the album. Putting in all these little things that would get your imagination going like we heard as kids growing up and listening to the radio."

I found Paul McCartney to be sensitive, highly entertaining and an all-around fun guy to be around. During the time of our interview, May 2002, he was about to marry Heather Mills. We were told she was around and in the building during the time of my interview, but we didn't see her. There wasn't even a glimpse of her at his rehearsal. I remember thinking how odd it was that his wife-to-be apparently showed such little interest in his work. I'm not sure it was a sign of things to come or not. When we were saying our goodbyes, I joked around with Paul about not receiving a wedding invitation. He smiled and playfully said, "It's in the post, Joe, it's in the post, man." We both laughed and I recall how happy he appeared to be.

Shortly after my interview with Paul McCartney, he and Heather were married. No, I never did receive my invite. It's probably just as well. I think we are all too familiar with the results of that unhappy union; a very public and messy divorce. Once in a while, I'll hear a McCartney or Beatles song on the radio and think back to how happy he seemed to be that night in 2002. I also can't help wonder what went wrong between him and Heather. Perhaps problems existed before they even wed? I'll leave that to the celebrity gossipers.

It was a privilege to be selected as one of five radio personalities from the state of Florida selected to share a mic with the superstar musician. Come to think of it, he loved handling my mic so much, I'm not sure he gave it back to me. Oh well. It was a thrill to chat with this icon of the music industry.

In the thousands of celebrity interviews I've been fortunate to conduct, interviewing Sir Paul ranks right up at the top of my list of personal favorites. Lesser known celebrities could learn a few things from this pop music mega talent on how to act and conduct themselves during an interview. Talk about being a pro! He was approachable and completely devoid of any out-of-control ego. Paul McCartney is a genuinely nice person, just like the guy next door who smiles and waves every time he sees you. He is living proof to the saying, "The bigger the celebrity, the nicer they are."

Before your interview, be prepared!
Judi Paparelli has been on the air for over twenty-five years, and has conducted thousands of interviews with world leaders, sports stars, authors and every type of celebrity. Judi believes the single most important factor in having a great interview is the host's interest in the subject matter. "When the host cares about the guest and the topic," she begins, "the listener cares to hear it. It's as simple as that. Guests are far more compelling when the host is fully engaged, prepared and enthusiastic. All of us, whether on or off the air, want to know the person we are talking to is interested in what we're saying. So I only interview people and cover topics that fascinate me," says Paparelli. "I also read every book by every author I interview, cover to cover, in advance. I find that my guest relaxes a bit, knowing that I have read his or her book. And I relax, knowing I am prepared and able to focus on, and react to, what my guest is saying. It's what works for me, and sets up a great dynamic within which exciting things can happen on-air at any moment with

the flow of those special unguarded, unscripted, fun candid moments—that's makes an interview great."

What to do, when an unannounced guest shows up and you don't have time to prepare?

This is why it's important to *read, read, read*. Make sure you're up-to-date on pop culture and what is happening in show business and in the world. Be current. Read newspapers, both local and nationally-syndicated papers like *USA Today*. The more you read, the more in the know you'll be and ready to handle the unexpected challenges that come your way on an almost-daily basis in radio. You need to be ready to handle sudden unexpected things that happen from time to time. That's the beauty of radio; the immediacy of it all. Try not to get upset. It's not brain surgery. Go with the flow and have fun! If you're uptight about having a guest on that you haven't had time to prep for, politely ask if they can come on at a later date.[11] If it's a major celebrity who is only in town that day, be gracious and thankful they want to be on your show. Suck it up! Give it your best shot! That's what winging it and ad-libbing are for! It's also a good test to see if you fit the mold as a real radio pro!

Longtime CBS reporter, commentator and editor-producer Edward R. Murrow was also a master at the art of interviewing, which he did so well and for so many years. Murrow was with CBS News for years, first on the radio side reporting to American families the horrors of WWII during the Nazi bombing of London. In one of those strange turns of events, the war actually made Ed Murrow a star. The popular radio personality later became CBS's chief news commentator and top interviewer on the program *Person to Person*, where he visited the homes of celebrities and chatted informally with popular personalities of the day, including Marilyn Monroe, Jacqueline Kennedy, Fidel Castro, John Steinbeck and many others.[12]

As far as how to interview, Murrow had his own words of advice for future radio wannabes, when he himself was the subject of an interview in May 1954.[13] People would constantly marvel at Ed's laidback style with the greatest figures of our time. He was seemingly at ease with famous folks from around the world, but actually beneath his poker-faced calm demeanor there was always a nervous and tense man. Murrow admitted that his own outwardly serene appearance came from years of self-discipline, and keeping in mind a piece of advice given to him by Judge John Bassett Moore of the World Court, who told him, "When you meet men of great reputation, your judgment of them will be greatly improved if you view them as though they were sitting in front of you in their underwear."

I wonder if this little-known Ed Murrow technique has been secretly passed on to other great interviewers in broadcast history, like Jack Paar, Johnny Carson, Mike Douglas, Merv Griffin, Barbara

Walters, Mike Wallace and one of broadcasting's best-ever interviewers, the late Tim Russett of NBC's *Meet the Press*. I always thought the ever-present smile on Tim's face was to project a warm, friendly demeanor to put the guest at ease. I'm sure that's partially true, but wouldn't it be funny if Tim and other interviewers were looking at their guests the same way Edward R. Murrow was told to do, just sitting there visualizing them in their undies? Makes you want to smile just thinking about it, doesn't it? So go for it, smile :-)

How to conduct a successful interview.

Celebrated broadcaster, **Sally Jesse Raphael** is another outstanding interviewer.[14] During her successful broadcasting career, she has interviewed thousands of celebrities, personalities and news-makers. Prior to launching her signature television program in 1983, Sally was a pioneering presence on radio. She served as a UPI and AP foreign correspondent in Europe and Central America, and holds the distinction of being one of the first females to accomplish a number of milestones in broadcasting, paving the way for other women on radio and television. Ms. Raphael had successful nighttime radio shows on the NBC and ABC radio networks; hosting her own radio call-in advice show for six years, on NBC's Talknet and for three years on ABC Radio. *The Sally Jesse Raphael Show* was the longest-running talk show on daytime television and the first nationally syndicated single-topic talk show hosted by a woman. Who better to ask about the art of interviewing then this two-time Emmy Award-winning talk show host?

I had corresponded with Sally in August, 2007, and asked her to share her thoughts on how to conduct a successful interview. "You have to find some area of mutuality," she begins. "Either they come from your hometown, or they're out selling their new book and you've read the book before that one. That flatters the author. You also have to find something that you and the person you are interviewing have in common. Your first few questions have to be unusual ones, because this person is probably on a publicity tour and has been asked the same things over and over again."

Sally has been interviewing guests for a very long time and therefore knows the nuts and bolts of what goes into making a good interview a great one. The well-known celebrity talk-show host stresses not being too unusual with your line of questioning. "If you do, you'll sound goofy. In other words, don't ask something dumb, like, what kind of pecan pie do you like? Or, if you were a bird, what kind of bird would you be? That's nonsensical. Instead, ask something that relates to them, but is out of the ordinary. That gets your guest involved and interested. It is important to always make your guest feel comfortable with you. One way to do this is to make sure near the top of the interview you plug their book or their movie; because that's the reason they're on your show…to sell something. And make sure they know that you know they're selling something. And, make sure you say it loud and long and clearly, or you'll never get booked by the same publishing house or same publicist again."

Sally Jesse Raphael has spent her broadcasting career doing what others said couldn't be done, *listening* and not merely *talking*. She left the air in 2002, but continues in syndication worldwide via the Internet.

Talk show host **Melanie Morgan** is another popular air personality. For many years, she hosted mornings on KSFO 560 San Francisco and today is the chairwoman of the pro-troops, pro-Iraq-war group, Move America Forward. Melanie believes the best way to handle an interview is to "Prepare, prepare, prepare. Then throw out all your research and interview from the gut. Thank God for Al Gore," she continues, with her tongue firmly planted in cheek, "since he invented the Internet to help in the research process, many future radio stars were saved from the fate of becoming doctors, lawyers, accountants, and Citadel Broadcasting CEOs."

My friend and former Boston radio competitor **Jordan Rich** is another outstanding radio interviewer.[15] Jordan hosts late night weekend talk shows on Boston's top-rated WBZ 1030AM, a station which has been a leader in its field since first signing on in 1921. Jordan has been on the air in Boston for over twenty-five years and has been hosting the weekend shows on 'BZ since 1996. He's warm, witty and conversational and one of the best one-on-one interviewers in the business.

I asked Jordan what advice he has for both future radio wannabes and seasoned radio pros alike, on how to conduct a successful interview. Here is his response, verbatim, from April 2, 2008: "Interviewing is an art form, one that I have practiced and studied for years. I have gained a lot by observing some extraordinary interviewers over the years, Jack Paar, Dick Cavett, David Suskind, David Brudnoy, Charlie Rose and others. You ask, what's the secret to a successful interview? Certainly doing homework before the interview, reading a guest's book, checking bios, literature and press materials are a must. Listening with interest to what your guest is saying is super critical. Listening is essential in building conversation with someone. Anyone can rattle off pre-written questions in sequence, but it is ONLY by listening closely that a true conversation will develop and one that is infinitely more interesting to the listening audience." Jordan Rich stresses the importance of letting the interviewee respond. "Don't make the interview focus too much on you and your feelings about the subject matter. It also helps to be naturally curious about a lot of things of course." The popular host says, "Going to the well and using that frame of reference you've built up by reading and exploring is a wonderful way to connect with both your interview subject and your audience."

Jordan has a feel for what the listener wants to hear. His program features an eclectic mix of actors, athletes, authors, musicians and other interesting personalities. He's been successful at handling both interviews and lots of open-line conversation with his callers on WBZ for the past fifteen years.

Radio pioneer Arthur Godfrey, who is showcased in chapter one, turned radio into an intimate personal medium. He was the leader in one-on-one conversational radio. He is another prime example of excellence in the art of interviewing. Interviewed in a 1950s *Radio-TV Mirror* article during the peak years of his air popularity, the master of the airwaves offered this advice for future radio stars on how to handle an interview: "Suppose you're my guest," said Godfrey. "I ask you a question. We then kick it around for a while and take it to a laugh. Now, it's my job to make you look good and to know when to cut away. Keep in mind," says Godfrey, "when talking with a guest, the listener is also participating by listening. He or she is either identifying with my view on the subject being discussed, or the guest's, or he or she may be arguing with both of them! But, the listener is sharing my interest in what the guest is saying."

Godfrey's casual style of interviewing always made for a relaxed atmosphere. His guests were at ease, resulting in lots of laughs or sometimes even controversy. He described the interview scene this way: "Our conversation is just as it may be in your own living room when friends come in, only in this case the radio is the living room and the radio and the listener become one." That's the good word on what goes into the art of interviewing from one of radio's true masters of the mic, Arthur Godfrey. [16]

There's no such thing as a bad interview or a really bad guest, unless you deem it so. You control the direction and the way the interview precedes. You also set the mood and tone of the interview, so leave your grumpiness outside the studio.

Several radio folks forewarned me '70s heartthrob **David Cassidy** was a bad interview: moody, tough to handle and wouldn't answer certain questions about his years on the TV series *The Partridge Family*.[17] The morning of the scheduled interview I was so uptight and concerned about how it would go that, before he even arrived at our studio, I was ready to blow off the entire interview. As so often is the case, David Cassidy turned out to be a great guest. He was fun, couldn't have been nicer, and is an all-around great guy. Once again, it just goes to show you shouldn't believe everything you hear! Usually what you waste time worrying about will never come to pass, so why worry about it!

Cassidy is like so many guests: treat 'em right and they'll be nice! Try to be flippant or ambush them with a line of embarrassing questions and I'm sure you'll succeed in ticking them off and wind up calling them a bad guest. There are times to go easy and slowly with a guest. If you know in advance they're touchy about certain subjects, treat them respectfully, win their confidence and *then* go for the Keith Partridge line, if you feel you must bring it up at all. Never ambush a guest by hitting then squarely between the eyes with an opening question you know will make them uncomfortable. If you want the shortest interview on record then go for it. Just have plenty of music ready to fill the time allotted when your guest suddenly vacates your studio. My interview with David Cassidy was in 2001, following the events of 9/11.[18] He was in West Palm Beach for a concert at the Kravis Center. He was so moved by the calamity of 9/11 and the terrorist attack on our country that he donated ten dollars of his own money for every ticket sold with the money going to help victims and their families. In my book, David Cassidy is top-shelf and a fine American.

Interviewing isn't brain surgery! Like most things in radio and in life, the more you do it, the better you will become. I did it for over 40 years and I can honestly count on one hand minus my thumb and pinky the bad interviews I've experienced and even in those few instances the guests probably came off sounding badly because I didn't do my homework! As David Letterman said, "If I can't make a guest feel comfortable for 2½ minutes then I haven't done my job." I totally agree!

Radio Pro Point to remember: As the program host, it's important to be conversant and express your opinion, but that doesn't include answering for your guest.

In summation: Here are a few pointers to keep in mind the next time you conduct an interview with the goal of making it great!

- Spend twice as much time preparing for the interview than the actual interview itself.
- Make the interview an enjoyable experience for you, the person interviewed, and your listeners. Make your guest feel welcome, comfortable and relaxed. You will learn more and get more if you do.
- Ask questions that your listeners might ask if given the opportunity. Try to ask questions that are new to your guest, especially if it's a major celebrity who has been interviewed countless times.
- Try to get something "special" - an exclusive out of the interview that may gather you some press and publicity. **For example:** So are all these rumors true about your upcoming nuptials? Guest: "Yes, I want you to know, we are definitely getting married. No rumors, it's true!" **BINGO!** Get online and e-mail or phone ALL the papers with your scoop and make sure they give credit to you and your station in their story.
- Don't stick to the order of your questions. *Listen to your guest's reply* and play off their comments

- While you're asking questions, you need to be a good interviewer and a good editor. You need to know when an interview is not going in the right direction and take control. If something said by your guest isn't clear you need to clarify their comment so that you understand what they say to be true…for example: "So, are you saying, that you never heard of this person's name before tonight?"
- Never forget that you are in charge. Sometimes, interviews can be a dud and even though a celebrity may be a major star doesn't mean they come off well in an interview setting. If you find yourself in an interview that is going absolutely nowhere, do yourself and them a favor and wrap it up, quickly! Great interviews can be a gold mine to you and your listeners and knowing how to handle them properly is truly an art. Hopefully, some of the ideas and suggestions gathered from the radio pros in this chapter will help you paint a masterpiece the next time you conduct an interview.

Notes:
1. This chapter is named for one of broadcasting's best interviewers, the late Art Linkletter. Read more on his career and interviewing style later in this chapter.
2. In Sept. 2010, unable to reach an agreement on a new contract, Bob Rivers left the station.
3. The legendary Paul Harvey is profiled in Chapter 16
4. LaPierre won several Edward R. Murrow Awards for Best Radio Newscast
5. To learn more about Lissa Coffey go to www.brightideas.com
6. Sally Jesse Raphael comments later in this chapter
7. Art Linkletter is also profiled in Chapter 1- Radio's First On-Air Personalities/Learn from the Masters
8. In April 2004, I was hospitalized with pneumonia. Doctors discovered three nodes on my vocal chords. I wasn't allowed to speak for 31 straight days.. In the past, I had bounced back from lung surgery and open heart surgery. There would be no come-back this time. My forty-one-year radio career was over.
9. Mike Addams comments in Chapter 20, Who Inspired the Radio Pros
10. A list of questions should be part of your pre-interview preparation, and if nothing else it serves as a security blanket if you run into trouble and lose your way. Questions should only be used as a guide. You should always listen to your guest and respond accordingly. Let the interview flow naturally like any conversation. Don't make it strictly a boring question-and-answer session.
11. To learn more about show preparation, see Chapter 7- The Importance of Show Prep

12. *Person to Person* was telecast "live" and was first seen on CBS-TV October 2, 1953. It remained on the air until September 1961.
13. Source: *Radio TV Mirror* Magazine May 1954
14. Sally also tells it like it is on the status of women in radio today in Chapter 13, A Woman's Perspective on Being on the Air.
15. You can listen to Jordan Rich every weekend on WBZ Boston, or his podcast on WBZAM1030.com. Jordan is also co-owner of Chart Productions, Inc., an audio production agency. Jordan's voice is heard on hundreds of narrations and commercials throughout the country. He also teaches voice-over acting, offering workshops and private training throughout the year.
16. It was once estimated that Godfrey was heard by 40 million listeners every week. At his peak, he was the best on-air salesman on radio and the most valuable single commodity at CBS Radio. In 1959, to support the claim, *Variety* reported Arthur Godfrey was responsible for $150 million in advertising billing for CBS. Read more about this radio pioneer in Chapter 1.
17. David Cassidy was trying to shake off his TV image as Keith Partridge. It wasn't because he didn't want to talk about those TV years, but preferred to move on.
18. 9/11 was the date, Sept.11, 2001, when America was attacked by terrorists

The Art of Interviewing • 207

Bob Rivers, Seattle morning-drive pro.

Ken Smith, air talent and former oldies PD X-M Satellite.

Judi Paparelli, Boston, Florida and nationally syndicated talk personality.

Dr. Joe Galati, Houston Liver specialist and weekend talk radio host, *Your Health*, first.

Les Jacoby, Paul McCartney and author.

Sally Jesse Raphael, popular radio-TV personality.

Jordan Rich, long-time popular Boston Radio Pro.

Jay Leno (Emerson College grad) with author, a fellow Emersonian.

Guests on author's Oldies show, montage #1. Top from left: Chuck Negron of Three Dog Night with author Paula Abdul and Cyndi Lauper with author, Davy Jones of the Monkees with author. 2nd row from left: Cousin Bruce Morrow with author, 1950's pop singer Eddie Fisher with author. 3rd row, left to right, 3rd row L-R, should read as follows, Eagle's Don Henley at Walden Woods MA w/ author, Donny Osmond and 50's pop idol, Eddie Fisher. Bottom left, Ben E. King of the Drifters w/ author, right bottom, foreground L-Howard Kayland of the Turtles, middle KLDE air staff, author, Linda Cruze and Allen Beebe, on right, Mark Volman. In background, author, listener, John the mailman and Bobby Vinton.

Guests on author's morning-drive shows, montage #2. Top row from left: author with Heather and Bob Urich, author with Bob Urich, author with Linda Ellerbee. 2nd row from left: author with Cindy Williams of Laverne and Shirley, author laughing with Mary Hart on mic, author with Lassie (best guest ever-let me do all the talking!) 3rd row from left: author with actor/producer Gary Marshall; group photo including Jerry Stiller, Boston Mayor Tom Menino, Estelle Harris (Stiller & Harris played George Constanza's parents on Seinfeld) and author. Bottom row: author with Drew Cary and Linda Cruze, Debbie Reynolds.

CHAPTER 9
Attitudes and Actions

"Fill these!"

– WKBW's Joey Reynolds alleged sayonara note to management which was attached to a shoe nailed to the PD's door upon his leaving the station in the mid-1960s.

How to develop a winning attitude

"When it looks like you're not getting anywhere, a real radio pro turns up the heat and keeps moving forward."

Shortly before his passing in 2001, my friend, actor **Robert Urich** gave me his definition of attitude: "Attitude is everything," he said. "It motivates action, which increases productivity and it improves morale, which perpetuates a positive attitude."

There is little doubt your attitude means everything if you are to be a success in anything in life, including as a radio personality. You MUST believe in your ability to get the job done and that you can make it on the air. Belief in yourself is the strongest single factor in developing a winning attitude!

"A real radio pro realizes nothing will work, unless you do!"

The difference in failing or being a success on the radio pro can be summed up in one four-letter word, WORK. That's not to say that another four-letter word, LUCK, isn't important, too. A little bit of luck certainly can't hurt, and can only help, but in any endeavor there is no substitution for good old-fashioned hard work! Radio Hall of Fame member **Dale Dorman** has been a fun fixture on the Boston radio scene for over 25 years. Dale believes work is the best advice for future radio stars. "Come in early, leave late, listen and watch all the talent at the station and learn from them," says Dale, who adds, "and don't be afraid to work!"

Cary Pahigian is the President and GM of Saga Communications' Portland, Maine, Radio Group. My friend Cary is a thirty-five-year radio pro who began his career while still in high school. He believes attitude and energy are the keys in being a winner on the radio and has a laundry list of questions for air-talent to ask themselves. "One, are you willing to work at it every day? Two, are you getting a little better at it every day? Three, do you really care about the station or is it all about you? And, four, do you consider being on the air, a profession, or just fun and an easy way to pick up a paycheck?" Pahigian also has strong words about ego. "Air-talent better have a good dose of pride to go along with their ego, or it isn't going to work."

Be a positive force!

Just think how great it would be to have your own cheering squad pumping you up with positive vibes every minute of every day! Someone constantly giving you an IV full of encouragement. It would be pretty cool, wouldn't it? Well, if you get in the habit of encouraging yourself, that's exactly what you'll have. A constant IV full of praise, directly wired to your brain and your heart! A good attitude begins with you. All day long, as you go about your business, you have the ability and the power within you to decide what your thoughts and words will be. Choose your words carefully to move yourself in a positive direction. If you choose to say your day will be bad because you tripped over the dog and spilled your coffee all over the new living room rug, more than likely your wish will come true and you *will* have a lousy day! One negative thought feeds another and another, until you find yourself drowning in a sea of negativism. On the other hand, you can take a negative incident in stride and turn it into a positive. Thank your lucky stars you didn't break your leg, or the dog's, when you tripped and fell! And the spilled coffee? Go get another cup, after you clean up the mess you made.

The point is really simple: A winning attitude feeds off positive thoughts. When you begin to feel yourself sliding into a negative mood and mentally begin beating yourself up, immediately stop! Instead, try giving yourself a few sincere words of self-praise and encouragement. You'll instantly feel more energized. You will project a more positive, happy feeling. In addition to encouraging yourself by being your own pep squad, try to get in to the daily habit of praising and encouraging others. Positive action and energy towards those around you will send even more encouragement right back to you. Some call it good Karma. It's one way you can move closer to a winning attitude, and proceed further along in your goal of achieving success as a real on-air radio pro.

Think like a winner, and don't be a whiner.
Instead of polluting your brain with negative thoughts that will wear you down and tire you out mentally and physically, choose to make your thoughts positive and encouraging. Start right now, by putting to good use the hundreds and hundreds of opportunities that come your way every day to give yourself solid words of encouragement. Remember you have a built-in IV that's filled with praise for you and nobody else.

Difficult times in life can help us grow.
There are times when we can't always explain the difficulties we face, but one thing is certain: we all face them at some point. There are some difficulties that shape us for a lifetime and some that leave us only momentarily changed. Some of us search deep within our souls for answers that we may or may not find. But in the search, we may find that our difficulties diminish, and we can come to accept not only what we've come through, but the pain we've experienced as well.

The difference between success and failure is the ability to get up just one more time after falling flat on your face and a few other parts of your anatomy! There will be times in radio when you're going to fall and fall hard! It's inevitable. It can't be avoided or side-stepped. You will fail! It's as predictable as a winter snowfall in the Colorado Rockies. When this happens, you must, as the song goes, "Pick yourself up, dust yourself off and start all over again!"[1] I know, you've heard it all before: "Real champions never quit," "When the going gets tough, the tough get going," all those great quotes that are supposed to pick you up and magically heal the hurt, squelch the anger within and fire you back up the ladder of success. But somehow, when you're failing, things are falling apart and you find yourself fading from the radar screen of life, it's not exactly the sort of thing you want to read, or is it?

Well, my friend, based on my own rocky radio road, I have learned that's just exactly when you do need a little positive motivational reading in your life. You'll find these little pearls of wisdom scattered throughout this book, usually at the top of a page. They are here to give you a lift when you may need it most. Please consider them as your own personal shot of positive food for your brain, your heart and soul. Sometimes, at just the right moment, it can be encouraging to read an inspirational word or two. If you find a few quotes that make you stop and think, well, who knows, maybe they will help pick you up and get you back on the right track in your radio career. If that doesn't work, I think you know who will be standing by with a helping hand.

I'm hoping and praying I won't lose a few of you on what I'm about to say, but it is my opinion the only way a truly inspirational, life-changing mini-miracle can occur is through faith in God and the power of prayer. Now hold on just a minute, ye of little faith, especially those of you who are about to close my own book on me! Please stay with me a little bit longer. When I failed several times in my life and career, and we're talking big-time failings, and I was so depressed it would take a dozen Doctor Phils to figure me out, someone much wiser than me advised the following. It was four simple, yet powerful words, *Let Go, Let God!* Now, please don't think of me as some sort of Jesus freak or religious nut-bag. I checked with my wife, Kimmie, and she assured me, I am neither, and pardon the pun, her word is gospel in my Book of Revelation.

Honestly, it is not my intent to become preachy. Well, maybe just a little. In all seriousness, that's not what this book is all about so fret not. I'm not about to sneak a sermon in between chapters on air-style and getting fired. However, while piecing this book together on how to become an air personality, dawn broke over my thick Italian skull. I came to realize what a significant role God has played in my life and career as a radio pro! I'm not in any way trying to sway you to my beliefs and feelings. I do believe you want me to be honest and speak from my heart in all things regarding my own radio career. Therefore, I would be less than truthful if I didn't disclose my feelings about how my faith in the Lord worked to help me. His guidance and inspiration picked me up and carried me through some trying times, both on and off the radio.

How to handle adversity and depression and to stay focused.
Faith and staying focused.

Radio Pro deals with what it takes to become a real on-air radio personality, much of which is based on my own personal journey and how I found my way to a successful 41-year radio career. One thing is certain: I am sort of an expert on the art of failing. Heck, I failed so many times I could easily serve as a poster child for failed radio talent. So, how did I combat the depression-filled days and nights of getting fired several times, coupled with the stress of being out of work, bills piling up, three major surgeries and the loss of my voice?[2] All this coupled with an unsuccessful first marriage and the wicked, seductive roller-coaster ride of an up and down radio career. How did I keep a positive attitude through all this? First of all, be assured I am no Superman but rather a mere mortal like you. However, when the bottom fell out and scattered my feelings, hopes, and dreams all other the countryside, and I honestly felt the whole world was turning away from me, how did I cope? Okay, just like a true radio sales person, here comes my commercial for God, as if He needs one. Then, again, given today's decadent society, maybe he could use a little help.

The power of prayer and my strong faith and belief in God carried me through life and my radio career. Without my faith and God's help in carrying some of my emotional baggage, I never would have made it. I thank Him for walking with me through some extremely dark nights and days. Whatever your religious beliefs, He'll be there for you, too, and will help carry your load, if you let Him. That's it! I'm stepping down from the pulpit now and apologize if my words constitute any sort of sermon.

Keep charging forward when life is trying to hold you back.
If you find yourself faced with a major disappointment in radio, please keep the following in mind, from someone who has faced similar situations. Don't retreat and give up! Stay focused and move forward! In May 2000, I underwent open-heart surgery in Houston. Finding myself off the radio and out of work again because the station didn't renew my contract, I was as depressed as an old dog without a bone. Houston Astros owner **Drayton McLane, Jr.**, sensing my feelings of despair, wrote me an inspirational letter. "You're a terrific guy with unlimited potential," he wrote. "Keep your nose to the grindstone and things will come together for you. You're a champion. We all go through dry spells but remember the rain will come and the refreshment it brings will be sweeter than ever before. Give Kim my best and I'll look forward to hearing from you. Until then keep charging!" I share his words of support and encouragement for one important reason, so that if and when you find yourself in a comparable situation, you will keep them in mind and "**keep charging!**"

How to handle getting fired.
There's an old saying in radio that you haven't arrived until you've been fired! If that's true, then I've arrived and departed several times during my long air career! Personally, it has happened to me a few times, including my very first on-air radio job at WFAU in Augusta, Maine, which is covered in detail later in this chapter.

Radio Lesson learned: Don't ever change the format of the station you're working at, without at least notifying management in advance. It seems they don't take too kindly to surprises! As far as being fired in radio, I'm afraid, as air-talent, the odds are not in your favor that you will avoid getting the ax at some point in your career. Remember, the one constant in radio is change and you may find yourself on the beach and off the radio through no fault of your own.

> *"There is no way you can experience real success without experiencing some failure."*

How to handle getting fired.
Top-rated Minneapolis morning drive guy, **Dave Ryan** at KDWB-101.3, says he clearly remembers the first time he got fired. "I had been doing mornings for about seven years and had heard the saying, 'You've never been in radio until you've been fired!' Well, I thought that I was above ever getting fired. I just didn't see that ever happening. Not to me!" At the time, Dave had been working for about a year at KZZP in Phoenix when the rumblings started that a format change was coming. "Strangers were seen at the station at odd hours

on weekends. My girlfriend saw my boss with an out-of-town radio friend we both knew and wondered what was up. Signs were subtle, but they were there." It was then that Dave Ryan decided to go right to the horse's mouth. "I went into the GM's office with the PD and said that if anything happened, I hoped that I'd still be part of the new format. I expected the GM to reassure me that everything was okay, but it didn't happen! Instead, he cast a look at the PD that gave away his thoughts, like, uh-oh, help me answer this."

Dave Ryan instantly knew he wasn't part of their new plan. Radio showfolk have a built-in antenna on approaching doom and gloom and Dave knew his own personal doomsday was approaching. "I don't remember how we knew the time was approaching," he says, "but we just knew. One weekend it all came down. I was out of town and called my voice mail. The first message I got was from my producer who was calling from the station. He said, 'Dave, there's someone here changing all the locks!' The very next call was from my program director, saying, 'Dave, give me a call. I need to talk to you.' I knew what he was calling about, but dutifully, I called his house and his babysitter answered. 'Oh, my gawd,' she exclaimed, 'is this really Dave Ryan?' It really wasn't what I was in the mood for, since I knew he was calling to fire me. Yes, I said, just have him call me back. And he did. And it hurt. And I felt screwed."

Later that weekend, as Dave continues, "I went by the station to pick up my headphones and other belongings, but they wouldn't let me in the building. Why? Because they were doing a dry run and didn't want an outsider watching what they were doing. In one day, I had gone from their star morning man to not even being allowed in the building. Needless to say, I was crushed, but things started to look up. First, when I did go back to pick up my things, I found a brochure for the station's clients that explained the format change by saying in part, 'even our new morning show, *Dave Ryan in the Morning*, was unable to draw the listeners needed to sustain our past format.' What! I thought, so they were pinning part of the blame on me? My lawyer didn't like that and instantly got $50,000 out of them to avoid going to court, plus I got the station to release me from my non-compete."

Dave says he had two job offers within days. He took one for more money than he had been making. Ultimately, his old station's format failed. "It's a little petty of me to enjoy seeing that," he admits, "but it sure was fun seeing it tank!" Dave says the station which let him go in such a callous manner is still on the air and back in its original format, but has never regained the popularity it had before the format change.

As radio luck would have it, Dave Ryan was let go from his next radio job, too! He says it was because it was a hip-hop station that played about ten songs an hour and just wasn't his style. Ryan was philosophical about getting canned a second time from radio, because of what was about to happen. "About the time I got let go, this amazing radio job that I've had for almost twenty years opened up at KDWB. I really have learned to have faith in the idea that the job you get after you're fired will most likely be much better than the one you got fired from." However, he quickly adds, "Getting fired, sucks. It hurts and it makes you question your talent and your future. But have faith; believe in your past accomplishments and how you will top them in the future. And most importantly," the popular Minneapolis morning show host adds, "remind yourself that you are valuable and will be an asset to the right station."

> *"It's important to keep in mind that failure is not the end of the world! Failure should be looked at as a challenge. If you don't get knocked on your butt a few times during your radio career, you'll never reach your level of excellence."* – Author

Radio Lesson learned: Attention, management: change for the sake of "change" isn't necessarily for the better!

Here are just a few reasons given to air-talent for being fired or released from their contract:

- Insubordination: management feels you are way too difficult to handle.
- Format change: management doesn't feel you fit the new direction of the station.
- A change in program directors or GMs. Call it radio paranoia, but many feel it necessary to bring their own team on board.
- A change in ownership, frequency, or call letters. Many believe it's time to make a clean sweep.
- You're making too much money. With the present economic situation this one seems to be topping the list lately. Senior air staff members find themselves replaced by talent making less.
- You totally went over the edge, locked yourself in the control room and played the same song over and over for two hours before security finally broke in and shut you down.
- You're getting a little long in the tooth and the station wants to project a younger, hipper image.

On a serious note: it appears that age discrimination is rearing its ugly head when it comes to competent air-talent getting fired, released, or not having their contracts renewed. Other reasons may be given, but in many cases it is simply a case of "age discrimination." Quite often, it is so blatant to both employer and employee that management will make the talent sign an agreement that in order to obtain their severance pay, they (air-talent) will not bad mouth or sue the station under any circumstances. This is one-way ownership and management avoids potential future lawsuits and litigation by providing buy-out packages to air-talent, with strong stipulations.

Getting fired

It's mentioned time and again in this book that as much fun as being on the radio can be, one of the pitfalls is the uncertainty that today may be the day you get "blown out!" Being canned, sometimes for unexplained reasons, is one of the harsh realities of being on the radio. It happened in West Palm Beach to my friend and former co-worker, **Sunny Quinn**. Her story is so compelling that I'm going to let her share it with you in her own words, complete and unedited:

"In my situation, a new GM had been brought in from CBS corporate right after our current manager was suddenly laid off. This new guy had been working there for over a month, and not once did he take a walk down the hall to even introduce himself to me. I was on the air from 10 to 3, Monday through Friday, so there was no excuse for that. Red flag! I knew there must be something in the works. I had been working at that station for twelve years with #1 ratings, so I was a bit curious as to why this man didn't want to know who I was. Then one day, an office worker was laid off. The next day our Production Director was laid off. The following day, I reported for work as usual, got out my headphones to go on the air, and my Program Director told me that the GM wanted to see me in his office right away. I froze, and just said, 'There goes my job.'

"The scene in his office wasn't pretty. I was determined not to lose it. I didn't raise my voice and I didn't cry. But here was this total stranger who knew nothing of my twenty-three-year history on the air in this town; who knew nothing of the seventy broadcasting awards I had accumulated; who knew nothing of the hundreds of charity events I had emceed or taken part in; who knew nothing of the loyal listeners who followed me from station to station for more than two decades. All he said to me was, 'Uh, we're uh, changing the direction of the station.' Yeah, right. I calmly accused him of taking part in age discrimination and wanting to replace me with someone younger and cheaper. He was quite defensive, of course. I had no interest in listening to anything he had to say. I made a few brief statements to him, asked him how he slept at night, and walked out. I never raised my voice, but I did slam the door, hard! The next thing I knew, the office manager was right by my side, escorting me back to the studio to collect my things, then to my locker to clean it out, and she then followed me to the elevators to make sure I exited the building. No goodbyes, no thanks, no nothing. Twenty-three years. Done. Finished. Over.

"I didn't quite make it to my car before the tears started. And once they started, they didn't stop for a year. It was like I was stripped of my identity and purpose. I felt so useless and so insignificant after having such a vital career for so long. I didn't get to say goodbye to my co-workers or even my listeners. I felt like a traitor to them. I became extremely depressed and angry. During that time, I even ripped all my awards off my walls. I threw them in boxes to take out to the trash, but my husband found them and stored them away in the attic. But I'll never put them up again.

"I loved my job in radio so, so much. I looked forward to going to work every single day for twenty-three years. I worked every shift around the clock, and loved every minute of it. In fact, I loved it so much, I started teaching it. I eventually became the Director of Education at the Connecticut School of Broadcasting for six years. But like everything else, the corporate world has taken over, and radio and television have changed dramatically. Radio today isn't what it was in the days that I got to experience it. Looking back, I feel very lucky to have enjoyed it when it was at its best. And today, I'm over it. It sure took a long time, and yes, I sorely miss it. But I miss the old days of radio, not so much what it was becoming. These days I spend my time mostly with horses. I find horses to be a much kinder breed than corporations."

– Sunny Quinn
West Palm Beach, Florida

How to survive getting canned. One way is to maintain a positive attitude.
One of America's true radio pros, **Dick Biondi**, says he was fired no less than **24 times** during more than half-a-century on the radio. As of this writing, May 2009, Dick is still entertaining his loyal listeners every weeknight from nine until midnight on Chicago's True Oldies station, WLS-FM. Giving up is not part of Dick Biondi's nature. During our telephone conversation, Monday, May 4, 2007, I asked Dick if he ever got depressed after finding himself on the beach and out of radio so many times. "Just once," the veteran radio pro replied. "I said the hell with radio, and I drove to California and visited my stepson. I also saw several other people that I knew. On the drive back, I started getting the feeling that I needed to get back on the air. I think what that trip accomplished was sort of like using plumber's aid on a clogged pipe. I got rid of whatever was inside of me and eating me up and pissing me off. I said, I wanna get back on the air."

What prompted Dick Biondi to take a year off was a combination of factors, including the sobering fact that he had been canned ten or twelve times. "It was 1973 and I was in Cincinnati," recalls Dick. "What happened was they brought me in because the guy who was doing mornings [Jim Scott] went to New York. So, they brought me in for I think several months and the guy didn't make it. He wanted to come back. So, I was out! That's when

I said the hell with radio if that's the way it's gonna be, and I took the trip to California." When Biondi returned to radio, it wasn't back to Chicago, or any other top radio market. He ended up at WNMB in South Carolina. Sometimes it's good to be the big fish in the little pond, even for a little while. The station became his home for a decade. He didn't return to the Windy City until 1983. After a year at WBBM, he was selected to be the "signature" voice at WJMK, which became Chicago's first oldies station.

Dick Biondi's passion for radio and positive action carried him through.

Dick Biondi's positive attitude has helped him make it through his twenty-four firings. "You know, Joe, for a skinny little Italian kid, I've done all right," he laughs. "When I was at my peak at WLS-AM in Chicago, Russ Regan and I were talking one day on my way to a record hop. [3,4] This was a long time ago, and he said to me, 'How come you're always so happy?' And, I said, 'Russ, if I get fired tomorrow I've had the best of it.' Think about it, Joe! How many guys got on a station and did as well as I have?" This past Saturday night [May 12, 2007], I walked out on stage at a doo-wop show at the Chicago Theater. Dale Hawkins was there and I went backstage to say hi. He opened the door and he hugged me and said, 'You know, Dick, if it wasn't for you, I don't know where I'd be today. You played my records and your station WLS, along with WLAC in Nashville did, too, and between both stations, you covered the country. Thank you and your station.' For a guy like Dale to say that, well, it just blew me away. Let's face it, "Suzie Q" was one of the greatest records ever. How many guys, Joe, would love to have someone as legendary as Dale Hawkins say nice things about him?"

In talking with fellow Biondi, his love for radio comes shining through loud and clear. "Radio is all I ever really wanted to do. From eighth grade in school through my senior year of high school," says Biondi, "I worked at a radio station. I spent more time at the radio station than I did at school," he laughs. "At the same time, for two years in a row, every time the sports editor at the Endicott [New York] newspaper went down to spring training, I took over the sports section each morning. How many guys can say they had that kind of training?"

Dick Biondi is one radio pro who very much appreciates where he's been and where he's at in his long, successful career. "There are so many guys out there that can't even get on a small station. We're so lucky to have our radio careers, Joe."

Today, at age eighty [2011], how does the "Wild I-tralian" stay pumped-up after half-a century on the radio? "I love what I do," says Biondi. "Wives and friends don't understand that even with personal issues going on, radio is the most important thing in my life. Friends will say let's go and do this and I'll say that I wanna work. I don't wanna take a day off. If it's gonna end, Joe, I wanna make sure I do it right up to the very end. I'd like to die with my earphones on, while introducing a song."

A real radio pro like Dick Biondi knows success is gained by working through challenges. In Dick's situation, those challenges meant coming back time and time again! To be exact, and in his own words: "After being fired twenty-four times in radio!"

Radio lesson to be learned:
Getting canned in radio is only a temporary ending to a brand-new beginning in your on-air career! What's done is done. The time and energy spent worrying and complaining about it will get you absolutely nowhere, except lots of continuing frustration and negative thinking! What's happened has happened! Instead of looking back, and worrying about the why, how or who may have been at fault, look forward and consider all the positive possibilities that are available to you. If you think you've been wronged, don't seek revenge. Seek success…seek fulfillment…seek to take what has happened and turn it into a positive force in your life and radio career. Don't waste time and energy looking back to the "what ifs," but look ahead to what can be!

Detroit radio legend **Dick Purtan** says he was fired after five weeks at WBAL in Baltimore. "The GM said I was 'too wild for the town.' We had three daughters at the time, aged 7, 5 and 2. They paid me $4,000 to cover the move and I moved back to Detroit and took a job at WXYZ Radio (now WXYT-1270AM). How did I cope with getting canned? My feeling, it was his problem [the GM's], not mine." Timing is everything in radio and sometimes it's not a good thing.

When I asked then-Phoenix morning man, **Bill Gardner,** if he had ever been fired, he replied, "There's a lot of irony in your question, Joe. A week ago [Feb. 15, 2008] I was summoned by the general manager and told I had done my last show on KOOL. I was 'terminated without cause.'" Talk about feeling badly. Out of hundreds of broadcasters, why I decided to reach out to Bill with that specific question at that moment is one of those true mysteries of life. ESP is not necessarily my forte, although sometimes, I really believe there's a piece of Carnac the Magnificent residing somewhere deep down inside me.

Gardner is a veteran broadcaster who has the right perspective on being fired. "We'll be okay," he said. "Phones are ringing pretty well and my e-mail box is filling up with nice inquiries, too. I'll walk away with over nine years' ratings consistently in the top five with 25-54 demographics at KOOL, with a format that's generally perceived to appeal exclusively to those over fifty. Now, my next assignment," adds Gardner, "is to find a GM and owners who have the luxury of preparing for next year's bottom line as hard as next week's. My favorite quote on the subject of firing comes from a journeyman jock I know who told the GM on the way out the door, 'I've been fired more times than a cannon.' Now, as far as aspiring broadcasters are concerned and how to handle the entire 'firing experience,' I have just three words for them," says Bill Gardner,[5] "**prepare for it!**"

Mary Blake is a longtime Boston radio news voice. We worked together at the original 98.5-WROR. Later, Mary moved down the hall to handle news on sister-station, WRKO AM-680. Her dismissal in radio came after 23 years at the station. It also came as a total shock, as Mary explains. "The first piece of advice I would give to anyone in radio is NOT to assume it will never happen to you. Always be prepared!" By being prepared, Mary Blake means have a current air-check of your work on file along with an updated resume. "It sounds like a no-brainer, but believe me, I was not at all ready when it happened to me."

Mary was laid off from WRKO Boston in November 2006, a week to the day before Thanksgiving. "I was actually in Atlanta at the time, and received the news over my cell phone. Station honchos had decided to do away with the entire news department, so I was actually one of seven who were terminated. On the one level," she says, "there was comfort in numbers, but it also meant that a lot of news folks would be looking for a job in what had become a shrinking news pool in Boston. Fortunately for us, management at WRKO generously allowed us time to return to the station to put together air-checks of our work on CDs, and I took full advantage of that."[6] She continued, "I had to scramble to come up with something. I had NOT been prepared." Mary admits one of her biggest mistakes was getting too comfortable. "I had been working at the station for 23 years and had gotten very comfortable with my news shift and my seniority level in the union and never thought I'd be fired. What a wake-up call! I was shocked and felt very vulnerable."[7]

She readily says she took time to do some soul-searching. "I thought about possibly teaching and then I realized that I still loved radio and wanted to continue in the field, if possible." Mary made the right decision to do what so many others do when they find themselves on-the-beach and out of work: You reach out to people. "I began calling people at other stations in town and found out quite pleasantly that after twenty-three years at the same station in the same market, I didn't have to do a lot of selling. People in the business knew me and knew my work." Within two months, Mary landed some freelance work at FOX radio in New York and also at the other Boston talk station, WTKK. Four months after being laid off, Mary received a call from WBZ, the all-news station in Boston. She has been working there for the past year and says she loves every minute of it.

Getting fired, even after a long tenure with the same station in the same area, can in many ways be a blessing. In Mary Blake's case, her firing proved that new doors can be opened for you. "There really was a great situation just around the corner. So, given my experience," she says, "I would tell tomorrow's radio stars to keep at it if they really enjoy radio. There's always one more phone call you can make when trying to land a job." Mary also passes along a warning to all radio wannabes. "If you find yourself fired or laid off, don't burn bridges! Don't give in to the temptation of burning bridges. It may make you feel better, but that's for the short term. Radio is a very incestuous business," she laughs. "I often joke that throughout my career, I've worked with the same thirty people. The only change is under different management or station ownership and different job titles! You should be able to shake hands and smile at all of your former bosses and co-workers when you run into them down the line and believe me, run into them you will!"

Mary Blake's advice is well taken about not burning bridges. During my many years on the air, I not only burned a few bridges, I blew them up. We're talkin' totally destroyed and blown to itty bitty pieces. Thanks to the grace of God, a very contrite heart by your author, and forgiving folks, I think, or at least hope and prayer, I have managed to rebuild most of those bridges. It wasn't easy and required a great deal of effort. The rebuilding process literally had to be done piece by piece over a very long period of time. No doubt, part of my self-destructive nature can be attributed to my volatile Italian blood which always seemed to be bubbling just beneath my outwardly warm, friendly demeanor. This hereditary "blow 'em up" gene, when coupled with my years of dealing with plastic explosives like C-2 as a member of the 10th Engineer Company, Marine Corps Reserve in Portland, Maine, was lethal![8] I'm teasing about the use of explosives. Believe me, I didn't need any help to find the target when I was on a search-and-destroy mission. I can sniff out a weasel in the haystack with the best of them!

The point is, burning or blowing up bridges is not a smart thing to do. Even though the momentary joy of telling off someone who you feel has done you wrong can be extremely gratifying and juice one's testosterone level, ***don't do it!*** Instead, back off about ten paces, take a deep breath, swallow your hurt pride, bite your tongue and live to find another radio job. As the saying goes, "Beware of the toes you step on today, because they just may be attached to the butt you'll have to kiss tomorrow."

In a weird sort of way getting fired in radio is almost like a badge of honor. Not that I'm condoning the action in any way, nor do I wish to see anyone go through such a difficult time. However, show me a real radio pro who's at the top of his or her game and I'll show you someone who has probably been fired at least once during their illustrious career.

Morning drive radio talent, **Bob Rivers** says, "I've been lucky. Early in my career, I was fired several times for various reasons and each time, I went on to a better job." How did it happen? Rivers says he had passion and that he worked really cheap! "In those days radio jobs were easy to find. If you were a decent announcer with a passable set of pipes, you got the job. However, at 98 Rock in Baltimore, my arrogance caught up with me and getting fired taught me a great lesson that all of this could go away! If I had not matured quickly after that, and polished my business and people skills, my whole career would have ended up in the dumpster."

Being fired from your first radio job.

Speaking about maturing quickly enough to save one's own radio career, I'd like to share a slice of my own radio life. It involves being canned from my very first radio job. My first full-time job in radio was in the early 1960s at WFAU-AM, a 250-watt pea-shooter in Maine's capitol, Augusta. Back then, Faust Couture owned two Maine radio stations, WCOU in Lewiston and WFAU-Augusta. Obviously, not being shy in the vain game, he took some of the letters from his own name and applied them to the call letters of his stations. You may want to do the same thing, only with appropriate letters from your own name when you grow-up and own your own radio station.

My weeknight air-shift at WFAU ran from 6pm until station sign-off at 11:15. The station was affiliated with CBS and carried the complete network programming line-up, including the hourly newscasts and many features. Music on the station was strictly adult standards; Frank Sinatra, Rosemary Clooney, Percy Faith, Ray Conniff, Perry Como, big bands and other non-rock artists. I loved Sinatra and couldn't wait to play him on my show. With the station's near-death format, Frank was the closest thing to an up-tempo artist I was allowed to play on the air. No complaints from this radio rookie. I was happy just to be on the radio anywhere, and whatever the music format!

After I signed off from my shift, I'd head on over to Doc's Tavern for a burger, fries and a coke. What can I say, the year was 1962 and that was the cool thing to do. Doc's was also about the only place in town still open at 11:30 on weeknights. It was the local hang-out for young people; the after- high school and before-married crowd, and the booths were usually filled by the time I strolled in, just before midnight. It didn't take long before I developed a friendship with many of the locals. It certainly didn't hurt in the "girls" department when they found out I was the new radio DJ in town. Even spinning tunes meant for old fogies didn't seem to bother them. Well, at least not during our initial, get-acquainted stage. Later, they would use their feminine charms to get me to play a few of their favorites on the air, a move that eventually would lead me down the road to radio ruin. One girl in particular caught my eye. Eleanor was really nice and we became good friends. She was well-liked by the others and became my one-person cheering section. With her friendly persuasion, she convinced many others to listen to my show.

In no time at all, requests became a regular part of my nighttime show on WFAU. I was still cautiously playing it safe and trying not to alienate the older listeners by playing many of the "less offensive" younger pop artists of the day, like Connie Francis, Brenda Lee and even a jazz clarinetist from England with the unusual name of Mr. Acker Bilk. You may remember he had a #1 hit in May 1962 with the haunting instrumental, "Stranger on the Shore." Even though my younger female followers liked "most of the stuff" I played on the radio, the highly testosterone-charged dudes of the town were hardly convinced to listen! The guys were a totally different animal. When I'd walk into Doc's, they'd be ready for me with their snide comments. "Hey, Joey boy, why don't you play more rock, like Elvis, Dion and the Four Seasons and lay off that soft crap!"

Once in a while, Eleanor would be seated in a booth at the far end of the restaurant. My long walk to where she was sitting was more like traversing a gauntlet, only instead of tomahawks thrown my way, it was a verbal assault. I'd smile, wave and proceed on down the aisle. It was quite apparent my appeal and newness had run its course. It didn't take me long to put in my own request to Eleanor that she sit a little closer to the front of the restaurant. She just smiled and said, "Don't you want a little more privacy?" What could I say? She had me. Most of the cat calls from the guys were friendly enough. I think it was motivated more by jealousy than personal animosity. Who could blame them? They were tired of seeing their girlfriends gathered around my booth, giggling and chatting away while scribbling down their requests on paper napkins and handing them over to me. Why do we guys act so stupid and juvenile at times! WFAU Augusta may have only been a small-town radio station, but I was still the guy on the radio playing songs for *their* girlfriends.

Usually our conversations at Doc's centered around music, specifically on why I didn't play more top rock artists of the day, like Elvis, Buddy Holly, Fats Domino, Eddie Cochrane and others. "Can't do it," I'd say, "it'll drive the older listeners away in droves." I wanted the guys to listen to the station and I guess a part of me longed for acceptance as the new kid in town. Slowly, over time, I began to capitulate to their requests. After a while, more kids who lived in town began listening primarily to hear their names on the radio. I soon developed my own little following. More teens began calling me at the station and making requests. After all, it was a nighttime radio show and kids tuned in while doing their homework. It was my first honest-to-goodness fan following, and I loved it! I began slipping a few more rock artists into the show, Elvis, Ricky Nelson and even Jerry Lee Lewis and "Great Balls of Fire." The once stodgy-sounding WFAU suddenly took on a hipper rock sound at night. Fewer and fewer Sinatra and Ella Fitzgerald records were being played and more Dion and the Belmonts found their way on the air, a bit more rock than the station's base of adult listeners were accustomed to hearing.

Warning: changing formats without management's prior approval will most likely get you fired.

I was having a ball. My nightly routine would be to head on over to Doc's immediately after my air-shift to have my ego stroked a little, and to grab a burger while taking as many requests as I could for the next nights show. It didn't take long before I had converted many local teens and young people to listen to the station. Up until that time, WFAU had been their parents' station.

Radio lesson learned: To appeal to the local teens in town, I made one of the biggest mistakes an air-talent can make. I took it upon myself to change the nighttime format of the station, deciding on my own to work more "rock artists" into a high-profile, adult-easy listening format. Of course, in defense of my own actions, I was fairly naive about different station formats at that early stage in my radio career and my only intention was to make the station more popular with young people. Right, sure, Joe!

Getting fired.

One night, I was rockin' away on the airwaves and having a great time! It was a little after eight, when all of a sudden, the studio door flew open and there stood the station manager, Norm Gallant. He was glaring at me with a look that told me everything I needed to know. He didn't stop by to say hi and congratulate me for increasing our teen listening base on his station at night. No, ol' Joe was about to get the heave-ho. I was about to be fired! Without saying a word, he motioned for me to pick up my records, grab my coat, and leave! Any compensation due me would be forthcoming in the mail. The entire scene took less than 15 seconds, but it played out in some sort of eerie slow motion. Norm was accompanied by his front office manager, Mona Toothacher. I'm not kidding, that was her real name! She was a nice enough lady, but she was also glaring at me. Standing right behind Norm was a little dweeb of a guy who was a part-time announcer at the station. He looked like the character Sherman on TV's *Fractured Fairy Tales*,[9] complete with over-sized, horn-rimmed glasses. And, yes, he was also glaring at me. They were all glaring! I guess Norm brought them both along just in case things got ugly. He didn't need to worry. I was too shook up and scared at the thought of being canned to do anything but follow his orders. I was summarily dismissed on the spot.

Talk about humiliated and embarrassed! I never even got to say goodbye on the air to Eleanor and the gang over at Doc's Tavern. I was replaced in the chair and on the radio by a kid who was a huge suck-up to the station manager. I was devastated. Driving away, tears rolled down my face. I had just been fired from my first radio job. How on earth, I lamented, would I ever get another job in radio, especially without a recommendation? Chills ran down my back and during that long ride home on that dark night in Augusta, Maine, I truly believed with all my heart that my days on the radio were over, even before they barely got off the ground!

Take note, all radio air-talent: It's never a good idea to change the format of the radio station you're working at without prior approval of station management! You may get canned! Getting fired for changing the music policy of the station without management's prior approval taught me a valuable lesson which stayed with me for the rest of my radio career; namely, talent needs to be talent, let programming and management decide what format will be in place, and whatever you do, don't deviate from it. Follow it to the letter!

It's important to remember when you get canned, for whatever reason, that change is a constant part of life and is expected in radio. People change, work conditions change, the world changes and even radio station formats change. Sometimes, in radio, when changes occur and through no fault of your own, you will find yourself on the short end of the stick. Of course, in my case, I screwed up big-time and deserved to be fired. When it happens, you need to keep in mind that being laid off or fired is not the end of the world! Becoming angry or resentful is not the answer. Being obsessed with placing blame will not solve the problem. Instead, take a step back, look in the mirror and see if there's anything you could have done differently. Try and look objectively at all the factors, at least the ones that you are aware of. Try and put everything in perspective. Difficult situations like getting fired, as hurtful as they may be, quite often come complete with valuable life lessons which will help you improve as a person and move forward with your career.

When and if you get fired, you have a choice. You can make life even more difficult for yourself and those who love you by throwing yourself a "pity party" that never ends, or you can deal with it and move on. Keep in mind it's not the situation, but your reaction to the situation that matters. You can't always control your circumstances, but you can control your own actions and attitude! Look at your firing as an opportunity! Getting knocked down is never fun and being counted out is not my style. The difference between succeeding as a radio pro and failing is not how many times you get knocked down but how quickly you get back up!

Successful Nashville radio talent and program director **Barbara Bridges** admits she has never been fired. "At least, not yet," she quickly adds. "Never say never in this business." Even though she can't give advice from the first-person perspective on what it's like to get canned, she does have sound words about "changes" in radio: "Firings and contract issues are pretty much a part of our daily life in this industry. Formats and budgets can change quickly and sometimes good people become the casualty. I would suggest that people pick themselves up by the bootstraps…and quickly." Bridges, the PD at MIX 92.9-WJXA, Nashville for the past eleven years, suggests that air-talent should keep their audio files current and be ready to dust their resumes off at a moment's notice. "I also would recommend keeping a list of contacts and making decisions about whether you are willing to move." She adds, "There are a finite number of radio positions in any given city. More cities, more opportunities. Depending on your skill level and desire to work in the industry," she forewarns, "it may be necessary to take something less than you wanted in order to get your foot back in the door. Be open to all options."

Skip Kelly is a well-known South Florida air personality who has been in radio since the days the "big yellow bird" flew the friendly skies of New England.[10] Skip grew up in Exeter, New Hampshire, and his on-air duties have taken him from Maine and New Hampshire to Massachusetts, West Virginia, and his current radio address, KOOL-105.5-WOLL FM in West Palm Beach, Florida. Skip doesn't mince words when it comes to getting canned in radio: "First of all, don't let it bother you," he says. "If you deserve to be fired, you know what you did. Take your medicine, swallow it and move on. Usually in radio," Kelly adds, "firing is for a selfish, internal reason and a goal the company needs to accomplish. It's NOT really about you. Ego plays a big role in the entertainment business, but you can't let your ego rule you. You have to realize and know you are a good person and good people will always survive even during the darkest days. If you dwell on being let go or if you dwell on the down side of the radio business it will destroy you! Just take a step back, analyze the situation, think about what your next move will be, then MAKE IT!"

A positive attitude is a must in radio, regardless of your job.

Whatever your job in radio, whatever size station you're lucky enough to find yourself working at, in whatever size town or city, *always* give it your best! A positive attitude is a must! If you happen to be fortunate enough to be on the radio, *always* approach your job with a positive feeling and with passion! Treat your time on the air as the most fulfilling position you will ever have in radio! Don't ever forget, being on the air is a privilege! Don't ever take it for granted!

In 1963, my second full-time job in radio was at WIDE-AM 1400 in Biddeford, Maine. My shift was from 6pm until midnight on the small, 1000-watt AM radio station.[11] WIDE reduced power to 250 watts at night and consequently its coverage area was also reduced. It made me wonder if my boss planned it that way. You know, put the unpolished new kid on when the station's total listenership could easily fit in a corner booth at the local Nutshell Restaurant. If that was the case, it didn't bother me. I was on the radio and that's all that mattered!

WIDE signed off at midnight, following 45 minutes of beautiful music on *Cozy Corner*. We even had a really snazzy sign-off, voiced by station manager and owner, **J. Alan Jasper**. He was a good guy, who always greeted me with a big grin and a cheery "Hiya, kid!"

A positive attitude is a must in radio, regardless of your job.

Alan Jasper had the most mellifluous delivery of any air-talent around. His voice was smooth and syrupy. He sounded big time and gave our little station's sound a major market air of professionalism. When he wished our audience "a pleasant good night" and urged them to sleep tight, you could actually feel his warmth and sincerity oozing all over the radio. Alan Jasper was also my on-the-job teacher. I will always be indebted to him for the time he took to show me the radio ropes.

As soon as the station carrier (transmitter) was remotely silenced for another broadcast day, the door to our second-floor studios and offices would fly open and in walked **Banjo Bowden**. Banjo was quite the character and fun to be around. He worked full time for the highway department and fire department for the neighboring City of Saco but also moonlighted by cleaning a few offices around town, including the offices and studios of WIDE radio.[12] It was easy to tell Banjo loved his job at the station. Every night, he, along with his son Everett and his wife, would promptly report for duty at the station, ready and willing to do their thing. They painstakingly did a thorough job of cleaning up after us less-than-tidy radio folks messed it up. Wastebaskets were overflowing with wire copy from the UPI news machine, empty pizza boxes, coffee cups, and other material. The control room window had finger and nose prints all over it from both small and big folks, who while visiting the station during regular office hours would press up against the glass to stare at the person on the air in that seemingly magic fish bowl. The floor was another story. It had enough dirt tracked in to grow a small garden.

Yes, every night Banjo and his small crew certainly had their cleaning work cut out for themselves. One night as I was cleaning up the studio area, gathering news copy for our morning guy and filing records away, I couldn't help noticing through the studio glass what a meticulous job Banjo was doing mopping the outer office floor. He had already been over it twice and was proceeding to do it again!

"Banjo," I yelled, so he could hear me through the open studio door, "you're working too hard. Slow down, you'll kill yourself!" Looking up at me and sporting his infectious grin he said, "Gotta make this place shine, Joey boy! After all, it's a radio station!" I smiled back and thought, here's an older guy, who holds down two other jobs, but he truly enjoys cleaning the station and making it shine. Even though it was none of my business, I was curious as to why he wanted to work nights cleaning the station. It wasn't just the extra income. It had to be something else which motivated him. Banjo had confided in me before that he did all right from his full-time work, so what was it that possessed this man to work so hard late at night at the radio station? Curiosity got the best of me and I decided to find out.

"Banjo, you told me you're doing all right working your other jobs, why don't you ease up a bit and quit cleaning this place?" The man immediately stopped mopping the office floor, leaned back on the mop handle and stared at me for what seemed the longest time, as if in total disbelief about my question. Smiling, and with an incredulous air about him, he replied, "And give up working in radio?"

There is much to be learned from the man's straightforward and totally honest reply. Many would look at his cleaning job as menial, but not to Banjo. He took pride in his work. In his eyes keeping the radio station clean was *the* most important job at the station and probably just as important as going on the air, or maybe even more so, at least to his way of thinking.

I never forgot that incident and to this day it makes me smile thinking about it. Banjo Bowden was one of the lucky folks who found the most meaning in life by giving the most to each of his jobs. If you want to get the most out of life and your work, then choose to be like Banjo. Approach every job in a positive manner. Whatever job in radio you find yourself doing, whether it's answering the phone, being on the air, or even mopping the floor, it's a job to which you can add value. As William J. Bennett said, "There are no menial jobs, only menial attitudes."

Notes:
1. Lyrics by Dorothy Fields from the popular song, "Pick Yourself Up," with music by Jerome Kern.
2. The author's health issues which resulted in his being unemployed and off the radio several times in his career are covered elsewhere in this book.
3. At his peak popularity at WLS-AM in 1961, Dick Biondi had a whopping 56% share of the Chicago radio market. A rating that huge is non-existent in today's radio market. In February 1963, Dick Biondi became the first American DJ to play a Beatles record on the air.
4. Russ Regan (born Harold Rustigian) is a longtime record exec who was President of both UNI Records and 20th Century Records. He also worked at Motown and other companies. In the early '60s, Regan recorded "Joan of Love," which was released under the name "Russ Regan."
5. When I checked in with Bill in 2010, he was happily doing morning drive on a group of Los Angeles-area stations
6. Quite often when air-talent is laid off or fired, management does not allow them to return to the station for any reason, let alone to work on audition tapes.
7. WRKO-AM was an AFTRA Union shop until May 2006
8. C-2 is a soft, putty-like compound. When combined with a blasting cap, it can be highly explosive.
9. *Fractured Fairy Tales* was a segment on television's *Rocky & Bullwinkle.*
10. One-time New England carrier Northeast Airlines flew between Portland, ME & Boston and called their planes yellow birds.
11. In the early '60s, and in some cases even today, many small market radio stations signed off the air at midnight or before, simply because they couldn't afford the overhead of operating 24 hrs a day.
12. The City of Saco, Maine is pronounced *SOCK-O.*

Attitudes and Actions • 231

Robert Urich, author and Andy Moes on So. Boston set of ABC-TV's *Spenser: For Hire*.

Dick Biondi, legendary WLS Chicago air pro.

Cary Pahigian, Group radio Mgr- Saga Comm. Portland, ME.

Dale Dorman, legendary Boston air personality.

Dave Ryan, Minneapolis Morning-Drive air personality.

Author with MIX-98.5, Boston morning team. Clockwise from left front: Jody Winchester, Amy Doyle, author, Mary Blake, Lynn Hoffman.

CHAPTER 10
Program Directors, Friend or Foe?

"Being program director at a radio station is the best and worst position in the building. You get to create and manage the #1 reason customers use the product. It's not so good on bad rating days!"

– Gary Berkowitz

ON THE CBS RADIO HOME PAGE, the role of a radio station program director is defined as "One who is responsible for the on-air product of the station, and who also controls production, talent and program schedules." A very nice description of a PD's position, but they left out one very important factor. It is also the *most thankless* position in a radio station. I should know: I was one!

The program director's position is multi-faceted. He or she plays psychiatrist and chief counselor to the highly charged and emotional air staff! The PD reports to upper management, who have only one thing on their mind: "Just get me numbers."[1] This middle-management post lends a whole new meaning to being stuck in the middle. It can be a less than desirable position to be the "go-between" upper management and air-talent. In the wrong set of circumstances, radio PDs can find themselves in a no-win situation.

Radio stations are often the scenes of battles for turf and control between managers, program directors, and talent. In the final analysis, it comes down to survival of the fittest. Since managers have the final vote on who goes and who stays, usually it's the GM who wins, but not so in every case. A top air-talent with solid ratings and a well-written contract can sometimes outlive an overly precocious manager. Warning to you radio newbies: don't go using my words as a ticket to go head to head with management. As I said, the GM has the ultimate power to hire and fire.

As air-talent, if you are perceived as a malcontent or troublemaker, even the best ratings in town won't save your butt if they decide your number is up and want to dump you! Keep it in mind that it may help to temper your emotions. There's no question that ego-driven, highly over-sensitive talent can drive a PD up a wall. This I also know to be true, since I have sat on both sides of the programming desk, as a PD and as talent. Now, on the other hand, program directors who are power-crazy, wishy-washy leaders without any backbone, who are unapproachable and devoid of any program creativity can drive talent nuts! Many PDs perceive air-talent as whining and complaining crybabies, and with good reason, we are!

Station managers are not exempt from driving PDs out of their squash! Many push their program people to the edge by insisting they are too easy on temperamental talent. They constantly press their PDs to ride air-talent harder, particularly when it comes to following the station format. Quite often, the end result is talent rushing to the GM to seek aid and comfort! Some air personalities are known for running to the GM for support at the first sign of being slighted or seemingly mistreated by their PD! When it happens, the GM must carefully consider how to handle the problem. Words spoken to show support for the talent can undermine a PDs position faster than butter melting on a stack of hot pancakes!

Advice for PD's: It's the emotion-filled air-talent who usually is *the best* air personality. Mood swings are part and parcel of what the real radio pros are all about. The really good PDs know this and even though it may be hard to accept and handle, it is part of talent's make-up and goes with the territory. Don't get me wrong, I am NOT condoning bad behavior by either air-talent or the PD, but sometimes, because radio is an emotion-filled business, things are said in the heat of the moment that can be quite regrettable later on. When sharp, angry words are spoken in haste, the best answer is to shake hands, forget it, and move on. Hopefully, both individuals will come away from the unfortunate circumstances with a better understanding of each other and will not repeat their bad behavior in the future. In a perfect radio world, cooler heads should prevail, but realistically, sometimes hot heads cannot be avoided or prevented!

Many PDs wind up in the difficult position of being nothing more than a mouthpiece for the GM. They have no real say in handling talent or the station's sound. They are merely glorified carrier pigeons and designated messengers who pass directives on from "up above." Never has the term "good cop, bad cop" been truer than in a radio station. Quite often it describes the roles of the PD and GM. Guess which one usually comes up smelling like a rose with talent at the expense of the PD! By usurping a PDs position, a general manager can do irreparable damage to the future success of the individuals involved and the radio station.

Air-talent needs to be mindful that in most cases, the PD is your immediate supervisor and reports directly to the GM. Be sensitive to the difficult job they face on a daily basis. Don't treat them like some sort of office flunky. **Cary Pahigian** is the President and GM of Saga Communications in Portland, Maine. He believes strongly that a PD must understand that he or she is first and foremost in the people business. "Many PDs can rotate music and write promos, but if you cannot lead you are dead. As GM," he continues, "I want the PD to keep me in the loop all the time on all matters. Not to okay everything, but the more I know, the more effectively I can do my job and be more helpful to the PD when needed."

A gentle suggestion to GMs: Allow your program director to do what you hired them to do, program and lead! Hands off!

It doesn't take long for air-talent to size-up a PD's make-up, good or bad! Radio talent has a sixth sense when it comes to figuring out exactly who is running the ship and who is really in charge. When all the pieces are determined, many strong-willed air personalities will run roughshod over a "weak link" in the management chain of command, like a PD. If a GM is a control type who won't allow his or her PD to have the freedom to direct programming and talent without interfering, it can be a most difficult and unpleasant predicament for everyone, but especially the PD. If as the program person you can't get the GM to see the errors of his or her ways and the potential damage he or she is creating, then I strongly suggest you look for another position and move on! Thinking things will change in time usually doesn't happen when working for a person who needs to be in control. No matter how willing you are to try and live with these stressful and distasteful circumstances, it is a one-way ticket to ulcer-land! Radio is and should be a fun business and no one should have to work in a stressful environment.

A word to PDs.

Nowhere on a radio station's employment application does it state you must be a martyr. Don't try to save the station at the risk of destroying yourself! Sound a little over-the-top? Your tune will change if you have the misfortune of finding yourself in such a position. Being jammed in the middle and taking heat from all sides is not easy to handle. It's noble to take one for the Gipper, but not all the time![2] There are no rewards for being a radio martyr, at least not in this lifetime! Try to discuss your concerns with your GM. If it looks like you're at a dead end and no one will listen to you, then it may be time to move on! Of course, before you decide to jump overboard, there are a few things you can do as a PD to make life easier for you and your air-staff. The first thing you can and should be doing is making time to listen to your air-staff. Dismissing their input and suggestions on how they feel the station can win is not only unwise but really dumb! It always seemed incongruous to me that air-talent expected to "cook" on the air was never invited into the station kitchen to lend a hand in preparing the meal. Let them speak their mind and *really listen* to what talent has to offer. Don't be condescending and only appear to listen as a gesture so as not to upset the station's sacred cash cow and prima donna.

Take a memo, PDs and managers:

No matter how busy you are, take time to listen, really listen, to the concerns of your air-staff! When they approach you with their thoughts and ideas on how they believe the sound of their show and your station can be improved, bury your ego and listen up. Talent may have an idea to save the day, the station's ratings and the all-important station cash-flow, which is directly tied-in to having huge ratings.

As mentioned, I truly believe the most thankless position in a radio station is the job of a PD. As a former PD, myself, I am well acquainted with the many trials and tribulation that a program director faces on an almost daily basis. Therefore, I tried really hard to understand the individual circumstances and difficulties imposed on the many PDs I worked for over the years, who numbered no less than eighteen during my forty-one years on the air. Many handled their positions of authority in a friendly, professional manner without being arrogant or too bossy. Other PDs were near-tyrannical in their approach. It was their way or the highway. A few of the more qualified and competent PDs knew what they were doing and carried out the mission statement of the station with concision and relative ease.[3] The really good program directors conducted day-to-day station programming business with air-talent with an air of mutual respect.

The program people I found myself in conflict with were those who were on nothing less than a major power trip. They were the PD and you're the talent, period, regardless of what you thought. It meant nothing! Whatever suggestions and input you may have about your show or what was uniquely your style and what you were all about as a personality made little if any difference to them. These power-crazed people were going to do it their way, come hell or high water, and woe to the talent who tried to stop them. It was a scenario for total disaster. Unfortunately, I was directly involved with some of them or witnessed their terrible behavior during the course of my own radio career. Power hungry PDs and ego-driven creative air-talent can be a volatile mixture and a recipe for failure. In my opinion, it is the primary reason for a breakdown in communication between talent and program directors.

Many PDs have never been on the radio, or if they worked an air shift it was for a very short period of time. It's sad but true to say these people were not very successful on the radio and often made the shift to the PD side of the business. It always seemed so paradoxical to me to take a person with no apparent air-talent who never made it as a successful radio personality and put him or her in charge of air-talent! Yes, whatever the nonsensical reason, known only to the "suits" in charge, it seems to be the norm in radio. It's just another example that life is stranger than fiction! Please don't misunderstand, there are many talented radio program directors who are excellent air-personalities, but for one reason or another choose not to be on the air! But, the really decent PDs who were also successful on the air are few and far between.

During my long radio career, I've worked for some really good PDs and some not so good! In the late 1960s at WGAN Portland, Maine, I learned a lot about personality radio from Dick Fixaris. Dick and I, along with a few other station staffers, also helped pay Tony DiMillo's mortgage on his waterfront restaurant by downing a few pops at his place after work. Another PD, Clif Hunter at the 50,000-watt clear-channel voice of the Midwest, WLW Cincinnati, gave me my first shot at big-time radio and let me "be me" on the legendary station. Clif allowed his air-staff to do their thing on the radio with little if any interference. While on the air in Boston, from 1979 until 1998, I worked for no less than a dozen PDs. By far, the best of the bunch was **Gary Berkowitz**.

My own personal criteria for the perfect PD, if there is such an animal, are this: first and foremost give me someone who has integrity, followed closely by compassion. As the song says, *"You gotta have heart!"* I learned that if a person has solid values, usually they are also a strong person and won't sway too much when the wind starts blowin.' And believe me, it can get pretty windy around a radio station with all that hot air, if you get my drift! Compassion in a PD is very important, because we all screw up, and when we do, we need someone to be a little understanding. Even though they may be chewing us out for a dumb move we made, we still want to feel loved. Another important quality in a program director is loyalty. You want and need to know your PD can be trusted when things get tough!

Every now and then, everyone can experience a bad ratings book. Ratings come and ratings go; there are so many factors involved. For example; what demo got the rating diaries, what zip codes did the majority of the books fall in, what was the sampling size of the listening audience, and so on. An air-talent can be busting his or her butt to do the best possible show, but sometimes there are other factors involved that are completely out of the talent's control! A good PD will give their air staff a break for a down ratings book! Not many will, but the good ones like Gary Berkowitz do. It's common knowledge in radio that if you work for Gary, which I did on three separate occasions, the chain of command is quite clear. He is the general and you're the soldier, but that's okay, because he took the heat that went along with being the leader. Whenever we had a down book at the original 98.5-WROR Boston, and we had a few when the station changed formats from Solid Gold to AC, Gary would say, "Don't worry, you did everything and more that I asked. This is my report card, not yours!" "Berko" always had a game plan and unlike some PDs who change course on a whim, quite often in the middle of a ratings book, Gary always stayed the course.

Another great quality about Gary Berkowitz, which is so important in a good PD, is that he did his best to keep things light. He tried to make you feel good, even when he was chewing you out for some bonehead thing you said or did on the air! He's the kind of guy you enjoy being around. Did I mention that another important quality in a PD is a sense of humor? If not, please add it to your list. It is important not to take yourself too seriously. After all, it is what it is, radio, and not brain surgery! It's also a known fact that if you were in the building at lunchtime, you got a free lunch on "Berko." Not a big deal, you say? I beg to differ. I worked for a General Manager, higher up the suit chain than a PD, and covered in the next chapter, who during the two years I worked for this person never invited me out for a cup of coffee, let alone lunch. Believe me, having a free lunch or dinner works wonders in getting a person to work all the harder, let alone making them feel wanted!

Lorna Ozmon is another program person I worked for during my nearly twenty-year Boston air-adventure. Lorna gets high marks from me as a PD for one simple reason: she put up with me! There were times our working relationship could be described as stormy. I admit it. I've had a few verbal exchanges with PDs that left the studio walls shakin' for days! I'm not proud of losing my temper and engaging in shouting matches with radio associates, but it happens. Radio is driven by emotions, and unfortunately there are lots of people in the business who don't understand that. Lorna isn't one of them. They take too many things personal. Lorna actually spoiled me for other PDs that followed. You could vent and rant and rave to her and present your point of view in complete and total honesty without ever fearing any sort of reprisals! Once you aired your feelings with her, it was over. On with the show! I think it was a heck of a quality in her. She stood up and took the heat and never, ever held a grudge. Well, at least none that I was aware of. For all I know, she could have gone home and spit at her doggie, Chiblee, pretending it was me! In all seriousness, I never felt Lorna Ozmon was on any sort of power trip because of her position. She was also my station manager, when she was promoted to that position at WROR. We also worked together a third time at KLDE Houston in the late 90s. I was in morning drive and Lorna was the station consultant.

A tip for PDs on how to further enhance a working relationship with your air staff:

When Lorna Ozmon wanted to drive home an important point she took you to lunch, and we're not talking Mickey D's either. Oh no, it was the best of the best, usually an upscale restaurant. So, take note, Mr. and Mrs. PD, air-talent loves free food and it's a lot easier to get their attention on an important matter over lunch or dinner on a full tummy than sitting in some stuffy office.

If you find yourself working for a PD or GM with some of the qualities I mentioned, consider yourself lucky. If you find yourself working for someone with ALL the qualities mentioned, consider yourself in radio Disneyland. I'm afraid the really good radio management types in radio are becoming harder and harder to find. Oh, they're around, you just have to look a lot harder these days! Every PD I worked for had their own unique brand and idiosyncrasies. Some were rubber-stampers for upper management, few had little backbone and even fewer were stand-up people. Many were follow-the-leader types instead of leaders who said, "Follow me!" A few were eccentric and borderline crazy and off-the-wall, others were angry and mean-spirited. Some had creative ideas and were innovative types, but most were simply button pushers and implementers of what others told them to do. One unique characteristic all PDs seem to share is a definite lack of a sense of humor, especially when it comes to following the station format. Break it and believe me, they won't think it's funny!

Well, you've read about some of the good PDs I worked for during my forty-one-year broadcast career. On the flip side, I also worked for some real stinkers. Stinko's! Lowlifes, mentally inept, who couldn't program a grammar school closed-circuit station comprised of second graders, let alone a real, honest-to-goodness radio station staffed by radio pros. We're talking about the shallow end of the creative gene pool, baby! The worst of the lot and the program directors you really have to watch out for are the ***nomads without gonads!***

These lowlife vermin, nomads without gonads, float at the bottom of the barrel moving from radio station to station with absolutely no regard for their own personal welfare, let alone yours as an air-talent! Why do they top the most dangerous list? Because these people are in search of one thing, the quick fix! Their one and only mission is to get some quick ratings, whatever the cost, pick up a good-sized bonus and with the flick of a Bic, they move out and on, looking for new radio prey to feast on! These PDs couldn't care less if you're an institution in your radio market and that your listeners love you! If you're having a down time in your career, and brace yourself for this, we all have 'em at some point, and you find your ratings are less than great, LOOK OUT! You are ripe for the picking, my friend, for this radio nomad's personal buffet! Keep both eyes peeled directly on this new "hired gun in radioville."

What can you do as an air-talent to protect yourself?

Try and find out as much about this person as legally possible without a wiretap. Check them out as much as they're checking on you! Take a long hard look at where this person's been. Did he or she butcher the air-staff at his last PD post? How many notches are on their gun belt from their last PD job? How many air personalities have felt the sting of this person and been blown away? Is there a blood trail leading directly to you and your station?

How many radio towns and how many stations has this PD worked at in the last year or so? Call the stations and find out all you can about their record. Don't panic and scream. Well, scream if you want to. They say it can lower your blood pressure.

How else can you protect yourself from these hired radio gunslingers?

There are many ways, a few of which I just mentioned. The most important thing is not to panic and call home and ask your spouse to immediately refill your prescription to Xanax; there's plenty of time to do that later on! One thing you should be doing if you're not already doing so is to *become more visible* at the radio station. Your routine of four and out the door has to stop! If you have a tendency to disappear immediately following your air-shift, start hanging around more at the station, if for no other reason than to see what "No Mad" is up to. I almost lost one job because I simply wasn't around to state my side on several issues that one program director embellished as being the truth. You don't want to be a pain in the butt and roam the halls being a total nuisance, but it doesn't hurt to be visible, either!

Radio rule to remember: being seen keeps the story clean.

Another point to keep in mind: there's nothing quite like first-hand information. It beats the heck out of gossip and second- and even third-hand idle chit-chat every time. It's important to note that these nomads without gonads, a name I have tagged them with because it seems to fit, are usually gutless wonders and lack testosterone. They will never do anything directly to your face, but behind your back, whoa daddy! This next point probably will not sit well with you on-air folks, but has to be said! All set? Here it is! You will need to work even harder on your show! I know, I know, you're spending all day, every day, and half the night on your show now and that's good, but it's not good enough! Work twice as hard on every aspect of your on-air performance! Strive for better content, and more relevant and hipper bits geared to the key demographic your station is trying to reach. Schedule more entertaining and interesting guests, work on tighter production and most importantly, work on how to improve your own delivery!

As silly as it may sound, the key to working around these nomads without gonads is to smile more and be cordial with everyone possible at work. No one likes a smart-assed, egocentric air personality, especially someone who is making five or ten times as much money as most everyone else at the radio station! There will come a time in your life where you will find yourself in need of support, whether directly or indirectly from your co-workers. Make it a point to always try and leave a nice impression as you vacate the station and head home for the day.

Attention, morning drive talent: You are only at the radio station for about an hour or two during the actual business day, while the person in the front office is around for a full eight-hour day. Strive to have as many people as possible at the station thinking and saying nice things about you during your absence. Of course, it's impossible to walk away with one-hundred percent support and approval but you'll be amazed what a kind word or gesture can do for your reputation. Believe me, it will pay off when the new PD goes poking around, asking questions of other staff members about you when you're not around to speak for yourself. Remember, it's hard to build support and sympathy for a mean and arrogant person. Kindness towards your co-workers is not only the proper way to behave but will go a long way in helping you when the chips are down and you find yourself in need of support from the troops. You want your likeability rating as high as possible when a nomad without gonads is trying to build a case against you!

Most air-talent, especially morning drive people, do 95% of their preparation for the air, or show prep, as it is more commonly known, for their next day's show at home.[4] This is common practice and completely understandable when you take into consideration the early hours morning-show folk keep. Besides, there never seems to be an extra file drawer, desk and computer space available around the station for the AM-Drive crew! I suppose management's reasoning is, they blow out of here every morning at nine or ten anyway, why take up space with a desk for them that will be unoccupied most of the business day!

Here is one important way you can protect your interests as an air-talent at the radio station and defend yourself against the prickly barbs of the nomads without gonads. There's an old saying that is particularly true in radio, "Keep your friends close and your enemies closer." Invite the PD to lunch, but also make sure your manager comes along for the ride. Your GM will likely feel obligated to pick up the tab, because after-all, it's a business luncheon and most GMs have an expense account while most air-talent do not! The primary purpose of the luncheon with the new PD and your old GM is to chat about positive things you've done at the radio station. It's your showtime! Don't come off as a blow-hard, but in a friendly, folksy, non-boastful way, remind your old boss and the new guy about a few things that have made you a success at the station and in town, like how loyal you've been through thick and thin in the ratings war. Be very careful not to gloat or be too boastful.

The whole luncheon can blow up in your face if it looks like you're trying to show your own worth, even though that's exactly what you're doing! I realize this next word is hard for we radio guys, but try and drop...here comes that word, **subtle** hints as to your value to the operation and the station!

Remember, the word is "**subtle**." Be as cooperative and friendly with this son of a serpent as humanly possible. After lunch, go home and chop wood and with every whack, pretend it's this dude's thick skull, but at the luncheon don't let on this new PD is getting to you! Whatever you do, don't allow this person to build a case against you as being totally uncooperative. Remember at all times that your general manager, the third party at your luncheon, hired this new PD. It was for a reason, and as tough as it may be to hear, that reason could be to evaluate your over-all performance, including your attitude! Don't give out anything but a warm, fuzzy, positive one!

Here are a couple of other good reasons for having this luncheon. First, and most importantly, to show the new guy in front of your boss that you're a pretty valuable commodity to have around. Secondly, to prove your worth as your own promotions person! Over the years, I worked at radio stations that had superb promotions people; to name a few, Arnie Kuvent at GAN in Portland, ME, Dave Milberg at WLW Cincinnati, Nancy Noveline, Marilyn DeMartini, Barbara Crouse and Nina Hughes at ROR-Boston, Tim Johnston in Houston and Patty Palmer in West Palm Beach.[5] Keep in mind that, they are busy promoting the entire radio station. They can't always do for you! You need to stay focused on promoting your show and yourself!

Here's something else to keep in mind during your luncheon with the new PD and your GM. Your GM hired the new PD. As tempting as it may be, try to refrain from using the luncheon as an opportunity to deep-six the new guy. If you take that approach, you'll also be attacking your boss as well, by subliminally questioning his hiring practices and sound judgment. Don't give the head honcho a reason to test his firing techniques, too. You could wind-up the victim. Now, conversely, if your new program director takes advantage of the luncheon to attack you and your air performance, then all bets are off and he's fair game! I suggest going straight for his jugular, although, his testicles can be a sensitive area, too.

Remember, you have one very important strength: You were at the station first! People know and hopefully like you! It's the new guy who's on trial. Don't let him push you out or give you reason to quit. If you're blessed with good ratings, this weasel will have to come up with another angle to move you out. There are ways to remove someone from a position. Insubordination is one; being late for your air-shift, being uncooperative with the staff and so on are others. Don't let your guard down for a minute. When radio station managers are looking to explore a new direction and course of action for their station they do the following: (1) hire a new PD (2) hire new consultants (3) ask for more research on the marketplace or (4) all of the above. The new PD has to justify his position and his cash call. He has to find something wrong, even if it means you have to go! It will be a tough sell for this nomad without gonads to get your dismissal approved by your GM, but it can be done even if you have top ratings.

I experienced it a couple of times during my own radio career and both times I was at the top of my game, ratings-wise and otherwise. Out of nowhere I was smacked upside my head with medical woes, which resulted in emergency surgery. The first time was in Boston in November 1995. I underwent emergency lung surgery. My second out-of-the-blue medical surprise was a triple bypass in Houston in 2005. In both cases, my contract wasn't renewed. Don't ever kid yourself into believing you can't be fired when you're out on sick leave. As ugly as it sounds, there are always ways to get rid of someone. Management will bury any health issue and give your reason for departure a new spin, like a format change. Believe me, if they want to get rid of you, they will find a way around any possible legal ramifications. It happened to me, and not to be the voice of doom, but it could also happen to you! In the meantime, try and be patient with your new set of circumstances, and don't become overly paranoid. Patience is not a virtue I was blessed with, but try and bide your time. Don't give the nomad reason to build a case against you. Do as he says, within reason of course. Hopefully, in time, your GM will see through the nomad's veneer and one fine morning when you arrive at the station, you'll read the memo that says it all, mister nomad without gonads has left the building for good!

In 1978, I was operations manager at WCSH in Portland, ME. The station had undergone a few distinctively different format changes. From its earliest years as one of NBC's original affiliates to music of your life, followed by all-news as a subscriber to NBC Radio's creative but short-lived News and Information Service (NIS). Next, I segued WCSH to an Adult Contemporary (AC) format.

Jon Lund had come to town as an outside consultant to evaluate the station and what changes we needed to make to be more competitive in the marketplace as an AC radio station. WCSH had been dead last in the ratings, but with the switch to AC, music personality had moved up to #3 in key demographics in just six months. I was ecstatic. Management felt differently. They wanted to be #1. As if that wasn't my long-term goal as well! Management, yours truly included, met for dinner with Lund to hear his report. Other than a few minor points, Jon said, he couldn't find anything wrong with the air sound or the air-talent. I wanted to hug him. On the other hand, my boss was inclined to slug him. He wanted the consultant to find something radically wrong with the station. In his mind, that why he was paying him. Not only was it classy on Lund's part, but he saved my bacon at the station. As air-talent, keep an open mind when it comes to dealing with PDs, management and consultants. Not all of them are mean-spirited and bad people. Just like you, they have a job to do.

Not all PDs are from the planet Uranus, but a few might be from Mars.

Many PDs have the charisma of a traffic light. They recognize two commands, stop and go! They are usually good technicians and can follow a game plan fairly well, for example: "Okay, we'll play nine songs an hour, stop for news on the hour and half-hour with traffic on the 3's, blah, blah, yeah, we'll add eighteen minutes of commercials to the hour, yeah, that'll work!" They practically salivate over how ingenious they feel about their own mundane game plans and can't wait to hear it put into action the very next morning in drive time. Only one problem: these pencil-pushing computer whiz kids have given no thought to where the show host will place show bits and have any time at all for "personality" that management insists they project! These PDs have no regard to the time restraints placed on the talent!

One program director had me so tight for time in AM-Drive that I couldn't sneeze without falling behind in the format. Each hour was jammed with nine songs, each averaging 3:30 minutes, with 21 minutes of commercials, news, traffic and weather. I didn't have time to say my own name! I kid you not! To give you an idea of how he conducted business, here are the instructions he left on my answering phone regarding the new format: "Now have fun tomorrow morning, do some really fun and relevant bits, take lots of upbeat and interesting phone calls and above all...let me hear that warm-wonderful Joe Martelle we all love so well!" Yeah, sure! It's no wonder many of us in the talent pool wind up drooling and talking to ourselves at a very young age! Drooling is good, though, it lets the venom out!

During my many years on the air, I worked for about twenty different program directors. Out of that number, I would only give half high marks. Like so many people you come in contact with in life, I encountered both good and not so good! In all honesty, I can only recall a few who were outstanding PDs. Names are not necessary, since it is not my intent to embarrass those who made the bottom of my list. Time, along with Mother Nature's aging process, has a way of changing folks and here's hoping some of the grumpy, mean-spirited ones have mellowed and changed over the years for the better!

As a former PD and Operations Manager myself, I know only too well the difficulties of the job.[6] A few PDs I worked for were really dedicated individuals. They loved their work and did their best when it came to handling air-talent. However, many PDs love the feeling of power. In many instances, their only mission seemed to be to make life as miserable as possible for those who worked for them. My advice: run away quickly from power-crazed PDs, or at least as soon as you find a new job! If you don't, I'm afraid you will find yourself in a daily battle and power struggle with them. It is impossible for these narrow-minded PDs to see the forest for the trees. They are too busy playing PD, instead of performing their duties as one and being a true leader! Trying to reason with these out-of-control PDs will either mean constant visits to the GM's office for you, or worse yet, a weekly visit with your psychologist. Trying to reason, let alone communicate your thoughts and ideas and what you truly feel is in the station's and your best interest, will be impossible and before long will have you thinking you're off your rocker!

Before taking off on your PD and dumping all over the guy or gal for not knowing what they are doing, take a moment to look at their set of circumstances. Try and appreciate what they are up against and cut them some slack. Perhaps they have been placed in a difficult situation and are not allowed to do much of anything, let alone lead. Many station managers are such control nuts they give little if any authority to their PDs, who wind up being little more than glorified babysitters for temperamental air-talent. Yes, I include myself in that description. As talent, take time to think of ways you can work with your PD and how you can help them carry out the goal of the radio station, which should always be to obtain top-ratings and be a winner! Trust me, winning is a lot more fun than losing for everyone.

"A real radio pro knows you learn a lot about 'character' when you have to show up every morning at 5:30!"

Some say radio talent are a breed unto themselves, and they're probably right. You can't go on the air every day in a broom closet-sized studio talking into a mic thinking people are going to hang on your every word and not be deemed a little "strange." Personally, I prefer the words "unique and special"! Every facet of radio has, shall we say, "original" types of personalities. None are more "original" than radio engineers. For the most part, they're brilliant people who are actually quite nice, but definitely a breed unto themselves. Radio station program directors are another special breed of animal.

WLW and my experience in dealing with a new PD, who may have been from Uranus.

In 1970 I left my home turf in Portland, Maine, and set out for big-time radio in Cincinnati, Ohio. I was offered and accepted the all-night show at one of America's greatest radio stations, WLW.

Like many others, I probably would have worked at the station without a salary. It was a heritage radio station with a legendary history and I was proud to be a part of it, but it also meant something personal to me. I remembered being a little kid, when my dad, who worked hard all his life and didn't have lots of extra money floating around, somehow managed to come up with ten shares in Avco stock. In 1945, the Aviation Corporation bought WLW from the station's founder, **Powell Crosley, Jr.** In 1947 the name was changed to Avco. Every year, when Dad would get his annual prospectus on the company, I'd grab it and spend hours looking at the pictures in the broadcast division and dream of being on WLW Radio one day. Twenty years later my dream came true. I was privileged to be on the "Nation's Station," as it was known.

As nervous as I was with half the nation listening, and shaking like a leaf the first time I cracked open the mic and did the top-of-the-hour station ID, thoughts of my dad checking out his ten shares of Avco stock so many years earlier made me smile! As host of the all-night show, from midnight until 6am, I had a ball. My shift was six hours, six nights a week, on a great radio station playing the pop hit songs of the day, mixed with oldies. As a bonus, taking calls and chatting with the night-owls was a hoot! The Big-700 covered 37 states, parts of Canada, and even reached way down to the deep blue sea of the Caribbean. One of my biggest thrills was having my dad listen while nice and comfy in his bed many miles away in Portland, Maine. Quite often Mom would tell me how proud he was to hear his son on "his" station.

I loved doing the all-night show on WLW and in the relatively short period of time of about six months, I built an extremely loyal following. My weekly mail numbered in the hundreds. Ego aside, I'm proud to say I answered every letter. To my way of thinking, if a listener took time to write and post it, then they deserved a reply! In the 1970s, before the advent of e-mail, snail mail was about it.

We began a trivia club, the *WLW Night Owls*. All-night radio is a very special time to be on the air. It was fun playing trivia and being host to millions who tuned in to the 50,000-watt clear-channel voice.[7]

Reaching out to college kids up cramming for exams, all-night shift workers, truck drivers and just plain old insomniacs made for one heck of an eclectic and active audience. In about a year, things changed dramatically at WLW and not for the better. **Clif Hunter**, one of the best program directors I ever worked for, left and moved further west to become manager of the Avco Station in San Francisco.

I enjoyed working for Clif and remember asking him one day for input on my show. His reply surprised me. "Joe, when I hire people it's because I like what I hear in them. Keep doing what you're doing." Talk about a confidence builder for a twenty-nine-year-old radio guy from Maine! I floated out of his office. Clif Hunter also said something else I've never forgotten. "At this level," he said, obviously referring to working in a top-25 market and on a 50,000-watt station, "I find talent knows what they're doing. I try to stay out of their way. My job is to make sure they have the necessary tools to work with and let 'em go!" Now you have some idea why we loved working for the man.

When Clif Hunter left WLW, we were happy for his continued success, but little did we realize that his replacement would be the second coming of Attila the Hun. It didn't take more than a few days of having the new PD in house that the writing began to take place on the radio station wall!

Why does it seem so often in life a really good thing is replaced by something, or someone, not as good? Such was the case for our new program director. My contract was coming up for renewal and the new PD began turning the screws tighter and tighter. He simply didn't dig me or my act even though I had been quite successful. Hey, sometimes it happens in radio. It's the tough part of the game that can be hard to handle. I definitely picked up the new guy's vibes and they weren't calling me to dinner to sign a new deal. No way, Jose. The new PD wanted a totally different approach on his radio station every night at midnight and like it or not, it was his call to make.

WLW's new Program Director didn't appear to like anything that I brought to the show, even though we were doing very well in the ratings and with advertisers.[8] It wasn't radio paranoia either, which I have to admit I've been known to suffer from on occasion. No, it's not radio paranoia, when a two-page, single-spaced critique begins with this opening salvo, "The following are the most significant examples of non-professionalism that I have ever heard. This is compounded by the fact that it was on the air at WLW Radio being broadcast to half the nation! Under no circumstances will this sort of sound be permitted on the air at WLW." This next part is what really grabbed my attention: "In view of your current contract situation I would suggest immediate attention to the following improvements." Ouch! He wrote that almost forty years ago and to this day it still stings!

My loyal following and great numbers didn't matter to the new PD. He didn't like the way I did the show, period! The few times we actually spoke (he preferred to write memos), we clashed more than Bill O'Reilly and Congressman Barney Frank I admit I was probably oversensitive to his brutal critique, but he was overbearing and straight from the mindset so many PDs have - his way or the highway. **Bob Martin** was on the air before me from 7 to midnight, and he advised me not to let the new PD drive me out. "Bide your time," were his words. "He'll be gone once Charlie gets wind of what's going on."[9]

I have to mention right here that in the mysterious Holy Grail known as the Program Director's Handbook, it must be written that to inherit someone else's air staff is tantamount to failure. Many PDs don't like to work with an air-staff that has been put in place by another PD. I think it has something to do with the size of one's manly jewels or something. It never really made sense to me.

Later in my career, after a little seasoning from a few more bumps and bruises, it became quite clear to me that WLW's PD meant nothing personal in his scathing critique of my air work. In his own mind, he was simply taking care of business. It's the way he and so many other radio people handle things. They cling to one thought: "It's nothing personal, it's just business." My question is, how can you separate the two? Any type of personal criticism of one's work is going to slice through to the heart. Simply saying, "You understand, this is nothing personal, just business," is to my way of thinking a way for those in charge to make themselves feel better about their own inept management. When you are being harshly critiqued and ripped apart for what you truly believe is best for the show, the station, and most importantly, your own air style, it hurts! There is a world of difference between trying to show an air-talent a different way of doing things and brutally destroying their ego by basically saying their entire approach to radio and their show is blatantly wrong!

As an example, **Howard Stern** and **Ryan Seacrest** take completely different approaches to their shows. Each has a totally unique and different air style, but it doesn't mean one approach is wrong or better than the other. They are just different. A good radio program director would never tamper with or try to change a successful air-talent's style, even if that talent's particular style doesn't suit the PD's personal taste. It's like telling a .400 Major League hitter to change his batting stance at the plate! What? A unique air presentation is what makes a talent stand out above the rest of the pack. It's unfortunate, but many PDs prefer to have a cookie-cutter-type personality on the air rather than someone who has a unique and special style.

I didn't want to leave WLW and blow a great opportunity. Being on the air at one of America's premier radio stations is what I always dreamed about. It didn't get much better than *The Nation's Station* --- **WLW Cincinnati.** However, after the new PD moved in, it didn't take long before I began thinking long and hard about moving back to Maine. The pressure of working all night was getting to me and my family and even though I loved working at the station, I had been wrestling with the idea of leaving for a while. As so often is the case in life, sometimes difficult decisions are made for us. Mine was helped by receiving the scathing critique about my air work. It made such an indelible impact on me that to this day I still have it in my possession. Later in my radio career, when I dabbled in radio programming and management for a few years, I'd occasionally dig it out and re-read it - sort of a quickie refresher course in how to really screw-up decent air-talent. If you're interested in a copy to learn how not to handle talent, send me a SASE and I'll drop one in the mail to you.

In no time flat, the new PD proved to be one of the most difficult folks I've ever tried to work for and with. I won't mention his name for a couple of reasons. For one, it was almost forty years ago and, thanks be to the Good Lord, people do change. I hope he has. Secondly, in writing this book, I decided early on to try and showcase only the nice folks who I met and had the privilege of working with in radio.

No two PDs hear the same thing

Another thing that has always blown me away about program people: seldom if ever do two PDs hear exactly the same thing. It is truly amazing how two people can listen to the same person and walk away with totally different opinions. The new PD's predecessor seemed to think I was taking care of business and liked my sound. Besides, the all-night show was sold out, with many national clients and a ton of loyal Ohio-based sponsors like Marathon Oil and Cassano Pizza King, based in Dayton. WLW was top-rated. I made sales calls during the daylight hours when I probably should have been sleeping, but I cared about making our all-night show a success and did everything I could to make it so, including client calls and making personal appearances. Why he and other PDs felt the need to mess with success is a mystery known only to the PD Gods. Why is it so difficult for a new PD to go along with the flow, at least until he or she gets to know the air-talent?

Air-talent, don't let PDs or anyone mess with your mind.

Don't allow any person's opinion to screw you up and play games with your mind. You need to be you on the radio. You have to be comfortable with who you are and what you sound like. Yes, scathing criticism can hurt and cut deeply, but you always need to consider the source and move on! I am so grateful I didn't allow one person's opinion to effectively change my air style.[10] You see, after leaving Cincinnati my best years on the air were ahead of me in Boston morning drive for nearly 20 years, and in Houston and South Florida, complete with my own unique style!

A wake-up call to PDs: change for the sake of change isn't always good.

To this day, it puzzles me how many program directors upon assuming their post at a new station feel they need to make changes. How stupid to blow up a winning formula, because pride and ego makes them want to do it *their* way. Unfortunately, putting one's stamp of approval on someone else's format isn't usually the norm in radio. Many PDs feel they need their own air staff to accomplish the mission! In many cases, when the new PD inherits someone else's air-staff, the innocent talent is deemed the enemy! I truly believe one huge misunderstanding is that many PDs think their newly inherited air-staff can only be loyal to the former PD and will never be loyal to them or be on their team. It may sound silly and stupid, but I've seen it happen! I suppose when a PD brings in their own air staff it is a move to support their own insecurities and bolster their own egos. They must believe that by surrounding themselves with hand-picked talent they can control their own paranoia!

Program Directors, don't always be quick to pull the trigger and make wholesale changes.

In fact, change for the sake of change can ruin a station, especially the all-important morale of the air staff. It's almost like some of these programming dudes picture themselves as gunslingers who are just dying to get another notch on their belts. PDs need and should take time to know their air-staff. Find out what each personality is all about and what makes them tick before making wholesale changes. Prejudging a person and their performance is wrong. One of the biggest mistakes PDs seem to make is not taking time to know the individual before pulling the trigger. In my case at WLW, the new PD came on board like a gunslinger. It didn't take long to realize I had a big bullseye painted right in the middle of my forehead, and believe me, I wasn't the only one in his sights. He made working at the radio station incredibly unpleasant.

Some insight for programming minds on the make-up and thinking of most air-talent.

If you find yourself in a position as the new PD on the block, go easy. Don't force senior air-staff members of your newly inherited team to take advantage of their working relationship with the GM. The scenario is all too familiar. The new PD comes on board and immediately places his or her thumb directly on top of the station's top-rated morning talent! Trust me on this one; as a former morning guy, let me tell you straight out that that ain't cool. It's definitely not the way to win friends and influence people, at least NOT in radio! If you create a situation like this, you can bet the mortgage that before the morning show host's spittle dries on the mic and the final break on their show is over, he or she will be flying down the hall to get the GM's ear. Believe me, if animosity towards the new PD is so acute that the GM decides someone has to go, well, I'll give you another sure bet. It won't be the station's top-paid and top-rated morning talent that will be heading out the door and down that long, lonesome highway. So, you PDs, be cool and think twice before making a really dumb move like alienating the talent.

PDs, always try the gentle touch, first.

Have you ever tried aggressive handling of a pit bull? It doesn't work. Ask Cesar Millan, the expert dog trainer. He'll tell you pit bulls are bred to fight back when handled in an aggressive manner. Not unlike a pit bull, some air-talent react to harsh treatment in the same way. You push them, they'll bite back. You'll accomplish more and get better results with kindness than with rough and aggressive handling.

The proper way for a new PD to handle air-talent.

A good solid working relationship in any field needs to be based on trust and loyalty. Radio station talent and management are not exempt from this belief and need to be on the same page. Sometimes, and I've seen it happen, an air personality who has a good working relationship with one PD, for whatever reason, can't seem to make the transition to the new person. It can and does happen. There are some relatively easy ways to avoid this from happening. **First and foremost,** if both parties could picture themselves in the other person's shoes for just a few seconds that in itself would help. Secondly, try humming or singing a few bars of Aretha Franklin's hit song, "R-E-S-P-E-C-T." Showing each other *just a little respect* goes a long way in kicking off a solid working relationship. Who knows, it may even lead to a friendship!

Joe Kelly was one of several managers I worked for at WROR - Boston. Joe would often say, "Relax, radio ain't brain surgery. It's made up of a bunch of talented people that need to learn to work together for the common good and ultimate success of the station. The secret is to be nice to each other. Treat the other guy with a little respect and watch how far it will go!" Lack of communication runs rampant in radio, a business that sells communication![11] Do your best to communicate effectively. Say what's on your mind and try not to deal from the shadows. Be upfront with co-workers, but as Joe Kelly said, do so in a respectful and polite manner.

Tip to PDs: it doesn't hurt to be nice!

It doesn't cost any more or take more time to be nice than it does being a hard-ass! Let's be clear on one important point: not everyone is going to get along with and love each other. There are times, given the nature of radio, loaded to the gills with strong-willed personalities, that inevitably two people will clash. When this happens, not even a room full of Dr. Lauras and Dr. Drews will ever get them to see eye-to-eye, let alone work together in perfect harmony! Many battles of the words can often be avoided if everyone would simply treat each other with a little civility and respect.

In the early 1990s, **Amy Doyle** was a member of my morning drive team at MIX 98.5 Boston, today WBZ-FM). At one point in her radio career, Amy was a radio programmer herself. She says, "Respect for everyone in the entertainment field is so important, no matter what their position, because sooner or later your paths will cross again." Today, Amy Doyle is VP of talent at MTV.

A direct message to Program Directors of America: *WAKE UP*! Get to know your air-staff.

Before you grab the talent and sit them down for an air-check session, why not take some time to get to know them? Try an old-fashioned bull session. Take time to know the cash cows at your station, the all-important air-staff. Treat them as individuals, not as a herd. Talk about everything, but nothing in particular. Radio talent loves free food. Feed 'em! After their show, take your morning-team out to breakfast. You may be pleasantly surprised what you'll learn. Get to know them on a personal level, so you know how they think, what their hot buttons are, what excites and interests them. Find out what they are passionate about, and why they love being on the radio. It will help you understand why they do the things they do on the air, so the next time you hear them do a bit on the radio, you won't be so quick to criticize and will know why they took the time to do it in the first place. The investment in your time with talent will pay off in huge dividends for you as the program director and also for the radio station. It'll go a lot further in developing an open dialogue and working relationship with them than critiquing and ripping their show to pieces your second or third day in-house.

This I can promise you, PDs: critiquing before seeking and knowing your air staff will lead you in one direction, and that's the furthest point away from having a decent working relationship with them! You can bank on it! Oh, they'll go through the motions with you during your air-check session, and *yes sir* or *yes ma'am* you to death, but the next time they hit the air, you better have the little purple pill handy, because I can almost guarantee you they'll be right back doing it their way on the radio and driving you one step closer to the Betty Ford Center.

Talent will respond to praise.

If you are the new PD at a station, give air-talent a chance before you jump all over them and form any opinions about the quality of their performance. The air-staff you recently inherited will work just as hard for you, if you treat them fairly and show them a little respect and kindness. Try to keep in mind, *respect and loyalty is love on a two-way street.* Give it out and you'll get it right back. It also wouldn't hurt to occasionally show them a little appreciation and thanks for what they bring to the table every day on their show. Even the best salary will never fully compensate for a sincere bit of praise. So after their show, when you see them in the hall, give 'em a big *atta boy* or *atta girl* for putting on a good show. Give it a shot and watch how it will work wonders for their confidence levels. You will help build station morale while putting a positive spin on your own reputation. The good word about your positive reinforcement will spread to the rest of the staff faster than a Kansas prairie fire. A sincere word of praise to talent can be worth more than all the bonus money in the world!

One other point for you, PDs: the next time you listen to your morning show and you hear them being a little too chatty and carrying on a little longer than you'd like, stop listening as a PD. Be a P1 listener for a few minutes and *really listen* to what they're putting out over the air.[12] You may be pleasantly surprised at what you hear and actually like what they're saying and doing!

Nobody became ill from receiving well-deserved praise.

These next few paragraphs are most important reading for program directors, so please take heed as to what I'm about to say. You may even want to **highlight this page** and show it to your station manager. That's how important I believe these comments are for everyone in a managerial position. Regardless of what you may have read somewhere in the PD Handbook, praise is not a word to fear, particularly when it comes to lavishing it on your air-talent! Somehow, somewhere, PDs and upper management have decided that it's not cool to give genuine praise or pass along compliments to talent! It has to be a throwback to archaic thinking that "If the help is praised, they'll ask for a raise." Wrong! Of course, cash is always needed, but one of the greatest gifts you can give anyone, especially a temperamental, sentimental, emotional air-personality, is a little sincere, honest-to-goodness praise.

Please allow me to clue in management, including program directors, that to the best of my knowledge, nobody ever became ill or passed away from receiving too much well-deserved, sincere praise. The next time you're ready to heap a critique on your talent, why not try passing along a few thoughtful words of encouragement and praise. You may be surprised at the positive results. As the saying goes, you reap what you sow.

Another pointer for you PDs on how to get along with your new air staff.

I know this will be a bitter pill for some of you program people to swallow, but here goes: try really hard not to disrupt the air-talent's comfortable on-air routine, especially if it's successful. Even if you think their show isn't hip enough for the station try extra-hard not to mess with success.

A lesson to all PDs on how NOT to get along with your new air-staff!

The following is an example of how the new PD should *not* act toward his or her air-staff. Please keep in mind this is merely a tongue-in-cheek example, but I have actually seen some program directors act in this incredibly callous and brainless way. Follow these suggestions as the new PD and you will surely create enough waves to sink any possible working relationships with your new air staff.

This lame-brained example is guaranteed to lead to problems between you and your air-staff. So, if you want problems, do the following!

Begin by telling your assistant to hold ALL your calls, unless it's an emergency. Next, head into your office and close the door. It helps to have a concerned look on your face, so when your curious air-staff members confront you, your assistant can honestly reply, "I'm not sure what's up, but, man, does he look upset! I wouldn't bug him (or her) right now!" Next, contact a morning show host you worked with in another market. You know the routine, just in case an opening should suddenly pop up here at your new station home. Radio folks across the country love to network and check in with each other all the time. In no time at all, your newly-acquired air staff will hear the word and think you've put out feelers to replace all of them. At least that's what the evil seed you planted will accomplish.

There are no secrets in a radio station. Let me, rephrase that, there are **NO SECRETS IN RADIO.** You can make a call to your favorite morning guy working in another city at ten o'clock in the morning, and I absolutely guarantee you before the noon lunch bell rings your present morning guy or gal will know about it. Someone, somewhere, will find out what you're up to and spill the milk! Trust me! The message will come full circle that you've been talking to your former morning talent. It will do all kinds of crazy things to your present morning talent. Of course, the very first thing that Mr. or Ms. Paranoia will assume is that they are being replaced.

PDs take note:

Air-talent has built-in radar on this kind of stuff, so don't think for a minute you're getting away with something, because you're not! In radio, it seems everyone knows everyone else, or at least someone who knows someone else. I'm sure it is also true in other professions, but in radio circles it's a given. There are no secrets.

How to raise the paranoia bar even higher.

Here's something else you PDs can do to try and raise the paranoia bar even higher with your air-staff: If your office has one of those ceiling-to-floor windows so staff members can peer in while waiting for you to summon them in, stay on the phone for long periods of time. Make them wait, worry and wonder. It also helps if you have a stern look of worry and concern. That will really get your air-talent's paranoia machine revved up and working in overdrive.

Now, if you really want to tick 'em off try this little technique. While they're gawking at you through that window, waiting ever so patiently for you to acknowledge their presence, shoot them a mean look and then quickly spin around in your chair, and turn your back on them. Man, they will be working overtime trying to figure out who you're on the phone with and what they did to tick you off! Can't you just hear them now: "Hey, it must have been someone important on the phone. He was on with this person forever!! I know it's about me, because, when he noticed me out in the hall, he spun around in his chair and wouldn't look me in the eye. I'm outta here, I just know it!"

Yup, want to start problems and dissension amongst the troops, that's a sure way to do it. Oh, one more point: If the talent makes eye contact with you and smiles, as if pleading, "You love me, don't you?" Never, ever return their smile! It drives them nuts to think that you as their PD may be upset and displeased with them for whatever reason. It's another way to really crank up talent's paranoia. This type of bad behavior in a PD is a fairly good indicator that something big is coming down! Talk about sending negative vibes to the air staff! In their minds it most likely means one or more is about to receive their walking papers and get canned. Trust me, the examples I've given are surefire ways to destroy potential relationships between you, as the new PD, and the already fragile egos of your newly acquired air staff. If you're stupid enough to try it, go ahead, give it a shot!

Program Directors, Friend or Foe? • 255

Lesson to air-talent in how NOT to communicate and get along with your new PD.

Enough on the actions of the Program Director and HOW NOT to interact with air-talent. Now, let's focus on a good path for you as air-talent to mosey on down if you really want to torpedo any potential working relationship between you and your new PD. Whenever the PD makes a suggestion about some of the content on your show, or perhaps urges you to try something new, here's how to respond. Without taking a breath or missing a beat, react this way in a surly tone, "Hey, we've always done it this way and it's worked fine, Okay? I see absolutely NO reason to change it." Now, if you really want to come off as a no-nonsense kind of talent who believes in putting their foot down with management just to let 'em know who is really in charge, you may even want to take a little more caustic approach with the new PD. So, try this approach: "Hey, pinhead, when I want your input and advice, I'll stop by your office and ask for it. In the meantime, we're doing fine, so butt out."

Now, air-talent can soften their words and verbal assault with this technique:

"We really appreciate your input and stop by the studio anytime, okay? Thanks so much for your time and take care, man."

One thing to definitely keep in mind, whichever approach you decide to take in *conversing* with your new PD, it always seems to help if you speak with sort of a defiant edge to your voice and in a surly manner. You know, cop an attitude. It will serve to make more of a lasting impression on the PD. One thing I can almost guarantee, he or she will remember *it* and *you* for a very, very long time!

Of course, both scenarios are mere examples of how NOT to behave. As ludicrous as they may sound, they are only meant to stress a point that this totally off-the-wall behavior is commonplace in radio. As sad as it may seem, what you just read is not out of the ordinary. In fact, it is the norm for commonly expressed dialog and bad behavior between some program directors, air-talent and even station managers. Is it any wonder that many radio stations wind up defeating themselves from within and eventually take a nosedive in both ratings and revenue?

More inside scoop for PDs about air-talent.

No air-talent wants to purposely torpedo their radio station, so the next time you hear something on a program that you think isn't quite up to the standards of the station and believe that's what's happening, clear your mind! Most air-talent I know would NEVER purposely do something on their show that they didn't think fit what the station and format is all about! Period, end of case. No talent wants to see the station's ratings go down the tubes for many reasons, not the least of which is personal pride and their own success.

Let me clue you in on a little more inside stuff and allow me to focus on the material side of radio for just a moment. No talent wants to see the station's ratings falter because of financial considerations. Usually, bonus structures are predicated on having decent ratings. It's fairly elementary: no numbers, no money! Not every air-talent looks only at the financial remuneration as a primary reason for being on the radio. Some do, most don't! However, it goes without saying, making a living has to be taken into account, but in many cases it's not the most important thing, believe me.

Money isn't always the sole motivating factor when it comes to real on-air radio pros.

Real radio pros love what they do and in most cases do it for a lot less than what they're worth.

Money isn't everything - being happy, having fun and being appreciated for what one brings to the mic every day rank right up at the top of the list, or at least for my money they do. My Boston radio partner Andy Moes would often tell me, "Joey, you scare me! You'll go across the street for a pat on the butt, rather than for more money." It may not be the wisest or most prudent way of conducting business, but to me being happy is more important than all the money Chase-Manhattan has to offer. Here's an example of what I'm talking about and putting my money where my mouth is:

In 1970, while hosting the all-night show on WLW-the 50,000-watt blowtorch of Mid-America, my weekly salary was $250. It wasn't poverty level, at least not back then, but I was light years away from being one of the best-paid radio guys in the country. The important thing to know is it didn't matter to me. Oh, to be sure, it bothered my wife that I wasn't taking home more money and that's the difficult thing about supporting a family and trying to live one's dream. There's a world of difference between making a living and doing what you love to do. Sometimes, a price tag just doesn't apply.

Like so many other personalities who absolutely love being on the radio, I probably would have taken the air shift at WLW for even less cash! To me, it was the ultimate position, my dream come true. My illustrious predecessors on the station included such notables as Fats Waller at the piano, sportscaster Red Barber, singers Andy Williams, Doris Day, the Clooney Sisters, Rosemary and Betty, and the Mills Brothers. Future *Twilight Zone* creator Rod Serling worked as a writer at WLW and comedians Red Skelton and Abbott and Costello broadcast some of their shows from the station. The long-running soap opera *Ma Perkins* originated in the studios of WLW. As Dick Perry points out in his book, *Not Just a Sound-The Story of WLW*, the station regularly sent talent scouts to New York to see if any of Manhattan's offerings were good enough for Cincinnati. It wasn't just a station slogan that

WLW proudly called itself "The Cradle of Stars." It was a fact!

I was honored to be behind the mic at this heritage radio station which had such a wide coverage area at night, reaching out to 37 states and Canada. At age twenty-nine, I was in fact my own network! It was a blast! On the other hand, I'm sure John Murphy, the President of Avco Broadcasting, along with the other powers-that-be, sensed this about talent.[13] They knew we loved being on the air at such a legendary station and I'm sure they loved how much money they were saving. Who could blame them? It was part of their job and responsibility to keep an eye on the bottom line, including saving a few bucks on salaries. I look at it this way: management was happy and so was I.

As an air-talent, you know you're in trouble when a program director begins telling you, as talent, what to say and how to say it! When talent fights back and balks at the idea, they are usually tagged with the bad rap of being *unmanageable*. That's simply not fair! When you're on the air, you and you alone are the quarterback! You can't have anyone second guessing your gut instincts as to what sounds right on *your* show; not the PD, GM, consultants, or anybody else! Your own unique and individual air style is one area where you must stick to your guns and not waver.[14] Read more on how to develop your own air style in Chapter Two.

Attention PDs: Hot-lining air-talent in the middle of their show is a definite NO, NO!

Most PDs and GMs, at least those with even a smidgen of common sense and decency, would never hot-line air-talent in the middle of their show.[15] This is an out and out NO NO! However, it can and does happen, and yes, much to my own personal displeasure, it happened to your friendly author. In fact, I can still taste the bile in my throat from the foul taste it created!! Not pleasant! If your PD or GM is consistently hot-lining you in the middle of your show, you need to put an end to that sort of bad behavior right away! Don't go off the deep end screaming at your boss and shouting profanities to "Leave me the ___ alone and don't ever blankety-blank do that again!" That sort of emotional display could definitely be deemed insubordination. If your bosses are looking for a reason to get rid of you, my friend, you have handed them your dismissal on a silver platter. Instead, respectfully request a meeting with your PD, GM or whoever is in charge to calmly discuss why their phone calls are so distracting and unnerving. Explain how hot-lining you in the middle of your show throws you off and takes you completely out your game.[16]

It also helps to explain that even a seemingly innocent suggestion creates a negative feeling. A good rule for all managers to follow is: If the suggestion is so innocuous in the first place, it can wait until the show is over. As talent, you also need to reinforce to the powers-that-be that you were hired for your sound judgment and nothing you ever say or do on the air will ever place the station license in jeopardy. Remind them that nothing is so serious that it can't wait until the end of your show to discuss. Also mention that second guessing your game-plan while it's in motion is another definite no-no!

When you're on the air you are the "acting" PD!

Over the years, I found that using sports analogies usually hits a homer with the guys in charge. Here's one I've used to successfully make a point. Former Denver Broncos quarterback **John Elway** was quoted as saying, "I don't care what the game plan is, when I walk up to the line of scrimmage and see something out of whack, the game plan is out the window and I'm about to ad-lib and call an audible." It's the same way in radio. No two shows are exactly the same, and that's the beauty of live radio. You never know what's coming your way in a phone call, a late arriving guest, a technical snafu, and so on. There will be many times when you, as the QB, will have to make an adjustment, make a call or implement a last-minute change. You don't have time to make a call to the PD or run it by a committee of radio experts. This is particularly true in morning drive with all the added elements of news, traffic, features, show bits, commercials, and so on.[17] You don't have time to waste thinking about how to handle a late-breaking problem on the show, whatever it may be! You need to call an audible! As stated elsewhere in this book, the only common denominator in radio and this applies to you and your show is *change!* You need to be flexible enough to go with the flow and, like NFL great John Elway, be able to call an audible when necessary.

A good PD will accept that you are the on-air quarterback of the show and will not flip out because you made an adjustment in the format, including, heaven forbid, "dropping" a song because an interesting guest went a little long. You need to make it clear to those in charge you are not on the air to deep-six your own radio show, let alone the station. Hopefully, they'll hear you!

LISTEN UP, AIR-TALENT!

This does not mean that you may abuse the power given to you as the QB of your show. Wanton dropping of songs if you have a fixed number to play each hour, or format violations, are not accepted. Running the show the way you are most comfortable doing it also does not mean you are not open for input or suggestions from your PD and management. Personally speaking, and in all honesty, listening to input from management was always a problem for me during my own radio career. I was from the school that I knew what was best for my program. **Don't follow my lead!** Always be open for input on how to improve on what you already do so well. It will make things a lot easier for you and others you work with. It will also save you tons of money on Pepcid and other antacids.

FOLLOW THE FORMAT, AND WHEN TALENT HAS A RIGHT TO SPEAK UP.

If you want live a happy radio life and make your bosses happy, you must follow the parameters of your station format. At the same time, as the on-air gal or guy in charge, you need to be you while on the radio. Anything less and it's a no-win situation for everyone. I can't emphasize enough the importance of being you and those in charge allowing you to be you on the radio!

When the big Arbitron ratings report card comes out, for better or worse, the numbers are yours to live or die by![18] Whether it's an "up" or "down" book, if you can honestly look back over the last few months of your shows and know you did your best to cover all the bases, then you have nothing to be ashamed about. You know in your heart you gave every minute of *every show* your all and did your best! On the other hand, if you feel your style or delivery was tampered with, or your PD shut you up way too much, or made a popular show bit disappear and you didn't question his or her moves, then in my opinion you have no one to blame for low ratings but yourself. Don't ever be afraid to challenge your PD in a respectful manner when it comes to what you feel is right for you on your show. Better to fight and complain now then after the fact, when a bad ratings book comes out and it's too late and the blame game begins with fingers pointed directly at you!

Radio Pro asked some of America's top programmers what they wish all air-talent, both radio newbies and seasoned pros alike, would keep in mind when dealing with their PDs.

Harry Nelson has spent many years as a program director in several radio markets, including Boston and Portland, Maine. During my on-air days in Boston, Harry was my PD on three separate occasions. Here's how he feels about the often thankless job of a radio program director: "Being PD today is not easy and certainly is not as easy as it used to be. Today's program director now implements a plan that is developed by a committee of consultants, research strategists, operations managers, GMs, and VPs of programming. The PDs of the 1960s and '70s were in total charge of their stations and implemented their vision, totally." Nelson, a one-time boss jock on WRKO-Boston during its highly successful Top-40 days and also on top-rocker of its day, KFRC- San Francisco, goes on to say, "You need to understand that most PDs are doing the very best for you as air-talent that they can, given these circumstances. Also, keep in mind that most programmers are responsible for two and even three or more stations in some markets. This is very stressful!" Harry Nelson concludes by putting out a plea to all air-talent: "Do everything you can to be positive and to help your PD accomplish his goals and those of the station." In 2008, Harry took a leave of absence from radio to start his own record label, Ride, with his partner

Steve Azar. In Harry's words, "I am doing great. The record label is starting to do well. Let's say a good beginning."

Barbara Bridges is the PD of Nashville's #1 rated radio station, MIX 92.9-WJXA. She says, "I wish all air-talent would keep in mind that PDs are looking at a much bigger picture than air-talent. Talent is looking at their show. We get to see the world from 10,000 feet, not ten feet. Therefore we are looking at everyone's show. We are also looking at music and perceptual research on the entire station and analyzing the whole market. It's like a giant chess game. We get to work with all the pieces on the board and we know how to put them together to make the best outcome. The talent needs to hyper-focus on making their show the best it can possibly be. Management wants talent to care and be concerned about the rest of the station, as well. We're all in this together! If talent begins by hyper-focusing on knocking their time slot out of the park, they'll be fulfilling their primary role on the team."

Peter Casey is Director of News and Programming at top-rated WBZ-AM 1030 Boston. [19] "As program directors, we understand that when changes are made some people just like to vent and have their opinions heard. No problem there. But I do wish that everyone would recognize that change is coming and change is here. Radio won't ever be like it was. The radio I grew up with exists only in my memories and it sounds better than ever there. This is still a fun business and is not like any other industry. We don't call it 'not a real job' for nothing. Many people I speak with who are no longer in the business insist they never had as much fun as when they worked in radio. It's true, but enjoy it today for what it is...even if it's not like it used to be."

These radio programmers share their expertise on what they look for in hiring air-talent.

Gary Berkowitz was a programming winner at PRO-FM in Providence and also at the original ROR-98.5-Boston. Today, as one of broadcasting's leading consultants and the programming mind behind many of America's top AC stations, including Greater Media's Magic-106.7 Boston, Gary believes enthusiasm and eagerness to learn are two key qualities he looks for when hiring radio talent. "You've got to love radio, and I know the ones who do and the ones who don't," says smilin' Gary. He feels radio will have a great future if we don't mess it up. "We cannot clutter the air with too many commercials, contests and other stuff. Today more than ever, it's about the music on music stations and we must be aware of too much clutter. Many people say it's what's between the music that counts and I often say it's what between the music that will kill you."

Tom Cuddy was VP of Programming for WPLJ and the ABC-FM Radio Station Group (now Citadel Broadcasting) for eighteen years. Here's the inside scoop on what qualities Tom looks for when interviewing someone for an on-air position: "A great communicator. Someone who can keep my attention without being too wordy. A talent with a love of radio and music that is contagious. Someone who is dependable and who is a team player." Tom Cuddy said his biggest challenge as a programmer was finding the up-and-coming Scott Shannons, Todd Pettengills and Rocky Allens. "I received half as many air-checks as I did ten years ago, and most of the ones I receive would not be great in a medium market, never mind the #1 market, NYC."

Paula O'Connor is a well-known programmer in Boston radio. She says the quality she looks for in hiring prospective air-talent is certainly their overall personality, but also has her eye on other things. "I look to see whether or not they have strong opinions, to be able to read between the lines, present their opinions with emotion and passion to evoke a response." Paula is known for her expertise in talk radio, so she looks for a talent's knowledge of local, national and world news and issues and a talent's sense of history. "In interviewing, they have to understand the importance of maintaining an entertainment factor," she emphasizes. As far as the best advice she can pass on to future radio stars, she says, "Don't believe your own press. Remember whence you came." Paula also believes an air-talent has to be able to relate to their audience. "In this day and age of ever-advancing technology and new media, radio is still an intimate experience. It's you and that person in their car, in front of their computer, or in their kitchen."

Lorna Ozmon describes the role of an air personality. Lorna is a former Chicago air-talent, and she was also in radio management. I affectionately refer to her as my triple-threat, since, at various times in radio, she has been my PD, manager, and consultant at stations in Boston and Houston. We know each other fairly well. One thing I liked about her as my boss was that if she had something to say to you, she didn't haul your butt into her office, no way! It was done in a more genteel and civilized way over lunch or dinner, talent's choice by the way, and always at a classy restaurant. No Mickey D's for Lorna or her air-staff.

Lorna Ozmon describes the role of an air.

In May 1987, I was in morning drive in Boston. Lorna was our PD. She described the role of an air-personality in a special way that I hadn't quite heard before. It made total sense and I tried to apply it to my own air role for the rest of my career. "The role of an air-personality," she began, "is more like the job of the host or hostess of a big party. With very few exceptions, the stage or screen performer presents to an audience, while the great radio personalities interact with their audience. A great host or hostess interacts with each individual guest, making each guest comfortable as well as entertaining them. That is precisely what your job is, making the audience comfortable with the station by being relaxed and friendly and by entertaining the audience with relatable and usable information. The only difference between you and that good party host (besides the food and booze) is that your guests are in a different room and can only hear your voice. That makes your job harder, but it also pays better than hosting parties."

One of the duties of a program director is to coach.
    Les Howard Jacoby has been a radio pro for over forty-five years. His radio career began in 1965 on a 10-watt college station, WVBC at Bethany College in Bethany, WV. Les first began programming radio stations in 1973, and has programmed radio stations in Raleigh, Peoria, Fayetteville, Memphis, and Myrtle Beach, along with Florida radio markets including Tampa St. Pete, Ft. Lauderdale, Gainesville-Ocala, and a successful ten-year run at WEAT Sunny-104.3 in West Palm Beach. I first met Les there in 2000, when he and then-GM Lee Strasser hired me to do morning drive at Sunny-104.3. During his tenure, the station was the market leader with total persons 12+, 25-54 and 35-64 for an impressive *fifteen* Arbitron ratings sweeps. Jacoby's PD responsibilities included handling a ten-person-air staff including yours truly, not an easy task. Les believes, "A good programmer needs to be a good teacher. I was fortunate to learn from some of our industry's best programmers, and I always attempt to apply their winning philosophies to those who work with me."
    He continues, "A radio on-air staff is very much like a basketball team. Each member of the jock team possesses different strengths and weaknesses. A good programmer, like a winning coach, is a teacher who works closely with each member of the air staff to improve their individual skills through weekly critique training sessions, which are designed to strengthen all aspects of the talent's on-air skills."[20] The well-known Florida broadcaster believes today's radio programmer must be a teacher and a coach as well as part-time psychologist! "For this strategy to work," he emphasizes, "talent must have a strong desire to learn and grow. It's all about positive attitude. I always tell my folks that when they've learned all they can from their current program director, it is time to move on to the next job. My greatest joy is watching the men and women I've had an opportunity to mold become the leaders within our industry."

How to score big with a PD when interviewing for an on-air position.
    Les Jacoby has solid advice for radio newbies on how to score big when interviewing for an on-air position. What does he look for in a prospective air-talent? "Again, using a sports analogy, during the interview process I look for people who work well within a team atmosphere. I'm not interested in an individual who refuses to pass the ball to another player, because in their mind they're more important to the squad than their teammates. There is no place on my team for a prima donna."

Jacoby also passes along valuable information to future radio wannabes heading out for that first radio interview, hoping to land an on-air shift. "I look for people who are unselfish, who possess a strong, positive attitude, take direction well, have a burning desire to win, are committed to constantly improving their on-air skills, are a student of the industry and understand that radio is more than 'four and out the door.' I especially like on-air people who are creative thinkers." Today (2010), Les Howard Jacoby is on the air in Sebring, Florida.

What important qualities do radio programmers look for in hiring air-talent?

Greg Strassell has been VP of Programming on CBS Radio in Boston for the past nineteen years. He was also my program director when I handled morning drive at WBMX (formerly 98.5), the original WROR Boston. Greg grew up like so many radio wannabes hearing the local voices on hometown radio, which in his case was Tell City, Indiana. He first got on the air when he was fifteen. "They gave me a pre-puberty shot on-air, but really stressed the less I talked and the more I segued, especially at night with only 250 watts, the better I sounded!! Okay, but seriously, it was a great hometown station that taught the values of serving a community with local content and respecting the FCC. It ended up being a great place to learn and to launch my career." In fact, Strassell adds that he and many of the station's former employees were so indebted to the station owners, the Brewer family, for giving their careers a jump start that they formed a salute to Jim Brewer in 2000 as a way of saying thanks.

Strassell says, "If you're looking for your first radio job you should know and appreciate the business side of radio." He also urges future radio stars to "Stay current on all technical aspects in this fast-changing environment, but also understand what will move the audience and create buzz for this industry. Overall, be real, be a student and stay focused on your goals. If there is no hometown station available like the one I learned at in Tell City, go to the Internet. That's where talent will come from," he predicts. "The next 'Jed the Fish' (KROQ) is about to crack open a mic on the Internet. Programmers need to find that talent locally and put them on the air." He also suggests, "Look in the hallways or outside the station for personality and talent, even if they've never been on the air before."

Chris "Mac" McGorrill shares tips on how to communicate effectively with your PD and how to audition for an on-air shift.

I look at the radio success story of Chris Mac with a great deal of personal pride and satisfaction. The first time Chris walked into my office was back in the late 1970s. At the time, I was managing WCSH in Portland, Maine. I instantly sensed that the high-school student had the right stuff to be a successful radio pro. We were looking for someone to answer the phones on our nightly sports talk show and Chris eagerly accepted the position, but I'll let him his story: "I grew up in a broadcasting family, both radio and television, my career in radio occurred because of opportunities I seized, rather than from an inspiration by a radio personality. While in high school, I was fortunate to have an opportunity to answer phones for a sports call-in show, *The Bullpen*, hosted by Bruce Glasier on AM-970-WCSH. [21] Thanks to Joe Martelle, that experience provided me a resume to take to a local radio station while in college."

"In January 1980," Chris continues, "I was offered the afternoon-drive slot on AM 730 WJTO in Bath, Maine. It was a great three-hour air-shift from noon until 3pm, when the daytimer shut down. It fit well with my college schedule and working 15 hours per week did not interfere with my studies. Being somewhat naïve, I did not understand that a daytimer expands its hours of operation as the year goes on and it remains lighter later. By August, afternoon-drive extended to become an eight-hour shift, from noon to 8pm."

Today, Chris Mac is the Operations Manager for the Saga Communications Group in Portland, Maine, working directly for the GM of the stations, my longtime friend, Cary Pahigian.[22] Chris' duties include overseeing the daily operation of seven radio stations while supervising three program directors. Chris offers some great tips on how future wannabes and seasoned pros alike can maintain a solid relationship with their program director:

1. *Communicate*
2. *Don't BS*
3. *Accept responsibility*
4. *Work for someone you respect*

Needless to say, broadcast technology has changed a great deal over the years. When this author auditioned for an on-air position back in the dark ages, most PDs preferred an audition tape to be on reel-to-reel tape and 3-to-5 minutes in length with some news, a quick song intro or two, and one or two commercial spots. I asked Chris how he prefers to hear how a prospective on-air hire sounds. "I prefer listening to them online while they're presently on the air somewhere. If that's not possible, mp3 format which is computer-generated. Email the resume and mp3 of the air-check. Another form would be on cassette," Chris asks with a laugh, "are they still available?"

Mark McCray tells it like it is on how to grab that on-air job!

Former South Florida Radio Pro **Mark McCray** is one of the nicest and coolest guys around, on or off the radio. Mark, known to his legions of loyal morning drive listeners as Mark "McCrazy" on X-102.3 in West Palm Beach, did double-duty and was also the top-rated station's program director. Working for the CBS cluster is where we first got to know each other and became fast friends, a friendship which continues to this day. I did morning drive on Sunny-104.3 and Mark was my neighbor right down the hall on X-102.3, blazin' away with 18 jams in a row! Since we both did morning shows, we would arrive at the Bell South Building around the same time every morning, usually about five minutes before air time! As we rode the elevator up to work, we'd share a few words and a couple of laughs as we both tried to wake up! I instantly liked the man. Then again, Mark McCray is easy to like, with his big broad grin and easygoing, polite manner and warm, giving nature, qualities which not only make him a natural on the air but also as a top PD.

Mark grew up in the Chicago area listening to Doug Banks and Tom Joyner on WGCI. "I also listened to Robert Murphy on WKQX," says Mark. His first break in radio came from the late Michael Spears and WGN Production Director/APD Todd Manley. "They were both wonderful mentors. I was in college at Southern Illinois University and headed home for the summer and an internship at WPNT-FM Chicago to get more experience. After about two weeks in the building, I played my tape for Michael Spears and he decided to put me on the air. I was only nineteen and enjoyed the experience and learned a lot from Michael and Todd. I later worked with Michael at KRLD-AM in Dallas." Mark McCray has some solid advice for future radio wannabes on how to go about landing that air job that you really want! "Be persistent, but not annoying," he advises.

"You also need to market yourself. If there's a job you *REALLY* want, go for it hard! Don't just send your resume and CD and follow up with a phone call or e-mail. Send your potential boss something that makes him or her go 'WOW!' Go the extra mile and make them notice you in a good way."

Critiques and air-check sessions! There is a better way!

"Show me an air personality who enjoys daily air-check sessions and I'll show you one lying sick individual who probably enjoys bamboo shoots shoved under their fingernails, too!"

Gary Berkowitz was one of the most brutally honest PDs I ever worked for, and he was also one of the best! We worked together on three different occasions during my long radio career. As PD, he first hired me in 1979 at the original WROR-Boston. Later, in 1997, as a consultant, he hired me at the New WROR Boston and, in 2000, hired me again in AM-Drive at Sunny-104.3 West Palm Beach.

Gary gave you your head as an air-talent, as long as it was within the parameters of the station format. Break it and the disappointed look he would shoot your way would be more than enough punishment. An air-check session with him, when you go over every minute of your show, was not exactly a trip to Disney World. As stated, he could be brutally honest when evaluating your air work. But, it was just that, an evaluation, which is a lot different than a critique. If you check with Mister Webster, "to evaluate" means to "find value or to appraise." "Critique," on the hand, is to "criticize or to find fault, disapprove, to knock, censure and complain." I always thought critique sessions were tortuous. Give me an evaluation session any day.

Program Directors take note:
You may want to stop referring to air-check sessions as "critiques" and use the more friendly sounding "evaluation time."

Evaluation meetings are important for talent, especially for those new to the radio business. Learning the proper way to handle station formatics is MOST important. Before continuing, please know, there are different stages of a radio personality's career:

Stage one is the radio newbie, who has much to learn and should be open to *everything* a good PD has to say and offer.

Stage two is the radio pro, who listens to everything the PD has to offer and agrees with most everything the PD says.

Stage three is the seasoned radio personality who has been around so long, about the only thing the PD tells him is where they are going to have lunch.

More on the value of lunch with your PD coming right up!

It is important for new radio talent to listen and take in everything your PD has to say, especially about how to handle the station format and how to carry it out effectively on the air! This is an acquired technique that can be taught by a qualified program director who is patient and takes time with raw radio talent, as long as the talent is willing to listen and learn. I was fortunate to learn from some of the best PDs and I hope you will be as lucky. A really good program director will help you as a radio newbie develop and enhance your style by offering suggestions about the mechanics of what you bring to the table. For example, your PD may comment by saying, "Your subject matter was right-on and fit our target audience, but it went a little too long in this particular area." Your PD is emphasizing a point for you, as the air-talent, to think about the next time you do a similar break on your show.

A good PD would NEVER try to change your natural style. You as the talent need to make sure you don't allow them to do so. Your uniqueness on the radio, whatever it is, is your personal ticket to success! It is the program director's job in evaluation sessions to help guide you not to change you. As a radio talent you put your heart and soul into each and every break on your show and it's difficult to hear someone, like your PD, find fault with that. No one wants to hear statements like "Why did you do that?" or "Why did you include that story on your show?" And, like so many before you, you may feel inclined to be upset, storm out of the office, or maybe even sit in total silence without replying. There's no question that sometimes air-check sessions can be brutal. Try to keep your cool, like it or not it comes with the territory.

For a moment, let's cover **Stage three,** air-check sessions for the seasoned radio pro.

Washington, DC, area radio personality **Cindy Maguire** says she honestly doesn't mind doing air-check sessions. "I do them so infrequently, maybe one in the past four years, that they don't bother me. I like the approach of a PD listening to a break, stopping the tape and then asking me if I was satisfied with that break. If I answer yes, he asks me why. If he disagrees, he makes a note of it and comes back at the end of the session with why he disagrees and how it could be better. Now, if he agrees," Cindy adds, "he just moves on. If I wasn't satisfied with the break, he would ask me how I thought it could be better and what I didn't like about it. It is kind of a self-help session."

Author's note: If I only had to sit through one air-check session every four years, I may have enjoyed it a lot more, too. Personally, I have never been a fan of air-check sessions. For the most part, I found them to be confrontational. It sets up a situation where the talent is put on the defensive and must explain why they said or did something that the PD probably didn't like. My question for program directors and management is this: Do you think talent would take time in the first place to say or do something on their show if they didn't think it was relevant, funny, entertaining, interesting or important? Come on! The answer is simple, of course not. So, the entire reason for an air-check session is moot, or is it?

Why have air-check sessions in the first place? I'm serious! Besides, sitting and listening to your show being played back and dissected bit by bit, piece by piece, is to my way of thinking tantamount to being publicly flogged! Well, maybe that's a bit of a stretch, but honestly, most air-talent I know believe listening to their own performance serves no other purpose than to embarrass the talent. Of course, a PD would say, "That's ridiculous! We would never purposely embarrass our stars. Our only intention is to help improve their overall performance," which I answer by saying that telling talent a particular break is bad or good is all relative. For example, as talent, I may think a bit is clever. You, on the other hand as the PD, may find it unacceptable! No two people will ever agree on everything.

Calling these sessions "evaluation time," rather than a critique denotes an entirely different message. The sound of evaluating their show sends a friendlier message from the PD to the apprehensive talent who is skeptical of having their show reviewed, dissected and "gone over" in the first place. Most air-personalities look at the entire air-check experience as less than pleasurable and view being critiqued as being publicly stripped naked and hung out to dry. With seasoned radio talent, why not try a totally different approach in discussing their air work? Discuss things over a cup of coffee or lunch, and preferably away from the station. One-on-one sessions with talent seem to work better over food. With morning folks who don't have time for lunch because it's their nap time, suggest a cup of coffee after their show. Meetings away from the station are paramount for both parties. Feeding your talent will go a long way in cementing a relationship and also remove you from the constant interruptions and emergencies that PDs face on a daily basis at the station.

Remember, your morning drive talent has been up long before your body leaves the mattress. Work around their weird hours! Don't pull rank and demand they see you when it's most convenient for you! Show a little respect and you'll get it back ten-fold. Sound like pretty basic stuff? It is, but you'd be surprised how many radio PDs and managers don't do it!

Oh, one other point about those show bits you think aren't very funny and don't reach out and hug your station target audience, at least in your mind. Let me share a brief story with you. Nationally known consultant Lorna Ozmon was my boss on several different occasions.[23] I remember quite vividly one instance where criticism was leveled at me and my show and how she handled it. Word filtered back to me that a competing PD was giving her a bad time about some of the content on my show. Apparently, Lorna stopped God's gift to radio in his tracks by saying, "Look, I don't always get what he does either, but I do know this: he's #1 and I ain't messin' with it!" Sage advice for the nation's programming minds.

How to survive air-check sessions and live to do another show.

The worst part for talent in going over their air-check is fear of the unknown. You never know what the PD will say about a particular break on your show. It could be good, bad, or indifferent. The worst reaction is when the PD leans back in his/her chair and yawns while listening - not a good sign.

Whatever the PD says, try not to overreact and become defensive. Trust me, it's easier said than done, but give it your best shot. Remember, it is just one person's opinion. You certainly can defend yourself and explain why you thought the bit or rap was relevant and why you included it! [24] Don't be shy about asking questions in response to their remarks. An air-check session should be two-way communication between the PD and talent. It should not be a session where you are not allowed to speak your mind.

If the PD asks why you included a story, answer by stating in polite fashion, "Why do you think it didn't fit our show...and please tell me why you have concerns about things on our show." Always try and refer to your show as "our" show to make the program director more of a participant rather than just a casual outside observer. Get them involved.

If you honestly believe your PD is way off-base and feel you are in the right about the content, by all means respectfully disagree. Be firm but polite and explain thoroughly why you disagree with their observations. Don't just say in a huff, "Well, I disagree!" Explain yourself and why you feel so strongly about a particular point. Being angry and upset will only lead to further frustration.

Valuable pointer for both PDs and talent.

If an air-check session becomes a heated exchange over program content and you are both feeling frustrated, agree to disagree and take a time out. One of you or both needs to smile and say, "You know what? Why don't we continue this tomorrow or the next day, when we both feel more relaxed and we can discuss it more rationally without being so upset?"

A special word to program directors:

Choose your words wisely and carefully when critiquing, or as I prefer, evaluating the work of your air staff. A real radio pro puts everything they have into their show, and contrary to what you may think, they would not include something which they didn't think was a valid contribution to the success of their show and the station! When you as the PD single out a particular break and question the whys and wherefores and display a negative attitude about why it was included, you automatically offend the talent. Even when it is not done in a hurtful way, it still comes across that way. It's like calling their baby ugly!

To air-talent:

It is important to remember that it's your work, not you, that is being evaluated. There is a huge difference. Honestly, during my own radio career I would have been a lot better off and made life a lot easier for myself and others if I only took time to heed my own advice. Instead, I would get angry if a PD didn't love every aspect of my performance and every bit on my show! Try as I did, I seemed to take it personally if any part of my show was questioned. I admit this was wrong, and as mentioned elsewhere in this book, talent must be open at all times to input from their PD, GM and consultant.

At the same time, it's extremely important for talent to recognize that no matter how forceful the PD's words seem to be, you, as the air-talent, are the final judge of what you create, say and do on your show! It is your air-work with your own special brand of personality. The person doing the actual critiquing, whether it be the PD, manager, or consultant may wish for you to do it their way, but in the final analysis you're the one who must feel comfortable in delivering the final product!

This is where many PDs and talent cross swords. Instead of a free flow of thoughts and ideas and what is best for the show, it dissolves into a personal attack and power struggle with both sides digging in their respective heels, if for no other reason than to save face. Take it from one talent who has engaged in these senseless cat and dog fights, it doesn't have to be this way if you apply some basic common sense rules.

> *"Let me never fall into the vulgar mistake of dreaming that I am persecuted whenever I am contradicted." - Ralph Waldo Emerson-*

How PDs and talent can live and work in near-perfect harmony by following a few rules.

First a few simple rules for air-talent to keep in mind during an air-check or evaluation session:
   1. **It's your show.** That's a given. Everyone realizes it, or should, but it doesn't hurt to listen to ALL who are willing to take time to comment on what you say and do on the air. It is *your* show, but it is *their* radio station. Sort of a 50/50 partnership and in any partnership or management, including the PD, has a right to monitor you and to give you their input as to what is said on the air. Now, I realize this is a bitter pill for talent to swallow, but just take it with a big glass of water and you should be fine.
   2. If you **keep an open mind** during your air-check session, and that means being open to some suggestions and new ideas, you may find that some of the ideas make sense to you and you can implement them to improve your show and your on-air skills and delivery.
   3. **Before each air-check session** and evaluation meeting, it will help to ease your anxiety if you silently repeat the following, "*The program director is my friend, he wishes me no evil or harm… the PD is my friend, he wishes me no evil or harm.*" You get the idea! Keep repeating it to yourself as you make your way down the hall towards the PD's office!
   4. **You may reject all of the ideas and suggestions** from the PD and management! But if you do, remember when you choose to steer the boat alone, without any help from the navigator and crew, you and you alone are solely responsible for either bringing the big ship safely into port or ramming it to pieces against the side of the dock! There is safety in numbers!

Accept some of the PD's ideas instead of rejecting them carte blanche. Think about this for just a moment. It's better to be partners with the director of the show, the PD, instead of being adversaries.

There is a little bit of job security and comfort in telling your manager that you tried it their way, especially after a down ratings book.

Suggestions for PDs on the best way to approach talent during an air-check or evaluation session:
   First and most importantly, before your air-check session with talent, silently repeat the following: *Air-talent, although seemingly egocentric and out of control at times, is not here to torpedo the radio station and to fail in the ratings war. He is my friend and wishes me no evil or harm.*" Keep repeating this to yourself over and over while waiting for them to show up in your office.
   Secondly, don't listen to station rumors about something your air-talent supposedly said on their show and be all-juiced-up and ready to take their

heads off, before listening to a recording of their show. For example, the sales manager stops you in the hall and with a gleam in his eye says, *"Hey, man, did you hear that raunchy bit on your morning show? Wow! I was appalled, bet we lose a couple of sponsors over that one!"* There is an undertone of jealousy which exists in many radio stations between programming and other departments. Don't ask me why, but it does exist, so be aware of it! It's one thing if you heard the bit yourself, but like many PDs during their morning commute, they use the time to monitor the competition and don't always listen to every break on their own station. This is why the good Lord invented tape and CDs, so you can play back every break over a cup of coffee, while sitting comfortably at your desk. As Rush Limbaugh would say, "Don't rush to judgment." It's important as the program director to avoid hearsay in the halls.

Everyone hears things differently and most only hear a portion of what was said. Quite often, people critical of something supposedly said by an air personality totally miss the all-important set-up and only hear the punch line. Therefore, they lose the real intent of the entire bit. A good rule for PDs to follow is to only comment, whether good or bad, on what you personally hear or observe. Period! Talent's air-check is the proof of what was actually broadcast on their program.

PDs should only comment on what they hear their talent say, not hearsay passed on about them!

As a program director, when you hear something that you feel went over the line for your station and format, here is a good way to open the subject: "The piece I heard while driving in this morning, you know the funny bit about a woman's chest...ah, the boob bit, around 7:20, just before traffic...now, we know our primary target audience is female. Ya know, mom driving her kids to day-care, with that in mind, please tell me how did you feel about that bit?"

Radio 101: Right away, your morning team knows you were listening, because you have the exact moment of impact down cold. They will immediately be thinking, "Oh s***, we're screwed!" At this point, nine times out of ten, your guys will start singing like canaries. The guilt of going over the line will be written all over their faces. They will either admit to screwing up, or become defensive at your accusation that the content was all wrong for their show and the station! The first reaction of any real radio pro will be to defend their actions with their life if need be! Either way, stand by and prepare yourself for a spirited debate on the subject! You have done your job as the station PD and their supervisor by dropping the ball directly in their court!

Most radio pros instinctively know whether a bit worked or didn't. As air personalities, we are our own worst critics! After a few minutes of discussion, accept your talent's reasoning if at all plausible, even if you strongly disapprove of what they did, and move on! It's important that both sides come out as winners! As PD, make your point and gently refresh in their minds the all-important target audience their show is trying to zero in on. Make sure they completely understand the goals of the station! It is important for everyone to know that a raunchy bit that would seem milquetoast on Howard Stern's show could and likely would offend a mom with two young kids in the car. Many PDs go beyond the sale, and frankly don't know when to shut up. Make your point, which as the PD you are entitled to do, and move on. Try not to preach and go on and on over the same single issue! Hope that they learn from it and move on! At the same time, don't let the personalities involved linger over the issue either. Gently move your sensitive air-talent off the touchy subject. It's important that talent does not constantly beat themselves up over one issue out of a three- or four-hour show.

Bottom line, it was said and it's gone out into the ionosphere! Sure, your talent needs to know they messed up and made a poor judgment call, but at the same time, it was only one bit in a jam-packed action-filled morning drive radio show, a show that most likely was loaded with excellent on-target material. As their PD, don't forget to acknowledge the good stuff that your morning team did on their show. It will NOT diminish your point made about the questionable comment. You've done your job by raising the issue. Trust me, your point has been made and received. Knowing how air-talent thinks, they will beat themselves up over that lone bit for the rest of the day and into the night.

One final thought after all is said and done - don't look pissed! Try smiling! It will help cool any hot embers left smoldering along with any hurt feelings. It will also send a signal that, as their leader, you still love and respect them even though they messed up! Oh yeah, handshakes all around are a nice gesture to signify it's time to move on, but hugs are better!!

A special bulletin to air-talent everywhere: Your Program Director should not be perceived as your enemy. Here are a few key points for air-talent to remember in how to work with your PD.:

Points for talent to ponder in how to successfully work with PDs:

1. Be open to his or her suggestions! Don't be from the school of "Hey, we've always done it this way and I've never done it that way before, nor do I intend on doing so!" Instead, try to be open to new ideas and to different ways of thinking. Suck up your pride and listen. It may just keep you from sounding stale on the radio.

2. Try not to deviate from the format! Do your utmost to follow it to the letter every time you're on the air. This may come as a surprise, but management and programming have (hopefully) put many hours in to developing the station sound and gone to great expense to implement the format. It is your responsibility as air-talent to follow the guidelines they have (hopefully) outlined for you. Ask questions if you're unclear, but don't ever willingly violate the format. If the station music format calls for you to play five songs in an hour in morning drive, give them their five!

I've found that most PDs will relax on show content and look the other way on a questionable bit, but drop a song and you're dead meat. There are always extenuating circumstances where dropping a song will occur, but try and make format violations the exception and not the rule.

3. It is NOT a mortal or even a venial sin to share your creative thoughts and ideas about future shows with your program director. Too many radio personalities feel it's tantamount to treason to converse intelligently about future show bits with their PD! Trust in their ability to give you solid input and positive feedback. It is also smart business and follows the PTA rule (protect thy ass) which says that if you get the PD involved, in a hot programming idea and it fizzles and flames out, you won't stand alone in the blame and accountability department.

A good PD should serve as a coach to help guide the air-talent in a positive direction. This does NOT mean to try and change the talent's air-style. From time to time and probably more than you'd like to hear, your program director and others will try to tell you how you should sound on their radio station. Perhaps they want you to be more upbeat, or to slow down your delivery a little. Maybe they want you to shorten the length of your calls on the air or to be a little more succinct with your guests. These are minor cosmetic changes and will not hurt in essence the "real you" on the radio. Your personality will still find its way to reach out and fill the airwaves. As mentioned, you also need to follow the station format, but where you need to draw the line in polite but firm fashion is how you sound and your own style. It is mentioned repeatedly throughout this book that you must stand-up for what is uniquely "you" on the radio. Only you know what is right and what works for you. Don't let anyone mess with your own special style and uniqueness in what you bring to the air! Your personality is your own personal ticket to success as an air personality and real radio pro!

"A good program director knows what it takes to get the job done...a really good assistant program director!"

Radio station program directors and air-talent should work together. However, quite often this is simply not the case. Basically, because radio is an emotional business saturated with huge egos and overly sensitive people, many PDs and talent find themselves at opposite ends of the radio spectrum. Instead of working together for the success of the station, they become adversaries. This should not and does not have to be the case. Keep in mind that both parties lose when they remain inflexible, will not change their ways, are not open to new ideas and suggestions and won't listen to each other. Hopefully, these pointers for PDs and talent to ponder will help both sides have a better understanding of what it takes to get along and work together.

Here are some dos and don'ts for both PD's and air-talent to try to live by:

POINTS FOR PDS to remember when it comes to getting along and working with talent:

- Don't criticize talent's show bits or content, unless you have something better to offer.
- Always try to temper your criticism so it doesn't appear to be coming from envy or a position of power. In other words, don't come off sounding this way: *"I'm the person in charge and you had better do as I say!"*
- Quite often it's better to offer a helping hand than to point a finger.
- The fastest way to lose talent's attention and respect is to say that something is for their own good.
- Don't become impressed with your own importance; everyone around you will become less impressed.
- Staring up to admire one's own halo usually only creates one big pain in the neck.
- People look to you as a leader. They gain confidence in you as they watch how you handle various situations. If you're in control, they feel they're in control, too.
- Sometimes talent does their best air work when you just let 'em go!

POINTS FOR AIR-TALENT to remember when it comes to getting along and working with the PD:

- When receiving criticism from your PD, keep this in mind: if it's untrue, forget it. If it's unfair, keep from becoming upset, and if it's justified, learn from it.
- When you're selling an idea to your PD, don't go beyond the sale.
- Nobody has ever listened their way out of a job. Listen up to what your PD is saying to you!
- You can't be held responsible for what you don't say (Gary Berkowitz drove that home to me 30 yrs ago).
- Try to accept that some things are not in your control, but in the hands of others, like your PD.

And finally, something for both PDs and talent to ALWAYS keep in mind... *"Humility is a virtue that will carry you far in radio and in life."* - Harry Harrison-legendary NYC morning radio pro

Notes
1. "Numbers" as in ratings.
2. The term "take one or win one for the Gipper" is in reference to one-time Notre Dame Univ. football player George Gipp, who was immortalized in a 1928 half-time speech by legendary ND head coach, Knute Rockne. Gipp died Dec. 14, 1920, of a strep infection. Rockne called him the greatest halfback to ever play on his teams.
3. "Mission statement of the station" refers to carrying out the station format, whether it's music, talk, sports, etc.
4. The importance of show prep is covered in detail in Chapter 7
5. The importance of radio promotion is covered in detail in Chapter 15
6. In writing this chapter about program directors, I did my best to be as fair as possible. My assessment of the PDs I worked with was based on their overall performance as far as leadership skills and working with people.
7. A clear-channel spot on the AM dial means that station usually does not share the frequency with other stations. There are exceptions.
8. Arbitron, the ratings service co. for radio, showed us #1 from midnight 'til 1am. At one point, our all-night show was ranked #1 in Chicago.
9. Charlie Murdock was the GM of WLW in the early '70s.
10. Your air-style is unique and special tyou and is covered in Chapter 2
11. How to communicate effectively is covered in Chapter 6
12. A P1 listener is a person who listens to the station all the time, almost exclusively. They know everything about the station.
13. During my time spent on the air at WLW in the early 1970s, Avco Broadcasting owned the station.
14. Read more on developing your own air style in Chapter Two.
15. Hot-lining refers to calling the air-talent on a direct line to the studio while they are in the middle of their show.
16. Note: Later in this chapter, I have outlined a few do's and don'ts for both program directors and air-talent to try to live by, or at least to co-exist and treat each other in a more civil way.
17. Read more about how to handle morning drive radio in Chapter 14
18. Read more about the radio ratings game in Chapter 18
19. Peter also wrote the dedication in this book to his friend and legendary Boston broadcaster, the late Jess Cain.
20. Note: Critique and air-check sessions are covered elsewhere in this chapter.
21. In early 2012, popular personality, Bruce Glasier, retired as Sports Dir. at Ch.-6 WCSH-TV - Portland, ME. A post he held for over 30 years.
22. Cary Pahigian comments in Chapter 9, Attitudes and Actions
23. Radio consultants are hired by management to help develop a format for the station and help see that it is properly executed by talent. Radio station consultants are covered in Chapter 12
24. "Bit" is a word used to describe either a pre-recorded or live element on a show.

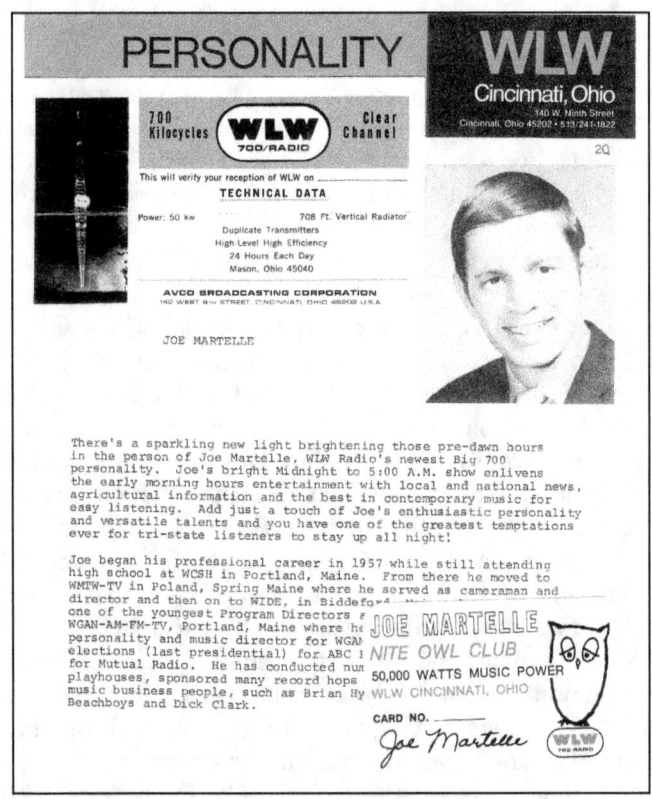

Author, publicity piece WLW Cincinnati, Ohio.

WLW Radio 700 Air staff in the early 1970s.

Barbara Bridges, PD and Air Talent Nashville, TN.

Les Howard Jacoby, former PD and Florida air talent.

Chris "Mac" McGorrill, air talent and Ops Mgr Portland, ME.

Mark McCray, PD and morning personality Florida and now Dallas.

Air-staff at WLOB-1310AM Portland-early 70's, L to R: Ray Bobby Ocean, Wally Brine, Author, Bob Anderson.

WCSH-AM 970, Portland, ME. air-staff 1978, left to right: Bill O'Neil, Dave Bailey, author, Dean Rogers.

Saddleback Ski Area in Maine in the late 60's with the air staff at WGAN-560AM (Portland)...left to right Dick Broderson(with skis), Author, Wayne "B" Bearor, Bud Sawyer (in glasses), Dick Fixaris.

WROR-98.5 Boston air-staff, 1980- left to right: Mike Waite, Andy Moes, author, Phil Redo, Gary Berkowitz, Joe (Jim Roberts) Noga.

CHAPTER 11
Inside the World of General Managers

"A GM's job is to run the business and not lose the license. It's like the captain of a ship without the nice uniform and the captain's dinner table."
– John Gehron, COO AccuRadio

The mission of the radio station GM.

Radio station managers are responsible for the overall operation of the station. All department heads, including the PD, operations manager, chief engineer, sales manager, promotions and office manager report directly to the general manager. In addition to determining the format and making sure the bottom line doesn't drift dangerously close to the red, the manager ultimately decides who to hire and fire and makes sure the station runs smoothly. In radio, you will report to a station manager, aka the person at the top of the food chain, aka "the boss." If a station is to survive and be successful in the competitive battle for ratings and sales revenue, competent, solid leadership is needed at the top of the chain.

During my years in radio, and having sat on both sides of the negotiating table as a manager and PD and as talent, I feel management would foster a more harmonious atmosphere if they went nice and easy with talent. Nowhere is it written that in order to get talent to cooperate you must constantly berate them, treat them with little if any respect, and run roughshod over them. Showing talent respect and being courteous to them doesn't cost anything extra.

Greater Media Chairman & CEO **Peter Smyth** and I worked together at the original WROR Boston in the 1980s. He was local sales manager and I was in morning drive. Peter believes "Respect is the keyword for all members of a station staff. Mutual respect between management and air-talent is essential for getting along."

As Ralph Waldo Emerson succinctly said, "Every human being, whatever origin, of whatever station, deserves respect. We must each respect others even as we respect ourselves." Everyone needs a little respect. You know when you have it and you certainly can sense it and feel it, when you don't have respect.

How managers can demonstrate respect at work to their talent:

- Always treat your staff, both on-air and off-air, with courtesy and kindness.
- Encourage your air-talent to express their opinions and to share their ideas on programming.
- Use their ideas to change or improve the station programming. Let them know you implemented their ideas, and let it be known to the suits higher-up.
- Don't take credit for their ideas.
- Never be rude or insulting or put them down, particularly in front of other staff members.
- Make time to listen to what they have to say. Never interrupt or cut them off.
- Treat your staff the same, regardless of gender, race, religion, or age. Treating individuals differently or playing favorites, will only create a hostile work environment.
- Praise more than you criticize.
- Do not constantly criticize them over little things on their show. Doing this continuously is just another form of bullying.
- Include all staff members in meetings and station events. Not every person can participate because of their own schedules and prior commitments, but invite them anyway. For example, morning show members who have been up since 3am probably won't be able to attend a luncheon or afternoon function, but invite them anyway.

There are no fewer points or gold stars for GMs who treat their air-staff kindly.

To be sure, there will always be a few ingrates who will try to take advantage of kindness, that's just the way it is in radio and in life. In general, though, most people respond favorably to kindness and personalities are no exception. It makes no sense for any manager to purposely try and ruffle the feathers of talent's already fragile ego. Many radio personalities who project a bigger-than-life persona on the air can be extremely insecure individuals off the radio. Of course, there are exceptions. There are some air personalities who are totally out-of-control egomaniacs who are insufferable to be around. These hombres should be pistol whipped into submission! All kidding aside, the point is there are many different types of radio personalities. Managers should treat them as individuals.

It is the station manager's responsibility to know each staff member, including air-talent. It makes perfect sense: if the boss knows each person on a one-on-one basis, it will be easier to make the proper judgment call in how to handle and communicate with that person if and when the situation warrants it. Make no mistake, though: As talent and a member of the manager's staff, you are in charge of your relationship with your boss. The quality of your relationship with the manager will determine how successful you are in your career. However, your manager can't effectively do their job or accomplish their goals without your help. So, your manager shares a critical interdependency with you. Whether you like it or not, you both need each other. If you don't succeed as a top air-talent, your manager will never succeed as a top-flight leader. As a manager, don't make the same mistake others have made and place all air-talent in the same box. They come in all shapes, sizes and are uniquely different and therefore require special handling.

Some things radio managers want talent to be aware of:

In 1979, **Tom Baker** was my GM at the original WROR Boston. Tom possesses that rare combination in a manager of projecting strong leadership in a kindly manner. Baker believes being humble is the key for talent to remember in developing a solid working relationship with management. "The first thing is humility. Realize as a talent you have been blessed with a gift and cherish it each day. Secondly," Baker continues, "talent should understand that radio is a vehicle to move products. Talent brings the audience to the radio and the commercials hopefully convince the audience to buy the product or service offered. Another key point for air-talent is they MUST have a good working relationship with sales.[1] I know of talent that call on clients on a regular basis to thank them for their business. When you have the sales team and programming in sync, there is no better formula for success." A forty-year radio pro, Tom Baker has managed stations in Boston, Portland, Oregon, San Diego and Santa Barbara. In 2009, he was back in Boston running the Greater Media Group and working with his longtime friend, Peter Smyth.

The GM establishes the chain of command in a radio station.

It is important for the manager to establish the chain of command! The GM's responsibility is to make it absolutely clear from the get-go what each staff member's role is and to whom those people report, including air-talent, the PD and other department heads and staff members. The chain of command is vitally important if a radio station is to operate effectively and efficiently. A good manager will lay down the law and set the parameters for both talent and programming people, including the station consultants. It's the only way to keep unnecessary and petty arguments from cascading into full-blown, out-of-control confrontations. Unfortunately, I found myself involved in more than a couple of these conflicts during my radio lifetime and they were not pretty. Do your best to avoid conflicts of any nature with everyone at the station.

How to develop a good working relationship with your GM.

Mark Hannon is the market manager of the CBS radio stations in Boston. He feels there is no "silver bullet" for a great working relationship between management and talent. "It requires commitment and investment on both sides," says Hannon. "In order to build trust and have partnerships that are effective, you must work to communicate as consistently and effectively as possible and really try to understand how each other's goals can be achieved through your collective efforts."

Station Managers need to plug the right people in to the right positions.

Nancy Widmann was the first woman president at CBS, Inc. and managed the CBS Radio Division for eight years. "At WCBS-FM New York City, I made the most significant appointment of my long career," she says. "I hired **Joe McCoy** as program director. Joe had a unique talent for hiring and managing air personalities. He was a talented personality himself, but his great strength was understanding that every minute of the day, the talent needed to relate to the city, to touch the pulse of New York, to talk about what everyone was chatting about at that very minute around water coolers in the building right outside our studio. Joe McCoy understood that radio is a personal, intimate, immediate medium. This is what has been lost over the years and radio has suffered because of it."

During my long radio career I worked for some managers who gave their PDs complete control, while others didn't want their program director "messing" with their air-staff in any way, particularly their high-priced morning drive poobahs. The role of radio program directors and how they interact with talent and upper management is covered extensively in the preceding chapter, so there is no need to rehash it here. However, one important point does bear repeating. Many managers believe they are the only one capable of handling their temperamental morning stars, and quite often it's true! At the least little sign of trouble the PD would be invisible as the GM handled the problem. When talent find themselves in the envious position of having the GM in their corner, it takes a pretty big person not to take advantage of the PD and scoot down to the big office at the first sign of trouble. Human nature being what it is, some insensitive talent pounce on any opportunity to make the poor PD jump through hoops.

It is extremely difficult, if not impossible, for a program director to maintain any sort of control over talent that has the luxury of running down to the GM's office at the drop of a hat. It's a difficult, gut-wrenching, no-win situation for the PD. Having been a PD myself, I feel for those who find themselves in such a pickle. As talent, try to understand and be a little sympathetic to their plight.

How to develop a solid working relationship with your GM.

Mike Haile is general manager of WDWS-AM and WHMS-FM in Champaign, Illinois. He is also VP of the parent company News-Gazette, Inc., and is the morning personality on WHMS. On May 8, 2011, Mike celebrated thirty-three years in morning drive, but when he is off the air he is the boss. Mike offered this advice to future radio wannabes on how to develop a solid working relationship with their boss: "The first thing is to check your ego at the front door. For example," he says, "we work as a team in our building. We have a lot of terrific stars on our air, many of them legends in the market, but they are all team players who do extremely well in our environment. Our newer talents are anxious to learn. Don't ever hold in problems or concerns until you reach a boiling point," urges Mike. "If you've got something on your mind, communicate with your boss. Don't play mind games with your boss! Communicate and reach out to your bosses (PD and GM) on a regular basis."

How talent can develop an effective relationship with their radio station's manager.

These tips will help talent develop a positive, supportive relationship with their manager or boss. Such a relationship will serve talent, the manager, ultimately, the radio station, well.

- Do what you say you will do. Keep true to your commitments.
- Focus on what is good about your manager. We all have both good and bad points. As you would like them to do for you, cut them some slack when they appear to be having a bad day.
- Never blindside your boss with surprises that you could have prevented.
- Keep your manager informed about all things involving your interaction with the rest of the staff.
- Take time to get to know your boss as a person and focus on what makes them tick.
- Be aware that success at the station is **not** all about you. Place your manager's needs first! Try to understand your manager's goals and priorities. Think in terms of the overall success of the station and not just about you and your show.
- Learning to read your manager's moods will definitely help you communicate more effectively. It will help you understand when to

stop by to say hi and when to stay away. If the boss is trying to make budget or just received word of bad ratings, it probably wouldn't be the best time to ask for a raise or to discuss a problem! It may be prudent to avoid the corner office.
- Remember your manager can't read your mind. Share how you're feeling about your show, the station, and even your personal life. Just keep in mind that timing is everything - be aware of your boss's work load and busy schedule. **Don't** bring in a laundry list of ideas and things to discuss. Stay focused on a few important issues.
- Remember that you can learn much from your boss. Remain open to their input and suggestions on how you can improve. He was promoted because someone in your organization recognized his leadership abilities and management style.
- Sometimes, you and your manager will clash over a difference of opinion. In a heated moment, don't make threats about leaving. You need to get a grip and realize your boss has more authority and power than you do. He gets the final vote. You will not always get your way. Don't hold a grudge. Get over it and move on. Keep in mind: disagreement is okay, discord is not.

Who is in charge of the radio station?

Quite often, the atmosphere of a radio station can be like a playground. You want people to feel free to have fun on the radio, but sometimes that playful behavior on the air is carried outside the studio to the hallways and offices! A little harmless office fun can lead to potential problems, especially when it comes to staff members losing respect for the folks in charge! Questions come up of who's running what, and who reports to whom. There's no doubt in my mind that the line "the inmates are running the asylum" had to originate in a radio station somewhere. Listen up, folks, don't act like children. Running down to the manager's office because somebody threw a little dirt in your face is kid's stuff and has no place in the grown-up world of radio or in any business. The manager is busy enough trying to keep the station afloat and solvent. You should always try to resolve your own problems first with your department head. Save the really big stuff for your GM.

One of the most important duties of the GM is to act as a mediator to settle differences between department heads and staff members when difficulties arise. There is a world of difference between the role of a mediator, who makes peace and acts as a referee and a go-between, and that of an arbitrator, who makes judgments or settles disputes between others. Managers should always try to mediate, rather than arbitrate.

All too often in radio the question of who is in charge becomes a power play between management and talent! Without a doubt management is in charge, or at least they should be, but who is actually in control of the air product?

Here is an example involving talent and the program director: The PD insists talent do as they say regarding *their* show, without listening to *talent's input or feelings* on the subject. Talent, on the other hand, wants to handle the show *their way*. The PD feels talent is out of control and needs to be reined in. Talent believes the PD is a control freak and is trying to micro-manage. Both sides feel strongly about their point of view and both are probably somewhat accurate in their assumption. **It's a stalemate! What to do?** Both decide to take their case to the GM. Now, here's where the problem becomes sticky and tricky: Who does the GM stand with and support? It all comes down to a position of power. The GM has to support her department head, or at least should, but at the same time she doesn't want to upset the talent. It's a tough call.

Remember, the mission of the GM is to act as a *mediator*, not an *arbitrator*. The GM should not be judgmental or appear to take sides. I believe it is not the role of a manager to serve as both judge and jury in disputes between the PD and air-talent. The GM should make every attempt to make both parties feel like they won. It's very difficult. No matter how you slice it, more than likely someone will emerge the injured party and walk away unhappy. So what to do?

Here's the bottom line: the problem never should have been brought to the attention of the GM in the first place. Getting your GM involved is risky business. The GM could look at the PD as not being in control of the troops, while at the same time looking at talent as a whining problem child. Neither party should want to be tagged in such an unflattering way. Having been down that slippery slope once too often myself, I know first-hand that bringing little problems to the GM is not acceptable. He is much too busy! Work it out! Your GM wants solutions from you, not problems!

First and foremost, as talent, try and work out everyday minor problems with your PD. Only under the most difficult circumstances and after all options have been exhausted should the GM be brought in to negotiate a settlement between talent and the PD. If you reach an impasse, request a meeting with the GM that includes you and your PD. Don't go barging into the GM's office demanding everything stop to handle your crisis! Make an appointment! Too many air personalities, and I include myself, place too many demands on their GMs. Keep in mind that your manager hired department heads for a reason. Use them!

Chicago and Boston radio GM John Gehron refers to the role of a GM as the captain of the ship, who is on board to assist when a serious crisis arises, but who for the most part should be left alone while you work things out with your immediate supervisor. Let your GM focus on their primary function: The overall operation of the station and keeping the bottom line out of the red!

A position of power in a radio station is a delicate balancing act between the general manager, programming people (including consultants), and air-talent.

As a manager, if you have tried your best to put out a fire between individuals and believe you have dealt fairly with both sides, then there's nothing more you can do. Well, there is something else you can do: hope and pray that in time things will resolve themselves. If that doesn't work and the PD and talent continue to bicker and be at each others' throats, as the person in charge you can fire them! Just remember, it may give you instant satisfaction and restore temporary peace at the station but you'll be faced with the new challenge of trying to find competent talent to fill two important positions at your station! There are no guarantees that you won't wind up in a bigger mess than you already have on your hands. It may mean more headaches for you in the long run. It's the old scenario; better to deal with the devil you know than the devil you don't! The easier answer may be to give them both a well-deserved boot in the butt along with a pat on the back and tell them to go have a beer and work it out!

Every manager walks a tightrope between supporting the duties of their program director and nurturing and keeping their air-talent happy, not an easy task! Unless the balance of power is handled extremely carefully and diplomatically, leaning in the wrong direction at the wrong time can usurp the authority the PD needs to maintain some sort of control over the talent pool. This is one reason why the manager has such a difficult role. There are no easy answers when it comes to handling various personalities. Every person and problem that pops up on a daily basis is unique and different. Truly, a program director who tries to operate without the complete support and backing of his or her general manager is doomed to failure. On the other hand, an unhappy air personality who is micro-managed to death by an overzealous, out-of-control, power-crazed PD is also doomed to failure! This is why a GM's primary responsibility, after keeping the bottom line out of the red, is trying to keep peace and harmony between the PD and air-talent. The most experienced and best GMs in the business admit it is one of the most difficult challenges they face!

Radio station managers come in all shapes and sizes along with all levels of skill, and some have more skills than others. Some managers are simply bad bosses. Trying to work with a bad boss can be taxing and stressful. However, over time, trying to work things out may be well worth your time and effort, especially if you enjoy being on the air at the station. Of course, off the radio may be an entirely different story that is driving you out of your mind.

Before you fly off the handle, it's important to know your manager may not view himself or herself as a bad boss. "Bad" depends on talent's needs, the manager's skills and the circumstances you both find yourself in. Your boss may be so overwhelmed and slammed for time by his job that he has nothing left over for you. During my time in radio, usually if I found myself at odds with a manager it was because we didn't share similar values, or we didn't agree on the direction of the station. If your values are not in sync with those of your manager then you have a bigger problem than learning to live with a bad boss.

You're fed up and frustrated with the lack of direction from your manager. Trying to work with he or she makes you uptight and frustrated. He or she is a bad boss. Dealing with a bad manager is a challenge many radio personalities face on a daily basis. Hopefully, these suggestions will help out and prevent you from experiencing too much stress:

- Talk to your boss. Explain that you need feedback, direction, and most importantly, support. Be polite and do not use an accusatory tone. You need to move slowly with an insecure manager, or they may feel you're stepping over the line.
- Ask your manager how you can help reach their goals. Listen carefully, and above all follow through on their thoughts on how you can help.
- Ask for advice from other station managers on how to cope with your particular situation. I would strongly suggest doing so in confidence. You don't want to break the confidence shell on an already fragile individual.
- If you've tried all of this and failed, it may be time for you to think about moving on to save your own sanity.

Time for managers to look in the mirror. Are you a bad manager? See if any or all of these 12 points fit you!

- Do you fail to communicate with your staff, using excuses like, "I'm slammed with work"?
- Do you change your mind frequently, leaving your staff wondering what's going on? A bad manager changes expectations without notice, throwing their staff totally off balance.
- Do you ignore the requests of air-talent until a problem arises, and then jump all over them?
- Do you give your staff time to respond to accusations?
- Do you blame your staff when things go wrong, rather than taking responsibility?
- Do you fail to praise while being quick to criticize?
- Do you fail to give praise and recognition for a positive performance?
- Do you nitpick, badger, and refuse to let go of a problem?

- Do you fail to accept constructive feedback from air-talent and the rest of your staff?
- Do you lack integrity? Are you less than honest and truthful with your staff?
- Do you break promises and never keep your word to your employees? For example, constantly breaking luncheon appointments because you receive a "better" offer.
- Do you lack the intestinal fortitude to handle difficult situations, knowing full-well the right thing to do?

If you think you have any of these unbecoming traits, it's time to do something about it. Self-evaluation can be extremely difficult. However, sometimes it's necessary to step away from the big desk in the corner office and do a little soul searching and reflecting on one's actions and behavior, if for no other reason than to prevent yourself from self-destructing.

Who make better managers, men or women?
During almost half a century of being on the radio, and in writing this book, inevitably one question keeps popping up: Who was better to work for, male or female managers? It's an interesting question, and a little complex to answer, but I'll do my best without offending either gender. Early in my career, I honestly believed women would be the better taskmasters. Why? Because, growing up in the late 1940s and '50s, I observed first-hand what women are all about. I was raised by a strong mom, smack-dab between two sisters. Three women with distinctively different personalities! My sisters and I were under the controlling thumb of our 5'2", hot-blooded Italian mom, who wasn't the least bit shy about displaying her emotional side to anyone! The expression, "Dynamite comes in small packages" must have come from someone observing our mother in action! Don't tell my mom women are the weaker sex—you're liable to get a few meatballs tossed in your direction!

Women were supposedly stronger than men, and my mom exemplified it. Men were taught to be tough, macho, never to cry, and not to let their sensitivity come through no matter what, because that wasn't what leadership was all about! At least, that's what men were told back in the post-WWII days.

We Baby Boomers were raised never to show our emotions unless it was to fight back against the school bully if he went too far in picking on us. Male managers were supposed to subscribe to one philosophy: "Get the job done no matter how many dead bodies lie in your wake!" Women, on the other hand, were raised to show their emotions. It was all right for them to be compassionate, considerate, sensitive and compassionate. Interesting, because they are all outstanding qualities in a leader! It is not my intention to make inflammatory comments regarding male or female managers and begin a round of *Battle of the Sexes*, but I do have my own theory on why female managers can be perceived as tougher than their male counterparts.

To their credit, women radio station managers have made their mark in a male-dominated business. Even if they didn't care to display toughness, women were forced to do so. It was either that or be eaten alive by the male egos which run wild in the radio game! I dislike drawing comparisons, but there are distinctive differences in styles between the sexes! Please allow me to explain. When and if problems arise, women managers seem to focus more on the how's and why's more so than men. I'm sure they do this for one very good reason, to try and ensure the same problem doesn't happen again! From what I experienced, female managers have a tendency to dig and dig some more for information on why a person screwed-up. Women seem to need to know the story behind the story! [2] On the other hand, their male counterparts for the most part (there are exceptions) seem to use fewer words, get to the point faster than women, and move on! Men may not be as diplomatic as women or as compassionate, but in most instances they get to the chase faster and to the heart of the matter a lot quicker.

One example of the differences between men and women radio managers:

Men and women managers even conduct themselves differently with employees at lunch. Most of my hour-long luncheons with male bosses would be ten minutes of business and fifty minutes of schmoozing about personal stuff, family, sports, whatever. Luncheons with female managers were totally different. Oh, they talk just as much, only their business luncheons are just that, business. They ask more work-related questions. Women managers, more so than men, seem to want to hear specifics of what is going on with the show, and all the nitty-gritty details of a problem that may be ready to rear its ugly head.

There are definite characteristic differences between the sexes in the way they handle various problems and situations, but there are also similarities. For example, both sexes can display explosive, emotional outbursts. I have always been from the school that a gentleman respects a gentle lady. Funny, I didn't cross paths with many genteel women station managers. Come to think of it, I didn't meet very many gentle men either.

One thing both sexes are guilty of is going over the same issue again and again with an employee who has made a mistake. Don't keep berating the person for screwing-up. As a manager and leader, express your opinion, listen to theirs, and move on! As a manager or department head, you may want to keep in mind that it's idiotic, stupid and pointless to beat a dead horse!

I was raised to believe women were superior to men in many ways. I was told that women had a more gentle touch; they were more compassionate, more caring, and more concerned about others than men were. I'm not so sure that's entirely accurate! During my broadcasting career, I worked for no less than twenty managers. Only *three* were women and I worked for the same one on three separate occasions. During the first half of my radio career, the early 1960s until the mid-'80s, there was a significant difference between the number of male and female managers employed by America's radio stations. Even today, radio management is still predominantly male.

One thing which became quite evident to me during my many years in radio is that most managers, both men and women, are cut from the same cloth - perhaps not in the physical sense, but definitely in their mindset about how to run a radio station. Both genders have one distinctive commonality: each has one eye on the ratings and the other fixed on the bottom line! I worked for some great managers, and some not so great.

So, who is better, male or female? Not to dodge the question, but it's really a tough call. Both have their good and bad qualities. I will say this: when I was going through some of my most stressful times in radio, I always seemed to be working for a female manager! Coincidence? Who knows? Maybe so.

Advice for both employees and management who have disagreements.
Each of us has our own take on almost every subject and situation, but we also have many things in common. Behind every difference of opinion and petty argument there is common ground. Finding that common ground does not mean giving in or forcing the other person to believe or accept another's point of view. On the contrary. What it does mean is finding that common thread where you can share a similar perspective. It is well worth the effort to find things that you can agree on and reach some sort of understanding. The next time tempers flare and you feel your blood pressure rising and a road block appears, try to find common ground and to see the other person's point of view. It doesn't have to be about winning or losing or giving in, it's about trying to see the other person's point of view.

How to get along with management.
Author's note: The best advice I can pass along to talent on how to get along with management is to keep an open mind and to listen to your bosses. It's something I didn't always do, which at times made my own radio career stressful and difficult. In fact, I was accused by a couple of managers and more than a few PDs of being rebellious and hard to handle. I won't deny that once in a while, I could be very demonstrative and stood up for what I believed was best for me. I detest labels, but rather than be tagged with the word "rebellious," I prefer words like "creative" and "innovative." Make no

mistake; there were times I definitely clashed with those in authority when I truly believed they were wrong and way off base on their views about my show and me. During the times management looked at what I was doing from a totally different perspective, I held my ground. I don't believe either side was entirely wrong, and who was right is up for debate. However, in radio the proof is in the ratings, and most often I was blessed with good numbers.³

America's radio managers and executives offer their advice to future radio wannabes.

Tom Baker, Manager of radio stations in Boston, Portland, Oregon, San Diego and Santa Barbara, CA

"Get started early. Intern if you can. Get in the door of a radio station as a part-timer. Once in, look for a programming mentor. If there is an opening doing overnights, take it! You want to practice, and practice some more. Volunteer for any on-air situation, weekends, vacation, holiday fill-in. Continue to ask for feedback from the PD. Do not be afraid of criticism! It is imperative to get feedback on your performance at all times. The **BEST** talent **ALWAYS** reviews their last show to see if they could have done it better. That's why football teams review film - to improve and be the best!"

Peter Casey, Dir. Of News & Programming-WBZ-Boston

"Write as much as you can, do as much voice work as you can, be as creative as you can. Use the word 'no' sparingly and the word 'yes' liberally. If you do not know computer, digital audio and Internet technology you will be left behind. Too many news people feel they shouldn't have to write, produce or voice material for the website or whatever content vehicle we use. This is wrong. We are content providers and since the future is here now we should not get so bogged down in what platform on which the user is consuming that content. I don't think I've ever had the thought, 'Hey, that's not in my job description.' We should all keep learning and embrace the new technologies, regardless of whether we like them or not, and forge ahead."

John Gehron, GM-WLS -Chicago, WRKO/WEEI Boston; Sr. VP-CBS also GM Harpo and Internet radio

"My advice to future radio stars: keep trying, but be realistic. Talent will cut through, but you must have talent. Find a station that has people who will encourage you as well as teach. Picking the right station is crucial to your success. I also think about how creative are they? Does their style fit the format and how do they relate to the audience? Can they move the ratings without losing the license, and will their act hold up over time? I also look for what kind of person they are. Will they fit our culture or be overly management-intensive? Will they be a positive or negative in the building?"

Dan Mason, Pres. & CEO CBS Radio

"Be persistent! Somebody will eventually put you on the air in some small town and in some day part. Respect a radio station no matter how small it is because it is your ticket to communicate with people. And above all, be a student of the business. Understand each generation of programming eras. It is shocking today to see new people in our business with little knowledge or interest of where the medium began and how it evolved."

Paula O'Connor, former Program Manager at several Boston radio stations, including WRKO & WTKK-96.9

"Keep coming back for more. If you are passionate and lucky enough to work at something you love, make yourself available. No task is too big or too small. Any setback can be overcome. You have to be willing at times to take a step back in order to get two steps ahead."

Cary Pahigian, Pres. & GM-Saga Communications/Portland (ME) Radio Group

"All you need to know is what we all learned when we were young. Radio will test your work ethics, people skills, integrity, ability to learn, dedication, patience and desire. Take responsibility and be honest. In hiring talent, the first things I look for are attitude and energy and whether the talent is willing to work at it every day! To me," adds Pahigian, "radio is the most rewarding thing I could ever dream of doing. If it breaks right, you can happily ask yourself each day, they pay me for this? What's better than that?"

Phil Redo, Manager of New York City and Boston radio stations

"Talent is the key in hiring. Great talent providing information and entertainment in a unique way."

Dave Robbins, VP& GM-CBS Radio-Chicago, Orlando

"Set goals. You can only achieve that which you set as a goal to achieve. Success is not by accident, it is the intersection of preparation and opportunity. If you are prepared when opportunity happens, you will be rewarded with success. Set your goals and make them very specific; ex: the type of job you want, etc. You can achieve anything you want to achieve. Any success I have achieved is due to my parents telling me all of these lessons at an early age. Where you are today, or your past, has nothing to do with where you can be in the future. Start today to build a better you."

Mollie Simpkins, formerly Director Of Operations-Metro Networks-Baltimore

"Regardless of the profession you choose, love what you do. As a manager, there is nothing more frustrating than a miserable employee. However, I must say in all fairness that I have seen some horrible managers who create a terrible hostile environment. I have been fortunate enough to be in an environment where I felt comfortable enough speaking my mind without fear of retribution. It is so important for everyone, managers and employees alike, to be able to have an open dialog."

Where do radio managers come from?

Radio is a business that prides itself on practical on-the-job experience, but seldom if ever does an individual land a management position in radio directly from "cap and gown day" at college. In fact, most radio station managers have been in the business for quite a few years. In radio, practical application and a philosophy of learning by doing is the best teacher. A college degree is important and can open the door and even set you apart from other applicants, but nothing beats hands-on experience.

A successful track record in sales or programming is what gets you to the management post in radio.

Quite often, radio station managers are recruited from the sales side of the business rather than from the programming ranks, although there are exceptions. Several successful managers who comment in this book actually rose from the programming ranks, including John Gehron, Dan Mason, Lorna Ozmon, Cary Pahigian and Phil Redo.

The reason more radio managers come from the sales side is because the GM's primary mission is to generate a profit. Station owners usually feel more comfortable hiring a person with a solid sales background. Therefore, three out four radio GMs at some point during their broadcast careers made a living selling commercial radio time. I believe solid programming people also make quality managers, but sales experience goes a long way in preparing a person to handle the budgets and bottom-line realities of today's radio.

During my earliest years in radio as a struggling air-talent trying to earn extra money, I attempted to sell radio time. I say attempted, because I found it to be one of the most challenging and difficult positions in radio. It didn't help that my sales list was randomly taken from the local Yellow Pages. Making cold sales calls, both in person and on the phone, taught me a lot about how to handle rejection. At the same time, it certainly didn't do much to help my fragile, sensitive side. My brief sojourn in radio sales did give me a deeper understanding and appreciation for the sales staff who work so hard on a daily basis to bring in the all-important dollars to the station.

As talent, if you're ever presented with an opportunity to try sales, don't turn up your nose at the idea. I strongly suggest you give it a go. You may not make a lot of money as a beginner in radio sales, but I guarantee you will learn valuable lessons and have a better understanding and appreciation for how important sales is to the overall success of a commercial radio station.

"A pat on the back, although only a few vertebrae removed from a kick in the pants, is miles ahead in results." Bennett Cerf, radio commentator

Here are a few pointers for managers to remember when dealing with air-talent

- Don't just point out what's wrong with talents' performance, take time to point out what's right! Positive reinforcement works every time.
- Don't use your position as head honcho and person in charge to allow yourself to become a bully.
- Be a real leader! Make positive contributions and inspire your staff to do the same.
- A manager with compassion wields more power than one with muscle.
- Hope for the best behavior but prepare for the worst.
- You can get air-talent's attention quicker with your ears than with your mouth. Don't let your ego and pride as the boss get in the way of being a good listener.
- Take time to listen to the input of your air-staff. Since they are on the front line with listeners, quite often they really do have a better feel for how the station sounds and the format is being received.
- One of the hardest things to give away is kindness…it usually comes right back to you!
- The golden rule of being a good manager is to listen attentively to others as you would have them listen to you.

Radio Station Managers take note: If you're not careful, you can suffer from acute paralysis through over-analysis of your air-talent's on-air performance.

Here are a few pointers for air-talent to remember when dealing with management:

- You can get your manager's attention quicker with your ears than with your mouth.
- Don't let your ego and pride get in the way of accepting solid input and advice from your boss.

- Listen more, talk less.
- Your manager will point you in the direction of the finish line, but you need to run your own race.
- Be yourself on the radio, but be ready to take the heat when your idea bombs.
- Spend some time thinking about what their job is and how tough it can be.
- Show your manager a little respect and you'll get it back ten-fold. Always be respectful.
- Managers are people, too, and if they trust you and depend on you, don't let them down. Do your job and do it well, every day!

60-second management course.

I am grateful to my longtime friend and former radio co-worker Doug LaVallee for passing along this meaningful story regarding a 60-second management course for would-be managers, especially of the radio variety!

A turkey is talking with a big ole bull out in the pasture.

"I would love to be able to get to the top of that big tree," sighed the turkey, "but I haven't got the energy."

"Well, why don't you nibble on some of my droppings?" replied the bull, "They're packed with nutrients." So, the turkey pecked away at a large lump of dung and found it actually gave him enough strength to reach the lowest branch on the tree. The next day, after eating some more dung, the turkey reached the second branch. Finally, after a fourth night, the turkey found himself proudly perched at the top of the tree where he was promptly spotted by a rancher who shot him out of the tree!

Moral of the story: BS may get you to the top, but it won't keep you there!

Notes:
1. Radio pros Steve Feldman and Steve Gilinsky share their thoughts on the importance of sales and talent being best friends in Chapter 19.
2. A familiar phrase borrowed from the late legendary Boston talk-master, Commander Larry Glick, who is saluted in Chapter 16.
3. During the author's time spent on radio in numerous markets, including medium to large cities like Cincinnati, Boston, Houston and West Palm Beach, the ratings service Arbitron most often showed him to be #1 in his demographic, which always placed him in the top five as most popular radio personalities in any given city.

Peter Smyth, Pres. and CEO Greater Media.

Mark Hannon, Boston radio group GM.

Tom Baker, radio GM.

Nancy Widmann, first woman Pres. CBS Radio

Dan Mason, CEO CBS Radio

L to R: John Gehron, author, Bob MacAleney (Sheraton Hotel Mgr) Andy Moes

CHAPTER 12
The Role of Consultants

"A real radio pro is disciplined and stays focused no matter what else is going on."

The role of a radio station consultant

It is no big secret in broadcasting circles that air-talent is suspicious of most consultants. Why?

Well, the primary mission of a consultant is to find out what's wrong with a radio station and fix it. Sometimes, in making those repairs, and if the situation is to be rectified, talent may be perceived as part of the problem and will have to go! It's a pretty good reason for air-talent to be jumpy and grumpy when they get the word the consultant is in town! Here's another thing that is worrisome for talent: Consultants are notoriously known for shutting up air personalities and cutting out what they believe is too much talk on the station. Consultants also have a lot of say on who gets hired or fired, therefore striking fear in the hearts of talent. Is it any wonder many air personalities tremble when they get word that consultants are in town - or worse yet, he's in the building!

I consider myself one of the lucky ones in radio. During my 41 years on the air, I worked with some of the best consultants in the business. However, that won't always be the case with you. Many of these ramrods and head-choppers can be brutal. They are ruthless in their approach and lack tact and diplomacy in handling tightly-wound and egocentric talent. Their summation on what's wrong with the station and the air staff and how to fix it can be tantamount to disaster. They don't mince words; they lay it on the line and shoot directly between the eyes! The end result: bodies lying in state all over the place!

The following memo, although written tongue-in-cheek, and from an unknown source, reflects how some consultants conduct business. In this scenario, the consultant has been hired by management to help Santa Claus. It appears the jolly ole gent's "Q factor" is dropping and something needs to be done to help improve his image![1] Hello! Make room for the man in black, the consultant!

"Hi, Santa, I'm your new consultant. The home office hired me to fly in here a couple of times a year to give you my thoughts on how you can boost some of those sagging ratings. Oh, sure, I know, you've maintained a pretty good rating with the 12-and-under demo for a long time, but Santa, babe, let's face it: it's not like you've had a lot of competition! Admit it, there are not many old guys running around dropping dolls down chimneys now, are there? Be honest! You're kind of winning in the share you have by default. If someone comes along and challenges you, it could mean trouble.

"Now, look: I've done a little call out research…and your share of 18+ adults is—well, to be honest, it's pathetic! Our focus groups show your credibility REALLY suffers with men and women, especially 18-to-49-year-olds, and your 54+ numbers are a total joke! Now, look: I've drawn up a few suggestions for you that I really feel are going to help a whole lot. First of all, let's get one thing straight, right from the get-go: LESS TALK. I mean, come on, Santa, how many times in any given conversation do you think it's really necessary to say, 'HO, HO, HO?' One 'Ho' is more than enough!

"According to my research, we're losing adults after that second 'Ho.' What we want to do is less 'Ho' and more music! And, Santa, when the kids are sitting on your knee? Do some kind of 'Santa relate' in 10 seconds or less, and don't feel like you've got to talk between every kid!! A quick 'Merry Christmas' is all you need, especially between siblings. What you don't want to do is risk boring them with a lot of superfluous chit-chat. The last thing we want are kids going over to the competition—if, of course, we ever have any, ha, ha, ha.

"Now, back to that music issue for a minute. When you're at the mall, I want you to get those part-time helpers, ya know the ones who take photos, to crank up the carols just a little louder. As a matter of fact, what I'm really thinking is 'ten carols in a row.' If we have to, we might even consider speeding up each carol by 10% so we can fit another one into each hour and then we can claim to play the MOST Christmas carols! Of course, we can't play just ANY Christmas carols and songs because some of them seem to test quite poorly. But, you know that 'Grandma Got Run Over by a Reindeer' song? Yeah, I know it sucks, but they love it, Santa. We'll put that one into a high rotation and hit it every 90 minutes or so."

The role of a consultant in dealing with Santa.

"I'm also thinking about a tight Christmas carol playlist comprised of, say, 43 records. What's that? Yeah, I know, there are hundreds of songs, but hey, I'd rather play only the stuff that tested well…and nothing with any negatives. What's that? What do you mean, you KNOW there are other songs that they like!? This is NO time for unscientific gut-reactions, Claus. Now, come on. If we're going to shore up your standing and image, we've got to go with what we know!

"Okay, next, let's get one of the elves to write up some nice signs with slogans like, 'LESS HO, MORE CAROLS, TEN-IN-A-ROW OR YOUR CHRISTMAS BACK! MORE MUSIC, LESS JINGLES.' Oh, by the way, that reminds me, did I mention the jingle bells have to go?! Yeah, people are really burned on those jingle bells of yours. How do I know? Well, I got five people together in a quiet room and conducted a FOCUS GROUP! Ever hear of one, Santa? You know, you talk like you've been living near the North Pole! Do you have any idea how valid five peoples' thoughts are compared to the whole population? I tell you, you get the right folks into a closed environment for three hours and what they tell you is almost like gospel!! NEVER doubt a focus group, Claus!! I'm a CONSULTANT!! I KNOW this stuff! What do you mean the last focus group told you to INCREASE the jingle bells?? He cited WHAT research? No, I never heard of that research. Well, I guess we'll just have to agree to disagree, Santa.

"So, that's pretty much it. Look, I'll be back in about three months to check on you and see how you've integrated these suggestions. I'd like to stay longer, but I've got to catch a flight to PA. I've got a little furry guy in Punxsutawney who's BLOWING his credibility with his predictions of spring. Oh yeah, one last thing…that will be $10,000!!"

A bit of an exaggeration? Perhaps. But, ask anyone who has been in radio longer than breakfast, and who has dealt with consultants, and I guarantee you most will identify with the Santa story.

The primary role of a consultant is to "fix" broken radio stations!

Guy Zapoleon founded Zapoleon Media Strategies in Katy, Texas in January, 1992. We have known each other for many years. I consider Guy one of the best consultants in the radio business, on a par with my longtime friends Gary Berkowitz, Walter Sabo and a few others. Guy credits WABC's Cousin Brucie as his inspiration.[2] "I was thirteen and my friends told me," says Guy, "if I wanted to be cool and attract girls than I'd have to know my music. I loved Brucie's show. He was a great personality, a lot of fun and you could tell how excited he was to be on the radio."

Over the years, Guy has consulted many radio stations in the biggest markets. He says his biggest undertaking was helping to launch WKTU in 1996, which he proudly proclaims went from worst to #1 in New York City.

"My job was to create the musical recipe and assimilate and create a formula for Evergreen's new radio station," says Zapoleon. "I first had to convince the station to buy WKTU from someone in New Jersey. Then RuPaul was actually my contribution to KTU, as my friend Marc Nathan suggested to me that we ought to have a morning show, *3 Queens from Brooklyn*, two women from NYC with RuPaul. Everyone at the station thought I was crazy, but eventually after trying out three other more traditional shows we went with RuPaul."

Zapoleon continues, explaining his role in working with air-talent. "I always feel a consultant's job with talent is to introduce, or reintroduce them to the **BRILLIANT BASICS,** one thought per break. Also, to help them understand where they hit the punch line in a topic and move on. How to tease on their show and recycle ideas, and so on. I also believe a consultant's role is to share 'benchmarked bits' for air-personalities that have worked in other places."[3] Guy feels strongly that a consultant can help an air personality with fine-tuning their act. "This can be done in monthly critiques, but if there is an issue with the personality, it may take a lot more than fine-tuning to help the personality get to the next level.[4] A qualified programming consultant can tell you, as the PD or GM, whether your air-personality can make it to the next level in his or her current state." Zapoleon says other aspects involving talent, such as voice quality and delivery, are best left to a talent coach. He strongly emphasizes, "If the personality has major talent issues, then at that point you need a qualified talent coach to evaluate the abilities and if they are capable of improving enough to reach the desired goal of the station or not."

What a consultant looks for in an air-talent.

Guy Zapoleon believes God-given talent is #1 in a person's make-up to be a successful air-talent. "You also need a voice, an engaging personality, either you have it or you don't, along with instincts about what people want to hear. Talent must always drive to excel and the desire to learn and improve."

Zapoleon has special words of advice for future radio wannabes.

"If you are a talent and especially have the qualities I've described, find a programmer or manager or even talent at a given radio station that is interested in nurturing talent and mentoring future radio stars. When you find that person, express your interest in working with them in any entry-level job that could lead to an on-air position even part time. Go to the radio station and DO THIS IN PERSON!! Stay in contact with that person via phone or e-mail, and if you don't get in the door the first or second time, continue to stay in touch with them and meet them in person. Develop at least a couple of people that could possibly help you. In other words, don't put all your eggs in one basket, although that one person might be the one that lets you break in."

In July 2003, Zapoleon commented on the declining popularity of commercial radio and stated some of the reasons. Here are his comments.

"The strategy to fix radio is so simple, but like all things in life there are no shortcuts; it will take hard work and a lot of patience because we've chased away many of the people who were passionate about radio. Radio has become irrelevant to a generation of listeners who have turned to other [media] for satisfaction." Zapoleon forewarned America's broadcasters about the disastrous direction in which radio was headed. "Most people desire brand-names with the best quality and have been taught to know the difference in brands. Now, we plan on giving them watered-down generic brands in radio and expect them to be happy about it. NO WAY! Do you ever feel like you're in a horror movie and just when you think things can't get worse something even more horrible happens!! Well, that's the way I feel. Looking at radio today," Guy solemnly swears, "if anyone had told that thirteen-year-old kid who listened to his transistor in the 1960s that radio would be dealing with this sad state of affairs I would have put my head in my hands and cried. I love this business and it's a tragedy to see it has come to this."

Guy Zapoleon's personal insights on the problems facing radio today.

What has happened to commercial radio?

Like many other broadcasters, Zapoleon believes the dire shape radio finds itself in today is largely due to consolidation on Wall Street. "Even former President Clinton commented in January 2002 at the R&R[5] convention how sad he was that he ever allowed the radio ownership limit changes clause to be attached and passed along with the Telecom bill. President Clinton was promised better format diversity and better radio overall, but instead," continues Zapoleon, "he commiserated with the radio programming audience that it had gone downhill."

According to Zapoleon, these are some of the serious issues facing radio:

- **Consolidation** - Wall Street creates a lack of tools and cookie-cutter strategies.
- **Too-tight playlists** - which means fewer songs played on the radio.
- **Top-40 radio out of touch** with passionate listeners
- **Diminished role of the radio personality**

"Owners who work for public companies are so focused on keeping Wall Street happy and delivering 10% cash flow growth," says the popular consultant, "that many have totally lost touch with the product and the listener. Little do they know that with radio they have an industry that should really be on life support and receiving all the best care and treatment. Instead, radio is being treated as if it is a healthy athlete still in its prime! Radio is being starved for research, outside programming experts, and very important consistent marketing dollars at a time when radio needs it most. It is hard to blame the owners since the outrageous prices that were paid for stations have caused a huge chunk of operating costs to simply be paid to cover that. As the old saying goes, we're killing the goose that laid the golden eggs!"

Guy Zapoleon first made these comments in 2003. During the same time period, a major focus group research company probed the reasons why so many listeners were dissatisfied with radio. The biggest complaints were:

- **A lack of variety** on station and format diversity in general
- **Unable to find** the music for their taste
- **Too much** meaningless DJ talk
- **Too many** commercials

"Radio better wake up," Zapoleon cautioned, "because mp3 downloading is attacking its youth base. As radio becomes much less important to the 12- to-24-year-old age group and they spend more time sharing music files with friends, because it is the way they discover music, radio will find itself in big trouble. They no longer depend on radio exclusively for their music source. XM-Sirius is making deals with major car companies to make satellite radio systems standard in new models. This will cause an avalanche of adults to discover commercial-free radio with a huge variety of channels and wide playlists of satellite services. The threat is upon us [radio] and the mass exodus has already started."

What has happened to commercial radio?

Too-tight music playlists is one of the biggest reasons for diminished radio listenership. "Everyone in radio programming, including we consultants," points out Zapoleon, "looks at our Cume and TSL, but has anyone looked at PUR [people using radio] over the past ten years?[6] The drop-off is astounding. One big reason is overly-tight music playlists on radio stations. As a consultant over the years, I have always seen in research that very few songs satisfy the majority of listeners and in an effort to find common denominator songs for a wide group of people, radio has played a very tight list. This creates a playlist of songs many of which test fairly well with a lot of people, but may NOT really test great with anybody. Also add to this the major problem that research companies are searching out P1's and Cume and aren't measuring the people that no longer listen.[7] What is so sad," he continues, "is that ARB [ratings service] success is as much based on TSL as CUME. People who grow tired of tight music playlists and do so extremely fast."

"For example," says Guy, "on oldies stations that cut playlists from 500 to 250 songs, the killer or most favorite gold songs like 'My Girl' and 'Good Lovin'' were played to death and as a result the listener passion for these songs has dropped for the core library.[8] Now, there is nothing left to replace them with except incompatible-sounding '70s songs that are creating challenges for the format."

Here is another example to further elaborate on Guys Zapoleon's point. The Temptations' "My Girl" is definitely a classic oldie, and deserving of its #1 status.[9] However, another song from the same group that I feel rivals "My Girl" in every way, is 1965's "Since I Lost My Baby," a beautiful song that barely made Billboard's Top-20, coming in at #17.[10] On a tight-playlisted station, you would never hear the song. The Temptations gave us many hit songs that never made it to number one, but have all that great Motown quality. These are songs people love, spent their money buying, and gave a home to on Top-40 charts. Hit songs like "Get Ready," which only got as high as #29, "Ain't Too Proud to Beg" at #13, and "The Way You Do the Things You Do" at #11.[11, 12, 13]

Tight music playlists have driven listeners away from commercial radio.

Many artists recorded great songs which may not have been #1 on the charts but were certainly #1 in people's hearts. Dick and Dee's [14] bestselling song, "The Mountain's High" charted at #2 in 1961, but they also recorded a haunting love song, "Tell Me," which only got as high as #22 in 1962, but is still a highly requested song by radio listeners. Have you ever heard the song played on your favorite oldies station? My guess is not! New Orleans' legendary R&B singer/songwriter Fats Domino will always be best known for his smash hit "Blueberry Hill," which in 1956 charted as high as #2, but the man had a whopping total of thirty-six other songs which made the Top-40 charts.[15] Seventeen placed within the Top-20, with eleven making the Top-10. Great soulful rock n' roll songs, like "I'm Walkin, I'm In Love Again," "Blue Monday," "Whole Lotta Loving," "Let the Four Winds Blow," and others. How many songs from the Fat man have you heard on the radio recently?[16]

Another example of not having many of their hits aired on radio is the pop group from New Bedford, MA with the smooth harmony, **Tavares**. The brothers, Ralph, Antone (pooch), Feliciano, Arthur and Perry (Tiny) are my friends, and also one of my all-time favorite groups from the 70's and 80's. Quite often, Pooch and Tiny would sit in with me during my Saturday Night All-Request Oldies Show. Tavares gave us many Top-40 hits which charted on Billboard, but usually, only two are played on radio: It Only Takes A Minute Girl (#10-'75) and Heaven Must be missing an Angel (#15-'76) Both super hits, but what about their other hit songs like, Check It Out, Remember what I told you to forget, Who Dunit, More Than A Woman and others.

How many have you heard on the air? Tavares is another example of so many music artists who are all but forgotten by radio.

Popular recording artists such as Elvis, Michael Jackson, the Beatles and Madonna have a combined total number of 215 hit songs which placed on Billboard's Top-40 music charts, according to Record Research expert, Joel Whitburn. Other than a few songs from each artist, how many of their numerous hits have you heard played on the radio? With tight music play lists in rotation on many of America's radio stations is it any wonder more and more listeners are turning away from radio in favor of other media, I-pods, internet and so on, in their search to find a wider variety of music.

Two of my longtime friends in the music business, **Bobby Vee** and **Bobby Vinton**, between them have proudly placed *forty-four* hit songs on Billboard's Top-40 charts![17] But, other than "Blue Velvet" for Mr. Vinton and "Take Good Care of My Baby" for Mr. Vee, how many of their hit songs have you heard on the radio? This is what happens when a station insists on a tight music playlist. Fewer popular hit songs get aired on radio!

Great oldies never get played and therefore never get heard. At the risk of sounding mercenary, these artists/songwriters never get the royalties they richly deserve because their songs never receive air play and are relegated to an occasional spin, if that, and are classified as "lost 45's."

Bobby Vee is best remembered for his hit "Take Good Care of My Baby," which was number one for three weeks in a row in the summer of 1961, but a dedicated "true-oldies" fan knows that Bobby Vee, who still plays to a full house in Branson, Missouri, with his sons "The V's," also placed *thirteen* additional hit songs on America's Top-40 charts. Classic gold hits, including "Please Don't Ask about Barbara" and "Sharing You," both placed at #15 on the pop music charts. Another Vee hit, "The Night Has a Thousand Eyes," got inside the Top-5, at #3. My favorite from Bobby, "Devil or Angel," got inside the Top-Ten at #6.

Bobby Vinton has amassed an amazing total of thirty songs on the Top-40 charts. Nine placed in the Top-10, six in the top five and four became number-one hit songs: "Roses are Red," "Blue Velvet," "There, I've Said It Again," and his last #1 hit, "Mr. Lonely." 1960s teen idol Rick Nelson had a string of top-ranking hit songs as well, including "Poor Little Fool," "Travelin' Man," and "Hello Mary-Lou."[18] If you love oldies, I'm sure you've heard these songs played over and over again on the radio. That is, *if* the program powers-that-be at your favorite oldies station consider Ricky to be one of their core artists. Many don't. The reason? Call them and ask, then let me know.

American music legends Bobby Vee, Bobby Vinton and Rick Nelson, with few exceptions, get very little if any air-play on radio today. In my opinion, these former pop artists do not receive air-play because many programmers believe they only attract a much older listener, like that's evil or something. Many programmers think these artists and others do not appeal to their prime Wall Street demo, a thirty-something. Someone needs to enlighten these uninformed radio minds that these former teen idols had hit songs because people enjoyed hearing them, and a whole new generation and not just oldie fans will love them, too.

A station with a tight playlist would never air Ricky Nelson's other hit songs like, "Young Emotions," which charted at #12, or the great rock-a-billy sound of "Waitin' in School," which only charted at #18. If a song didn't achieve number-one status, or at least top-five on the survey charts, chances are slim-to-none of ever hearing it played on your favorite oldies station or anywhere on radio. As a matter of fact, these songs are played so infrequently on radio that when they are aired, these all but forgotten golden gems are referred to as *"Oh, Wow!"* songs, a phrase coined by listeners who are so thrilled to hear one of their forgotten favorite songs on radio that they excitedly proclaim, "Oh Wow! I haven't heard this song in ages!"

Before moving on to the next important reason radio consultant Guy Zapoleon believes listeners are leaving commercial radio by the boatload, the diminished role of the air-personality, let's look at another music group, The Young Rascals, or as they were later known, The Rascals.[19] "Good Lovin'" was one of their biggest hits, hitting number one for one week in March, 1966. It is played constantly on radio! However, their biggest hit was "Groovin'," which was #1 for four weeks in a row in May 1967, one year following the release of "Good Lovin'." The Rascals also had hits with "You Better Run," "I've Been Lonely Too Long," "A Girl Like You," "How Can I be Sure," "Beautiful Morning," "People Got To Be Free," and others. How many of the Rascals songs, other than "Good Lovin'," have you heard on the radio? Few if any, I bet. You can thank tight station playlists for this abysmal situation.

When stations only play one song from an artist over and over in high rotation, like "Good Lovin'," it causes listener fatigue. People actually go from loving a song to hating it! They also begin to dislike the artist without giving any conscious reason why. Constant repetition of the same songs causes loyal listeners, or P1's as they are called, to tune out and away from the station. I'd like to have a dime for every time I tried to convince my PD or GM that our listeners were growing weary of hearing the same twelve songs over and over again in morning drive. Here's how the conversation usually went:

> Me: We're driving our listeners away by playing the same few songs over and over!
> PD or GM: How do you know that?
> Me: Duh, because we're getting complaints on the listener-line to the studio.
> PD or GM: Oh, that's just the regular P1 listeners who are calling. You guys are too close to it. You have to play these songs over and

over, every day and therefore YOU are the ones who are growing tired of hearing them and getting burned out on them, NOT the listeners. [Logical, eh?] The listeners don't hear the same 100 songs over and over, like you do. We spend big bucks on focus groups and test these songs over and over. We pay you to be entertaining around these songs. Just play them and don't concern yourself with music rotation, thanks for your input and have a nice day!

That's basically how the conversation went, minus a few descriptive adjectives. I'm sure it still takes place today between concerned air-talent and program people. It was so frustrating when programming and/or management refused to listen to the input of their frontline troops, the air-talent. Who better to know and feel the pulse of the listener than the air staff? We as air-talent could actually feel our listeners leaving by the bus load and our ratings along with them. Sadly, it was such an easy fix to play more music, but the simple solution often fell on deaf ears.

Short song playlists on the radio need to be a thing of the past. **Dick Clark** said it best at the 1972 *Billboard* convention in LA, which I attended. At one of the sessions, a heated debate was going on about which songs to play on the radio. I was seated directly behind Dick Clark when he stood up and proclaimed, "If it's a hit, play it! If a song made the charts it's because lots of folks heard it, liked it and bought it! Radio programming is not brain surgery, play the hits and folks will listen." The popular radio and TV pro received a thunderous round of applause.

As mentioned, our song playlist from the 1950s and '60s on the original WROR and *Saturday Night at the Oldies* consisted of any song which charted on Billboard's Top-40 and even a few below that magical "40" number. We were not handed a list of songs to play, nor were we restricted to playing only songs from our regular station playlist. We had free reign to play whatever we wanted. It made total sense. After all it was an "all-request" oldies show. As long as the listener requested a song from the '50s, '60s, and early '70s, and if the song and sound fit, we played it! It proved to be the winning formula. For twelve consecutive years *Saturday Night "Live" at the Oldies* was Arbitron-rated #1 in double-digits across all demographics!

We took pride in adding songs to our thousand-plus playlist every weekend and would proudly announce songs we added: "Guess what little golden nugget we dug up for you tonight? How about 'You Were Mine' [20] by the Fireflies, a doo-wop group from Philly, the classic, haunting instrumental 'Rumble' [21] by guitarist Link Wray, 'Baby I'm Yours' [22] by Michigan-born Barbara Lewis, and 'Believe Me' [23] by a group from Fort Lee, New Jersey, the Royal Teens." Even the Beatles, "And I Love You" [24] only charted as high as #12 in 1964. None of these songs made the Top-10, but that doesn't mean people didn't love them, bought them, and want to hear them again on the radio.

Author's Note: Many thanks to Joel Whitburn for allowing us to borrow some of his chart information on various artists from his well-researched book, The Billboard Book of Top 40 hits (2000 edition)

The diminished role of the radio personality has hurt radio.

Radio consultant Guy Zapoleon strongly believes another reason radio listening is off is because of the diminished role of the personality. In an uncanny way he made these predictions in July 2003, but they could easily be made today in describing the present state of radio here in America.

"Another big reason we've suffered TSL loss may be the most important of all," says Zapoleon, "is the decreased role and diminished content of the air personality. There was a time when the air personality was allowed to consider the day part he worked on his or her own show and was encouraged to create compelling content. They were encouraged to host the show like it was theirs and introduce music on a one-on-one level with the listener, sharing a play list that was specially constructed for their day part; upbeat-wake up songs in the mornings, mellower songs in middays, and so forth. *The air-talent sold the music like it was their favorite music* and built up the artists by telling the listener behind-the-scenes information and tidbits about their lives. The radio personality passionately sold all the station benefits. They made the contests appear to be larger than life."

Without personalities, radio is just a jukebox.

"Today, we tell radio personalities that it is NOT their show and to simply concentrate on selling the station. When radio went to this approach in the '80s, it began losing its personality in every day part except in morning drive where that type of mindset is still allowed." Zapoleon continues, "The great on-air radio pros made you feel like you were missing something if you turned the radio off or tuned to another station. Their presence made every single other element on the station better. Without them radio is just a jukebox and the listener might as well be listening to downloads or the 'jockless' formats on cable radio."

Former radio personality **Joe Desimone**, who today is in the advertising business, rocked Portland, Maine's airwaves in the early '60s as Johnny Dollar. Like Guy Zapoleon, Joe feels strongly about the important role personality plays on radio. "Radio personalities looked at their time on the radio as *their* show. They spent years to come up with a unique style and honing it to get ready for the big time!" Desimone believes the lack of personality radio goes back to shortly after the FCC deregulated broadcasting. "Large companies began buying up thousands of independent stations, and one company could own practically an unlimited number of stations. Broadcast corporations bought as many stations as they could to blanket a market. They hired outside format consultants and reduced the air-staff by overlapping talent to cover more than one station, and there you go. With the exception of morning drive," adds Desimone, "most stations run 25- to 30-minute segments of uninterrupted music. How can a 'personality' truly be a 'personality' when they hardly are heard on the air!"

Joe Desimone began his on-air career in 1959 at WARE in Ware, Massachusetts, before moving to New Orleans under the air-name Allen All Night. Needless to say, he was on the all-night shift but later moved up to days. He laughs when remembering the wild story the station's publicist dreamed up and released to the press. "He said, I refused to take a day shift because I came from a long line of nocturnal creatures! The story went national and *Ripley's Believe it or Not* got hold of it and wanted to put me in their book and newspaper circulation." Joe moved to WLOB in Portland in the early '60s under the air-name Johnny Dollar. "To get a little publicity as the new guy on the radio in town, I threw dollars from the roof of a downtown Portland building. It stopped traffic at rush hour on Congress Street, one of the city's major thoroughfares, and caused half the police force to rush to the scene along with hook and ladder fire trucks. The crowd loved it! Of course, I got arrested and WCSH-TV filmed it from the roof of their studio across the street for the 6 o'clock news. Radio stations today just don't do really exciting things like we did in the past," asserts Desimone.

Sometimes even in the coveted AM-drive slot, less personality is almost the byword. Many programmers perceive "personality" as "talk" and on a music-intense radio station, talk is an evil word and is not encouraged! In 2004, while in morning drive at Sunny-104.3 in West Palm Beach, I was so frustrated by how little personality I was allowed to project on the air, I actually counted the total amount of minutes I spoke on the radio in one hour! Between 8 and 9 am, it came to around two minutes for the entire hour, which included intros for news, traffic, and the six or seven songs I was required to play in the hour. Pathetic, I say. My advice for radio wannabes: if you have a personality and want to use it on the air without constantly being at odds with management, learn how to project it in an entertaining and informative manner in ten seconds or less, or opt to go into talk radio!

How to fix radio's problems.

Okay, so now that you've heard some of the challenges facing radio today, so how do you go about fixing them? Once again, let's turn to our "go-to Guy" for this chapter and his solution on how radio gets out of its current state. Guy Zapoleon says, "Do compelling radio. The programming side of radio, air-talent, PDs, consultants and other creative forces need to be like the newscaster in the film *Network* and scream from the rooftops, 'I'm mad as hell and I'm not going to take it anymore!!' All of us in programming need to keep on screaming until the radio owners and Wall Street listen or we'll be working in another industry in five years!"[25]

Radio consultant Guy Zapoleon's eight basic steps to fix radio's woes.

The solutions are easy, he says, but the road back is long and hard and starts with eight basic steps:

1. Admit there is a problem and take a hard look at ourselves.

"It is critical to do research not just on individual stations, but on radio as a medium and how we can get back the people we've lost and how to make current listeners more satisfied. If anyone doesn't think this is possible, take a look at the cable TV industry. It was on the ropes and faced with extinction due to the explosion of satellite TV. Cable took a hard look at themselves and what their viewers wanted, which was better quality programming and more variety. Sound familiar? What they came up with was the digital cable solution. This was right out of a Ries and Trout book on marketing basics - they covered every advantage satellite had and cable offered the same variety (the same channels), then they took on an aggressive TV campaign to reposition the satellite industry and preyed on their weaknesses. For example, system unfamiliarity and the limitation of one TV set per setup. Again, the same kind of advantage radio has over either satellite or the Internet."

2. Build a brain trust to create and execute your strategy.

"More important than any single aspect of a great radio station are the people who create the product and staff and manage it. As Nationwide Communications President **Steve Berger** always said, "Only the BEST people." If you want greatness you have to have the best money can buy. It's like the all or nothing principle - if you don't have someone excellent in a given department then you have a weak link and your chances to be great are slight. With two or more weak links and your long-term success - even your chance to succeed at all - is greatly compromised. I agree with John Gehron who always told me, you can't have a programmer devoted to programming two radio stations and expect the same quality. It also extends to air-personalities. You can't have voice-tracking and expect the creativity and immediacy that a live air-talent provides when reacting to local events and connecting with listeners. Your brain trust should include outside experts to provide an outside perspective. It's so easy to lose sight about what is really right or wrong with your station.

"A good consultant who works with a particular format can boil it down - the keys to success or failure. Many times, the PD or GM already knows the answer, but they don't have the credibility from the inside, often perceived as making excuses. A noted consultant can come into the situation at the station and lend credence while getting the local team the tools and understanding they need. Most consultants have had the experience of working with many different research companies and have seen different ways of putting a questionnaire together with many different interpretations of the same results. The wrong interpretation of a study has the potential to destroy a station. A good consultant has the programming expertise to interpret and read between the lines. The average programmer cannot match knowledge with a consultant - someone who has been in the radio business for years and has seen many stations and formats in different markets and in competitive scenarios. A good consultant is the radio station's insurance policy in getting the strategic plan executed with excellence. The consultant should be looked at as a filter for programming to help the PD and GM understand programming and marketing issues that they generally have not faced."

3. Get to know your listeners and ask them what you can do to be better.

"You need to do research all the time. Most station operators who do one perceptual study a year or even every few years and act like the competitive landscape is not changing may be 'penny wise and pound foolish.' Everything is changing all the time.[26] The format of radio is evolving and there is always new competition from other media. Australians and German broadcasters get it so much better than we Americans. They have their own research departments and a research consultant with monthly perceptual tracking to compare the ratings. They can tell exactly what caused a decline in a given month in the ratings, instead of waiting and letting the problem linger and damaging the station further. At this point, it's probably too much to ask, and the radio station can't afford it, but two perceptuals a year will give you time to fix mistakes before they can do permanent damage. In a cluster of stations, you need to do a market format viability study for the stations every year to measure market changes and desires of the individual formats. Hire a researcher who tells you the truth you need to hear and not what you want to hear. Someone who will help you design a custom strategy that will produce lots of success stories."

Some research names Guy Zapoleon respects most are Mark Ramsey of Mercury Research, John Coleman at Coleman Research, John Parikhal's Joint Communications and Ted Ruscitti of Ted Ruscitti Associates. "As the radio exec in charge, you don't need cookie-cutter strategies and a researcher who will avoid the brutal truth in order to not upset the client. We're in a time where radio is so competitive with all mediums, and you always need to hear the truth about your stations if you are going to win and, more importantly, if you are going to be an important part of your listeners' lives."

4. Create custom solutions for listeners.

"Take your excellent brain trust and interpret the research for the radio station looking for custom solutions, not rehashed ideas that have been used in a thousand markets. Wipe the slate clean and see if you can come up with something new and creative. When you brainstorm, don't put a numbered limit on the amount of ideas someone can write down because the more ideas you have, the more likely you will find at least one GREAT creative idea! When more and more people are removed from the creative process there are less unique ideas - that creates 'sameness' and breeds stagnation. The best ideas come out of a free idea exchange with judgment withheld; that interaction of people's ideas creates new creativity."

5. Make a promise and deliver on it RELENTLESSLY.

"Use the research to find listeners' needs, desires, and expectations, then make a promise to your listeners and never stop delivering on that promise. Tell the listener about how you listened to them and how you improved the air-sound, both on the station and most especially with outside marketing. All the time, MARKET, MARKET, MARKET! At the end of my tenure as National PD in 1991, I worked for some incredible radio companies, like Nationwide Communications. These companies knew it was a dogfight every day and gave you the budget necessary to staff, create, and market a great radio station. These stations had a FULL staff, not one we shared with two other stations, and our staff was dedicated to creating a great on-air product and giving the listener gratification with promotions."

6. Give the consumer (listener) better variety and a better product.

"This has a lot to do with great promotions and great personalities. Where do we start to find answers to today's problems? Search out history when radio was successful. I grew up loving radio from the time I was 13, with my little transistor tucked under my pillow listening to Cousin Brucie on WABC," reflects Zapoleon. "I hung on every word, as did every teenager in the New York, New Jersey, Connecticut area back in 1965. We were thrilled to listen to WABC with the best music, presented by great air-personalities in all day-parts with exciting jingles and ABC News to let us know what was happening in the world. Then I moved to Los Angeles when I was 15 and grew-up listening to KHJ, another great station for a different reason. KHJ had seamless production making every song sound better than on any other radio station I've heard before or since. KHJ was a combination of Bill Drake with his tight format and 12-second jock raps and PD Ron Jacobs, who was the creative force. Ron created the non-stop contest concept. There was an incredible contest every one to two weeks on the station. Everyone who is looking for a mirror on the great radio of the past should pick up the KHJ book from Ron Jacobs."

7. Music-based stations should test their music often, listeners want a variety.

"Most radio experts will agree that a tight playlist is the answer to better ratings, and it is in the short-term, but unless the music titles are tested three or four times a year that strategy has long-term ill effects. At many oldies stations, playing Roy Orbison's 'Pretty Woman' and The Rascals' 'Good Lovin'' every five hours for five years has single-handedly burned the core music library![27, 28] Strategies like that have chased all passionate oldies TSL-delivering fans to their CD collections and turned a foreground music format to a utility format that is primarily used for ten minutes in the car or as background (*way* in the background). If it can happen to oldies, it can happen to other formats. **Greg Strassell** at WBMX (MIX-98.5) Boston developed about 25 great 'Oh Wow' titles that had low familiarity but high potential-playing.[29] These titles over the years have created more gold titles to fall back on versus most Hot AC stations. Listeners want variety and the way to get around a tight core library is the right features and the right 'Oh Wow' titles for your passionate TSL listeners!"

8. Create a unique radio station with GREAT live personalities.

"The main job of most PDs in radio's heyday was focusing on the jock, talking everyday to see what they had planned for the next day's show, filling them in on late- breaking entertainment or hard news and spending time critiquing their show. The time it took air-personalities to prepare their three-hour show was as long as the show itself." [30]

How radio can dig itself out from the black hole it's dug for itself!

Zapoleon says that "fixing" radio can be accomplished one radio station at a time. "Some people think that the model that great companies of the past used is no longer relevant. That is completely wrong," he says. "It's a model that still works and will work again. Learn from the great companies of the past and take out an insurance policy. Spend money on people, resources and marketing to maintain your success. The time to start using this reinvestment strategy and these tactics isn't when the ratings are in the toilet. Cutting off the money supply necessary to keep this strategy in place is like wondering why your car won't start when you don't put gas in it! It's plain and simple; it takes a large consistent investment every single year of its existence to maintain success. The alternative is to not spend the money and wait until your station is in huge trouble and it's too late to build it back up to high ratings and profitability. Then you will have to spend five times your normal budget to launch a new format and spend years rebuilding the relationships you have with advertisers. It doesn't seem like much of a choice," suggests Zapoleon. "Invest enough money in your radio station every single year and you will more than make that back in ratings and revenue increases.

"Even without a huge budget you can take all the basics from a great station like KHJ. Become a totally local targeted radio station that is ALWAYS on top of what is happening in your community, a station that is plugged in to local events as well as what is happening nationally in news, entertainment and pop culture. Find young talent - are you paying attention radio wannabes - and teach them how to entertain using an economy of words." Zapoleon says, "Give every air-personality a job and make them feel part of your success. Train the programming and marketing staff in strategy and tactics so that you have a brain trust of seven to ten great minds. Use this brain trust to create excitement on the air in every way possible; through personality, promotion and production values. Borrow a page from Ron Jacobs at KHJ Los Angeles and create the non-stop contest brand that captures the listeners' imagination."

In conclusion, Zapoleon believes owners and managers need to make their radio station a friend. "Your station needs to have connections to get your listeners into events and give them prizes they can only dream about. Make the station production values totally plugged into what is happening today. Find cost-effective ways to market outside and create a ton of events and personal appearances. Build P1 listeners one at a time. Make your radio station a well-crafted brand that is intimate with listeners and the local community. Do that and you create an unbeatable winner!"

Note: The author is indebted to well-known radio consultant Guy Zapoleon for sharing his views along with his in-depth analysis and insight on the problems facing radio and some of the solutions.

Walter Richard Sabo, Jr. is a leader in media programming, marketing and management. He has the distinction of being the youngest Executive VP in the history of NBC, having landed the position at the age of 26. He is the only media executive to have been the chief of a station group and of a radio network. Since 1984, he has been President of Sabo Media, a New York-based programming and management company. Sabo Media consults on all programming on Sirius Satellite Radio, now merged with XM, and even has an on-site office to facilitate interaction with the staff. Sabo Media was the first to program talk successfully on the FM band for a younger audience. His other innovations include the creation of the format known as AC, Adult Contemporary, which many believe is the financial backbone of American radio. Many of today's best-known personalities were discovered by Mr. Sabo, including Sally Jesse Raphael. [31]

Walter Sabo comments on the qualities he looks for in a future radio pro.

"When I listen to an audition CD for the first time," says Sabo, "I listen for three things: first, an intelligence in the voice. Not intellectualism, but intelligence. The voice is being controlled by a brain that is in charge. Next,

I listen for an understanding of the science of radio. There is nothing harder to do in all of show business than a live radio show," insists Sabo. "Many stars from other media fail after a few weeks on radio, because they simply do not have a script or a staff of writers and producers at their beck and call. Radio performers know how listeners listen. They know how Arbitron works. They are proud and clever about how they incorporate the name of the station and other basic elements into their show. Thirdly and most importantly, are we having a good time? Is the personality being a personality who would engage you in a restaurant, at a party, or in your home? All radio stars have clear, consistent opinions. Whether they are doing a comedy show or a daily events-based talk show, they know how they feel about every subject and they express their opinions with confidence, without compromise. The confidence to give an opinion and never change that opinion is the result of preparation, endless preparation. Preparation results in passion and passion results in ratings!"

Walter Sabo believes there are two common traits to every radio pro and mega star, he has had the priviledge to work with. "The first trait about radio people," says Sabo, "they spend all day preparing their next show. They do nothing else - they prepare and prepare and prepare! They are obsessed with their show. They are never happy; they know every show could be improved and the next show will be improved! It drives them! They are never satisfied with their show and always look to improve their performance. Despite this," he continues, "they are oddly grown-up. Usually performers that are this obsessed are childlike, but these radio people are not! They are very grown-up in confronting their work. They are sober and decent. They treat their co-workers extremely well. The jerks don't last. Radio," he emphasizes, "unlike the movies and television, does not coddle its stars. That has drawbacks, but the result is that the jerks are banished. The second characteristic that these radio folks have in common is that they have an off-air partner. They have one or more mentors who keep their egos level and their demons in check. This can be a gifted program director or general manager, but it is more often their lawyer or agent."

Before founding Ozmon Media, Inc., a radio air-personality development company, **Lorna Ozmon** and I worked with Walter Sabo at the original WROR Boston. Are you getting the feeling that radio is a small club, and the same people wind up working together again and again? You're right. Another good reason to speak kindly about everyone you meet in radio: You never know when you may need to cross over that same bridge again. Lorna has worked with great air-personalities across America. Danny Bonaduce, Laurie DeYoung, Dick Purtan, and John Tesh are just some of the many great air-personalities who have garnered much from Lorna's coaching.[32] In addition to her personal air-talent coaching work, Lorna offers a wide variety of training seminars and workshops. She has done group presentations or workshops for many organizations, including Citadel Broadcasting, the Country Music Association, Maine Broadcasting Association, the Public Radio Program Directors Association, and NAB-USA. In 2008, she completed her first annual Ozmon Media conference, *Creating Outside the Box... a Creative Radio Programming Workshop Convention*.

How to be an effective coach of air-talent.

With Ozmon's experience in coaching and dealing with air-talent, I asked her to explain her particular style. "Regardless of our level of experience in radio, all of us hear the same things when we listen to an air-personality. We can all easily differentiate between what sounds good and what sounds bad about the performance. We are all particularly good at finding faults and negatives," she says.

"Coaching," Ozmon explains, "by definition, involves advice and instruction. Without these elements, you are simply managing, which by definition, involves direction and control. The difference between just saying something to air-personalities and getting positive results on the radio is how the message is delivered. The biggest mistake many managers make in their attempt to control or develop their air-talent is to do so through negative input. But, to attempt to improve an air-personality's performance only by giving him or her a litany of negatives and don'ts without plausible and credible do's and how-to's is rarely an effective tactic."

To become a more effective radio talent coach is to change your mindset about the process.

"Stop thinking in terms of *telling* and start thinking in terms of *selling* your coaching points," advises Ozmon. "Appeal to the talent's desire for greatness by stressing how and what you want him or her to do and how it will impact the show's ratings position. For example, try this approach; to me, this coaching point will make the difference between your show being number four and number one. Imagine just how great it will feel to be on top in the market! You'll make yourself much more valuable to the station when you make these improvements to your show." Ozmon says it's important to show respect and that you admire the air-talent for their accomplishments.

Here is another one of her approaches, which as a coach you may want to try: "There's a reason why you've been in this market for so many years. We just have to get you back to what made you a market name in the first place, when you do these things there isn't anybody better than you."

Ozmon emphasizes that understanding the talent you are coaching is critical to succeeding in the air-personality development process. "When you strongly appeal to your air-talents' self-interests, you are much more likely to coach meaningful changes in their performances." Lorna has these words for future radio wannabes: "Be willing to work harder than anyone else at the station and resist the temptation to resent those that get ahead by doing less. Focus only on what you can change and shut out those you cannot. In the end, great talent and hard work do win. Sometimes, it just takes longer than we'd like it to." Reach out to Lorna at ozmonmedia@aol.com.

Consultant **Joe Lou Josephs Buczynski** and I worked for Lorna Ozmon and Walter Sabo at WROR Boston in the 1980s. Yes, radio is made up of the same people in a very tight circle. Keep it in mind. Lou was born in Northern New Jersey and that meant he grew up on WABC and WOR-FM. But because Lou had a radio that could pick-up just about anything, he found a station in New York City that he really liked, WNYW Radio New York Worldwide, owned by Bonneville International. It was the first station to employ Lou's talents. It was just a gopher gig, but just out of high school it was the perfect summer job. At the same time, its sister station was doing its first beautiful music FM dial card-campaign and Lou was involved in that. Later, he worked as a traffic gopher at WOR-FM. [33] Upon leaving the station, he walked out with the station's format clock which he promptly handed over to Gary Berkowitz, Lou's PD at Emerson College station-WERS-FM in Boston where they were both students at the time.[34]

Lou actually got on the air at WKOX, a day-timer in Framingham, Massachusetts. During his senior year in college, he scooted over to do production and weekends at sister station, WVBF- F-105 (today the new ROR-FM). After graduation, Lou joined Gary Berkowitz at WROR-FM as production director, traffic guy and later assistant PD. ROR-FM is where he and I first met and worked together. As a consultant, Lou has been involved with Massachusetts stations WXLO, WFGL, WIZN, WLKZ and WMAS.

Lou Josephs' comments on where tomorrow's radio stars will get their first break.[35]

"College radio may be about the only place for new talent to break in," says Josephs, "although you just never know where good air-talent will be found. Longtime radio programmer George Johns had this amazing ability to pluck someone from the streets and put them on the air, and so was born classic rock-jock Atom Smasher. Comedy clubs are another venue for budding would-be air-talent. The sidekicks that Opie and Anthony use on their syndicated morning show came right from the comedy clubs. Howard Stern's done the same thing for years, so it's another area where the next great air-talent may suddenly emerge."

Lou Josephs agrees with other broadcasters that starting out in radio in a small market used to be the way to go up the ladder, but that's no longer the case. "If you can locate a radio job when first starting out, the pay and the hours are discouraging. Radio can't continue to be a low-paying kind of business. It has to pay better than McDonald's or Wal-Mart." Lou claims that finding the next air-talent isn't as easy as it used to be. "Time was, you could drive four hours from your market and search the small stations in very small towns and cities. Now, it's a voice-traced world where the midday person may be halfway across the country and not in the same town. The local information and weather may have been pulled from the Internet and added to the voice-tracking computer program just before the show airs, so it still sounds local, but the knowledge a local air-talent has about where he or she lives is not going to be the same as some voice-tracked jock from within a corporate radio empire. Sure, it saves a few dollars here and there," according to Josephs, "but it's not worth it in the long run, and is why more and more radio listeners are turning off their sets."

Note: College kids, develop your comedy routine. See if you can pick up a night at the local comedy club. Radio folks love to frequent comedy club and you just never know who may be catching your act.

A final word about radio station consultants.

It is a misnomer to believe that radio station consultants only pick and select which music is played on a station. They do a lot more, at least the ones I was privileged to know and work with, including designing formats and working with air-talent. Qualified broadcast consultants can be a valuable asset to radio stations in need of specialized expertise on a format. A good radio consultant can provide important skills for stations seeking ways to plan, develop and carry out new programming or to freshen up an existing format. A good radio station consultant can be an important liaison and link between all departments in a radio station: management, programming, air-talent, promotion and sales. And finally, a good radio station consultant can and should increase ratings and revenue for a station by addressing the needs and goals of the station and to see that the format is carried out in all day parts. Whether you're a radio wannabe or a seasoned pro, you can learn much by listening to a good station consultant.

Notes:
1. Q Factor refers to the popularity of the celebrity with the public.
2. Cousin Bruce Morrow kindly wrote one of the introductions for this book.
3. Benchmarks are regular features on a show and are covered in detail in Chapter 14: How to Win in Morning Drive.
4. You can read more about air-check and critique sessions in Chapter 10.
5. R&R or Radio & Records was an industry publication.
6. TSL stands for "Time Spent Listening" to radio.

7. P1's refers to "preferred listeners" who usually are loyal to their favorite radio station.
8. "Good Lovin'" by the Rascals was a hit on Atlantic Records.
9–13. All hits on the Gordy label for The Temptations.
14. Dick Gosling & Dee Dee Sperling recorded for Liberty.
15. Fats Domino recorded on the Imperial label. In 1963, his last charted hit song, "Red Sails in the Sunset," was on ABC-Paramount
16. **Author's Note:** During my years as host of *Saturday Night "Live" at the Oldies* on the original WROR-98.5, one of the reasons our show became the all-time most popular all-request oldies show in the history of Boston radio was for one simple reason. We played MORE oldies. If a song from the 1950s and '60s charted on *Billboard's* Top-40 charts, we played it. We did not restrict playing songs that were only survey-rated #1 or just in the Top-10. By the way, I never would have thought about going on the radio without a copy of Joel Whiburn's Billboard book of Top-40 Hits right by my side. I often referred to his well researched book while doing my show. I consider it the Bible of chart info. and highly recommend it. Every air personality should have a copy readily available to double check artist and song info. Don't leave home or go on the air without it!
17. Bobby Vee recorded for Liberty, and Bobby Vinton on Epic
18. Rick Nelson's early recordings in 1957 were on Verve. In late 1957, he was on Imperial and stayed with the label through 1963 when he was on Decca including his '72 hit, "Garden Party." "Poor Little Fool," "Travelin' Man," "Hello, Mary-Lou," "Young Emotions" and "Waitin' in School" were all on Imperial.
19. All the Rascals hits mentioned were on Atlantic.
20. "You Were Mine" on Ribbon records charted as high as #21 in Sept. 1959.
21. "Rumble" got as high as #16 in 1958 on Cadence.
22. "Baby, I'm Yours" peaked at #11 in 1965 on Atlantic.
23. "Believe Me" reached the #26 spot in 1959 on Capitol.
24. "And I Love Her" #12 in '64 for the Beatles is on Capitol.
25. Guy Zapoleon made these warnings about radio's future and how to fix the problems facing radio in July 2003.
26. Remember, what is repeated over and over throughout this book is that the one constant in radio is *change*.
27. "Pretty Woman" by Roy Orbison is on the Monument label.
28. "Good Lovin'" by the Rascals is on Atlantic.
29. Greg Strassell comments in Chapter 10, PDs, Friend or Foe.
30. **Author's note:** Rule of thumb from one of Boston's best air-talents, the late Jess Cain, to whom this book is dedicated: preparation time is at least one hour off the air for every hour. In my case, sometimes I would spend

two hrs. for every on-air hour. I guess, you could say, I was slower than the average radio pro!
31. Sally Jesse Raphael comments in Chapters 8 and 16.
32. Laurie DeYoung comments in Chapters 4 & 14. Dick Purtan comments in Chapters 6, 14, 15, as well as the Afterword.
33. Being a "gopher" is a great way to break into radio. Eventually, depending on your attitude and ability, you may get hired full time.
34. Consultant Gary Berkowitz specializes in the AC format and comments throughout this book.
35. Radio consultant Lou Josephs has also programmed stations in Europe, including putting the first FM station on the air in Kazakhstan's capital city of Almaty, and was involved with Metromedia's Radio 7, an English-Russian broadcaster transmitting from a former Moscow jamming station. Lou also worked with several stations in the Netherlands, including Radio 2, and helped do a live broadcast from Iraq for Radio Veronica.

Guy Zapoleon, nationally known radio consultant.

Walter Sabo, Jr. another nationally known radio consultant.

CHAPTER 13
A Woman's Perspective on Working in Radio and On the Air

"I grew up bold. Survival made me bolder."
– pioneer radio pro, Jean 'the Queen' Steinberg

"When a man gets up to speak, people listen, then look. When a woman gets up, people look; then if they like what they see, they listen."
- Pauline Frederick, radio news reporter in 1948 she became the first woman to report network TV news.

A brief history of pioneer radio women.

One much overlooked aspect of radio talent is the important role women have played on the air.

Reaching back to the early 1920s and the birth of radio broadcasting in America, the list of successful women in radio, both on and off the air, is lengthy and impressive.

Vaughn De Leath was a famous female jazz singer who gained tremendous popularity on the radio. Her first break came in January 1920, when radio inventor Lee DeForest brought her to his studio in New York City and asked her to sing before his radio transmitting equipment.[1] She sang "Swanee River." Her performance is said to be the first live singing broadcast on radio, although some historians dispute the accuracy of the claim. Nevertheless, she became known as "The Original Radio Girl" and "The First Lady of Radio." In 1921, during the formative years of commercial broadcasting, she began singing on WJZ in Newark, New Jersey.[2] In 1931, De Leath sued Kate Smith for using the "First Lady of Radio" title. Smith stopped for awhile, but resumed using it after De Leath's death in 1943.

Judith Waller was another first lady of radio. Not only was she a pioneer in the field, but as an executive dared to try many firsts in broadcasting. In 1922, when she put Chicago's WGU on the air (later WMAQ), her efforts led to several innovative educational programs. Miss Waller's introduction to radio happened one night in 1922. Walter Strong, then business manager of the *Chicago Daily News,* called her and said, "Judith, I just bought a radio station. Come on down and run it." She replied, saying she knew nothing about running a station. "Neither do I," replied Strong, "but come on down and we'll find out." She did and they did and Ms. Waller spent twenty-five years running the station.

Aimee Semple McPherson, also known as Sister Aimee, was a Canadian-born evangelist and media star in the 1920s and '30s. She was a pioneer in the use of radio as a forum for religion and founded the Foursquare Church in Los Angeles. McPherson was the first woman in history to preach a sermon on radio. With the opening of Foursquare's radio station KFSG (now KXOL) in Los Angeles on February 6, 1924, she also became the first woman to be granted a broadcast license by the Federal Radio Commission, which later became the Federal Communications Commission.

Edythe Meserand began her broadcasting career in 1926 at NBC, but her greatest influence in radio was felt at WOR in New York, which she joined in 1935. At WOR, she achieved a number of firsts in broadcast history, including founding the first radio newsroom, producing the first radio documentary, and organizing the station's enduring Children's Christmas Fund Drive. Edythe Meserand was also a founding member of American Women in Radio and Television and served as the organization's first president from 1951 until 1952.

Alma Kitchell[3] was a pioneering radio talk show host. In 1917, six years before regular broadcasts began, she sang for an experimental radio station established at the base of the Statue of Liberty. The first time she walked into New York's WJZ in 1927, she literally sang her way into a job. For the next two decades, Alma was known as the Golden Voice of the Golden Age of Radio. When she retired from singing in 1940, she began a new radio career as host of a series of talk shows focused on women's issues. Alma Kitchell's *Let's Talk It Over* and *Women's Exchange* were on radio from 1938 until 1947.

Marjorie Mills was a favorite radio fixture on Boston's airwaves, beginning in the mid-1920s on WNAC (today WRKO). Later, she moved to WBZ and remained on the air through the 1950s.

Bertha Brainard made broadcasting history in 1928 when she became the first head of programming at NBC Radio. Her primary duty was to fill the airwaves with shows in whatever way she could. By 1937, Brainard was chairman of the board at NBC and had built a programming service and personally supervised many of the top names and programs of the day.

According to a 1937 *New York Times* article, she reportedly commanded a salary that was rated the highest in radio for either men or women. Her persistence and vision shaped many a successful show on NBC, including *The Rudy Vallee Hour,* radio's first family sitcom *The Goldbergs,* and one of the longest continuous-running programs in the history of network radio, the Saturday-afternoon Metropolitan Opera broadcasts. Brainard had definite opinions regarding women's impact on radio and encouraged program managers to present better and more interesting programming for women.

A native of New Jersey, Brainard was a Red Cross ambulance driver in Europe during World War I. Upon returning to the U.S. she planned on a career in movies. Her brother owned an early crystal radio set and when she heard what was being presented on the air, she was so appalled that she decided to enter radio and make some changes. She suggested a program of theater reviews to station WJZ and was hired. Her weekly program *Broadcasting Broadway* made her one of the first theater critics in the history of radio. Like many early radio talent, she was not paid for her air work. By 1922, Brainard was assistant manager at WJZ. When NBC bought the station in 1926 and moved it to New York City, she became the manager. Her gender had been cause for great criticism early in her career. Brainard's manager at WJZ did not believe in female announcers and said he would have fired her from her *Broadway* program if it hadn't been for her critical reputation. Throughout it all, she maintained a positive attitude and served as an inspiration for the women who came after her in radio.

In a 1927 interview Brainard remarked, "A woman can fill practically any position in radio, providing she is willing to concentrate her energies on it and do exactly as a man would do." Bertha was an executive at NBC until 1946, when she retired from radio after marrying advertising executive Curt Peterson. She died later that same year of an apparent heart attack.

Ruth Reeves, known to her devoted radio listeners and later television viewers as Ruth Lyons, began her radio career in 1929 on WKRC Cincinnati. She then moved to WSAI and WLW in 1942. Ruth was a natural air personality with a gift for knowing what the common woman and man wanted to hear on the radio. Sponsors did not get equal time on her show, although they paid equally. Ruth alone decided what and when the spots would run and what they would say and how they would sound. More than once during her ninety-minute broadcast did the show feature eighty minutes of non-stop Ruth with ten minutes of commercials jammed in at the end. Advertisers didn't mind. They knew that if Ruth Lyons said something good about their product in one of her mostly-adlibbed commercials, it would fly off the shelves. If she said something negative, it died a quick death. Case in point: Royal Gelatin. Royal was a popular gelatin and a big advertiser on Lyons' show. When the sponsor came out with watermelon-flavored gelatin, Ruth reportedly said on-air that she tasted it and it didn't taste like watermelon at all. The product was quickly pulled from the stores within hours and never mentioned again. On the other hand, if she talked about a specific type of perfume she was wearing, later in the day, it would be sold out in virtually every department store in the area.

Ruth Lyons possessed the power to make or break products with one sentence. The waiting list of advertisers on her show was measured in years! Her power as a personality and communicator was unbelievable. As host of her popular *50/50 Club* on WLW Radio and Television, she enjoyed five decades as one of the Midwest's most beloved air personalities. Ruth Lyons passed away on November 7, 1988, but her impact on broadcasting lives on and serves as a shining example of how a successful air talent performs. Her legacy lives on to inspire future radio stars on what it takes to be a real on-air pro.

Kathryn Elizabeth Smith, known to millions of loyal listeners as **Kate Smith**, debuted on radio in 1929 and became one of radio's first great personalities. Kate was the same on the air as she was off, *herself* - something for future radio stars to keep in mine. She was a warm-hearted girl from Greenville, Virginia, who spoke to her listeners like they were family and everyday good ole folks. Her friendly demeanor came across on the radio so sincere that when she opened her show with, "Hello, everybody, this is Kate Smith. Thanks for listenin,'" you got the feeling she was speaking directly to you.

Kate's big radio break came on May 1, 1931, when she began her long association with CBS in an early-evening 15-minute program of songs. For the next sixteen years, Kate Smith was one of radio's biggest and brightest stars. One of her greatest coups took place in the fall of 1938 when she obtained exclusive rights to Irving Berlin's song, "God Bless America." Kate sang it on her show every week and brought so much attention to the song that its popularity grew tremendously. At one point, there was even talk of making it our national anthem. She was a great patriot and during WWII she raised millions for orphanages and war bonds and pushed the American way every chance she had! In her later years, Kate often sang before home games for the Philadelphia Flyers, since she was a huge hockey fan.

Her theme song was "When the Moon Comes Over the Mountain," the lyrics of which she helped write. Kate Smith was also one of radio's first talk show personalities. In 1938, she signed on to do a noontime feature, *Kate Smith Speaks*. The program of down-home chatter, news and her opinions on different subjects became a longtime listener favorite. The show was broadcast from her Park Avenue apartment in New York City. Her longtime mentor/manager Ted Collins read the news and the twosome chatted back and forth about life. The show became one of radio's top-rated programs with an estimated daily audience of around 10 million listeners. The talented songstress, who never married, passed away in 1986.

Jessica Valentina Dragonette was, appropriately, born on St. Valentine's Day. The year, however, remains a mystery. Many accounts give the year of her birth around 1905, but it's impossible to know for sure, as her original birth records were destroyed in a fire. Orphaned at a young age, Jessica found solace in her music. She was sent to the Philadelphia Girls Catholic High School where her devout faith was nurtured by the Sisters of Charity, who encouraged Jessica in developing her musical talents. Blessed with a superb soprano singing voice, the curly-haired, petite blonde was destined to be one of radio's biggest stars. In the 1920s, after being on the radio for little more than a month, she signed a five-year contract with WEAF. In 1930, she joined the cast of radio's *Cities Service Concerts* on NBC and her success as a radio star really took off. In addition to singing in English, Jessica sang in French, German, Italian, Russian and Spanish. She never used printed words from music and it's estimated that she memorized over 500 songs and 75 operas.

In 1937, she earned a reported $2500 dollars a week as the star of NBC Radio's *The Palmolive Beauty Box*. Jessica Dragonette was a superstar even by today's standards. Her drawing power was tremendous! In the summer of 1938 more than 150,000 fans gathered at Chicago's Grant Park to hear her sing. In 1952 she wrote her autobiography, *Faith is a Song*. Within the pages of her life story, Dragonette revealed many aspects of her personal life and radio career that she had heretofore kept very secretive. The premiere radio performer passed away on March 20, 1980.

Helen Sioussat was Director of Talk and Public Affairs programming for CBS Radio from 1937 until 1958. In her role, Helen oversaw as many as 300 radio broadcasts a year. In 1941, she created and hosted *Tube Talk*, the first round-table discussion show on television. If you'd like to read more about radio from her perspective, she wrote a book about broadcasting, *Mikes Don't Bite*. It was published in 1943.

Mary Margaret McBride is credited with leading the way for talk programming on radio. Born to a Paris, Missouri, farming family, she launched a new type of personal broadcasting in 1934, when she joined WOR in New York City. Her air-name was Martha Deane and her role was that of an elderly grandmother who chatted about the goings-on of her family. In reality, Mary wasn't a grandmother and had never even been married. She quickly tired of the charade and said so. "I'm not a grandmother, don't have grandkids and from here on out, I intend to be me on the air." Since she spilled the beans about all this live on the radio, the decision was irrevocable.

Radio 101 advice for all air-talent:
Actions like Mary's are not advisable and could easily result in being canned, unless, of course, you own your show or a piece of the radio station. Mary continued as Martha Deane, but without the grandkids and her

grammie persona. In 1937, CBS hired her to do a 15-minute talk show under her own name. She also continued with her Martha Deane broadcasts on WOR until 1940, when she quit to devote her full time to her CBS show. In 1941, NBC offered her a 45-minute time slot and she jumped at it, remaining with the network for a decade. In 1950, she moved to ABC for a daily half-hour program.

Mary Margaret McBride is considered one of radio's first and best women broadcasters. Her on-air salesmanship of the sponsor's product was compared to Arthur Godfrey's, which was a huge compliment since Arthur raked in millions for CBS pitching Lipton tea and soup and other products on his own top-rated radio show. [4]

The advertising trade magazine *Printer's Ink* once described Mary Margaret's influence over her listeners "as perhaps the most outstanding reliance upon the word of a human being in the commercial field." She had a genuine *homey* way about her and was known for her spontaneity, natural style, and warmth. Her special gift at interviewing and placing her guests at ease resulted in a large loyal following. Her tenth anniversary broadcast from Madison Square Garden attracted 20,000 listeners. On May 31, 1949, a crowd of 35,000 gathered at Yankee Stadium to pay tribute to Mary Margaret McBride as she celebrated her 15th year in radio. The gregarious radio pro passed away in April 1976. **There are many other achievements and firsts in radio credited to women. Here are just a few:**

- **Sybil Herrold** was the wife of radio pioneer Charles "Doc" Herrold and as early as 1912 was on the air at her husband's station playing phonograph records and doing some announcing. She was so adept at Morse code that she taught courses at the "Herrold College of the Wireless" in San Jose.
- Around 1918, Eunice Randall was one of radio's first female engineers. She not only operated her own amateur station, which she built, but went on to be one of the first female announcers in Boston at station 1XE, later WGI.
- **Mary Texanna Loomis** was the first woman to be director of a radio school. She operated the College of Radio Engineering in Washington, DC, in the early 1920s.
- **Marie Zimmerman** was the first woman to own and operate a radio station. WIAE in Vinton, Iowa was on the air for a year from July 1922 until July 1923.
- **Mary Costigan** signed on KFXY Flagstaff on December 5, 1925, and operated the station from her theater until she sold it in 1932 and the station moved to Yuma.

Note: credit goes to Barry Miskind for information on the above mentioned women. For more info on Broadcast History contact him at barry@broadcast.net

Pioneer Radio Women.

Louella Parsons was an internationally known Hollywood gossip columnist who brought her chit-chat to the airwaves in 1928 reporting celebrity news. She and another Hollywood gossip reporter, **Hedda Hopper**, who began in radio on Rudy Vallee's show in 1929 and tattle-taled until 1951, had so much power in Tinseltown that they could make or break a star by merely mentioning their name on-air. Both popular columnists and radio celebrities were followed on radio in 1949 by **Sheilah Graham**, who continued the tradition of women reporting celebrity news on radio.

Gertrude Berg, born Gertrude Edelstein in Harlem, New York, was an American pioneer of radio's earliest days. She was one of the first, if not the first, women to create, write, produce and star in a long-running radio sitcom, *The Rise of the Goldbergs,* later *The Goldbergs*, which debuted on NBC on November 20, 1929. When the program first began, Gertrude was paid $75 a week. Less than two years later, she allowed the sponsor to propose a salary and was told, "Mrs. Berg, we can't pay a cent over $2,000 a week." Gertrude became so closely identified with the character she played so well, Jewish mother Molly Goldberg, that fans forgot her real name. *The Goldbergs* remained on radio until 1954. Gertrude Berg was among the earliest examples that women in broadcasting could transcend acting and exert their versatility behind the scenes as well.

In 1931, The Kellogg Company sponsored *Irene Wicker, The Singing Lady*, which was billed as the nation's first network radio program for children. As the writer, producer and star of the show, Irene had originated the show about six months earlier on WGN-Chicago. In 1937, she told *Radio Stars* magazine, "I loved being a child. I never wanted to grow up! It gives me a kinship with children." For 45 years, Irene Wicker was one of radio's most successful children's show hostesses.

The longest running cooking program on radio is credited to **Mary Lee Taylor**. Her program began on CBS Radio on November 7, 1933, and concluded on rival network NBC on October 9, 1954.

Fania Borach, known to radio listeners as **Fanny Brice**, played the on-radio part of a bratty toddler named Baby Snooks. *The Baby Snooks Show* debuted in February 1936 on CBS, moved to NBC in December 1937, then back to CBS for Maxwell House Coffee and finally back to NBC in November, 1948. Brice was so meticulous about her program and the character Baby Snooks that she often appeared in costume as a little girl, even though her character was only seen by the studio audience.

Bea Johnson began on the air in 1936 as Joanne Taylor on KMBC Kansas City broadcasting from a department store. Twenty years later in 1956, she was the only female broadcaster in Kansas City and was featured in *Who's Who in Radio & TV*. Bea proudly boasted in the report that she was the only woman who owned up to her real age! In a March 1956 *Radio-TV Mirror* interview, Bea said, she really learned most about how to do radio when she got married and took time out to raise a family.

As a listener, Bea Johnson said she found people on the radio were talking down to her and "only one man, Arthur Godfrey, seemed interested in me." When she returned to the radio, she adapted Godfrey's style and applied it to her own delivery.[5]

From 1937 until 1950, **Adelaide Hawley Cummings** was host of her own program. In 1949, she was hired by General Mills to assume the persona on radio and TV of Betty Crocker. Adelaide continued in the role until General Mills, seeking a more sophisticated image, dropped her.

Irene Beasley, because of her height, was known as the long, tall gal from Dixie. She was a composer, singer and radio personality. Irene is best remembered for her long-running musical quiz show, *Grand Slam*, which aired weekday mornings on CBS for Continental Bakers from 1943 to 1953.

Network daytime dramas, or soap operas as they are lovingly called, opened many doors for women on radio. There were so many talented actresses that a special volume would be required to list them all. Here are just a few female stalwarts of radio and their accomplishments.

Minetta Ellen played Mother Fanny Barbour on NBC's popular soap *One Man's Family* for the entire run of the program, 1932-1955. In 1933, Virginia Payne was an ingénue of twenty-three when she first played Ma Perkins on WLW Cincinnati. She played the role continuously through radio's entire Golden Age until its final broadcast on CBS in 1960. Radio listeners knew Anne Elstner as the well-known character Stella Dallas. She starred in the title role for the *Stella Dallas* show's entire eighteen-year run on NBC Radio from 1937 until 1955. Vivian Smolen played Veronica on *Archie Andrews*, and Laurel on *Stella Dallas*, but is probably best remembered by soap fans as the title character on *Our Gal Sunday*.

Popular Mary Jane Higby was known as the queen of daytime serials for having starred on several soaps, including *The Romance of Helen Trent*, *This is Nora Drake,* and her long-running role as Joan Davis on *When a Girl Marries,* which ran on network radio from 1939 until 1958. An excellent first-hand account of what it was like to act on radio's daytime dramatic fare is *Tune in Tomorrow*, written by Higby in 1966. Another familiar radio voice was Jan Miner. She was featured on several soaps, including her role as Julie on *Hilltop House* on CBS from 1948 until its final broadcast in 1955. You may remember Jan best as Madge the manicurist from the old Palmolive commercials on television, a role she played for over twenty years.

Gwen Davies was a cast member for twenty-three years on radio's popular children's program, *Let's Pretend*. She was also heard on the soap *Aunt Jenny*, and appeared on numerous other radio programs, including *Easy Aces, Fred Allen, The Goldbergs, Gangbusters,* and *Mercury Theater of the Air*. Later in her career, Ms. Davies was the voice of Casper the Friendly Ghost in hundreds of cartoons. Talented Nila Mack was the driving force behind *Let's Pretend*. She joined the program in 1930, when it was first called *The Adventures of Helen and Mary*, serving as both writer and director.

Wendy Warren and the News arrived at CBS Radio in the summer of 1947 with Florence Freeman in the title role in one of soap-land's most interesting formats.[6] Wendy was a news reporter for the *Manhattan Gazette* who also did a CBS newscast at noon. The program opened with three minutes of current news of the day read by real-life newsman Douglas Edwards.[7] At the conclusion of his newscast, Edwards would segue to Wendy saying, "And now, Wendy, what's the news today for the ladies?" Miss Freeman, in character, would give her report from the women's world. The entire report took about four minutes and was followed by a commercial for Maxwell House Coffee. Listeners would then rejoin Wendy, who was just stepping out of the control room and continuing on with her life and dramatic episode for the day.

Other popular female radio voices featured and heard regularly on both daytime and nighttime programs include Joan Banks, Bea Benaderet, Fran Carlon, Mary-Jane Croft, Rosemary DeCamp, Elspeth Eric, Louise Erickson, Verna Felton, Betty Garde, Betty Lou Gerson, Virginia Gregg, Abby Lewis, Barbara Luddy, Charlotte Manson, Mercedes McCambridge, Agnes Moorehead, Claudia Morgan, Jeannette Nolan, Rosemary Rice, Ann Shephard, Marion Sweet, Sybil Trent, Lurene Tuttle, Vickie Vola, Lucille Wall, Janet Waldo, Jane Webb, Miriam Wolfe and countless other talented actresses whose performances made radio so popular.

From 1941 until 1944, **Jean Ruth Hay** woke up millions of American troops during WWII with her upbeat radio show, *Reveille with Beverly*. The program originated at KNX-AM in Hollywood and was broadcast to foxholes, cockpits, and military outposts around the world. Her effervescent voice opened her show with a friendly, "Hi there, boys of the U.S.A. We're ready with the stuff that makes you swing and sway." Her program reached an estimated 11 million people.

Mary Marvin Breckinridge was the first woman employed by CBS as a foreign correspondent. World War II had just begun and Mary was working as a freelance photographer in London. That's where and when Edward R. Murrow, London bureau chief for CBS News, hired her. Like Murrow, she knew Europe. When Germany invaded Poland in September of 1939,

Murrow suggested she do a radio report on the effect of war on a typical village. She did the report and CBS felt she had a natural voice for radio and a gift for reporting. Before her broadcast, Murrow gave Breckinridge a little advice: "Keep your voice low and, remember, you're an American...speak like an American." What he meant was that she shouldn't take sides, since at the time, 1939, the US was a neutral country.

Arlene Francis was born Arline Francis Kazanjian on October 20, 1907, in the Boston suburb of Brookline. She was one of radio's first female stars beginning in 1932 on the soap *Betty & Bob*, which was the first daytime serial for the prolific husband and wife team of Frank and Anne Hummert. The couple went on to produce many popular radio shows, including *Easy Aces, Mr. Keen, Little Orphan Annie, Mary Noble, Just Plain Bill, Lorenzo Jones, Our Gal Sunday, The Romance of Helen Trent, Stella Dallas,* and many others. In 1938, Ms. Francis starred on the daytime soap *Central City* on NBC, and in 1946, starred as a private eye on *The Affairs of Ann Scotland* on ABC. In 1943, she was host of radio's *Blind Date* and was host of several other shows.

On television, like radio, Arlene Francis was a pioneer for women broadcasters. She was one of the first women to host a program that was not musical or dramatic. It was a daytime magazine program called *Home*, which ran on NBC from 1954 until 1957. Arlene was also a regular panelist on *What's My Line?* throughout most of the program's network run on CBS from 1950 until 1967. Arlene Francis was also a popular New York City radio personality on WOR. She passed away from Alzheimer's and cancer on May 31, 2001, in San Francisco. The witty and entertaining Ms. Francis was 93.

Martha Roundtree was another pioneer broadcast journalist. She was the first moderator and co-creator, along with Lawrence Spivak, of NBC's *Meet the Press*. She was the only female moderator in the 61-year history of the show and served as the program's moderator on the TV version from 1947 until 1953, when Roundtree reportedly sold her share of *Meet the Press* to co-creator Spivak for $125,000 after a coin toss.

Long before **Delilah**'s syndicated nighttime radio show there was *Lonesome Gal*. The show was created by Jean King. After a tough time finding a lucrative on-air radio job, Jean came up with the idea for *Lonesome Gal* in Dayton, Ohio. She was perfect for the part. In the show, she played a lonesome gal who spun romantic songs and cooed to all the lonesome guys in radio-land. When making personal appearances, she wore a kitty mask to further the mystique of her sexy radio persona. She began her dream of syndicating *Lonesome Gal* on four stations. Her listener base grew and she was carried on over 50 stations across the country. She personalized each show for the local stations - not an easy thing to do in the 1940s, before today's digital age. Sometimes, her efforts required over 300 recordings a week. Talk about a tired, lonesome gal! Eventually, she recorded her show in her home studio which made life a lot easier. Jean King stayed behind her kitten mask until 1953, when she finally revealed her true identity. She is credited with creating one of radio's first and earliest recorded music syndicated shows.

Donna Douglas was born in Paris, Ontario, Canada. She was on the air in the 1950s at WTOP Washington DC. She is credited with saying, "Be yourself on the air and worry more about what you say than how you say it!" Donna had a stimulating yet relaxing air-style.

Long before *The View* with Barbara Walters and her lady friends came to television, radio was first with a similar program. *Leave it to the Girls* was the creation of Martha Roundtree, whose credits include being one of radio's first female moderators as the co-host of radio's version of *Meet the Press* with Lawrence Spivak when it debuted originally on Mutual in 1947. *Leave it to the Girls* was a serious panel discussion among four career girls who discussed problems submitted by the listeners. At various times, the panelists included Lucille Ball, Binnie Barnes, Constance Bennett, Robin Chandler, Eloise McElhone and Florence Pritchard. *Leave it to the Girls* aired Saturday nights, from 1945 until 1949 on Mutual Radio.

Special mention goes to two additional first ladies of song on American radio, **Dinah Shore** and **Rosemary Clooney**. Shore, born Frances Rose Shore in 1916, debuted on CBS Radio in March 1939 on a Sunday afternoon with Ben Bernie's Orchestra .She then became a featured vocalist on the NBC program *The Chamber Music Society of Lower Basin Street,* which featured blues and Dixieland music. Next, Dinah became a regular on Eddie Cantor's show and in 1943 had her own show, *Call to Music.* She then moved to another radio program, *Paul Whiteman Presents.* During World War II, Dinah was a big favorite with U.S. Troops and had a major hit with "I'll Walk Alone," the first of her string of #1 hits. Dinah Shore was a popular singing star on radio throughout the '40s, before moving to television in the '50s and finding more success as hostess on *The Chevy Show.*

Rosemary Clooney's radio career began in 1945 when she and her sister Betty won a singing audition at WLW Cincinnati. They were hired for a regular late-night spot at $20 a week each. In 1954 radio made a strong bid to challenge the growing magnetism of television by signing big Hollywood names to variety shows. Rosie signed to host a 15-minute weekday morning show on CBS.

On November 5, 1950, NBC Radio launched what many radio historians believe was network radio's last gasp at trying to lure television viewers back to radio. *The Big Show* was hosted by

Tallulah Bankhead, a celebrated stage veteran with a husky voice. Ms. Bankhead, with her deep voice and ultra-sophisticated campy style, began her show-business career at age fifteen by winning a movie magazine competition and a trip to New York. After many years of playing minor roles on Broadway, she achieved stardom in well-received plays like *The Little Foxes* and *The Skin of Our Teeth*. [8,9]

Bankhead won the New York Film Critics Award as Best Actress for her role in Alfred Hitchcock's 1944 film, *Lifeboat*. On radio, Tallulah appeared on shows like *Fred Allen, Screen Guild Players, Screen Director's Playhouse, Theater Guild of the Air* and *Lux Radio Theater*. During World War II, she was heard frequently on Armed Forces radio, including *Mail Call* and *Command Performance*.

The Big Show had a big budget of nearly $100,000 per broadcast, which is almost a million in today's dollars. NBC designed the expensive, star-studded extravaganza in an effort to reclaim its former dominance with Sunday night listeners, which was decimated by both the rising popularity of television and talent raids by rival network CBS.[10] *The Big Show* presented a weekly mix of drama, comedy, and music during its 90 minutes on the air. The guest stars were some of the biggest names in show business, including Fred Allen, Eddie Cantor, Jimmy Durante, Judy Garland, Bob Hope, Ethel Merman, Rudy Vallee, and others. Music Man Meredith Willson conducted a 44-piece orchestra and led a 16-piece chorus. The popular Ed Herlihy was the show's announcer. *The Big Show* received glowing reviews, with critics calling it "perfectly wonderful and the fastest, funniest ninety minutes in memory." During the second season, the entire cast was flown to Europe for remote broadcasts from London and Paris. In spite of enthusiastic reviews and the expensive price tag, the program could not compete with television. It was a tremendous effort by NBC, but even with all its stunning window-dressing the show barely made a dent in the ratings. After two years on the air NBC had lost a million dollars on *The Big Show* and both Tallulah and the show got the heave-ho!

Radio Pioneer **Vida Jane Butler**, known on the air as Janie Joplin, was an announcer at WHER-Memphis in the 1950s. The station was then billed as the first all-female radio station in the nation. Radio producer and legend Sam Phillips came up with the idea for the format. During her 17 years at the station, Janie Joplin would sign-off with a phrase that her family says could have been her personal motto: "Be good and you'll be happy."

Martha Jean "The Queen" Steinberg was a true radio pioneer whose influenced extended far beyond the medium in which she became famous. Her radio career spanned forty-six years, beginning in 1954 as an R&B DJ on the legendary black radio station WDIA-AM in Memphis, and in her later years becoming an inspirational on-air personality and radio station executive owner in Detroit. From her earliest days on radio, Martha Jean exemplified the power the radio personality has as a leader and spokesperson for the community. Looking back on her Memphis radio days, she once said, "At that particular time you have to understand that you didn't have any black politicians. No black judges and very few black lawyers. You didn't have any 'so-called' black leaders, so we were the ones who spoke out." At one point, she used her on-air position to help quell social unrest and wield influence on local politicians. Her preacher-like air-style endeared Steinberg to her family of Detroit listeners for forty years! So vitally important were her words to the community as a whole that the station broadcast repeats of her programming for several years following her death in 2000.

According to her *Contemporary Black Biography* entry, Martha Jean Steinberg was intimidated when she first went on the air. She was self-conscious about her grammar and diction but also her race and gender. "Being a black radio pioneer and being a woman was hard," she told the *Detroit News* in her later years. "I always used to say, to be a woman in radio, you have to think like a man, act like a lady and work like a dog." Her extraordinary career spanned six decades and Steinberg transformed herself from a tentative, insecure R&B DJ into one of the most prominent people of any gender or race in radio. In 1972 she became an ordained minister and founded a church called the Home of Love. Her radio programs on WJLB, one of Detroit's first FM powerhouses, began to focus more heavily on gospel music and her own homespun brand of inspiration and self-help aimed particularly at women. She spoke about God, civic duty, and moral issues like staying away from married men. She came up with signature catchphrases like "live, love, laugh," "be cool," "fight for happiness," "pray for peace and above all, be kind." Her regular sign off was "God loves you and I love you, too."

Martha Jean became a Detroit icon, revered by her listeners and courted by politicians. In 1982 she joined with several partners to create a new gospel and talk station, WQBH. In 1997 she bought the station outright and continued to perform on the air until her death three years later. Ms. Steinberg played a key part in the evolution of both popular music and the relationship between air personalities and their community of listeners. Jean the Queen was inducted into the Black Radio Hall of Fame in 1993 and the Rock and Roll Hall of Fame in 1998. Her greatest talent may have been her ability to touch the souls and hearts of her listeners, empowering them with her message of redemption, self-reliance and self-respect.

Alison Steele, the first lady of rock 'n' roll and an inductee in the Rock and Roll Hall of Fame, was known as "The Nightbird" to her dedicated New York City listeners. She got her first break in radio in 1966 on WNEW-FM. It was the time AM & FM split, she explained in an interview and subsequent article written by Kathleen Warnock[11] called "The Nightbird's Final Fling": "I was on the air at WNEW-AM, one of the leading independent stations in the country, when they split AM & FM programming. So, WNEW-FM debuted as Sexpot Radio with an all-female air staff." Steele, who had been working in radio and television since the late 1950s, was one of the few women hired with any broadcast experience.

"The original format was Frank Sinatra, Steve Lawrence & Eydie Gorme middle of the road music and it didn't last long," as the Nightbird further explains. "By September 1966, WNEW-FM switched its format to progressive rock. All the jocks were fired except me. They found that 90% of our listeners knew my name and liked me, so they asked me to do overnights and I said, what do I do? They said, 'Do your thing.' I was thinking about my thing. I am a night person. I hate to get up in the morning. There are larks and there are owls and I've been an owl all my life, so I decided to be the Nightbird, because of the duality of a nocturnal bird and being a girl."

Talk about going the extra mile to get the job done, **Alison Steele** personifies the definition. "I knew nothing about rock 'n' roll," she says, "they had a library of about 500 albums, so I'd take them home, listen to them and study them. Eventually, they made me music director."

The first night Alison was on the air at WNEW-FM, she opened with some poetry she had written, with some Incan flute Temple music in the background, followed by the Moody Blues' "Nights in White Satin." "The switchboard lit up," she recalled. "I knew how to do a program that was more conceptual than anyone else. I always started with poetry, something inspirational to demonstrate that we all have tremendous potential."

"Things will always get better" is the message Alison Steele tried to convey to her listeners, even later in her radio career when she was undergoing several surgeries and chemotherapy for cancer. On her nightly program, Alison used the Bible, Shakespeare, Longfellow, Camus, and music related to those works. With her inspirational words and music to guide her flight through the night, she developed a loyal following of night-owls and was on the air at WNEW from 1966 until 1979. Alison moved on to play jazz on a New York City AM station, from 1981 to '86, and then in 1986 moved to WPIX. She left when the station changed ownership. During her time away from radio, Alison Steele opened a boutique, Just Cats, with her sister, and continued operating it even after she returned to all-night radio at K-Rock in NYC in 1991.

When asked her opinion about why there was a higher percentage of women working overnights in radio, she responded with, "The pay is lower. They hide you on overnights. They don't trust that women can do what men do." Funny thing is, they couldn't hide Steele and her talent. Even working overnights, the Nightbird became a huge favorite with the all-night listening crowd. Alison Steele was just 58 when she died on September 27, 1995, after a long battle with cancer.[12] She left behind a rich legacy in the form of radio as a pioneer in all-night personality radio. Jimi Hendrix even titled his song, "Nightbird Flying," for her.

Yvonne Daniels was the First Lady of Chicago Radio, with a powerful voice that echoed throughout much of the U.S. and Canada thanks to the clear-channel signal of Chicago's WLS. Yvonne was a real radio pioneer, a woman on the air at a major Top-40 radio station, when a female on the air-staff side wasn't quite as commonplace as it is today. During an interview about her success at WLS, Yvonne said, "I decided that I had to make good there (WLS) because If I didn't cut it, they might never hire another woman." Not only that, but there was another barrier to break: she was African-American. Thanks to her talent and positive personality, Yvonne Daniels rose above it all to become one of the most legendary DJs of the Top-40 era, finding her fame at the Big 89 in the 1970s. In 1972, she left WLS for her first love, jazz, and was hosting a jazz show on WNUA when she passed away from cancer in 1991. Yvonne Daniels was inducted into the Radio Hall of Fame in 1995.

During radio's formative years, many women worked hard to get their feet in the door. Like other professions dominated by men, they found the door closed, or worse, slammed shut in their faces. Those who did manage to get a toehold were often subjected to bigotry, sexism, and dead ends with few if any chances for advancement. A quick look at a list of prominent network radio announcers from the 1920s through the '50s will prove my point. You'll be hard-pressed to find a woman's name anywhere on the list. There were plenty of women in soaps, dramatic and comedy fare, but few as announcers or newscasters. But, that was then, what about today?

Has radio today changed in its acceptance of females on the air?

For the most part, is radio still a business primarily controlled and run by men? What is the most difficult thing about being female and trying to be successful in today's radio world? For these answers and more, we turned to some of America's leading broadcast talents, from on-the-air and off-the-air positions in radio.

We begin with consultant **Donna Halper.** Her radio career includes over twenty-five years as a consultant and thirteen as an announcer. I asked Donna if she feels it's easier today for a female to break into radio than in years gone by, considering the industry is still dominated by males. She responded, "Yes and no. I was the first woman at many of the stations where I worked. I encountered varying levels of sexism from men who absolutely hated the idea of having women on the staff and actively made my life miserable. What has changed since I first got hired is that society in general has become more accepting of an expanded role for women." Halper goes on to explain that "Today in radio, there are more women on the air, and outside radio, there are more women in all aspects of the professions. There are more women doctors, lawyers, engineers, and yes, traditional professions like nursing and teaching.

Halper believes society has changed. "Look at how the language today is different from how it was only 30 years ago. When I was growing up, a female doctor was so unusual that she was in fact called a woman doctor. Normally, doctors were male, so a woman was the exception," she says, "but today, few people talk about a 'woman doctor.' There are plenty of women who are doctors and it's no longer considered strange. The same is true in many levels of radio. We no longer talk about a woman reporter. Yes, women news anchors are still rare, but there are many news reporters who are female, just as there are lots of women in radio sales, management, doing a morning show or midday air-shift. Women announcers used to be buried on the late night or the overnight shift, no matter how good they were. People don't think much about it anymore. It's no longer the case that the only woman at the station is the receptionist. In fact, at some stations, the receptionist might be a guy," smiles Halper.

Halper says it's only really the upper end of radio that is still dominated by men. "The head of the NAB, and the RAB, along with the majority of station owners of the biggest broadcast groups, are still pretty much all men, with one or two exceptions. The majority of radio station general managers are also men, although there are many more sales managers who are women." Does she believe there are still more men in the lead role on morning radio shows today then women? "Yes, on most morning shows," she says, "the host is the man and the sidekick might be a woman, except even there, I know a few women who do a morning show so that too may be changing.[13] The point is, yes, it is still true that the radio industry's major decision-makers still tend to be white males, but it is also true that women are no longer arbitrarily excluded the way they once were."

Commenting on the male-dominated business of radio and how tough it was when she was trying to break into the broadcast business, Halper continues: "When I was first seeking radio work, station managers came right out and said to me, 'We don't hire women.' These days, although certainly some men still have old-fashioned attitudes, many have grown-up with a woman as on-air-talent and as sales managers, so it doesn't seem quite as strange anymore. I'm sure some cities are more old-fashioned, but I am also sure that if you are committed to breaking into radio, your gender will not stop you! It may slow you down in some cases, but there are more places now where woman can and do get that first opportunity. My advice," confides Halper, "don't be surprised if you encounter sexism, but don't expect that you will find nothing but sexism. Times really have changed and if you have talent, there will absolutely be someplace, somewhere, that will hire you. It may not be immediate, but, hey, even guys don't get hired immediately these days! So, have a plan, have a good presentation and get out there and let people know why they should hire you!"

Linda Smith worked with me as our producer at the original WROR-98.5 Boston. From the late 1980s through the early '90s, she produced our popular morning drive show, *The Joe and Andy Family*, and our top-rated, all-request weekend oldies program, *Saturday Night "Live" at the Oldies*. Linda was asked if she believes gender is an issue today in radio, particularly as far as advancement is concerned.

"Great question. I have had three successful careers and I honestly don't feel that being female has ever been a disadvantage. In fact, it can be an advantage. You just need to recognize the landscape and become part of the infrastructure. Of course, working for the right people who never allowed gender to be an issue is helpful. But, as a woman," she continues, "you can't let gender become an obstacle to career progression and success. If you're smart and have something to say, don't be reluctant to do so. But," she adds, "also be aware of the professional environment. Being an important piece of an integrated puzzle is not something to be ashamed of. Understand the culture of your workplace and learn to peacefully coexist with it, support it and thrive in it. Think of every interaction, every project, every undertaking, as an opportunity that will enhance (or not) your ability to progress. Because that is the reality."

Smith's advice works for either gender, but she specifically directs these examples, based on her own experiences in the work place, towards women. "I conducted myself the same way in radio that I did in high tech. I just packaged it differently. In high tech," she explains, "I traveled in business suits, if that's what worked for the clientèle with which I was dealing. But, when I dealt with clients down south, I softened my look." Smith insists that's not giving in, but just being smart and in her words, "If you owned a bakery and someone ordered an éclair, you wouldn't give them a turnover. Think about it. You don't want the package to negatively influence those who are receiving your message. Don't give them a reason," she adds, "to ignore your message, and your presentation. Above all, be real!

"All of this may sound like I'm living in Pollyannaville, but I will issue this disclaimer: I have and continue to work for very smart people who have considered my contributions to be valuable and completely gender-neutral. But, remember this," she cautions, "as a woman, you have a responsibility, not only in the workplace, but in life. Grasp every opportunity for what it is. Give it your all. And put it in context. So make sure there is substance, but fit the style to your workplace. Deliver the goods and package it appropriately.

"The advantage to being a woman aspiring to a career in radio is that radio is a cutting-edge business that currently trends strongly toward reflecting the targeted demographic. If the target is men, many programmers will prefer a female voice, alone or paired with a male partner, especially in certain day parts on the station. And if the demographic is primarily women?

Again, many programmers will prefer a woman reflective of the audience and desired demographic. There will continue to be many opportunities for women on the air as well as off," predicts Smith, "as women become more prevalent in radio management." Today, Linda Smith works in the telecommunications industry.

"The cable giant by whom I am now employed, for all intents and purposes, no longer has a glass ceiling," she says. "Being female should not stand in your way of success. You will deal with men on various levels every single day. You will travel with them, you will have dinner meetings. And there can always be that 'sexual tension' thing. It's another facet of business life and life in general that just is! Here's some advice that worked for me and which I discovered quite naturally. I grew up loving sports. I was at my dad's knee," she explains, "watching football, baseball, basketball, you name it. So I was always interested and always stored away knowledge and trivia the same way I stored that kind of information on music and artists." Smith feels it's easy to be brilliant and conversant on a subject when it's studied as a matter of true interest and not force fed. "Knowledge of sports became an indispensable component to my own success, because when dealing with men, the minute you begin talking about one of their favorite subjects you are magically transformed into something other than a subject of 'sexual tension' and 'a woman.' You become psychologically an equal, and even better, more like their sister than a potential companion. The relationship becomes relaxed, natural and generally successful."

It worked for Linda Smith and she urges women to try it! "Peruse the sports pages," she says. "You don't have to be an encyclopedia, but a working knowledge of that world can reap bountiful benefits down the road. Opportunities for women in radio exist in even greater numbers simply because more women have on-air experience than ever before. Quite often a prerequisite for becoming a music or program director is on-air experience and a greater number of women than ever before now have that experience as part of their resumes. Consider this, one of the most successful radio stations in Boston, the sixth largest radio market in America, is WEEI-AM, a sports talker. The GM is a woman, Julie Khan. Yes, a woman running a sports talk station. Yes, the opportunities do exist today for women in radio and are more readily available for those who have prepared themselves."

Los Angeles news and traffic air personality **Stacey Cohen**, who also heads her own creative agency in Redondo Beach, California, believes strongly that radio needs to recognize women. "It's not just males that have a problem with that, but there are women in our industry that don't see the potential in the young women who are currently on the air. Radio is a tough business," says Cohen. "You have to have thick skin to be a part of it. I always saw myself as an equal to my on-air male partners. I never felt that there was something they could do and I couldn't. As a woman, you can't be afraid to take risks and accept challenges. Never compromise who you are. Stand up," shouts Stacey Cohen, "and let your voice be heard!" You can reach out to Stacy at go4it@roadrunner.com.

Nancy Widmann started out in sales and rose to the Presidency of CBS Radio. She has extensive knowledge and experience in leadership and management. With over twenty-five years experience in broadcasting and marketing, Nancy knows what its like to be female and trying to break into radio. She started out in the 1960s in the advertising business in New York City. Her first job was an assistant in the media department. "That's where and when I fell in love with radio. I recognized that radio was amazingly effective in selling products for my clients. The connection between the listener and the air personalities was so powerful, so immediate, so personal, that I spent the next several years convincing all who would listen that radio was the most effective way to move products."

Nancy Widmann's next move was selling radio at CBS. "I was the first woman in radio sales in New York and I think the first in the country to do so. That was the beginning of my long career at CBS. Over the next twenty-five years, I moved steadily upward, assuming more and more responsibility." In 1980, she became the GM of WCBS-FM and proclaims it was her favorite time at CBS and proudly says, "We took that station to the number-one oldies station in the country. It was the position I enjoyed the most and as I moved up in the company, I looked back at those six years at 101-FM as my favorite time at CBS."

As the former President of CBS Radio, Nancy Widmann has an interesting perspective on whether or not it's easier today for women to break into radio than it was five, ten or even twenty-five years ago.[14] "I think it is far easier today in every business than it was when I was making my way up the ladder. First of all, we have seen women achieve success in every area of the radio business. Women now have templates and role models. In addition, with more critical mass women are helping women. They are developing a network of support quite like men have had for years. I think the progress has been slow and it seems to be stagnating a little as the business slides into economic distress," says Widmann. "My daughter is selling radio in San Diego. She is managing a household, raising a baby, and doing remarkably well. I have been impressed at the understanding and support she has received from her management. This is a new day, and I believe that everyone, women and men, will be better off if we make work a more accommodating place for families."

Paula Street has been the midday voice on Oldies-103-Boston for the past twenty-three years and is one of the Hub's favorite radio personalities. Paula thinks gender is still an issue in radio, "simply because fewer time slots are available to females on the air. It's changing slowly as PDs are willing to give the main drive-time slots to whomever can get the best ratings, male or female! It's about being a person on the air, not a woman on the air. It makes me crazy," she continues, "when PDs and GMs decide to put a female on in an unusual shift, like morning drive, afternoon-drive or a talk show that doesn't work so they conclude that women don't work! I say, NO, you just put the wrong person in that shift, not the wrong gender. I have never felt held back in radio because I am a woman," says Paula. "I work at Oldies-103 in Boston. We have Karen Blake on in morning drive, a Boston radio icon, and then me in the middle of the day. Our listeners don't think, 'Wow, they have two women back to back?' They think, Paula's on or Karen's on, it's really all about content, not who's wearing pants or a dress. There are many great talented females in radio and ten years from now, there will even more!"

Melanie Morgan is a former host at KSFO-560 in San Francisco. She previously worked as a reporter at KGO-TV. Today, she is Chairman of Move America Forward, a non-profit organization that supports U.S. Armed Forces and the current mission in the War on Terrorism. Melanie says there isn't a lot of room in radio today for men or women. "Unfortunately, there isn't much room for anyone, due to consolidation of the industry. It's quite disturbing that so many young people are locked out of the smaller market jobs, because syndication is eating the airspace that previously belonged to local programming. But," Morgan adds, "for the determined, focused young woman or man who loves radio, my advice is to follow my path, target a station you want to work for, and get an internship." Melanie Morgan's first internship was at KUDL-AM in Kansas City. "I was sixteen, and I'm pretty sure I lied about my age, but I was very fortunate to have some very talented people who taught me the ropes in radio, production, traffic, music and news, even as I did the gofer work: go for this, go for that. Don't ever turn up your nose at being a gofer; it can be the path to your future success in radio."

Johnnie Putman and her hubby Steve King have spent the better part of twenty years together as Chicago's #1 nightly radio habit. Johnnie co-hosts Chicago's number one all-night show on WGN. Her experience in broadcasting is as impressive as it is extensive. After graduating from Columbia College in 1977, she joined the staff of WMRO-AM and WAUR-FM in Aurora, Illinois. "Sadly, when I was hired, no one even listened to my audition tape which I had made at the college radio station. In retrospect, that may have been a blessing," she laughs. "Point is, I was hired because the station needed a woman. It was a time when the government was requiring a better representation of women and minorities in all industries, including radio." As Putman explains, "I was invited to the station to meet with the manager and got the job the same day because he needed a woman on the air. The guy who was on the air and who would be losing his job was told that he would have to train me over the next few days. It was incredibly stressful. I was painfully aware of just how unfair the business can be that this newlywed would be unemployed. I made up my mind on the second day that I had to make this guy proud, because he was trying to teach me everything possible in a short amount of time. I also firmly believed I had something to prove. I loved the job from day one and wanted to be more than just a warm body filling a quota."

"Today," Johnnie Putman says, "both males and females looking for a career in radio have the challenge of finding a place where they have an opportunity to get hands-on training that is so necessary. For women in particular, I would recommend being well-informed and having a wide comfort zone. Be strong, sound strong and learn to express yourself. It can be challenging, since there are still those who feel that a strong woman is 'bossy' or overbearing. Keep in mind," Johnnie emphasizes, "that it's not necessary today to settle for being a giggly sidekick in radio or the airhead who's the butt of jokes. If a chance to be on the radio comes along, seize it then go about making it your own. Being the BEST traffic reporter news or sports reporter or producer who's given a chance to be heard on the air are all chances that could get you heard by the person who could ultimately make your radio dreams come true!"

Since 1982, **Nancy Quill** has been the midday personality on Boston's Magic-106.7, which makes her show the longest-running and most listened to program on Boston radio. As far as being a woman in the radio business, Nancy refuses to label herself as a "woman announcer." "I always felt that first and foremost I was a radio personality and that being a woman didn't enter how I approached the job. If I was good, I was good. Period," she says. "There would be no special rules for me. If someone liked my work, it was because I was good at delivering the product. However," Quill quickly adds, "that's not to say you won't find people that still play the gender card. Just remember, be a pro and the right people will recognize that."

Here are additional comments about women in radio, from women radio pros I worked with during my forty-one-year broadcasting career. Their comments are based on the questions: "**Do you believe gender is an issue today in radio?**" "**Is it easier for women to break in to radio today?**"

Before going national, **Judi Paparelli** hosted talk shows in New Hampshire, Charleston, Atlanta, and Boston. We worked together at the second incarnation of WROR-Boston. "There are certainly more opportunities for females in broadcasting today, and it is great to see so many talented women breaking new ground, both on- and off-air. It's also encouraging to see visionary men and women in powerful radio positions now offering opportunities to the most talented broadcasters, whether they happen to be male or female. That, to me, is real progress. Male or female, I just want to hear the best."

Linda Cruze worked alongside me in morning drive at KLDE in Houston in the late '90s. "I do think it's a bit easier for women to break into radio these days. Years ago, I think many on-air positions for women simply called for them to be a 'cheerleader' for the boys. That limited job openings. I think we've seen change in the past 10 to 15 years. It now seems like management is more likely looking to hire relatable authentic personalities whether they be male or female."

Lindy Rome was my on-air partner for two years, from 2002-2004, at Sunny-104.3 in West Palm Beach, Florida. "Unfortunately," she begins, "radio still remains a man's world for the most part, so all of the usual male vs. female stuff applies. However, I really don't believe there is a huge difference between the tough things that a female goes through in radio as opposed to a male. I've seen men get 'beaten with a stick' as many times as I've taken a beating, so to speak. GMs, PDs and listeners can all certainly be tough on both genders."

Mollie Simpkins, aka Kristy Kramer was with Metro Traffic in West Palm Beach and was an integral member of my morning-drive team at Sunny 104.3, from 2000 until 2004. "I can honestly say while I was with Metro gender was never an issue," says Mollie. " f, it was the boys, Dave Klahr, Walt McDonald, Gary Lawrence, John Frawley, Jeff Brown and Jim Purther deserve Oscar nominations. In fact," she continues," I thank all of them for helping me grow and who made my job a joy. I did not find being female an issue during my many years with Metro," says Mollie," while working in Florida and later as Metro Market Chief in Baltimore. At times it was challenging while dealing with affiliates," she admits. "Every now and then I encountered someone I feel may have thought I had no idea what I was doing, but for the most part, I believe most saw that I was competent and had a small clue what I did."

Advancement for Women in radio.

While most broadcasters, male and female alike, agree that radio has come along way when it comes to gender and hiring, a report from *Inside-Radio/M Street Corp.* tells a different story, especially when it comes to female programmers in radio. The report states that, "Opportunities for women to program radio stations of any format are exceedingly rare." That's the conclusion of a Most Influential Women in Radio Program Director Gender Analysis Summary. The study is based in updated information provided by MStreet publications.[15] "The analysis, which includes all groups in all markets who own 12 or more radio stations, shows that there has been little growth in the ability for women to become PDs since this analysis was first published in 1995," remarks MIW spokesperson/Nassau Media Partners President Joan E. Gerberdine. "Only 10 percent of all PDs are women, up from eight percent eight years ago. Approximately 53% of all the radio station programming in this country is skewed toward the female listener, yet females are not in the positions to program those radio stations."

- 17% of all GMs and 31% of GSMs (general sales managers) are women.
- Some of the companies who own 50 or more radio stations exceed the average. Entercom has the highest percentage of female GSMs (35%) and also has the highest number of female PDs (13 or 20% of their PDs).
- 14% of ABC Radio's (today Citadel) PDs are females.
- Most station groups with 50 or more stations are below the norm. Women account for 8% of programming teams at both Clear Channel and Infinity (today CBS Radio); 7% of Cumulus' programmers are female.
- In companies with less than 50 stations, Multicultural has one of the highest percentages of female PDs (17%), followed by Emmis (14%), HBC (13%) and Greater Media (13%). MIW is dedicated to using its influence and resources to help put more women in positions of leadership in radio.

Note: It's important to know that this study was released in 1995. Hopefully, today, more women have found an easier road to advancement in broadcast programming and management.

Notes:
1. Dr. Lee DeForest, often referred to as "The Father of Modern Radio" invented the 3-element electron tube in 1906 and named it "audion." As a detection amplifier and oscillator (generator of radio waves) his invention made radio broadcasting possible.
2. WJZ, originally located in Newark, New Jersey, was later designated a New York City radio station.
3. Alma Kitchell's programs on NBC's Blue Network (later ABC) and Mary Margaret McBride's on NBC's Red Network are regarded as radio's first talk shows.
4. Arthur Godfrey is profiled in Chapter 1.
5. Read more on how to develop your own on-air style in Chapter 2.
6. **Note:** During radio's earliest days, female newscasters were extremely rare and just as rare was a woman newscaster covering a national political convention. A first for women on the air in the radio news business was in 1940, when Elizabeth Bemis of Cincinnati interviewed Wendell Wilkie at the Chicago GOP convention.
7. Douglas Edwards is profiled in Chapter 16, Radio Formats – News
8. 1939 Lillian Hellman.
9. 1942-Thornton Wilder.
10. NBC lost air-talent like Amos n' Andy, Jack Benny and others.

11. Kathleen Warnock is a playwright and freelance writer. Her work has appeared in *New York Press*, *New Directions for Women* and *Literary Cavalcade*. Reach out to her at kathlen@rockrgrl.com.
12. To learn more about Alison Steele, read Gillian G. Gaar's comprehensive, "*She's A Rebel, The History of Women in Rock & Roll*"(Seal Press-1992).
13. Laurie DeYoung has been handling morning drive in Baltimore for years and comments in Chapter 4, how to be a successful on-air radio pro.
14. Today, Nancy Widmann is a motivational speaker and consultant who has co-authored the book, *I Didn't See It Coming*, a practical guidebook for executives, published by Wiley in April 2007. She commented for Radio Pro in June 2008.
15. Thanks to Inside Radio/M Street Corp. 365 Union Street Littleton, NH 03561 1-800-248-4242 www.insideradio.com for permission to reprint this report.

Melanie Morgan, nationally known talk host.

A Woman's Perspective on Working in Radio and On the Air

Montage, pioneer women in radio.
Top row (L to R) Kate Smith, Vaughn deleath; middle row (L to R) Mary Margaret McBride, on CBS mic, Jean Ruth Hay on MBS mic and Jan Miner; Bottom row, (L to R) Virginia Payne (glasses) as Ma Perkins, Bertha Brainhard and Soap Opera Queen, Mary Jane Higby.

CHAPTER 14
How to Win in Morning Drive

"He treated each day as a fresh day to entertain"
– Bob MacAdorey about the late Al Boliska, former CHUM morning man, as quoted in *The CHUM Story* by Allen Farrell

"*The forecast for a great morning show: Mostly hot and partly funny.*"

MORNING DRIVE IS THE KEY SPOT on any radio station. The saying, "So goes mornings, so goes the rest of the broadcast day" is so true. A solid morning show is important to the overall success of the station, especially commercial radio, because AM-Drive is where the all-important advertiser spends big bucks.

Longtime Boston broadcaster **Don Latulippe** agrees. "The morning drive person is the most important person of the program day. He or she leads the station into all that follows. They set the pace. The most important thing a morning personality has to do is to be prepared. Two of the best morning drive persons I have known, Jess Cain and Joe Martelle, were at the studio long after going off the air, preparing for the next day's program." Latulippe, a 2009 inductee to the Massachusetts Broadcasters Hall of Fame, has this advice for future radio stars: "Don't abuse your night life so that you will be well-rested and ready to go in the early morning."

The problem is that morning-show people can't seem to find the time to get enough shut-eye! It's one of the toughest things about doing morning drive radio - finding time to get enough rest, a problem which seems inherent with the wake-up people at every radio station. Talent always feels tired! For many years, **Dr. Don Rose** was the morning drive voice of KFRC San Francisco. He frequently said, "The hardest part of the job is at 4:22a.m., when the alarm goes off, and being able to get up, and being able to function enough so you can make it in to do the show." [1]

As an AM-Drive person it is important to try to keep a regular schedule. Taking naps is a necessity if you plan on staying up past nine at night like most adults! However, catching a nap during daylight hours is virtually impossible if you plan on living a life! Many things come up, and if you want to have any sort of life outside radio, you constantly will find yourself pushing the envelope trying to do just one more thing, which is usually followed by another and another. One frustrating thing about being in morning drive is that other station personnel, especially management, seem to forget how *early* the day begins for the morning team. Here's some friendly advice to the troops in suits in charge: think twice before scheduling an afternoon sales call involving your morning drive people. Take into consideration their weird hours before scheduling any meetings or appointments for them late in the day. A noon luncheon may be conducive to your work schedule but totally out of whack with theirs! Early afternoon is nap time for most morning show folks.

The morning drive shift is the toughest in radio. It is also the most lucrative, but also carries with it more stress and pressure than any other time slot. In every radio format, including music-focused stations, morning drive talent play fewer songs and lean on their personalities to keep a smooth conversational flow going throughout their shows. Radio management knows a station gathers a large listening audience through a strong morning drive show. Without a top-rated show to kick-off the broadcast day, it is nearly impossible to have a successful station. This is not to diminish the ability of the other air-talent in any way; it is simply the cold, hard fact of the matter.

There are many different types of morning shows. Some shows have little personality and focus more on music. Other programs emphasize personality and are heavily laden with features: news, traffic, sports and entertainment. Regardless of the type of music played, most AM-Drive programs have informational features aimed at the commuter. In this chapter, the focus is on the format the author is most familiar with, AC (Adult Contemporary). Many AM-Drive shows I quarterbacked were heavy on personality and jammed with information, including traffic updates six times an hour, news at the top and bottom of each hour, and weather and sports. We did play music around our features, but usually not more than four songs in each hour. In December 1983, when I was teamed with the late Andy Moes on Boston radio's *Joe and Andy Family*, our station consultant, Walter Sabo delivered this edict: "The only time I want to hear a song on your show is when you are preparing another bit!"[2] We were lucky; most consultants want to hear MORE music and LESS talk!

"The Good Lord gave us two ends, one to sit on and one to think with. Your success as a radio pro and personality, particularly in morning drive, depends on which one you use. Heads you win! Tails you lose!"

In addition to my own input drawn from thirty-plus years in morning drive, I reached out to some of the best morning talent in the business on how they approach AM-drive radio. What a super line-up of radio pros! **Harry Harrison** was the "Morning Mayor" of the #1 radio market in the world. For 35 years, warm n' friendly Harry woke up New Yorkers, first at WABC and later CBS-FM; legendary Dallas morning man **Ron Chapman** spent 32 years at KVIL-AM and KLUV. **Capt. Dan** is now in his 34th year as the wake-up voice on KKLI-FM in Colorado Springs; **Laurie DeYoung** is in her 25th year in morning drive at WPOC Baltimore; **Bill Gardner** has been in the wake-up chair for 45 years, including AM-Drive at KOOL Phoenix; Seattle's **Bob Rivers** spent 20 years in mornings with nine under his comedic belt at KZOK-FM; **Dave Ryan**, since 1993, a total of 18 years as the morning-voice at KDWB-Minneapolis; and **Mark Wallengren**, 24 years waking up Los Angeles at KOST-FM. These eight radio pros have a combined total of **233 years** in morning drive! Future radio stars have a wealth of knowledge and experience to draw from thanks to the input of these highly successful radio pros. Their time spent in the prestigious morning drive slot more than qualifies them as experts on the subject. Their insightful, instructive and humorous comments are found later in this chapter.

What type of person does mornings?

First, a word of caution for future morning drive wannabes who long to be in the prestigious position: morning drive radio carries with it more pressure and stress than any other shift in radio. And don't kid yourself, morning drive radio personalities feel the pressure of getting up early in the morning and handling the most important time slot in radio. We worry about getting to work on time, ratings, and so on. You name it, we'll fret about it. So what kind of personality does it take to handle a morning drive air-shift? How different from everyone else is the radio wake-up pro? Is the type of person unique? Speaking as someone who was in morning drive for many years, I believe you have to be a certain type of individual, a person who does their best work in the early morning hours. In a June 1978 article, *R&R* (Radio & Records) reached out to several top-rated morning drive personalities for their takes on the subject.[3]

My friend Harry Harrison, who reigned supreme in morning drive in New York City for 35 years feels that morning people are a different breed. "I feel that they are special, because I don't think everybody can roll out of bed at 4a.m. in all kinds of weather and be pleasant and happy on the air, day after day, year after year. I think people who do morning shows or morning jobs of any kind are unique, maybe a little crazy, but unique."

Los Angeles radio legend, the late **Dick Whittinghill** was KMPC's wake-up person for twenty-eight years. He felt discipline was the key to handling morning drive. "You have to have a lot of discipline in order to get up at 4:15am, and then be 'Happy Sam' for a few hours."

One-time Houston radio pro **Bill Bailey** minces no words about being on the radio. "Either you can cut it or you can't. It takes a special kind of person to be on the radio, especially in the early morning. No amount of schooling will do it for you. I think the same thing is true about working morning drive, either you're a morning man or you're not!" It's the only shift in radio so far as I'm concerned," says the former Houston country radio personality. "The only thing I have to give up is rest. Morning is the prettiest time of the day. There's a certain solace and beauty to a sunrise. I enjoy participating in the town waking up. I can do my job without interference from sales, secretaries or executive row. The time slot is almost hassle-free."[4]

Lee Sherwood, formerly of WMAQ-Chicago says, "Biologically, I think there are morning people and others who are not. If your mind works well in the morning, you can do it. I've always found my mind is clearest in the morning and I can relate better to the audience at that time."

"Three wishes of a morning-show host: (1) more creative freedom (2) more money (3) more sleep!"

No matter how much you love being in morning drive, who really enjoys getting up at 3am!!

There is a misnomer that most morning radio people *are* morning people! WRONG! Now, it's true that MOST morning drive people enjoy being on the radio early in the morning. If they don't, the odds of doing well are considerably less. However, that doesn't mean most morning drive talent don't enjoy being grown-ups and staying up late just like you! Let's face it, no one in their right mind likes getting up at 3am. Add to that the adventure and thrill of climbing out of a warm bed on a cold winter's morning with 60-mile-an-hour gale force winds whipping around and snow drifts up to your ying-yang and you get the picture. T'aint easy being a morning drive person and having to deal with all this *before* arriving at the studio to do your show while most normal folks are still asleep!

Chicago radio legend **Wally Phillips** said it best in his book, *The Wally Phillips People Book*: "One of my least favorite activities is getting out of bed at 3:30am. It is also one of my more frequent activities. At the risk of sounding like a social dinosaur, I am a morning man! Not a morning person. That is someone who enjoys running around the block in a monogrammed, day-glo sweatsuit and solving three or four of the world's major crises before breakfast! I consider both these activities demonstrably irrational behavior!"

Phillips believes there are two basic kinds of people in the world. "There are larks, who like to tweet amidst the early morning dew, and there are owls, who like to hoot under the moon." Wally placed himself in the latter, an owl, only with the schedule of a lark. "I think," said Phillips, "there are many more owls than larks in morning drive radio!"

In a June 1978 article in R&R, another Chicago morning drive radio legend, **Larry Lujack**, was brutally candid about why he was in morning drive. "I do mornings not because I like to do mornings. I don't like getting up at two o'clock in the morning better than anyone else. I do mornings because that's where I can make the most money, and being the basic shallow, greedy person that I am, that's why I do mornings."

Nashville morning drive radio personality **Anna-Marie Ritter** emphatically states her case on how tough it is to get up early. "The ABSOLUTE hardest thing about working morning drive, for me, is GETTING UP! I have to get enough sleep, or I can't think quickly enough to be my best on the air. It means bedtime is 6:30 at night. You will lose a lot of your friends," she laughs, "or they will start working you into their lives for lunch and afternoon get-togethers. It's hard to hear, come on over for dinner tonight, or come out and hear this great band, and have to say, repeatedly, no, I can't on a school night. I once heard a morning radio guy say he quits his job every morning when his alarm goes off at 2:30. Then, he gets up, gets his coffee and he's okay, that's about the size of it!" (laughing)

One of the toughest things about doing morning drive radio is finding enough time to get rest and not feel constantly tired and wiped-out! When I handled morning drive, I was *constantly tired!* Many mornings, I would put so much energy into our show that I'd have little left over for much of anything else except sleeping! A lack of sleep seems the norm with the wake-up show at any radio station. It's so important to *try* to keep a regular schedule by taking naps.

Being a morning drive radio personality carries a lot of responsibility.

As a morning drive personality you need to keep yourself in shape to handle the weird hours and the stress and strain on your body that seems to accompany being on the wake-up shift. If you don't take care of yourself, you'll soon find yourself down for the count, perhaps even seriously ill and out of the game. As the key player on the radio station, in the most important time slot, you can't afford to be off the air! Not only is your own good health at risk along with your career, but the success of the entire radio station.

How to increase your energy level for your show and all day long.

Research shows you can predict what your energy levels will be like in the afternoon by knowing what you do in the morning.[5] If you crash and take a nap every afternoon there are reasons. When we spend mornings rushing around, like on a morning-drive radio show, our bodies run on stress hormones instead of "real energy." Stress hormones send flight or fight responses through your system causing you to temporarily have more energy. The problem is that stress hormones run out. When the stress hormones are gone, say "bye bye" to your energy!

The **key to increased energy** is to start your day off right and fuel your morning with "real" energy instead of stress hormones. Starting your day off right is like warming up your car on a cold winter's morning before driving it! **Awake to music,** instead of a jarring alarm. Don't hit the snooze alarm. Give yourself enough time to wake up, but don't lie in bed, get up. **Turn on the light**. By exposing our bodies and brains to light, we increase alertness and energy. Take a few deep breaths when you first get out of bed. Drink water. It will refuel your body with water lost during your sleep.

Exercise before leaving for the studio. Even just five minutes on an exercise bike will kick in your metabolism which sets you up for increased energy during the day.

Eat breakfast. Studies show that people are more productive when they eat breakfast.

Think positive! When you think positive about your show and the day ahead you increase your mental and physical energy. Instead of being stressed-out about an upcoming guest or anxious, which causes a release of stress hormones, thinking positively that everything will be fine sends positive energy to your body supplying you with sustained energy.

Keep in mind: From the moment you wake up you are dictating how much energy you will have during the morning for your show and throughout the day. With each activity, you choose to increase your metabolism…your energy and your health. A great start to the day will result in a great show and a great day for you!

How do you keep your mind and body in shape to handle the daily rigors of morning drive radio?

Here are a few suggestions

- Keep a positive attitude…most days are tough, but hang in and give it your best shot.
- Exercise regularly, if possible, before you go on the air …even five minutes on the exercise bike helps.
- Eat healthy. Don't allow Ms. Krispy Kreme and Mr. Dunkin' Donuts into your studio.
- Don't rely on drugs or booze to reduce your stress level…run or take a walk, instead.
- Get enough rest. You can't function effectively without enough sleep - three or four hours won't do it!

- Be assertive instead of aggressive, assert your feelings instead of becoming angry and defensive.
- Learn to manage your time more effectively - don't let the computer run your life. Learn to say no!

Morning Show Survival Kit

- **Band-aid** - to remind you to heal hurt feelings, either yours or someone else's on your team.
- **Candy kisses** - to remind you that everyone needs a hug or compliment every day.
- **Chewing gum** - to remind you to stick with it, no matter how many things may go wrong.
- **Eraser** - to remind you as QB that everyone makes mistakes and that's okay, we can learn by them.
- **Mint** - to remind you that your family of listeners is worth a mint to you.
- **Pen** - to remind you to list all the things that went right on your morning show.
- **Rubberband** - a reminder to be flexible. Things may not always go the way you planned.
- **Slice of bread** - to remind you what a fun job you have while making good bread.
- **Toothpicks** - to help keep your eyes open at 5:30 in the morning.
- **Tea bag** - to remind you to take time to relax daily and go over your list of God's blessings.

Morning drive radio ain't for sissies or for those who enjoy sleeping in.

One morning I happened to turn on the RFD Channel, not just because we live on a ranch in Colorado and feel a special kinship towards cattle, sheep and horses, but because I wanted to see what was new with **Don Imus**.[6] The "I-Man," as he is known to his loyal radio listeners and cable TV watchers, is truly a radio icon. Unfortunately, he was out ill that morning and not on the air! Evidently, and according to his longtime producer Bernard, who was holding court, the I-Man's son Wyatt had brought home a few unwanted germs from school and infected his dad. It got me thinking about how difficult morning drive radio can be to one's body. For over 35 years, I got up every morning at 3:15, and know how tough the "early call" can be under normal circumstances, let alone when you're not feeling well.

In Boston, while doing the morning drive show with my partner Andy Moes, station consultant **Walter Sabo** told us we were great morning show talent. Before Andy and I had time to puff up our chests and suck in his compliment, he added, "Yes, you're great, because you show up." Showing up to do your morning show at 5:30 or earlier is one of the prerequisites of being a top-shelf morning radio pro. Regardless of circumstances, including bad weather, the old adage "the show must go on" is so true when you're on the radio!

On the morning of March 24, 1993, Boston and New England got hit with one of those late winter/early spring nor'easters. To paraphrase a popular song, the snow was as high as an elephant's eye.[7] I wasn't sure I'd be able to make it down our long driveway, let alone through the snow-covered streets of our little bedroom town of Boxford, MA. It was only a few miles from our home to the interstate. I thought if I could make it to I-95, it would be almost clear sailing until I made it across the Mystic-Tobin Bridge to my exit on Storrow Drive in Boston. Of course, the streets of downtown Boston would present a whole new set of problems, but I figured I'd worry about that if I made it that far. The snow was at least three or four feet deep and still coming down.

One of the problems of heading into work at 3:30 in the morning in a snowstorm is that you are usually out before the plows. Most major highways are not cleared, let alone the secondary roads. This was one of those mornings where the plows on the interstate had a difficult time trying to keep up with the blowing, drifting snow. I managed to drive over snow-covered I-95, but at the Danvers exit, where I had to get off to take Route 1 the rest of the way into Boston, it happened. I got stuck. Even though I had left my house early enough to make it to the station, or so I thought, it took me an hour and a half to drive about 20 miles. The more I tried to get my Chevy Blazer out of the snow, the deeper it got stuck and me along with it. I had a cell phone and called my friend Skip Trombley, who had a wrecker service. He was willing to come and tow me out, but with the difficult weather conditions, coupled with the fact he was at least a half-hour away in good weather, I knew it would be a while before I saw his smiling face.

It was now almost 5:30 and I was due to go on the radio. I called the station and told Sam Montillo, the overnight control board operator, to "pot me up" after the next song.[8] For the next 45-minutes, I did my show on-the-road, from my Blazer stuck in the snow. The morning commute was beginning to take place and the few cars that were out were passing me ever so slowly. Many honked their horns as they drove on by. One listener pulled into a nearby Dunkin' Donuts and brought me a cup of joe. He joined me in the front seat of my vehicle and we chatted on my cell and out over the air about how crazy we both were for being out in the middle of a blizzard.

I share this story for this reason. Where there's a will, there's a way. Being in morning drive and the "wake up, get 'em up" time slot on any radio station carries with it a great deal of responsibility. You must have an attitude that nothing, even a New England blizzard, will keep you from being on the air! **Passion** and **dedication** are the bywords for being a successful morning drive radio personality![9]

> *"Every day is a precious gift that should be opened and enjoyed"*
> – Harry Harrison, NYC AM-Drive radio pro.

One of the most passionate and dedicated broadcasters ever to do a morning-show is my friend, **Harry Harrison.** For thirty-five years, Harry was the top-rated "Morning Mayor" of New York City radio, first at WABC-Music Radio 77 and later at WCBS-FM. Harry shares a similar incident involving an overnight snow storm! It is a prime example of dedication to your listeners and show, even when Mother Nature hits you full-force with an over-night blizzard! "I was doing mornings at WABC when we got hit by a terrific snowstorm," recalls Harry. "I got up earlier than usual and with the snow drifts, I couldn't even get the car out of the garage. It was so bad and it was like three o'clock in the morning and I remember my wife Patti was in the garage with me and the lights in the garage were shining down on the freshly-fallen snow and I said to Patti, 'You know what, I'm going to start walking' and she said, 'What?' I repeated it, 'I'm going to start walking on foot. The cops in our little town of Norwood, New Jersey, about 25 miles from NYC and the station, will pick me up. They'll take me to the next one, and I'll get to the George Washington Bridge and then I'll make it all the way.'" As he walked away, Harry says he remembers seeing Patti standing there under the garage lights, yelling, "You're crazy, you're craz—y!" People did pick him up along his snowy journey and he eventually made it in to the station.

Harry Harrison wasn't there for the beginning of his show, but was there for the end. In fact, he wound up filling in for Ron Lundy who followed him on the radio, because Ron couldn't make it in. Looking back on the experience, Harry says, "Maybe it was crazy, but as you know, Joe, people depend on you. I remember later, people told me, 'I turned you on and you were there, Harry, on the radio, and figured, he made it, I can do it, too.'" Harrison truly believed he had a responsibility to his listeners to get to work to get on the radio and deliver the goods! On that morning, his show was service-oriented information about the storm, weather updates, school and business closings, and so on. Harry Harrison's dedication and determination to get to the radio station to be there for his family of listeners is a shining example for future radio wannabes on what it takes to be a real morning drive radio pro!

Time management is the key to success in handling morning drive and also being a PD.

Mark McCray, like so many PDs in radio today, multi-tasks. Mark was also the morning drive guy at X-102.3 in West Palm Beach. His advice to those PDs who find themselves doing double duty with management responsibilities and a morning drive air-shift: "Make sure you surround yourself with a good team of people who are also targeting the mission you have for the station.

I have learned," adds Mark, "that good managers surround themselves with passionate hard-working people, because it is impossible to do everything by yourself. Prioritizing and time management are also important."

Brian deGeus Foxx is Music Director at KSFI-FM Salt Lake City. He is also in AM-Drive. Brian agrees with Mark McCray about handling your time wisely. "It's all about time management, knowing what needs to be done and setting up schedules to get the tasks completed. Collectively," he says, "it's a wide variety of tasks, from show prep and music scheduling to planning ahead and making time for people." Brian also says an important part of being successful on the radio, in or out of the morning drive and whether you're a radio newbie or seasoned pro, is to be respectful of the program director. [10]

"He or she has a job to do, just like the rest of us. It seems that within the industry, there are many fragile egos. Listen to what the PD has to say and learn from it. Thicken up your skin. Most PDs are simply guiding you to be what the station needs you to be without changing your style."

How does a future radio star wind-up in the coveted seat of morning drive radio?

Boston radio pro and all-around good guy **Dale Dorman** sums it up with one four-letter word, "Work"! Detroit's **Dick Purtan** is regarded as Michigan's most respected air personality, and agrees with Dale. "Work harder than the next guy. Study the air-talents that have gone before you, and what made them successful. There is nothing wrong with 'borrowing' some ideas and even a little bit of their style," he says with a grin. "Remember, copying from one person is plagiarism; copying from six people is research."

The author finally makes it to big-time radio and on the air in Boston.

Boston is where I always dreamed of being on the radio. When at long last the opportunity presented itself, I grabbed it like it was nothing short of my life support system. My previous seventeen years of sweating my butt off in radio and constantly dealing with rejection finally paid off! Countless frustrations while struggling to make it in a business I loved served as my personal motivation to keep going! My goal was to make it as a radio pro on the air in one of America's largest radio markets. When I finally made it to the top and #1 in Boston, it was especially sweet. Growing up just 90 miles to the north in Portland, I could pick up great Boston stations like BZ, HDH and RKO, all AM powerhouses long before FM hit the scene. The hub was home to some of America's greatest radio personalities, several of whom have graciously given their time to comment in this book. It was such an honor to work with them. It goes to show, if you want radio badly enough, go for it! You will succeed! I joined WROR in the fall of 1979, working the night shift. Never in my wildest imagination did I ever imagine I would wind up in the coveted morning drive seat.

Initially, **Gary "Berko" Berkowitz** hired me do fill in air work at ROR, I guess to see how I'd sound and fit in. Oftentimes, he'd call me at home in Maine at the very last minute and say, "Hey, man, can you be down here to do the ten-to-two pm shift?" Down here was a two-hour drive one way *without* traffic, but I'd jump at the opportunity. I'm sure it was his way of testing me to see how much I really wanted to be on the radio in Boston, but more importantly, to find out how willing I was to follow direction and do what he asked, when he asked. Following directions and showing loyalty rank really high on Gary's wish list. He needs to know you are a team player and whether or not you want to be on *his* team! For me, auditioning for Berko's team was almost like going through Marine Corps boot camp for a second time.[11] That's probably a stretch, but at least mentally there are definite similarities. He will test you at every turn, but once you pass the *Berko Boot Camp* you are a member of his inner circle for life. Ask anyone who has worked with him and I'm sure you'll get the same response. I speak from first-hand experience. When I'd find myself off the radio and out of work, Gary was always the first to call. During my forty-one-year radio career, he hired me on *three* separate occasions. More details on those circumstances are found elsewhere in this book.

Berko, along with Tom Baker and Sales Manager Peter Smyth, must have liked what they heard, because my fill-in air work led to a full-time air-shift from 7pm to midnight.[12, 13, 14] A few months later in early 1980, I was handed the reins to the prestigious morning drive slot vacated by a true radio pro, Frank Kingston Smith.[15] Our excellent ROR wake-up team featured news-director Rod Fritz and Carolyn Murdock on news, Traffic with Dick Syatt, Ted Sarandis on sports and meteorologist Harvey Leonard.[16, 17, 18] For the next 17 years, I had a blast in AM-drive at WROR (later MIX-98.5). I worked solo from 1980-83 and again from 1992-95. In between, for nearly ten years, the late Andy Moes was my air partner on the *Joe and Andy Family.* It was radio utopia! I felt I was at the top of my game.

Just before Christmas 1983, WROR's GM **Tom Baker** had the foresight to put Andy on my morning show on a trial basis. Andy had been my traffic guy but the reports became secondary to our chatter in and out of his commuter updates. So, Andy left his warm, comfortable ROR Accu-traffic van and came into our studio for a two-week trial basis! His story is not unlike the wild n' crazy, somewhat eccentric but lovable uncle who pays a visit and ends up staying forever! His two-week trial wound up being almost a ten-year stay as my radio partner.[19] We had a ball! We were blessed with super-high ratings and became one of Boston's favorite morning radio drive-time teams. In '92, Andy left to solo mornings on competing station WEEI, while I continued in AM-Drive at ROR for the next three years. In November '95, emergency lung surgery ended my many years on ROR. It was a time in my career when I would face some serious challenges, but first, a bit about my radio life with Andy Moes.

My radio partner, Andy Moes.

For those of you who weren't privileged to know or hear Andy, describing the man is like trying to put lightning in a bottle, but I'll give it a shot! If Andy were here now, I'm sure he'd say, "Joey, make that shot Jack Daniels!" Andy was a rascal and a rogue, and he loved upsetting the apple cart. When he learned that male members were excluded from joining Boston's prestigious "Women's City Club" on fashionable Beacon Hill, Andy, said, "Whoa, wait just a minute, we're talking about a case of reverse discrimination here!" So, he pushed the envelope to obtain membership. As far as I know, he was the only male member of the club. Quite often after our morning show, he would invite me to join him for breakfast at the classic brownstone, halfway up Beacon Hill. The view overlooking Boston's scenic public garden was spectacular. As we enjoyed eggs, croissants, and freshly-squeezed orange juice, which Andy insisted on, the mostly-elderly ladies peered warily at the two men amongst their midst.

Andy could also be conniving and cunning, a little eccentric (aren't we all), delightfully demented, and extremely adventuresome. Andy Moes dared to be different and he was. He also possessed a rapid-fire mind which bordered on genius. He could also be loving, caring, and possessed a heart almost as big as his girth. Andy could also be sensitive, but his manly man's persona usually kept it well hidden. He enjoyed fine cuisine. Several of his close friends were well-known Boston chefs, including Lydia Shire and Jasper White. During his drinking days, Andy favored a bottle of Dom, but was not opposed to a glass of port or a shot of Jack. He also had a special taste for the ladies, and was definitely a guy's kinda guy. Jokingly, on our show, he would often boast that he was a man's man, a manly man, a man's sort of man!

Andy was naturally funny and it was my natural style to be the set-up guy for him! It was easy to set Andy up on our show and let him deliver a punch line, which often was ad-libbed and delivered right off the top of his outrageously funny mind. We clicked as a team because we were so different. Thankfully, we were able to mesh our differences in an entertaining way for our listeners. It was fun being the voice of reason, because that's really who I try to be off the radio. Andy was gifted as being one of the funniest guys the good Lord ever placed on this planet. He looked at all things in life as being funny and seldom missed an opportunity to poke fun at any situation. Most anyone and everyone was fair game, including himself.

On our show, Andy constantly made reference about his slightly rotund size.[20] A favorite line of his was comparing himself to a popular Hollywood film star. If a female caller asked Andy to describe himself, he would often reply, "Madam, I look just like actor Richard Gere!" Then, quickly add, "If Richard Gere had a hooked nose and was grossly overweight!" Yup, that was our Andrew H. Moes!

Andy enjoyed staying at some of Boston's finer hotels, no doubt a throwback to his college years at Emerson when he worked as a security guard at the Boston Sheraton. He was friendly with many local innkeepers, like the Sheraton's Bob McAleney and Tim Kerwin, former GM at the Bostonian, two of our favorite places to hang out. Andy also enjoyed sharing the hotel good times by making reservations for his friends for special getaway weekends. It wasn't just any old hotel room either, but usually the Presidential Suite! Nothing but the best for my pal Andy and his family and friends. He was extremely generous to those he loved.

Radio Pro lesson learned: To get the real inside scoop on what's happening in your town, cozy-up and become friendly with a few managers at the city's top hotels. They know the real movers and shakers in town and can provide plenty of juicy gossip on who, what, where, and when for your show.

On the radio, Andy Moes often said what every guy wished he could say and get away with! He definitely displayed a "devil be damned" attitude! He couldn't care less what people thought about him, and the loftier the perch of someone in authority, the more deadly Andy's aim became! He specifically targeted pompous, arrogant folks. You know the type; people who are just plain full of themselves. They would bear the brunt of Andy's more caustic barbs!

The Joe n' Andy Family – Winners in morning drive radio.

Certain folks were taboo with Andy and off his target list, notably seniors and small children. They received special dispensation from Sir Andrew, who had the build of a fire hydrant; our little round mound of sound, as I affectionately called him. Because of his rather diminutive height and chubbiness, he could be the quintessential little angel in the presence of religious clergy. It was a kick for me to watch radio's little bad boy become so reverent whenever former Boston Cardinal Bernard Law was a guest on our show. Watching Andy curtsy and bow and be ever so polite to his eminence would truly make you believe pious little Andy was in reality just a choirboy and masquerading as "Peck's little bad boy" on the radio. It wasn't an act! It was simply another side of the very complex Andy Moes. His unique personality is what made the man so human and lovable. Andy was unafraid to reveal every aspect of himself on our show, as was I. We let it all hang out for our listeners to hear and take in. In doing so, emotionally, they got a sense and feel for what Joe and Andy were all about.

Unlike many of today's air personalities, Andy didn't have to dig down in the gutter to be funny. Once, when a consultant suggested he be more like Howard Stern, Andy, obviously annoyed by the reference, shot back, "I'm not Howard Stern, I'm Andy Moes." That quickly ended that discussion! Andy was one of those gifted performers who thought funny. His thoughts were humorous. His unique voice and infectious laugh served to enhance his on-air delivery. He was truly an original and special in every way. In no way am I trying to canonize the man. Like each of us, he was not without his own demons and faults. What I am trying to do is paint a complete mosaic to show you the interesting and complex personality mix he brought to our radio show everyday, and in so doing made Andy so popular.

Jerry Lewis is one of my all-time favorite comedians. As a solo performer he enjoyed much success, but with **Dean Martin** as his partner, it was a once-in-a-lifetime comedic dream team! Unselfishly, Dean relinquished the spotlight, not easy for another talent to do, and set up the wild and crazy Jerry so he could play out his comedic shtick! As a youngster, I went to the movies faithfully to catch the latest Martin & Lewis films! In addition to their big-screen popularity they also were stars on their own radio shows and helped pioneer the early days of television.[21]

During the tube's formative years, the late 1940s and early '50s, I was front-row center peering at the small, black-and-white Sylvania TV in our family den. My eyes riveted on one of my favorite shows, NBC's *Colgate Comedy Hour*, which aired Sunday nights from 1950 until 1955. The hour-long variety program competed quite successfully with CBS-TV's popular *Ed Sullivan Show*. Every week, the *Comedy Hour* featured different comedians as hosts: Eddie Cantor, Jimmy Durante, Bob Hope, and two of my favorites, Martin and Lewis. Jerry's outrageously funny behavior, constantly mugging for the camera, and running wild all over the set was the perfect partner for the laidback, easy-going Dean. I ate it up!

Martin and Lewis, like my other favorite comedy team, **Abbott and Costello**, presented a special type of humor that the entire family could enjoy and watch together without fear of being embarrassed by either language or content. Their routines were loaded with lots of innocent double entendres. The adults loved it while it sailed right over our innocent kids' heads. It was a more placid type of comedy which was devoid of the meanness which is so prevalent in much of today's so-called humor. Much to the delight of our own personal egos, Andy and I were often compared to great comedy teams like Martin and Lewis and Abbott and Costello. We knew we weren't close to being as talented as them and certainly not as successful or popular, but it was cool to be thought of in their company. One thing I believe we did have in common with some of the great comedy teams was our impeccable timing. Andy and I had an uncanny ability to know exactly where each other was headed during our show. It was like reading each other's mind.

The fifties, the era of my growing-up years, seemed to be a kinder, gentler period. A somewhat naïve time, if you will, which was reflected in comedy - especially on the air. It's the type of humor I was raised with, and later in my adult life became part of who I am, which was reflected in my air style.

I unashamedly admit some of Martin & Lewis' and Abbott & Costello's style and sense of timing rubbed off on me. My partner Andy also enjoyed their humor, but because of the ten-year difference in our ages, he was schooled more in the *Saturday Night Live* generation and the comedic styles of Chevy Chase and John Belushi. Therefore, his humor was a little hipper. When our two styles were brought together on the radio, they worked beautifully! The so-called "Joe and Andy Magic" on the radio, which other broadcasters kindly referred to and worked so well for us, came down to one important thing: we had fun working together! We made each other laugh and would often say, "Geez, I hope our listeners are having as much fun as we are and laughing just as hard!" Andy and I laughed a lot. We really did entertain ourselves and, thankfully, our loyal family of listeners went along for the fun ride.

Andy and I didn't report to just any job every morning at 5:30. It was a special gig and we knew it! Neither of us enjoyed getting up at 3:30 in the morning, but when we hit the air a'runnin', it was showtime and fun time! We looked forward to going on the radio and having a good time with our family of listeners. When I'd set Andy up for the punch line, he knew exactly when to deliver it and get off, and I knew enough not to step on him, or to try to out-funny him. We knew our roles and stuck to them. It is so important to know your role on the radio. [22]

The Saga of the Head Brothers.

When we took to the air every morning at 5:30, we knew management wasn't up that early. One morning, Andy happened to mention on our show that no one in management listens to the earliest segment of *The Joe and Andy Family*, which we referred to as "the 5:30 Club." He also gleefully added, "So we can pretty much say and do as we damn well please!" To prove our point, the next morning at 5:30, during the segment of our show which ran from 5:30 to 6am, over our theme music we came on and introduced ourselves this way, "Good Morning and welcome to the 5:30 Club on 98.5-WROR. Joe and Andy have the day off and filling in, we're the Head Brothers, I'm DICK and here's my brother, PIN." We opened the show like that for a solid week! Right after the intro, we'd go right on taking care of business without laughing or saying anything else about The Head Brothers. Laughing would have brought attention to the bit and ruined it. For it to work, we had to drop it ever so gently on the listener and let subliminal humor do its thing. During the half hour, we would refer to each other only as Dick & Pin without any further mentioning of our last name, HEAD!

Listeners would come up to us and mention the Head Brothers and think it was the funniest thing they ever heard. The suits never said a word. Either they really weren't minding the store at that early hour, were too slow to pick up on it, or because we had such high ratings simply turned a deaf ear. Silly and sophomoric humor? You bet! Anything for a chuckle and a fun time! That's what Joe and Andy were all about. To this day, whenever I think about the Head Brothers, juvenile humor or not, it still makes me laugh!

The Joe n' Andy Story as told in the words of David Kruh.

David Kruh was an engineer at RKO/ROR in Boston when Andy and I were a radio team. Dave is a friend who was a loyal listener to our show. I asked him to share a memory of Joe and Andy on the air that he felt would best describe what we were all about on the radio. Here is Dave's complete and unedited reply: "I am flattered Joe asked me to contribute to his book. You see, I was one of those people who, even as a child, was afflicted with a love, an obsession, really, with radio. Growing up in the 1960s and early '70s meant the great old days of Top-40 AM radio, when disc jockeys did the impossible; they entertained and informed and made us laugh out loud, all within the eight-second instrumental intro on a record before the singer began to sing. I was a true radio geek, someone who would tune the radio dial not to find music, but to hear the disc jockeys and their patter.

"Growing up in New York, I got to hear true radio legends, like Dan Ingram, Ron Lundy and Don Imus, back in the days when the I-Man played music. Naturally, I had to give it a try myself, which I did after college (sorry Dad) and quickly found out how really hard the job is. If I got nothing else out of the experience, other than the meager salary small stations paid, it was my increased respect for those who do the job well. Like so many things, it is tougher than it looks."

"Before I get to the Andy story Joe would like me to tell, I'd like to share a little piece of Joe's Boston radio life and how passionate and dedicated he was to his profession.

"After my own on-air career ended in 1981, I landed an engineering job at WROR-FM in Boston (it was good parental advice to have something to fall back on). Joe Martelle was the morning man, and he also did a show called *Saturday Night "Live" at the Oldies,* a five-hour program that was a certifiable smash. I mean, you heard Joe's show everywhere, coming out of windows in college apartments, from cars and taxis, even parties where *SNL at the Oldies* was the entertainment. It was huge! Now, you have to remember that in the early 1980s FM radio was still battling with AM for music listenership. Hard to believe today, but even as late as the mid-1980s most AM stations still played music and got more than half of the radio listeners. Shows like Joe's were important in helping FM in its drive for music listener supremacy, which I want to reiterate was never a slam-dunk. Want proof? Even the Westinghouse Corporation took FM's potential for granted when they sold their Boston FM for peanuts, a decision they would later come to regret.

"Being even a small part of *Saturday Night "Live" at the Oldies* was something special. It was radio the way I heard it growing up, and Joe was a practitioner of the highest order. He could bond with thousands of people at once, while each and every one of them knew, yes knew, that Joe was speaking to them personally. You can call it a gift, but I saw how much work went on in that studio to make it sound so effortless. Joe must have lost five pounds every Saturday night. He was literally dripping with sweat as he raced around the studio to find requested music, cue up songs, take requests, play the commercials, and read copy. And, as the low man on the staff totem pole who got 'stuck' with Saturday night shifts, I had a ringside seat to many of those programs. Stuck? Ha! I was in radio heaven.[22]

"Okay, now for the story Joe wanted me to tell in the first place. A few years after Joe got the morning show at WROR, they paired him with Andy Moes. Andy...well, I'm sure Joe has had plenty of things to say about Andy, so all I'll say here is that Andy was one of the most unique human beings there ever was, or likely will ever be. Andy Moes burst upon the Boston scene in the 1970s when he famously sued the Metropolitan Transit Authority, what we call the 'T' in Boston, for false advertising. You see the 'T' called their delay-ridden subways 'Rapid Transit.' Andy was one of the first radio bad boys, a brilliantly funny man who invented many of the stunts and bits that have become the staple of every morning zoo radio program. Andy pushed the envelope of radio comedy to the breaking point, and the story I am going to tell you now is about the morning Andy Moes tore open the envelope. I have never laughed harder!

"It was 1984 and it was Joe Martelle's birthday. Andy decided to buy Joe a few gifts that he would present to him on the air, which sounds like a nice thing for someone to do for their on-air partner, right? Of course, it does, but this was Andy Moes doing the gift giving. You see, Andy went shopping not on Washington Street at Filene's or Jordan Marsh (which were then Boston's premier department stores), but a few blocks away near Essex Street, an area that was then known as the Combat Zone, Boston's red light district.

"Andy decided to broaden Joe's horizons by purchasing some, ahem... reading material. He also purchased, how shall I put this...a 'battery-operated device' that he intended to give Joe live on the air. That's where I come in. One of Andy's quirks (they were countless) was his complete and total aversion to technology. The man couldn't even change a typewriter ribbon. So, installing batteries in this device presented an insurmountable technical problem.

"So, in he came to the engineering shop, where I happened to be working the morning shift that day. 'I need you to install batteries in something,' Andy said. 'What kind of batteries do you need?' I asked. 'I think D,' he said as he whipped out this...thing in front of me. I can still see it wobbling as he shook it in front of me. I can also remember thinking that maybe my dad was right,

I should have gone to law school. Anyway, I took the item from Andy and installed the batteries.

"'How do I turn it on?' he asked (like I said, Andy was technologically clueless, even when the on switch was staring him in the face). I pushed the switch and the device buzzed to life. By this time it was past 7 o'clock and other station employees were beginning to show up in the company cafeteria, which was next to the engineering shop. The buzzing began to attract a crowd. I looked at Andy and asked, 'Are you really going to give him this thing on the air?' 'Sure, why not?' he said. I had no answer. Andy switched off the device (I give him credit for figuring that out) and began putting it back into its package. 'Thanks,' he said, and headed down the hallway to the on-air studio, followed by the crowd from the cafeteria.

"Now, imagine the scene. Live, on the air, Andy announces that it is Joe's birthday and begins to hand him his gifts, starting with the magazines. Now, what you have to know about the Joe and Andy team was that each had very defined roles. Andy was the bad boy and Joe was the good boy, the conscience; married, a father, a Catholic and a former Marine. So, Joe unwraps the first magazine and without even hesitating, reads the title: *Enema Digest*. Just like that, as if he were reading the headline of that day's *Boston Globe*. In the studio, the crowd that had followed Andy down the hall burst into laughter. Yes, part of the humor was in saying this filthy title ON THE RADIO, but what made it funnier was that it was JOE who was saying it. That was Joe's genius; he knew his part, but also knew the right moment to stretch his character to get the most laughs from it. And laugh we did, as Andy bestowed the rest of the printed material he had bought on the birthday boy."

Finally it was time for Andy to present Joe with his final gift…all live and still on the air.

"I was still in the engineering shop," recalls David Kruh, "listening over the air (the studio was very crowded at this point) and I heard Andy say, 'Joe, you know we love you and you're the captain of our team, and we have a final gift for you' and Andy hands him the…device. I have the tape of this show somewhere in my basement and remember listening to it a few years ago. You can actually hear Joe take the gift out of the bag. 'That's a fine Doc Johnson product, partner, nothing but the best,' you hear Andy say. 'I had engineering put some batteries in it, Joe, let me show you how it works' and with that reached over and flipped on the switch. Joe knew he didn't have to say a word. That was part of his gift, knowing when words were not necessary. He simply held the device close to the microphone and let it do its thing. Now, I can't swear to this, but I have to believe that this was the first time this sound was heard on Boston radio. Maybe on radio in any town. Clear as a bell, that distinctive buzzing on 3,000 watts (50kW e.r.p.) of major-market FM radio.

And I recall sitting in the engineering shop thinking that somehow, in my own small way, I had a part in radio history, and how proud Dad would be if I were to ever tell him. I listened to the laughter in the studio as it finally died down. There was silence for a few seconds, and then Joe spoke. It was, and still is, one of the funniest things I have ever heard uttered on the air, and it was the perfect ending to the bit. 'Boy, have I got a surprise for my wife tonight!'"

Saturday Night "Live" at the Oldies.
As former RKO Engineer David Kruh kindly mentioned in the preceding pages that in addition to co-hosting morning drive on ROR-FM, I also was also the host of an all-request oldie show every Saturday night on the station. For just a moment, I'm going to divert from morning drive radio to give you some idea why *Saturday Night "Live" at the Oldies* was so special to me and thousands of New England listeners.

In November 1979, PD, Gary Berkowitz and I launched *"Live"* on ROR. It was set up in a phone call. Gary called me at my home in Maine and asked one simple question, "Do you know anything about oldies?" "Do I," I shouted, "I love oldies!" I quickly filled him in on how I had played drums in a rock band while in high school back in the '50s, The Rhythm Rockers, and how I'd filled in for the regular radio DJ at our high-school record hops when he'd take a break. "Heck," I said, "I played today's oldies, when they were newies!" That's all it took! The very next Saturday night, we kicked off *"Live"* from 7 to Midnight. It became a twelve-year love affair with one of the most exciting programs I ever had the privilege of hosting! The show became a huge hit with Boston and New England listeners.[23] Thousands listened and called in to request their favorite oldies from the '50s, '60s and early '70s. Many became stars in their own right with their lively conversation. What a party! It was one big happy family reunion every Saturday night. My extended family of listeners made my time on the radio very special.

Unfortunately, space does not permit naming everyone, but some of the regulars include a loyal contingent of listening friends from Revere; Bobby and Stevie Rosetti, Carol & Freddie, Benny Mara and a couple of likable Mikes, Chella and Messina.[24] Another regular was Sandi in Haverhill, who billed herself as Roy's "Blue Angel."[25] She was joined by Dottie in Canton and Georgia and Jan in New Hampshire, along with fun guys like Big Tony from Everett, Chuck Raymond, Mike Cooley and the friendly toll-taker, Mike Paulicelli, who called in requests from his post high up on the Mystic-Tobin Bridge spanning the majestic Charles River. These folks and so many others tuned-in and called in every Saturday night or showed up at our various remote broadcasts, including the Revere Bandstand, Fort Devens, and Canobie Lake Park. They were the reason the show became so popular and such a huge Boston and New England hit! I will always be appreciative and grateful for their support. These dedicated listeners kept the show rated #1 for twelve years, from the fall of 1979 until February 1991.

Radio Pro lesson learned: If you find yourself surrounded by loyal listeners never, ever take them for granted. On days you're feeling down and out, they will be there for you through thick and thin.

Many calls to our oldies show stand out in my memory, but one call was very special. To this day, it makes me smile just thinking about it. It was the night a miracle happened on our show. The call was from Ritchie Conigliaro, the younger brother of former Red Sox outfielder, the great **Tony Conigliaro**. I had known Tony and his brothers Billy and Ritchie for years. Ritchie and I became close friends and for a while we lived in the same apartment complex in Malden, MA. For those of you not familiar with Tony Conigliaro's story, please allow me to share a little slice of his life and baseball career with you.

Tony was a local kid who went on to become a star athlete with the Boston Red Sox. In his rookie season, 1964, he batted .290 with 24 homers and 52 RBIs in 111 games and was a leading contender for Rookie of the Year honors, but he broke his arm in August. The next season, 1965, Tony C. led the league with 32 home runs. In '67, he was selected to play in the All-Star Game. In August of that year, the Sox were playing the California Angels at Fenway Park. Tony was batting against Jack Hamilton when he was hit on his left cheekbone. He was carried off the field on a stretcher, suffering from a broken cheekbone and a severely damaged left retina. The batting helmet he was wearing was not equipped with the protective ear flap which is standard today. It was a miracle he survived.

The night a miracle happened on *Saturday Night "Live" at the Oldies*.

Tony C. did survive and made a miraculous comeback in 1969, hitting 20 homers with 82 RBIs and earning "Comeback Player of the Year" honors. He played a few more seasons with the Sox and one with the Angels in '71, but his sight was so severely affected by his injury that he was forced to step aside from the game he loved! His playing days were over, but because of his outgoing personality and good looks, he was a natural for television. Tony was a guest on various TV shows, including Merv Griffin, and eventually landed an on-air sports position on TV in San Francisco.

In early January 1982, Tony's love for New England brought him back to Boston for an audition. It was the break he had wanted; a chance to handle color commentary on the Red Sox broadcasts. However, fate was to dictate otherwise. After the interview and on his way to Logan airport, Tony suffered a heart attack. He was only thirty-seven years old. The loss of oxygen and blood to his brain affected him so much that the one-time star athlete was incapacitated and restricted to his parents' home in Nahant, MA, for the rest of his life. Tony's loving parents Sal and Teresa, and brothers Ritchie and

Billy, devoted much of their time to "T," their nickname for the popular Boston slugger. They spent hours talking to him, holding his hand, reassuring him that he would get better, and hoping and praying for the miracle that, somehow, Tony would regain full use of his body and be able to speak again. Almost daily for eight years, Tony was subjected physical and/or speech therapy. Nurses, therapists, and family members worked on him, moving his limbs, doing their best to help him regain use of his muscles and his voice. They never gave up on him and Tony never quit trying!

I would often visit Tony at Sal and Theresa's home in Nahant. Tess, as Tony's mom was called, was a gracious and generous lady who must have thought I looked undernourished, because she always made meatballs and macaroni for me. Of course, she didn't have to beg me to have a seat at their table. Many times when Tony would see me, he would grip my hand tightly and begin crying. Since he was unable to speak, it was his only way of communicating his thoughts. I felt badly that my presence seemed to upset him so much. After one such visit, I mentioned to Ritchie that "maybe 'T' becomes emotional because he recognizes me as 'Joe on the radio' and it upsets him to know he can no longer be on the air, too." Ritchie just shook his head. We never did learn why my presence seemed to affect Tony in such an emotional and sad way.

Tony Conigliaro was extremely popular. The handsome athlete was loved by his fans, especially the ladies. The mega-celebrity even recorded a few popular hit songs, including one of my favorites, "Why Don't They Understand." In December 1957, the song was a hit for George Hamilton IV and got as high as #10 on *Billboard's* music survey. A few years later, Tony also recorded the song and it became a big Boston-area hit! I'll always remember the Saturday night I played Tony's recording of "Why Don't They Understand." It was memorable for me because a miracle happened! As soon as the song finished playing, the station hotline rang. An excited Ritchie Conigliaro was on the other end. His voice filled with emotion. "Joe, a miracle has happened," he cried into the phone. "Tony just sang every word to his song which you just played on the radio!" It's important to know that up until that time, Tony had been unable to speak, let alone sing, and now the man who could only utter a few almost unintelligible sounds had actually sung along with his own song! Yes, it was one of those mysteries of life, proving once again that miracles can and do happen. It may have been for just a couple of minutes during the length of one short 45rpm record, but those precious few minutes gave a burst of new hope to Tony's family and his millions of fans around New England. Maybe T would make a full recovery after all.

Sadly, it never came to pass. Tony Conigliaro passed away in February 1990, one month after his 45th birthday.[26] During my twelve years as host of *Saturday Night "Live" at the Oldies*, we received many wonderful calls, but none can compare with the night I received word that a miracle had occurred with Tony C. It was a very special moment for me that I will cherish for the rest of my life.

The sweet highs and bitter lows of being in morning drive radio.
    The early '80s were a mixture of fabulous highs and terrible lows in my life. On the downside, after nineteen years of struggling to keep our marriage together, my first wife Janet and I went our separate ways. We married young; she was eighteen and right out of high school and I was twenty-two going on sixteen. We were just a couple of good kids searching in vain for a little piece of happiness and stability that seemed to elude us in our marriage. There is little doubt, at least to my way of thinking, that the instability radio created did not help our roller-coaster ride, and did little to solidify things. If anything, it created more tension, anxiety, and stress. My own immaturity didn't help matters, and not to make excuses, but in my own way I honestly tried to make things work. I know she did, too, but it almost seemed like the harder we tried the more difficult it became. Janet is a kind-hearted person and deserves all good things in life.
    One of the positives in my life was my radio career. It was pretty darn good and my years at WROR were some of my happiest in radio. I was at the top of my game as a radio pro. My pal and air partner of almost ten years, Andy Moes, was fun to work with and from day one, we hit it off! We were double-stuffed Oreos and a glass of ice-cold milk! We complemented each other and with modesty aside, we had a special magic other morning radio teams would die for. Andy and I made each other laugh and our loyal listeners laughed right along with us. We got paid for having fun on the radio! Great work if you can get it and the radio angels blessed us, because we got it!
    Midday talk show host **Dick Syatt** was our buddy and worked right down the hall from us, on sister station 68AM-WRKO. Occasionally, after our show, we'd bump into him in the hallway. Andy and I would always be laughing about something that had happened earlier on our show. One day, Dick stopped us and smiling, said, "You guys are working in radio Disneyland and are so lucky, but one day it too shall end!" We chuckled and thought, "Poor, Dickie, he's so miserable over on AM. Listen to how negative the poor lad is." Little did we know how prophetic his words would be. In retrospect, I guess we must have thought we'd go on together, forever, that somehow we were bulletproof. After all, we reasoned, we were Joe and Andy and we had top ratings to back us up! The station could be and would eventually be sold, but so what?! We had survived several programming and management changes in the past, big deal. We were Joe and Andy.
    Radio Pro lesson learned: Don't ever let your ego get so far up your butt that it blinds you to what's going on around you."[27]

One thing all morning drive shows have in common, they all had to begin somewhere.

Here are a few examples on how to launch your morning drive show. The ideas were exchanged between the author and other morning-radio pros during his many years on the air.[28]

Radio Pro Bert Weiss says the first and most important thing to do in AM-Drive is to share the excitement and anxiety of your new move with your listeners. Most of your listeners will be able to identify with a move and even empathize with you. When **Weiss** and his team went on the air at Q100 in Atlanta, they took a novel approach to their first time on Atlanta's airwaves. They didn't try to sound like Atlantans right off the bat; it wouldn't have been real. Instead, he made a real connection with his audience by forming a committee of listeners. He gave them the station hotline and urged them to call in whenever they heard them make a mistake on the air, whether it was butchering the names of streets or towns or any mistake they made about the city of Atlanta. They put the callers right on the air to make the correction. Listeners want to help you settle in. It's sort of the big brother or sister approach. Let them help you. It's a great way to learn all about your new town, and to let listeners help you succeed. They love helping out and knowing they helped in your success.

Kicking off a new morning drive show is just like starting in a new school in a new town. What did you do to make yourself popular and accepted in class and hopefully, become popular? It's all about defining what they think is cool and then adapting. Everything you do on your show during the first few weeks and months should spell out who you are and what your personality is all about; warm and fuzzy, Ms. or Mr. Friendly, a lovable rascal, well-informed and so on. Find out who the community movers and shakers are and have them on your show. It's a way to have them endorse you and give credibility to your show. Fill the air with the voices of your listeners welcoming you to town.

Popular Chicago radio personality, **Matthew Erich "Mancow" Muller**, a Kansas City, Missouri, native, takes a different approach to being on a new show. He feels you should do nothing your first week. "Come into the market and get a feel for your new listeners," says the radio pro. "The way you present yourself the first week on the radio is the way your listeners will look at you forever. A slow build is better than trying to play 'can you top this' for the rest of your career. The really cool stunt you planned to kick-off your new show with and get attention often times will raise the ire of too many people. Take it from me," laments Mancow. "I blocked the bridge in San Francisco. It cost me two and a half million bucks and made me a felon."

Radio Pro lesson learned: Be careful about doing stunts or engaging in outrageous behavior early on in your show. Ask yourself, do your listeners care enough about you yet as the new kid in town to have a stake in the outcome? One thing I learned, your listeners need to know and love you first before you can begin taking potshots at people.

Consultant **Walter Sabo**, who comments extensively in Chapter Twelve on the role of consultants, advises radio folks in a new town "To get out of the radio station and spend as much time as possible with the people you're going to talk to. Listen to what they talk about with their friends, and talk about that. Don't worry about radio people, what radio people think, or what's going on in other markets. Radio people can't fill out rating diaries."

Commenting in *The Morning Mouth* , a media magazine for morning talent, veteran radio pro **Bill Whyte** at 95-WSM-FM-Nashville says one ole bit that worked well for him was the old line, "I don't have any pens...send me your company pen and if I mention it on the radio, you'll win a prize." Another way is to do it with coffee mugs and put a photo of all that are sent in on your website. You need to endear yourself to the listeners and the market before you can be funny and outrageous.

Author's helpful hint: When I started in a new radio market, I asked the PD and staff to respond to a questionnaire about the city; for example, worst traffic spots, correct pronunciation of towns and streets, well-known local celebrities and leaders in the community, and even high-school sports rivalries. You will find it most helpful on the air. Here's another tip; make friends with local police officers. They can clue you in on lots going on in town so you can sound like you're in the know and well-connected.

How to build a successful morning drive show from the ground up.

Here are a couple of additional ideas that will help popularize you and your new morning drive show. Host a weekly or monthly "breakfast broadcast" from a hot local restaurant or hotel. Invite your listeners in for a free breakfast. Folks will always show up for free food! It's fun to interact with a live audience. Besides, there's nothing better than having your listeners put a face with their new morning talent, unless of course you look like Quasimodo; then I suggest you stay locked in the studio.

If you find yourself in the position of replacing a popular personality and morning show (I found myself in that position more than a few times), pay homage to your predecessor. Don't try to hide the fact that she or he never existed. Don't be afraid of callers or you mentioning them unless they are now your competition. It will make you look like a BIG person for acknowledging their favorite radio personalities. Suck up your pride and eat your ego. Take baby steps and with a little bit of luck and a few prayers, maybe in a few months your new listeners will love you just as much as the last team.

Creating and producing a successful morning drive show.
Prepare for your radio show well in advance. It's the only way to succeed!

Prepare for every hour on the air. The late Boston air-talent **Jess Cain**, to whom this book is dedicated, once told me and other Emerson College students, "You need to spend at least one hour preparing off the air for every hour you spend on the air." I found it to be a good rule to follow. I would add one additional suggestion; show prep should be foremost on your mind all day, every day![29] The first break on your show should be strong. Set the table for your listeners. Let them know what's coming up that morning on their favorite radio show. If you start strong and finish strong, usually the middle will take care of itself.

More tips on how to produce a successful morning drive show.

Buffalo New York AM-Drive personality **Joe Chille** has worked for Gordon McLendon, American Radio Systems, and CBS, and has been with WJYE since August 1978. In addition to co-hosting *Buffalo's Morning Show* with Cheryl Hagen, Joe is Operations Manager for Buffalo's Regent Broadcast Group. *Radio Ink Magazine* also named him one of the best program directors in America. Joe Chille is well-qualified to offer his advice on how to be a "winner" in morning drive. "**Prepare, Prepare, Prepare,**" he says, "and I'm not just talking prep services. Read the local paper, be involved in the community. When you leave work, jot down, or keep an audio journal of things to do. You would be amazed how much is relatable to your audience that you experience in your everyday life. Be the same person on the air as you are off," Buffalo Joe points out, "because it makes it a lot easier to transition. If you have quirky listeners that call you all the time, consider making them a part of your show. It's important to be relatable, and also to be interesting, and to be a good storyteller. Another major ingredient to be a success in morning drive," says Chille, "is to be a 'sounding board' of sorts for things going on in your community. It helps weave you into the fabric. Volunteer. Don't just have your hand out when a talent fee is involved. It's all part of being a winning radio personality."

The biggest mistakes air-talent make in developing their morning show.

Alan Burns of Alan Burns Associates has been one of America's leading radio consultants for over twenty years. He says that "Too often the talent's focus is on themselves and on other morning shows, instead of thinking about the audience and working to understand entertainment. 'What do I find funny?' and 'What are other morning shows doing?' Both are important, but many if not most morning talent spend too much time copying other shows or doing things without really thinking about them. Instead," Burns suggests, "there needs to be a strategy and a plan for actually 'developing' the show.

The questions air-talent should ask themselves: How is this show going to be different? How are the characters different, what are their dimensions and how do they interact? What are the values of this show and how does that fit with the audience's values? Looking at the big picture for the show and over the long-run is important, says Burns. "How is the first six months of this show different from the second six months? What does year one look like versus year two? Where do we want to be after two years? What do we want to be known and remembered for with our morning drive show?" Alan Burns has provided programming and marketing research and advice to AC, CHR, AOR, Country, and News/Talk stations in over 100 markets, including Z-100 in New York. He believes that "Ideally, the air-talent would know what major lessons to take and employ from *American Idol, Seinfeld, Fear Factor, Survivor, The View,* Leno and Letterman, the circus, and Disneyland." **To learn more about Alan Burns Associates go to** www.burnsradio.com.

Creating and producing a successful morning drive show.
Avoid Narcissism.

Don't fall into the trap of making your show all about you! It should be about your life, but presented in such a way that your listeners feel included and can identity with your own personal slices of life. Remember, your listeners are the real stars of your show! Most importantly, talk about what you're passionate about. Share slices of your own everyday personal life with your extended family of listeners. Talk about your family, in-laws and out-laws, your friends, the overrated lousy movie you and your wife shelled out twelve bucks each to see. Talk about your kids, especially the bright one, who at the ripe old age of thirteen seems to know more than you do on every subject, yet is failing religion at the Christian Academy they attend; the noisy, out-of-control kids next door, your dog with the flatulence problem, the neighbor's dog who hates you and tries to take your leg off every time you step out of your car. Talk about the rude cashier at the local market, or the friendly one; the guy who cut you off in traffic, or the person who graciously let you merge onto the expressway.

On the air, share "real-life" experiences that happen to you. How about the marmot and his family of six who have made a permanent home under your front porch? You want to evict them, but your wife says in no uncertain terms, "They stay! They are now part of the family!" She even has names for all of them, including Einstein for the head of the household, because he is so smart. Bring it up on your show and toss it out to your family of listeners. I'm sure they will identify with your dilemma. They may not have prairie dogs living under their front porch, but you may be surprised at the sundry critters, both domestic and wild, that some folks may be sharing their living quarters with! Some invited, others definitely uninvited, but nonetheless living under their roof. Relate to every day life! Your listeners will bond with you!

During my lengthy time in morning drive, I seldom if ever had a listener tell me how much they enjoyed the cool segues on the station. Instead, they would often comment that we played the same songs over and over. How many times have you heard that line? Makes you wonder when management will wake up and start listening. But, that's another chapter in this book. What listeners did comment on were the funny bits, or the weird phone calls, but usually what they enjoyed was the "slice of my life" that I shared with them. Give your listener an emotional link to you and your show! Be consistent in your role, because that's why your listeners like you on the radio. Talk to your family of listeners whenever and wherever you can. The more you get to know them, the easier it will be for you to learn first-hand what they want to hear on the radio. A loyal listener base will help you win every time!

Being in morning drive is prestigious, but the position carries with it responsibility and stress.

Irish playwright and critic **George Bernard Shaw** is credited with saying "There are two sources of unhappiness in life. One is not getting what you want; the other is getting it." One of my wife Kimmie's favorite expressions has always been "Be careful what you wish for, you just may get it." Make sure being in the pressure cooker and stress-filled slot of morning drive radio is where you want to be! Keep asking yourself one important question: how badly do I want it? Do I desire it so much that I'm willing to give up almost anything and everything to achieve success as a top-rated morning radio personality? Being in morning drive radio requires so much focus and extra attention to detail that quite often, many other important things in your life will be left by the wayside.

Morning drive is the epitome of having made it on the radio. The shift itself offers so many perks and benefits, not the least of which is usually a fat paycheck, but it is also demanding in so many ways. Think carefully before accepting the position. It will mean a tremendous lifestyle change for you *and* your loved ones!

> *"Don't make decisions because they are the easiest, the cheapest or the most popular. Make your decisions because it's right!" - Former Notre Dame University President Fr. Ted Hesburgh.*

A morning show needs to have a lead person, a designated quarterback. Only one person at a time can lead the team, and that's the quarterback.

Someone has to be in charge. You need to have a lead person, who I like to think of as either a quarterback or a bus driver. I cannot emphasize this enough; you can NOT run a top-rated radio show by committee. At least, not while you're on the air producing a product. Only one person can steer and drive the bus! Only one person can call the plays that lead the team to victory! As the lead person in morning drive, you are ultimately responsible for the ratings. It's a stressful business and you're fighting for *your* survival and those of *your* morning team. You need every team member supporting you and that means *everyone* pulling in the same direction and that's towards you! Your team members are passengers on your bus and go where you drive it. As the driver, you have the right to throw a disgruntled passenger off your bus! Be a strong leader, but lead by setting a good example, so others may follow. Keep in mind that even the most passionate quarterback can't win the game all by himself.

It's imperative that every member of your morning show team knows their role and why you as the QB need and expect their support. They need to understand your needs, goals, and priorities and how they fit in with their areas of responsibility. It is also your job as the QB to magnify the strengths of your team members and to minimize their weaknesses. You need to put people in a position to do their thing and help them accomplish that! **Remember**, they can't be held responsible or accountable for what they don't know and what you neglect to tell them.

The role of the morning show quarterback.

As the quarterback of your morning drive team, you always need to be upbeat and show up at the studio in a positive frame of mind, even when you have a migraine and don't feel like it! Your job as the show's QB is tough! You are not only faced with the difficult challenge of making sure your own act is together but also those who work with you. Your attitude, good or bad, positive or negative, sets the tone and is sure to be picked up on by those around you, so make sure you show up each morning with a good one! When you show up happy, they're happy. When you're uptight, they're uptight. As the key person on the show you must show leadership qualities! Your team members must look at you with confidence and respect. If you're in control and don't overreact when things go awry, they'll always believe you are capable of making the right call in difficult situations and will hardly ever question your decisions. They'll stick with you through thick and thin. Loyalty plays a big factor in your quest for success in morning drive. Very little is said about the importance of loyalty between co-workers in radio, but believe me, it can make all the difference in whether you and your show are a hit or a flop. When it's show time on the radio, all parties on the morning drive team have to put disagreements and ill feelings aside and make it work for the success of the show!

Legendary Alabama football coach Paul "Bear" Bryant said this about team work, which so aptly applies to morning radio teams: "In order to be #1, your team must have a feeling of unity. Every member of your team must put the team first, ahead of personal glory and ego!"

The bottom line as the morning show leader.

As the morning show quarterback, you are not only responsible for your own success, but that of your team members. You cannot avoid responsibility. It goes hand in hand with the position. You are responsible for the on-air product and success of your show. You have two choices: ignore the responsibility and lose, or accept it and enjoy the benefits you will receive. Responsibility gives you the power to control the make-up of your show and to make changes if necessary. It should not be viewed as a burden that is haphazardly thrown your way. It is a *powerful tool* to help you move your show in the direction you choose, which is hopefully to the winning side. Your success in morning drive isn't a matter of chance. It's a matter of choice, *the choices you make.*

Creating and producing a successful morning drive show.

There are five basic rules to be a successful morning drive radio personality. You can't sit back and wait for success to happen. It's something you can make happen with consistently hard work.

The first golden rule is to be energetic.

The second rule is to focus your energy in the right direction and what is important to your listeners and the station's demographics.

The third rule is to stay focused, no matter what!

The fourth rule is to gather all your resources to be the very best radio pro ever!

And **the fifth rule** is be passionate and always appreciate that being on the radio is a privilege.

In radio, there are no guarantees about winning, especially in the most competitive time period on any station, *morning drive.* Success on the radio is not found by getting lucky on a one-shot deal. That usually only happens on television's *American Idol.* Almost anyone can do one good radio show, but to do a quality show, consistently, day in and day out, is the mark of a real on-air radio pro. Real success in morning drive is achieved by weaving all the little positives into your daily performance. It just makes sense; if you do your best on a daily basis, you stand a better chance of being successful on the radio. Here are a few solid tips on how to enhance your chances of being a winner on the radio, whether your shift is in or out of morning drive time.

Follow the Six C's to success...

- Concentration - stay focused on topical and relevant issues of the day.
- Consistency - always approach your show in a prepared manner – do your show prep.
- Confidence - believe in your ability to get the job done, but keep your ego in check.
- Control - maintain control at all times over what goes out over the air on your show.

- Composure - stay cool in unexpected, difficult, and stressful situations.
- Communication – communicate to your listeners what you and your show are all about.

Popular Boston air personality **Matt Siegel** has consistently and successfully been driving the KISS-108 bus since 1981, back when he and I were friendly competitors. Today, thirty years later, *Matty in the Morning* is still the leading FM morning show in Boston. As his show's quarterback, how does Matty maintain peace and harmony amongst the talented co-workers on his morning show? He is well-aware that someone has to lead the team, and as a vet of the early AM-Drive slot he knows only too well that when times get hectic and chaotic, things can get out of hand. Even well-meaning folks can have short fuses and get a little grumpy. With so many egos and sensitive folks hanging out in a confined space, all trying to be creative, what's Matty's secret for getting everyone to pull together, let alone get along?

"This is a great question," says Matty. "If you host a show with a good-sized staff you must remember you all win together and you all lose together. The idea is to focus on the ratings, regardless of the format. This may sound obvious, but it really isn't. Lots of people go into the business for the little perks we get, such as a little fame, the rush of being on the air, the fun of doing the show and so forth, but lose sight of the point of the whole endeavor, which is to win! This is not your hobby," emphasizes Matty, "this is how you feed your family. So once this is made clear to everyone, the show becomes greater than its parts. If a member of the team cannot grasp this, they need to be replaced," he insists, but quickly adds, "If you, the host, make your staff feel unappreciated or uncomfortable, then the problem is you. Trust me, when you win, everybody is happy. Is this easy?" asks the 2001 Marconi Award-winning personality of the year. "Of course not. But then, how many shows win?" A hint on how to be a winner with your team in morning drive, from Kiss-108's Matty in the Morning, "Stop yelling," smiles Siegel, "and, oh yeah, one more thing, the host always buys breakfast."

As a member of the morning show team, your role is to support the quarterback.

Dave Ryan, the longtime morning drive guy at KDWB-101.3-Minneapolis, jumps in with his thoughts on how to explain nicely that a morning show newbie is there to lend support to the show's quarterback. "Years ago, a friend of mine said, 'Yeah, you wouldn't believe our new morning guy. He told the rest of us on the show to think of him as the sun and we're the planets, rotating around him. We were there to make him look good. Can you believe the ego on this guy?' Well, 'this guy' turned out to be Glenn

Beck; the same Glenn Beck had a hugely successful syndicated radio show and nightly television show on Fox. Glenn might have seemed egotistical in telling his show how to be successful," adds Ryan, "but you cannot argue with success. Glenn knew that for his particular show to be successful, he needed a central character, himself!"

As far as team members supporting the driver of the morning show bus, **Dave Ryan** says to look at it like this: "One of the most successful comedies of all time was *I Love Lucy*. The cast understood that Lucy was the show. Fred, Ethel and Ricky were all supporting cast. Now, can you imagine," asks Dave with a smile, "if Ethel decided SHE should be the star of the show? Can you see the look on the producers' faces is she stormed into their offices and announced, 'I'm the STAR of this show. I want equal billing and as many lines as Lucy!' Well, it would never happen, because good old Ethel understood her role. She was grateful that she got to work with Lucille Ball instead of singing at a crappy dinner theater in Lexington, Kentucky. The show needed and required a star! Lucille Ball wasn't an egomaniac for being the star. Lucy was the star and obviously it worked and everyone was grateful to be part of such a successful show."

Minneapolis radio pro Ryan gives another example of how team members on a successful morning show need to know who the key person is. "Take Howard Stern. Robin Quivers knows it's the *Howard Stern Show*. She's knows she's there to make him look good, and granted, he makes her look good, too. Robin recognizes that without Howard, she'd be making $50K in Salt Lake City. Maybe. She knows her role is a supporting one. The trick for everyone getting along in the pressure cooker, ego-driven atmosphere of morning drive radio is getting the point across to the supporting cast. Someone needs to tell them in no uncertain terms they are not the star; they are not going to be the star and at the same time, impress upon them how important their role is. The best person to do this is the PD. He/she has to lay down the law at the beginning of the show and let everyone know who's in charge."

How to get along in morning drive.

Bill Gardner has been in radio for over forty-four years. Much of his airtime has been spent in morning drive, including nine years waking Phoenix up at KOOL-FM. Today (2011), he wakes up the Los Angeles area on several stations. How to win in morning drive with the phones? "Every incoming phone call," says Bill, "is answered, recorded and filtered in my head with the thought is there any of this that would sound great to others who could hear it on the radio?"

As far as getting along with your morning drive crew, Bill Gardner offers first-hand experience. "Getting along probably comes from my basic philosophy of take the cards you're dealt and play them. You can't ask for a new hand, but you can still beat the others in the game. I tell myself I'll beat my competitors no matter what they deal me and that includes sales, management team, or even my morning-team members. I like to find my coworkers' 'on buttons' and strengths and play to them. As the quarterback, forward momentum, brevity and energy are **my** responsibilities. They are also the responsibilities of every lead person in the chair in AM-Drive. I try never to forget that, regardless of who's talking."

How does Seattle morning drive radio pro Bob Rivers keep peace and harmony amongst his group of talented coworkers?

"Boy, this is a tough question. Like a good book or a movie, a good radio show is an evolving story with a cast of characters," says Rivers. "Ours is unscripted improvisation, based on the true stories of our lives. There needs to be some friction and tension in order to make the story interesting. At the same time, we do want to enjoy working together over the long term." Rivers emphasizes that it's important to reward your friends and co-workers, but not to be phony about it. "The most important positive trick is to remember to give out praise wherever and whenever you spot great things," but cautions, "be specific, friends can smell BS. We have an e-mailed 'atta boy' that our producer puts out everyday. He mails it to us in the afternoon and puts it on the website. He calls it the 'Quote of the Day.' Every one of us looks forward to opening it and remembering a fun moment from our show that morning." Below is a sample of some great line from a member of his morning team, "Downtown Joe, " in a conversation about the Kirkland brand that included Joe's defense of his $14-dollar jeans, a call from Bob's niece Sara in Connecticut, and the Quote of the Day:

> **Joe**: The thing about Costco is, it's quality everything. They've got the best big shrimp. They got good cheap inexpensive clothes of good quality.
> **Sara**: Yeah, but you shouldn't buy your pants in the same place you buy your shrimp.
> **Bob**: Get your wife some Amish furniture. I think she'd really be into it. You don't have to go to
> Pennsylvania.
> **Joe**: Well, you don't go on the Internet, do ya? I wouldn't trust any Amish on the Internet.

The role of being the driver of the bus and "coach" of a morning-show can be difficult.

"Joe knows I love him," says Bob Rivers. "We have a lot of fun, but we've had a rough moment, too. A couple of years ago, after a hard night of NFL football partying, he was too drunk to make it to work. The Seahawks won the championship playoff game that sent them to the 2006 'Big Game.' I decided on-air to let everyone know that I was concerned with his drinking, and that I was worried and not going to put up with it anymore. As I did this," recalls Rivers," I knew I was setting myself up as the bad guy, and pissing a lot of people off. None of this was contrived and I felt afterwards that I had gone over the line. When you make a mistake, I think you should apologize. And I did. The very next day, on-air. Joe hasn't had a drink since and has lost over 60 pounds. Last year, the whole show, led by 'Downtown Joe,' walked the Portland Marathon (26.2 miles) and raised enough money to build a brand new school in Ethiopia."

Rivers believes it's hard to know the right way to handle people and situations because everyone is different, but believes, "As the show's coach, I am responsible for the health and well-being of the team. It's both personal and business, whether I like it or not. I try not to be too harsh on people, and at the same time I must set standards, be firm, and earn their trust in me. It's a delicate balancing act for me and I do make mistakes."

Doing a morning show with an equal partner can be a delicate balancing act of egos.

Mark Wallengren, the longtime morning personality on KOST Los Angeles, says, "Doing a morning show with a partner can be a delicate balance." For more than twenty years he co-hosted the morning show with his former partner, **Kim Amidon**. Mark reflected for our book on those years and what it's like to work side by side with an equal partner in morning drive. Mark admits he was "professionally married" to his former morning show co-host, Kim, for all that time. "It definitely had its ups and downs," he laughs. "It's not easy. I think the strength that we had is that we got to know each other's strengths and weaknesses. I knew what she couldn't do and what I needed to help out with and vice versa. There becomes a time those weaknesses become so weak that you want to throw a life preserver. It's a delicate balance. One could argue that getting into this business of radio for any of us, to a certain degree, is an ego-driven thing. A lot of people think ego is bad. Ego is bad if it's misdirected and it interferes with you doing a good job."

Wallengren continues, "I think any radio pro could find an example where somewhere along the line their own ego got in the way of them trying to do something." He refers to these ego moments as "speed bumps." "As far as morning teams are concerned, to help control one's ego," he points out, "it does help when you are equally billed and equally paid! But in all honesty," Mark quickly adds, "there still becomes an issue over time on mic, and it goes both ways, where one of you feels like the other is getting too much time or you're not getting enough air-time, or where you're putting more into the show than the other person. You always struggle through those kinds of things. I had to recognize that I was better with her than without her and that's the delicate ego balancing act. At the end of the day, I'm worth more to the company with her than without her because of the amount of time we've spent together on the radio."

"Maybe it's part of my own insecurity," says Wallengren, "as my on-air partner Kim was an incredible, unique individual. There were times when she would be furious with me. It would bubble and then boil over - that's how we worked together for twenty-plus years and I think that's human nature. She just doesn't really edit herself all that much, which could be disastrous. She'd be so gall-dang direct it knocks your breath out. You put up, put up and then it takes a little thing to blow it all out of proportion. Sometimes you need a shock to come down to the real world, and I know that while I may consider something in my partner as a weakness it's really not, because her other strengths so overpower her weaknesses."

Today, KOST's Mark Wallengren is getting adjusted to his new on-air partner and enjoying it. He offers these words of advice for morning radio partnerships: "The bottom line is, when you start hitting home runs with the paychecks, no matter what your frustrations may be with each other, those golden handcuffs still fit pretty nicely and you put up with each other's faults."

> *"Even if you think you're the best thing that ever happened to radio, keep it to yourself"* - Detroit radio pro, Dick Purtan.

Radio Pro lesson learned, a few words about ego.

Ego is the drug for fools. An out-of-control ego cuts you off from everyone. As the star of your morning show it's really easy to let your ego fly out of control sometimes, without even realizing it. An out-of-control ego is not a pretty picture and can derail your climb to success faster than a falling star. There will come a time in your radio career when your ego will do its best to convince you that nothing is bigger and better than you. It's so important to be well-grounded and have a good handle on your own self-worth, but there's a huge difference between self-worth and self-importance. Being concerned and focused on your own individual performance and achievement can be a good thing. Feeling good about what you do as an air-talent is important for your own well-being and self-esteem, but allowing it to cloud your good sense and conduct with others is not.

Radio pro **Casey Kasem's** signature statement said it all; "Keep your feet on the ground, but keep reaching for the stars!" Don't project an attitude that you're better than anyone else and bigger than your show and the radio station. This is a fool's goal and if you follow that path, your future as a radio personality will be doomed to personal failure. Don't let ego rear its ugly head. If it does, cut it off and replace it with kindness. Actions always speak louder than words. Alter your ego and your attitude.[30] Your success or failure as a radio pro depends entirely on your own attitude and your control over your ego. If you keep the following in mind, it should help to keep your ego in check: "No one deserves the right to be on the air—it's a privilege."

Radio pro **Alpha Trivette says,** "I've never understood the big ego thing. I know, we all have to have some ego in this business, but that pertains only to your professional behavior." He has these insightful words of caution about ego for both newbies and seasoned radio pros: "You have to be egotistical enough to want the best performance from yourself and those around you, but once that studio light is off, remember, you're just a guy who turns on a mic and talks for a few hours each morning. You work hard to get people to trust you enough to give you a few minutes each morning."

Continuing with his personal feelings about ego and self-importance, Trivette says, "Your listeners may consider you a friend and rely on you to provide info and entertainment, but you must keep in focus that there are people who really are important, who shape, change, or save lives, and there are those who fight for our country, those people are the really important ones. We're just friends helping friends get up and get to work with a smile."

You need to figure out what your role is and where you fit in.

Trivette, the one-time WSB-FM Atlanta drive guy, whose radio career has taken him from Charlotte to St. Louis and other major cities, has this advice for radio newbies who may be trying to blend into an established morning show: "Chances are there are some defined roles already. You should figure out precisely what you're going to be doing. That does not mean your role or persona can't grow as you become part of the team, but that will require paying attention, playing the part, and playing along 'til you earn your shot at expanding your role."

The DJ and former stand-up comic says, "It's always important to remember as a comic that you are part of the show that generally consists of an opener, a middle act and a headliner. Most times, you will start out supporting the show headliner. As you work to hone your act and get funnier, you add, edit, and fine-tune your act. As you add more time, you become a middle act and with more fine-tuning, you become a headliner. It is important to remember," he emphasizes, "as an opening or middle act, do NOT exceed your time! If you are the middle act and you are hired to do 20-30-minutes and you decide to do 45, you are not proving that you are ready to headline! Instead, you are proving that you are not ready to be a good middle act! Figure out your role on the show. Fulfill your role, expand it where you can, and look for ways to make the entire show better. With time and effort, you will be ready to headline your own morning show."

Shelly Dunn's first "real" job in radio was in 1982 at KATT in Oklahoma City. She moved to San Diego in 1990 as a member of the KGB-FM morning team. How does talent keep their ego in check? Shelly answers, with her tongue firmly planted in cheek, "Well, isn't that what morning men are for? The point of being a sidekick is to support the main man, even if he's a she. You act interested and laugh when he or she tells a joke. Know that your feelings may be hurt once in a while," says Shelly, "but try not to take it personally. Do not bring up a topic or opinion you are not ready to support or argue about until you either back down or lose…and make no mistake, you will lose sometimes. Just learn to take it. It is okay to disagree, but learn to lose your battles." Shelly Dunn uses former *The View* TV talk show host Rosie O'Donnell as an example: "Rosie did stand up for what she believed in, but it was a battle that cost her job. Be prepared to lose the job. If you are smart, you will learn to walk the line between opinion and humor. Keep your sense of humor. Keep in mind; you have a job in a fun field that most people envy."

The important role of second bananas and sidekicks.

Call them second bananas, sidekicks, or as they are sometimes lovingly called, *side-chicks,* most supporting roles in morning drive are filled by women. It is one of the toughest assignments an air-talent can face. It can be a thankless and difficult position on a morning drive radio show to be placed in a supporting role to the quarterback of the show. More often than not, the co-host or sidekick will have to be big enough to park their own ego in support of the leader of the pack. This is not easy, especially for gung-ho talent looking to establish themselves as a bona-fide air personality. It takes a very giving person to suck it up and not want to be bigger than the lead person. Many sidekicks simply don't measure up because their fragile egos will not allow them to do so. In my own situation as the QB on several different morning drive shows, I never cared who got the best line off or ad-lib, as long as the listener was being entertained or informed in some way.

"As a member of the morning show team, your role is to support the quarterback."

Sharing the spotlight is the name of the game in AM-Drive. The bottom line is to win in the battle for ratings and when the show wins, everyone is a winner! Supporting team members need to know that only one person can lead the team, and that's the quarterback, not the sidekick. However, it is extremely important for the morning show lead person to make team members believe they have a helpful and constructive role in supporting their leader. It's a known fact that the lead person on the show will get most of the credit when things go right and the ratings are smokin,' but the same person will also take most of the heat and blame when things go belly up, too!

Team chemistry is so important to the overall success of the morning show. Leave petty arguments, sniping comments, and jealousy outside the studio door! The old saying, 'One rotten apple can spoil the whole bunch' definitely applies to a morning radio team. The quarterback needs to keep peace and harmony amongst the troops, which is not an easy thing to do. Getting along is essential to winning. It's a lot easier to have fun on the radio if you like one another and enjoy being around each other. I'm not saying you need to set up house and live together 24/7, but it does help if you get along.

Author's note: I was involved in some touchy situations where it was less than comfortable trying to interact with a person for three or four hours a day on the radio. Getting along is difficult. If you have a spat with your spouse, you can take a much-needed time-out, perhaps going a few minutes or longer without speaking to each other. This is impossible to do with an on-air partner when a show is in progress. When the bottom falls out of the relationship between the show host and a team member, usually for stupid petty reasons, you can't afford the luxury of taking a "sanity break" or *a time-out*, even though you'd love to! The show must go on! Trust me on this one, even the most dedicated radio pros have trouble working their way through difficult moments, when for whatever reason tempers are short.

Thank God for commercials and news breaks to calm troubled waters. It gives one or both parties a chance to leave the studio for a few moments to calm down. Of course, ideally, explosive tempers should never be allowed to reach the out-of-control state. It is imperative that the lead person tries to maintain a cool perspective at all times. If a member of your team is constantly losing it and being an irritant to others, take the guilty person aside *after the show*, and in a one-on-one have a serious conversation about bad behavior and that you expect a better attitude. Don't mince words. Lay it on the line, shape up or ship out. Don't let the one bad apple ruin the bunch and don't kid yourself into thinking that after things calm down, they will get better. It seldom happens. Continued bad behavior by a member of your team will not improve by itself. In fact, usually, things will only get worse. As the QB, you need to lay down the law. You can't always be a nice person. Sometimes, someone else's out-of-control ego will bring out the worst even in the nicest people.

How to create and produce a successful morning drive show.
Benchmarks and fixed bits ^{on} your morning drive show are important.[31]

Benchmarks are important. It gives the listener a reason to make a date with you and tune in to hear something special on your show at a fixed time. I won't list all of them, but here are a few regular features that worked well for us on *The Joe and Andy Family*, along with a brief explanation, so you can use them if you like. However, I'm sure you have your own ideas and know what works best for you and your target audience.

Mondays were "Preggo Predictions" - Pregnant moms would call in and Andy in his bad boy role would listen to the baby's heartbeat and make a prediction on whether it would be a boy or a girl. He would also give the expectant momma a little advanced "inside info" on how the child would act as he or she grew up. To say the least, most of Andy's predictions were out to lunch and for some unusual reason, his comments on what the baby would grow up to be like were always somewhat devilish. Lots of fun!

Tuesdays, "Mr. Manners" was front-row center, played by Andy with tips on etiquette - yeah, sure!! Since Andy was the bad boy of our team, he was a natural to be the imp and I tried my best as the straight man to keep the loose cannon "somewhat" under control.

Wednesdays, it was **"Name that Disease."** Boston has a huge medical community and we thought this contest would be a winner - it was! My friend and neighbor at the time, and everyone's friendly pediatrician from Everett, Dr. Peter Masucci, would pick a disease of the week and give its symptoms. The person who correctly named the disease got a highly coveted Joe and Andy coffee mug and a dozen roses sent in their name to Children's Hospital in Boston.

Thursdays it was **"The Kollege of Musical Knowledge,"** where, inspired by 1930s and '40s radio legend Kay Kyser, I played the professor and asked musical trivia questions based on artist or hit songs. It also gave us an opportunity to plug my all-request oldies show, *Saturday Night "Live" at the Oldies*. Andy would do the intro and it usually went something like this, "Yes, friends and neighbors, children of all ages, it's time once again for the Kollege of Musical Knowledge with Professor Joe Martelle and I am his unworthy, inattentive, worthless, good-for-nothing student, Andrew Q. Moes! Professor…" (cue to Joe!).

Fridays, we wrapped up the week with **"Dating Do's and Don'ts,"** which were tips on dating, as we eased our listeners into the weekend.

"Fun with Foreigners" was another semi-regular feature. Foreigners were invited to call in and answer three multiple choice questions about America to see if they qualified for citizenship, along with a highly prized Joe and Andy coffee mug. It was a lot of fun talking to newcomers to our country about their impressions of their new home. Some of their answers to our questions made the bit work and were outrageously funny.

"Amnesty" was another semi-regular bit. We would take a call from a listener who was in badly need of a day off. They would make an impassioned plea for us to call their boss, which we would do, conferencing the two together on the air. Quite often, we would make the boss person feel like a lowlife if they didn't oblige their employee's request and give them the day off. We ran this on Fridays or Mondays for obvious reasons. We were trying to get someone out of work for the day, either to start their weekend early or to give them an extra day off and recuperate from a wild n' crazy weekend.

Listeners are not loyal to just one radio station. Radio has successfully developed a mentality of "sameness." Competition for the listener's ear is tremendous. Therefore, you must offer them a compelling reason to listen to you. If they hear something they like, a song or bit, they'll stay with you, increase their time spent listening to you and your show, and boost your ratings!

Where to place your best bit on your show.

If you play music on your morning show, hook your best bit to your strongest or most popular song. The music will command your listeners' attention. Right after your call letters or station slogan, your name, a time check, temp & condition, do your best bit! Do it before going into any elements like traffic or a commercial stop set. Research shows the biggest hour in AM-Drive with the most listeners available is **7-8a.m.** That's when you need to use your best material. However, it goes without saying that every minute you're on mic should be a great break with your best effort. Don't be afraid to recycle a well-received bit later in your show. For example, a bit aired at 7:20am could easily be replayed at 8:50 for new listeners.

How to create and produce a successful morning drive show.

Live phones can be an important part of your morning show. Listener calls about topics, answers to trivia questions, contests and so on, are great, but pre-recorded bits lessen the chance for error. Live calls also open yourself to all sorts of problems, including a bad line, a flat performance or, worse, salty language. You never know when a caller will make slip of the tongue. For instance, November 10 is the official birthday of the United States Marine Corps. As a former gyrene, it's a big deal in my book. One year, I thought it would be safe to put a Marine Captain on our show live. Wrong! Never in a zillion years did I expect him to drop the "F-bomb," which was practically the first thing out of his mouth. Looking back on it, what was I thinking? Most Marines' favorite descriptive adjective is the f-word. Play it safe. Record all your phone calls. With today's equipment, like the short-cut, you can speed edit and air just part of a call you want and dump the rest.

Don't let bits run away with your morning drive show.

Bits are great, but don't let the fun of them run away with your show. Constantly ask yourself if you're including the basics; the all-important necessary elements, time, temp and brief weather! What will they need to wear today? What's traffic like? Run your elements at the same time. Listeners familiarize themselves with certain elements like traffic updates and come to expect them at specific times. Don't disappoint them. One caller told me she knew she was running late for her train, when she heard the traffic sounder at: 20 past the hour. As the show host, you have a tall order to fill every day.

You need to spoon-feed basic info, but in an entertaining way. Remember, there's a fine line between preparation and spontaneity. Give yourself enough elbow room to ad-lib and allow for the unexpected that will often occur in morning drive. After all, the beauty of radio is that it's live, or should be!

Humor is an important element.
Radio pro **Don Imus** is quoted as saying, "Humor is most often discovered in true tragedy. Funny is what's serious. Many of us take a certain amount of perverse enjoyment in the misfortunes of others, especially celebrities." The bigger the name, the bigger the target. Double entendre is funny. It allows the listener to decide which way to take it. Humor is relevant to where you are! You need to know the city and your audience. Your listeners want and need to laugh. Create character voices. They allow you as the good guy to take opposite points of view. Former Boston radio pro **Charles Laquidara's** alter-ego was Duane Glasscock. He got away with saying things Charles never would! Self-deprecating humor and poking fun at yourself will always be a big win for you with your listeners. True-life situations are all around us. Find a way to bring them to your show in a humorous way and your listeners will love you.

Humor doesn't mean jamming into your show as many bits as you can. Balance is the key! In morning drive, your listeners want a little distraction to help get them moving and make it through a tough commute. Helping them begin their day with a chuckle should be part of your job. Famous comedian Red Skelton, who began on radio in 1937, lived by the credo, "Have a little laugh and look around you for happiness instead of sadness. Even in your darkest moment, you usually can find something to laugh about. Laughter always brought me out of unhappy situations."

Always respect for the laugh buffer zone!
Enjoy your own bits, especially the funny ones. Don't be afraid to laugh at your own joke while setting your audience up for the punch line. If you sound like you're having a good time, your listeners will too! Have respect for the laugh buffer zone! Let me explain: If you told a joke to someone face-to-face, after the punch line you wouldn't simply turn and walk away. Of course not! You'd give the other person a chance to laugh. Well, it's the same way when delivering a punch line on the air. Wait a second or two before playing the next element. Give the listener time to digest what you said and fully appreciate the punch line before you throw something else at them. Use a transition jingle or even your own laughter. A traffic sounder is always a good bridge - it gives your reporter a chance to laugh or respond to the line.

How to build a successful morning drive show from the ground up.
Pre-promote everything on your morning-show! Coming up, coming

up! If you know in the 7-8 hour you have a killer call or prepared bit, don't be afraid to pre-promote it! You've put time and energy into the bit off the air, writing and producing it for your show, so don't throw it away. Capitalize on it, set your audience up for the pay-off with a big build-up!

Your AM-Drive audience is constantly moving, so keep your show moving, too.

Whatever the format, keep your show moving, because that's exactly what your AM-Drive audience is doing, moving! They're going helter-skelter all over the place as they try to wake up! I don't really subscribe to the theory of one thought per break, but when you consider the miniscule attention span of your average listener, there is some credence to it. Although, it is so difficult to give your listener everything they want in one break: time, brief weather, information and entertainment news, a funny line or two and, oh yeah, don't forget to promote the station, all in 10 seconds! Impossible, you say? Of course! But, as insane as it may sound, that's what many programming minds expect from their morning show talent. It often leads to big battles between talent and management. The secret in keeping your sanity is to follow their direction and use creative license when and where you deem it necessary to succeed in running a good show.

When you feel compelled to share a story and a slice of your life with your listeners, try not to make it a long break. Radio experts say listener fatigue sets in around the two-minute mark. They'll get bored and restless, and, God forbid, turn you off unless you're in the middle of one doozy of a story! The more personal your tale, the more *life experiences* you share with your audience, the more your listeners will bond with you and look forward to your next saga.

Self editing is important! Know where to cut to the chase and get to the meat of your story. Make sure it has a strong beginning to grab their attention, include a little anecdote and a funny *you wouldn't believe it* ending! Most importantly, get to the point quickly, and before you lose their attention. It sounds like a tall order and it is, but it can be done. Just keep working at it.

Attention-air-talent: As much as it may come as a total shock to your enormous ego, your P-1 listeners are not hanging on to your every word with bated breath. Unless your listener is madly in love with your voice, if you drone on and on they'll be gone…to your competition!

During the morning rush hour commute, your listeners have many things on their mind and can't always stay tuned to your dulcet tones. There are many distractions. I can almost guarantee that even with top-shelf material, many listeners will totally miss most of your story because of all the little interruptions they face each morning. By the time they share your slice of life story later at their work-place, trust me, "it" will have a new spin on it. The good part is, your story will transcend one of their own which they can identify with, and they'll be talking about you and your show with everyone within earshot of the water cooler. Congratulations! Take a bow, you've completed a really tough morning-show task - reaching out and communicating directly to the ears and hearts of your listeners.

Charles Laquidara, one of my former friendly Boston competitors on the old WBCN, described the best thing about being in morning drive this way: "When you wake up, you have people in the palm of your hand. You can make somebody's day by just really being high energy and having a good time and a great sense of humor."

Listen up, radio programming people!

Many creative, top-shelf talent in morning drive are told by management to shut up and play the hits. I believe the salvation of commercial radio is bringing spontaneity and personality back to the airwaves. Let 'em open the mic and have some fun.

> *"As host of a morning drive radio show, you should generate more light than heat!"*

How to build a successful morning drive show from the ground up.

Chuck Igo is in morning drive at Oldies 100.9- WYNZ in Portland, Maine. His radio background covers many years on the air in all size markets and formats, giving him extensive knowledge on how to handle morning drive. "In building a successful morning show, keep in mind the format of the station and the target audience. From that point forward, think and act as a median-aged member of that audience. Immersion into lifestyle interests is key. Being relatable in a casual, off-the-cuff manner keeps it all together," says Igo. He suggests some elements to augment the goals of a station where the key product is the music: "Most listeners depend on hearing the basics in the morning; time, temp, brief weather, and news. Keep the elements' overall tone in line with the music format. Weather should be short n' sweet. On an E-Z-listening format, the delivery would be a bit more subdued than a CHR, Contemporary Hit Radio. On a rock station, the news might be more lifestyle or off-beat variety while toning down the more serious news stories of the day. Inclusion of sports varies depending on geography. If the area's Major League team is part of the community, then more than passing lip-service should be paid."

Continuing with his philosophy on how to win in morning drive, Igo says, "Daily contests should be kept simple. The harder the contest with an adult audience, the greater the likelihood of an adult not taking the time or chance to call in and win. Adults do not wish to be thought of as foolish. I use this benchmark today for daily contests," says Igo. "I'm often chided by a select few who take me to task for using multiple choice answers at times or painfully obvious clues as part of the challenge. To those listeners, I remind them that on the days when the question is a bit more challenging, we get few if any calls. There is a time and place to turn up the heat, so to speak, on the level of difficulty regarding a question. If you're giving away a box of donuts or tickets to a comedy club, keep it simple. If you're giving away thousands of dollars then you need to apply serious thought to a more difficult question."

Interviews: Igo admits to personally not being a big fan of regular interviews on a music format morning show. "The occasional opportunity to speak with someone regarding something timely or topical lends itself well to your show. On the other hand, once the interview becomes part of the formula, the bulk of such interviews sound strained and forced. That said, the ability to stretch a bad interview into a thing of beauty is the benchmark of a great morning talk-show host. That same ability allows for the chance to turn a listener phone call into a tremendous thought-starter which can take any planned show and place the scheduled agenda on the back burner to be used at another time."

Listener interaction: "A morning drive show strives every single day to get any interplay with the audience. It sounds like it's just one more thing to do before we play another song, but when dealing with an audience whose P-1 [preferred regular listener] is a forty-something parent trying to get ready for work and get the kids off to school, they simply do not have the time to stop, pick up the phone, call and wait for the chance to chime-in that they prefer boxers over briefs. But, on occasion, when the right button is struck, it can be pure on-air gold." [32]

Play to your station's strengths "If you're on a music station, then remember the listeners are there for the music. The on-air person is just the icing on the cake! Okay, as talent, we'd like to believe that in our history's great moments, first came sliced bread, followed by me on the air." Igo recommends "creating elements that directly relate to what your station does on the air. How about a daily trivia question based on the music format of the station? Spotlight an artist coming to town for a concert, if the artist is part of your station's playlist."

Chuck Igo concludes his comments about how to win in morning drive: "As talent, there will be times when you will need to stand up for what you believe is right for your show. At times, stand up to those who have ideas on how to make your show better, when such suggestions merely dictate 'my-way or the highway.' Keep in mind," says Chuck, "there's a time and place for a morning-show host to stand his or her ground in regards to artist integrity. Pick those battles carefully. For example, if sales wants six units per morning break instead of the three and you've fought for flow and continuity, then find the compromise.[33] Point out that 18 minutes of commercials are already crammed in, and going to 24 units would be tantamount to running an infomercial! Sometimes it will work and you will be heard, and when it doesn't, play lots of short Beach Boys songs at 1:53 or less."

Speaking of Commercials!

If you've got a case of the *"Too Many Commercials Blues,"* read on! Let's face it, commercials equal money for the station and that translates itself to mean an easy ride for you as the on-air-talent! It's a doubled-edged sword. If the station is selling you and your show it means things are going well, for both you and the station. No one smiles more broadly around the station than the GSM when the station is sold out and filled with all those wonderful commercials![34] Let's be real: The life blood of commercial radio is commercial advertising that brings revenue to the station. The downside is that too many commercials will turn your listener base off faster than a cold shower! Commercial overload is nothing new and until some brave and creative radio suits decide something has to be done about it, I'm afraid it's not going to change.

One way to cut back on commercial clutter on radio would be to sell portions of a show to a single sponsor. This throwback to the way network radio was sold during Radio's Golden Age appears to be working today for nationally syndicated talk-show host Glenn Beck. Basically, at the top or beginning of a designated hour on his show, you will hear a disclaimer proudly stating, that, "This portion of the Glenn Beck program is brought to you by (sponsors name) and commercial free." It immediately sends a signal to the listeners that for the next segment, however long it may be, they will not be bombarded with a zillion commercials. It's a great way to give listeners more of a program and fewer commercials, while at the same time spotlighting an individual advertiser. Until more creative ways and moves are made to reduce the spot load, like the one Glenn Beck instituted on his program, the same maximum number of commercials, usually 18 to 20 minutes, will air each and every hour.

In the early '80s at WROR-Boston, our station GM **Joe Kelly** had a philosophy about buying commercial time on our morning drive show: "If you want on their show you'll pay a premium." You'd be surprised how many advertisers did just that! The station made money, and the advertiser's sales message was not jammed in with a ton of others. The station kept the total number of commercials in each hour of our show to a maximum of 10 or 12 minutes. By charging the client a premium rate their advertising message was spotlighted and special, and not lost in a big bunch all grouped together in a dumb "let's air 'em and move on back to music" philosophy. The client was happy because their spots, usually ad-libbed, were showcased and not lost when grouped with other advertisers.

Today, most commercial radio stations *cluster* their spots, grouping them all together, running four, five or even six minutes back to back before returning to more music or talk programming. This concept always makes me shake my head in total disbelief. It is so illogical. Do radio sales managers really believe advertisers are that stupid and are not aware their commercial message is being wasted and tossed away out in to the ether? And radio advertisers, I ask you, what kind of logic is behind allowing your sales message to be buried in the middle of a six-pack of commercials? We all know that the moment a listener hears any break in programming, it's button-pushing time. Maybe, just maybe, they'll punch back to your station in about five minutes, *if* they don't find something more interesting to listen to in the meantime.

How to fix commercial overload.

An important note to air-talent: Your best ally at any radio station can be the sales staff. [35] Get to know them. Offer to accompany them on client calls to meet the sponsors. This is one important way of making yourself more valuable to the station. My late radio pal Andy Moes and I would often say that if the advertisers love us and are willing to pay premium advertising rates to be on our show, then we don't have to live and die by the ratings. Our GM would insist that all advertisers on our morning drive show be locked in to a one-year-minimum contract. It was a win/win for the station and air-talent. There was no need too worry about those all-too-common fluctuations in ratings, and station management was assured of guaranteed revenue, whatever the ratings picture, to keep the lights on and pay their high-priced morning talent. Take time to get to know the sales staff. They can be your ticket to job security in a business that doesn't offer much in that way!

Legendary Dallas morning radio pro **Ron Chapman** adds his invaluable insight in how to win in morning drive radio: "When you are on the air there is only ONE listener, talk to her or him. Don't address a large group. There is nothing personal in that. And as consultant King George Johns taught me, there is only ONE break that's important, and that's the next one! George also taught me the one most important thing an air personality could learn: don't go into anything you don't know how you're getting out of! Know your out 'Q' before you open the mic. Otherwise, you'll wander aimlessly trying to think up a closer. It's called preparation. If you're not into it, stay off the air."

The role women play in morning drive radio.

As we enter a new decade (2011), most lead roles on radio morning shows are still held by men.

It's a sad commentary, but true. Very few women are cast in the lead role on morning shows. There are exceptions like **Laurie DeYoung,** who has been in morning drive on WPOC-Baltimore for over twenty years and comments later in this chapter. Women for the most part are still cast as sidekicks. It is important to know that more and more are being hired as co-hosts with equal responsibilities and hopefully equal pay. To define the role of women in AM-Drive radio, we turned to some of the best in the business for their input: Los Angles news/traffic reporter and former AM-Drive personality, Stacey Cohen; Mix-92.9-Nashville's Anne-Marie Ritter; April Sommers of Star-101.3 San Francisco; radio consultant Donna Halper, and two of my former Florida on-air partners, Pam Triolo and Lindy Rome.

We begin with **Donna Halper,** who comments elsewhere in this book. She has had a successful twenty-five-year career as a radio programming and management consultant. We go all the way back to my time spent on Boston radio. I value Donna's input about all phases of radio, particularly her take on women on the air. She's been there and experienced it first hand. "Yes, on most morning shows the host is a man and the sidekick might be a woman," she says, but quickly adds, "I know a few women who do a morning show, so that may be changing. But as for doing a morning show alone, we are running up against history. Historically, the morning drive show was the most important show on the air and it went to a guy with a deep voice who was supposed to be up-beat and funny. Howard Stern showed that you didn't need the deep voice, but the idea of the male doing mornings has been a truism for generations. I can think of a few women who did the shift, but very few.

"One example," says Halper, "was in Chicago. There was a former journalist whose name was Halloween Martin - her real name- she was born on Halloween, who in 1929 began doing a very successful morning show on station KYW which was in Chicago in those early years. Halloween, you gotta love that name, was on the air with her show *The Musical Clock* throughout the 1930s with no negative reaction from the audience at all. In fact, the listeners loved her. When KYW changed owners and let Halloween go, people were outraged and kept up the pressure 'til another station put her back on in the morning. She was the exception, however. Most stations would not take a chance on a woman in morning drive.

"These days, women in the lead position in morning drive radio may slowly be changing," says Halper, author of three books, the most recent of which is *Invisible Stars: A Social History of Women in American Broadcasting*.[36] "Today, there are more women announcers, and we are finding a few more women doing morning shifts. One who comes to mind is Stephanie Miller. She is syndicated by the Jones Radio Network and does political humor.

"Another problem holding women back, in addition to tradition, is on lots of stations the morning show niche has turned into something crude and vulgar over the past several decades, and women tend not to be comfortable with lewd jokes or talking about sex the way Howard Stern or others of that style do. Our culture is struggling with its own ambivalence about the role of women, look at how women politicians are held to an impossible. If they act in a manner that is considered too strong, they are called aggressive and accused of 'acting like a man.' If they try to downplay their strength and perhaps show some emotion they are accused of being weak and called a 'typical female.' Strong women are damned if they do and damned if they don't. Ditto for women TV news anchors. The standard that was set many years ago was the older white male with a deep voice who never showed much emotion even if the studio was on fire. A woman who tries to act that way looks artificial, but the fact is we [women] haven't developed any archetypes that a woman can follow.

"On radio, there are plenty of women who co-anchor the news, even the morning news," continues Halper. "NPR, National Public Radio, has a number of women in these important positions and even heritage radio stations like WBZ-Boston have a woman co-anchor in morning drive. On news and news-talk stations, it's no longer a sidekick position. Women report on news and do commentary and whatever else, right alongside the male co-host." The question is, will there be more women doing morning drive on Top-40 and other music-formatted stations? "I don't know about that," is her reply, "but I do believe we'll hear more female voices in the all-news and news-talk format and perhaps in Adult Contemporary. Time will tell, but I am encouraged to hear women in most of the other air-shifts, even including some in afternoon drive."

Stacey Cohen has been actively involved in the radio business for thirty years. She began her career as an air-talent at KNIX Radio in Phoenix, Arizona. Stacey's background includes extensive experience at several major-market stations as morning host, news person, and sidekick, as well as hosting a daily talk show at KOGO in San Diego. Stacey was one of the first women in the country to co-host a morning show with another female while at KOMP in Las Vegas. Today, she is on the air in Los Angeles, handling news and traffic reports.

Cohen cautions all future radio wannabes, "Radio is a tough business and you have to have thick skin to be a part of it. I always saw myself as an equal to my male on-air partners. I never felt that there was something they could do that I couldn't. You can't be afraid to take risks and accept challenges. One thing that is so important," she adds, "is timing on the air. You have to be in harmony with your partner in order to make it work. Find the key that will make both of your voices sound the best and work from that angle. To be successful on the radio, especially in morning drive, you need to learn as much as you can and read every single thing about pop culture that you can get your hands on. It is also important to know what the radio business is all about, and to understand how it works. As a woman," says Stacey Cohen, "never compromise who you are. Stand up and let your voice be heard."

The difficulty of being a woman and "making it" in morning drive radio.

Laurie DeYoung has been in morning drive in Baltimore at WPOC for the past twenty-four years. Her program is consistently rated #1 with adults aged 25-54. "One of the most difficult things about being a female in the radio business is trying to make it in morning drive and putting up with all the 'second banana' roles you usually have to play before getting a chance to do your own show," says Laurie. "Women generally are relegated to play roles that support a male lead by laughing or chastising his every thought - good girl vs. bad boy. This is a generalization, but it was my experience. Most male-female teams," she continues, "are controlled and directed by the male. I think women are bored with the roles they're being offered. Lorna Ozmon says, 'All the smart women go to public radio.' That's because," DeYoung adds, "they don't have to 'play the game' there. I was part of three different morning teams before I ever did my own show. I think one reason my show works and has a large female audience is that they, the listeners, really feel represented in an authentic way, not in some contrived way that some radio consultant has decided 'really works.'

"I'm pleased that there are more women programmers now, but it took me thirty years of working in radio to get a woman PD," proclaims DeYoung. "I work for Meg Stevens now and years ago I had a woman general manager, but in all of this time only one of each."

Women on the radio and the difficulties they face.

In 2001, **Pam Triolo** worked alongside me in morning drive at Sunny-104.3 in West Palm Beach. We only worked together for a short while, but had fun on the radio and clicked as a team. At the time, she was in business for herself and decided to go in that direction. The New York native began her radio career right out of Emerson College-Boston in 1989 at WFGL in Fitchburg, MA.

"Growing up as a child, my parents always told me there was nothing I couldn't do so I believed them," says Pam. "WFGL, along with most radio stations at the time, had strictly male personnel so I was one of the first 'newsgals' in the area. Fortunately, Marty McNeil was one of the best in the biz and she promoted me. I had a scanner and Marantz recorder with me at all times and chased fire engines and drug busts looking for a story in the sleepy tri-city area. Eventually, I tried to create my own special on the Leominster Fire Department and what it takes to get the job done. I spent the night in the rec room of the fire department alone, waiting in anticipation for the alarm bell to ring, so I could suit up and get my story! It never rang. I fell asleep and woke up on their uncomfortable sofa, defeated and went home. Later in the day, when I called to reschedule my story, I was told my access was denied. I was given strict orders that I was not to come to the fire station after 11pm to collect news information ever again. What happened? Apparently," recalls

Pam, "the wives of several firefighters were upset that I had 'slept' with the fire department. Are you kidding me?" she says in jest. "I started looking for a new city to move to. And this time it was going to be warm and welcoming. Hello, West Palm Beach! My first job offer from Florida came from a PD who forgot to tell me before I moved to West Palm Beach that he had changed his mind and was going to hire a woman he had a love interest in."

A note to future radio wannabes: Always get your deal in writing! Two years after landing a job with the newly opened Metro Traffic Control, Pam Triolo joined WEAT-Sunny as the morning-show co-host, and eventually as news director. She was the first full-time, on-air female the station ever had. "Back in those days, women really weren't equal to men in radio. It's not like there were mules plowing the field and I had to walk eight miles to work with no shoes on, but we just weren't equal. I couldn't accept that and almost lost the job on my own several times until I got tough and reached down deep. I decided I was going to do everything humanly possible to find my own voice, to become a visible part of the community, win industry awards, work harder than anyone else, take every outside gig, paid or not, and be the best I could ever be. Along the way, I worked with a Tom, Dick, Chuck and Rob and was the only consistent player on Sunny-104.3 for many years.

Triolo eventually took her first solo on-air position in middays, moved to afternoon-drive and then moved to television for a decade. "I left the business to open my own marketing and PR firm, First Impressions Creative Services, Inc.[37] I was tempted to reenter the radio field back in 2001," says Pam, "when Joe Martelle joined Sunny in morning drive, but my business was lucrative and women still weren't drawing the type of salaries that men did and it just wasn't the right time. Today, women have more opportunities than ever and I'd like to think I and the thousands of other women in radio helped pave the way."

Pam has this advice for women in morning drive: "First, have four alarm clocks strategically placed around your bedroom to ensure you wake up on time. Make sure only two of them are plug-ins, just in case power goes out overnight, and the others are wind-up or from a cell phone. Secondly, remember that ratings are the key so do your homework and make sure you are always out in the community. With the invention of Sirius and iPods, the reason people tune in to their local radio station is for community information and topics that suit the way they live, and finally, have fun and be yourself. No one can resist an authentic talent."

Roles in morning drive radio need to be defined.

Lindy Rome also worked with me at Sunny-104.3 in West Palm Beach. We teamed up in morning drive in 2002 and were top-rated, until I lost my voice in 2004, which ended our on-air partnership and my forty-one-year radio career.[38] Here are some of Lindy's thoughts on roles in morning drive radio for women: "My best advice would be, *know your place*. Whose show is it? Get this question answered from the start. Better yet," she laughs, "get it in writing! If it's your show, great! Do what you want and ask for lots of money. However, if you are the co-host, sidekick, news gal, or whatever they call it, learn to submit to the guy making more money than you. Yes, he WILL make more than you," she insists. "People get all freaked out when I talk about submission, but it's really very powerful." Lindy goes on to explain: "If you play into it as the one who gets picked on and even bullied a little once in a while, then you will endear yourself to the audience for life. That doesn't mean you don't speak your mind - you do, just do it without being arrogant. I wish I had a dime for every phone call that came in from a listener that said, 'Stop picking on Lindy!' THAT made me a star. If you want power, respect, more money, learn to be humble. It works every time. I was fortunate to have worked with some awesome talent that took much joy in cracking me up. God bless them all!"

The importance of knowing your role as a member of the morning show team.

As far as roles in morning drive are concerned, **April Sommers,** who works side by side with longtime radio pro Don Bleu on STAR 101.3-San Francisco, says, "It's all about maintaining perspective and understanding your role. Each member of a solid morning show understands their role on the team. I suppose it's the same for any team. In baseball," April points out, "if the pitcher tried also to be the catcher, they would lose the game. As for keeping the ego in check as a supporting player, personally, I always keep in mind where I am. I am working with a legend. I have the opportunity to learn sooo much about doing great radio. I'll always be grateful."

Anna-Marie Ritter has been in morning drive at Nashville's top-rated Mix-92.9 for about twelve years. She is the station's news director and morning show co-host with Kim Leslie. Anna says "The better the roles are defined, the easier it is to do your job. I have also found that some people think they're the funny one and end up killing a lot of bits because they just won't quit talking until they get the last word in. So, it's important to have a great program director like we do in Barbara Bridges, who can guide each talent into their strengths."[39]

Working together! If a bit fails on your morning show, everyone fails! Make it work!

Anna-Marie Ritter says, "Sometimes, no matter how hard you work on the show, you're teamed with someone who can't, or won't, do the work required to make each bit its absolute best. Then," she says, "you have to make choices: do I want to put in the EXTRA work, to carry the load that they're not doing, and MAKE this work, or take the option, 'it's NOT my job. If the bit fails, it's HIS fault. I did my part.' But, did you really? Let's face it," she says, "once the bit makes it past the idea stage, the brainstorming, the prepping and the mic opens, I have a motto, *make it work!* No matter what anyone else brings, or fails to bring to the table, I try my absolute best and you should do the same thing, to make it work."

It's Ritter's view, shared by all successful morning drive radio pros, that "Being part of a morning show team means EVERYONE should be on their toes ALL THE TIME. If two or three members of a radio team are all ready to play, to volley, to hit the ball and catch it when someone else drops it then there's never a bad on-air bit. It's when they're standing there, looking at each other, sending instant text messages to their wives, or just not 'plugged in' that the ball drops and the bit fails! When everyone is tuned in to their show, even if one person messes up, the others can make it work. When a bit fails, that means everyone fails, not just the person who dropped the ball."

Producing and running the board is a critical component of a successful morning drive show.

Julee Mara says that radio was something she knew she always wanted to do, no doubt highly influenced as a child by her dad's love of listening to oldies on the radio. Every Saturday night, her dad Benny would call my all-request oldies show and make a dedication. Over the years, Ben and I became friends, so it is with a great deal of personal pride that I follow his daughter Julee's development as a Boston radio pro.

After graduating from Lynnfield High School in 2001, Julee was accepted at Boston's Emerson College, earning a Bachelor's Degree in Media Arts. The hard-working Ms. Mara offers this advice for high-school students who dream of being on the radio, and eventually being part of a morning drive show: "Take advantage of every opportunity your school has to offer that will give you experience in public speaking, even if it means reading the school announcements over the PA in the morning. That was the closest I could get to 'real-world' radio experience in high school," Julee laughs, "but it was a start. If your high school has a radio station, get involved! My major at Emerson was designed specifically for students looking to work in radio. I obtained invaluable on-air experience at the college station, 88.9-WERS, hosting *Gyroscope*, a world music show.

"During my sophomore year, I got an internship at a Boston station," something Julee suggests all future radio wannabes do. "If you work hard and are determined, you can move up quickly in radio." In 2003, after interning at Boston's former Star 93.7 with *Ralphie & Karen's Morning Show,* Julee was hired. She quickly moved up the ranks in the programming department as a producer. One year later she was on the air, weekends. For the past five years, using her air-name, "Jewels," Julee has been heard on several Boston stations, including Magic-106. She has also been a radio producer at 93.7-Mike FM, WTKK-96.9 and WKLB 102.5.

The important role of the board operator and producer of a morning drive radio show.

At the time of this writing, Julee produced overnights at Oldies-103 and was also technical director for Zito & Karen Blake's morning show. "My biggest challenge in producing their fast-paced morning show is making sure I can turn around the audio fast enough for the next break, because we don't air live calls, and I have to make sure I have made the proper edits to turn around the bit that's going to air next. You only have a few minutes to get it done and it gets hectic. Often times, there are only a few minutes to go through a three-minute piece of audio and make the necessary corrections."

Radio newbies should start out small, before jumping in as producer of an AM-Drive show.

As technical director on a morning drive show, Julee emphasizes, "It's important to keep in mind you're in charge of how the talent sounds and to follow their instructions on the direction of the break and how the show hosts want it to sound." Julee shares this advice for future radio wannabes who aspire to be part of a morning drive radio team: "My advice for those looking for a position like mine would be to start out small. Learn to run live remote broadcasts. I worked for years producing a weekly Saturday night broadcast which required a lot of recording and editing, but didn't necessarily need to be turned around as fast as audio for the morning show. Learn how to operate the on-air control board. [40] Learn how to use editing equipment. Practice editing bits in a fast way, taking out audio that is unnecessary and leaving in the 'meat' that enhances the sound bite or phone call to make it sizzle and sparkle for the air." As producer for one of Boston radio's top morning drive shows, Julee Mara feels radio today has moved to a "'get in-get out' momentum where quality bits and pieces are better than quantity."

The inside scoop on being in morning drive in any size radio market.

Captain Dan, on KKLI-Colorado Springs, shares his insight about doing mornings in a medium market as opposed to the major cities.[41] "John Lodge was the guy who really taught me how to do mornings; I owe much of who I am today to John. During the year I was his sidekick at KVUU, we'd occasionally get John to talk about his years in the majors and he would always say, 'The only difference is there are more zeros.' The spots cost more, the promotions are bigger and the jocks get a larger check. They do the same thing we do; our show would be successful in any number of major markets!' When I first came to Colorado Springs almost thirty years ago," says Dan, "my first book as PD of KYSN produced an 18-share 12+, and we were #1 across the board. Today, the number one station here would be lucky to see double digits with only tenths of a percent separating the top five stations and perhaps a first place ranking in only one or two key demos.

"During my tenure in the Springs, we've added about ten new radio signals to the market" and, adds Dan, "we've become fragmented and very competitive! The big markets no longer have a monopoly on competition or pressure. There are plenty of places you can prove yourself on this level. With that said, there has been a time or two over the years when I wondered what it would be like to be on a big stick in a big market. The one time I vocalized the thought to Willie & Jojo, Willie Fisher & Jojo Turnbaugh, the morning guys in the studio next door, they said, 'Are you nuts? You've married the market; nobody gets to do that anymore. I know a hundred guys who would kill to be you.'

"I can't argue with that," says the longtime radio pro on KKLI-FM. "I make a very good living, have a loving family, close friends, comfortable home and live in a city at the foot of Pike's Peak where the majority of people think I'm an okay guy, enough so they invite me into their homes every morning! How many major market guys can say that?"

Whatever size radio market you're in do ordinary things consistently and exceptionally well.

One big mistake many morning show radio personalities make is that they are so fixated on making a major impact and scoring a big hit on their show, they overlook the basics of handling their show. To win in AM-Drive, you need to remember to include the basic elements your listeners need to know to start their day: time, temp, and what's the weather doing right now! Some personalities are so into scoring the big one with a creative bit they neglect to include the basics. Let's face it, it's more fun to punch up a creative bit or phone call than to keep repeating the time and temp, but it has to be done!

Scotty Brink may not care to admit it, but he is a tried-and-true American radio legend. His on-air, programming, and radio management experience covers fifty eventful years. Don L. Brink's radio career began in 1958 at age sixteen, in his hometown of Williamsport, PA. At nineteen, he became the youngest jock ever in the history of popular Philly radio station-WIBG, affectionately known to listeners as "Wibbage."

In 1965, he moved west to the City of Angels and middays at powerhouse KHJ. The station had been Boss Radio for about four months when he arrived, and because *The Real Don Steele* was doing afternoon-drive, Don L. Brink had to undergo a name change. He became Scotty. Six months later, he was drafted and spent time with Armed Forces Radio in Vietnam. Upon returning to the States, he joined WOR-FM -New York, the first Drake FM station, and then was asked to return to sister station KHJ. A few years later, Scotty moved to Chicago and WCFL and recalls, "After a couple of exceptional books, I was wooed over to competitor WLS." From Chicago he moved to the Pacific Northwest and was on the air at KJR-Seattle. Next, he moved across the country to Boston as PD at WRKO. In 1977, he jumped to the Big Apple and WNBC to do morning drive. Richard Belzer became his comic sidekick and the duo gave birth to Brink & Belzer. In 1981, the well-traveled Scotty Brink did a morning talk show at WCAU Philadelphia and then moved to KHOW-Denver as Operations Manager. As you can see, Scotty Brink's radio credentials speak for themselves. He has worked at some of America's greatest radio stations and is more than qualified to offer his input on what it takes to be a successful radio personality, including in the most prestigious shift on any station, morning drive.

"I may not be the best person to tackle this," Brink humbly begins, "but I will tell you what I think. Some things like brevity, savvy, and a realization that the listener is more important than you, along with an understanding of what the listener needs from you and a genuine desire to see that he gets it, are timeless. However, the way content is presented in AM-Drive is changing, and will likely soon change drastically. Because of the financial state of the industry, which is dire at this point, morning drive radio teams such as those we've been so familiar with for the past couple of decades will not be budget-friendly, and as I understand it, are losing a lot of their appeal anyway."

So, what does the future hold for morning drive radio talent? Brink believes we can expect to hear more solo players in the morning and soon. "That means a whole different way of presenting content, and a lot more attention given to common sense programming. Local information and content will be of paramount importance. It's the only advantage radio really has," he exclaims. "Community involvement has to make a comeback." He believes the role of morning talent in the future is as follows: "The morning drive person will be more of an anchor, and a self-styled producer of the various pieces of content, primarily pre-produced and often from outside sources that he or she will be presenting. This will require talent who can think as well as speak. A morning radio pro must really love people and want to please them, and this is very important. Talent must have an analytical understanding of new media and how consumers use it. As most radio operators have been learning the hard way, other radio stations are no longer our most important competition. Radio needs get personable again."

Today, you'll find Scotty Brink in his studio in Edmond, Oklahoma, working on a project-by-project basis. Now and then he goes to Nashville for a music session, which he admits is his favorite thing to do. "I work well with musical talent and I can think of nothing more gratifying than contributing to a great musical moment." You can reach out to the legendary radio pro at scottybrink@att.net.

It goes without saying that to win the battle of the ratings and bring more listeners into your tent, you need to be compelling, entertaining, interesting, and unpredictable and that includes featuring fun, entertaining and even emotional content.[42] Just keep in mind that in doing so, you don't lose sight of doing the basics, which also includes your station call letters as part of your total presentation.

Speaking of giving the call letters, in the event one or more of your listeners become an Arbitron family and receives one of those precious little rating diaries, you want them giving YOU credit by writing down your call letters and not those of your competition.[43] Many talented radio personalities come up short in the ratings game by simply not identifying their station's call letters or frequency often enough on their show. Repetition is the name of the game if you want to win. Give your station's slogan or call letters often!

Do the basics well and consistently and you will be on your way to winning in morning drive and in any other air-shift on the radio!

The secret in developing your morning radio show and being successful is plain and simple: Work harder than your competition.

Your success as a morning drive air-talent does NOT come from everything going well…real success comes when you're willing to move forward no matter what stands in your way! Your goal as a winner on the radio in morning drive or any other shift should be to shoot for the stars, because if you fall short of your mark, you'll wind up on the moon, and when last we checked, there weren't too many people, let alone radio personalities, living there!

Variety always will be the key to radio's success. It is imperative in morning drive.

One word, "sameness," is the reason listeners are turning away from terrestrial radio. Radio needs to get back to being a source for creativeness and entertainment, particularly in morning drive where the most listeners are. Stations that play the same songs over and over again, which made Top-40 radio so appealing for the past 40 years, had better wake up. Today there are numerous other sources for music that aren't radio.

Radio management specialist **John Gehron** says, "Music on radio is no longer special. Thirty years ago, you got music in two places, record stores and radio. Now music has become a commodity and is available everywhere. From phones to iPods to the Blackberry I'm using to write this. Radio will not abandon music, but will have to look for content that cannot be copied or is unique to radio."

Here is a list of 35 suggestions on how to make your journey as a morning drive talent more successful. Circle those you feel you need to work on; they may help you reach your goal.

1. Be passionate about being on the radio every time you open your mic and on EVERY break.
2. Don't just listen to your boss. Listen to what they're saying and why they are saying it.
3. Share your knowledge. It's a way to achieve immortality.
4. In disagreements with your co-workers, only deal with the current problem. Don't bring up the past.
5. Judge your success by what you had to give up in order to achieve it.
6. Be assertive instead of aggressive. Assert your feelings and opinions instead of becoming angry.
7. Learn the format inside and out, so you know how to properly break it.
8. Remember that not always getting what you want is sometimes a stroke of luck.
9. Always be open to new ways of doing things on your show.
10. Be willing to reinvent yourself to change with the times.
11. As good ratings and success come your way, don't rest on your laurels. Keep working just as hard.
12. In contract negotiations ask for more program control and not money. It will pay off in your future.
13. Be willing to go the extra mile to gather info on a guest for your show.
14. SHOW PREP, SHOW PREP, SHOW PREP. Never lose focus or skip preparing your show.
15. Control your urge to squeeze the living snort out of your PD or GM.
16. Never stop working to promote yourself, your show, and your station.
17. Always be nice to your listeners, even when they become demanding and in-your-face.
18. READ, READ, READ. Suck in all the info you can. Read everything, including the classified ads—you never know where you'll find a funny line. Just ask Jay Leno.
19. Watch as many new TV shows as you can without vomiting, especially those geared to your demo.
20. Run tape, CD, or DVD on the news and entertainment shows. You never know when you'll get a perfect sound bite for your show.

21. Set your standards high but not so high that you fail to accomplish anything.
22. Open your mind to change, but don't let go of your values.
23. Great accomplishments are derived from numerous small achievements.
24. Be inspired by perfection but don't let it stop you from reaching your goals.
25. When your goals are achieved, like being top-rated, set your sights even higher.
26. Control your ego! An out-of-control ego is something that can kill even the greatest air-talent.
27. Live with the knowledge that your character is your destiny.
28. Don't ever think that just because you drive the bus, you're bigger or more important than the team.
29. Always make sure your brain is in gear before engaging your mouth.
30. Learn from the mistakes of others. You won't live long enough to make them all yourself.
31. Don't fall into the trap of making "your show" all about "you."
32. Get enough rest. You can't consistently sound your best for long on three hours' sleep.
33. Eat healthy. Do not allow Ms. Krispy Kreme to set foot in your studio.
34. Exercise regularly. I know you're mentally and physically drained after getting up at 3am and running a hot show, but try at least to get a walk in every day.
35. Finally, keep this old Chinese proverb in mind: "If you always give, you will always have."

CKEY-Toronto Canada radio personality Mickey Lester would end his show with these parting words: "Take it easy 'n' friendly and you'll last longer and finish a whole lot stronger."

Notes:
1. Source: The Method to the Madness- The American Comedy Network, copyright 1985.
2. Read more about consultant Walter Sabo in Chapter 12 .
3. *R&R* or Radio & Records was a weekly music trade publication which began in 1973. It followed the radio business and tracked current songs by format. It was mostly available through subscriptions to people who worked in the radio and music industry. For a few years, the magazine was consolidated with *Billboard Magazine*, but on June 5, 2009, parent company A.C. Nielsen ceased operations.

4. Houston's Bill Bailey left radio in 1982. Today, the native Texan works as a Constable in East Harris County, Texas.
5. Information on the subject of stress hormones and how they affect the human body was obtained from several sources, including the Harvard Medical School Special Health Report on Stress Control, a US Army study, www.hooah4health.com/mind/stressmgmt, and other publications.
6. In Oct. 2009 the simulcast on TV of the I-Man's morning radio show moved to the Fox business channel.
7. Lyrics from "Oklahoma!"
8. The term "pot me up" means put me on the air, as in turn up the switch or volume that controls voice input.
9. Passion is one of the 7 Powerful P's and is covered in Chapter 5.
10. The role of radio program directors is covered extensively in Chapter 10.
11. The author graduated from USMC Boot camp at Parris Island, So. Carolina, in the summer of 1960- Plt 248 I Co. 2nd Battalion.
12-17, Gary Berkowitz, Tom Baker, Peter Smyth, Frank Kingston Smith, Rod Fritz and Dick Syatt all comment elsewhere in this book.
18. Following Ted's departure, Roy Reese handled sports, followed by former Red Sox players Rico Petrocelli & Dick Radatz.
19. Andy Moes and I were together as the morning drive wake up team on WROR-98.5 from Dec. '83 until the spring of '92.
20. Because of an ongoing heart condition, Andy lost a lot of weight a few years before his passing at age 51 in Feb., 2001.
21. If you're interested in comedic timing, especially on the radio, I strongly suggest you listen to Martin & Lewis or Abbott & Costello on their radio shows to hear how the real pros pulled it off. DVDs and CDs are also available of their television shows and film work.
22. **Author's note**: Thank you, David, for your kind words which were totally unsolicited, but nice to hear. From Christmas 1983 until the spring of 1992, my role as Joe on Boston Radio's *Joe and Andy Family* was one of the highlights of my 41 years on radio. It was one of the most enjoyable and lucrative times in my entire broadcasting career. I'm proud to have worked with Andy. There isn't a day that goes by that I don't think about him and smile. My late radio partner and friend Andy Moes took me places I never would have achieved on my own. It was truly a righteous ride!
23. Based on Arbitron, the radio ratings authority, *Saturday Night "Live" at the Oldies* was rated #1 in double digits, across all demographics for most of its twelve-year run -Nov 1979 until Feb. 1991. Because of its high ratings and popularity it became the most popular all-request oldies program in the history of Boston radio.
24. Benny Mara's daughter, Julee, now on the air in Boston, comments later in this chapter on the role of a producer in morning drive.

How to Win in Morning Drive • 407

25. "Blue Angel," on the Monument label, was a Top-Ten hit for Roy Orbison in October, 1960.
26. Today, the Tony Conigliaro Award is presented annually to a player who best overcomes an obstacle and continues to succeed. In 2007, the Boston Red Sox added a new 200-bleacher seat section on the right field roof. The section was named "Conigliaro's Corner."
27. ROR & RKO were eventually sold and radio Disneyland became more like *land of the lost*. It was a difficult time in the careers of Joe and Andy, and eventually we would split and go our separate ways. The break-up is covered elsewhere in this book.
28. During my years on radio, I subscribed to Bob Hamilton's *Morning Star*, which was an excellent exchange of programming ideas for morning talent. Bob comments on the importance of show prep in Chapter 7.
29. The importance of show prep is covered in Chapter 7.
30. Attitudes and Actions are covered in Chapter 9.
31. The fixed-bits were written and prepared in advance but we always ad-libbed around them. Nothing on our show was set in stone.
32. **Author's note:** As one who presented a "topic or thought starter" in AM-Drive on a daily basis for over 30 years, I believe it is imperative that you choose your subject matter wisely in order to receive maximum caller input and achieve that "pure on-air gold" that Chuck mentions. It can be done. One other note: there are always listeners who will willingly call your show, like folks who arrive home from working the all-night shift, others who may be stuck in traffic, folks who are already at work with time on their hands and nothing to do. Listeners will take the time to call in, and NOT necessarily to win something, but just to have fun and voice their input, *if* the subject material is interesting and compelling and warrants their time and effort. **TIP:** Choose your subject matter wisely!
33. Six units in a break refers to how many commercials are aired at one time during a "break" in the show.
34. GSM in radio is the General Sales Manager.
35. Why sales and air-talent should be best buddies is discussed in Chapter 19, Some Things to Know about a Career as a Radio Pro.
36. *Invisible Stars* by broadcast historian Donna Halper documents women broadcasters whose presence made a difference, who overcame great obstacles and persevered in their chosen careers. Her book is highly recommended by this author.
37. You can reach Pam Triolo at www.ficreates.com.
38. My voice loss was due to pneumonia and three nodes on my vocal chords. Thanks to a great speech pathologist, voice rest and the grace of God, with lots of prayer, my voice has returned.

39. Barbara Bridges comments in Chapter 10-Program Directors: Friend or Foe.
40. One of the prerequisites to being on the radio is that first and foremost, even before thinking about turning on a mic switch, you MUST know how to run the control board.
41. Read more on how radio pros are found in cities and towns of all sizes in Chapter 19: Some Things to Know About a Career as a Radio Pro.
42. Read more about radio ratings in Chapter 18.
43. Arbitron or ARB is the ratings service company radio stations subscribe to.

Harry Harrison, legendary NYC morning air personality.

Brian deGeus Foxx, MD and air-talent, Salt Lake City.

Anna-Marie Ritter, Nashville morning-drive personality.

Joe n' Andy with pound puppies a regular weekly feature, The Critter Corner, where shelter animals were placed up for adoption.

Joe n' Andy PJ Party "live" on-air with guest, fashion maven, Yolanda.

Author on phone taking requests on his oldie show Sat. Night 'live' at the Oldies -WROR-98.5 Boston.

David Kruh, former RKO Engr. Boston.

How to Win in Morning Drive • 411

Oldies show montage A.

Tony Conigliaro, one of the Red Sox most popular players.

Joe Chille, long-time Buffalo, NY morning air pro.

Bill Gardner, Phoenix, Las Vegas and LA morning-drive personality.

Matt Siegel, popular morning-drive personality KISS-108, Boston.

Mark Wallengren, long-time Los Angeles AM-Drive air personality.

How to Win in Morning Drive • 413

Casey Kasem, legendary nationally syndicated radio personality (host American Top-40).

Future radio wannabee, Julee Mara, riding high on her daddy Benny's shoulders while talking with author during anniversary broadcast from Revere Beach Bandstand on 98.5-ROR-FM. Also Julee today as Boston air talent.

Scotty Brink, former air personality, now voice-over talent in Oklahoma.

Capt. Dan, long-time Colorado Springs morning-drive talent.

CHAPTER 15
Radio Promotion: Marketing & Publicity

"Attack the market. Be on the offensive all the time."
— WABC Music-radio PD, Rick Sklar

"Radio's earliest on-air promotions"

PROMOTIONS AND RADIO have gone together as smoothly as peanut butter and jelly since broadcastings' earliest beginnings. From the 1930's through the early 50's, popular children's programs like Little Orphan Annie sponsored by Ovaltine, Tom Mix on the air for Ralston cereal and Jack Armstrong-the All-American Boy for Wheaties would feature rings, maps, booklets and other premiums. All it took to receive these little goodies was a box-top or a jar label from the sponsor's product and a thin dime.

We kids could hardly stand the wait for our radio premium to arrive in the mail! Rushing home after school, we raced in the house, tearing through the pile of mail to see if the little brown box from Chicago, 77 Illinois or Minneapolis, Minnesota had arrived! Spying it, we nervously opened it and gazed lovingly at our little gem. Even though the secret compartment in the ring wasn't quite as big as we imagined it to be, we still enjoyed every minute of holding the ring and showing it off to our friends. So what if your ring turned green to match the envy your pals were feeling. Long before radio ratings, the radio premium offers were an excellent way for radio programmers to determine how many kids were listening to the shows. It was also an ingenious way for advertisers to entice the kids of America to buy and try their product.

One of the cleverest marketing ideas for kids came from the advertising of Quaker Oats cereal which sponsored Sergeant Preston of the Yukon.[1] The promotion was a Deed to one square inch of land in the Yukon. Some ambitious kids, probably coaxed by their mom and dad amassed quite a few copies of the certificate and tried to consolidate them into a claim for themselves. It was later reported in the Wall Street Journal the land was never owned by the Quaker Oats people and was not their's to give away. The deeds say so in small print. Quaker leased the land for ten years to use in their radio promotion. A million deeds were stuffed in boxes of Quaker Puffed Wheat and Rice and then later offered in ads.

"One of radio's first promotions"

One of the hi-lights of my successful radio career was my time on the air at "the Nation's station," WLW Cincinnati. In 1921, just as a hobby, Powell Crosley, Jr started WLW with 20 watts of power. He got interested radio after he was prompted by his young son to build his own wireless set. It was Crosley's earliest stages of developing and building a radio station that would go on to become an institution...the mighty 700AM -WLW Cincinnati! In Dick Perry's well documented book *'Not Just A Sound-the story of WLW*, published by Prentice Hall in 1971, he points out that during it's earliest days on the air, the staff at WLW were constantly trying to determine how far their station reached. It was easy to "pick up"WLW even though it was only broadcasting with 100 watts of power, since at the time, there were only 28 stations broadcasting legally in the entire United States.

In January 1923, in what was one of radio's first promotions, WLW offered a free box of candy to the first listener from each state to send in a telegram. Entries were received from forty-two states and Canada. Fifty-seven years later, (1970) when I sat behind the mic at WLW,[2] hosting the all-night show, we continued with station tradition, to see who was listening the furthest away. I urged listeners to send us a letter with a self-addressed stamped envelope and we'll mail you back a "Nite-Owl" trivia card. In days, we received thousands of letters from listeners in 37 States, Canada and the Caribbean.

"The purpose of radio promotions"

Promotions should generate publicity for you, your show and your station. Most major and medium sized radio stations have a marketing department, but I discovered in my many years in radio their primary function is to promote the station first—and that means ALL day parts, not just your air-shift. Secondly, promotions has to assist sales with ideas to generate sales, and thirdly, if there is any time or cash left-over they promote individual personalities. Now, realistically, how often do you think there is any time or cash left over to help promote you and your show (other then the prime morning-drive shift). Secondly, have any "cash" left over for you? Did I hear NOT very much? Give that person a used CD from the station prize closet!

"The role of the Radio Promotions Director"

Today in radio, the station promotions director promotes the image of the radio station, the programs and personalities, or at least that's way it's supposed to work. They do this through contests, events, activities and both "in-house" and "outside" advertising or "marketing." The radio promotion director works with the program director and the sales department to develop promotional and marketing ideas and hopefully, find advertisers to help co-promote the idea. It is also the job of the promotions person to obtain prizes to be used with the promotion.

It's important to remember, if your radio promotion or "contest" doesn't "sizzle" it will soon "fizzle" out and flop! On-air radio station contests and promotions need to grab your listeners by the ear. They need to sound exciting and most importantly be fun.

Remember as an air-talent, your station promotions director isn't working solely for you!

I can't tell you how many times, over the years, I've heard air-talent complain that they are not getting enough publicity from their station promotion people. Sometimes, the complaint is justified. I worked at one station, where management promised they would spend 100,000 dollars to promote me and my morning-drive show. Since I was the new guy in town, in a highly competitive major market it was a necessity to promote me and the show. I went to great lengths to emphasize the importance of promotion during our contract negotiations, long before discussing salary terms. Management promised that money would be used on "outside" promotion, meaning television, buses and billboards. It never happened! The money that was guaranteed never materialized. It was "supposedly" slashed from their operating budget. However, I think it was channeled to a major station promotion or to another station in our cluster. When I approached my GM about it, she coolly remarked. "We're NOT going to promote you, because people will listen and they won't like what they hear." Why on God's good green earth, I didn't demand to know why she felt that way is beyond me. Guess, I must have been feeling a little too charitable that day or something. Maybe, her comment took me so much by surprise, I didn't know how to react, at least not in a civil way! Funny thing is if that had been a male GM making those kind of comments I probably would have laid him out in his fruit salad.

Radio Lesson learned: once again it is so important to get as many things—like promotional money spent to promote you and your show in writing and in your contract. It's charitable to think management will keep to their word on every thing, but that's not realistic. They can promise you the moon one day and then the next, look you right in the eye the next and say, "hey, sorry, we needed the money elsewhere. No offense, bub, it's just business!"

Radio is a pressure-packed, changeable, emotional business and things can change in a heartbeat! It's not that "the suits" don't mean what they say, or don't intend to keep their word. It's just that the playing field can change and if the bottom line dictates certain dollars need to be spent to improve the picture elsewhere, you can kiss your "promised" promotional money goodbye. It won't be easy, but everything you can in writing.

"Talent needs to promote themselves!"
When I joined the staff at WROR-Boston in the fall of '79, radio pro Frank Kingston Smith[3] took me aside and said, "don't think they are going to promote you! You'll have to do MOST of it on your own."

It was good advice that is worth passing along. The promotional staff at most radio stations have more than a full plate. As a talent, you need to help them and in turn help yourself by creating your own promotions and contests that will run exclusively"inside" your own show. It is always good to run your ideas past your PD, first. He or she will bring them to the attention of the promotions person and if need be, sales.

"Regular weekly meetings with talent and promotions is important"
It is a good idea to have regular weekly meetings with both your PD and the Promotions people to discuss the promotional concepts you have come up with to promote your own show.

Including other staff members about your ideas will automatically make them accountable to follow through for you. Don't be one of those malcontent air-talents who goes around saying, "promotions never does anything to promote me or my show." Of course, the promotion staff need to help you promote your show, but keep in mind, ultimately they need to focus on the overall imaging of the station and EVERY day-part. You, on the other hand are only responsible for your 3 or 4 hours on the radio station. Help them and you will find they in turn will help you! Weekly meetings are important with your department heads, if for no other reason than to exchange ideas and keep the lines of communication open.

"The promotions person can be an air-talent's best friend"
Tim Johnson is Intranet Director for Clear Channel University in Houston, Texas. In the late '90's, he and I worked together at the Oldies station, KLDE. Tim was Marketing & Promotions Director and I was in morning-drive. Tim says the promotion and marketing team for a station or cluster is talent's conduit to money and resources." Looking for cash through appearances and endorsements," he asks, "look no further then your station promotions and marketing person. "Work with the promo team," he suggests," and go above and beyond on your first project together. They'll

rave about you to everyone and soon other Account Executives will clamor to have you next. If you're looking to improve your on-air contests, or have some marketing dollars spent on promoting your show" Johnson says, " it's the Marketing Director who will often carry the majority vote on marketing campaigns and will be the one to design "on-air" sweepstakes. Inviting your Marketing Director out for a "brainstorming" lunch could result in thousands of dollars of marketing support for your ideas. Pick up the tab," adds Tim Johnson, "it will pay you back later!"

Brad Wallace[4] is Director of Marketing & Promotion at WLS 890AM, the talk station in Chicago.

He has kindly provided us with his job description at WLS and exactly what his job entails. It is listed on the next page.

Brad says, the relationship between "on-air" talent and the marketing/promotion department is important for a station's overall success. "On-air talent, must understand the unique combined responsibilities of the marketing department to programming (ratings) and sales (revenue)," he begins. "This two-pronged effort will rely heavily on the talent's ability to carry out promotional programs on-the-air, on-site and internally." In fact," he says, "speaking from a marketing director's point of view, this department would do well to have a great relationship with talent. As in all business and personal relationships," adds Wallace, " it is best NOT to assume you know the other person's job, even if you've had that person's position at another station. Open communication, based on goals results and results should typically start with a question, as opposed to a potentially uniformed statement of "supposed" fact. Brad Wallace concludes with these thoughts, "it is imperative that most AM show hosts(referring to the talent at WLS-AM but it pertains to all talent) have a close relationship with the marketing/promotions department. Just as the promotion director should find out how they can service the AM show's needs, the AM show host must be able to rise above their own show and understand how it fits into the entire product (the station) for which the promotion director is responsible for marketing purposes."

"The role of a Marketing and Promotions Director/Manager"
Brad Wallace-Dir. Of Marketing & Promotion-WLS-AM Chicago

Brad Wallace defines in his own words, his job description at WLS-AM to give you further insight into what the position entails.

"I manage the marketing, advertising and promotional activities for the station designed to create brand awareness, generate audience, build audience consumption and foster audience loyalty. I contribute to station revenue and ratings by successfully designing promotions that match the station objectives and direction with client needs."

"What you do"

While the scope of the position varies from station to station," says Wallace," it can include the following…"

- **Marketing**- development, care and feeding the Marketing Model, a statement of document that clearly defines the station's target audience, product description (air sound), position in the marketplace and supporting promotional activity.
- **Advertising**- Strategic and/or tactical messages, directed at the target audience, designed to define the product and create audience trial.
- **Promotions**- Campaigns and tactic used on-the-air to stimulate/manipulate listening AND while offering clients unique opportunities to position their products and services.
- **Research**- working in tandem with consultants or research companies, designing projects to determine audience perceptions, needs and feelings of radio. Working with sales, positioning the radio station to clients as a unique, results-oriented solution for advertising.
- **Management**- of a staff to execute the specific promotions or programs as well as cross-functional management of departments.

"How You Do It"

Brad Wallace further describes in detail *how to accomplish* the above goals as a radio station Director- Manager of Marketing and Promotion.

1. **You need to be creative** and lead the creative process to solve problems and address challenges.
2. **Be able to lead** a free-flowing, problem-solving discussion without straying too far from the goal.
3. **You need to be grounded in rational thought.** With all this creative thought flowing around, you need to be grounded in rational thought with a keen eye to fiscal responsibility. Managing a budget is important. Note: Besides payroll at a station, the marketing department can be the MOST expense oriented part of a station operation. It is also the most visible when cost-cutting becomes part of the solution in lean times! Because of that, expenditures should be positioned as investments…in the brand, in the audience and in the position of the radio station.
4. **A general business sense.** You need to read people, and quickly. This goes for in and out of the station. Sizing up the motivations of a potential marketing partner is key to getting the best deal and creating a genuine situation that benefits both.

At the station, the marketing department deals with more than just programming and sales.

The above comments are attributable to Brad Wallace-Director of

Marketing and Promotion at WLS-AM-Chicago. We are indebted to Brad for his time and for sharing his knowledge and expertise.

"Always be on the look-out for creative ways to market the station, your show and yourself"

One of the cleverest and probably MOST expensive radio station promotions and publicity stunts I ever heard about has to go to **WBZ Boston**! Hollywood went Boston way during the summer of '59. WBZ's talented on-air line-up of Carl DeSuze, Dave Maynard, Norm Prescott, Phil Christie and Alan Dary all stepped before the movie cameras to produce their own Cinemascope Technicolor extravaganza entitled *"Meet the WBZ Disc-jockeys."* The film—a one of its kind---was shown throughout New England as a short subject and was featured on th same bill as *Hercules*. How much do you think that little gem cost the BZ promotions department? Today, you could save yourself big bucks and reach the same amount of people—if not more by producing your own video for YouTube.

Important reminder to all talent: keep all clips of any "outside publicity" you receive. Whenever you or your show makes the news, whether it's a blurb in the newspaper or magazine, but especially television coverage of an event on your show. Later, make a montage of what you have done and post it on YouTube. It is also a video resume when the needs arises to shop yourself around to a perspective new employer. It is import to ALWAYS have a current up-to-date CD of your air-work ready to go. In radio, the only *constant* is *"change,"* and you never know when you may be part of that change!

"Develop your own band for live music! We even had our own band"

Andy and I had little time to play songs on our show what with all our bits, interviews and commercials! Factor in a "live" audience when we did a remote   broadcasts and it was even more difficult to squeeze 4 minute songs in. I came up with the idea of having our own band. They could play 2 minute instrumentals. Thus, was formed the world famous *"Joe and Andy "G-string band and "C" Note orchestra."* Our band was recruited from our own listeners. A few were students at Boston's famous Berklee School of Music, but most were folks who just enjoyed playing an instrument. At one time, our band grew to 14 in number. Whenever and wherever we went on location for a remote broadcast our band showed up! Total number depended on how many mom's had to drive their kids to school that day. We usually would wind-up with between ten and 14 band members. They sounded great under the personal supervision and direction of Revere school teacher Frannie Sacco.

"Great contest: In search of the typical "Joe and Andy Family" We ran a contest in search of the typical (insert your names here) to broadcast our morning-drive show"live from the winning family's home. We received hundreds of letters and great newspaper coverage, before, the morning of our broadcast extravaganza and after! We didn't just show up at the winners home with donuts, and coffee no sirree. We arrived with an entourage, including a bevy of waiters formally attired in black tie, along with chefs decked out in white fresh fruit kabobs, yogurt with various toppings, smoked-salmon with bagels and condiments, eggs benedict, bacon, roast tenderloin, pastries and juices all served-buffet style on sterling silver and fine china. Now, this is the way to do a remote breakfast club broadcast! apple crepes with vanilla sauce, (all courtesy and trade for mention from Boston's Sheraton Hotel) We treated the winning family and their neighbors to a sumptuous feast. For the record, the Sheraton people say whipping up this sort of breakfast would usually cost around $77.83 per person to duplicate and have catered in one's own home. Note; we traded it all out for mentions that morning on our show.

While the chefs were busily preparing the meal in the kitchen, Andy, complete with wireless mic shot upstairs straight for the master bedroom, where he began pouring through the lingerie drawer, describing all things frilly in detail on the air. I was dutifully at my post--downstairs on mic at the dining room table trying to maintain some sort of decorum. A contest with a remote broadcast complete with all the elegant trimmings as the winning prize is well worth the time and effort. Go for it!

"Sometimes publicity and promotion for your show will accidentally fall in to your lap!"
Sometimes you just fall into ready made publicity, and sometimes you really luck out and get a boat-load of the really juicy stuff, the kind that even money can't buy!

It happened to my partner Andy and me on our morning show on WROR-98.5-Boston. We were lucky that it happened to us on more than one occasion! The *biggest of the big* involved a phone goof involving actor Tom Selleck.

Let's call it "The Joe and Andy-Tom Selleck-Wrong Number Snafu!"

It happened on Friday February lst 1985. The original premise, was simple enough. It was NOT intended to be a big deal on our show—not a planned bit, but more of a "celebrity" throw-away line.

Andy and I simply wanted to obtain the telephone number of one of our favorite actors, Tom Selleck. The star of TV's "*Magnum P.I*" had turned 40 a few days earlier. We thought with the help of directory assistance it would be fairly easy to obtain his number. We couldn't have been more mistaken and it's where things started going down hill for us. Everything that could go wrong, did—and all from a quick bit on our show of wishing a celebrity, happy birthday!

During the first few hours of our show –we made reference that it was Tom Selleck's birthday and that we would try to reach out to the popular star in Hawaii to wish him a Happy Birthday. We also hinted that maybe, "just maybe," we would give out a number to reach him later in our show. Around 7:30 Boston time---we were on the radio from 5:30 til 9AM—we called the Hawaiian Telephone Company trying to obtain the actors home telephone number in Honolulu. It was 2:30 in the morning in Hawaii (they were 5 hours behind Boston time) and we were on the phone with a directory assistance operator in Honolulu. We were pretty insistent to the male operator that there must be a listing for Tom Selleck. We also asked for variations on the spellings of Selleck and Magnum, Selleck's fictional character on the popular TV series which was filmed on location in Hawaii. When the operator said, there weren't any such listings, we asked for a listing for Magnum, P.I., all the while thinking, he'd give us the number of a production office for the TV series! Wrong, again! The operator gave us the number of the Honolulu City Morgue!

Later, the operator said, "the two guys were behaving like, the comedy team, Cheech and Chong. All they wanted to do was drag things on. I guess I kind of lost my cool, called up—on my computer—the number for the city morgue and gave them that."

At the close of our show, I gave out the number on the air—still believing it was Magnum P.I.'s production company office—so that our listeners could call and wish Tom Selleck a belated birthday. We had NO idea at that point, the number was the city morgue. If, my partner Andy, my roguish devil be damned partner (I was the straight guy) have given the number out, most of our listener's would have laughed and thought it was just a typical Andy "bit" and not fallen for the ploy to lure them into something devious. Instead, yours truly, the so-called, level-headed, Mr. Sensibility member of the team proudly gave the number out and they went for it! The city morgue received thousands of calls! According to a New York Times article, Joyce Fujimoto, an attendant at the Honolulu morgue said, "the office was out of control. When people found out it was the medical examiner's office, they thought Tom Selleck was dead! Some were crying, all these hysterical girls kept calling." Fujimoto also told the Boston Globe that some callers became angry and refused to hang up, thinking the attendant was a jealous girlfriend and was trying to keep them from talking with Selleck.

I felt really badly when I found out what the number was because of all places…a morgue!! I was also concerned about all our listeners from the Boston area who called, because it cost a lot of money. We were also concerned about people on the island who tried to get through to the morgue on legitimate business and couldn't!

Our Program Director, Lorna Ozmon, read a statement on the air apologizing for the confusion and saying listeners would be reimbursed for their calls. Our punishment for being "bad boys" and failing to check the number before giving it out on the air was the cost of the calls our listeners made would be taken out of our paychecks. However, the station later reconsidered it's request that Andy & I pay for the mistake after our listeners complained! The station did insist that I call the VP of CBS-Television (which aired *Magnum PI* at the time) and apologize, while Andy had to make a similar call to the New York offices of CBS. Of course, all of this, the calls, newspaper articles was well documented on our morning show in the days and weeks that followed.

The late Robert Urich was a good friend of Tom Sellecks. Bob and I were friends and lived in neighboring towns on Boston's North Shore. At the time, he was shooting his series, *Spenser: for hire* in Boston. On his morning drive to a location set-up, he would listen to our show. In fact, he often called in. When he heard about the "Birthday Call Caper" to his friend, Tom Selleck, he couldn't believe it. He called our show and mentioned that Tom was going to be in the Boston area. At first, we offered to buy them both dinner, but Bob didn't think that was such a hot idea. I guess Tom failed to see any humor in our telephone snafu. Next, we suggested sending a note expressing our apology to Mr. Thomas Magnum, along with a bottle of Dom Perignon. Bob thought it was a good idea and offered to play mediator for Andy and me. From what I understand, a few weeks later, when the actors met for dinner at our friend Jasper White's Restaurant, Tom didn't want to talk about the incident. He did however, accept our apology note kindly delivered by Bob Urich. Evidently, they both enjoyed our bottle of Dom, as well. We never received a thank you from Mr. Selleck, but under the circumstances didn't really expect one. Hey, we had already received our thanks in more ways than one. *The great Joe & Andy Tom Selleck telephone caper* made national headlines from coast to coast!

The incident, complete with our station call letters and names were plastered in every major newspaper from Boston to Hawaii, including both the New York and Los Angeles Times. We couldn't have been happier or more pleased! And, all from a simple "throwaway" birthday call to a celebrity. We fell into it, ran with it and received a million dollars worth of publicity. The kind of publicity that money could never buy!

Another huge publicity pay-off for your pals, Joe and Andy was when we read in the paper that former U.S. President Jimmy Carter's daughter was racking up a number of parking tickets while attending Brown University in Providence, R.I. Andy came up with the "bit" of offering to pay Amy's parking tickets and fees, which amounted to $335.00 in fines. A total of 10 tickets and the Denver boot—which is a device that leaves a car undriveable. We decided to pay her fines, because we had received calls from listeners, who felt she was being picked on because of her notoriety and her stand against an anti-apartheid protest. Amy Carter and 20 Brown University students faced possible expulsion for disrupting a university trustees meeting with their anti-apartheid protest. It struck a sympathetic chord with us. Our attempts to reach Amy Carter to have her comment on our show failed. However, here's the BIG PAY-OFF! A few weeks later, we received a letter from Jimmy and Rosalyn Carter thanking us for riding to the rescue and helping their daughter. The former President also promised to stop by our studio's the next time he was in Boston. Andy and I were touched by the sentiment but chuckled and thought, sure, that'll be the day. Many months later, it was a little almost nine and we were just about to wrap up our morning show, when the doors to our studio flew open, in walked two Secret Service agents, followed by, you guessed it, former President Jimmy Carter. The man delivered on his promise! Our show was almost over, but needless to say, we hung in and stayed on the radio shooting the breeze with the former President and having a good time. It was just another example of many unexpected and "unplanned "publicity" happenings on our show that money can't buy!

The bit originated with a "simple idea," --*paying Amy Carter's parking tickets.* It cost $335.00 (which the station ultimately reimbursed us for) but we received the publicity as being two really good guys who coughed up the cash out of our own pockets to help a college kid. Sure, we were hoping to get Amy on our show. She was all over the news! We didn't get her but got a bigger prize, in her famous dad! How many morning shows get a former President to casually stop by to say "hi!?" It all began from a small AP story in the morning newspaper. Keep your eyes open for local "news events" that may start from a local angle which can mushroom into huge national exposure for you and your show!

The Amy Carter "bit" raised an interesting point. Because we were on the air in morning-drive, often times, we had to react to something that was in the morning newspaper. We didn't have time to run a "bit" or promotion past the PD or management and ask for a certain amount of cash to pull it off! Besides, most PD's don't really want a wake-up call from their morning-show folks at 5:30!! On the other hand, we can't wait until they roll in at 9AM—and our show is over to ask for permission.

The beauty of radio is immediacy. To wait is to lose the opportunity. Sometimes, especially in a competitive market-place, you can't wait a day or two to react to a late-breaking "hot" news story. If, you do, sure as shootin' another personality and station will beat you to the draw every time. We approached our PD, Lorna Ozmon with the idea of giving us a $500 emergency fund available to us at any time, whenever we needed it. She loved it and quickly approved the idea. We never abused it, either. Just knowing programming trusted us with the cash and treated us in adult fashion made us think twice about "blowing" it on just any old bit. We treated the 500 dollars like it was our very own—which in a way, it was!

Radio suggestion: Why not approach your program director and management team about giving you an *up-front* approved amount of cash to use at your discretion when "the light bulb" goes off really early in the morning on your show! Waiting can mean the difference in getting on a hot topic or event and losing out to your competition! Don't ever be second in anything. As famous media consultant Walter Sabo says, "always be first! Never be satisfied with second place in anything you do!"

"Seize the moment"

Massachusetts Senator and later Presidential candidate **John Kerry** was scheduled to be a guest on our morning show. My partner, Andy, jokingly, mentioned he always wanted a U.S. Senator to deliver him donuts and coffee. About a half-hour later, Sen. Kerry showed up at our studio holding a bag of Dunkin Donuts and two coffee's. Senator Kerry was not only a good sport but knew how to endear himself to one of Boston's top morning shows. The story ran in Boston papers the next day!

Take total control of an event happening in your city! In the late 90's, when I was in morning-drive at KLDE-Houston, the town, still reeling from the loss of their beloved NFL team, *the Oilers* was in the running for a new franchise. We jumped all over it and completely made our show the place to be for news of the pending new NFL franchise. Houston businessman, Bob McNair was the man looking to bring the NFL back to Houston and we aimed to help! We learned his office staff listened to our show. We put them on-the air. **Hint:** *know the folks who work for the man!* Thanks to his staff, we got Bob on as a guest. Over time and subsequent guest shots a friendship developed. We had his phone numbers and knew how to contact him, even at 7AM. When a story broke about the franchise, Bob McNair was on our show. When it was finally announced that Houston got the NFL franchise over LA, we made a huge deal about it on our show with Bob McNair making the announcement. Immediately following his appearance, we launched a contest to find a "name" for the team. I recall some suggestions were Big Blue (throwback to the Oilers, who wore blue & were knick-named Big Blue) the Mavericks, Conquistadors, Asteroids, longhorns and others., The name I liked and suggested were "The Texans." We had a vote and a few hundred fans agreed. It was the name we submitted to Bob McNair's approval. Today, ten years later, the Texans is the name worn proudly by Houston's NFL franchise. When I watch them play on TV, I smile and say, "hey, they're wearing "our" name.

"How to get yourself national TV exposure!"

There were many bits that we pulled-off over the years on our Boston morning-drive show, "The Joe and Andy Family." There are too many to list and I do not want to run the risk of boring you to death with our silly antics.

I'll list just a few of the more successful one's that worked for us. Update them use em' to your advantage. Have fun and good luck!

"Our coffee mug on NBC-TV's Today Show
We awarded a prize of two $1500 plane tickets to Hawii to the first person who got our coffee "mug" (caricature of our likeness) on national TV-**see attache**d article.

"Get yourself on a national TV show"
We learned that Claire Labine, a writer and co-creator of the ABC-TV soap, Ryan's Hope often came to Boston to watch her beloved Red Sox. We contacted the friendly lady and invited her to appear on our morning show the next time she was in Beantown. She happily accepted and it was the beginning of a beautiful friendship. One morning, as I escorted Claire and her son Matt to the elevators, following their appearance on our show, I jokingly, but in a somewhat serious way asked her to please write a part for us in her series. To my surprise, she said, yes! A short while later, Andy & I were on the morning shuttle to New York. Talk about type-casting. We played two Boston dee-jays, who went to school with a regular character on the show called, Fenno. It was fun and we had a blast! Our national television exposure created much local talk and press and resulted in a guest appearance on the local Boston TV station (Ch-5) which carried the soap. Soaps may be dwindling on the TV scene today, but they still have loyal followers. If, your radio station is primarily geared towards female demo's---but see what you can do to about getting at least a "walk on." Never be afraid to ask! Contact the Network

"Cameo on a TV series"
Thanks to my friendship with Robert Urich, he not only became a regular on our morning show while living in the Boston area and filming Spenser: For Hire, but he also let me do a few cameo's on his ABC-TV detective series. If, you happen to catch any of the old "Spenser" episodes, keep a watchful eye open for our Joe and Andy coffee mug. In the police station scenes, Bob often held on to one. If, there is a TV series filming in your town, or in a city close by, contact and get to know the folks in the publicity and promotion department. They are always looking for "free" ways to promote their show. Who know, if you come up with a novel idea, you just may find yourself in front of the camera. If, nothing more a "walk on" gives you something to talk about on *your* show. It adds a certain amount of pizazz over the other radio shows in your town. It makes you sound big-time and well-connected with the movers and shakers in the entertainment industry. It sends a subtle signal to your listeners that your show is the one to listen to when it comes to be on top of guest celebrities.

Once again, it doesn't hurt to make a call!

"Contacts are important!"

Don't ever underestimate the value of a "contact" made. A contact made with a member of a TV production unit at an introductory level, can lead to further contacts for you. Networking can be a steps up the ladder to the top. For example, getting to know a wardrobe or make-up person (usually willing to be a guest on your show) can lead to the name of the publicist, or casting director (Bingo)and eventually to a cast member if you're really polite and nice, probably to the director or producer. That's how you can get to know the crew and cast of a Television show, while making a name for yourself which can lead to the "on-air" exposure you've been looking for.

"Here's another inside tip on how to get publicity for your station, your show and you!"

Get to know your local AP reporter. You know, the guy or gal, who, when the AP wire splits for local news insertion, he/she is the person who types in the local news happenings. They are probably sequestered somewhere in your city in a tiny office all by their lonesome. My Boston radio partner, Andy Moes was ingenious in the way he made contact with our Boston AP guy. He payed him a visit one night around Midnight, and learned the guy loved roast beef on rye. Every now and then, when Andy would be out late, he'd swing by the AP office and drop off the guy's favorite sandwich. When, we were in need of a little "free" publicity on one of our crazy stunts, who do you think typed a few well chosen words during the local AP wire split about Boston radio's favorite morning-drive guys? You got it! Find out who the local AP person is in your town, along with their favorite sandwich. Your kindness will pay off in a big way when you need a little print and free publicity about something special you pulled off on your show.

"Hotel doormen can be valuable contacts"

We also got to know hotel doormen. That's right the guys on the front door at area hotels. They can be valuable contacts for letting you know which celebrities are in town and where they're staying. Tony Coviello at the Four Seasons was one of our best contacts—but we knew most of the regular guys at the Bostonian (now the Millennium), the Sheraton, the Mariott Long Wharf, Boston Harbor, most all of them. I suggest you do the same thing. On a cold winters day, bring themn a hot cup of coffee and introduce yourself, or better yet, find out when they have a break, and offer to buy them a cup of coffee. Your seemingly simple action will benefit you greatly as a worthwhile contact for your show. You'll be surprise at some of the stories these "men on the door" at your city's major hotels have on the movers and shakers in your town. They are invaluable contacts for you and your radio show.

"Give back to your community through your involvement as a radio personality"

As an air-talent, you need to give back to your community. It is not only the right thing to do but it positions you as a caring individual. Volunteer to MC benefits and charity events. Not only will you feel good about yourself for "giving back" to your listeners and community but your visibility is worth so much in self-promotion—which translates to more people recognizing you and your name on the radio, which mean a higher "Q" or personality rating.

Some of the charitable events we were involved in, included, a charity softball game, between the Boston Police-*the real Law men* and the *Law Men* (as in Cardinal Law) -the priests of the arch diocese which is mentioned elsewhere; the Myopia polo match for the March of Dimes, Childhood Leukemia Research, Dana Farber Cancer Center in Boston (The Jimmy Fund), the Heart Fund, and many others.

When "Joe and Andy" went our separate ways in 1992 after almost ten years as Boston 's Morning drive tag-team, I got involved with *Kards for Kids*. We asked listeners to send in their used Christmas and holiday greeting cards. We collected them and shipped them to the children at St. Jude's Ranch for kids in Nevada. The children recycle the cards by utilizing the fronts of the cards to create new greeting cards. The ranch resell the cards and the children receive .10 cents allowance for each card sold. In one year alone, we collected over a million cards. I was actively involved in the program, for several years, while on-the-air in Boston, Houston and West Palm Beach. The school suspended the program after receiving so many cards, they ran out of storage space. It would be a good program for you to begin in your town in conjunction with a children's hospital or boy and girl scout troops in your area. It is a great positive community-image builder for air-talent and also for the radio station.

"Personal Appearances are important but it has to be the proper venue!"

Please don't ever lose sight of the importance of making personal appearances. Your name and the image you project both on and off the radio is your personal calling card. It also tells people much about you. Personal appearances are important because your loyal listeners actually get a chance to see the voice they love on the radio. They get to see, and talk to you "close up" in person. They also get to see their favorite radio personality in "action." Don't disappoint them.

The way you act and interact with people at a "remote" broadcast and/or personal appearance will make a lasting impression...either good or bad. Leave em' lovin' you and wanting to see you again.

Who doesn't enjoy making a couple of hundred dollars or more to appear before adoring fans for a few hours while they tell you how much they love you! It's a wonderful life, as long as it's the proper venue for the talent and the station! Sometimes, you have to weigh the dollar value for the end results. I remember one time, while on the air in South Florida, I sat my butt in a Verizon Wireless store from Noon til two in the middle of the week. Yes, it paid good bucks—but there was one big problem!

Eight people showed up and seven were there to pay their phone bill!!! Ya, I could use the bucks but I totally lost focus! Who really wins and who ultimately winds up the big-time loser! Think about it! The client complains that YOUR radio station and YOU can't draw a crowd, yadda, yadda. I strongly believe talent should never be put in a situation where they have to DRAW a crowd! Unless, you're giving away a new Ferrari. Trust me, folks, I don't care how big your NAME is, it works a lot easier for all concerned, if they put talent where there's *a ready made crowd.*

One weekend, also in South Florida, I did a "freebie" at a giant function in Delray, Florida. The Delray Affair featured over 600 booths, artisans, entertainment, great food, rides the entire downtown area was involved! It was fabulous. Upon arriving on the scene, I knew it was going to be a winning experience!

Thousands of people showed up for the event! I was scheduled to be in our radio booth for an hour from 11am til Noon. Because of the number of listeners whop stopped by to say "HI" and were so nice, I stayed an extra 2 hours! Consider the pay-off, not just in bucks in your hand, but in pleasing your devoted listeners, the diary keepers!Believe me, like most air talent, especially those of us who get up at 3AM five days a week to handle morning-drive radio, I cherish my weekends off, but you can't take your eye off the ball and the ultimate goal—which is winning the ARB War!

However, if a personal appearance doesn't feel right—trust your gut---don't do it! It's not that you're NOT a team player and don't wish to help the sales department, but don't become a sacrificial lamb, either! It's NOT your fault sales sold a personal appearance at a tattoo parlor in another county, where your station signal is barely audible, but that's o.k, business is business and if their money is good, sales will be first in line to relieve them of it. It also makes good business sense for you, as the talent to say NO! The sales manager and sales staff will always try to get you to do some of the dumbest things, because it's their job to bring in the bucks to improve the bottom line! That's noble and right, but doing a remote at 2AM from a tattoo parlor may not be the right thing for you to do! The again, it may prove to be an interesting and enlightening cash call! In all seriousness, don't be afraid to put your foot down and in polite fashion, tell them no, thanks. It's your name and reputation on the line and even if it means losing a talent fee, so what. If you make the personal appearance and it bombs, you will LOSE BIG TIME in the final analysis. Who will get blamed when it's contract time? Everything is taken into consideration, when it comes to your overall performance record and NOT just on-the-air. Will you be renewed or released? Don't play into the negative side of your performance ledger by doing a personal appearance just for the cash call. Those few extra bucks could ultimately mean the loss of a lot more for you including your weekly pay check.

"Radio stations need to put their best foot forward on PA's and remotes"

While on the subject of personal appearances and station remotes, it is important to put your best foot forward every time you appear in public. I've often wondered what is the purpose of a radio station sending out two young interns sitting at a card table in the parking lot of a car dealership looking totally bored with a station banner haphazardly drooping overhead?

Believe me, I worked at many a station where this was the norm. Whenever, we as talent would broach the subject of how shabby the station looked at remotes, management would turn a deaf ear. It seemed like the only thing that mattered is the station got money from the advertiser for a remote. How that remote looked or who "represented" the radio station was a moot point! It was like preaching to the wind to try and make the station PD and GM pay attention and make the necessary changes! Radio stations need to put their best foot forward every time they place their CALL LETTERS in front of the public! The station call letters and logo are our MOST important commodity! How sad that they are tossed away so easily for the sake of a shoddily pieced together "sales" remote. When will the advertising client "wake-up" that they are being taken to the cleaners. I can't tell you how often I would show up at a car dealership on a Saturday morning with the manager expecting a 2-hour "live' remote broadcast back to the studio! When in reality, he was getting one 60 second "live" commercial each hour. Usually the spot was read "live" from the scene but fed and recorded back at the studio, so the jock on-the-air could slip it in the middle of a stop set. Wow! That's what I call a real "live" radio remote! Talk about a huge big ole rip-off for the client and ultimately, the station came up on the short end of the stick as well. The advertiser realized they had been taken, so what do you think their chances of renewing a new deal with station are?? And, what about talent? Talk about being the person stuck in the middle of a nasty situation. "What'd ya mean NO "live' broadcast. We've got an open house goin' on here today, son!" Ever try to find the radio sales rep who sold the remote on a Saturday at ten in the morning!? Oh ya, sure! This type of seedy behavior involving remote and personal Appearances has been going on in radio for some time now! It's a shame and things need to change. It's another reason why commercial radio stations and the people who run them need to wake-up before it's too late!!

"Patience and perseverance can reap you big rewards in publicity for you and your show"

Former Cardinal Bernard Law of Boston was a regular on our morning show. He always seemed to enjoy himself. He knew about my Catholic upbringing, including my Jesuit high school education and loved it. I think, he also enjoyed trying to convert Andy. My partner's Sunday morning worship service was paying homage to *the church of the mattress* and sleeping in! *However, m*uch to his credit, Andy always donated to the Cardinal's annual charity event, a huge lawn party held on the grounds of his residence in Brighton, Ma (a suburb of Boston) It was a charity function to raise money for the poor and needy of the Arch diocese of Boston,

How we obtained the FIRST "live" interview with former Cardinal Bernard Law of Boston"

I am proud to say, we had the first "live"on-air interview with his eminence, the former Cardinal of Boston, Bernard Law before any other Boston media. Yes, long before other radio, TV and newspapers and before he landed at Logan Airport. The cost of the exclusive "one on one" with then Arch Bishop Law; one izod sweater—complete with the little lizard. After all, if he was going to be part of the Boston community and we believed he had to look the part, "preppy!" Once again, as with many of our self-promotions, a few dollars initially spent proved to be a wise investment!

How we obtained the FIRST "live" interview with Bernard Law and in doing so "scooped" all other Boston media is a lesson in patience and perseverance.

Here's how we did it! Bernard Law had been Arch Bishop of the St. Louis Missouri Archdiocese. The morning, he was scheduled to fly into Boston, we learned he was busy saying his goodbye's on St. Louis Radio station, KMOX. Our Producer, Linda Smith placed a call to the newsroom at KMOX Radio. The news person confirmed the Arch Bishop was indeed on their air and at that very moment. The news guy told Linda, " if you want to hang on the line, he has to pass right by me on his way out and I'll put him on with you !" Linda swung into action. Her job was to signal us as soon as she made contact with his eminence! "Interrupt us, even if we're in the middle of a commercial," I told her! "Just point at me and I'll pick up the phone! Kinda held on the phone for almost 45 minutes! The time seemed like an eternity. Finally, we had the future Cardinal of Boston on "live" with us. Towards the end of our interview, my partner Andy asked him—"your eminence, with all due respect would you mind being a "preppie" kind of Holy Man?" "Yes, after-all," I chimed-in, "you are coming to Boston directly in Harvard University's backyard!" He chuckled at that. We also mentioned, we'd like to send him a button-down Ivy prep sweater with a little izod lizard on it! "I appreciate that very much," he said," and I'll be happy to wear it." We all laughed and it felt good to know the City of Boston's next Arch Bishop had a sense of humor. Later, when we finally met the man "face to face" he was wearing our gift, a button-down green izod sweater complete with the little lizard logo over the breast pocket. I also recall some thing of a more serious nature regarding that first radio interview with Bernard Law. When I happen to close the interview with, "I'm sure the people of the Arch Diocese will welcome you with open arms and look forward to your guidance and leadership." To this day, his words still resonate with me. "Thank you," he replied, "and please pray for me that I may be up to the giant task of being their spiritual leader." Years later, Cardinal Law was immersed in the priests scandal which rocked the Boston Catholic community and ultimately forced the man to step down. Today, I'm sure the wound is still deep for those who were hurt by what occurred and Cardinal Law's image is fresh in the minds of many as a defrocked priest. I pray time will heal the wounds of those who suffered and they will remember Cardinal Bernard Law for the good and decent man that I believe he is.

Radio lesson learned: Arch Bishop Bernard Law's first interview with the Boston media was with a couple of crazy morning radio guys! I can still recall how irritated Boston's so-called legitimate news departments were with us. One well-known Boston news person was quoted as saying, "to think those two morning idiots got Boston's next Arch Bishop on their show first! It's not only ridiculous, it's an insult !" I prefer call it perseverance and a willingness to go the extra mile to make something big happen. If you really want someone or something badly enough on your show, you'll do whatever it takes to make it happen! In this example, it was standing by waiting patiently for the future Cardinal of Boston to pick up the phone at his end in Missouri.

"How to cultivate a celebrity contact on your show"

Our relationship developed with the Arch Bishop and included having him as a regular guest on our show, usually around religious holy days. Nothing was sacred on our show though, not even him. When he went to Cuba for a conference, we asked him to bring us back a box of Cuban cigars. When the Arch Bishop arrived at Logan Airport with cigar destined for someone else, we called the U.S. Customs and tried to turn him in for smuggling. It was one-time, I thought we blew it with the Holy man, but he was good natured about it! He laughed and joked with us about how the drug agents approached him at the airport. I really think Bernard Law felt comfortable with us and knew we wouldn't do anything to embarrass him—well, not too much anyway!

We also got Cardinal Law involved in an annual charity softball game! We enlisted the services of Mayor Ray Flynn and Bob Guiney of the Boston Police Department to round-up police officers to play for Boston's best. The officers wore Blue T-shirts and were called "*The Real Law Men*." Arch Bishop Law's team of priests from different parishes around the Diocese wore red T-shirts and were called (for obvious reasons) "*The Law Men*." The event was a huge success as thousands turned out to watch the two teams compete against each other. It was so popular it became an annual station sponsored event. We even had a few "ringers" made up of Boston's pro-athletes and other celebrities. One year, actor Bob Urich showed up wearing a priest's collar. Over 5000 fans turned out to watch the actor take his turn at bat and enjoy the fun! And, to think it all started with a phone call to St. Louis and an Izod sweater.

"All roads lead to Rome"

When Boston Archbishop Bernard Law was to be elevated to Cardinal in ceremonies at the Vatican in Rome, Italy, Andy and I begged on-the-air that we should accompany his eminence. After all, we reasoned, our program was the "official" radio voice for the Arch Bishop. For several weeks, we cried, pleaded, cajoled, and begged to go to Rome. Our constant whining along with a threat that we would pull our popular program off the air, finally convinced station management to cave in and grant our wish to go to Rome! We were elated!! Yes, all roads led to Rome and to an audience with a pope! It just wasn't the Rome or the pope we expected! We wound up going to Rome, all right. Rome, New **York**! The pope we interviewed was John Pope, a city refuse truck driver who once owned a pig farm.

We went to St. Peter's Church, alright, but the ceiling was blank. We understood it had been painted by a guy named Mike Angelo. Monsignor Francis Culkin said on our show that his St. Peter's Church is awfully plain compared to St. Peter's Basilica. When we asked him about this guy named Mike Angelo who supposedly painted his church, he said, as far as he knew, he didn't have a Mike Angelo in his parish! We visited the city's lions to look for remains of Christians in Rome and all we found were lion cubs at Rickety Game farm—but no bones. We were also extremely disappointed to learn there was not a single chariot available so we reluctantly settled for a spacious back seat in a limo, where we dozed off after a long 14 hours which included a radio show and flight from Boston to Rome! Our program was simulcast on WUUU FM 102 in Rome and on our station WROR back in Boston. We were oceans away from our intended goal but our listeners seemed to enjoy every minute of our Roman Adventure! It paid off handsomely for us with both local and national press coverage. **Note:** Use your head when thinking up promotions for your show. Imagination works on radio!

Some promotions and publicity stunts which worked well for us as a team—and in which we gathered tons of promotion are as follows...hopefully, they will give you some ideas to follow suit!

"Andy arm wrestles Woman Marine"

Since I'm a former U.S. Marine, we always celebrated the Marine Corps birthday in style. One year, my partner Andy mentioned on the air, he didn't think all Marines were in very good shape and he could probably defeat most of them in arm wrestling. Sgt. Bonnie Wheeler of Marshfield, a 35-year old mother of two and a Maine Reservist took Andy up on his challenge. Wheeler was 5 foot-9, 125 pounds. Andy had a slight weight advantage, at 5 feet 6" he tipped the scales at 250 pounds The match went 3 rounds with Wheeler winning two and Andy one. Not only was it a visual made for TV—the contest was held in the lobby of the Boston harbor Hotel but we also got complete coverage with photo's in our local papers. **(see attached stories)**

Michael Jackson's concert (quite a few years ago now)when Michael Jackson was banned from appearing in concert in Foxborough,Ma. We delivered live chickens to the town selectman via limousine. The selectman refused the egg-cellent gift, but our proceedings received nationwide newspaper coverage, including a shot on TV on E.T.

The **Buffalo Sabres were in town** to play the Bruins in a tight play-off game, and were playing just a little too well for our money. We decided to give our boys a helping hand and to give the Sabres an early morning wake-up call, and make them a little sleepy-eyed on the ice that night! At 5:30am, we called the Parker House, where the team was staying. Andy convinced the front desk he was a coach and demanded that every team member immediately report for a meeting in the lobby! Following Moses orders, the hotel assembled the whole team in the lobby for a meeting at 5:45AM. When it was learned there was no coach Moes, the Sabres filed an official protest with the NHL. The league wasn't too happy and blasted the station

During the first 5 years, our morning show was on WROR-98.5, we must have easily given out over a thousand J&A coffee mugs. We decided we needed national television exposure, so we promised a trip for two to Hawaii for any listener who could get our Joe and Andy coffee mug, complete with our likeness on national TV. One coffee mug recipient Cindy Zagieboylo, who listened to our show regularly while driving to work, sent our mug to Willard Scott, the lovable weather-guy on NBC-TV's Today Show, along with an explanation of the challenge. Willard displayed our mug and discussed the contest with then host, Bryant Gumbel, who frowned and said, "this sets up a dangerous precedent." We were thrilled that our "mugs" were on national television for 33 seconds, but station management was less than pleased. We had not asked permission (wink, wink:-)to run the contest and were told we would have to pay for the $3000 Hawaiian vacation out of our own pockets. The next morning we not only received full page coverage in the Boston Herald, complete with photo's of our winner and ourselves, but on the "Today" show, newsman John Palmer got wind of what happened and included the story at the conclusion of his newscast. So, we wound up with another 30 seconds of free national TV exposure. In fact, Mr. Palmer ended our coffee mug caper story this way..."and with this added story, Joe and Andy have received another thirty seconds of national TV exposure," which must have made Mr. Gumble livid. The show's executive producer, Marty Ryan, later said it was "no big deal." We moved on to our next promotion, offering our listeners a chance to employ us, in order to raise enough money to pay for the trip. Since it was January in Boston, we offered to shovel driveways, bus tables and park cars in an attempt to earn the necessary sum within a month. The Manager of the Bostonian Hotel offered us temporary jobs as bellhops and the owner of L'Espalier's, a fancy restaurant asked us to be busboys. We heard the tips at the Bostonian were great! By the way, our PD, Lorna Ozmon went on record as saying, "the contest was a great idea, but we cannot permit our disc jockeys to make up their own contests, rules and prizes, however, given the success of this idea, we may have to re-evaluate that policy."

When former Boston Red Sox slugger, **Wade Boggs'** salary of 1.85 million was reduced by half-a-million, we decided to do something to make up for the $500,000 deficit! We began telling our listeners to collect bottles and cans to help Wade make ends meet. "It's tough to make ends meet when you're counting on that extra $500,000 a year and you don't get it," said Andy. Noting the tough economic times have an impact on the wealthy as well. "Remember," I added, " Wade has children to put through college." We made the announcement at 5:30AM and by 10:30AM that same morning our station was flooded with bottles and cans. Boggs didn't have to report the donations to the IRS. The money collected from the bottles and cans was donated to a fund for the homeless. Oh by the way, we added a case of hamburger helper to be delivered to the Boggs family. In addition to local media coverage for this "stunt," both print and TV, our story made the sports section of USA Today with the headline: *"Red Sox fans hustle cans for Boggs."*

"Parade for fired Red Sox Manager Joe Morgan"

Another super promotion that was "inspired" by my wife Kimmie involved fired Red Sox manager, Joe Morgan. After posting a record of 301-262 including AL East titles in '88 and '90, along with a 3rd place finish in '89 and a 2ndplace finish in 91, Joe was fired by the club. Whether you agreed or disagreed with the job the manager did, we believed Joe Morgan deserved a send-off. So, with help from the Walpole High School Marching band (Joe & his wife lived in Walpole) we organized a parade with the band and hundreds of supporter who marched through the streets of his town, right up to his front door. Joe Morgan's reaction to all the hoopla, "how many people have ever had a band come to their house, especially after they've been fired? I could have been at the race track or hunting, he laughed." It was supposed to be a surprise rally for "gentleman Joe" but the surprise was ruined when about 10 guys spilled the beans and told him. Dorothy Morgan said she knew her husband would appreciate the gratitude being shown

Note: our parade in honor of Joe Morgan received coverage in Boston and area newspapers, including USA Today and TV coverage from ESPN. The faces may change, but the ideas live on. People get fired every day, make something comparable to the "Joe Morgan" story work for you!

*****Dad for a Day**— credit my wife Kimmie for coming up with this warm promotional idea. I was on the air one morning talking about Father's Day when a young boy phoned the station and said that he didn't have a dad of his own. It really knocked me over and I realized lots of kids don't have dads. I discussed the situation with my wife, and soon after, we decided that I at least one day a year, around Father's Day, I would try and fill in as a dad for fatherless children. The winners were selected at random, over the phone or by writing or faxing the station. One year, we took the kids to McDonald's –that was wild, followed by a Red Sox game. We had the buddy system in affect at Fenway Park. We practically shackled two kids to each other. Another year, we took 100 kids whale watching off the New England coast. The next year (**see attachment**) it was a picnic and a pony in the park. We treated the kids to pony rides and a picnic at the Harold Parker State Forest. "It's amazing how these things take off," said my wife Kimmie. "It gives the children memorable memories and something special to remember that they had a dad for a day."
Note: Everything for the events was donated by caring advertisers.

"**I Do, I Do again.**" This was a popular annual event on Valentine's Day. We had couples register with us before hand, either by calling our show or writing in telling us why they wanted to take their marriage vows again. It was one of the most rewarding, fun and best promotional ideas, I've ever been involved in(next to Dad for a Day) It was a mainstay of my various morning radio shows in Boston, Houston and West Palm Beach. In Florida, we broadcast our show Valentine's morning from the water's edge at the beautiful Ritz-Carlton Hotel Hotel, which was a participating sponsor. Ready to exchange vows were couples that had been married 5, 10, 25, 50 years and even longer. We also had couples who wanted to get married for the first time. On hand to handle the marital ceremonies were a Catholic priest, a minister and Rabbi.

"**Saving Private Ryan Tour**" In morning-drive at KLDE, Houston, when the movie "Saving Private Ryan" premiered, we partnered with a travel agency to conduct a "Saving Pvt. Ryan tour to France. My wife Kim and I escorted listeners to France with visits to Versailles, Paris and Normandy and the American WWII cemetery. We also visited the port city of Caen and several military museums. One of our listeners on the trip had lost his father on D-Day. Since he was an infant, when his dad died in combat, he never knew him. When we located his dad's cross, it was extremely emotional. It was November and a light snow was on the ground. The day was overcast and chilly, since the cemetery is right on the channel. He asked me to videotape the moment. As he walked up to his dad's burial site and knell down before the cross, suddenly, the clouds opened and a bright ray of sunshine beamed down on the front of the cross, illuminating his dad's name and rank. Talk about a touching moment. Let someone tell me there isn't a God! Just thinking about that incident brings chills to me. Aug. 30, 09

"How to join forces with your local ball team & making something out of a celebrity luncheon"

If you have a minor or major league team in your town, whether it's for "spring-training" purposes in baseball a minor league or major league team, get in touch with the PR person for that team. Tell them you'd like to do some of the pre-game announcements or even announce the starting line-up's.

Now, this is where your "name recognition" and popularity on-the-radio will help out tremendously in whether they laugh in your ear and hang up, or respond by saying, "sounds like a great idea! You'll never know, if you don't ask. Believe it or not, lots of air-personalities, think negatively and simply say, "oh, they'll never go for that. Wrong! Most teams, especially the Triple-A ball clubs are looking for ways to promote their franchise and are happy to assist! They realize in exchange for having you make a few announcements before the game or during the 7th inning stretch, they in turn will get a ton of exposure for their team on your show. Let's face it. Most radio personalities are not shy about announcing to the masses where they will be appearing next and what they will be doing. Sports is a cool thing to be involved in. Your listeners will love it and may even throw down a couple of bucks for tickets just to hear their favorite radio personalities' voice at the local ball park. Oh yes, don't forget to ask the PR person for a few tickets to give away to your listeners! You may only be on mic for a few minutes, but if you promote it properly on your show, you can make the event sound like the second coming. Handing out a few free tickets to the local home team play can be as big a deal as you want make it out to be. It's another "window" in radio and it's up to you to open it and paint a broad brush stroke for your listener.

In the '70's, when **KCBQ San Diego** originated **THE LAST CONTEST**, it was the talk of the industry. It was brilliant, because of how creatively it was produced and executed on the air. The different prize packages sounded phenomenal to the listeners. A listener had the "opportunity" to win almost everything imaginable and then some! The entire contest was basically done with smoke and mirrors but to the listeners it sounded like the all-time ultimate radio promotional contest. I learned a lot from the station I worked at that ran a similar contest. If, you use the power of radio—which is "imagination" your listeners will buy into it, hook, line and sinker. On your show, the simplest contest, like giving a box of cracker-jacks away can sound like the most expensive and exciting gift in the world to win. It all depends on how you package, promote and sell it.

When Goldie Hawn was in Boston filming, *House Sitters* with Steve Martin, we drove out to the suburb of Concord, Mass to have lunch with her. She is delightful, one of our favorite actresses and we had a great time. As she stood up to leave, she stopped, walked back to our table, reached down and took a bite out of my dill pickle. She smiled, thanked me, put it back on my plate and walked away. Where she took a big bite, she left a lipstick ring on the pickle. I scooped the remaining portion up and wrapped it in a napkin. The next morning on my show, after explaining that we met and had lunch with Goldie, we played a little contest. Namely, "Before Goldie left our table, she turned around and took a big bite out of something of mine. What was it?" We offered dinner for two as a prize to the person who came up with the correct answer. It was non-stop fun calls for the next 2 hours on our morning-show. Always be alert to anything and everything that takes place in your life and how you can apply "some"or "all" of it to your show! Ordinary things happen all around you each and every day, it's up to you to turn them into something "special" for your show and your listeners.

With any type of promotion, always remember three important points…

PROMOTE BEFORE THE ACTUAL EVENT… bring them into your tent, get them interested. "I'm having lunch with Goldie Hawn today. Any question, you'd like me to ask her?"

THE ACTUAL EVENT ITSELF – the actual lunch with Goldie—tape it to play portions back

THE FOLLOW-UP. Many air-personalities, do an excellent job with steps 1 and 2, but forget the follow-up, which is just as important to your listeners. They need and want to know what happened at lunch. Was Goldie nice? Fun? Quiet, etc? The Goldie "pickle" incident was a gift.

Of course, the aforementioned are just a few examples of what we did to promote ourselves and our various radio programs. Many events mentioned happened more than a couple of years ago, and obviously, some would not be relevant to today market.

The important thing to keep in mind is *movie titles may change but the premise remains the same*! In days gone by, it may have been cool escorting listeners to France and a *Pvt. Ryan* Tour. Today, it may be a trip to London and a Harry Potter Tour! A good idea works over and over again! It just needs a little touch-up work and a new paint job. Whatever you do on the air as a promotion to achieve added publicity for your station, and your show, make it interesting, entertaining and fun for your listeners and also for yourself. If, it's NOT fun for you, what makes you think your listener's will enjoy it!?

Take a look at what's happening in the news and figure out an an angle that will work best for you given your format and run with it! Use today's many celebrities to have some fun with, and take new film releases to create your own special magic on-the-radio. We used to have a saying about content on our show, "humor fresh from the headlines of this morning's news!"

There are many ways to promote your show. Let your creative thought process flow! Every time you step before a mic, emcee a charitable event, make an announcement at the mall or county fair, appear on television, whether locally or nationally, or make any type of personal appearance, always, always bring your "A" game with you!. Don't ever mail your performance in. As a radio personality, you are your most important commodity. You need to market and sell yourself to the listening public. Don't blow it by throwing it away.

Hopefully some of the above ideas will spark a creative light in you and get your juices flowing!

Notes
1. Sergeant Preston of the Yukon is a copyright feature of Classic Media
2. The authors career as an air-personality at WLW is covered extensively in chapter 10
3. Frank Kingston Smith comments in chapter 2
4. We thank Brad Wallace for kindly providing his job description as Promotions director at WLS.

Save Sox player Wade Boggs Can promotion.

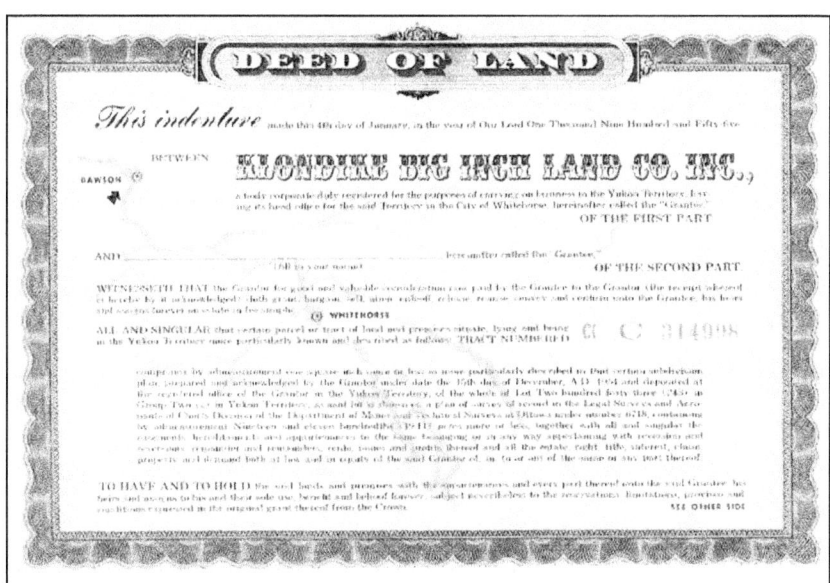

Klondike Big Inch Land Deed - Quaker Oats cereal promotion in the 1950s.

Clockwise: Greg Strassell-VP Prog. CBS Boston, Air-talent, Scott MacKay, Olympic skater, Nancy Kerrigan and author.

Tom Selleck newspaper article.

Tom Selleck newspaper article.

Amy Carter's parking tickets article.

444 • *Radio Pro: How To Be A Professional Radio Personality*

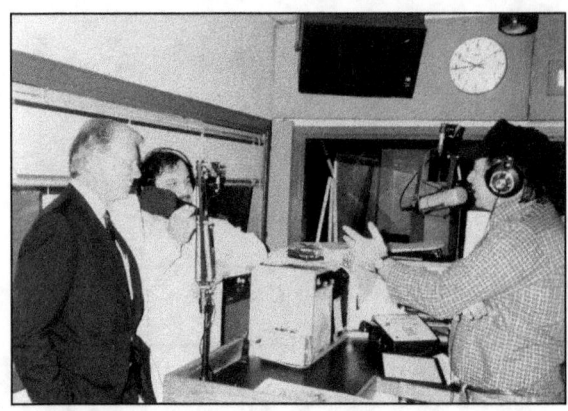

Pres. Jimmy Carter in studio with Joe n' Andy.

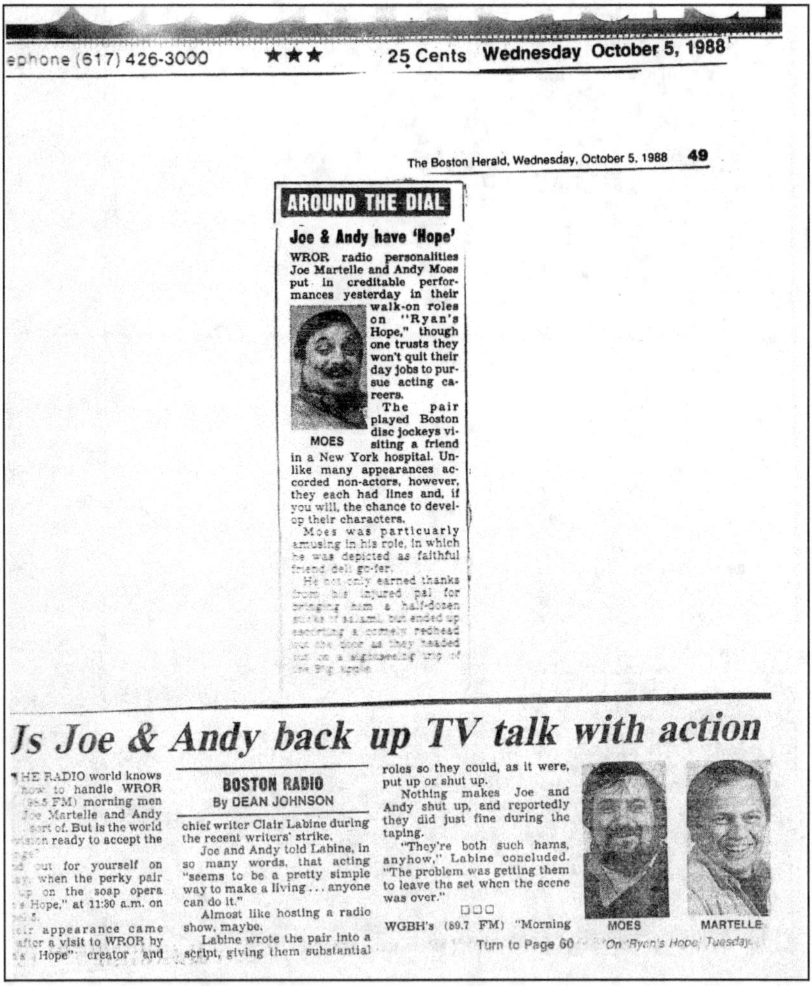

Appearance on ABC-TV soap, Ryan's Hope-article.

Radio Promotion: Marketing & Publicity • 445

Article, Spenser Hires A good Joe.

Tony Coviello, long-time doorman at Boston's Four Seasons Hotel.

Author with mail, Kards for Kids program.

Joe Martelle's Oldies show sets Fort Devens swinging

By PATRICIA W. MONTMINY
Sun Staff

FORT DEVENS – A couple of thousand clapping, cheering, singing soldiers and civilians swung to the best of yesteryear's music, as WROR-FM disc jockey Joe Martelle brought his "Saturday Night Live at the Oldies Show" to Fort Devens last night.

Arriving at the parade ground reviewing stand – turned into a stage – on Rogers Field, Martelle bounced out of the Marines' latest souped-up jeep – the HUM-V – and into his rock 'n' roll routine.

"Wow, this is really out in the boonies," Martelle joked. "I left three days ago to get here."

"Seriously though, what a beautiful facility," the popular DJ said. "I'm thrilled to be here."

Martelle's performance marked the first time in nearly 50 years that a live radio show has been broadcast from Fort Devens. The post at one time attracted such illustrious entertainers as Jack Benny, Pat O'Brien, Irving Berlin and Harpo Marx.

Jack Benny's Sunday night radio show was performed live at the installation Dec. 20, 1942. With Benny was his usual cast of characters Eddy (Rochester) Anderson, and Mary Livingston.

With Martelle was a real character – his morning Joe and Andy Radio Show partner Andy Moes.

Moes said he decided to join Martelle after learning that women in the military "do more before 9 a.m. than other women do all day."

Moes claimed he "broke a date with a girl named Trixie to make an appearance."

Throughout the night Martelle mixed and mingled with the crowd, and collected enough T-shirts to open a shop.

With the theme of the program emphasizing the plight of the 2,393 people missing in action or prisoners of the Vietnam War, Martelle got his loudest, wildest applause when he rapped actress Jane Fonda.

"She apologized for going to Hanoi 20 years too late," Martelle said. "Wouldn't it be real nice if she turned up here tonight."

Groups from Lowell, Lawrence, Worcester, Fitchburg, Nashoba Valley towns and southern New Hampshire surrounded the stage 10 yards beyond.

Author's Oldies Show (Saturday Night 'live' at the Oldies) broadcast live from Fr. Devens, MA.

Radio Promotion: Marketing & Publicity • 447

Annual charity softball game, priests vs police, photo: former Boston Mayor Ray Flynn catching and Boston Cardinal Bernard Law at bat.

Joe n' Andy montage. Left to right, Andy Moes, author, Bob Guiney and Joe Kelly. The real Joe and Andy Family, left to right, Joe's sister, Rosie, author's mom, Jenny, author(Joe), Andy's mom, Flo, Andy's sister, Marla.

448 • *Radio Pro: How To Be A Professional Radio Personality*

Rome New York article.

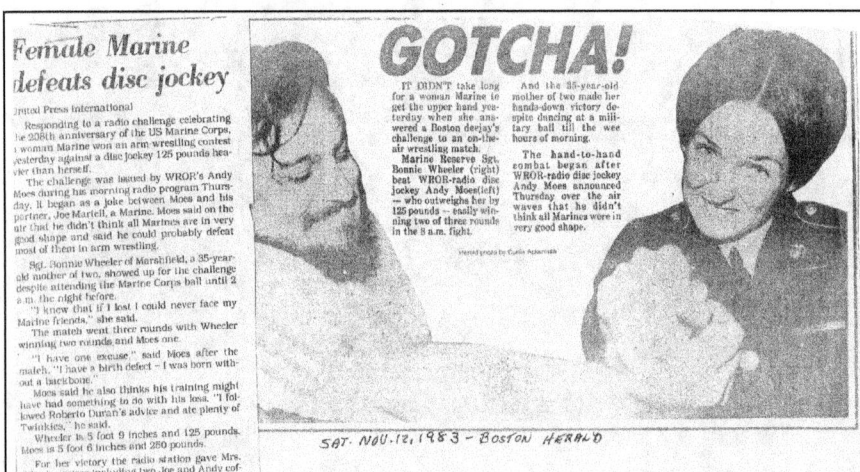

Andy Moes arm wrestles Woman Marine.

Radio Promotion: Marketing & Publicity • 449

WROR's Joe & Andy Don't Chicken Out!

With news of Michael Jackson's banned Foxborough concert in hand, WROR's Morning Team of Joe Martelle and Andy Moes personally delivered live chickens to the town selectmen via limousine.

Joe explained that the Jackson's show "is not just a concert. It's an event. It's the biggest thing since the Beatles."

The selectmen refused the egg-celent gift, but the proceedings reached newspapers nationwide.

WHO'S CHICKEN? – Boston station WROR-FM morning personalities Andy Moes, left, Joe Martell, right, and Linda Brescia, show producer, center, show the three live chickens they intend to deliver to the Foxboro Selectmen who vetoed a Jackson concert there.
UPI photo

FOXBOROUGH CHIEF OF POLICE John Gaudet (left) points to door, Foxborough Town Hall, Thursday, ushering out Boston station WROR-FM morning personalities, Andy Moes (right, fore), Joe Martell (right, rear) and Linda Brescia (extreme right) show producer, who attempted unsuccessfully to present 3 live chickens to the Foxborough selectmen. The selectmen voted Wednesday night not to allow the Michael Jackson concert at Sullivan Stadium. (UPI)

Daily Times & Chronicle   June 22, 1984

WROR's Joe n' Andy press release - Don't chicken out (Foxboro selectman wouldn't allow Michael Jackson to perform at the Sullivan Stadium.

Mug shot Cindy Zagieboylo wins trip to Hawaii for getting Joe n' Andy's mug on national TV.

Article: parade for fired Sox manager, Joe Morgan.

Radio deejay Joe Martelle plays 'Dad for a day' in forest

By Michael B. Pierce

Thirty children recently got something they didn't have, even if it was only for one afternoon — a father.

The children were treated to pony rides and a picnic at the Harold Parker State Forest thanks to the efforts of Mix 98.5 morning radio personality Joe Martelle.

Several years ago, Martelle was on the air discussing his plans for Father's Day when a young boy phoned the station and said that he didn't have a dad of his own.

"It really knocked me over," Martelle said. "I realized that a lot of kids don't have dads."

After that, Martelle decided that he would try to fill in as a dad for fatherless children at least once a year.

He has brought children to a Red Sox game and whale watching during the past few years. While only eight children went to the Red Sox game, 100 went whale watching last year.

"It's amazing how these things

See photos on page 7 of this week's *Citizen*.

take off," said Martelle's wife, Kim. "It gives them memories and something to remember; that they had a dad for a day."

The winners were picked either over the phone or by writing or faxing the station.

Martelle said it was difficult to pick only 30 winners.

While mostly parents contacted the station, one boy took the task upon himself.

"Mitchell called on his own," said his mother, Cheryl Jackson. "He thought nothing of it because he is very outgoing. This is the greatest that they do this for fa-

therless children."

Tracey Gray called the station because she thought her daughter, Whitney, would enjoy the event.

"I finally got through with some persistence," Gray said. "So many promotions are for adults. I thought this was great because it was for kids."

Everything for the event was donated, including the ponies from J & J Pony Rides and the food from Cardoos Catering.

Also, Martelle's Mix Morning Crew partner, Jodi Winchester, as well as Jennifer Markham of the station's marketing and promotions department, worked on their own time.

Caterer Robert Cardoos even changed his schedule to help Martelle, as he already had several other events planned for that day.

Martelle said an afternoon a year for children was not a lot to ask.

Dad for a Day promotion.

I DO, I DO again promotion (married couples renew their vows). Nun on mic with author from musical, *Nunsense*. To Joe's right, members of Sunny morning-drive show, Lindy Rome and Kristy Kramer.

Joe n' Andy's moms guest on Mom's Day- author's mom, Joan wearing headphones, Andy's mom, Flo.

CHAPTER 16
Radio Formats: News, Talk and Sports

PART 1 OF 3—NEWS

"to be persuasive, we must believe; to be believable, we must be credible; to be credible, we must be truthful"
– Legendary pioneer broadcast journalist, Edward R. Murrow

"Before radio, Americans depended on newspapers to get the news of the day. But, in the 1920s as radio found its way into more and more homes, Americans became accustomed to getting their news instantaneously from radio."

NEWS RADIO
Birth of Radio News.
  Radio News has always made a major contribution in keeping Americans informed. According to an article, *The Evolution of Radio News*, Americans first tuned in to radio to hear breaking news in November 1916. Dr. Lee DeForest, the inventor of the three-element vacuum tube which became the essential tool in modern radio, broadcast returns of the Presidential election between Woodrow Wilson and Charles Evans Hughes.[1] It was estimated that an audience of several thousand within a 200-mile radius of New York City, listened in their own homes as DeForest relayed reports from the offices of the *New York American* newspaper.[2] The news coverage signaled the beginning of radio as the first electronic news and information super highway.
  From its earliest beginnings, news has always been an important component of radio. On August 31, 1920, radio station 8MK (later WWJ) in Detroit broadcast a Michigan primary election. A few months later, Warren

G. Harding's win over James Cox in the Presidential election was broadcast over KDKA, the Westinghouse-Electric Company station in Pittsburgh. In 1921, President Harding's Armistice Day address was broadcast live from Arlington Memorial in Washington to crowds of listeners in New York and San Francisco as telephone circuits carried the message across the country.

In June 1924, radio news was on the scene as the first political convention was broadcast on radio when Republicans gathered in Cleveland, Ohio. Later that year, Democrats held their convention at Madison Square Garden, New York City, and once again listeners were able to have a front row seat, thanks to radio news. The inauguration of President Calvin Coolidge was broadcast on March 4, 1925, over 21 stations across the country from Boston to San Francisco. An estimated fifteen million people listened in thanks to AT&T's network service.

Radio news was given an added boost with the birth of America's first nationwide network, the National Broadcasting Company. NBC was launched on November 15, 1926, with WEAF in New York City as its key station and with nineteen affiliates, using more than 3,500 miles of special telephone lines. By 1927 there were more than eight million radio families in the United States, many depending on the new medium for news and information. That same year, the Columbia Broadcasting System (CBS) was established under the guiding hand of twenty-seven-year-old tobacco heir William S. Paley. CBS went on the air with WABC, today WCBS, as its key station in New York City and was supported by a network of forty-seven stations. By 1928, NBC had split their network into two separate services, the Red and Blue Networks.[3]

In 1927, radio news was such a feared competitor of newspapers that the American Newspaper Publishers Association warned members that advertising on radio would mean less revenue for newspapers. The fear was so great that many newspapers refused to list program schedules for radio stations and the word "radio" itself was forbidden in news columns. Old fears die hard. In the early 1960s, as program director of the only radio station in a one-newspaper town, I found that the local paper, *The Biddeford/Saco Journal*, would seldom, if ever, mention our call letters. It was only after many meetings and lunches and by giving their sports staff members air time that the newspaper somewhat reluctantly mentioned our station in print.

History of Radio News-Wire Services Versus Radio.

In the twenties, much like today, radio presented capsule news headline summaries and stations took pride in having the capability of immediately broadcasting late breaking news stories. Today, radio networks like ABC, CBS, CNN, and FOX provide a few minutes of news at the top of each hour, leaving the bottom of the hour for local newscasts. Early network radio, much like today, focused on the world and national news scene while leaving local and regional news, weather, and sportscasts up to their affiliated stations to cover. It made perfect sense then, as it does today.

Radio Networks did not develop effective news bureaus and staffs of their own until the mid-1930s. Until then, they relied on the national wire services, like AP, the Associated Press, to provide news copy for many of their newscasts. Competition for reporting the news between newspapers and radio stations became quite evident when AP warned its subscribers as early as 1922 against providing news stories to radio stations. Since many radio stations, like WGN Chicago, whose call letters stand for "World's Greatest Newspaper," were owned by newspapers like the *Chicago Tribune*, it was difficult for newspapers to adhere to AP's request. In 1925, AP conceded that radio stations should be allowed to report the most important wire service stories, hoping the listener would read the full story by buying newspapers. In other words, to get the full and complete story behind radio's headline version, listeners would have to buy the paper.

In 1928, the wire services AP and UP agreed that radio stations should be allowed to read the wire service reports at least twice daily.[4] One year later, the wire services allowed radio stations to actually subscribe to their services, with or without using the services of an affiliated newspaper as an intermediary.

The Great Depression made things difficult for wire services, networks, and newspapers.

Newspapers strongly suggested to their advertisers, who were sponsoring radio newscasts, that if they continued to do so, they would not run their ads in their newspapers. In some cases, they hinted they would even charge them higher rates to be included in their papers. The wire services united and denied all network radio stations the use of their news copy. At the same time, they required all non-network radio stations to pay for rights to broadcast their wire stories.

In 1933, CBS fought back, and in an intelligent way. Rather than engage in long and costly court battles, the network decided to establish their own news department and no longer use the wire services. The network opened news bureaus in most major American cities and dispatched correspondents all over the world. It didn't take long for the wire services to realize the error of their ways and the bold move by CBS to gather their own news seriously threatened their dominance in the news-gathering business. The wire services decided to negotiate with CBS and, in December 1933, a compromise was reached. Basically, with a few restrictions, the wire services allowed the network and stations to subscribe to their wire service.[5] One proviso restricted network news commentators to comment only on news stories that were more than twelve hours old. Many network affiliates and regional networks refused to accept the compromise and elected to gather their own news stories with the help of independent news services and contractors. The competition was fierce between print and radio media for news.

Some newspapers began buying radio stations and combined the news efforts of their broadcast and print outlets. It became obvious that the wire services could not control the dissemination of news. They would have to allow radio stations and networks to buy their services just like they did to the newspapers.

The Twenties and Thirties were an exciting time to be involved with America's newest innovation, radio! Listeners were infatuated and tuned-in as exciting events developed and unfolded around the world, like Charles "Lucky" Lindbergh's 1927 solo flight in the *Spirit of St.* Louis, when he flew across the Atlantic to Paris. The nation went wild and when he arrived back home to a hero's homecoming in the nation's capital, Graham McNamee was on the scene to describe it all for radio listeners.

The Stock Market crash of 1929, followed by the Great Depression, did not depress radio but added substantially to its growth and popularity. People could hardly afford food and their mortgages, let alone go out and pay for entertainment. They stayed home, and while nightclubs and movie theaters closed, radio boomed. Radio was *free* and provided entertainment in the privacy of one's home. Many families who had purchased their household belongings on credit and could no longer keep up with the payments gave up their vacuum cleaners, furniture, and cars, but kept up their payments on their radios. Radio as a source of entertainment, and especially news, had become an important part of their lives and something which they simply could not do without.

Some of radio's most memorable pioneer news personalities:

One of radio's first news reporter/commentators was **Floyd Gibbons**. He began his journalistic career as a war correspondent during the First World War for the *Chicago Tribune*. In France, at the Battle of Belleau Wood, Gibbons lost an eye after being hit by German gunfire while attempting to rescue an American Marine. When machine gun fire opened up, the troops dropped into the fields. One man did not and as Gibbons moved towards him to pull him down he was hit three times in the arm, shoulder, and head. A white patch covering his injured left eye became a trademark of the daredevil lifestyle that Gibbons portrayed. In August 1918, for his courageous actions under fire, Gibbons was awarded France's greatest honor, the Croix de Guerre with Palm, for his valor on the battlefield. Later, on June 21, 1941, Marine Corps League State Commandant Roland L. Young posthumously awarded Gibbons a gold medal, making him an honorary member of the U.S. Marine Corps. It was the first civilian honor ever made in the history of the Marine Corps League.

The popular CBS news commentator fancied himself as both a journalist and adventurer. Gibbons would often travel to where the news was actually happening. Gibbons went to war-torn places like Manchuria in 1931, to cover the invading Japanese Army, and to Ethiopia in 1935, when the Italians invaded that country. His fifteen-minute news program and his rapid-fire delivery, clocked at the speed of over 215 words a minute with as many as 5,000 words per program, were described by *Time Magazine* as a "machine-gun stream of syllables."

Floyd Gibbons was probably the most popular radio newscaster on the air until one night in 1930, when a young man from Cripple Creek, Colorado, **Lowell Thomas**, filled in for him.

Radio Pro Lesson learned: Always be mindful that when you take time off from your air shift, someone filling in may be just a little better and could spell imminent trouble. Don't be paranoid, but keep your antenna up and don't be taking too many vacation days.

The audience response was so favorable that Lowell Thomas was hired to do a regular broadcast. He did his best to step into the huge shoes left by Gibbons. During the next quarter of a century, like his predecessor, Lowell Thomas became one of the most popular news commentators in the history of radio. Students studied Thomas's diction in speech classes. Lowell not only covered the news, but uncovered it as well. The audience came to believe that if Lowell Thomas wasn't on the scene reporting it then it wasn't worth hearing about. He was a travel lecturer turned roving reporter. His 6pm nightly news program, *The Sunoco 3-Star Extra* on NBC, aired until 1947, when he moved to CBS. *Lowell Thomas and the News* spanned five decades and became a "must-listen" for Americans. He was a permanent fixture on radio for fifty years, commenting on news of the day. His final broadcast came in 1977 at age 84, and when he signed off for the final time with his regular closing signature, "This is Lowell Thomas…so long, until tomorrow," it marked the end of an era in radio news broadcasting commentators.

H.V. Kaltenborn began broadcasting in 1928 and was another of radio's first news personalities. Hans Kaltenborn was born in Milwaukee of German descent and was proud of his heritage but hated Nazism, which he viewed as contrary to traditional German values. He was fluent in German and French and often interviewed world leaders without the need of an interpreter. He trained himself in the art of total recall, which allowed him to quote the speeches of political figures after only hearing them once. H.V. gained national attention during the Munich crisis of 1938. Kaltenborn did not leave the CBS mic for the duration and went on the air 85 times with updates, analyzing the news which flowed in from Europe. It was the first time in radio history that a news program gained a larger audience than an entertainment show. It also gave importance to radio's position as America's primary source for news.

The importance of radio spot news coverage began to take shape in 1927 with **Ted Husing,** who specialized in covering sporting events but was so well-rounded that he could handle any radio assignment. He broadcast the arrival of the *Graf Zeppelin* over New York in its first transatlantic flight.

Radio news on-the-scene coverage really hit home on May 6, 1937. WLS Chicago reporter **Herb Morrison** was on hand in Lakehurst, New Jersey, to cover for radio the arrival of the German dirigible *Hindenburg*. What happened to the giant airship is legendary. It exploded and burned as it approached its mooring. Morrison, emotional and near tears, gave radio listeners one of the most emotional and riveting eyewitness accounts ever broadcast.

The March of Time was one of the best-known news documentary programs on the air. It first aired on CBS, March 6, 1931, and continued until 1945. The program dramatized current news events highlighted by the words of the narrator. **Ted Husing** and **Harry Von Zell**[6] were the earliest voices on the program, but best known was **Westbrook Van Voorhis**. His staccato delivery resonated from radios all across America. *March of Time* moved to NBC in 1937 and was last heard on ABC in 1945.

Boake Carter was also a pioneer radio journalist. His radio career began in Philadelphia working for the CBS affiliate and later moved up to the CBS Radio Network. His series of programs and commentary on the Lindberg baby kidnapping in 1932 made him a household name and a favorite with listeners all across America.

Longtime CBS anchor **Robert Trout** was born Robert Albert Blonheim in Wake Count, North Carolina. He added the Trout name early in his radio career. Bob began his radio career in 1931, as an announcer at WJSV in Alexandria, Virginia.[7] He did everything at the station from reading poetry to giving hunting and fishing advice. When CBS bought the station in 1932, Trout was part of the sale.

Bob Trout was behind the mic for many firsts in broadcasting: the first to report live congressional hearings, the first to transmit from an airborne plane, and the first to serve as an anchorman on a daily news program, a role many broadcast historians credit Trout with creating.

News commentator **Elmer Davis** was born in Aurora, Indiana. He first hit national attention by filling in for H.V. Kaltenborn in 1939. His nightly commentaries were always insightful and no matter how bad things appeared to be, he always seemed to be calm, cool and collected. His relaxed air style made listeners feel comfortable and gave Americans hope during the dark days of World War II that everything would be okay. At different times, Elmer Davis reported the news on CBS and ABC. In 1942, he was appointed by President Franklin D. Roosevelt to head the newly created Office of War Information Bureau. Davis continued on radio, reading the news of the day until he retired.

Dorothy Thompson was one of radio's first female reporters and commentators.[8] She was heard on the Mutual Radio Network from 1937 until 1945. Dorothy was also a popular newspaper columnist and magazine writer. Her weekly radio news and commentary program was estimated to have been heard by over six million listeners. For many years she was married to popular novelist Sinclair Lewis.

The War Years of WWII and Radio News personalities.
A 1939 poll showed that more than 25 percent of Americans depended on radio for most of their news and the majority of listeners believed radio was more objective than newspaper. During World War II that number increased to over 70 percent of those surveyed who said they received most of their news from radio. To see the full impact of news related programs on radio, one only needs to look at FDR's popular fireside chats during WWII.
[9] In May 1941, declaring an unlimited national emergency in the wake of increasing Nazi sub attacks in the Atlantic, President Roosevelt delivered one of his chats to one of the largest radio audiences to that date. Some 85 million people, according to the Hooper ratings service, were tuned in to hear the President - that's 70% of all radio homes in the U.S. His radio news address to the nation had a terrific impact on Americans everywhere. The NY Telephone Company reported a 50% drop in calls during the time of his speech. In movie theaters, audiences left their seats to hear the speech in the lobby. At New York's Polo Grounds, the game between the Braves and Giants was momentarily suspended after seven innings so the crowd of over 17,000, including the players, could hear the speech over the PA system.

According to a 2006 *Radio Today* annual report, issued by Arbitron, the radio ratings company, 93.7% of people age twelve years and older still listen to traditional radio each week, with news remaining a major attraction.[10]

In 1935, broadcast journalism came alive and would never be the same again. **Edward R. Murrow**, credited as the founding father of broadcast journalism, joined CBS as Director of Talks and Education. In 1937, he became director of CBS's European Bureau in London. Murrow's rich, expressive voice first came to the attention of the American listening audience when he intoned, "Good Evening, this is London" as Nazi bombs exploded in the background. Murrow's rooftop broadcasts during the Battle of Britain and the London blitz brought the dramatic events leading up to WWII into the homes of America's radio listeners. He reported the experiences of the war in Europe as he eyewitnessed and lived them. Ed Murrow often used the airwaves to popularize many American symbols of truth, freedom of speech and the individual liberties of all mankind. Bringing these issues to light while Nazi bombs rained down on London during his broadcasts hit home with freedom-loving Americans and served as a grim reminder that war was ever-present in the world.

After the war, in the late '40s and early '50s, Murrow found equal success on the television side at CBS, as host of two popular programs. *Hear It Now*, which he hosted on radio and was retitled for TV to *See It Now,* ran from 1951 to 58, winning four Emmys. Murrow also was host of *Person to Person*, which began in 1953 and continued until 1959. Later in his career, some say, because of his outspoken ways which created controversy for CBS, Murrow fell from grace with the network's hierarchy. After a career of twenty-six years with CBS, he left the Network in 1961 to head the U.S. Information Agency. Edward R. Murrow died at age 57 in New York on April 27, 1965. Ironically, the same network that turned its back on Murrow today proudly displays a plaque in his honor in the lobby of its headquarters in New York City.[11] It contains his image and the inscription, "He set standards of excellence that remain unsurpassed."

During the days leading up to WWII, CBS news correspondents reported from around the globe. In addition to Ed Murrow in London, Eric Sevareid covered the China-Burma theater. Winston M. Burdette and Charles Collingwood reported on the North African campaign, while Farnsworth Fowle reported on Italy. Other popular pioneer news commentators include Richard Harkness, who covered the 1944 Presidential election for NBC, Edward P. Morgan, John Cameron Swayze, who found additional fame after his newscasting years as a pitchman for Timex watches, Bob Considine, Alex Drier, Fulton Lewis, Jr., Roger Mudd and of course, radio's perennial iron man, Paul Harvey.

Howard K. Smith, a Tulane graduate, set out for Germany in 1936 with $100 to study Nazism. In 1939, he was based in London for United Press when war broke out in Europe. CBS hired Smith as a correspondent because of his expertise on Germany and dispatched him to Berlin to cover the war close-up. In 1941, he was banned from Germany for his prediction that Nazism would lead the world to war. Smith turned his findings into a bestselling book, *Last Train from Berlin*. He continued covering the drumbeat of war in Europe for CBS by moving to neutral Switzerland. After the war, Smith, considered the dean of network news anchors, was a fixture at CBS and later ABC. Howard Kingsbury Smith passed away in February 2002. He was 87.

Sidebar to Howard K. Smith with **Melanie Morgan**. Before closing this chapter on the late Howard K. Smith, fast forward to 1976 and Kansas City, Missouri. Melanie Morgan, who today is a noted conservative radio talk show host and chairwoman of the pro-troops, pro-Iraq war group Move America Forward, was an intern at ABC News during the Republican Convention at the Kemper arena in Kansas City. "I was assigned to the tape-unit, "says Morgan, a Kansas City native. "I was ultimately shuttled off as an assistant to the late Howard K. Smith, one of Edward R. Murrow's brave and talented reporters who illuminated the world about the Nazi regime from Europe during World War II. Behind the scenes, there was plenty of drama taking place. Tension was building because Barbara Walters, the first network female co-anchor in broadcasting history, was sent to join her new colleague, Harry Reasoner. Miss Walters, as we were instructed to call her, swept into the cramped quarters wearing designer clothing and trailed by her personal assistants. Immediately the chatter of typewriters stopped and conversation halted while the newsroom personnel sneaked a peak at the Famous One. Even Bob Furnod, later a Vice President at CNN, and his slant-tracktape editors peered around the corner of the makeshift walls.

"So, naturally," Melanie Morgan continues, "I decided to approach Miss Walters. As a gawky, shy eighteen-year-old, I wanted to express my admiration for her accomplishments. After she summoned me inside her 10x15 office, I stammered out my rehearsed praise, telling Walters how her rise to the top was very inspirational for me. Miss Walters gave me a cold look, and asked me to leave, immediately! Hugely embarrassed, reeling and my confidence completely undermined, I went on to make a horrible career mistake. At the end of the Republican Convention, at which, by the way, Ronald Reagan lost the GOP nomination in '76 to Gerald Ford," recalls Melanie, "Howard K. Smith offered me a job as his personal assistant with the Washington Bureau of ABC News, but I turned him down. Many years later, I learned that was the career path for aspiring reporters."

Melanie Morgan goes on to explain her reluctance to accept Howard K. Smith's job offer. "At the time of his generous offer back in 1976, I simply felt inadequate after my exchange with Barbara Walters to deal with inflated egos that dominated the world of television and broadcast news and the East Coast media elites. It took me a while," she confesses, "but I got my mojo back, went back to radio and escaped from my nearly unremarkable radio career choices. Other than that, I sacrificed nothing in my grasping ambition fueled ascension down the career ladder."

Lisa Sergio was a pioneer news broadcaster in Mussolini's Italy during World War II, and became a dedicated anti-fascist commentator for WQXR New York. Once known as the "Golden Voice of Rome," she translated the dictator's speeches into English until her modification of propaganda commentaries got her promptly removed from being on Italian radio.

NBC war correspondents who risked their lives to cover the news during the Second World War included Francis McCall, Wright Bryan, David Anderson, W.W. Chaplin and Tom Traynor, who was killed in action. Other war correspondents for CBS Radio included Larry Lesueur, Charles Shaw, Richard Curt Hottelet and Harry W. Flannery, who was the Berlin correspondent for CBS in 1940 and '41 and the author of the bestseller, *Assignment to Berlin* (1942).

The war years of WWII and after, radio news personalities.

During World War II, Americans were kept informed by radio with reporters at home and in the field. Ned Kalmer, William L. Shirer, Albert Warner, Bill Henry, and Elmer Davis reported from the home front, while in the field were Henry Cassidy, Frank McCall, Merrill Mueller, George Hicks, George Thomas Tolster and Bert Silen. It was Silen who broadcast the beginning of the Japanese attack live on NBC from Manila. He remained steadfast at the microphone until Japanese soldiers broke in and hauled him off as a prisoner of war. Several years later, when the Philippine POW camps were liberated, former NBC News

Director Abe Schechter was on General MacArthur's staff and located Bert Silen. After a debriefing, the newsman was allowed to go back on the air for NBC. His first words were, "As I was saying the last time when I was rudely interrupted…"

Morgan Beatty began his broadcasting career while attending high school in Little Rock, Arkansas. He became nationally known for his eyewitness account of the Mississippi flood in 1927. In 1941, Beatty joined NBC News as a military analyst and at the end of the war, in 1946, became a major commentator on the news of the day "roundup" program.

Drew Pearson wrote a syndicated column, *Washington Merry-Go-Round,* which was a behind-the-scenes look at politicians in our nation's capitol. He began as a newsman on radio in 1935 and became an expert of sorts at predicting political races.

Gabriel Heater was a network news commentator who began his broadcast with, "*Ah, there's good news tonight,*" regardless of how dreadful the report. He gained national fame in 1935 with his stirring account on radio of the electrocution of Bruno Hauptmann, the accused kidnapper of the Lindbergh baby. Almost overnight, Gabriel Heater rose from the ranks of newsman to a $3,500-a-week commentator. His "voice of doom" approach delivering the news during the Second World War really established him as one of the country's favorite radio personalities.

John Charles Daly was another pioneer radio journalist. He was President Franklin D. Roosevelt's official radio announcer in 1940 and later became a newsman for CBS Radio. It was Daly who was on the air that infamous Sunday of December 7, 1941, and broadcast to all Americans that Japanese war planes had bombed Pearl Harbor, Hawaii. In 1953, John C. Daly became moderator of the TV quiz show *What's My Line* and remained with the popular program for thirty years.

Douglas Edwards began practicing to be a newscaster by speaking into a telephone when he was twelve. By age fifteen, he was on the air on Troy, Alabama's 100-watt station, WHET. Edwards first real radio break came in 1935, when he was a regular reporter with WAGF in Dothan, Alabama. His next radio jobs were at WSB-Atlanta and WXYZ Detroit. Edwards joined CBS Radio in 1942, later moving to the television side as anchor of the evening news. In 1962, he was replaced in the anchor's chair by Walter Cronkite and subsequently moved back to CBS Radio, where he delivered the evening news on the network's flagship station for many years. Until his retirement he maintained a small role with CBS Television, anchoring a five-minute midday *Newsbreak*. Douglas Edwards remained with the network for 46 years until retiring on April 1, 1988. He passed away from cancer just two years later, at age 73, on October 13, 1990.

Walter Cronkite, referred to as the "Dean of News Broadcasters," was born in St. Louis, Missouri, in 1916. He began his radio career in 1935 as an announcer at WKY in Oklahoma City. The next year, he was a sports announcer for KCMO (AM) in Kansas City, Missouri, using the air name Walter Wilcox. In 1939, Cronkite joined United Press International as a war correspondent covering World War II. He became one of the top American reporters in World War II, covering battles in North Africa and Europe, including the Battle of the Bulge. He joined CBS Radio in 1950, becoming the network's senior TV news anchor in 1962. Walter Cronkite remained with the network until retiring at age sixty-five, on March 6, 1981. In an interview regarding his retirement, he described himself as being like a "comfortable old shoe" to his audience.

One national network news program that deserves special mention is the popular *CBS World News Roundup*, which is still heard today on many CBS affiliated radio stations. When the program first aired on March 13, 1938, at 8pm Eastern time, it was a one-time radio news special in response to growing tensions in Europe. The first program was hosted by longtime CBS news personality Robert Trout, who is profiled elsewhere in this chapter. The first program gave American listeners the voices of Edward R. Murrow and William L. Shirer. According to CBS sources, it was the first time Murrow had broadcast a news report. The program was a 35-minute special report from around the world as the pre-war crisis intensified. It was also the first time reporters in the field were hooked up with a central anchor in New York City for a national news broadcast. The program met with such favorable listener response that it was repeated the following evening and then revived later that year and eventually evolved into a daily news program.

In addition to the weekday morning news edition, CBS also broadcasts a late-edition at 7pm Eastern time with Bill Witney. The morning program host for many years was Christopher Glenn who passed away in 2006 and was succeeded by Nick Young. The longest tenure of one news anchor on the program was Dallas Townsend, who hosted *Roundup* for 25 years. Townsend was followed by Reid Collins and Bill Lynch before Glenn took over. Douglas Edwards, who is featured elsewhere in this chapter, also had a long tenure hosting the program in the 1970s and '80s when it was *The World Tonight*. Christopher Glenn took over as nighttime anchor after Edwards retired. Today, the *CBS World News Roundup* with anchor Nick Young remains an active part of the CBS Radio Network lineup. Now in its seventy-third year, it is America's longest running radio network newscast on radio or television. The 10-minute newscast airs every morning at 8am Eastern time.

Charles Osgood (born Charles Osgood Wood III) is another CBS broadcast journalist who is still heard and seen on the network today. While at Fordham University, in the '50s, he worked at the university's FM station, WFUV. In 1967, he anchored the first morning drive shift at WCBS-AM in NYC after the station's format switch to all-news. Among his personal trademarks are his bow-tie and his weekly Sunday Morning TV sign-off, *"Until then, I'll see you on the radio,"* words which bring a huge smile to the faces of we radio folks.

I had the pleasure of meeting Charles Osgood once during my own radio career. It was the mid-1980s and I was handling morning drive at WROR in Boston. Osgood, in town for a function, was preparing his daily CBS program, *The Osgood File,* from one of our studios. As I hurried down the hallway to grab a cup of coffee during one of our five-minute newsbreaks, he stopped me and asked if it would be all right if he cleared the AP wire. He was looking for a kicker story for his morning network broadcast. I smiled and said, "Sure!" There was no pretentiousness about the man and he was a living lesson that no matter how important one may be, politeness is still a necessity. It also can help get you whatever you want. In the case of Charles Osgood it was finding the perfect kicker story from our newswire. I'll always remember our brief but pleasant meeting in the hallway at the RKO studios in Boston. The well-deserving radio pro was inducted into the Radio Hall of Fame, class of 1990.

Walter Winchell was a radio commentator who shattered the journalistic mold when it came to exposing the private lives of public figures. He permanently changed the shape of celebrity journalism.

Born in New York's Harlem in 1897, Winchell began his journalistic career by penning a celebrity show-business column about Vaudevillians while still in his teens. In 1925, his writing career really took off when he joined the *New York Daily Mirror* as a reporter. He was first heard on radio in 1929, when his news program was sponsored by Gimbel's Department Store on a 42-station hook-up.

Winchell, with his brash, in-your-face, staccato, rapid-fire delivery, once claimed that he was clocked at 220 words a minute - the average for Americans is about 165 words per minute - complete with the sound effects of a chattering telegraph key inserted between stories first aired on NBC's Blue Network in 1932. His popular Sunday night news and gossip program ran for more than two decades and began with his signature opening, "Good Evening, Mr. and Mrs. North America and all the ships at sea…let's go to press! FLASH!!"

Walter Winchell was showmanship personified. His success was not entirely due to the celebrity secrets he revealed on his weekly program. Other gossipers, like Louella Parsons, Hedda Hopper, Sheilah Graham, and Jimmy Fidler, were offering much of the same fare. No, Winchell's success was also due to the fact that he was one of a kind. His unique on-air style and delivery was impossible to mimic. He strongly disliked flowery words and instead developed his own telegraph style that was filled with slang and incomplete sentences. Winchell was responsible for introducing into the American language such now-familiar words and phrases like, "pushover," "scram" and "belly laughs."

His language was filled with new expressions…to be expecting a baby was "infanticipating," and to marry was to "merge." He was known for originating some now memorable quotes, like, "A friend is one who walks in when others walk out," and "Never above you, never below you. Always beside you."

Walter Winchell's program was one of the most dynamic 15-minute shows ever broadcast on radio! He was extremely popular and his weekly listening audience was estimated to be over 20 million. It was well known in show-business circles that a few well-chosen words on his program about an actor or actress could easily make or break a star's career.

The radio news commentator was a master at self-promotion and became as big a celebrity as the stars he plugged on his program. He often appeared as himself in movies. He was often seen at Sherman Billingsley's Stork Club and always sat at table 50. When threatened with a lawsuit, Winchell would often shoot back, "Wanna sue me? Well, the line forms to the right, mister!" From the mid-1930s to his final ABC broadcast in 1955, he was never found guilty of slander. Walter Winchell was his own worst critic. He never thought anything he did was quite good enough. His network viewed him differently! He was such a hot commodity that in 1950, ABC radio (NBC sold its Blue Network and it became ABC) signed him to a lifetime contract. The deal guaranteed the journalist $10,000 weekly for as long as he was mentally and physically able to provide a quarter-hour Sunday night broadcast. If he could no longer perform his duties, per terms of the contract, he was guaranteed $1,000 monthly for the rest of his life. Not a bad deal for over half a century ago.

At the peak of his popularity, Winchell's combined audience in print and on the air was more than fifty million. The $800,000 salary he earned in one year made him the nation's highest paid American. As with all things in life, sooner or later they come to an end. Such was the case with Walter Winchell's high-rolling and successful career. After sixteen years on the air for Jergens Lotion, he and the company parted ways after a falling out over a deodorant commercial that he felt was beneath him to do. He finally fell from grace with his longtime network, ABC, as well. When he tried to get the network to indemnify him against future lawsuits, ABC said no and Winchell resigned in a huff. In doing so, he gave up his lifetime contract with the network. He believed they would never accept his resignation and was shocked when they did.

After his departure from ABC, Walter Winchell later joined Mutual, but left the network in 1960. It was the first time in twenty-eight years that the popular radio journalist was without a microphone. Walter Winchell often had no credible sources for his accusations. He really didn't have any incentive to be accurate in his on-air or printed comments, because for most of his career his contract with his newspaper and radio employers required them to reimburse him for any potential damages he had to pay, should he be sued for libel or slander. Even when friends accused him of breaking a confidence, Winchell would respond with, "I know, I'm just a son of a bitch."

Winchell was well known for being mean, cruel, arrogant and ruthless. With a string of show-girl mistresses, a son who later killed himself, and a daughter whose life he almost ruined, his personal life was a mess. Of little help in preserving his public image, the *New York Post* published an expose that further damaged his reputation. It was around this same time that, because of his verbal confrontations with various celebrities and politicians, Winchell was getting a reputation as a troublemaker and networks wanted to distance themselves from the man.

When his hometown newspaper, *The New York Daily Mirror*, for whom he worked for thirty-four years, closed up shop in 1963, Winchell faded from the public's eye. For five seasons, beginning in 1959, he did receive $25,000 an episode as narrator of the ABC-TV series *The Untouchables*. Winchell's easily-recognizable voice as narrator of the television series is better remembered today than from his many years as one of radio's most popular and listened-to news personalities.

Towards his final days, shunned by the media he loved and worked for and unable to find work at a newspaper for his column, Winchell allegedly would type up the daily news headlines on mimeographed copies and pass them out to passersby on a street corner. Allegedly, Walter Winchell's final two years were spent as a recluse at the Ambassador Hotel in Los Angeles. He was 74 when he passed away from prostate cancer on February 20, 1972. Although, his obituary made the front page of *The New York Times*, his star had long since faded, and sadly, only one person showed up at his funeral, giving testimony to the fact that fame is fleeting.[12] Enjoy what little may come your way, but never, ever, abuse it or take it for granted.

Paul Harvey was one of the most listened-to radio personalities in the history of broadcasting!

Born Paul Harvey Aurandt, in Tulsa, Oklahoma, on Sept. 4, 1918, he got his start in radio while still in high school. His speech teacher was so impressed with his voice that she took him to KVOO Radio and told the program director that Paul belonged on the radio. The station hired him on the spot to clean the floors and read announcements and news. A year later, he began getting paid. Later, Harvey worked on the air in Salina, Kansas, and from there he became a newscaster at KOMA-AM in Oklahoma City, followed by a stint at KXOK-AM in St. Louis.

It was at the St. Louis station that he met Lynne Cooper, whom he married in 1940 and referred to on the air as "Angel." She was her husband's strongest supporter and his professional collaborator. Besides serving as a director, writer, and editor on his daily fifteen-minute news and commentary program, she edited *You Said It, Paul Harvey*, a collection of broadcasts released by the family company. Paul and Lynne worked closely together on his shows and he often credited his success to her influence. She was inducted into the Radio Hall of Fame in 1997, seven years after the same honor was bestowed on her husband. Lynne Angel Harvey passed away in May, 2008.

Paul Harvey's daily news programs, *Paul Harvey News* and *Comment*, five minutes in the morning and fifteen minutes at midday, six days a week, were consistently ranked first and second in the nation among network radio programs. Equally popular were his five-minute *The Rest of the Story* broadcasts, in which Harvey shared historical stories with surprise endings.[13] It's been estimated that Paul Harvey's various programs reached 24 million radio listeners for more than fifty-eight years on more than 1200 radio stations and 400 Armed Forces stations.

According to Michael C. Keith, communications professor at Boston College and author of *The Broadcast Century*, part of Paul Harvey's enduring appeal was his writing style. Keith stated, "It had a down-home flavor with a sophisticated quality. It grabs you and holds on to you." Harvey's program and on-air delivery were a definite throwback to radio's golden years, when fifteen-minute network radio programs were commonplace. . .

Paul Harvey's on-air style was reminiscent of the great broadcasters of the past, which made him a unique sound on contemporary radio. But, Paul Harvey was always relevant to what was happening today. He was never out of date, out of fashion, or out of place. From the moment he hit the air, he commanded your attention. His unique on-air style was centered around exaggerated pronunciation and pregnant pauses at just the right time to emphasize a story or to accent a point. His air style has been classroom study material for several generations of future radio pros. Tom Taylor, editor of *Inside Radio*, said, "Harvey was a reminder of living words on the radio, and of silence. Most air-talent rush to fill dead air-time, but Paul understood the value of just the right pause at the right time. You would sometimes literally hold your breath to see what the rest…of the story was all about." Harvey always said his trademark pauses were originally developed as a "lazy broadcaster's way of waiting for the second hand to reach the top of the clock," but they quickly became part of his on-air style.[14] "I've always felt the pregnant pause is more useful for emphasis than shouting," he said, "but it can't be done deliberately. It has to just happen."

My friend and former radio co-worker Mike Matoin worked in the ABC mailroom in Chicago in the late 1950s. Not wishing to sort mail forever and aspiring to be on the radio himself one day, Mike had an opportunity to ask Mr. Harvey, whose programs originated from the ABC studios, how someone should prepare for an on-air radio career. Without missing a beat, the congenial radio icon looked up, smiled, and said, "Dramatics, young man, study dramatics." If you ever heard Paul Harvey on the radio, you know exactly what he meant!

Paul Harvey enjoyed saying he was raised in radio newsrooms. In 1988, he told CNN's Larry King, "I can't wait to get out of bed every morning and rush down to the teletype machines to pan for gold." And rushing on down to the ABC studio's on Michigan Avenue is exactly what this legendary news commentator did for more than fifty-eight years. Up at 3:30 each morning, he ate a bowl of oatmeal, and then commuted by limo from his 27-room River Forest, Illinois, home, arriving in the pre-dawn hours at his 16th-floor downtown Chicago studio, high above a street sign that reads "Paul Harvey Drive." His office is where he would prepare his daily news programs, each day sifting through mountains of wire copy and speaking with news editors around the country in search of unique stories of Americana. A typical Harvey broadcast would include a mixture of news stories, humor, commentary, celebrity updates, and special stories of everyday Americans, including salutes to senior wedding anniversaries. He loved telling human-interest stories in order to satisfy, as he would say, the public's hunger for a little niceness. Harvey is credited with coining such words as *Reaganomics, bumpersnickers, and guesstimate*.

Harvey's ability to move and sell products by doing his own ad-libbed commercials made him one of the greatest on-air salesmen in the history of radio. His sponsors (only one in fifteen was accepted) stayed with him for decades, and were required to sign on with him for a minimum of one year. Harvey boasted that he would never endorse a product that he didn't truly believe in. In 1988, he told, CBS, "I can't look down on the commercial sponsors of these broadcasts. Too often they have very, very important messages to put across. Without advertising in this country, my goodness, we'd still be in this country what Russia mostly is: a nation of bearded cyclists with b.o."

Paul Harvey's impact on American radio was so great that many small stations nationwide intentionally affiliated with the ABC Network just to have exclusive rights to air him in their markets. I did it myself when I was a program director, and I know for a fact we weren't alone in our decision!

Broadcast consultant Walter Sabo once ran ABC Radio and for all intents and purposes was Paul Harvey's boss. I asked Walter how he handled such a major-league talent. Without missing a beat, Walter smiled and said, "Easy, this way: would you like that with two sugars or one, Mr. Harvey?"

When the legendary news commentator celebrated his 82nd birthday in 2000, ABC Radio, his sole employer for all his network years, signed him to a ten-year, $100 million contract. Rival networks who lost out in the bidding battle for his services told him they'd be back at the table in 2010.

Beginning in 1951, and for more than half a century, his radio listeners were greeted by Harvey's trademark staccato delivery, punctuated by his patented and deliberate pauses. "Hello, Americans," he'd boom into the microphone, "this is Paul Harvey! (pregnant pause) Stand by for News!" I guess we expected Paul Harvey's rich baritone voice would go on sharing the news of the day with us forever! However, as with most things in life, nothing lasts forever. Radio's legendary news voice was silenced on February 28, 2009. The end came for Paul Harvey at his winter home in Phoenix. The man who ended his broadcasts with a distinctive and cordial "Good Day" was 90.

David Brinkley was one of America's best-known and respected newscasters and commentators. During his successful career, he was associated with both NBC and ABC News. Born in Wilmington, North Carolina, on July 10, 1920, he began writing for his hometown newspaper, *The Wilmington Morning Star*, while attending New Hanover High School. He attended the University of North Carolina, and Emory and Vanderbilt Universities before entering the U.S. Army in 1941. Following his discharge in 1943, Brinkley moved to our nation's capital hoping to land a job with CBS News. Instead, he joined NBC News and became the network's first White House correspondent. Even though Brinkley's journalistic roots began with newspaper and radio writing, his greatest broadcast achievement was in television. In 1956, he began co-hosting NBC-TV's top-rated *Nightly News* with Chet Huntley. *The Huntley-Brinkley Report* was America's most popular television newscast until it was overtaken in the late 1960s by the *CBS Evening News* with Walter Cronkite. David Brinkley remained with NBC News until 1981, when he moved to ABC. Every Sunday he hosted *This Week with David Brinkley*, a post he held for the next 15 years. He stepped down as host on November 10, 1996, but continued with weekly commentaries for the next year. He completely retired in 1997.

For over fifty years, David Brinkley was an electronic journalist. He hosted a daily or weekly national TV news program for over forty of those years, longer than anyone else. His career spanned the earliest days of broadcast news to the hi-tech information era. During his broadcast career he won numerous awards, including ten Emmys and three Peabodys. In 1992, President George H.W. Bush awarded him the Presidential Medal of Freedom and in presenting the prestigious award called David Brinkley "the elder statesman of broadcast journalism." Many quotes are attributed to the late broadcast news-journalist, but one of my personal favorites is this one: "Numerous politicians have seized absolute power and muzzled the press. Never in history has the press seized absolute power and muzzled the politicians." David Brinkley passed away on June 11, 2003, at his home in Houston, Texas. The elder statesman of broadcast journalism was eighty-two.

Postscript David Brinkley.
A fun moment for me during my radio career happened during the presidential elections of 1996. David Brinkley was anchoring his Sunday morning program on the road, from a diner. He was looking for local reactions to the various candidates. I called the diner and offered to buy him a cup of coffee, or "cup of Joe," if you will. I didn't get to speak with my journalist hero—after all, he *was* on the air, but I did speak with the owner of the diner, who promised to relay my good wishes to Mr. Brinkley. He also said that he would be more than happy to personally hand deliver him a steaming hot cup of coffee. I had no way of knowing if either my message or the cup of coffee were ever delivered to Mr. Brinkley.

I received in the mail the photo with inscription shown at the end of this chapter. To this day, it is one of my prized processions! When I look at his picture, it brings to mind another Brinkley quote: "Washington, DC, is a city filled with people who believe they are important." David Brinkley was one who lived and worked in Washington for over fifty years, and, make no mistake, he may never thought of himself as being important, but I'm positive his friends and fans felt quite differently.

Mike Wallace, like the late David Brinkley, is a true broadcast icon. For thirty-seven years he made his mark as an investigative reporter on CBS-Television's top-rated *60 Minutes*. But, like so many before him, Wallace's broadcast roots were firmly entrenched in radio. Born in Brookline, MA, on May 9, 1918, Myron Leon Wallace, known to millions of listeners and viewers as Mike Wallace, began his radio career in 1939. After graduating from the University of Michigan, he was an announcer on WOOD-AM in Grand Rapids, Michigan. His pay was twenty dollars a week. By the end of the year, Mike was making seventy dollars a week and his radio career was on a roll. In 1941, as a staff announcer at WXYZ in Detroit, his salary jumped to $200 weekly. Those were big bucks in the years prior to World War II. Later that year, Mike's income received another boost when he auditioned in Chicago and won a job announcing the CBS soap *The Road of Life*. During the Second World War, Mike left radio to serve in the Navy. Following his discharge in 1946, Wallace returned to the Windy City and more network radio announcing work including, pitching the creamy goodness of Peter Pan peanut butter on the popular children's adventure series, Sky King. Even with all his radio work, Mike still felt unfulfilled.

In a *Radio-TV Mirror* interview, Wallace explained his feelings: "It always disturbed me that I was just reading other people's words. It just didn't seem like much of an accomplishment." He wasn't complaining, but was searching for greater accomplishments in radio. The money was good, but he felt his creative side was stagnating. "I made very good money, but think I felt trapped by it. I liked being successful, but I wasn't satisfied!" A year after his return to Chicago, Wallace finally got the opportunity to do something worthwhile in radio. He became a newscaster on the *Air Edition* of the *Chicago Sun Times*. Mike wrote the news and even chased a few stories. Later, he left the news business for a while and hosted several successful TV game and quiz shows. In 1963, Mike joined CBS News and in 1968 was named as one of the original correspondents on CBS-Television's top-rated *60 Minutes*. He remained a well-respected reporter on the program for thirty-seven years, until his retirement in 2005, at age eighty-seven. Mike Wallace was one of the best interviewers ever; always showing a tremendous amount of self-control and discipline even when interviewing a difficult person and dealing with sensitive subject matter. Mike Wallace passed away April 7, 2012. One of broadcasting's finest hard-hitting investigative journalists was 93. His interviewing style should be a lesson to all broadcasters, not just news reporters.[15] Ask the whys, wherefores and how comes. Go to the core of the person and get a full discussion of his or her subject. And, whatever you do, don't put a lid on it.

Audio advancement for radio news coverage.
During the Second World War, listening to radio network news increased ten-fold. Following the war, in 1945 and '46, the NAB, National Association of Broadcasters, conducted focus groups across America (yes, they were around back then, too). Their purpose was to determine radio interests. One of the most important topics discussed was local news. Two technological advancements changed radio forever and significantly helped news-gathering efforts, both on the national and local level. These new inventions were the tape recorder and the transistor. They helped reduce the size of bulky recorders to make them portable.[16, 17] This was an invaluable asset for news reporters in the field and gathering news actualities. In 1954, because of mounting pressure from television programming, radio felt the need to change. CBS made a bold move into the future of radio news by introducing a program based on news actualities.

Night Watch debuted on CBS Radio in 1954 and ran for a year on the network. Reporter **Dan Reed** accompanied two Culver City, California, detectives as they answered police calls. There were no scripts. Reed recorded on-the-scene reports using a portable tape recorder. For radio news wannabes wanting to hear one of radio's first news actuality programs, the entire run of 47 episodes is available.

Around 1964, a major audio development found its way into radio station news and control rooms, the *audio tape cartridge*. I remember quite vividly that prior to this great new audio invention, we worked with a recording/playback machine called a MacKenzie repeater.[18] It sounds like a relative of the Gatling gun, but is far from it. This unit was an amazing recording device and set the standard for the broadcast industry in the 1950s and early '60s. We also used a piano roll device called the Gates ST-101 Spot Tape Recorder. I am indebted to former radio chief engineer **Graham Newton**, who kindly helped me remember the name of this device. Today, Newton runs a digital audio restoration service in Ontario, Canada. He is well-acquainted with this playback/recorder. "I knew it well. The ST-101 would accommodate 101 spots up to a maximum of 90 seconds in length, on a 13" wide ribbon of tape which was a single, wide piece of tape." Newton first used the unit in 1960 as a 19-year-old, operating the master control console at CFCF in Montreal. "The time required for this rewind process meant that you could not play spots back-to-back from the ST-101," he continues, "and that was a problem. You would 'ready' the spot by sliding a switch on the bottom front of the unit to a desired number."

The Gates ST-101 spot tape recorder, or piano roll as we called it, was an amazing invention for its time. It was used for recording commercials, station jingles and promotional spots. The downside, as Graham pointed out, was that the machine was only capable of playing one spot at a time. If a 30-second commercial was called for, immediately followed by a second spot, you would have to wait the full 90 seconds for the unit to play to the end and come to a complete stop before sliding the switch to the next required number. Sometimes, in haste or panic, the board operator would jump the gun and not wait for the piano roll to stop and hurriedly slide the switch to play the next event. What usually happened was total disaster! The ST-101, not knowing which command to follow, would flip nosily around, resulting in a loud bang accompanied by a puff of smoke. The wide piece of tape, just like a piano roll, would come flying off the take-up roll, which led to all sorts of problems.

The coming of the tape cartridge machine.

The tape cartridge machines we first used were Gates, Collins and Spotmasters. They were an exciting innovation for radio. In 1964, as the PD at WIDE, Biddeford, Maine, the station bought two Collins cart machines. We were gathered around the new toys like little kids on Christmas morning as **Dick Dunn**, our chief engineer, installed them and explained how to use them. It was like magic, watching the continuous tape loop immediately start on command by pushing a button and silently stop at the end of the announcement, thanks to an inaudible tone at the end of the tape. The audio cartridge used a continuous tape loop of various lengths. Initially, the carts came in 60-, 90-, and 120-second lengths, but later, when we no longer viewed the little gems in such a mystical way, and were not so intimidated by them, we learned how to load the tapes ourselves. We made carts as long or as short as desired. Many were only 20 seconds long and ideal for station jingles and news sound actualities. Sometimes during a newscast, as many as ten individual carts would be stacked on top of each other ready to be inserted in machines at the appropriate time as a story called for a piece of sound. Cart machines were quite an advancement for radio, and a masterful engineering achievement. They significantly changed radio operations for the better and were used extensively for about thirty years until computers took over in the 1990s.

The evolution of radio news.

In the 1960s and '70s, there were a lot of Top-40 radio stations across America. Many were searching for special programming that would make them stand out amongst the crowd to attract a larger listening base. Local news filled the bill. A strong, solid local news department was the answer for many stations. There were hundreds of news positions at radio stations across the country, with many stations competing against each other for the best local news coverage. Unlike the early days of network radio, when newscasts were heard infrequently, now newscasts were heard hourly, airing at either five minutes before the hour, "live at :55," or at the top of every hour. More newscasts were added in the key listening slots of AM & PM drive.

In the early 1970s, Sony introduced the TC-110 cassette tape recorder. In no time at all, it became the workhorse for radio station news departments and remained so for the next decade. It was great for taping interviews and press conferences as reporters covered their daily beat assignments. As mentioned throughout this book, the one constant in radio is change, and, in the 1970s, AM radio began losing listeners to the new kid on the block, FM. AM stations felt their audience slipping away and sliding over to FM, just as TV had siphoned off listeners from AM radio twenty-five years earlier.

Once again, AM radio needed to reinvent itself. News on radio was one of the tools AM radio used to keep and maintain its audience, in some cases even dropping music altogether, like perennial Boston powerhouse WBZ AM-1030.

The birth of all-news radio.

The all-news format on radio began in California in 1960 at KFAX San Francisco and a year later at EXTRA in Los Angeles. Soon, every large city had at least one all-news station, including WINS in New York City, WBBM in Chicago, KNX Los Angeles, and KYW Philadelphia. In the 1970s, news was the fastest-growing format on AM radio. NBC Radio offered all-news programming to stations in every size market with the formation of NIS, The News and Information Service. NIS provided 47 minutes of news and information every hour of every day. Unfortunately, the enterprising effort failed to attract enough advertisers and the innovative concept only lasted two years. At the time, I was on the air at 970AM-WCSH in Portland, Maine, which was one of the original NBC affiliates and one of the first stations to sign with NIS.

Today, major networks have cut back on their commitment to news or it has totally disappeared into the ionosphere altogether, like two of America's first radio networks, Mutual and NBC. Networks like CBS, CNN, FOX, and NPR seem to have made a commitment to radio news and air hourly newscasts. NPR, National Public Radio, which went on the air in 1971, today boasts one of the largest news organizations in the U.S.

The FCC/Fairness Doctrine/news and broadcast operators.

In 1987 the Fairness Doctrine was repealed by the FCC. The requirement that broadcast licensees present controversial issues of public importance was perceived as a deterrent to free speech.

Author's note: I have mixed emotions regarding the repeal of the Fairness Doctrine. Granted, saying so long to the fairness doctrine has been a big boost to talk radio, but, on the other hand, the FCC deregulation removed a number of requirements that had been imposed on broadcast license holders for decades, going back to 1927, including that stations provide news, public affairs and locally-produced programs. Without the requirement, many stations cut back on their news coverage or completely eliminated entire news departments and the staff along with it. Consequently, competent radio news journalists, many of whom were my friends and co-workers in the business, found themselves out of work. This is why I have problems with the repeal of the Fairness Doctrine.

In my opinion, I believe the FCC, in redefining its role and quite frankly abandoning its responsibility to oversee stations to insure they broadcast in the public interest, is partly responsible for the lack of news and other quality programs on radio today. They are also partly to blame for the loss of many jobs in radio.

The original byword of the FCC clearly states that radio stations will serve the public and broadcast in the public interest. The FCC's short-sighted decision has undercut news and other public service programming in America's towns and cities. Without Big Brother keeping a watchful eye on radio station owners and operators, many broadcasters have simply forgotten that the primary mission of stations is to broadcast in the public interest and to serve the needs of the listeners within the station's primary coverage area. At least, that's the way it used to be and it seemed to work well for 60 years!

Once the rules and regulations were lifted and the FCC was no longer the watchdog for quality broadcasting in America, many radio station operators elected to go with the cheapest way possible to program their stations - more music. The FCC's notion that the marketplace will take care of the public interest, in my opinion and based on my own 41 years in all aspects of broadcasting, including on-air programming and management, is total bullcrap. I truly believe, based on what I have seen and experienced in radio, that many broadcast companies will never serve the public interest and are only interested in selling commercials and serving themselves.

Today, radio news has eroded even further, almost to the point where there's little news available on the commercial dial outside of news and talk stations. The problem was further compounded in 1996 with the FCC's decision to greatly relax ownership limits in radio, resulting in a huge number of consolidations, which meant fewer and fewer air positions and more and more talent being cut loose, laid off and fired. Downsizing and cutbacks in radio are not just restricted to the talent side, but in all aspects of radio employment.

In December 2007, the FCC concluded a series of public hearings on local radio. Radio pro Bob Edwards spoke at one of the hearings on behalf of AFTRA, the American Federation of Television and Radio Artists' union. He strongly urged commissioners to resist allowing further radio consolidation and asked the FCC to tighten, rather than loosen, ownership restrictions. "The drive to consolidate ownership of media seems to ignore the disaster that consolidation has brought to local news and public affairs on radio in this country," Edwards said, referring to the 1996 deregulation. Speaking before commissioners of the FCC, he raised an excellent point about the common practice of using one air-talent to voice-track other air shifts, which meant a loss of even more jobs. Bob Edwards also spoke about the negative impact of syndicated programming which is produced in a distant market without any regard for local input and tastes of the local community.

Bob Edwards also brought up a serious incident which occurred on January 18, 2002, in Minot, North Dakota. A train derailed and emergency officials were trying to evacuate an area of the city. One company, Clear Channel, owned all six commercial radio stations in Minot, but officials were not able to reach anyone at any of the stations, causing an unhealthy delay in the emergency process and obviously bringing attention to the negative impact multiple-radio-station ownership can have on a community. It speaks volumes about the need for a return to locally-owned radio stations by individual owners, or as they are sometimes called, "mom and pop" operators. I agree with radio host Bob Edwards; if commercial radio operators are given the freedom and opportunity to abandon their obligation to serve the public interest, they will do just that. So, the next time you hear discussion of multiple ownership in radio, downsizing, FCC deregulation and the Fairness Doctrine, please sit up, pay close attention and think long and hard about everything involved. It involves far more than simply insuring free speech on the air. It's about serving the communities and hometowns of America with local news, public affairs, and quality programming, but most importantly, it's also about jobs and people.

You and your future in radio news.

With all the cutbacks by radio stations today, including in radio news, what's in store for you as a future radio news journalist? Are you worried about entering a field in such a state of flux and obvious turmoil? Well, as mentioned elsewhere in this book, the one constant about radio is change, and once again, the face of radio is changing. Even though the present state of radio is uncertain, I believe the pendulum will eventually swing back to the positive side of the ledger. As a matter of fact, as I write this, change in radio is already underway. Whether it's all good is yet to be determined.

We begin with my former co-worker in Boston, radio news personality **Bob Schuman**. Bob is a veteran news personality who is presently the news director and part of the morning team at WOMC-104.3 Detroit. He begins with an ominous warning for future radio news wannabes: "I hate like hell to say this, Joey, but I cannot recommend that somebody set out to be a radio news person in this climate. Radio news people on music-driven formats are extremely rare," says the longtime radio journalist. "Even stations with big news departments continue to cut back," Schuman explains. "I used to run WJR here in Detroit and I probably had ten full-time people and several part-timers. Today, the station is down to probably three full-timers and a few part-timers."

Not to be the complete voice of doom for enthusiastic future radio news journalists, Bob Schuman assuredly adds, "If anybody wants to give radio news a shot, here's my advice. Sure, you can learn some of the tricks in high school and college, but I'd advise folks to LISTEN carefully to radio news. Pick out talents you can relate to, but don't copy them. Pick up on their good points and blend them into your own style. And above all else, if you want to give radio news a go, be flexible." Schuman supports his claim by using his own experience as a good example. "I can do serious news with the best in the business. I can host a morning news wheel [format]. I can also belt a great 60-second news package on a rocker written in a creative way. It's because of my flexibility that I've been employable over the past forty years." Bob Schuman is a heavyweight in the radio news field, and knows what he's talking about. His extensive radio news background includes on-air work at major stations in the following large markets; Detroit (WHYT, WJR, WOW-FM and currently at WOMC), Boston (98.5-WROR), Dallas (KLIF), New Orleans (WNOE), Atlanta (Z-93), Minneapolis (WYOO), Cincinnati (WSAI), Tampa (WFLA) and Jacksonville (WOKV).

Let me present you radio wannabes with a question: is a career as an air-talent, whether it's in news or hosting a talk or music program, any more dubious than perusing any other profession during a sagging economy? I think not! If radio news is your passion, then go for it! Things will eventually turn around; they always do! And, there will always be a need for qualified, dedicated, hardworking news journalists in radio.

How to prepare for a career as a radio news journalist.

This book is dedicated to **Roger Allan Bump**, known to his many listeners and friends, including this writer, by his air-name of Roger Allan.[19] The man lived and breathed broadcasting, especially radio news, for many years. Roger Allan had a long, successful career as a broadcast journalist in Boston and New England. He was born in Brockton, Massachusetts, graduated from Brockton High in 1949, served two years in the Navy, and in 1952, graduated from Curry College. In addition to his lengthy career in broadcast news, Roger also taught at several colleges in the Bay State, including Curry. One of his former students, Jordan Rich, today a popular talk show host on WBZ Boston, has high praise for his former mentor and friend. "I think what Roger did best was inspire people to be better broadcasters. He gave people the kind of support that no classroom could ever provide."[20]

In June 2007, I asked Roger Allan to share his feelings about his many years as one of radio's best news journalists, and to pass along his thoughts on how future broadcasters should view a career in radio news. Here are Roger's own words, exactly as he typed them on onion-skin paper on an old Royal typewriter, dated June 22, 2007. Would you expect anything else from an old-line radio news guy? It was difficult to read the words, because in his own typed words at the very top of page one, he wrote, **"Hey Joe!! Yeah, I know, I need a new ribbon…tomorrow!"** Today, reading his words once again, they still make me laugh. Roger had the ability to make you laugh. His son, Jeffrey, says his dad's sense of humor was infectious. He had a running communication with a lot of his friends, this writer included, where they would call up and exchange jokes. He would leave jokes on my answering machine all the time.

Roger was definitely a throwback to old school journalism in so many ways. For one thing, he didn't use a computer. Not that he didn't recognize their need in today's society; he just didn't feel like using one, that's all. He figured, why spend money on a piece of expensive equipment when his old, reliable typewriter was still serviceable? That, in a nutshell, is what Roger Allan was all about. He was his own man. For those interested in pursuing a radio career, whether it be as an air personality or radio journalist, Roger Allan strongly suggested a college education. "If at all possible, go to college," he urged. "You must also be self-motivated. You really must want radio! Live it, every hour of the day! Listen critically to those on the air you enjoy, what he or she says and how they say it. Inflections, tone of voice, etc. And above all, don't copy anyone!" Roger underlined those last few typed words to emphasize his point that you should always be yourself on the air. [21] "You alone are a special human being with an instrument [a voice] made up of a body which can utilize the air you breathe and a head that can always think straight. Some may not believe this," Allan continues, "but your presentation uses your body's muscles, nerves, and thoughts of creativity, all blended to bring a response within anyone listening to you. Now, that's communication. That's the biz! It's fun to communicate and to watch others respond to words used to describe facts as we communicate one to another."

The legendary Boston newsman believed the key to success for future radio journalists was to learn a second language. "Actually, I majored in broadcast journalism in college, but in high school I enjoyed learning Spanish. I wanted to use it somewhere in the world as a correspondent. Obviously, it just didn't work out that way. If there is one thing our journalism business needs now," says Roger, "it's more broadcasters who speak languages of other nations, so we could learn more about that nation! Hello! The world is getting smaller, and broadcast journalism is lacking in this regard."

The 29-year veteran of WRKO Boston felt strongly that a radio news pro needed to be "4-letter men," explaining, "Yes, a 4-letter man as we used to say among sports enthusiasts. He or she could play several sports. A radio news person must be able to be versatile, too, and be able to converse during any situation. He or she must never forget the person listening to the radio cannot see what's happening and critically needs to hear all about the news story you are describing. You must be able to ad-lib in any situation, and if you are only vaguely familiar with the story you've been assigned to cover, you should go to the proper source, the library, etc., to get helpful information. You need to understand the story you will cover from start to finish. A radio news pro can describe anything," emphasized Allan, "ANYTHING!"

"If you are on duty," said Allan, "and 'it' happens, you, and only YOU, are there to describe the situation. The real radio news person is the communicator from the story to the ear. A real news radio pro LOVES the job," he stressed. "They eat, sleep broadcasting. They put in more hours than any broadcast executive can imagine."

Bump related that some meteorologists can't wait for a frightening storm to develop, "So they can really get that challenge to develop the story for listeners. Real radio news pros can't wait for a really big story to pop up, so their knowledge will be put to the test and they will be recognized for their skills and creativity. You won't have to assign them to the story, either," Roger said, "they'll be off and running at the sound of the FIRST bulletin bell in the newsroom!"

A year before his passing in July 2008, radio journalist Bump took time to share his feelings about the future of radio news. "I worry about the future of radio news," he lamented, "because in many instances, the owners of broadcast outlets are not broadcasters. They want to own 'cash cows' and that's it. They seem to forget that the station's success is because of talented employees. These owners don't want to pay the talents' health insurance or any other benefits. They don't want 40-hour weeks for obvious reasons. I also worry about the Federal Communications Commission. Where are the broadcasters on the commission? We are supposed to broadcast in the public interest, convenience and necessity, and I simply don't hear this on a daily basis anymore."

There's little doubt Roger Allan was the quintessential old-line radio news guy who longed for a time when news on the radio was given high priority to the listener, a time when being a radio journalist was considered by many as a highly-respected and admired profession. He raises some thought provoking questions on when and where did radio news coverage, especially on the local scene cease to exist. "Where is the radio station float in the local parade," he asked. "Why don't radio stations broadcast parades any longer, or for that matter other community events? Apple pie and broadcasting…gone." In closing, Roger Allan made a direct plea to colleges and universities. "Utilize broadcasters, current or retired, to teach," he urged. "Colleges want people with doctorate degrees, but real broadcasters have very little time to study for doctorate degrees. It's time for colleges and universities to get talented airmen and women on their faculties and let the reality set in. Only then will students realize not anyone can sit and talk or play CDs or other digital sources for radio listeners and be entertaining and informative. If we don't get back to what radio was and is, the theater of the mind, I'm afraid radio listeners will be playing their own CDs, because the thrill and excitement that radio once provided will be gone forever. Radio, long may it last."

Roger Allan Bump was 79 when he passed away in July 2008. I miss hearing his voice on my answering machine sharing one of his favorite jokes; radio lost a very special one-of-a-kind voice in him.

Radio pros speak out about your future in radio news.

Mary Blake is another familiar radio news voice to Boston listeners. Mary has worked in radio news since 1979 and began her broadcasting career in Lowell, Massachusetts, at a small community-oriented station where she was able to learn a little bit of everything about radio, including how to turn the transmitter back on when it got knocked off the air during a severe thunderstorm! She next joined another Lowell station, WCAP, where she cut her teeth as a broadcast journalist. "I was responsible for three daily news features along with anchoring the morning news," says Mary. The news feature allowed her to go out into the community, where she learned to appreciate what an industrial city like

Lowell had to offer. Mary worked at WCAP for four years and then Boston radio beckoned.

Mary Blake joined RKO General in 1983 and that's where she and I first worked together. Mary anchored the news on my morning drive show at the original Golden Great 98.5-WROR. She is not only the consummate radio pro, but also one of the nicest people I worked with during my forty-one years on the air. Niceness and being talented are not often found together in many radio personalities, but Mary is the exception. She is highly qualified to pass along advice to future radio news journalists.

The UMass graduate with a concentration in Communication Studies has been a news anchor on Boston airwaves for over twenty-five years, working on the air at WROR, WBMX, WRKO, and most recently at WBZ.

Over the years, Mary has won more than two-dozen awards from AP, UPI and RTNDA.[22] I asked Mary to share her feelings about being female and trying to make it as a radio pro in a field still dominated primarily by males.[23] "I think being taken seriously is still a battle with some program directors, news directors, and station managers, and even listeners at times," she says. "I've fielded calls in the newsroom where a listener would begin by saying, 'Tell that girl reading the news-blah, blah, blah.' I went to a job interview once," she confides, "where the news director asked me if I was planning to have a family, because he didn't want to worry about maternity leaves!"

Mary Blake has some strong opinions about "voices" on the radio. "I think even women are more critical of higher-pitched voices. I tend to hear more complaints from people about the sound of women's voices on the radio than men's, even though there are many more male broadcasters." As far as how women broadcasters are perceived by some industry workers, Mary shares a personal story that was quite upsetting to her. "I'll never forget it. I was covering a New England Patriots event when a new coach was named. At the time there were no cell phones and you had to file your story at a payphone. Well, a Boston TV sportscaster actually yelled at me to get off the phone because he had a story to file, *as if I didn't!* It was rude and uncalled for, and as I said, I've never forgotten it."

She offers this advice to women seeking a radio news career and looking to break into broadcasting: "I would recommend going to a small station first, if you can find one. I know that these days they are harder and harder to find, and to make matters worse, the pay is usually abysmal! However, they do allow you to be a jack-of-all trades and you can learn the ropes quickly and then move onward and upward. I'd say push hard, especially at stations where you're not hearing female voices, and put that observation in your cover letter. The general manager at the last station I worked at bemoaned the lack of female voices on the station. Always try and save your good work," she advises, "so you can send out a resume and air-check at a moment's notice, and remember, your air-check is your ticket to the next step - an interview - it needs to be the best it can be. For all broadcasting wannabes, you'll need to be flexible," warns Blake. "Radio has crazy hours and sleep deprivation seems to be the norm rather than the exception for most of us who work in the business, but," she adds with a smile, "you meet great people and it truly is fun!"

Another well-recognized voice in Boston radio news circles is **Rod Fritz**. Like Mary Blake, Rod and I also worked together at the original WROR Boston. In 1979, I was the morning drive guy and Rod anchored the news. Rod has a unique style and delivery and it was fun playing off him on the air. I learned much about the news biz by observing and listening to him and his choice of news stories.

Rod admits to being a Navy brat and grew up all over the country from Pennsylvania and New York to Illinois and California. "I used to sit in my bedroom at night when I was between twelve and fifteen, and listen to any AM radio station that would come in, from as far away as possible. I always listened to Dick Summer on WBZ and Dick Biondi on WLS. [24] In 1962, it was listening to Biondi and his antics that got me hooked on radio. I dreamed of the day I could be a radio disc jockey just like him," laughs Fritz, "never realizing that I would end up as a newscaster."

Talk about a long prosperous radio career! Rod Fritz has had one, from his first on-air job in 1971 at WCRV in Washington, to later stops in Allentown, PA (WEEX), St. Petersburg, Florida (WSUN), Philadelphia (WPEN), Denver (KIMN), and several Boston radio stations: WHDH, WEEI, WROR, WMJX, ten years at WRKO, and his current radio home, WBZ. With a long and successful radio news career, Rod Fritz knows what he's talking about when it comes to a career as a radio journalist.

"Study hard in high school and college," urges news veteran Fritz. "Study English and take any drama course that you can. You will find that being a good actor can really help you when you get into radio. In college, study communications and other general subjects that interest you, like political science or history. The more general your education, the more varied topics you will be able to fall back on when you're finally on the air." He also feels that it is very important to get that degree. "You will find that the longer you are in broadcasting, the more that degree will help you pursue your career." He also urges future radio news journalists to be sure current events is something that interests them. "News is changing every day. It can be very, very exciting. Covering a news event in person -whether it be the inauguration of a President, the swearing-in of a city council, the Super Bowl, or even a tragic accident - it's all part of history, so to speak, no matter if it's happening in your community or a world event."

Rod Fritz believes you need to be interested in the world around you to be a good news person.

"You also need to remember to be fair in your reporting," he adds. "If you begin to offer opinions, and many news people do, then perhaps a talk show host may be more to your liking. In any event, you still need to be interested in what is going on around you in your town, state, and country."

'How does this experienced radio news pro feel about seeking a career in radio news today? "I think it is very difficult to break into any aspect of the biz today," says Fritz. "BUT RADIO WILL NEVER DIE! It will always be with us. For sure, the business has evolved a lot over the last several decades. Corporations have more control in programming, share holders are demanding more profit and fewer and fewer stations actually have local news departments, which is a big mistake, in my opinion. One place to break into radio news," he suggests, "is at your college radio station, or small-town station, if there is one. Otherwise, you are pretty much left to the luck of the draw. You must be persistent, though, to succeed in getting a job in radio, news-wise or as a personality, in a major market. The important thing is DON'T GIVE UP! Constantly work hard to improve your on-air delivery and gather your experience in the radio game. The more you know, the better chance you will have at landing that big-time job," stresses Boston news radio pro Rod Fritz.

If there ever was such a thing as the "voice of New England radio news," it had to belong to **Gary LaPierre.** For more than forty years, Gary informed listeners around New England every morning on WBZ-Boston. He joined WBZ News radio as a general assignment editor in the early 1960s and two years later took over the morning news anchor post, a position he held for forty years. During his tenure, LaPierre won dozens of local, regional, and national news awards, including several Edward R. Murrow Awards for Best Radio Newscast and Investigative Journalism. LaPierre's ability to communicate is legendary throughout the broadcast industry. On several occasions he filled in for Paul Harvey on the popular commentator's network *News* and *Comment* broadcasts.

I asked LaPierre to pass along his experience and knowledge to those desiring a career in radio news. "Well, to begin with and in my opinion, a future in radio news is dubious at best. Take Boston, for example," he says. "If you want a job in radio news, you're either working at BZ or you're not working. It's pathetic. The attention span of the public equals that of an ant. Radio stations don't bother with grooming local reporters anymore. They plug in the networks. Now, having said all that," Gary adds, "if you're a news junkie, a solid liberal arts background is the best. Sprinkle in some political science courses because the whole world is political and all politics is local. Learn who the players are in the community where you want to work, and start scratchin'!"

Gary LaPierre does feel that the chances of making a good living in any city in America right now are minimal. "Yes, you'll find work in radio," he says, "maybe 40 to 60Gs, but make big bucks? Fuhgeddaboudit. Radio today, not unlike the big newspapers in America, is splintered, dumbed-down, and left impotent in many ways. The world is fascinated with itself, with e-mail, picture phones, text messaging, and everybody's even got their own blog" - even Gary LaPierre! To read what he's been doing lately, go to www.lapierrecommunicates.com.

Ed Walsh was Gary LaPierre's replacement at BZ when Gary retired. Ed has a boatload of credentials in the radio news profession. He joined WBZ Boston from sister station WCBS Newsradio in New York. He also anchored the news at All-News 1010 WINS, and at ABC News Radio. He has hosted the morning news talk programs at New York's WOR and at KFYI in Phoenix. For Ed Walsh, returning to Boston and joining WBZ means he has come full circle in his career. He began in broadcast journalism at Boston's WRKO, where he was also news director, a position he carried with him to stations in New York and Phoenix. The winner of dozens of national and regional journalism awards, including the Edward R. Murrow, Walsh has been recognized for best newscast in New York, Boston and Phoenix.

Ed Walsh is on the same page with his predecessor at WBZ, Gary LaPierre, when it comes to the future of radio news. "Regrettably, radio news is an ever-shrinking market, so you'd better be good!

Many places have turned to syndication companies like Shadow/Metro to provide traffic, sports, and even news reports. News departments are not even under the direct control of a local station's news director or program director. They tend to be less experienced," he explains, "and are paid far less and they're on the air in major markets like Boston." Walsh, a Holy Cross grad, believes the best way to prepare for a career in radio news is to have the benefit of at least some exposure to liberal arts.

"Journalism as a major," says Ed, "isn't as critical as is having some familiarity with it as well as with the classics, philosophy, science and political science. In radio news, you will be expected to be a generalist," points out Walsh, "endlessly fascinated with the world in all its aspects and conversant in enough of them to hit the ground running when encountering stories that run from the theft of famous art works to the collapse of a major investment bank to a sports steroid scandal. Plus, politics, crime, human interest, everything!"

Ed Walsh leaves future radio news journalists with this solid piece of advice: "Be prepared to be flexible, be able to fill in on talk shows and newscasts, be ready to work off-air in editing and writing positions and be ready to assume middle management roles as news and program director and don't be reluctant to follow opportunities in new markets." [25]

My sincerest thanks to WBZ radio news journalists, past and present, Mary Blake, Rod Fritz, Gary LaPierre, and Ed Walsh, for their contributions to this chapter.

David Brinkley

News montage. top row left: CBS pioneer news commentator, Floyd Gibbons (with eye patch), Lowell Thomas who replaced Gibbons. Center row from left: H.V. Kaltenborn, Walter Winchell (with hat on ABC mic), Edward R. Murrow, Douglas Edwards. Bottom row, from left, Robert Trout, Gabriel Heater and Walter Cronkite.

Radio Formats: News, Talk and Sports • 485

Cart Equipment Archive

MacKenzie

Louis G. MacKenzie developed his "repeater" in 1955. Using a silver coated tag applied to an endless tape loop (to provide a "cueing" function, the single and "five pack" machines could provide instant starting of desired spots. The tape cartridges were square metal boxes, with the tape loop hanging out.

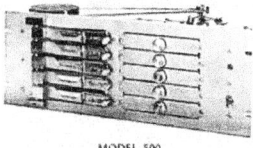
MODEL 500

The MacKenzie program repeater was offered in numerous configurations - with as many as 10 decks in a unit. The popular Model 500 (shown) featured 5 decks and independent audio outputs for each. The unit used a common capstan, much like the ITC 3-Deck cartridge machines that became so popular in the '70's. A front panel volume control was provided for each deck. The tape itself was mounted in a metal "magazine", and sat on a hinged deck secured with a thumbscrew. Loosening the screw allowed the deck to "swing open", providing access to the magazine.

Collins to Gates

Criterion Compact

Criterion Compact III

Gates Radio

When Bailey and Jenkins approached Gates with their design, Gates Radio was already developing the ST-101. The ST-101 found its way into many stations, but it was not practical to run more than one spot at a time. Eventually, Gates changed and built machines that could utilize individual cartridges.

ST-101 - 1960 - $995
This unit featured a 13-inch-wide tape belt and moveable head. It could run 101 different tracks, but only one at a time.

AMPEX
601

The portable recorder you specified

now the famous Ampex portable fits your professional recording needs exactly

ITC - International Tapetronics
SP - 1970 - The workhorse for thousands of stations.

Spotmaster 405 reproducer - The first of the famous ones with the "hand crank" to bring the pressure roller up for use. The case on this one is made of wood!

Spotmaster 500A recorder

Spotmaster 500B recorder
1963 - $695 - to switch from record to play you had to rotate the knob on the lower right.

www.oldradio.com/archives/hardware/carts.htm

Radio equipment montage.

Boston radio news voices. Top row from left, Barbara Quill and Rod Fritz; WROR 98.5 Boston news staff from the 1980's Susan Nardone, Bill Smith, Bob MacNeil with Mary Blake (seated). Center row from left: Don Latulippe; long-time WBZ News anchor Gary LaPierre interviewing Boston Mayor Tom Menino. Bottom: Ed Walsh – present-day WBZ morning drive news anchor.

RADIO FORMATS—PART 2 OF 3—TALK

"If you don't abuse your position, you have an opportunity to do a vast amount of good. If you do abuse it, you'll soon find yourself talking to yourself."
– Pioneer news commentator, Lowell Thomas from a 1949 interview with Radio-TV Mirror.

Talk on radio is a winner because it's foreground listening and not relegated to the background, which is often the case with most music-intense stations. People listen to music on radio primarily as a background to whatever they're doing. Talk, news, sports, and a personality with something to say on radio is foreground listening and requires upfront attentive listening. Simply said, it forces listeners to pay attention to what is being said, or they may miss something!

Real talk radio consists of spellbinding rhetoric and dramatic exchanges between the show host and the caller, along with tough but polite interviews with newsmakers of the day. *Excellent* talk radio should focus on something of importance, whether it be local, national, or the problems of the world affecting all of us!

Pointers on how to be a successful talk radio host.

First and most importantly as a successful talk host or show host in any radio format, you need to entertain your listeners and keep them interested in what you have to say! Talk radio doesn't have to be a place solely for serious discussion, at least not all the time. Grave, serious talk radio can quickly become boring. Pepper your show with what listeners are talking about, including celebrities with huge, out-of-control egos. Your audience cares about the big picture and what is happening in our tired old world, but they are also talking about trivial, gossipy things.

Your goal should be talking about what your listeners are talking about. As a talk show host the last thing you want to happen to your performance is to become predictable. It's important to stick with and espouse your core values, feelings, and beliefs, but that does NOT mean that to do so you will become predictable in your delivery. You occasionally need to shake things up. Work on saying the same thing, only in a different way. It's not an easy thing to do, and requires hard work on your part.

As the show host, if you find yourself saying to a guest, "Well, there are some people who think this and that about that, what do you think?" If you do that, then you're not doing talk correctly! You need to *voice your opinions* and make it clear where you stand on a subject. It's important so your listeners know exactly where you stand on a specific issue! Let your callers challenge you; it makes for compelling radio. In fact, you should hope and pray they come after you with flames shooting from their nostrils. Always have an opinion! It makes for better talk radio. There's nothing more uninteresting than a show host without an opinion. Disagreement and conflict presented in a civilized way make for interesting and compelling talk radio!

Boston talk programmer **Paula O'Connor** says, "The qualities I look for in a prospective talk talent are certainly their overall personality, but also if they have strong opinions, to be able to read between the lines, present their opinions with emotion and passion to evoke, a response from the listener."

The "B-12" list for talk show hosts.

Talented and well-informed talk radio hosts will do well and their audiences will grow if they keep in mind a few basics while on the air. We call these basics the "B-12" list.

1. Be respectful of your callers and guests - disagree in polite fashion without being disagreeable.
2. Be responsible - remember that you have a vast listening audience. Keep your facts straight.
3. Be reasonable - take time to listen to what your caller and/or guest is saying, even if you disagree.
4. Be civil - debate a guest intelligently but always be civil, even if you don't receive the same courtesy.
5. Be hard hitting - but not in a mean-spirited way.
6. Be sensitive to others and always remember there is no place for bigotry, on or off the air.
7. Be yourself - There is only ONE Rush Limbaugh.
8. Be entertaining to your listeners.
9. Be a champion for your listeners—represent them well in controversial issues that arise.
10. Be controversial, but have fun doing so. Remember, radio is show business.
11. Be interested in what you are talking about. If you're disinterested, so will be your listeners.
12. Be unpredictable with your topics and show content. Politics are fine, but your listeners need more.

Talk and information programs have their roots in radio's earliest days.

During radio's earliest days, talk and information programs, not unlike today, presented contrasting views of topical issues of the day. Programs of this type allowed listeners to hear the views of the host and experts. In the late '40s, listeners got to call in to speak out and express their own views, thereby giving birth to two-way talk radio. Today, talk is one format that has found a lucrative home on radio, first on AM in the late '70s when music made the shift to FM, and today on both AM & FM.

One of radio's earliest and most powerful political talk-radio voices was not a journalist but a Catholic priest. **Father Charles Edward Coughlin**, the mellow priest with a bit of a brogue, was from a small parish in Royal Oak, Michigan. He first took the airwaves by storm on WJR Detroit in October 1926 with his weekly broadcast of inspirational and personal commentary. The "Fighting Priest," as he was called, captured the imagination of millions of Americans following the dark years of the Depression with his visions of a better future. Throughout the 1930s, the radio priest had a listening audience estimated at around forty million. Mail poured in to his Shrine of the Little Flower in Royal Oak, Michigan, at the rate of around 50,000 letters a week.

Father Coughlin was a strong opponent of Presidents Herbert Hoover and Franklin Delano Roosevelt and attacked both on his program with equal fervor. Eventually, the fighting priest offended so many people that in 1933, CBS refused to renew his contract because he would not submit his scripts in advance of his broadcasts. Not to be dismayed, Coughlin, with donations and support from his legions of loyal listeners, established his own network of radio stations. Soon he was back on the air with an even larger listening audience than before. The Fighting Priest became so popular that he was able to form a third political party. In 1936, his Union Party even produced a presidential candidate, William Lemke of North Dakota. Father Coughlin accused President Roosevelt of being a "great betrayer and a liar," referring to FDR as a "scab President." As the radio priest's rantings became more outrageous, he came under fire from Catholic leaders, including the Holy See. Many of the priest's loyal supporters and listeners tuned out and turned away. In April 1940, no longer able to afford the air-time, Father Charles Edward Coughlin's voice disappeared forever from radio. On May 1, 1942, the Archbishop of Detroit, the Most Reverend Edward Mooney, ordered the priest to stop his political activities and to concentrate on his duties as a parish priest, with a warning that he would be defrocked if he refused.

He complied and remained pastor of the Shrine of the Little Flower until his retirement in 1966. Coughlin refused most interviews and continued writing pamphlets denouncing Communism until his death at age 88 in Bloomfield Hills, Michigan, on October 27, 1979.

At the opposite end of the radio spectrum from Father Coughlin is a brash radio personality from Roosevelt, Long Island, New York. **Howard Stern** is one of radio's most controversial morning show talk hosts. Like his priestly predecessor Stern basks in controversy, but that's where the similarities end. Stern's graphic, in-your-face descriptions of various sexual activities, peppered with profanity and vulgarity, has not detracted from his popularity. Before his move to Sirius Satellite, the FCC persistently tried to quiet him down and fine him for his lewd on-air content.[26] I don't subscribe to his type of radio, nor do I endorse it in any way. I acknowledge that others enjoy his style and as vulgar as it may be to some, that's the gift of free speech in America. Many find his humor offensive and less than appealing, and you can include me as one of that group. Interestingly, those who are often the most shocked by his outrageous behavior on the air also defend his right to do so. Count me in as one, again. The old adage still applies: if you don't like what you hear, don't listen. Like him or not, there is only one Howard Stern. For you future radio stars who wish to emulate his style, go for it. Just know Howard Stern is a tough act to follow. He is uniquely himself and an original on the air. Some said he had a short shelf-life. Let's look at his numbers. He first began on radio in 1976. As of 2011, he is still around and doing his morning shock show on Sirius Satellite. Short shelf-life? You do the math.

Shock radio vs. nice guy on the radio.

A word of caution to those of you who wish to pursue "shock" radio as your own air-style: It has been my experience, based on many years on the air, including morning drive, that you will have a longer shelf-life in radio if you come off as a nice person. Your listeners need to like you before you can get away with dumping on them even in a fun way. Howard Stern is one of the exceptions to the rule.

When my former Boston radio partner **Andy Moes** first joined me in mornings, he was a loose cannon. He would spew forth anything he felt like saying and doing! Andy was naturally funny and clever. I urged him to temper his raunchy comments and to capitalize on his wittiness, rather than being crude and lewd. Andy didn't have to dig down in the sewer for his comments to be funny. I constantly reminded him that he had to be liked before he could get away with insulting our listener base. He just smiled, shrugged it off, and attributed my comments to being good ole Puritanical Joey. That is, until our ratings began to plummet. Being a bright boy, Andy came to his senses really fast. His role developed into radio's quintessential bad boy, while I played the big brother. My role was to try and keep him in line, to reel him in, when he would begin to stray beyond the limits of good taste. As he controlled his output and focused on self-deprecating humor, which our listeners loved, it was an automatic win for us. Our ratings on *Joe n' Andy* shot through the roof.[27] It worked for us and we went on to enjoy a long, successful run as one of Boston's favorite and top-rated morning drive radio teams.

When Andy chatted about being overweight and the dumb things he did everyday, which everyone could identify with, it clicked with our listeners.

By placing himself in the "poor soul" role, it allowed him to get away with projecting his rascally, bad boy side. Whenever he began to let his personality on the radio sound the least bit over the top and out of control, our listeners automatically thought, "Oh, that's just Andy. He's really a good guy, and if he gets too far out of line, Joe, the voice of reason, will rein him in, you just watch!" We had our roles down pat and so did our listeners. They came to know what to expect from us and it paid off handsomely in so many ways for almost ten years. A word of caution to future radio stars: if your listeners don't like you, they won't listen, and without a loyal listener base, your ratings will quickly fade away like some distant AM station and you will, too!

A word about sexual humor. There is a world of difference in *sexual innuendo* and being *sexually explicit* and letting it all hang out all over the radio. A creative air-personality will always find a clever way to say something. Anyone can be lazy and make sexually crude comments. Finding a way to say it with double entendres and allowing the listener to draw their own conclusion is the mark of a real radio pro. Adults are pretty savvy. They'll figure it out!

Some of America's best-known talkers look at talk radio. (Their comments were made for NewsMax.com.)

Bill Bennett, a Reagan conservative, whose morning radio show is on over 135 stations, prefers to call talk radio, "listening radio." He said, "Americans and international listeners, too, are smart and informed people and are tired of being talked down to, tired of being lectured at by the mainstream media."

Mike Gallagher, another Reagan conservative who is on over 200 radio stations and is a regular contributor to the Fox News Channel, described talk radio this way: "I've always loved the description of talk radio by the late Boston talk radio personality, David Brudnoy. He referred to talk radio as the last great neighborhood. We're like a huge configuration of picket fences in backyards that neighbors use to convey what really matters to them. Sometimes we fight, sometimes, we laugh, sometimes we sell each other something, but we're always shaping ideas and sharing opinions. With the war on terror, world-wide turmoil and uncertain political times," Brodnoy added, "we need those picket fences and neighbors more than ever."

Michael Medved, a one-time liberal turned conservative who is syndicated on almost 200 stations, says he loves talk radio "because the medium is about ideas and argument."

According to *Talkers Magazine* publisher Michael Harrison, "Talk radio is the most accurate bellwether of American public opinion in the mass media today."

A brief history of talk radio pioneers.

In 1925, Bernard McFadden had a radio show in New York City, but not for very long. One morning, McFadden failed to show up for his daily program, which gave a young studio engineer, John Gambling, the opportunity to sit in on the air and ad-lib for a solid hour, thus becoming one of radio's first talk-masters. His efforts resulted in the radio station, WOR, giving Gambling the morning announcer's job. John Gambling stayed on the radio at WOR[28] for over forty years before turning the mic over to his son, who in turn, turned it over to his son, all named John! The *Rambling with Gambling* program on the 50,000-watt powerhouse station at 710 on the AM dial attracted tri-state (New York, New Jersey & Connecticut) audiences in record numbers for over seventy years!

During radio's formative years, commentary and round-table discussion programs played an important role in developing talk programming. Discussion programs included *The American Forum of the Air*, which debuted on NBC in 1937 with Theodore Granik as moderator. It enjoyed a nineteen-year run. Other talk programs included *America's Town Meeting of the Air* with George V. Denny, Jr., as the host. It presented opposing political views by panelists and took questions from the audience. In 1934, Bob Becker passed out useful info on how to care for your dog. His program aired for ten years until 1944, on NBC and then CBS. Victor Lindlahr dispensed health advice for seventeen years, from 1936 until 1953, on Mutual. Beginning in 1937 and airing until 1944, John J. Anthony offered advice to people with problems on *The Goodwill Hour*, first on Mutual and later, ABC from 1937 until 1944.

During radio's early days, women talkers stood shoulder to shoulder with the men. Even though they were usually relegated to hosting cooking or gossip programs, women nevertheless made an indelible mark on radio. One of America's most popular fictional homemakers was Betty Crocker. She debuted on NBC in 1926 and was later heard on CBS and ABC during her remarkable run of 26 years, through 1952. Zella Layne, among others, played Betty Crocker on that long-running radio program. Ida Bailey Allen was host of Radio's *Homemakers Club* on CBS from 1928 until 1936. Ruth Crane began on radio in 1929 and was known as the First Lady of Radio in the nation's capital. Other female radio talk show hosts included popular songstress Kate Smith, who hosted a noontime talk show, *Kate Smith Speaks*, on CBS from 1938 to 1947, sponsored by General Foods.[29] In 1957, Smith's daily talk show aired on Mutual. Mary Margaret McBride began on WOR- New York in 1934 under her air-name, Martha Deane.[30] In 1937, she joined CBS for a 15-minute talk show and in 1941, moved to NBC, when the network offered her a daily 45-minute timeslot. The first half-hour was a celebrity interview and the last 15-minute portion was Mary chatting about her sponsors. Her program ran for ten years at 1pm EST. McBride moved to ABC in 1950 for a daily half-hour show. She left radio in 1954.

In the 1930s, cooking programs were on network radio's menu. *The G.E. Home Circle* on NBC in 1931 featured a daily noontime homemaker program hosted by Grace Ellis. Frances Lee Barton was on NBC from 1932 until 1935 as host of the daytime cooking show, *Kitchen Party*. Mary Ellis Ames, with her 15-minute cooking program, was on CBS. Edythe Fern Melrose was first heard on radio in Cleveland in 1930. In the 1950s, her *Charm Kitchen* was on WXYZ in Detroit. Popular Mary Lee Taylor had a 30-minute Saturday morning cooking program which aired for 17 years, from 1937 until 1954, on CBS and later NBC. In 1936, Bea Johnson was *Joanne Taylor the Happy Homemaker* on KMPC Kansas City. Margaret MacDonald played *Betty Moore* on a 15-minute home decorating show originally on NBC and later CBS, sponsored by Moore Paints from 1931 until 1943.

Astrology also played a significant role on network radio in the 1930s. Astrologer Madame Sylvia was on the Blue Network (ABC) with a 15-minute show, while Belle Barte was on Mutual from 1936 to '37. She was followed on the same network in 1937-38 by Myra Kingsley with astrological advice.

Emily Post and her 15-minute program on manners was heard on CBS, later the Blue Network, from 1930 until 1933. *Child's World* was on ABC from 1947-49, hosted by well-known educator Helen Parkhurst, who interviewed children on subjects from God to death and dying. *Ask Eleanor Nash* debuted on the Blue Network (ABC) in 1941 as a 15-minute daytime fashion and beauty program. *What's Your Idea*, hosted by Imogene Walcott, was another quarter-hour morning program on Mutual and aired from 1943-45.

Movie critics and gossip columnists also talked it up on radio in the thirties. *The Nellie Revell Show* was a 15-minute interview program hosted by the variety columnist. It aired on NBC from 1934-36. Popular Hollywood columnist Louella Parsons was on CBS and later ABC with a gossip show that ran from 1931 until 1951. She was followed by another well-known Hollywood reporter, Hedda Hopper, whose voice was on CBS and later NBC from 1939 through 1951. Film critic Radie Harris and her 15-minute program aired on Mutual from 1938-39. Newspaper columnist Dorothy Kilgallen was host of the *Voice of Broadway*, another 15-minute gossip program, on ABC in 1949. Another favorite gossip columnist, Sheilah Graham, also debuted on radio the same year.

One of network radio's first female political voices was Eleanor Roosevelt. She began on CBS Radio in 1932 in a 15-minute format. Eleanor hosted several radio shows during and after the time her husband Franklin Delano served as President. After her CBS years, until 1949, she was heard on NBC and ABC. Maggie McNellis and her interview program first began on NBC in 1944, and later moved to ABC, continuing until 1948. One of radio's first political round-table programs, NBC's *Meet the Press*, began in 1945. The popular program, still going strong today after sixty-five years, was created by Martha Roundtree. She co-hosted with Lawrence Spivak.

Aline Kazajian, better known to millions of radio listeners and TV viewers as Arlene Francis, was one of radio's first female talk hosts and personalities. Arlene began her radio career in 1935 on WOR New York and concluded her career on the same station some 40 years later. In that time, the popular star was featured on a dozen radio programs and as many TV shows, including a long association as a panelist on *What's My Line?* Ruth Lyons, a broadcast institution in Cincinnati and throughout the Midwest, joined WLW in 1942 and remained on radio and TV for a quarter of a century until she retired in 1967.[31] To this day, the mere mention of her name brings a smile to those who remember her as host of the *50/50 Club*.

In the '40s and '50s, morning drive time had its share of talk-teams on radio, some of whom are covered in Chapter One. In the 1950s, Mary Jones was more than a chatty radio personality on WFIL-Philadelphia. She was a leader of the city's most popular women's civic groups. The Mary Jones Club served as an inspiration for 3,000 women who shared in charitable work.

Pauline Frederick holds the distinction of being the first woman network news analyst and diplomatic correspondent on American radio. For many years, she covered the United Nations on both NBC Radio and TV. *Breakfast with Paula* aired weekday mornings in the '50s on WIRE-Indianapolis. Paula Karr was the host, also holding the distinction of being the first woman on the Indianapolis Speedway Network broadcast. In 1955, Patty Cavin hosted her daily radio show, *Capital Bylines*, on WRC-Washington. She also contributed to NBC's weekend magazine program, *Monitor*. These are just some of the women who pioneered talk on radio and paved the way for others to follow.

Long before Glenn Beck, Alan Colmes, Laura Ingraham, Rush Limbaugh, and the rest of the current crop of talkers were chatting away on America's airwaves, yesteryear's radio featured many talk-masters. New Yorkers and Barry Farber mixed political jargon with offbeat topics, like guests who were taken prisoner by space aliens. Another Barry, also based in New York on WMCA in the nighttime, was Barry Gray. He, along with Boston's Jerry Williams, is credited with creating two-way talk radio.

Legend has it that it all began for Barry Gray in 1945. He was on the air at WMCA and apparently bored with playing music, not unlike many of today's air-talent, held a telephone up to his mic to interview bandleader Woody Herman. The exchange was later followed by listener call-ins and two-way talk radio was born on America's airwaves. In 1948, Alan Courtney began a call-in program in Miami, first on WGBS and later on WQAM and WINZ. Alan, along with the two Barrys, Farber and Gray, helped pioneer talk radio in the U.S., but two-way talk radio which is so popular today really came into to its own in the early 1950s. Early talk-masters Jerry Williams on WMEX-AM 1510 Boston and Long John Nebel in New York City on WOR popularized two-way talk radio.

I got to know the late Jerry Williams, the Dean of Talk Radio, when we both worked for RKO Boston. I was in AM-Drive on the FM side at ROR, while Jerry masterfully handled talk in PM-drive on the AM side at RKO. Williams and other early radio talk hosts were highly opinionated, and that's what made them great![32] Their shows were thought provoking, interesting, and entertaining. They could be acerbic to the point of being insulting to their callers, and listeners ate 'em up! The new breed of radio talk hosts in the '50s made no attempt to play nice-nice with the callers. In fact, controversy was the word for talkers like Joe Pyne in LA and Jerry Williams in Boston.

Talk saves the day for radio!

In the early 1950s, when listeners were leaving radio by the boatload in favor of the television, talk programming saved the day for radio. Talk shows began building new audiences late at night, when most TV stations were off the air. Midnight-to-dawn personalities, like Long John Nebel and Candy Jones on WOR, discussed way-out topics like the occult attracting a large audience and becoming big business. "Big Joe" Rosenfeld and his *Happiness Exchange* aired the heartbreaks and troubles of his callers and was another listener favorite. WOR New York is credited with developing one of radio's first all-talk formats, having evolved on the station over many years dating back to the 1940s. Radio pros like Jean Shepherd, who hosted a late-night show on WOR NYC from 1956 until 1977, had tapes of their shows syndicated to both large- and small-market stations around the country.

In 1955, NBC Radio created a unique program concept called *Monitor*. The extended weekend program service was the network's attempt to rekindle the spark of radio's glorious days of the '30s, '40s and early '50s. NBC created the weekend programming service for its network affiliates in the form of an audio magazine of the air. The ingenious 40-hour weekend show represented a new concept in radio, including news, interviews, remote pick-ups, and brief comedy bits from NBC stars Fibber McGee & Molly and Bob & Ray, along with musical segments.[33] Well-known broadcast personalities of the day hosted various segments, including Hugh Downs, Arlene Francis, Morgan Beatty, Frank Blair, Barbara Walters, Dave Garroway, John Cameron Swayze, Henry Morgan, Ed McMahon, Bill Cullen, Gene Rayburn, Joe Garagiola, and others. *Monitor*, with its opening billboard, "Monitor, a continuing service in sound ... going places and doing things, you're on the Monitor beacon." NBC's innovative program enjoyed a nineteen-year run until 1974. *Monitor* is credited with being the first extended talk programming on network radio.

In 1960, two radio stations, KMOX-1120AM St. Louis under station manager Robert Hyland and KABC 790AM-Los Angeles managed by Ben Hoberman, adopted all-talk formats. WBZ Boston has programmed talk at night since the early '60s with *Contact* and host Bob Kennedy, followed by a sports talk show, *Calling all Sports*, with Guy Manilla and later Bob Lobell and Upton Bell as hosts. Bill Balance was the nighttime personality in the late '50s and early '60s on top-rated KFWB, Los Angeles. In 1971, he moved to KGBS and became well known as host of the *Feminine Forum* radio show where he mixed topics with callers and in-studio guests.

Bill Balance is considered the forerunner to "shock jocks" Howard Stern, Tom Leykis and Opie and Anthony. Balance left LA in 1978 and joined KFMB-San Diego, where he was on the air for fifteen years. He retired from radio in 1993 after more than fifty years in the business.

At first, talk radio only flourished in major cities like New York, Boston, Philly and LA, but little by little, in town after town, local personalities began popping up and became huge hometown favorites. In the 1960s, one of Maine's favorite radio talk show hosts was Craig Worthing.[34] He and I broke into radio at a small southern Maine station, WIDE-AM-1400 in Biddeford. Craig's talk career began at the station with a daily interview show, *Seacoast Kaleidoscope*. He next moved to nearby Portland and WPOR-AM-1490, followed by a cross-town move to WGAN-560AM as the host of one of Maine's first call-in talk shows, *Maine-Line*. Worthing's name became well known to listeners up and down Maine's southern seacoast. Later, his talk career took him to Utica, New York, and South Florida.

Herb Jepko was another of radio's first talk personalities. In the '60s and '70s, he had a huge, loyal following across America. Sadly, today, he is mostly forgotten. I hope to change that and let readers know what a tremendous impact he had on talk radio. Future talk hosts can learn much from Jepko.

Born in Hayden, Colorado, on March 20, 1931, Herb Jepko later moved to Arizona with his dad and graduated from high school in Phoenix. He attended Phoenix College with hopes of becoming a doctor, but ran out of money and was drafted into the Army. While serving in the military, Herb discovered his life's work, radio, and during the Korean War he worked in Armed Forces Radio. After his discharge, he worked at several stations in the western United States, including KVNA-Flagstaff, AZ and KFI in Los Angeles. While working in promotions at KFI, Herb became highly influenced by popular late-night personality Ben Hunter. Herb was impressed by how loyal the late-night audience can be. Herb stayed in LA through the rest of the '50s, married Patsy Little, and in the early '60s they moved to her hometown, Salt Lake City, where he worked at several stations. In 1962, he was hired to do middays at KSL and in '63 moved to morning drive. Herb couldn't believe that a powerful station like KSL signed off at midnight. He knew how successful Ben Hunter's show had been in LA and believed there was a similar late night audience in Salt Lake City that was not being served. He set out to convince management to put him on from midnight to 6am.

On February 11, 1964, *Herb Jepko's Nitecap Show* debuted on KSL and soon found an enormous following. By 1975, Herb's nightly show became the first nationally syndicated talk show when the Mutual Radio Network agreed to syndicate it. Jepko's show was laidback and consisted primarily of listener calls. Outside of politics and religion, any subject was fair game, no matter how big or how small. As the show became more popular, regular callers were limited to one call every two weeks of no more than five minutes' length. Herb ran a recording of a music box version of the song "Never on Sunday" to signal the callers time was up. In a world of angry talkers, Herbie, as his listeners called him, was known for being friendly, warm and definitely non-controversial. He was the perfect person with the perfect voice for the midnight to 6am timeslot.

In 1965, in an interview with the *Ogden* (Utah) *Examiner*, Jepko told an interviewer that he hoped his program would contribute to "good will and understanding" and that his listeners would feel like they were part of a family. Jepko's show was more than just a radio show. It was a club. "Nitecaps," as they were called, formed local chapters called "Nitestands." Nitestand clubs were encouraged to do charitable work in their communities and took Herbie's message about spreading good will to heart. They volunteered their time helping the elderly, hospitalized and ill persons, and shut-ins. Herb Jepko's show had its own magazine called *The Wick* and even its own theme song, chosen by listeners from an on-air contest. The program also had its own travel agency, insurance company, and listener-created recipe books. As a forerunner to today's talk hosts who offer merchandise on their websites, Herb offered a host of merchandise for members to buy.

In time, Jepko found himself at odds with Mutual on how to "sell" his show and how things should be done. The network was having problems getting affiliates to carry his program. Ultimately, they decided his audience was too old, too rural and, *here's the bottom line*, not large enough to bring home a profit to the network. Even though his family of listeners adored him, he was dropped by Mutual and syndication in May 1977. His fans were upset and insisted that he stay on the air. Herb put together a few stations, including KSL, which became the *Nitecap Radio Network*. Unfortunately, by this time, unlike the early '60s when his show debuted, Jepko found himself faced with lots of competition from 24-hour television and 24-hour radio stations. When KSL dropped his program in 1978, he continued the show on a handful of stations, using all his personal assets to keep it on the air.

Jepko contributed much to broadcasting in America as an influential radio talk show host from 1964 until 1990. Today, while many of his faithful listeners still remember him fondly, he is all but forgotten. He shouldn't be. During a time when talk radio was becoming more in-your-face and show hosts sounded angry, Herb Jepko proved that a talk show host who is kind and gentle can still attract a huge audience. In 1970, when I was most fortunate to host the all-night show on the 50,000-watt voice of 700AM-WLW-Cincinnati, I unashamedly borrowed some of Herbie's friendly style for my own delivery. To my way of thinking, he was a shining example of how to communicate on a one-on-one basis on the radio, whatever the format. Herb Jepko passed away in 1995.

When Jepko's Mutual Radio Network contract was terminated in May 1977, he was replaced by Long John Nebel and his wife Candy Jones. The husband-and-wife team had been successful talk personalities on WOR-New York. Six months later, following Long John's untimely death, Larry King was hired!

Long before the King Kong of talk joined CNN in June 1985, **Larry King** was a popular radio personality in Miami on WIOD. From 1978 until 1994, the King's voice was heard by millions of nighttime listeners on the Mutual Radio Network's *The Larry King Show*. In June 1994, Larry created the first daily radio/TV talk show by simulcasting his nightly program on Westwood One radio stations across America. In 2010, King celebrated his 53rd year in broadcasting as host of CNN s *Larry King Live*, the first worldwide call-in television talk show.[35] His estimated nightly viewing audience was over one million. The Emmy Award-winning King is author of multiple books and has been labeled "the most remarkable talk-show host ever on TV" by *TV Guide Magazine*. He has also been inducted into five of the nation's leading broadcasting halls of fame and is the recipient of the prestigious Allen H. Neuharth Award for excellence in journalism. Both his radio and TV shows have won the George Foster Peabody Award for excellence in broadcasting.

Described as the "Muhammad Ali" of the broadcast interview, night after night for more than four decades Larry King consistently made headlines with high-profile guests like Billy Graham, Tony Blair, Michael Jordan, Marlon Brando, Prince, Barbara Bush, Nancy Reagan, and every U.S. President since the Ford administration. Guests on Larry King's programs not only included celebrities but anyone who has ever found their fifteen minutes of fame. He has been asking famous people questions throughout his career, and has accumulated more than 40,000 interviews.

Some critics have characterized King's style of interviewing by saying he asks "softball" questions which allows him to reach guests who would hesitate to be interviewed by "tough" talk-show hosts. In response to the "softball" accusation, Larry King answers his critics, "I've never understood that. All I've tried to do is ask the best questions I could think of, listen to the answers, and follow up. I've never not followed up. I don't attack anybody; that's not my style, but I follow up. I've asked people who make that comment, 'What's a softball question'? They'll say, 'You say to a movie star, what's your next project?' To me, that's not a softball. To me, that's interesting, what are you doing next?"

As a fellow broadcaster, I would not describe Larry King's questions as being softballs. In fact, I believe his questions are the type that a typical everyday person would want to ask a celebrity if given the chance. Actually, I think Larry's style of interviewing is masterful. If you listen or watch King, you will get the feeling he enjoys being around celebrities, that he finds them interesting and enjoys their company. His guests sense that about him, love the adulation, and consequently open up to him. Larry's laidback, easy-going style puts his guests at ease, and relaxes them. They therefore trust him and reveal many little-known facts that so-called "tougher" interviewers would never get.

I have known Larry King for more than a few years, going back to when we were both blessed to be represented by super agent Bob Woolf. I always found Larry to be approachable and friendly. In 1995, I was in Newton-Wellesley Hospital outside Boston, recuperating from emergency lung surgery, not knowing if I would ever return to the air. Larry took time to send me a note, which I still have. It reads, "Joe, You will get better. They need you. Love, Larry King." It was the perfect pick me up that I needed at that time in my life and career. I'll always be grateful for his kindness.

With Larry King's warmth and caring nature, is it any wonder why celebrities stand in line to be a guest on his popular show? Long live the King! May he always reign supreme as the leader in interviewing and talk broadcasting.

A note to future radio stars: Take a tip from the King.[36] The secret to being a good interviewer in talk radio, or indeed in any format, is to gain the confidence of the interviewee, to get them to open up and converse with you in an open and frank manner. As a future radio interviewer, you will learn much by watching Larry King in action. Another excellent talk-personality who seems to get little recognition for his superb work is Jim Bohannon. He was King's fill-in during the '80s, when Larry hosted his all-night national radio show. Jim took over as permanent host in 1994 when King moved to his CNN show.

In the 1970s and '80s, many listeners abandoned AM music stations for the stereo sound of FM. It was another chapter in radio history when the medium had to reinvent itself. AM radio did so by developing the talk format. Many former successful music stations, like RKO-Boston, WLS-Chicago, WLW-Cincinnati, and WABC-New York, made the switch to all-talk. The most successful talk radio host in the '90s was political conservative Rush Limbaugh. Today, El Rushbo still leads the talk brigade as America's most listened-to talk radio personality. Other top-rated talk hosts, in addition to those mentioned elsewhere, include Neal Boortz, Hugh Hewitt,[37] Carl Jeffers, Mark Levin, Michael Medved, Dennis Miller, and Michael Savage.

Talk Radio doesn't mean it always has to be politically directed.

Talk radio is an extremely broad category and covers a wide variety of subjects, not merely two-way conversations on issues of the day. Talk radio is not just a bunch of older guys talking politics. On the contrary! Art Bell had a huge and loyal listener base because of his fascinating UFO stories. Morning drive radio with glib guys doing bits, taking phone calls, and conducting interviews on FM is also a form of talk radio. From the early '80s through the '90s, Andy

Moes and I were very successful with the talk-music format on our program, *The Joe and Andy Family* on ROR-98.5-Boston. We played little music, and on some mornings none, depending on how hot the phones were on a topic or bit we had going! Walter Sabo, our consultant at the time, told us in no uncertain terms, "The only time I want to hear a song played on your show is when you're trying to line up the next bit!" Whether it's a morning drive person talking about last night's winning couple on ABC's *Dancing with the Stars* with host Tom Bergeron, how the home team fared, or how you tripped over the coffee table in the dark while trying to find your car keys, it's still talk-radio.[38]

Here are some examples of syndicated shows outside of the political and current news genres. All are syndicated by Premiere Radio Net, with the exceptions of Bob Brinker and Bruce Williams:

- **Handel on the Law**, Bill Handel's program, is a unique presentation of useful legal advice.
- **Dr. Laura Schlessinger** tries to steer her listeners through difficult life decisions.
- **Dr. Dean Edell** has been handling talk radio for years on a variety of health-related topics.
- **George Noory** explores the world of UFOs, strange occurrences, and other unexplained phenomena.
- **Leo Laporte** - The tech guy is radio's go-to gadget guy.
- **Gary Sullivan** gives home improvement advice for do-it-yourselfers.
- **Kim Komando** serves up a generous helping of computer information and
- two highly popular financial advice programs, **Bob Brinker** and Money Talks, syndicated by ABC, and **Bruce Williams** on Westwood One, who in February 2010 announced his retirement from radio

Talk radio experts give advice on how to prepare for a career as a talk-show host.

    Alan Tolz became executive producer for WWDB-FM in his hometown of Philadelphia in 1979. One of his duties was producing *The Jerry Williams Show*. Alan and I later worked together at RKO Radio in Boston. I was on in morning drive on the FM side at ROR-FM, while he produced *The Jerry Williams Show* on the AM side at WRKO. Today, Alan is Executive VP and CEO for Marlin Broadcasting and lives in Bedford, New Hampshire. Because of his vast experience in talk radio, I asked Alan to comment on the following: As far as talk radio is concerned, what do you personally feel are some of the important attributes for a future radio talk show "wannabe" to possess in order to be successful on the air? Here is his reply: "Since 'talk radio' now encompasses more than simply being a mirror for those who wish to react to the news of the day, the most important attributes in my view are the following:

- **Creativity** - the ability to expound about various topics you choose on which people will want to express their opinions.
- **Storytelling ability** - Experiences you have daily, both positive and negative, about which you can tell a story and elicit responses from your audience.
- **Radio savvy** - The best and most successful talk hosts are consistently those who have prior radio experience and understand formatics.
- **A dynamic personality** - not necessarily polarizing, but you'll need a strong, unique presentation to cut through the radio clutter."

Tolz was also asked how high-school or college students should prepare themselves for a career as a future radio talk master. "Study history. Learn to love it," he replied, "it's the key to your ability to relate to people of all ages and to have a firm understanding about why current situations are the way they are. Read everything and anything. The broader your base of knowledge, the more interesting you'll be to your audience."

In their talk-radio book, *Burning up the Air*, Alan Tolz and Steve Elman point out that Williams was one of the originators of two-way talk radio.[39] "Jerry perfected it," says Tolz. "He loved it. Every fiber of his body and personality was invested in it. He wanted to continue doing talk radio to his last breath. It was him and he was it. Jerry's formula for success in talk radio is as follows: 'Take phone calls and do interviews, build them around the show host, someone who is street-wise and funny and who represents the interests of the little guy in a big uncaring world.' Jerry believed a talk show should be fast-paced. Listeners need to feel the excitement of your show that something is always just about to happen. As a talk-show host, you need to be outspoken. There has to be an edge to interviews and finally, dramatic exchanges must happen between the host and callers."

KTSA-San Antonio midday talk host **Jack Riccardi** offers this solid advice for future talk radio wannabes: "Talk about what you actually care about and talk about it just as you would off the air."

Kevin Straley is a twenty-year radio pro and independent media consultant. He has successfully launched start-up talk stations in northeast radio markets, including Boston and Providence. From 2000 until 2008, he was Senior VP of News/Talk/Sports Programming at XM Satellite. Kevin shares his vision on how future radio-talk wannabes can prepare for a career in talk radio: "**Listen, produce, prepare, and practice.**"

Listen "to become a connoisseur of good talk radio. Listen to different hosts each week to try and observe what makes them great talk-show hosts.

Listen for pacing, production, monologues, topic selection, story telling... each successful host has developed a blueprint for success, which might have some relevance to your future show." A good way to begin in talk radio, Kevin points out, is as a **producer/call screener/intern.** "Be a talk-show host in training. A producer's job is great on-the-job boot-camp. You get to see the execution of a daily show from the other side of the glass and observe each day the ingredients for a good or bad show."

Prepare. "A good talk show host spends every hour they are off-the-air preparing for the show. Start to get into that mindset. Take notes when you are off the air on thoughts and observances that would be relevant if you were doing a show the next day."

And lastly, Straley emphasizes, **Practice.** "Do a daily show even before you get a gig. Practice doing a long-form talk show in an empty room each day for at least one hour per session. The naked feeling of being in a studio for the first time with no records to play can be crippling for a first-time talk show host. Start to tape these sessions and after a while," Straley suggests, "develop a short- or long-form demo. Within a couple of months start to deliver your show to an Internet radio station, or podcast it yourself, or take a weekly gig with a small station."

Pam Triolo has spent her lifetime in the entertainment industry, including on-air positions in both radio and television. Pam went from high-school plays to majoring in acting at Emerson College in Boston. Her on-air posts include co-hosting morning drive at WEAT in West Palm Beach, Florida. Her passion for writing led to writing and hosting the TV program *What's for Dinner?* Pam was asked how high-school or college students should prepare themselves for careers in talk radio. "Everything in radio is topical, so a student really needs to be well-rounded," advises Pam. "For example, to relate to current-day politics it's best to learn civics, history, social studies, etc., and be sure to keep up on current events. Start reading newspapers daily! The Internet gives you the ability to read thousands of papers at the touch of a button. And don't forget," urges Triolo, "the serious stories are most important, but you never know when you'll have to be up on O.J.'s latest arrest, so pay attention. Think of how many broadcast hours were devoted to the tragedy of Anna Nicole Smith."

"On to more schoolin' stuff," says Pam. "English would be important, ya think? Master it and do everything possible to increase your vocabulary. We are really becoming a bilingual society, so learning another language with all the nuances of its culture will help you see news stories from another perspective. If you're interested in controversial issues, try out for debating in school. Public speaking is at the heart of your future talk radio career. Get in front of an audience as much as you can. Try out for plays, volunteer to narrate your school's upcoming events, make the daily announcements, or lecture at your church. Get comfortable with it and please, oh please, learn to speak sentences without the utterances of the words 'ummm,' 'like,' and 'okay.' There are many great colleges and professional schools that specialize in radio and communications."

Triolo graduated from one of the best, Emerson College in Boston. "As a freshman," she recalls, "I called my mother crying after getting pulled aside after class by my voice and articulation professor who bluntly stated that I had one choice: lose my Long Island accent or fail the class! I told my roommates to listen to me read the newspaper and stop me when I said anything 'wrawng' or 'tawked' funny."

Author's note: I can't help wondering if Pam had the same speech professor, at Emerson, I encountered years earlier, who strongly recommended, I transfer to TV production because I would never make it on the air.

To prepare for a career in talk radio, Pam Triolo recommends one should "find an internship. Listen to your favorite talk show host and explore what you like or don't like. You have so many new choices I never had," she emphasizes. "Utilize new media by creating your own station online, post your work on YouTube, and while imitation is the greatest form of flattery, you need to develop your own style and find your inner voice. Experience will bring the real you to light so practice, practice, practice."

Words to ponder from two of America's top talk-radio pros.

Mark Williams is a freelance talk show host who has worked for ABC, Clear Channel, and Westwood One. Mark lays it on the line for future radio stars interested in talk radio. "It depends on what you love about radio," he says with a grin. "The radio I loved and got into was personality intensive, community involved, and as much a friend as any person. It was the social networking MySpace of its day without the predators. My radio was very different from the radio my parents knew and loved. Their radio was when entire families sat around to hear stories of the Lone Ranger or the trials and tribulations of Ma Perkins. The radio you love and want to get into today is not going to be here soon, any more than Fibber McGee is around today. Remnants will linger, like Old Time Radio today, but as a force, it will be very different. Where radio is going has the entire industry in froth right now. The owners of the major consolidated groups declared that they no longer believe in the viability of their own product and are selling out. On the way out the door, they fully intend to see that less is left standing than Sherman left in Atlanta.

"The important thing to remember," urges Williams, "is that radio is not dead, but it will be nearly unrecognizable soon. To prepare for a career as a traditional radio talk show host today is like training to host a radio serial in 1955, or to be a silent film star in 1928. The jobs were still around, but in a blink of an eye they were obsolete and people with those skills and training had to adapt or they wound up driving cabs. You are not a radio talk show host; you are in the content delivery business. The medium is irrelevant. You will likely be swimming in the waters of the New Media so learn as much about that as you can right now."

Sally Jesse Raphael is a true pioneer in talk radio and television. I asked Sally what advice she has for future radio stars, particularly women, who desire a career in talk radio. Her candid reply may surprise some of you. "Go to television," she says without hesitation. "You think I'm kidding, that's where the money is. If you are female and starting out in radio today and want to be a talk personality, you would have to go to your local talk station. You would have to convince them they need a local talk show done by a woman. Then they would take your idea and give it to a man, and that would pretty much be it. You might be able to get some guy to go on the air with you, and go under his skirts as it were. Then you hope something happens to him and you get the gig.

"I would discourage any woman who thinks she is going to get started in talk radio at this particular time," says Raphael. "It's not going to be so bad when this thing shakes itself out, but not right now. Radio, particularly talk radio, is in such flux with the buying and the selling and the fear that everyone has. Executives are terrified and no one is willing to take the risk of thinking independently." She continues by saying, "There are fewer women involved in talk radio now than there were fifty years ago, so it's all bad news and I don't see anything that'll make it better. The old guys will die off and some of them did have respect for women, so I think it'll get worse. The young guys don't know what they're doing. They come up through sales, and I don't see a lot of them directed toward trying to lure women on the air. They are so mired in what they are doing, attracting men, that they don't particularly care. The only thing that would make it better is if they fire some of these guys and bring in new people.

I've been out selling radio in the current market, [and] I have a very low opinion of those in positions of power now.[40] But, radio hasn't sunk as low as it needs to sink for it to come up again. Today, most of the stations are controlled by two or three companies, or the shows are syndicated by two or three companies, so I'd tell somebody not to go into this as a way of life. They'd have to be crazed to do this. Go into television." Sally Jesse believes with conviction that there is no creativity in radio today. "There is only the bottom line. The old guys are just waiting a couple of years to retire; they don't want to rock the boat. And the new guys are afraid to make any changes—it's easier to just let the ship sink than to try to save it, because if he's wrong, he's out. People have learned to be extremely cautious. The same people are afraid to help someone in trouble on the street - they might sue you! If I sound angry, it's because I am. I'm angry at the lapse in federal regulation that allowed the power to fall into a few hands."

The vital role of political talk radio today and in the future.
   In April 2009, syndicated talk show host **Hugh Hewitt** wrote an insightful article, *Now You're Talking*, on how political talk radio is a vital part of 21st-century democracy. His comments are printed here with his permission. Hewitt believes nationally syndicated talk radio is entering an era of explosive growth, as he goes on to explain: "This development will deliver great benefits, not just for conservatives but for the journalism profession, the government, and for the country. Ratings for political talk are surging, partly because my colleagues and I are attracting new listeners and partly because the old ones are being counted more accurately. One reason for the latter," Hugh adds, "is Arbitron's move to a much more precise audience-measurement system, Peoplemeters, which are replacing the old diary system, which many conservative broadcasters thought underreported our audience of higher-educated, higher-income listeners who did not have the time to write down everything, and every radio personality, they listened to.[41] In an age of fractured media, the new Peoplemeter-driven data tell advertisers, who need to reach business owners, professionals, married couples with children and influencer's generally, where they can find them. These folks are listening to Rush Limbaugh and Sean Hannity, the titans of the industry. They are also listening to my colleagues and me at the Salem Radio Network. As a result, the revenue picture for syndicated talk is better then any other format, with the possible exception of sports talk."
   Radio talk-master Hugh Hewitt continues with his analysis on the future of political talk radio. "A growth in audience and revenue is not automatic. A great talk show requires two important ingredients, quality programming and hard work." Hewitt specifically uses two of America's top talk talents to prove his point. "Rush Limbaugh and Sean Hannity are examples of successful professionals who have not rested on their laurels but continue to build new elements and new approaches to their shows." Hewitt believes the biggest threats to talk radio are actually indirect ones. He believes two in particular stand out. "First, the recording industry is pushing for a law that would extract royalties from radio stations for the on-air playing of music. This would be a ruinous new tax on an industry that is already reeling, along with its cousins in television and print, from shrinking ad revenues. It would likely force the collapse of some radio companies, and abandonment of the music format by hundreds of stations that couldn't pay the new fare. This performance tax would be a boon to talkers, since our format would be virtually untouched by the new tax," but, warns Hewitt, "it would cripple the broadcast industry as a whole."
   Author's note: Los Angeles AM-Drive radio host **Mark Wallengren** says, "I have heard small market numbers would be taxed close to $5,000 a year. If so, that would really cause them to go broke. If the money were distributed to JUST the performers I'd be all for it. But when you read the fine print, most of the money goes to the labels!"

Chicago-based broadcaster **John Gehron** also believes that radio should not have to pay a performance fee, but thinks radio hasn't made a strong enough argument against it. "If it passes," Gehron believes, "non-music formats will grow in appeal. This is already occurring because music on radio is no longer special. Radio will not abandon music but will increasingly look for content that cannot be copied or is unique to radio."

Hugh Hewitt continues.

"More serious than even the killer performance tax is the danger of deserved caricature," says Hugh Hewitt, "which the broadcast industry will invite if it neglects the paramount importance of fairness and decency of making the effort that's needed to be accurate and informative. I'm not talking about the standard political sniping that we've all come to expect: Rush attracts the biggest share of this, yet he has remained invulnerable through two decades of attacks because his attackers are never honest about who he is and what he does. Year in and year out, he has been informed, funny, entertaining and news-driven, which is why his audience keeps growing, and why occasional attempts by hard-left interest groups to pull a joke or a paragraph from his 15 hours a week on the air and distort it always falls flat. Anyone who listens in good faith knows that Rush understands exactly where the boundaries are and respects them, while delivering entertaining and informative radio built on a passionate core of conviction and fact. All good and talented broadcast journalists do the same thing. We have all been attacked relentlessly by lefties for many years," he exclaims, "and still our audiences grow."

Hugh Hewitt fires this warning shot across the bow of all talk radio hosts: "We could lose that audience if we stop serving it with excellent programming and guests and a continuing commitment to fairness. A marginal host with extreme views may provide fodder to our critics, but he or she will not compromise our mission - as long as such programming remains an exception and not a rule among syndicated shows." The conservative talker says, "It's important, for radio and for the cause of informed debate, for radio talk hosts to stay reasoned and responsible instead of adopting the methods of the extremists."

Hugh Hewitt concludes with his thoughts on the secret to talk radio's success. "Our shows are the last places in America where genuine, sustained, intelligent debate can occur on-air, where left and right - whether guests or callers - meet, argue and listen. Americans since the time of the Revolution have always loved political debate. And they like it hard-hitting, but not vulgar; pointed and passionate, but not extreme or bigoted. My colleagues and I continue to provide that kind of debate as do the best of the cable TV shows. Rachel Maddow is showing that the left can do the same thing."

The writer of this article, Professor Hugh Hewitt, is a graduate of Harvard College and the University of Michigan Law School. He has been teaching

Constitutional Law at Chapman University Law School since it opened in 1995. Hugh is best known as the host of his radio show, which has an audience estimated at more than 2 million listeners every week. He writes daily for his blog, HughHewitt.com, which is among the most-visited political blogs in the U.S. His nationally syndicated radio show can be heard every Monday through Friday from 6-9pm EST via the Salem Radio Network. Podcasts of his program are also available there, and he can be reached at the same place I contacted him, hugh@hughhewitt.com

Talk radio needs to be careful of over-commercialization.
The fastest way to kill even the most popular talk show is overloading it with too many commercials! Let's use **Sean Hannity's** popular program as an example. In listening to Sean, you'll hear a few minutes of relevant content, a caller or two and then hold on! Here they come, lots of back-to-back commercials. Then it's back to Sean for meaningful dialogue followed by another break for more commercials. The next time you catch his show, listen closely as he approaches the top of the hour. You will hear five or six minutes of spots followed by a quick tease from Sean, usually promoting what's coming up in the next hour or on his Fox News show that night. The "tease" runs no longer than 20 to 30 seconds. This is followed by more commercials, usually the news adjacency is where local stations have an opportunity to sell commercials and make money before rejoining the network feed for Fox News at the top of the hour.

Running too many commercials is not only frustrating for the listener, but for the air-talent as well! Believe me; the person on mic knows exactly how much or how little time he or she is spending on mic. It irritates them just as much as it does you, the listener; probably more so, when the host needs to break every few minutes to run another commercial stop-set. It must really bug Sean. The way his program is structured these days, he is little more than a centerpiece surrounded by a table full of commercials.

Over-commercialization is not exclusive with Hannity's show by any means. His program is merely used as an example. Unless the host owns their own program, he or she usually has little or no control over how many commercials are aired. So please, no finger-pointing at the host. It's the same old problem in radio. The more popular the show, the more advertisers want to be a part of it! Success can easily lead to over-commercialization. The danger is when sales allow more commercials to be added to an already oversaturated spot load on radio programs. When it happens, you may as well rent a bus and drive what's left of your loyal listener base over to commercial-free satellite radio or another outlet where listeners can obtain information without being commercialized to death.

Talk radio, unlike most music programming, is foreground listening. It means the attentive listeners are acutely aware of how many commercials they are being force-fed while waiting to hear their favorite host. I am fully aware of management's need to run more inventory to cover the high cost of talent like Hannity, Limbaugh and the rest. Here's my question: is over-commercialization worth the risk of lowering the quality of a program and integrity of the host? The answer should be obvious. The solution is simple. *Increase* the spot rate and *decrease* the spot load!

The way talk-radio is headed it is evolving into a glorified infomercial, surrounded by quick comments from the host, sprinkled with a few quickie listener calls. Wake up, free radio folks! I made a nice living on commercial radio for over forty years, and understand the importance of the advertiser. But as it stands now on many radio formats, and not just talk, those in charge are smothering the life out of what's left of a good product on *free radio* by running *too many commercials.*

The solution to preventing over-commercialization is an easy fix. Radio sales should go back to what worked so well during radio's golden years. Sell hourly or even half-hourly program segments at a bonus price, with a ten-second sponsor billboard at the top and bottom of each half-hour. Insert one or two premium-priced spots in the body of the show. To his credit, Glenn Beck has been doing this on his national radio show for some time. It seems to be working well for him. It's a win-win for everyone. The advertiser's important commercial message is not lost in a five-minute cluster of spots, the listener doesn't suffer from over-commercialization, and the show host can do what he or she does best, talk on the radio. Talk radio is too vital a format in keeping the public well informed on what's happening in our ever-changing world. Don't ruin its potential by over-commercializing it.

Boston talk radio pro Jordan Rich speaks out on how to be a successful talk show host.

My longtime friend **Jordan Rich** is the host of his own weekend program on WBZ-Newsradio 1030 Boston. In addition to working live on the air for almost thirty years, Jordan is co-owner of Chart Productions, Inc., an audio production agency. To fully understand his passion for radio, one must take a sneak peak at how it came to pass for one of Boston's native sons.

Jordan says he came into this world just as Sputnik was leaving our atmosphere in 1958. "Growing up just south of Boston, radio was an integral part of my childhood. Oh, I certainly loved television, but for a kid who snuck a transistor radio into bed and stayed up well past lights out, nothing was as imaginative and alluring for me as the radio. A staple was tuning to Red Sox baseball on the old WHDH-AM-850 with legendary announcers Ken Coleman and Ned Martin.[42] They painted elegant portraits of what was happening on my field of dreams. I would start each day before school," recalls Jordan, "listening to an amazing talent named Jess Cain who for nearly forty years made getting up so much fun for everyone in my household. Jess had a stable of hysterical characters, all of his own making. He got us through storms, recessions, national tragedies, and was the perfect companion when we had to stay home with a fever.

"At a young age, I got hooked, not on rock n' roll countdown programs, but on talk shows," says Rich. "WEEI Boston back in the 1960s featured talk-masters such as Paul Benzaquin, Howard Nelson and Jim Westover, true masters of conversation, wise men who seemed to know just about everything. And they all professed a love of language that we pine for today. There was also the irascible talk show legend Jerry Williams, New England's favorite weatherman Don Kent, and long-distance radio friends, like Jean Shepherd, Barry Farber, and my all-time radio hero "Uncle" Norm Nathan. Norm hosted a show called *Sounds in the Night*. I stayed up much too late on many a weeknight, listening to Norm play cool jazz tunes and chat with fascinating personalities and celebrities coming through town, all the while making us chuckle with his self-deprecating New England-style wit. For me, it was a rainbow of personality," says Jordan, "the serious newsmaker, the play-by-play announcer, the quick-thinking DJ, the storyteller, they all sparked a flame inside me that continues burning brightly to this day."

Jordan Rich's advice for anyone starting out in radio hoping to become a personality on talk radio, or on any other format, is pretty basic but directly on target: "Be willing and ready to work long and hard. When an opportunity presents itself, go for it! Breaks do happen, but you often will need to nudge the break along with some desire and enthusiasm. Perhaps, most importantly," Rich adds, "I learned early on never to listen to others with concerns about my chances for success. There were some who tried talking me out of radio, including a few veterans of this very industry, I didn't listen and you shouldn't either. I discovered then and it's still true today, that I have never been competing with others; I have always competed with myself. It has always been up to me. It is definitely up to you." You can reach the personable radio pro at www.jordanrich.com and www.chartproductions.com.

A great talk show host needs a great support staff to win.

Perry Michael Simon is editor of *The Letter*, a weekly media internet column for *AllAccess*. It deals with News-Talk and Sports radio programming. His column from February 26, 2010, focused on the importance of qualified radio pros "behind the scenes" on talk radio. The information is so relevant for both future radio talk wannabes and current show hosts we decided to reprint most of Perry's text. With his gracious permission, here is a transcript of his comments:

"How do you as a talk-show host do an entertaining and informative show? You need a competent call screener and a great producer. They are critical players in creating great radio and invaluable to the success of your show. A radio show that takes calls needs a gatekeeper who can recognize the robo-callers, who can quickly get a caller to distill what he or she wants to say into a quick, effective comment, who can weed out the phonies and the talking points readers on either side.

"A caller-driven show is only as good as the calls that get on the air, so the screener may be the most important person in the building. That's why most stations just stick some intern or newbie in there and treat him or her like a peon. Oh, wait, that doesn't make sense, does it? Yet, that's how radio treats producers and call screeners. There are notable exceptions," says Simon, "especially on the biggest syndicated and local shows, but too many stations economize in the support staff department. It's been like this for years; in my programming days, there just wasn't a budget for it. I ended up with some excellent screeners and producers, but I got lucky.[43] And when you don't get lucky, the result is obvious, right there on the air."

Perry Simon believes management is not totally at fault. "How many shows assign an allegedly 'wacky' name to the screener and the producer and use them as punch lines? Morning shows have done it forever, and, of course, once there was 'Baba Booey,' every 'edgy' show had to have their own. How many really sharp, smart, capable people who could have done those jobs very well never even applied for the positions because they just didn't want to be a joke? It doesn't matter how well you treat that screener off the air. Nobody with any ambition or, for that matter, self-esteem aspires to be someone's punching bag, not even for comedy's sake. Most shows shouldn't be talking to, or about, the screener anyway. It's a crutch. Leave some things behind the scenes. And a producer shouldn't be there to get you coffee. Get your own coffee and let the producer develop material, book guests, and plan your show. In other media, 'producer' is the top of the heap.

"A movie or TV producer is royalty. In radio, we don't offer that kind of respect to the position. We should. I know that radio stations are strapped for cash like everyone else, but if they want to do talk radio, they need to start treating the screener and producer positions seriously, and the people doing those jobs as professionals. A good screener keeps those organized callers off the air and makes the callers that DO get through sound better, and keeps the prank calls from sneaking through, too. A good producer is invaluable to creating great radio, something you really learn when you don't have a great producer, or, in too many cases, any producer at all. Great shows have great staffs. It's not that hard to grasp."

Author's note: Thanks to Perry Michael Simon for sharing some of his expertise on talk radio. Read his latest comments by going to psimon@allaccess.com. Or tweet him at www.twitter.com/pmsimon.

As a talk show host, you don't always have to be negative. You know the type, when the host is constantly talking about the ineptness of the current administration in the White House. Don't *always* paint a negative picture for your listeners no matter where you, as the host, stand on a particular issue. After a while, even the most popular radio talk show host will begin to fall out of favor with their listeners if you constantly paint a doom and gloom picture!

You need to cover the lead story and biggest news events as topics on your show, that's a given, but constantly painting a crash-and-burn scenario in the minds of your listeners is wrong. They need to be reassured there is light at the end of a very dark tunnel. Their lives are full of worries and troubles. Many talk show hosts believe it is their sole duty to inform the listener. This is true, but listeners want it presented in an entertaining way. This is why they pay you, the show host, the big bucks. You need to find different ways to basically go over the same material every day without making it sound mundane and boring. It is not an easy assignment, but to keep a solid listener base you need to make it happen, day in and day out. You can not take a day off from doing a successful top-rated radio show whatever the format, and talk is no exception.

A salute to one of America's greatest talk-show personalities.
On Thursday, March 26, 2009, we lost a true talk radio personality in **Larry Glick**. Larry passed away at the Boca Raton Community Hospital in Florida, after eight hours in the OR during valve replacement surgery. He was 87. Larry, who was retired from radio, had been working as a greeter at a Boca restaurant, Legal Sea Foods, owned by our mutual friend, Roger Berkowitz.

Larry Glick was a friendly voice in the nighttime on WBZ-Boston for twenty years. Because of the station's 50,000-watt signal and tremendous nighttime signal which covered 40 states and eastern Canada, Larry's loyal listeners, "Glicknicks," as they were called, numbered in the millions. When callers to his show would ask Larry how he was doing, his predictable reply would be, "Wait a second, let me check [he'd whistle] and say, "Not bad!" Everyone listening would laugh! That was vintage Larry Glick, always putting people at ease and having a good time on the radio. Larry had fun with callers, but never in a mean-spirited way. With his warm personality, quick wit and infectious laugh, Larry "Commander Lorenzo" Glick was pure listening joy. Part of his attraction was that a piece of Larry always remained the inquisitive little boy.

A frequent bit on his program would be a call to someone, some place, who had an unusual story to share. It was the Commander's way, as he put it, of learning *the story behind the story*! If Larry thought a caller was worthy of a prize, he would hand out a Glick University T-Shirt, emblazoned with *E Pluribus Glickus*. There was just one condition; Larry made them promise to "Keep it clean!" For first-time callers to his show, Larry warmly greeted them with "Let's give them a round of applause!" His cast of characters included the Champagne Lady and Boston cabbie Charlie DiGiovanni, who would often croon a song or two for nighttime listeners. One of Larry's funniest bits was when callers would beg him to shoot them off the air. He laughingly would oblige. Larry also didn't hesitate to good-naturedly shoot boring and '"dud" callers off the radio. When he read the news headlines, he would identify himself as Streeter Glick, a reference to longtime BZ newsman Streeter Stuart.

El Glicko would read sport scores on his show this way: 3 to 2; 4 to 3; 5 to 1!

It's impossible to do a chapter on talk radio without a few words from one of talk radio's all-time best, El Glicko. All I had for information was that he lived in Florida, but I was determined to locate him. Thanks to Peter Casey at WBZ, I caught up with the Commander by phone in 2007.

I don't recall exactly what Larry's comments were about, but I'll always remember how he made me laugh the entire time we chatted. For almost an hour, which was not nearly long enough to talk with a true radio legend, Larry told jokes and related funny incidents that had happened to him. It was almost like he was doing a radio show on the phone for an audience of one, me! I loved it. When Larry Glick passed on, his one-time program director at WBZ, Dave Martin, aptly described The Commander's on-air performance: "Larry created his own unique and special playground and leaving the door ajar, he invited the world to come in and play. He was a gentleman and a mensch! Let's give him a round of applause."

Fr. Edward Coughlin, one of radio's first talk personalities.

Radio Formats: News, Talk and Sports • 513

Larry King, legendary radio/TV talk personality.

Jerry Williams (on mic) the dean of two-way
talk radio in America.

Alan Tolz, former radio producer for talk-master Jerry Williams, co-author of book about Williams with Steve Elman, Burning up the air.

Kevin Straley, radio manager, most recently with X-M Satellite, now VP Programming with TuneIn.

Radio Formats: News, Talk and Sports • 515

Larry Glick, legendary Boston talk-radio personality.

RADIO FORMATS—PART 3 OF 3—SPORTS

> *Radio is to TV as a book is to a movie. With radio and the book, the listener and the reader uses his imagination.*
> *– Legendary baseball play by play announcer*

Sports broadcasting launches radio as a source of entertainment in the early 1920s.

In 1921, the heavyweight boxing match between American boxer Jack Dempsey and French challenger Georges Carpentier was billed as the "Battle of the Century." Thousands of fans gathered to see the big fight on July 2, 1921, which produced boxing's first million-dollar gate. Dempsey won in a fourth-round knockout, but the big news for many was that it was the first time a boxing match was broadcast to a mass audience. The blow-by-blow action described at ringside and relayed over the new radiophone system enabled hundreds of thousands to listen throughout the northeastern United States. An August 1921 story in *Wireless Age* magazine referred to the radio broadcast as "History in the making."

In addition to the 88,000 fans gathered to view the live action, tens of thousands gathered in various public venues, restaurants, barrooms, theaters, and halls, where ham radio operators or radio hookups had been installed. The various locations included Lowe's New York roof top at Broadway and 45th Street in NYC where some 1,200 fans gathered. The fight became big news across America. Many radio historians see the fight as a key to opening the golden age of sports broadcasting that boomed during the 1920s. It signaled the start of radio as big business entertainment in the United States.

Other sports broadcasts followed. In August 1921, the first broadcast of a Major League baseball game on radio was carried on Westinghouse's station, KDKA-Pittsburgh. Announcer Harold Arlin, a 25-year-old Westinghouse foreman and nighttime studio announcer, took his place in baseball history. From a ground-level box seat in Forbes Field and using only a converted telephone as a mic and some equipment strung together behind home plate, he called balls and strikes in a game between the Pittsburgh Pirates and Philadelphia Phillies. Arlin later reflected that the broadcast was just an experiment and that many staff members at KDKA felt that baseball on radio would never be commercially viable. "Baseball is too boring to be a hit on radio" was the consensus of many. Who could have foreseen how wrong these doubting Thomases were, and that baseball and radio would go on to be a match made in heaven! There is much conjecture by many radio historians as to whether or not the broadcasting of sporting events helped sell more radios. One thing is for certain – early sports broadcasts certainly didn't hurt radio as a form of entertainment, and in fact almost certainly helped radio take off and sweep across America, capturing the imagination of virtually the entire nation.

Radio's Pioneer sportscasters.
The birth of baseball on the air and some of radio's first sports voices.

At first, baseball team owners feared broadcasts of their home games would keep fans away and that they would rather stay home and listen than pay to see the games at the ballpark. They soon realized that local broadcasts not only increased fan interest in their teams, but also increased interest in the game of baseball, dramatically increasing ballpark attendance.

According to the website askville.amazon.com, **WJZ Newark**, today WABC, was the first station to broadcast the 1921 World Series between the Yankees and the NY Giants. Tommy Cowan actually recreated the games from reports that were phoned in from the two stadiums. Journalist Grantland Rice broadcast the first game of the series on KDKA-Pittsburgh. The next year, 1922, Rice was the lead announcer as WJZ broadcast the entire series for the first time. The game was relayed to WGY Schenectady.

On New Year's Day, 1923, the first radio broadcast of the Rose Bowl was beamed from Los Angeles over KHJ. In 1924, WMAQ Chicago pioneered daily home games of the Cubs and White Sox. Hal Totten called balls and strikes and was later joined by Pat Flaherty as they broadcast directly from the baseball park.

Some other memorable sports firsts on radio/

- **On October 28, 1922,** hundreds of young men gathered around Western Union offices and in the physics lab at Princeton University to hear the first ever cross-country broadcast of a college football game. Telephone lines carried play-by-play of the formidable Chicago Maroons (in those days, a Big Ten team) and Princeton at Chicago's Stagg Field. Athletic contests were among the first to be broadcast on radio and they always guaranteed great listenership. Early football games were almost always local and they weren't exactly live, but almost. A reporter would be in the press box at the field and would telephone details of the action back to the radio studio, where an announcer would reenact the game, complete with sound effects, for the radio audience.
- **On March 22, 1923,** *Toronto Star* reporter Foster Hewitt broadcast his first hockey game on radio from Toronto's Mutual Street Arena. Nearly ten years later, Hewitt was handling regular Saturday night broadcasts of Toronto Maple Leaf games. On January 1, 1933, NHL games became one of the first programs to be broadcast across Canada, when a patchwork of stations carried the games coast-to-coast.
- **The first "live from the field" broadcast of a college football game** didn't happen until 1924, when announcers Edwin "Ty" Tyson and

Leonard "Doc" Holland broadcast the Michigan-Wisconsin game live and direct from the stands at Ferry Field.
- **1935-** William Wrigley, owner of the Chicago Cubs, became the first owner to allow his team's entire schedule of games to be broadcast.
- **1938-** The New York Giants and Yankees allow broadcasts of home games. Mel Allen is hired.

Radio's first major sports star was **Graham McNamee**. He helped create America's golden age of sports on radio in the '20s and '30s. In 1923, McNamee, who began his career as a concert singer, broadcast the first World Series game on WEAF Radio, later WNBC and today WFAN, live and not phoned in, from the Polo Grounds. McNamee's vivid descriptions of the event before a live mic were characterized by a combination of informality and warmth, making him an instant fan favorite. He and his on-air partner Phillips Carlin created a one-two-punch style for broadcasting games that is still in use today. One person covers the play-by-play, while the second person provides color commentary and spells the lead guy on the air, usually by taking the middle three innings. The second banana also gives the lead guy or play-by-play person someone to kibitz with during a slowdown in the action. In 1927, Graham McNamee called the play-by-play of the Rose Bowl on NBC as the New Year's Day classic went coast-to-coast for the first time. McNamee set many broadcast standards throughout his lengthy career, from 1923 until his passing in 1942.

Radio's Legendary Sportscasters.
Graham McNamee was followed in network sportscasting by Ted Husing, who, from 1923 until 1946, called almost every sport for CBS. His preparation for future sportscasters is textbook straightforward: arduous preparation before going on the air, purposeful word usage, and a measured style of calling the action.

Some of radio's earliest sportscasters and play-by-play broadcasters, in addition to McNamee and Husing, include Grantland Rice, Red Barber, Don Dunphy, and the colorful Bill Stern. Each gave the world of sports a solid place in radio programming.

In 1929, Harry Hartman, handling play-by-play of Cincinnati baseball, became the first announcer on radio to coin the phrase, "going...going...gone!" Next on the sports mic in the Queen City was Red Barber. After reading a school newspaper on a campus radio station at the University of Florida, Walter Lanier "Red" Barber decided he liked radio better than college and dropped out. Red joined WLW in Cincinnati and on opening day 1934, the twenty-six-year-old redhead broadcast the first Major League baseball game he had ever seen. From 1939 until 1953, he was the voice of the Brooklyn

Dodgers. During his thirty-three-year career Barber was recognized as the master of baseball play-by-play. Listeners liked his down-to-earth style and loved his folksy colloquialisms, like "pea patch," "rhubarb" and "in the catbird seat," which gave his broadcasts a special flavor. Pioneer sportscaster Barber once said, "Being on the air for three hours for half-a-year demands patience, imagination, perspective and intelligence." Not bad advice, if you plan to enter the field of radio sports play-by-play.

Don Dunphy was born in New York City in 1908. After graduating from Manhattan College he gained broadcast experience by covering baseball, basketball, and track. In 1937, he became sports director at WINS-New York. Two years later he began broadcasting local boxing matches, and in 1941 began calling the fights on radio for Gillette, a post he held for the next nineteen years. As the voice of boxing it is estimated that Dunphy described the blow-by-blow action of over 2,000 boxing events. He was one-of-a-kind in describing boxing on radio. As late as 1981, Dunphy sounded just as knowledgeable and just as intense calling the blow-by-blow account of the Thomas Hearns / Sugar Ray Leonard fight as he did forty years earlier in 1941 for the Joe Louis / Billy Conn match. Don Dunphy was inducted into the Radio Hall of Fame in 1988.

Bill Stern began on radio in the 1920s as a sportscaster in his hometown of Rochester, New York. In 1934, he joined popular Graham McNamee covering football on NBC. Bill graduated from the school of "give 'em what they want." His broadcasts were filled with plenty of thrills and excitement, even if he had to fabricate some of the action that was supposedly happening down on the field. From 1939 until 1951, Bill Stern's *Colgate Sports Newsreel* was one of radio's most popular programs. During each 15-minute show, Stern told thrilling tales of athletic heroism, some legend, some hearsay, but all very interesting and delivered in his exciting, authoritative, and smooth delivery. Bill continued doing a nightly show on ABC until 1956, and concluded his radio career on Mutual with a regular sports show along with play-by-plays of college football. Bill Stern passed away in 1971 at age 64. His story, *A Taste of Ashes*, is excellent reading for anyone contemplating a career in sports broadcasting.

Pioneer sportscasters like McNamee, Husing, Barber, and Stern influenced dozens of others who came after them, like Russ Hodges, the voice of the Giants both in New York and San Francisco, and

Mel Allen, whose exclamation, *"How about that!"* after Yankee home runs became his trademarked expression. Allen landed his first Major League baseball assignment as radio color commentator on the 1938 World Series. He joined the Yankees on radio in 1939 and eventually called 22 World Series on radio and television, including 18 in a row from 1946 until 1963. Allen called 24 All-Star Games and was inducted into radio's Hall of Fame in 1988. He passed away on June 16, 1996.

Other early sports voices include Jack Drees, Jimmy Powers, Red Grange, and Chris Schenkel, who began his radio career at WBAA and later at WLBC in Muncie, Indiana. His warm, baritone voice and smooth delivery became famous in 1952 as the TV voice of football's New York Giants. He also called horse racing's Triple Crown, the Masters golf tournament, and for thirty-six years was the voice of the Pro-Bowlers Tour. Christopher Eugene Schenkel earned a pre-med degree at Purdue but still pursued a sportscasting career. He passed away in September 2005, at age 82.

Another longtime voice on radio belonged to Tony Roberts, who for twenty-six years called Notre Dame football on the Mutual Radio Network.

Lindsey Nelson began his radio career calling high-school football games at WKGN in Knoxville, Tennessee. Legendary coach Robert R. Neyland called him one day to praise his work and added a few words of advice: "If you go to Howard Johnson's," said Neyland, "you'll have a choice of 27 different flavors of ice cream. I always get plain vanilla. And that's the way I like my football broadcasts, plain vanilla." Lindsey never forgot the words of the coach throughout his sportscasting career which spanned thirty-five years covering Major League baseball, NBA basketball, PGA golf, and both college and NFL football. He always gave listeners and viewers a straight vanilla account of the action. In one of his speeches about sportscasting, Nelson remarked, "The game is the important thing," and passed this bit of advice on to future sportscasters: "The announcer should never get in the way of the game."

After an unsuccessful stint at Harvard Law School, **Robert Ferris Prince** turned to his love of sports with a daily fifteen-minute program. Since his first encounter with a mic, the legendary radio sportscaster admitted he never had an urge to do anything else but to holler into that little ole microphone. In 1941, he won an audition to host Case of Sports on WJAS- Pittsburgh. He soon became a fan favorite because of his colorful, opinionated style.

In 1948, Bob Prince was named the radio sidekick to beloved Pirates play-by-play man, Rosey Rowswell. Both men shared similar air styles and saw themselves as entertainers. Each coined his own set of memorable catchphrases. Rowswell's included "Oh, my aching back," when a Pirate rally didn't materialize. Prince had his own home run call, "You can kiss it goodbye!" A close out was called "Bs close as the fuzz on a tick's ear." Prince worked alongside Rowsell for seven baseball seasons. When Rowswell passed away in February 1955, Prince took over as the Pirates' #1 broadcast voice and remained with the team until October 30, 1975.

When Westinghouse broadcasting shocked Pirate fans by announcing that Prince would not return for a 29th year behind the mic, sponsors complained and fans were outraged. 10,000 fans lined the streets of downtown Pittsburgh in a parade to show both appreciation and a rally for his return to the broadcast booth. Prince did not handle the firing well and sank into depression. He made a comeback handling Houston Astro broadcasts and was also featured on *Monday Night Baseball* with Bob Uecker and Warner Wolf, but Prince was used to being in the starring role and it was not a good fit for him. During the final decade of his life, he remained highly visible on the Pittsburgh sports scene, including a return to WJAS as sports director, where his sports career had started some forty years earlier. Prince remained a popular after-dinner speaker and continued his charitable work while broadcasting a few Pirates games on cable TV. In 1985, Lanny Frattare, Prince's successor, had the idea to bring Prince back to the broadcast booth. After undergoing surgery for mouth cancer, Prince dragged himself from his hospital bed to attend a press conference at Three Rivers Stadium, announcing that he'd signed a three-year contract to broadcast Pirates games.

On May 3, 1985, Prince returned to the Pirates radio booth but only lasted through two of his three scheduled innings. His voice wasn't clear but fans could still hear the uniqueness that made him so special calling Pirates baseball games. He handled just two more games before being hospitalized again, this time for pneumonia. On June 10, 1985, he lapsed into a coma and passed away. Bob Prince, the royalty of Pittsburgh baseball broadcasts, was just 68.

Harry Caray was born Harry Christopher Carabina, on March 2, 1914, in St. Louis, Missouri. He broadcast Major League Baseball for four different teams, beginning with his hometown St. Louis Cardinals and ending as the announcer for the Chicago Cubs. In between, he also was an announcer for one year with the Oakland A's and for eleven years with the White Sox. One of Caray's trademark expressions was "Holy Cow," which is also the title of his 1989 autobiography. For 14 years, his broadcast partner during Cubs broadcasts was former Cubs pitcher Steve Stone.

In his book, *Where's Harry?*, Stone mentions that on Valentine's Day, 1998, Harry was celebrating with his wife Dutchie in Palm Springs when he collapsed and was rushed to nearby Eisenhower Medical Center. Caray never regained consciousness and passed away four days later. Harry's son Skip followed his dad to the radio booth as a baseball broadcaster with the Atlanta Braves until his death on August 3, 2008. Harry Caray's sports broadcast legacy extended to a third generation, as his grandson, Chip Caray, replaced Harry as the Cubs' play-by-play announcer from 1998 until 2004. In the early '90s, Chip returned to work with his dad, Skip, on Atlanta Braves broadcasts.

Vin Scully has been calling Dodger games since 1950 and is still at the mic to this day. Vincent Edward "Vin" Scully was born in the Bronx in 1927 and has primarily been the voice of the Brooklyn and Los Angeles Dodgers, An association that goes back to 1950. Vin was inducted into the Radio Hall of Fame in 1995 and in 2000 was named Broadcaster of the Century by the American Sportscasters Association.

Down through the years, we've heard and seen many outstanding sportscasters and play-by-play broadcasters. It's impossible to list them all here. The ones mentioned are some of the best.

As a future radio wannabe, who grew-up in New England, I got to listen to some of radio's best play-by-play voices, such as those of Ken Coleman, Ned Martin, Curt Gowdy and the present voice of the Red Sox, my longtime pal Joe Castilgione. Later in my own radio career, I got to know each of them.

Ken Coleman was a radio and television sportscaster for thirty-four years. Born on April 22, 1925, in Quincy, Massachusetts, Ken broke into broadcasting with the Cleveland Browns in 1952 and stayed with the team until 1965, calling every touchdown that Hall of Fame running back Jim Brown ever scored. In 1965, Ken was hired by the Boston Red Sox to Curt Gowdy. Ken was at the mic for the 1967 World Series which the Sox lost to the Cardinals. From 1975 until '78, Coleman worked with the Cincinnati Reds TV crew. In 1978, when popular Red Sox radio combo Ned Martin and Jim Woods were fired, Coleman returned to Boston and broadcast the Sox 1986 World Series, which was another loss for Boston. He remained in the Red Sox broadcast booth until his retirement in 1989. He was inducted to the Red Sox Hall of Fame on May 18, 2000, at the age of 75. He passed away three years later in Plymouth, Massachusetts. Ken was the father of the late Cleveland sports and newscaster Casey Coleman, who passed away in 2006.

Edwin "Ned" Martin was born in Wayne, Pennsylvania, on August 9, 1923. The former WWII Marine Corps veteran was well known throughout New England as another popular voice of the Red Sox. Martin may hold the distinction of having watched more Red Sox games than any other person, having spent thirty-one seasons with the club's broadcast team, meaning he saw more than 5,000 Red Sox games. For those of us who longed to enter radio as a career, Ned Martin was more than an excellent play-by-play voice on radio; he was a teacher in so many different ways. Known for his passion for words and literary references during broadcasts, we radio wannabes learned literary passages from him while enjoying the game of baseball. Quotes from Shakespeare, Dickens, and Hemingway were not uncommon during his broadcasts and many fans relished rain delays, as they gave audiences a chance to hear Ned Martin share little-known stories about baseball, the players, and the game.

Ned Martin's delivery was cerebral and low-key. Ned Martin had a special way of calling the game in an expressive array of words and phrases that colored each game, even when the Sox were losing, and any die-hard Sox fan knows there were plenty of long-suffering losing games and seasons! Ned was also known for his signature comment, "Mercy," which he exclaimed on both good and bad plays by the BoSox. During one game when the Sox split a double-header with the White Sox, winning the opener and losing the nightcap, he began, "It was the best of times, it was the worst of times," referring to Dickens' *A Tale of Two Cities*. Another night, when a bad bounce gave Boston a win, Martin quoted Shakespeare, saying, "And so, ladies and gentlemen, as Shakespeare once wrote, fortune brings in some boats that are not steered. Good night from Fenway Park." Martin was pure magic on the radio.[44]

On July 22, 2002, after attending a memorial service for Hall of Fame slugger Ted Williams at Boston's Fenway Park, Martin was returning to his home in Clarksville, Virginia, when he suffered a massive coronary while on a shuttle bus at the Raleigh-Durham International Airport. He died there at age 79. Ned Martin was inducted into the Red Sox Hall of Fame in 2000.

Another favorite Red Sox voice belonged to **Curt Gowdy. Curtis Edward "Curt" Gowdy** was born July 31, 1919, in Green River, Wyoming. Play-by-play broadcasting for the man began in 1944, when he sat on a box with his mic perched on another box and called six-man football game in sub-zero temperatures in Cheyenne, Wyoming. It was my privilege to share a mic with the legendary broadcaster for a full hour when he was a guest on our show in 2004, when I was in morning drive at Sunny 104.3 in West Palm Beach, Florida. Curt's daughter Cheryl is a friend and she helped convince her dad, then eighty-three, to appear on my morning show. I am indebted to her and that's how I got to meet another of my boyhood radio heroes.

Advice from broadcast sports legend Curt Gowdy on how to be a play-by-play person.

Curt Gowdy spent fifteen years as the voice of the Boston Red Sox and I grew up listening to him. I was ten years old in 1951, and my dad and I loved listening to Curt call all the action. His friendly voice sounded almost musical. You could sense that he loved being on the air. Curt Gowdy was gifted with a smooth, folksy way of telling a story on radio and no one did it better! He brought a warm, friendly feeling to the broadcast booth and his descriptive calling of the game was full of interesting anecdotes, good humor, and lots of enthusiasm.

When Curt was a guest on our morning show on WEAT-Sunny-104.3, a station he once owned, he described the way he approached sports play-by-play: "I tried to pretend I was sitting in the stands with a buddy, poking him in the ribs when something exciting happened. I never took myself too seriously. After all," he chuckled, "an announcer is only as good as yesterday's performance." He also passed along this word to future sportscasters: "If you want it bad enough, just do it."

In 1960, Curt Gowdy did play-by-play of the first five seasons of the American Football League on ABC-TV. In '65, he left the Red Sox to join NBC Sports, where he called MLB telecasts on the *Saturday Game of the Week* and *Monday Night Baseball*. Gowdy also handled the All-Star game and post-season play-off's, along with baseball's fall classic, The World Series. After the '75 World Series, he was removed from NBC's baseball telecasts when sponsor Chrysler insisted on having Joe Garagiola, who was their spokesperson in many commercials, be the lead play-by-play voice. Curt was in the press box for Carlton Fisk's legendary home run in game 6 of the '75 World Series, but the actual call went to two of his Red Sox successors, Dick Stockton on TV and Ned Martin on radio. Curt continued as NBC's lead NFL voice through the '78 season, with his final broadcast being the memorable Super Bowl XIII between Pittsburgh and Dallas. He next moved to CBS to call football and baseball on radio.

An avid outdoorsman, Curt Gowdy also hosted the popular ABC-TV series *American Sportsman*. Curt was proud of his Wyoming heritage and loved the outdoors. He boasted he was "born with a fly-rod in one hand, and a sports mic came a little later." "The outdoors was a way of life for me," smiled Gowdy, "I should have paid them to host the *American Sportsman*." On March 27, 1972, a new state park opened in Wyoming and was officially named for him. The 11,000-acre Curt Gowdy State Park is halfway between his hometown of Cheyenne and the college town of Laramie. More land was acquired for the park in 2006. Proud of the honor bestowed on him, Gowdy remarked, "It has two beautiful lakes, hiking trails, camping, boating, fishing and beauty. It has everything I love. What greater honor can a man receive." [45]

When the award-winning *American Sportsman* was canceled in 1985, Curt Gowdy retired from broadcasting. While working for three major television networks, he announced a record sixteen World Series, eight Super Bowls, twelve Rose Bowls and eight Olympics. For two decades, he also hosted the *American Sportsman*. He has been named America's top sportscaster seven times. In 1970, Gowdy was the first sportscaster to receive the coveted Peabody Award for excellence in broadcasting and in 1981 was elected to the National Sportswriters and Sportscasters Hall of Fame. He was selected to the Red Sox Hall of Fame in 1995. Additionally, in 1984 he was presented the Ford C. Frick Award from the Baseball Hall of Fame and in '93, the Pete Rozelle Award from the Pro Football Hall of Fame. He also received a lifetime achievement Emmy in 1992. Curtis Edward Curt Gowdy passed away on February 20, 2006, after an extended battle with leukemia. He was 86. In a fitting tribute to his many years as the voice of the Boston Red Sox, his funeral procession circled Fenway Park. He was interred in Mount Auburn Cemetery in Cambridge, Massachusetts.

Advice on being a play-by-play voice from radio pro Joe Castiglione.

My longtime friend **Joe Castiglione** has been the voice of Red Sox for the past twenty-eight years. Joe was born in Hamden, Connecticut, and graduated from Colgate University. As a student, he was the voice of Colgate baseball and football. He received his MFA from Syracuse and worked a variety of broadcasting assignments, including at WSYR-TV (today WSTM-TV). Joe began his play-by-play career in Youngstown, Ohio, in 1972, calling football games for WFMJ-TV. He pay was fifteen dollars a game. As is often said in this book, you *don't go into radio for the money*! Castiglione's first Major League job was in 1979 as a sportscaster in Cleveland where he called Indians games. He joined the Red Sox in 1983 as Ken Coleman's partner. After Ken retired in '89, Bob Starr became the lead announcer on Sox games. When Starr left the next year, Joe took the helm and has been calling Red Sox games ever since.

Joe Castig's advice for play-by-play wannabes? "Whatever sport you choose to specialize in and hope to call all the action for on radio, play the game as long as you can. Learn everything you can about the game, including its rules. Be as proficient at is as possible; it helps if you have played the game, particularly the sport you want to call the action for. If you lack athletic ability, then make sure you are at least acquainted with the rules of the game. Basically, you should be aware of strategy, rules, and so on. You should read, and read some more about the history of the sport. Knowledge of the sport you are covering ranks right up there with having played the game. Read up on the regulations and the rules regarding the sport. Talk to as many people as you can, both coaches and players, who are involved in the game, to help you to have a better understanding of the rules. Be up-to-date on rules changes. Rules are constantly being scrutinized and changed in all sports. It's impossible to be really comfortable calling play-by-play for any sporting event if you are unfamiliar with the rules of the game. You'd be surprised," Castiglione says, "how few sportscasters know the basics when it comes to sports. Example: the dimensions of a basketball court, or the distance from home plate to the pitcher's mound."

Castiglione continues, advising radio sports wannabes to reach out to people who know the game, "You should also talk with sports people, like scouts and coaches and ex-players. It's also important to remember that the play-by-play broadcaster becomes part of the listener's family. The primary on-air voice of any sports team becomes the spokesperson for that team. It is an awesome responsibility." In 2004, Joe Castiglione published his book, *Broadcast Rites and Sites: I Saw It on the Radio with the Boston Red Sox*, which is a collection of stories from his days covering baseball. I highly recommend it for future radio play-by-play wannabes and for every baseball fan!

During my rookie years in broadcasting in the early '60s, and learning my craft in small-town radio, where you did it all, I did color commentary, along with Frank DeFrancesco, who did play by play, on high-school football and basketball games. The $15 extra per game fee came in handy. When I moved up to the play-by-play spot, my pay doubled to $35 a game. I found calling play-by-play of basketball games relatively easy, because you only had ten players to watch down on the court. You were indoors, out of the elements, and fairly comfortable. Football was a different story. I found it difficult to call and be accurate with an on-air account of the game. In foul weather jerseys got muddy and numbers became hard to read, especially when sitting in the back row of the bleachers during a snowstorm. Now I know why legendary radio play-by-play sportscaster Bill Stern would occasionally fabricate what was taking place down on the field. As great as he was, he probably couldn't read the obscured numbers either and to keep the action moving took the liberty of ad-libbing around the play.

There have been so many super sportscasters and great play-by-play voices over the years. They have provided us with unforgettable and many memorable moments. It is impossible to list them all here. Each of us has our own personal favorites. A couple of mine which come to mind are the following.

Who could ever forget Al Michaels' call, "Do you believe in miracles" as the USA Hockey team beat the Russians to win the Gold Medal at the 1980 Winter Olympics? For Celtics fans, we'll always recall the voice of the late Johnny Most, who called play-by-play for the Celtics for years. He sounded like he gargled with razor blades, but what a champion for the Celts. Remember the game he yelled into the mic, "Havlicek stole the ball!" Do you miss the familiar voice of Jim McKay, who covered the Olympics on ABC for over forty years? I do. And a voice I'll always remember, Sherm Feller, the Red Sox PA announcer for 26 years, whose resonant pipes intoned, "Ladies and gentlemen, boys and girls, welcome to Fenway Park in Boston."

Gil Santos was the morning-sports voice on WBZ-Boston for thirty-eight years. He has also handled play-by-play for the New England Patriots on radio since 1966. In a 2009 *Boston Globe* interview, just prior to his induction to the Massachusetts Broadcasters Hall of Fame, Santos made it clear that broadcasting sports on radio is not easy work. "The research and preparation that goes into each broadcast is the hardest part. You just can't show up and start talking." Take note, to those of you interested in a play-by-play career: Gil takes at least four hours to prepare for every hour he's on the air. He reads about opposing teams and memorizes names and how they're pronounced. He also learns the heights and weights and other stats of the players, such as the number of years they've played in the league, the schools they attended, and other tidbits of information to make the game interesting for the listener.

Many radio play-by-play announcers practiced over and over for their big day in a real broadcast booth by doing "phantom" games. Bob Murphy, Al Michaels, Dick Stockton, and countless other sports radio wannabes began their radio careers by sitting high up in the stands and speaking into a tape recorder. They pretended they were broadcasting the game for real. Many great sportscasters say it's the best way for would be play-by-play people to get a real feel for what the game is all about … practice, practice, practice, and when the big day comes, you'll be able to swing into action for real, whatever the sport may be! Today, you can tape yourself calling a game, pop it on YouTube and let the world see your work!

Tips from sports radio pros if you plan on a career as a play-by-play person.

When calling a game, visualize one or two people listening to you and speak directly to them, conveying what is happening on the field of play. Don't try to be overly descriptive with adjectives or cutesy-cutesy. Be natural and conversational. If your style is enthusiastic, like a rabid fan, let it come across. Always be yourself, but keep in mind that on radio, unlike TV, you need to constantly describe to the listener what is taking place.

Hockey is one of the fastest sports follow on radio. **Mike Emrick** does an excellent job of following the puck and describing where it is at any given moment. I got to know Mike when we both worked in radio in Portland, Maine. He was calling play-by-play action for the Maine Mariners of the AHL. I think Mike is one of the best hockey play-by-play people in the business. I'd put him right up there with two of Boston's best, **Fred Cusick** and **Bob Wilson,** who handled Bruins games for years! Emrick has called games for the Flyers and the New Jersey Devils. He is also a familiar voice on Stanley Cup playoff games. His knowledge of the game of hockey has been deemed encyclopedic. He is known for his eloquent vocabulary, using words during his broadcasts that are not commonly used in sports play-by-play. During line changes, Mike will often mention interesting facts about a player's personal life. He is living proof that a broadcaster must be comfortable with their own style. Mike Emrick is a founding member of the *NHL Pronunciation Guide*, a handbook for all NHL broadcasters to assist them in pronouncing hockey's most difficult names. Hockey play-by-play is tough because the action is fast and following the puck can be difficult. On television, you have the camera to assist you; on radio, you are the eyes and the camera for the listener

Women sportscasters on the air have had to overcome many obstacles.

Women have come a long way in sportscasting since the late 1930s and early '40s when the wife of Harry Johnson, a sports announcer in Omaha, Nebraska, provided color commentary on his broadcasts. She is believed to be the first woman sportscaster on radio. Unfortunately, her first name appears to be lost out in the ether.

Jeannie Morris and **Jane Chastain** are pioneers as women sportscasters. According to an article from *American Sportscasters Online* by Lou Schwartz, Chastain began her sportscasting career in the mid-'60s and was the first woman to work for a large network (CBS). It is also believed that she was the first woman to do play-by-play. Jeannie Morris had journalistic skills and a reputation as a writer, yet was not afforded the same press box facilities as men. In the early '70s, assigned to cover the Vikings and Chicago Bears game at the Metropolitan Stadium in Minnesota, she was not permitted to work in the press box because she was a woman. Bound and determined to cover the game and get her story, she reported the game seated above the press box, outside in a blizzard. Talk about a pro!

In the mid-'70s former Miss America Phyllis George worked at CBS. Later, her replacement was Jayne Kennedy. Leandra Reilly was the first woman to do play-by-play of an NBA game.

Suzyn Waldman was born in Waltham, Massachusetts, and has been a sports reporter for more than twenty years. Since 2005, she has been the color commentator on Yankees broadcasts on WCBS Radio in New York City, working side-by-side with John Sterling. Waldman, a former actress and Broadway singer, sang the song "There Used to be a Ballpark" in the documentary, *Local Heroes: Baseball on Capital Region Diamonds*. Waldman is noted for her early achievements in the male-dominated field of sports broadcasting. Suzy is the third woman in Major League baseball to handle full-time color commentary on a regular basis. She is right behind Betty Caywood, who in the 1960s did color for one season for the Kansas City Athletics, and Mary Shane, who called balls and strikes for the White Sox in 1977. In the mid-'90s, Suzyn handled play-by-play for the Yankees local telecasts on WPIX, which made her the second woman to serve in that capacity for a Major League team. In 2007, Waldman and Sterling signed contract extensions to continue as the Yankees radio team at least through the 2011 season.

In 1985, Yankees owner George Steinbrenner sent his GM to fire Yogi Berra. The move upset Berra because in all his other times being fired the owner personally made the move. In Yogi's own words, "George never even called." Yogi vowed never to visit Yankee Stadium again and not to participate in any Yankee function as long as Steinbrenner owned the team. In 1999, Suzyn Waldman brought the two men together with an apology from Steinbrenner to Yogi. Thanks to her efforts, the fourteen-year feud between the two was finally over. Later, in the 1999 season, Steinbrenner declared a Yogi Berra Day to the thrill of Yankees fans everywhere. On that special day, Don Larsen threw the ceremonial first pitch to Yogi and David Cone pitched a perfect game against the Montreal Expos.

Female trailblazers in sportscasting faced many more problems than men in breaking into the field. Take well-known CBS Sportscaster **Lesley Visser**, who has been covering sports for almost thirty-five years. She remembers a time when credentials specifically barred women and children from press boxes and women's restrooms were nowhere to be found in the press area. Players and coaches were rude and threatening and refused to allow women reporters access to locker rooms. Through it all Lesley persevered and went on to be the first female beat reporter to cover the NFL, MLB, and NBA. She was also the first female member of the Monday night football announcing team.

Born on September 11, 1953, in Quincy, Massachusetts, Lesley Visser has been a sports fan since she was a child. At age twelve, she decided to become a woman sportswriter, but there was just one problem: back then, the job didn't exist - not for women, anyway. Her family never discouraged her. Her parents didn't say "girls can't do that" and Lesley's mom told her, "Sometimes, you have to cross where it says 'don't walk.'" Visser believes the three most important things for any sportscaster to remember are knowledge of the game, a passion for sports, and the professionality and the stamina to struggle!

Gayle Gardner, the first female sports anchor on a major network, says, "No one is just going to hand you a job. For women especially, this profession will never stop being a struggle with constant blows which must be taken." As for today's would-be women sportscasters, Gayle Gardner senses a backward trend in female sportscasting. She says that after years of women struggling to be accepted, the NFL shows today are back to hiring men or male former athletes instead of professional women sportscasters. Jeannie Morris blames the culture. She believes feminists today are not as aggressive as they were in the '70s. This translates to less pressure for the networks to hire females, because the women are not really fighting for the jobs anymore. All sportscasters agree on one important thing, whether it be male or female, you must be prepared, know the game, and remember that real sports fans know what is real and what is not.

Lesley Visser, Gayle Gardner, and so many other women blazed a trail that eased the way for today's generation of female sportscasters, and also for tomorrow's radio wannabes.

Author's note: Today, things have changed dramatically in broadcasting for women, particularly in the NFL and NHL, as more and more have a presence on televised games as sideline reporters.

Quotes and words of advice for future radio play-by-play wannabes from some of radio's all-time great play-by-play sportscasters.

> **Red Barber:** "When I'm talking to a large audience, on or off the radio, I imagine that I'm talking to a single person." Barber also told legendary sportscaster Vin Scully to "never be a homer." That is, not to openly display a rooting interest in the team that still employs you. Barber also told Scully, "Never listen to other announcers and keep opinions to yourself."
>
> **Harry Caray:** "My whole philosophy is to broadcast the way a fan would broadcast."

Dizzy Dean, Baseball Hall of Famer and post-career broadcaster with Mutual, ABC, and CBS: "Practice, work hard and give it everything you have." Known for telling it like it is, once while calling a game on CBS Dean said on an open mic, "I don't know why they're calling this the Game of the Week. There's a much better game, the Dodgers and Giants, over on NBC."

Ernie Harwell, fifty-five years calling ML Baseball games, 42 of them with the Detroit Tigers: "Baseball is a lot like life. It's a day-to-day existence, full of ups and downs. Make the most of your opportunities in baseball as you do in life. I owe thanks to the people who have listened to me over the years, who turned on the radio. They have given me warmth and loyalty that I've never been able to repay."

Bob Murphy, fifty years doing MLB play-by-play and best known as voice of the NY Mets: "The game is to be enjoyed. Seek out the joy in the game to bring to the fans."
Lindsey Nelson, thirty-five years covering the NFL, MLB, NBA, and college basketball and PGA golf: "The game is the important thing. The announcer should never get in the way of the game."

Whatever format you choose to do on-radio, always choose your words wisely. They may come back to haunt you later in your career.

NBC sports analyst Chris Collinsworth was reminded of just that. In 2009, an interview popped up on YouTube that was conducted in the '80s, when Chris was a receiver with the Bengals. His sophomoric comments about dating young girls (teens) were callous and insulting. Even though he claimed his remarks were made in jest some 20 years ago, they nevertheless were made on camera and didn't paint a very flattering portrait of the clean-cut image he has always projected. A word to the wise, always choose your words and actions wisely...especially if you plan on being in the public's eye, or ear.

Bill Stern, legendary NBC, ABC and Mutual Radio sports personality.

Mel Allen, radio-TV sports personality and long-time voice of the Yankees.

Curt Gowdy with author, baseball's Jim Palmer and Jared, "the Sports Kid"

Author broadcasting for the Childrens Christmas Fund, from lobby of the Pru with long-time friend, Joe Castiglione-the voice of the Red Sox for over 30 years.

Frank DeFrancesco, former GM, WIDE Radio, Biddeford, ME with author. Together, they broadcast hundreds of high school football & basketball games on WIDE Radio in the 60s and 70s.

Notes:
1. DeForest referred to the three-element vacuum tube as the "audion."
2. *The New York Journal American* was a newspaper published from 1937 until 1966. The *Journal American* was the product of a merger between two New York newspapers, owned by William Randolph Hearst: *The New York American* (originally the *New York Journal*-renamed the American in 1901), a morning paper, and the *New York Evening Journal*, an afternoon paper. Both papers were published by Hearst from 1895 until 1937.
3.. WJZ was the key station for NBC's Blue Network and WEAF for the Red. On Oct. 14, 1943, NBC sold its Blue Network to Edward J. Noble and the new network became ABC - The American Broadcasting Company.
4. UP was United Press, the competitor to AP, the Associated Press. Later, UP became UPI (United Press International). In 1998, UPI sold its broadcast operations to AP Radio.
5. The restrictions were about the same as in 1928, which only allowed stations and networks to read their news copy on the air twice a day.
6. Harry Von Zell is best remembered for his announcing role on *Burns & Allen* on radio and TV.

7. Today WJSV is WTOP in Washington.
8. Read more about women on the radio in Chapter 13- A Woman's Perspective on Working in Radio.
9. FDR's fireside chats, which began eight days following his inauguration, inspired the nation following the dark days of the Depression. President Franklin D. Roosevelt spoke to Americans informally on the radio almost as if he were in the same room with the listener.
10. Source: Arbitron, Radio Today: How Americans Listen to Radio; 2006 Edition, February 14, 2006.
11. Source: The Museum of Broadcast Communications.
12. Reportedly, several of Winchell's former co-workers wanted to attend his services but were allegedly turned away by his daughter.
13. Edited by his son, Paul Harvey, Jr.
14. How to develop your own air style is discussed in Chapter 2.
15. The art of interviewing is covered in Chapter 8.
16. Magnetic tape recorders were developed by German engineers during WWII and seized by Allied soldiers. The technology returned home with the GIs, and soon tape recorders like Magnecorder and Ampex were seen and heard in radio studios across America.
17. Three Bell Lab engineers in New Jersey, John Bardeen, Walter Brattain and William Shockley, received the Nobel Prize in 1956 for their discovery and development of the transistor.
18. MacKenzie program repeaters were around during the 1950s and offered numerous configurations with as many as ten decks in a unit. One popular model was the 500, which featured five decks and independent audio outputs for each. The unit was much like the ITC-3 deck cart machine which became so popular in the '70s. A front panel volume control came with each deck. The ¼ inch magnetic tape was mounted in a metal magazine. MacKenzie repeaters were used extensively in the 1950s by Top-40 radio stations prior to the loop cartridge machine. Interestingly, hundreds were used at Disneyland in 1955, because they provided "accurate and dependable" synchronization of external devices with the audio program at the Haunted Mansion and other rides and exhibits.
19. Radio Pro is also dedicated to another Boston personality, Jess Cain.
20. Jordan Rich comments elsewhere in this book.
21. Read more on how to develop your own on-air style in Chapter 2.
22. RTNDA is the Radio-Television News Directors Association.
23. Mary Blake also comments on the subject of being fired in Chapter 9, Attitudes and Actions.
24. Legendary radio pro Dick Summer comments in Chapters 17 & 20 and Dick Biondi in Chapters 4 & 9.

25. Ed Walsh retired from broadcasting in 2010.
26. The Broadcast Decency Enforcement Act of 2005 increased FCC fines to stations violating decency guidelines 20-fold.
27. An example of sexual humor handled in "adult" fashion on the Joe and Andy Show is covered in detail in Chapter 14.
28. WOR is credited by many broadcast historians with pioneering talk radio in America.
29. Read more about pioneer broadcasters Kate Smith and Mary Margaret McBride and their accomplishments in Chapter 13.
30. Read more about the radio career of Mary Margaret McBride in her book *Out of the Air*, published in 1960.
31. Ruth Lyons is profiled in Chapter 13.
32. Read more about Jerry Williams in Chapter 5.
33. Bob & Ray are profiled in Chapter 1.
34. Craig Worthing's earliest days in radio are covered in Chapter 6.
35. After a much celebrated and successful broadcast career, Larry King stepped away from his CNN mic in early 2011.
36. Read more about Larry King and how to be a good interviewer in Chapter 8, The Art of Interviewing.
37. Hugh Hewitt comments on talk radio later in this chapter.
38. Tom Bergeron comments in Chapter 2.
39. Broadcasters Alan Tolz and Steve Elman have written an absorbing biography about Jerry Williams. *Burning up the Air* was published in 2008 by Commonwealth Editions-Beverly Massachusetts. The book is a fascinating read about the "Dean" of talk radio.
40. **Note:** Sally Jesse Raphael commented for Radio Pro in August 2007.
41. Peoplemeters are passive electronic sensors that capture every radio signal the participant encounters during his or her day.
42. Boston sportscasters Ken Coleman, Ned Martin, and others are profiled later in the sports section of this chapter.
43. **Authors note:** I, too, was blessed with having some great producers and call-screeners. They were team players with super attitudes. There's no doubt at all that they were not paid their worth.
44. Future sportscasters wanting to hear how a real radio pro handles play-by-play of a Major League game, pick up a copy of either *The Boston Red Sox-Impossible Dream Album-1967* or *Super Sox '75*, both from Fleetwood Records (Revere, MA) and available on CD. Some of Ned Martin's memorable play-by-play calls have been preserved for future generations of sports radio wannabes.
45. Note: On October 12, 2006, the United States Postal Service in Green River, Wyoming, was officially designated the Curt Gowdy Post Office Building in honor of the place of Gowdy's birth.

CHAPTER 17
Radio Formats – Music

"He loved radio and when you listened to him, you could tell he loved it."
– Alan Freed's son, Lance

1906 WAS THE YEAR. Brant Rock, Massachusetts, was the place! Located on the Atlantic Ocean about ten miles north of famous Plymouth Rock is where **Reginald Fessenden** played his violin, sang a song, and read Bible verses into a wireless telephone of his own design. This is acknowledged by many broadcast historians as the first radio broadcast and acknowledges that Fessenden was one of radio's first DJs. The purpose of the Christmas Eve broadcast was to find financial backers for radio.

Shortly following Fessenden's broadcast, Lee De Forest broadcast well-known opera singers to an audience of reporters. **Charles Herold** in San Jose presented wireless phonograph concerts to amateur radio operators in the Santa Clara Valley. These three radio pioneering men and their efforts were some of the first on record to broadcast to an audience of more than one person. Radio's first personalities to broadcast music and talk on a regular schedule were Herold's students in San Jose, California. These regular broadcasts took place between 1912 and 1917.

Following WWI, when the ban on wireless broadcasting was lifted, inventor **Lee De Forest** set up a station in High Bridge, New York. He was using his invention of the vacuum tube as a transmitter to broadcast music and news. The federal government shut him down, saying the air was no place for entertainment! In 1918, most believed that radio should only be used for two-way communication and there was a general agreement that the US Navy would be in charge of all radio. De Forest responded by packing up his tubes and radio gear and moving to San Francisco, where in 1919 he set up another station and began broadcasting daily.

Meanwhile, back east in Pittsburgh, Westinghouse engineer Frank Conrad had received governmental permission to be on the air during the war in order to develop the De Forest vacuum tube into a transmitter for the war effort. Conrad used a phonograph record to test audio. He received calls from other radio experimenters who were in defiance of the government order and were listening illegally to his tests. Conrad began playing records every Saturday night for his clandestine audience. His company, Westinghouse, asked him to go on the air on a regular basis and play music. They in turn would sell radios for his service. The company applied for and received the first official commercial radio license in November, 1920 and KDKA was on the air! Within a few years, hundreds of radio stations were on the air, entertaining thousands of people who had either bought a radio or built their own crystal set receivers and listened with earphones. Read more on Westinghouse and KDKA's contribution to the birth of broadcasting in chapter 21.

Since broadcasting's earliest beginnings, music has always played an important role on the radio. In 1927, during radio's formative years, a survey of New York City stations showed that almost 75% of their programming consisted of some sort of musical content. In fact, music historians believe radio was directly responsible for the development and growth of popular music in the United States.

In the late '40s television arrived, and by 1952 the new media all but surpassed radio as the primary source for comedy, drama, and other programming. Soon, all the major radio stars, along with their programs and sponsors who made radio's golden age from the '30s to the early '50s so great, left network radio and defected to television. This forced the face of radio to change, and change it did by playing records and featuring music programs. Among radio's first pop music disc jockeys was **Fred Robbins**. The popular New York City radio personality joined WHN in 1942. He later moved to other NYC stations, WINS, WABC, and WNEW. With his smooth delivery, Robbins was known as "the man with the spectacular vernacular," and with good reason. Fred first rose to fame because of his original approach to introducing records and his special talent for coining unique phrases that captured the distinctive personalities of many recording stars of the day. One example of the many phrases attributed to him is "the merry old soul" for Nat King Cole. Commenting in the October 1959 issue of *Radio-TV Mirror*, Fred Robbins stated that he believed it was the responsibility of the DJ to work with the radio station to decide what type of music should be played. He also felt strongly that just like a good editor is needed for a newspaper or magazine, a good personality must carefully pick the music for his show and not rely solely on Top-40 lists.

Today's radio formats and personality.

During the 1930s and '40s, not unlike today's music-intense radio formats, commercial radio stations required a personality, a specific type of music depending on the format, and lots of commercials, and they were in business! The big difference between music stations of today, compared to those of years gone by (the 1920s through the early fifties), is that back then music on radio was live and provided by an orchestra. Today, music on your favorite radio station may sound live but it's really on CD and computer-generated.

According to Arbitron, the media and marketing research firm that serves radio, there are no less than fifty-eight different radio station formats. The various formats range from music-based, like adult contemporary, active rock, country, jazz, and oldies, to Latino urban and Mexican regional, Spanish adult, Christian, and nostalgia. Additionally, there are all-news, talk and sports formats and even an "other" category to include formats that are not covered by the 58 listed. Space does not permit a detailed explanation of every radio format. Instead, we will endeavor to paint a broad brush stroke of some of the basics which apply to most music formats.[1] Keep in mind, different radio formats require numerous styles.[2] As a radio personality, you have the option of selecting the format with which you are most comfortable and which properly suits your style. Whichever format you feel is right for you, AC, country, progressive, rap, rock, sports or talk, it's important to communicate on a one-on-one basis![3]

Radio communicates to the masses, but to be effective as a real radio personality, you need to talk and *relate to just one person.* Communication is the key! Whatever station format or air-shift you find yourself working, keep in mind that you are unique, so think and act like it. Play to your strengths on the radio. You are capable of achieving greatness as an on-air radio pro, if you will passionately and consistently be yourself on the air. Don't allow anyone, whether it be a GM, PD, parent, sibling, girlfriend or boyfriend, define who you should sound like on the radio! You need to be happy with who you are on the air. You possess something valuable that no one else has and that is the unique perspective of being you, of seeing life in a way that can not be duplicated. My own on-air style is "warm n' friendly." It seemed to work well for me on the radio for over forty years. When you're warm n' friendly on the radio, folks will want to spend time with you, just like in real life.

Communication is a means of speaking, but being an excellent communicator is more than just speaking words. Talking on the radio is meaningless, unless you *communicate* your thoughts into words meaningful to the listener! You need to convey your thoughts through your words on a one-on-one basis. Here are a few tips on how to communicate effectively on the radio:

- Be expressive…speak with emotion, especially when selling an all-important commercial.

- Say what you feel and mean - be your own person and bring your feelings to your show.
- Don't be afraid to share slices of your life with your listeners - they will come to know you better
- Speak with style—don't speak in a monotone or sing-song delivery.
- And above all, don't be a communication hog! Share your mic and show time. Give your guests time to speak *without interrupting*. Listen to how they respond to your questions. Being a good radio communicator means speaking effectively, but it also means being a good listener!

My friend, **Dick Summer,** with his comfortable, friendly voice, is a great teller of stories, both on and off the radio! Dick was a popular radio pro in Boston and New York City. I first heard him back in the early '60s when he was hosting his all-night radio show on WBZ-Boston. He quickly became one of my radio favorites. Summer's Night-light show, complete with his Venus Flytrap plants and personable one-on-one delivery, was must listening for insomniacs and all nighters. His inimitable style greatly influenced my own decision to pursue an on-air radio career.

"Take the personality out of radio and you're not left with much" - Radio Pro Dick Summer

Dick Summer is an original who was made to be on the radio, although, he feels that in today's radio world of intense "more music" formats he would be an utter failure, "I simply wouldn't fit," he explains. "Actually, I don't fit today's talk radio format either. But then, neither would William B. Williams. He's dead, and I don't care about radio anymore, because it doesn't seem to care." Strong words and hard to fathom, coming from one of America's most popular radio personalities who in the 1960s was heard nationally on NBC radio's weekend talk magazine, *Monitor*.[4] Summer believes the norm in radio today is more music. "I'd rather chat with folks than try and jam ten seconds of information over the intro to song," he exclaims.

Today's talk formats are not his bag either, not when it comes down to who can out-shout each other. Summer always took a kinder, gentler, more civil approach when on the radio. "I love talking with people. Not to people—that's with people," says the native New Yorker. "I love talking with people in the middle of the night when strange faces look out of the dark and the only other sound is your own breathing. That's why today I do my *Good Night* podcasts. Some people do care and that's what I care about." Dick Summer's *Good Night* podcast will put a smile on your face.[5] He tells grown-up bedtime stories to crowd out the day's problems and tuck you in for a safe, sound, good night's sleep. "That's how one reviewer put it," says

Summer. "It's basically what I loved doing with my huddle, when I was on the radio. I especially loved being in the air at night, because there were fewer people listening, but the people who were tuned in were really listening. It always seemed like I was a quarterback with his team gathered around him for protection and working out a way of achieving a goal together. The goal, most of the time," he adds, "was making it through the night."

When asked what insightful words of advice he could pass along to future radio personalities, Summer answered reflectively, "Learn to tell the truth. Then trust the people who listen to you to care about the truth. Believe me, it's not as easy as you might think to tell the truth, especially, all the time. And trusting somebody else with your truth," the legendary air-personality says, "is about as easy as dropping your drawers on New Year's Eve in Times Square. I don't know if radio is going to do that ever again. But that's what Willie B did… and I tried."[6] These words from one of America's greatest communicators and real radio pros, Dick Summer.

Author's note: When I asked Dick for his advice on how to go forward in writing this book, he replied with just three words: "**TELL THE TRUTH!**" Whenever I would get bogged down in writing and wonder if I should make mention of a private matter or delicate situation in this book, Dick's words jumped off my computer screen and hit me squarely between my perplexed eyes: tell the truth! Just like you, Dick, I have tried. Now, only time and the readers will tell if we succeeded.

The major differences between a DJ and a radio personality.

There is a difference between a disc jockey (DJ) and a radio personality. A DJ may be deemed a radio personality, if they are allowed to use their personality on the air, but a radio personality is not necessarily a DJ. In today's world, a DJ is someone who plays music no matter where the venue; clubs, halls, or even a stadium. This does not mean the disc jockey, whether on radio or off, is devoid of personality! On the contrary. If he or she wants to be a successful DJ, it would benefit them greatly to possess an award-winning personality. The old saying, "It's what's between the music that counts," still rings true.

A great disc jockey is also a great entertainer. Today, since the term disc jockey has also become commonly referred to as a club DJ, the term "radio personality" has actually become more appropriate for hosts of radio programs whatever their format. A personality on talk radio is someone who discusses issues on the air. A personality on a music radio station presents the music and does not merely play it. A DJ on a music-intensive radio format can also be a personality, but is limited to how much personality, or talk, if you will, they can project because of time restrictions. In such a format, they must think of clever ways to say something funny or relevant over a ten-second song intro or during breaks in the music flow, which usually happens before a commercial cluster or an element like traffic or news. If you think projecting your personality in ten seconds is easy, give it a shot some time. It is one of the most difficult things an air-talent faces and it takes a real radio pro to master.

Whether air-talent are referred to as radio personalities or DJs, their primary goal is to entertain or inform the listener. This is accomplished by talking *to* the listeners, not at them.

Personality is the key to radio's success regardless of the format.

I'd like to take a moment to clarify a point on a controversial subject between radio talent and programming minds. The hotly contested question is what is more important to a radio station, the talent or the music? It has been an ongoing debate that many of us as air-talent have had and still have with PDs, managers, and consultants. Sometimes the exchange can become quite heated! Who is the real star of the station? In a talk format, the answer is a no-brainer! On a music station the scenario is quite different. It has been my experience that most programmers strongly believe music is the star. I hotly challenged their philosophy and will explain why in a moment. It almost goes without saying that on a music-intensive radio station, music is a key to the mix as long as the right format-fitting songs are played. Naturally, since I'm from the talent gene pool, I believe personality gets two thumbs up, but let me support my claim with the following. My contention is that air-personality is more important and in a special way. I believe you can train any chimp to spin records. It's even easier today with hi-tech equipment. All Bonzo or Cheetah has to do is touch his index finger to a computer screen and "poof!" a song will magically play. The key to a successful music station is not simply the music but the personality showcasing the songs and selling the product on the air. As radio pro Dick Summer says, "Take the person out of personality and you're not left with much!"

When I first joined RKO's Boston FM, WROR-98.5 in the fall of 1979 on the 7pm 'til midnight shift, the station was converting from an automated oldies sound with voice-tracked announcers to a live AC, adult personality station.[7] With live talented personalities on board like Frank Kingston Smith, Bob Stuart, and later Jim Roberts, Phil Redo, Lou Josephs, and this author along with Boston radio legends Larry Justice and Sean Casey, ROR-FM became a bona-fide player in the market.

Whatever the format, music or talk, *personality does make a difference*. To further support my claim, let's take a page from radio's history book. From 1935 to 1959 one of radio's all-time most popular programs was *Your Hit Parade*. Long before radio's Top-40 format, *Your Hit Parade* featured a ranking of the week's top fifteen songs sung by a cast of regular singers. At first, the songs were the stars; the singers didn't even receive a credit mention. It all changed when a young, skinny crooner named Frank Sinatra joined the cast of singers. Free tickets to sit in the audience were scalped to teenage girls outside the CBS studios. Sinatra's voice and personality made the difference. Would the program have been as successful without him belting out the top tunes? Who knows. The show certainly was loaded with other talented pop vocalists of the era, including Buddy Clark, Ginny Simms, Dinah Shore, Martha Tilton, Dick Haymes, Doris Day, Andy Russell, and others, but there was something special in the minds and ears of the radio listeners about the way "Ol' Blue Eyes" phrased the lyrics that sold the songs on *Your Hit Parade*.

In the '50s and '60s, would New York City radio station WNEW-1130AM have been as successful without great air personalities like William B. Williams, Art Ford, Jazz Beaux Collins, Stan Shaw and Jim Lowe spinning their magic between the songs? My vote is emphatically NO! In the late '50s, Albany, New York's WPTR, reaching out to the Great Northeast with its 10,000 watts, would have been just another rock n' roll radio station playing the hits of the day without super personalities like Boom Boom Branigan, Charlie Brown, Bob Badger and a friend who helped point me in the right direction with my radio career, the late Tom Shovan. In the 1960s, a giant radio station along the Niagara frontier was WKBW Buffalo. KB would have been just another hit-bound station without super personalities like Dan Neaverth, Jeff Kaye, Sandy Beach, and Jack Armstrong.

New York City radio station W-A-Beatle-C was a legendary rock station in the '60s, but would it have been as successful without Harry Harrison's reassuring voice that it would be a great day and Cousin Brucie Morrow in the nighttime sharing stories with his radio cousins up and down the eastern seaboard, I think not. Do you really think radio's popular countdown show, *American Top-40*, would have been as popular without Casey Kasem counting 'em down every week while urging future radio stars to "Keep reaching for the stars but keep your feet on the ground!" What about non-music formats. Today, would ESPN Radio be as popular without the personalities of *Mike and Mike in the Morning*? How many consumers do you honestly think would pay for satellite radio if Howard Stern weren't part of the package?

I hope I'm making a strong case that any radio station can play music. It's the personality that makes it go. Radio programming people will try and convince you that the small sampling at the recent focus group says they listen for more music and not the person on the air. This is simply false. Of course, listeners pick a certain station to listen to because they like the music, but they also listen because they want to be entertained and informed by their favorite air personality. It's what's between the music that is so important. In today's new competitive media world with music available from so many different sources, radio programmers need to back off from their misguided thinking, and stop telling air-talent to "shut up and just play the music!" Radio management needs to step back from this antiquated policy of "more music, less talk."

The radio station disease called *musicitis*!

Now is as good a time as any to warn you about a disease that runs rampant through many stations. No matter where you go, or where you hang your headphones, you will undoubtedly come in contact with the number one disease that all too many radio stations seem to be afflicted with, and that's *musicitis*, which in radio jargon means being obsessed with playing too few songs in music rotation. This ugly disease found living in radio stations spreads like E. coli bacteria, from radio station consultants to managers, program directors, and eventually air-talent. The fatal blow is when it spreads to the station's listeners, which will in turn infect the station's ratings.

Musicitis is lethal, and in many advanced cases the only known cure is to do away with the air staff, along with a change in station call letters and format. However, if the same disease-carrying management team is kept in place, burying the air staff and changing the station's call letters are only temporary fixes. Such treatment should be viewed by most intelligent people as nothing more than a band-aid on the real problem, which are the nimrods in charge who believe that fewer songs played in the rotation is a winning formula. More often then not, even when the old format has been surgically removed and a new one inserted, if the same *infected* management types are kept in place, usually it's only a matter of time before musicitis once again rears its ugly head and the infection begins to spread all over again! Your radio board of good health strongly advises all air-talent to be on the lookout for telltale signs your management may be suffering from musicitis.

Personality is the key to radio's success, regardless of the format.

Carriers of the radio disease musicitis can usually can be spotted acting quite peculiarly, even more so than usual. They appear to be very excitable and anxious, their eyes bulging and swollen as they excitedly examine their new playlist of *only 150 songs*, a list they plan to place in constant rotation, 24/7, to be played over and over again on their radio station.[8] In severe cases of musicitis these "suits" will be drooling profusely from the corners of their mouths as they excitedly point to specific song titles on a page. This is accompanied by rapid chatter and hysterical laughing, as though they're intoxicated. These are obvious signs that musicitis is in its advanced serious and can be highly contagious.

When you observe management and their underlings in this condition, beat a hasty retreat and stay away from them! Under no circumstances should you approach them, let alone try and open the subject of music and station playlists, while they are in such a state of bizarre behavior. They have been infected with the disease and are sadly incapable of any rational thinking, let alone intelligent communication! They have lost any common sense, assuming they had any in the first place. The welfare and well-being of their air staff is the furthest thing from their demented minds. They have been infected with musicitis. The best advice for both radio newbies and senior pros is to immediately give serious thought to tearing up your contract and severing your ties with these lost radio souls. Once the disease seeds its deadly roots and pollutes the brain, there is no communicating with these people, let alone getting them help. It is too late to change their minds about the deadly acts they are about to commit; cuts to the station's music playlist are imminent! Just the thought of musicitis setting in is frightening! Air-talent and listeners forgive them, for they know not what they are about to do. It is the disease of musicitis which has taken over their misguided minds.

Any human contact with these obviously disturbed characters, on any level, could destroy your spirit and kill your chances of survival and success as a radio pro. At the first sign of musicitis, you need to act quickly. Even though I was acutely aware of the signs of this insidious disease when it first began to spread through our great radio station, KLDE, I neglected to heed my own advice. I turned my back on the problem and ultimately paid the price. Don't let it happen to you. Musicitis has destroyed the heart, soul, and spirit of more air-talent than any other disease known to radio-kind. Don't be the next victim. Fight back against musicitis. Insist that your station expand and broaden its tight playlist today, before it's too late! Grab management's ear today, before musicitis beats you to it!

Author's Note: The preceding was a dramatization. The poetic description may be a bit of an exaggeration, but don't miss the message, which is dead on. More than a few radio managers and programmers operate in the frightening manner described.

Cars will always be a home for Radio

In my opinion, one of the last places where personality radio can still succeed is in-car listening. Consider for a moment a future where every car radio gets iPod and Internet streaming. Commercial radio needs to encourage more "live-local" personality to differentiate themselves from a service that provides a steady stream of music, music, and more music!

One additional point: when PDs and GMs tell you, as talent, that music on your station is the star and not you, don't get all upset and toss your cookies. It's their way of keeping your ego in check. They are doing their best to keep you off-balance to prevent you from demanding too much of an increase during your next contract negotiations. Don't kid yourself, management knows your worth.

Some radio programmers and consultants, like my friend Gary Berkowitz, strongly believe that it's what's between the music that will kill you! I guess it all depends on who is positioned between the music. Sorry, Berko, but I have another example of why I believe in the theory that it's *what's between the music that counts.*

It's radio's Good Guys story.

From 1960 until 1970, WMCA -570AM was one of New York City's great Top-40 radio stations. In 1958, Steve Labunski, a former Todd Storz executive, was the station's GM. He had been in Kansas City prior to joining WMCA and had worked with a talented program manager, Ruth Meyer, who had evolved into an expert on Top-40 radio. Despite much opposition in hiring a woman program director, Ruth was hired in 1958 to work with Labunski to create a Todd Storz-type Top-40 music radio station in New York City. Todd Storz and his contributions to radio are discussed later in this book.

In the late fifties, the station had been playing Top-40 music, but Meyer consolidated the format in late 1960. It was the definition of "team radio," where all the air personalities worked together as a cohesive group. Meyer did not coin the term "Good Guys," but she perfected it and the use of the legendary phrase began on the air at WMCA in 1963. Other radio stations, including rival WABC, had used the term Good Guys, but no other station ever promoted its use to the extent WMCA did. Everyone on the air at the station worked together in promoting the idea of Good Guys on the radio at WMCA. It caught on with the Baby Boomers at their teenage peak and the station handed out thousands of sweatshirts with smiley-faced logos to an enthusiastic audience that pushed the station to the top of the ratings. WMCA became one of New York City's highest-rated Top-40 stations.

The station took pride in its promotion of the station, saying "Its success was built on showmanship." The original WMCA Good guys were popular personalities that made the station a success. They were Joe O'Brien, Harry Harrison, Jack Spector, Don Davis and Jim Harriott. In the fall of 1961, Dan Daniel was hired and Ed Baer joined a few weeks later. During the next year, a number of changes were made, but the air-talent lineup that most New Yorkers remember as the *WMCA Good Guys* started with Joe O'Brien at 6am, and continued through the day with Harry Harrison, Jack Spector, Dan Daniel, and B. Mitchell Reed, with Johnny Dark on overnights. Ed Baer and Frank Stickle filled in and did weekends. In 1965, Gary Stevens replaced Reed at night and Dean Anthony did overnights. During that period, talk radio was also part of the WMCA lineup. One call-in program, hosted by Barry Gray, aired weeknights from 11pm 'til 1am.

In 1961, WMCA's biggest competitors were WINS, WABC and WMGM. WMCA beat WMGM, was the one-time radio home to Ted Brown and Peter Tripp, who was known on the air as "the curly-haired kid in the third row." The station shifted to the "Beautiful Music" format. In 1965, WINS went all-news, leaving only WMCA and WABC in the Top-40 race. **Note:** It's important to know that WMCA was only a 5,000-watt radio station, where WABC had 50,000 watts! As a result, 77-WABC had a much greater reach to Long Island, the suburbs of New Jersey and Connecticut, and most of the rest of the Atlantic seaboard. In the city itself, where it had a strong signal, WMCA did extremely well in the ratings. The ratings war between WABC and WMCA has been described as a donut, with the center hole representing the area where WMCA won, and the donut itself indicating WABC's top territories.

In the late '60s, things changed. WABC dropped a lot of network programming in 1968 and behind the genius of PD Rick Sklar and a new jingle package. The station was built around the theme of "the most music."[9] FM stations began to have an impact, especially WOR-FM. FM became a bigger problem for WMCA than for WABC, because of its lower power. The emphasis on personality changed at the station.

In 1968, Harry Harrison moved to mornings at competitor 77-WABC, replacing Herb Oscar Anderson and joining an already killer lineup of radio pros that included Ron Lundy, Dan Ingram, Charlie Greer, and Cousin Brucie Morrow. Meanwhile, Gary Stevens moved to Europe.

In 1969, Joe O'Brien moved to mornings at WNBC. New WMCA personalities included Frankie Crocker from WWRL and Murray "The K" Kaufman, who was hired as the station tried a mix of talk and music, but nothing seemed to click. It was in the fall of '69 when WMCA switched back to The Good Guys with the return of Ed Baer, Jack Spector, and Dean Anthony, but even their presence didn't seem to help. By 1970, New York radio was changing. Music on FM was hurting WMCA. WABC was able to continue setting ratings records because of its powerful 50,000-watt signal. A 5,000-watt AM station like WMCA could no longer compete. The Good Guys and music radio faded away on September 21, 1970, when the station changed to a talk format. Anyone who listened to Radio's Good Guys knows what they said between the records was just as important as the music they played!

Rock n' roll radio's celebrated Moondog.

In the fifties, when radio was losing its biggest stars to television, **Alan Freed** with his strong on-air personality revived radio with music he labeled "rock 'n' roll." On July 11, 1951, Freed took the nickname "Moondog" and began hosting a program of rhythm and blues on WJW-Cleveland, where he coined the term "rock 'n' roll." Within a year Freed became a local sensation, with a loyal audience that crossed racial lines. In 1954, he moved to Ten-Ten WINS (1010AM) in New York City, where he featured rock 'n' roll's early performers on his nightly show, including Chuck Berry, Bo Diddley, and Frankie Lymon and the Teenagers. He also emceed a string of legendary *Big Beat* stage shows at the Brooklyn and New York Paramount Theaters, was heard nationally on CBS Radio, and starred in several rock 'n' roll movies, including *Rock Around the Clock* with Bill Haley and the Comets. In the spring of 1958, when violence occurred outside the Boston Arena following one of his stage shows, local authorities indicted him for inciting a riot. The charges were eventually dropped, but WINS failed to renew his contract.

In 1958, Freed joined 77AM-WABC NYC and also hosted a TV dance show. His on-air endorsement of rhythm and blues and his popularity with both black and white teens made him a lightning rod for both racists and musical conservatives who weren't thrilled with rock 'n' roll in the first place. The popular radio personality's career ended in November 1959, when he was caught up in the payola scandal, in which he was accused of accepting bribes to play certain records on the air. Freed claimed payments he received from record companies were for "consultation," and not as an inducement to play their records. He was fired from his radio and television programs.

Next, Freed was hired by a Los Angeles radio station but when management refused to let him promote his live rock 'n' roll shows he left and returned to Manhattan to emcee a live twist revue. When the twist craze cooled, he joined WQAM in Miami. Realizing that his dream of returning to New York radio was just that, Freed's drinking was alleged to have increased. His job in Miami lasted just two months.

In December 1962, Alan Freed was back in New York again, not on the air but on trial. He pleaded guilty to commercial bribery and was fined $300. Living in Palm Springs, the one-time "King of Rock and Roll" was a broken man. He died there on January 20, 1965. Those closest to him swear he died of a broken heart. Alan Freed was just 44. Despite his numerous personal tragedies, his innovative contributions to radio helped make rock n' roll and the Top-40 format permanent fixtures on radio. In 1986, he was part of the first group inducted into the Rock and Roll Hall of Fame, which was built in Cleveland partly in recognition of his involvement in the promotion of the genre when he was on the radio at WJW. In 1988, Alan Freed was also posthumously inducted into the Radio Hall of Fame.

Ranked right up there in popularity in rock radio legends with Alan Freed is **Murray "The K" Kaufman.** Kaufman was another influential rock radio personality from the '50s through the '70s. While Freed introduced rock n' roll to AM radio, Kaufman launched rock on FM.

Rock radio legend Murray "The K" transformed music radio on FM.

Murray the K's big break in the Big Apple happened in 1958, when he joined WINS New York. His all-night show was called the *Swingin' Soiree*. When Alan Freed's contract was not renewed, Murray moved into his old time slot, 7-11pm, which he held for seven years. He reached the zenith of his popularity in the mid-1960s, as one of New York's top radio personalities. Murray became a big supporter and friend of the Beatles, and often referred to himself as the 5th Beatle. In 1964, WINS was moving toward an all-news format. Murray found out and resigned on the air, breaking news of the pending format change before the station released the news.

In 1966, the FCC ruled that AM & FM stations could no longer simply simultaneously broadcast the same programming, opening the door for Murray to become the leader of the pack in rock FM radio. He joined WOR-FM New York as the PD and primetime DJ. The station became the first FM rocker. He created a groundbreaking FM radio format that transformed music radio. He called it attitude music and played all types of music. It was a free-form format that featured the long album versions of hit songs, which became known as FM cuts. Murray also played cutting-edge album cuts rather than singles. He also featured live, in-studio guests, and played the album versions of hit songs by artists such as Bob Dylan and Janis Ian. Kaufman's WOR-FM format was a first for FM and for radio. The air-staff line-up at WOR-FM included Rosko and Scott Muni. WOR-FM's format was a first for FM and for radio.

The station's format was a cultural phenomenon and commercially successful, but management wanted more commercial appeal. They tried to force Murray to use a station playlist and to cut back on the less-familiar album cuts. He refused and the stress resulted in a heart attack. WOR-FM switched to an oldies format and Murray, who had left the station, moved to Toronto where he had a program on CHUM. His show was also carried on WHFS in Washington, DC. In 1970, he returned to New York and the night shift on WNBC. Even though his air-work at NBC was more laidback, he was still the quintessential Murray the K, complete with pairing song cuts by a theme or word association. In early 1975, he joined Long Island alternative rocker, WLIR. His final NYC program was on WKTU-FM. Already in ill health, he moved to Los Angeles where he hosted the syndicated *Soundtrack of the '60s* until his health forced him to resign. Murray "The K" Kaufman, the first person to bring rock to FM radio, passed away from cancer one week following his 60th birthday on February 21, 1982.

Another broadcaster who was a leader in formatting album rock on radio is **Lee Abrams**. As a founding partner of Burkhart/Abrams, the Atlanta-based consulting giant, Lee invented and built album rock. He also designed numerous other highly successful radio formats, including the first classic rock format at San Francisco's KFOG and the first urban/dance format at New York's WKTU. Abrams joined Tribune as SVP/chief innovation officer in April l, 2008, but left the position in early 2011.

Founding fathers of rock n' roll and who helped perpetuate the sound on radio.

Les Paul - Without his innovative engineering, rock wouldn't have developed. His contributions to rock n' roll include the solid-body electric guitar, the reverb and echo chamber, electromagnetic pickup, and the first 8-track recorder, among many others.

Norman Petty helped invent rock n' roll by producing artists like Buddy Holly, Roy Orbison and others at his studios in Clovis, New Mexico.

Sam Phillips' Sun label in Memphis gave birth to artists like Johnny Cash, Charlie Rich, Jerry Lee Lewis, Carl Perkins, and a very young, Elvis

Presley. Phillips sold Elvis's contract to RCA for just $35,000.

Berry Gordy, Jr., the founder of Motown records in Detroit, one of rock's greatest record companies. Motown turned out soulful hits for Smokey Robinson, The Supremes, The Temptations, and The Four Tops, by spectacular songwriters like Brian Holland, Lamont Dozier and Eddie Holland.

Ahmet Ertegun, along with his brother Nesuhi and partners Jerry Wexler and Herb Abramson, built Atlantic Records and gave us Ray Charles, Aretha Franklin, Solomon Burke, Wilson Pickett, and others.

Jerry Leiber and Mike Stoller, songwriters who perfected the two-minute pop song with hits written for The Coasters, The Drifters and others

Phil Spector and his Phillies label, whose slogan was "Tomorrow's sound today." Spector's huge "wall of sound" featured many different instruments in a voluminous effect on hit recordings by The Ronettes, The Crystals and The Righteous Brothers, which were easily the most well-produced pop music ever.

Brian Wilson perfected the Beach Boys' harmony with hit after hit, and with "Good Vibrations" gave birth to the psychedelic sound long before it became popular.

Paul Drew was another founding father of rock radio. He witnessed the birth of Top-40 radio and helped it grow to mammoth proportions by programming and directing one of the most successful radio groups in history, RKO Radio. During its glory years, RKO Radio claimed #1 stations in Boston, Detroit, Los Angeles, Memphis, New York, and San Francisco. Paul's greatest legacy is perhaps the success of those he hired, including Les Garland, Bob Hamilton, Walt "Baby" Love, Dave Martin, Harry Nelson, Bobby Ocean, Dave Sholin, Charlie Van Dyke, and so many other talented broadcasters.

A word about **Mike Joseph's** Hot Hits stations of the late 70s and early 80s: Hot Hits stations only played current hit songs, no oldies, in a repetitive fashion with fast-talking personalities and loud station jingles. The first Joseph station to use the term Hot Hits was WFBL Syracuse, New York, in 1979. Known as "Fire-24," the station played its Top-14 Hits in tight rotation. Other stations, like WTIC-FM-Hartford, WBBM-FM in Chicago and KITS-San Francisco, followed suit and were instantly successful.

More proof that a "real" personality wins every time on the radio.

In the 1950s, '60s, and '70s, every city and town across the fruited plain had "name" radio personalities who showcased the music they played, along with their unique style and personalities. Space doesn't permit us to list them all, but here are a few of the "major" players.

In **Albany, New York**, JW Wagner, Roy Reynolds, Boom Boom Branigan and the all the great personalities on 1540AM-WPTR. WTRY was home to Lee Gray and Jay Clark. In **Atlanta**, it was Dick "Dickie Doo" Blanchard on

WPLO. In 1960, Bob Mckee, Larry Brite, Stan Richards, Russ Knight and Bill Drake were doing their thing on WAKE.

Boston: in the 50s and 60s on the more adult-sounding WNAC-680AM, home of the Yankee Network, with Roy Leonard, Gus Saunders, Louise Morgan and the velvety voice of Bill Marlowe caressing the mic. Color-radio 1510 WMEX was J.J. Jeffrey, Mel Miller, Ed Heider, Arnie Woo Woo Ginsberg; holding court on WBZ was Carl DeSuze, Dave Maynard, Jay Dunn, Jim Holt, Jefferson Kaye, Ron Landry, Bruce Bradley, Dick Summer, and later, Larry Glick. WHDH was home to Bob and Ray, Ray Dory, Jess Cain, Alan Dary, Dave Supple, Tom Kennedy, Sean Casey, and Norm Nathan; in the '80s on 680-RKO were Charlie Van Dyke, Dennis Jon Bailey, Harry Nelson, Mike Addams and Scott Burns.

Buffalo, New York, in the pre-rock days of 1955, on WKBW, it was Frank Ward and in '59, George Hound Dog Lorenz. In 1961, Jay Nelson was the wake-up guy, followed by Russ Syracuse, Johnny Barrett, Jim Taylor, Tom Shannon, Sandy Beach, Ted Hackett, and all-nights with Bob Diamond. In 1965, on KB, it was Stan Roberts in AM-drive, followed by Fred Klestine, Rod Roddy, Dan Neaverth and nights with Joey Reynolds.

Chicago radio in the pre-rock era featured Howard Miller and Wally Phillips, who had a 42-year run in mornings at WGN. Later came Art Roberts, Larry Lujack, Fred Winston, Dick Biondi, Bob Sirott, Steve King, and Yvonne Daniels. In the late '70s, Steve Dahl and Gary Meier were #1 at WLUP, and from '81 to '86 continued that success at WLS-AM and WLS-FM in PM-Drive.

The Queen City of **Cincinnati** was a hotbed of radio talent, including Jim Scott on WSAI. On WLW in the '70s, it was James Francis Patrick O'Neal in AM-Drive, followed by "Jockey" Joe Kelly, the music professor, Jim Labarbara in PM-Drive, along with Bob Martin and a guy named Joe Martelle on overnights. In 1981, Gary Burbank joined WLW and remained with the station until his retirement in 2007. **Cleveland** radio immortals include Bill Randall, Alan "Moondog" Freed, Ernie Anderson, Norm N. Nite and in 1959 Pete "Mad Daddy" Myers was radio's famous bard of the air on WJW with his kooky jargon and offbeat, wavy gravy, record sounds. Everything was done in off-the-cuff rhyme.

In **Dallas,** Ron Chapman was king of the kilocycles, along with Russ Knight "The Weird Beard," Chuck "Baby" Dunaway, Ken Dowd, Charlie and Harrigan, and Rex Miller.

Denver in the '60s found John Rook at KTLN. 950AM; KIMN was the heritage Top-40 rocker with great personalities like Gary Owens, who went on to join the cast of NBC-TV's *Laugh-In*; Pogo Poge, who jumped a pogo stick to Boulder; Roy "The Bellboy" Gunderson, Steve Kelly and Jay Mack.

Detroit radio in the early '60s found Lee Alan at WXYZ and WJR's J.P. McCarthy who joined the station as an announcer in 1956 and when Marty McNealy left in 1958 for WKMH, J.P. Took over the *Morning Music Hall*. J.P.'s show was #1 for thirty years until his passing on August 16, 1995, at age 62. Dick Purtan is another Detroit radio legend. Robin Seymour on WKMH and across the big lake in Windsor, Ontario, was mighty CKLW where former KBW-Buffalo personality Tommy Shannon was on-the-air.

Hawaiian radio was home to Hal Lewis on KGMB, better known to his listeners as Akuhead Pupule or simply, Aku. Another popular radio fixture was Ron Jacobs. In the '50s, he was still a teen but doing Top 40 radio at KHVH. In '59, Ron was also one of the original Poi Boys at KPOI.

Houston radio in 1950 is when legendary Paul Berlin arrived at KNUZ 1230AM. Later, it was Bill Bailey and two radio pros I was privileged to work with at KLDE in the late '90s, Joe Ford and Barry Kaye.

Jacksonville, Florida and WAPE Jacksonville with its distinctive Tarzan-like ape call on-hour station I.D. was extremely popular, and featured popular personality Dan "Dusty Discs" Brennan, one of three brothers who owned the station in the 70s. Also on air were John Ferree, Ken Fuller, Jack Mock, Dino Summerlin and others.

Kansas City WHB is the second-oldest station in KC and, in the 50s and 60s, rocked with its air-force led by Johnny Dolan and Phil Jay. KCMO and WDAF also featured outstanding air personalities.

Los Angeles radio in the '50s found Hunter Hancock counting down the hits on K-POP on Gower Street in Hollywood. Some say he was the first to play rhythm and blues on California radio and one of the first to broadcast rock n' roll. Jim Hawthorne was on KFWB. "The Emperor" Bob Hudson hit the radio scene in the mid-fifties and was consistently voted one of the Top 10 DJs in Southern California. His radio career took off in 1963, when he replaced Bob Eubanks in AM-Drive at KRLA. In the early '70s, he teamed with one-time WBZ-Boston personality Ron Landry. They worked at KGBS and the two became a potent morning-drive team in LA. Popular Sam Riddle was part of KRLA's line-up in the early '60s. In '65, Riddle joined KHJ as one of the original Boss Jocks. In May of 1965, "The Real" Don Steele became one of the first personalities on Boss Radio-KHJ. Robert Smith, better known as Wolfman Jack, syndicated his oldies show from LA. B. Mitchell Reed, one of the original WMCA-New York Good Guys, was on several LA stations. Dick Whittinghill spent almost three decades on KMPC. His long tenure was followed by another LA radio favorite, Robert W. Morgan (later on K-Earth). Other LA radio pros include Wink Martindale, Sonny Melendrez and Jim Ladd on KMET, known as "The Mighty Met" during the '70s and '80s. **Memphis** has the distinction of presenting the first all-girl radio station in the US in 1955 with WHER-AM. Memphis also found Martha Jean "The Queen" Steinberg, one of the first R&B dee-jay's in the nation on WDIA-AM.

Top-40 radio in **Miami** was a battleground between AM giants, WQAM and WFUN. The city had super radio talent. To name just two, Doc Downey, yes, the same Morton Downey, Jr., of later TV talk show fame, and Rick Shaw, whose voice covered the beaches for over 50 years until his retirement in 2008.

Minneapolis radio is home to Dan Donovan, who zipped into the Twin Cities in 1979 and never left. Chuck Knapp has been on-the-air in the city for over forty-five years. Name the format and he's probably done it.

Montgomery, Alabama, in 1953, WBAM 740AM signed on with a 50,000-watt booming voice which covered much of Alabama, Georgia and Florida. During its Top-40 heyday, The Big Bam, known as the Voice of the Deep South, was loaded with super air talent like Bill J. Moody, Bobby Brennan, his brother Dan "Dusty Discs" Brennan, Coby Shubert and Joe Cook.

Nashville, on WLAC it was Gene Nobles from the 1940s through the '70s, playing R&B before Alan Freed and fellow WLAC personalities, John R. Richbourg, Bill Hoss Allen and Herman Grizzard, the four WLAC personalities played R&B, soul and gospel music. Who could forget legendary Ralph Emery?

In **New York City** in the '50s and '60s it was John Gambling and Martin Block on WOR, Bill Cullen on WNBC, and before WCBS-AM became Newsradio-88, Jack Sterling breezed through mornings. WNEW was the longtime home of Klaven and Finch and William B. Williams. The Big Apple was and is the home to so many talented personalities including Harry Harrison, Big Wilson, Dan Ingram, Don Imus, and many others mentioned elsewhere in this book.

Oklahoma City is home to legendary Top-40 radio stations, WKY at 930AM and KOMA at 1520AM. One of the popular d-j line-ups on WKY featured Danny Williams, Wilson Hurst, Don Wallace, Jimmy O'Neal, Chuck Boyles and Ronnie Kaye. KOMA, had equally talented personalities including, Paul Miller, Johnny Dark and M.G. Kelly.. In **Phoenix** in the late 60's on KRIZ it was Doug Cornet, Pat McMahon and Joe Light; on KRUX it was Lucky Lawrence, Norm Seeley, Dick Gray, Kit Carson and Bob Shannon. Long-time radio personality, Bill Heywood entertained Valley listeners for 45 years on KOY, KTAR and KFYI. In **Philly,** it was Boss jock "Long John" Wade on WFIL, and Jim Nettleton. Former Portland, ME, talent Ken Garland was on mornings on WIP for twenty-two years and then spent another five years on WPEN. On WIBG, Hy Lit and Joe Niagara were top cats; and Jerry Blavat, "The Geator with the Heater" was as popular as a Philly cheese-steak sandwich! In **Pittsburgh** it was Bob Tracey and Art Pallan on KDKA. In 1958, KQV was home to Chuck Dougherty and Herb Oscar Anderson. In '73, Jackson Armstrong, the fastest talker on Top-40 Radio, took the town by the ears shouting, "It's your leaddderrrr on 13Q."

In the '50s, in **Portland Maine,** the author's hometown, we only had three AM stations to choose from, but what talented personalities! Will Whitten was the witty morning man on WCSH, followed by Ken Whitmore, Bob Shaw, and my longtime pal, Doug LaVallee. Waking up to WGAN was Maine's favorite country personality Ken MacKenzie and his wife Simone, "The Missus." Ken was followed by *Chuck Sanford's Early Risers Club*. Also on

GAN were Jay Dunn, Jim Winters, Jay Maher, Dex Card and Arnie Kuvent and his *560 Revue* playing hit songs of the day. Congenial Ray Mercier and his *Alarm Clock Club* were the morning voice on WPOR, followed by Howie Leonard, *Matinee Frolic* with Ralph Fenno, Frank Sweeney and Mike Norton in the afternoon with *Teens, Topics and Tunes;* Bob Armstrong and all nights with Bob Mowers and *Spinners Sanctum.*

In 1956, **Portland** picked up its fourth station and first official rocker, WLOB at 1310 AM. What a line-up of air talent: Seth Larrabee, Jim Mack, Russ Blood, Bob Raleigh, smooth-sounding Jack McDermott and Pat Matthews. Even the station's Chief Engineer, Dick Dunn, had a weekend show, complete with his own theme song, *Open the Door, Richard.* For a while, WLOB was home to Dick Johnson, who became the long-time familiar wake-up news voice on WGAN-560 AM. In the early 60s, WLOB featured the popular *Live-Five,* Allen E. Allen, Bob "Doc" Fuller, Jim Sands, Dick Fixaris and Charlie Brown. Later came Joe "Johnny Dollar" Desimone, Bob Anderson, Surfer Joe Shevenell, Lil Jeff Weinstein and a hubby-and-wife team, Snyder & Snyder (Rick & Mary-Jo). Portland's second rocker, WJAB-1440AM, a 5000-watt daytimer, signed on November 8, 1959. The original Mister-Jab DJs were Jim Sands, Frank Fixaris, J. J. Jeffrey and, later, Bob Caron, aka Jon E. Dee, and Bob Raleigh. For a medium-sized radio town, Portland, Maine, had a host of major-market air talent.

San Diego gave us Bobby Ocean and the station that made radio history with The Last Contest, KCBQ. Other popular air personalities, include, Buzz Bennett, and Shotgun Tom Kelly, and Boss Radio, KGB.

San Francisco had Dr. Don Rose and other longtime bay area radio favorites Don Sherwood, Don Bleu, Jim Lang and Dan Sorkin, who made Bay area listeners laugh for over fifty years. In 1965, Gene Nelson and Ed Hider were on KYA.

Seattle and KJR is where Richard (Rick) Johnson was heard. Better known as Bwana Johnny, he also worked at WUBE-Cincinnati and other radio markets. In 1966 on KJR, it was Lan Roberts, Tom Murphy and Pat O'Day.

St. Louis was home to one of the city's first black DJs, Spider Burks. He began on-air at KXLW in 1947 and stayed with the station until 1956. He was also on-air with St. Louis stations, KSTL, KADY, KADI-FM and KATZ, before leaving the business in 1969. Robert BQ Burris was the morning radio personality at KATZ. In 1964, he became the station PD and gained a reputation for KATZ as a power in African-American radio. KXOK was a favorite pop music station and Jim Irwin (aka Peter Martin), who joined the station in 1954, became a listener favorite in the midday hours. Reed Farrell was on KWK and in 1958. Jack Carney was the legendary mid-morning voice on KMOX. After two years at the station and with top ratings, he got an offer to join WABC in New York. It was a bad move and he left after a few months and went off, in his own words, to find himself. After a West Coast stint, Jack returned to St. Louis and KMOX, where he worked until his death in 1984.

Syracuse radio talent in the '50s included Jim Deline (WFBL), Deacon Doubleday on WSYR. Dean Harris on WHEN was the Dean of Morning Radio with a big voice. Denny Bracken was on WOLF. By the late '50s, WOLF had a powerful line-up for a 250-watt radio station with morning guy Gene Nelson, Charlie Featherstone, Ted Hackett, Dusty Rhodes and Tommy Saunders. Other Wolf alumni from that era include Ted Jones, Ron Roberts, Andy Andrews and Larry Light (C. Truman Wigglesworth). WNDR 1260AM was the Rock 'n' Roll powerhouse in the late '50s and early '60s in Syracuse. The station line-up was Dandy Dan Leonard, Ross Mad Man Morton, Jolly Rolly Fowler, Terry Mann, Gary Van, D.J. O'Day, Joey Reynolds, Gene 'Yours Truly' Robinson, Bob Dell, and Peter C. Cavanaugh.

Washington, DC, featured Harden and Weaver and the "Joy Boys," Willard Scott and Ed Walker. At WPGC in '63 was Harv Moore, "the boy next door," and Bob 'Tiger' Raleigh (Rolle Ferrar) who went on to handle all-nights at WBZ Boston for 20 years. Some other outstanding radio personalities who handled music and talk were Howard Hoffman, who worked almost every market from the Northeast to the left coast with a few stops in between like Detroit and Houston. Last we heard (2008) he was production director at KABC in LA.

The above-mentioned cities and radio personalities are just the tip of the iceberg on the thousands of air-talent who have entertained listeners in markets of every size over the last sixty-plus years!

Author's note: Who were some of your favorite hometown radio personalities? Drop a note to the author mentioning their name along with the call letters of the station and city. Proper credit will be given to them and you in a future edition of Radio Pro.

The Birth of "Underground" radio in San Francisco.

In 1967, FM rock pioneer Tom "Big Daddy" Donahue at KMPX San Francisco created America's first alternative radio programming. By playing album cuts and reintroducing "live" radio broadcasts, Donahue founded "underground radio." On the verge of becoming general manager and part owner of KMPX, Donahue died of a heart attack on April 28, 1975. He was just 46.

The birth of Top-40 radio.

In 1947, radio legend **Gordon McLendon,** credited as one of the fathers of the Top-40 radio format, started KLIF in the basement of the Cliff Towers Hotel, located across the Trinity River from downtown Dallas in the suburb of Oak Cliff. McLendon was in his late thirties and had an active imagination that won listeners with the wildest on-air promotions imaginable. For example, he promoted a treasure hunt with a grand prize of a hidden check for $50,000. He paid Lloyds of London to insure the contest, just in case a listener found the check. KLIF gave out clues on the air as to where to find the check. A listener did locate it, Lloyds paid the $50,000, and McLendon's million-dollar promotion had cost him a mere $5000, the cost of the insurance. It was an ingenious radio promotion from a radio genius. McLendon hired great radio personalities like Bruce Hayes, Don Keyes, Ken Knox, and Art Nelson, who spun records, played cool station jingles, and ran wild station promotions with fun prizes awarded to the winners.

Bostonian Bill Stewart went to work for McLendon in 1954. He saw KLIF jump in the ratings from tenth place to first in just two months. The McLendon magic and sound had done the trick! By 1955, KLIF was the highest-rated metropolitan radio station in the United States! The McLendon magic and sound had done the trick! But wait! There's more.

Some say **Todd Storz** pretty much invented Top-40 radio and that he was the guy McLendon, Bill Drake, and all the rest copied. While the idea was new, the concept was simple: play the most popular songs from a tight playlist over and over again in a defined format. In a 1973 interview in *Billboard*, Bill Stewart, who worked for both Storz and McLendon, told writer Claude Hall how they 'invented' Top-40 radio.

One night, as the story goes, Storz and Stewart, who ran Storz's Omaha station, were in a bar discussing business.[10] They were there for four or five hours and it began to dawn on them that the same record was being played over and over again from the forty selections on the jukebox. When the bar was closing, the waitress, who had endured hearing the same songs all night long during her shift, put money in the machine and played the same record two or three more times! Here was a favorite record, being played over and over by choice. The two men decided right then and there that people would rather hear a record they liked over and over again, rather than songs picked by disc jockeys. Now, here's where the story becomes a little more like which came first the chicken or the egg?

One version of the story is that the idea clicked with Stewart and helped him sell McLendon on starting a station format that played the Top-40 hit songs of the week, over and over again in rotation. KLIF began surveying Dallas area record stores for weekly sales figures to compile the station's weekly music playlist and Top-40 radio was born. Sounds reasonable, right? But wait…there's more!

In the meantime, Storz hired Bill Stewart away from McLendon to run his Omaha station. Storz and Stewart applied this formula to the programming of KOWH-Omaha and the Top-40 radio format was born, again! Some say the format originated when Stewart shared his concept first with McLendon, but even McLendon said that Storz actually conceived the idea of Top-40 radio and he merely borrowed it. The real facts of the story may never be told, since both Storz and McLendon have passed on.

The day Top-40 radio came to Detroit and the battle over personality vs. music began.

In **Dick Osgood**'s book *Wyxie Wonderland: An Unauthorized 50-Year Diary of WXYZ Detroit*, Osgood talks about the day Top-40 radio came to Detroit: "In 1958, six air personalities were summoned before Hal Neal, the VP of radio programming at WXYZ. He informed the group of anxious announcers that Top-40 was working well at KLIF in Dallas and at KOWH Omaha, both owned by Todd Storz, the father of the format. Neal said they were going to try it in Detroit. He also said in no uncertain terms that everyone was to cut down on the talk."

"What people want to hear is the music, they tune in for their favorite records," insisted Neal.

"Fiddlesticks, "chimed in Ed McKenzie, one of the personalities. "Music's part of it but they tune in to a deejay because they like him!" Neal agreed. "Personality is important. It's not to put personality down at all. But they don't tune in to listen to a disc jockey talk about inane, ridiculous things that he and only a minor segment of the audience might be interested in. The object," continued Neal, "is to get a mass appeal and a consistent sound going, so that the listener, no matter what time of day he tunes in, he can depend upon that station for that type of sound. And WXYZ is going to be that station with that sound. Someone asked, you mean we'll be playing the same 100 songs over and over again, all day? All day and all night," said Neal. "And the most popular ones will go on the air once every hour. Remember, less talk between records, more music. We're going to tighten things up." The meeting ended and the six men, their egos soundly slapped, left the office. And that's how Top-40 radio, fast paced and with a cap on talk and personality, was introduced to Detroit.

Bill Drake, another founding father of rock radio, built upon Storz and McLendon's foundations to create a variation of Top-40 called "Boss Radio." This format of less talk, shorter (shotgun) jingles and more music launched in 1961 in Stockton, California, at KSTN, followed by KYNO Fresno, KGB San Francisco, and finally to KHK Los Angeles in May 1965. The Drake format spread to stations across America and it was later presented by American DJs on *Swinging Radio England*, or pirate radio as it was called due to its being broadcast from on board a ship anchored in international waters off the coast of England. At that time there were no commercial radio stations in England and the BBC offered little in the way of Top-40 music programming. Boss radio spread from San Francisco and KFRC to Boston and WRKO.

"My definition of a radio pro is to get from one end of the show to the other without quitting"-Fred Weiss, WXYZ Detroit personality commenting on how he felt in the '50s about handling the new Top-40 format.

Balancing your show is the key in any format.
   Balance on your show is the key. Keep in mind, there are many other topics that your listeners will find compelling, interesting, and entertaining outside the political beltway! Don't get caught up in being predictable. It is the kiss of death for any radio personality, regardless of whether you're on a music or talk format! In the '80s and '90s, when I was on the air at RKO-General Boston's 98.5-ROR-FM, each air-personality was given a guide book to formatic rules. You were to follow these rules while on the air. Failure to do so could result in death, or worse yet, immediate dismissal. In preparing this chapter, I dug the booklet out of mothballs to check it out. It was most interesting to see that the basics of radio formatics from over twenty years ago still apply to this day. .

The following is a list of some of the basics to keep in mind, regardless of the station format.
   Here are a few examples from the RKO Radio formatics booklet, dated April 1990:

- **Desire:** you must have the desire and passion to be on the best on the radio.
- **Discipline:** it's fairly easy to do a great show when you're up and everything feels great. It's tough when you're not feeling well, or when things are lousy in your personal life. It takes discipline to be positive and push aside the negative. Maximum effort is needed every time you're on the air regardless of how you personally feel.
- **Excitement** comes from energy. You must generate an air of excitement on your program. I have often said, "A real radio personality does not depend on spontaneous combustion, you need to set yourself on fire." You also need to project positive energy both on and off the air.
- **Be real:** you need to sound real on the radio. Consistently, show after show, be yourself.

In handling a music-based format:

- Make sure your segues are smooth. Are you inserting promos and sweepers where they belong?[11]
- Remember, station liners which help promote your radio station need to be "told" and sold in your own words. The basic information on a station liner card must be creatively delivered in your own style and words. If you are reading a liner over the intro to a song, be creative and tie it in to the song. Are you following the station music playlist in order, or playing songs you want to hear, which

is a GIANT NO, NO! It's something almost every air-talent has done at one time or another.

While on the subject of music: The music you play must always be showcased in a positive manner.

Never make a negative comment about the songs you play!

Proper formatic execution.

Regardless of the radio format, in today's world of broadcasting one thing that appears to be missing is proper "formatic execution" by air-talent. Many air personalities, whether handling music, talk, or other formats, simply do not pay attention to formatic execution. I'm talking about the basics of good on-air execution. .

The basics of proper formatic execution.

For example, are you giving the call letters or station slogan enough airtime? Are you selling the radio station call letters with pride, or simply throwing them away? If you're hosting a nationally syndicated talk show, are you mentioning the call letters of the station and the city your callers are from? Are you mentioning who your guests are frequently enough? Quite often, talk show hosts simply do not identify who they are they are talking with. It is frustrating to the listener, who often tunes in and out at various times during the show. You must identify your guest repeatedly. Is your show content reflective of the demographic your station is reaching out to? For example, taking time to talk about a 1940s romantic movie you watched last night would have little if any significance to the 18-24 core male audience on a hard rock station. On the other hand, if the movie was about a boxing legend it might fly a little better with that audience.

Sometimes, you will need to defend your right about calling a shot on your show.

There will be times when you'll have to go with your gut about including something on your show. During the 50th anniversary of the classic film *Gone with the Wind*, our morning-show quiz was a question about the movie. When I got off the air, our station consultant was all over me like a cheap suit. "What possessed you to ask a question from a film that is fifty years old? What were you thinking?" He went on and on. "How does that relate to your audience?" Hmm, let me see…well, to begin with our target audience is women, 25-54. *Gone with the Wind* is not only a classic film, but an important piece of Americana. Does the fact it was shown this week on television matter? Most importantly, the subject matter pertains to our primary demographic, women. Many females love the romantic story between Scarlett O'Hara and Rhett Butler, played to the max by Vivien Leigh and Clark Gable. "*Frankly my dear, I don't give a damn"* - no, those were not the words of the consultant, but could have been. His contention that half our listening base doesn't remember a movie filmed in 1939 is simply wrong. The film remains a classic. Who cares how long ago it was filmed? I still think he was out to lunch for coming down on me about asking a trivia question about the film. Sometimes, you need to defend your right about calling a shot on your show, especially when you feel in your gut it was the correct one! Maybe the consultant had a late flight, got in late, and needed a nap.

In the case of *Gone With The Wind*, I believed that if I let the consultant think his accusation was right, it could lead to future questions - not just about my choice of trivia questions, but other show content. If management begins to believe you lack the ability to call the right shots on your show and lose confidence in you, look out. You will constantly be under their watchful eye and thumb. Believe me, it's a royal pain to have to run all content by the PD or consultant before your show. I've been there, and it's no fun! Word to the wise: choose your battles with management wisely. You have to be selective and let some things slide. If you don't, you will constantly be at odds with them and no one needs that kind of stress, neither talent nor management.

Know your audience and who you are trying to reach, and play to them. Have fun on the radio. Always strive to entertain or inform. Always follow the format, which includes doing the basics and doing them well, every time you open the mic!

Notes:
1. Non-music formats, like news, talk and sports formats are covered in the Chapter 16.
2. How to develop your own style for the radio is covered in Chapter 2.
3. How to communicate effectively on the radio is covered in Chapter 6.
4. In 1955, when network radio programming was winding down, NBC attempted to bring back the glory days of radio's golden age with a weekend radio service called *Monitor*. The 40-hour magazine program aired from Friday nights through the weekend. "Going places and doing things with NBC's *Monitor*" and "You're on the Monitor Beacon" were regular on-air slogans. The series of beeps that identified the program were comforting to hear. Listeners to *Monitor* knew that wherever they traveled on weekends, NBC and its network of affiliated stations around the country would be their sound companion. *Monitor* ran on NBC from 1955 until 1974, and featured comedy, news, talk, sports and music.
5. Dick Summer's podcast can be heard on the Internet at www.dicksummer.com/podcast/latest.
6. Willie B refers to NYC radio legend William B. Williams. who for many years was a popular radio personality on WNEW 1130AM.

7. **Author's note:** No finer company did I work for during my 41 years in radio than in my years spent on-the air in Boston working for the General. We were paid well and always worked with state-of-the-art equipment.
8. Playlist refers to the music songs that are in rotation and aired on a radio station.
9. Rick Sklar was a radio genius. At MusicRadio-77-WABC he created an excitement level never seen before in music radio. Rick was a master at promotions and always made sure WABC capitalized on what was "happening," whether it was the arrival of the Beatles or distributing 14 million promotional buttons around the New York area. He also had a gift for knowing music, jingles, and how to handle air-talent. Rick Sklar was one of a kind and an amazing radio success story. Read more about his radio career in his book, *Rocking America*.
10. Some radio insiders, like Richard Fatherly, who was production director at Storz's KXOK-St. Louis, believe the legend of the barroom discovery is just not true. What is true is that some time in the '50s, Todd Storz, pioneered the practice of surveying record stores to learn which singles were popular each week. He gradually converted his stations to an all-hits format.
11. Quick-voiced station promos, usually recorded and inserted between two songs, with no talk from the personality.

Fred Robbins, legendary and nationally syndicated radio personality, late 1940s and 50s.

William B. Williams, legendary NYC air personality.

Dick Summer, popular WBZ Boston and NYC air personality.

Alan Freed, granddaddy of Rock n' Roll radio pros.

WMCA Good Guys – NYC in the 1960s.

Radio Formats – Music • 563

Montage 2-A. Growing up with Portland ME. radio in the 50s. Dick Johnson in cap and Howie Leonard holding record.

WLOB 1310 AM-Live-5- left to right, clockwise: Bob Fuller, Jim Sands, Dick Fixaris, Charlie Brown, Allen E. Allen.

J.J. Jeffrey, popular Portland (ME) Boston and Chicago air talent.

Surfer Joe Shevenell, circa early 60's, was classmate of author at Cheverus High School, Portland, ME.

Rock and Roll Reunion WROR-98.5 Boston, author with guest air personalities. Front row kneeling (L to R) Mel Miller-RKO-MEX Boston; Ed Hider-Boston-LA; Freddie Boom-Boom Canon; Arnie Woo Woo Ginsburg-Boston. Standing L to R, Author, Dan Donovan-KS-95 Minneapolis; Joe Kelly-GM-ROR Boston; Lorna Ozmon, PD-ROR; Mike Addams- RKO ROR; Charlie Van Dyke, Chuck Knapp-KS-95 Minneapolis.

CHAPTER 18
Attorneys, Agents, Ratings and Contracts

"In contract negotiations, both sides (management and talent) have to walk away feeling good about the deal. If one side feels low-balled or unhappy, it will usually surface somewhere down the road and you don't want that to happen."

– Randy Vataha, agent and former Patriots player

Should air-talent have an agent or attorney?

The question of whether air-talent needs an agent or attorney comes up time and time again. During my own broadcast career, I worked with several different attorneys and agents. My first dealing with a lawyer was in my hometown of Portland, Maine. My family was friends with attorney Sumner Bernstein. He rode to my rescue when I was fired from my first air job in radio. As described in Chapter 9, "Attitudes and Actions," I took it upon myself to change the music format on my shift without management's prior approval. Talk about a really bright move on my part! Stupid me. My biggest fear was that I would be banished from the kilocycles, never to work in radio again. Sumner was extremely sympathetic, but basically told me to get over it and move on! It was probably some of the best advice I ever received from an attorney!

During my on-air years in Maine and Cincinnati, I didn't have legal representation. When I made the move to Boston radio while still maintaining my residence in Saco, Maine, attorney Barry Hobbins handled my first contract at WROR Boston. Barry was a former high-school CCD student of mine, who went on to law school and earned his degree.[1] My next agent representative was John Amato, who is based in Boston. He is not an attorney. John is a super guy who does a great job primarily booking bands and singers at various venues. He represented me as far as booking personal appearances at area clubs. In my many years on the air in Boston, my station contracts were managed by different lawyers, including Jack Sands and Charlie Speliotis. During my final days on Boston radio, when faced with some contract difficulties at the new WROR, Bob Gilman represented me. My friend, attorney Jeff Schreiber, also did some legal work for us during my time spent in Boston. In 1975, when I was in management at WCSH Radio, Jeff was a student at nearby Bowdoin College in Brunswick, and interned in our news department.

My longest association with attorneys and agents in Boston was while I was represented by the firm of the late Bob Woolf. You will read more about my association with the super agent coming up. Bob and his associates Jill Leone, Randy Vataha, and Gregg Clifton were excellent representatives. Greg Clifton comments later in this chapter.

During my time spent on radio in Houston, Texas, I tried a long-distance working relationship with longtime Boston agent and attorney Ken Fishkin. It was difficult and not something I would necessarily recommend. Ken is a great guy and knowledgeable attorney, but distance was a problem.

He was based in Boston and I was in Houston, so we never met in person, eye-to-eye, to hash things out. We tried to deal with important contractual issues strictly over the phone. All things considered, we both did our best to keep the lines of communication open, but it was extremely difficult. My bout with open heart surgery, and the station deciding not to pick up my option year, didn't help our situation. In Florida, I decided not to be represented by an agent, primarily because my boss at the station, Lee Strasser, preferred to deal directly with talent. Good enough reason for me. However, it did not preclude me from employing the Services of contract attorney, Don DuFresne of West Palm Beach, to make sure things were in order with the language of my contract.

All of this brings us to the question, when do you need an agent or legal representation? Below you will find a few questions to ask yourself to help determine the answer.

Here are a few questions to ask yourself to help determine the answer.

1. First and most importantly, do you think your station GM will deal directly with an agent, or would he prefer to deal with you directly on all matters involving your contract?
2. Are your ratings consistently above those of your competition in your station's key demographics?
3. Are you prepared to test the waters as to your value with your current employer and other stations?

4. Does your station refuse to hear your requests for salary raises? Would it affect your relationship with your manager to continually ask for same?
5. Do you honestly feel when it's time to make a change to a new station, or you've been fired, is an agent better equipped to do a job search on your behalf?

If you answered yes to most of these questions, than I would suggest it's time you spoke with an agent.

Why I believe every air-talent needs an attorney.

Like most air-talent, I always did a decent job of espousing the value of other broadcasters, but when it came to verbalizing my own worth, I was a walking disaster. I never seemed to know my own self-worth or what to ask for salary-wise. I never wanted to appear to be greedy and was shy about asking for a certain salary. Perhaps this is part of your MO as well. If so, read on.

As you just read, during my forty-one years on the air, I dealt with several different agents and lawyers. The best advice I can pass along is this: every air-talent should have a strong attorney *read every word of your contract*, preferably someone who specializes in contract law. There is legal language that laypeople (that's us) may read one way but because of the legal jargon may in reality translate to something totally different, and as the signer of the document, guess who's in trouble! My advice: always have a lawyer, preferably a contract attorney, read your contract before you sign it! One-time Boston Celtics star **M.L. Carr** told me, "Joe, use an agent but always be present at any meeting when they're talking about you and your future." It's good advice.

When I first approached Bob Woolf for representation, I'm sure the last thing he needed was another fresh-faced, exuberant radio guy in his stable of high-profile, talented folks. At least, that's what I was thinking. I couldn't have been more mistaken. Bob Woolf was a super-agent to be sure, but he treated all his clients, whether they were top NBA stars like Larry Bird or upstart radio guys like me, the same as far as respect, concern, and what was right for you and your career. Bob Woolf was well-connected and well-respected, not just in Boston but nationally, in all fields of sports, media, and entertainment. It is important that when and if you decide you need an agent, to select someone like the late Bob Woolf, who can do the most for you and your career. Make sure you have an agent who not only has the contacts but also the respect of the people he is shopping you around to.

In all honesty, with his huge portfolio of talented sports and entertainment celebrities, Bob Woolf didn't need me, but I needed him. I'm grateful he took me on. There's a little piece of me that still believes the reason he decided to represent me is because we both grew up in the same town. Oh, I'd like to think he thought I had talent and was a fairly decent radio personality, but I'm sure the fact that we both had roots in the port city certainly didn't hurt.

In the many years that I had the privilege of having Woolf's firm represent me, I never got the feeling I was less important than some of his "big buck boys" like Larry Bird and Carl Yastrzemski, and just about *everyone* who was *anyone* on the Boston sports scene and on radio and TV. Come to think of it, there was one time I felt brushed aside by his firm and got my nose out of joint, but I'll save that story on what turned out to be a humiliating experience for me for a little later in the chapter. It may help to give you a little insight into the kind of man Bob Woolf was.

Super-agent Bob Woolf.

Bob Woolf was a master at what he did, simply the best. He was a lawyer who didn't sound like one. Like so many successful people, he was passionate about what he did. He loved putting solid deals together and once told me, "Joe, I work hard, but I love what I do! When I can help you or others to a decent, fair contract and see that you will make sensible investments for your future, well, it doesn't get much better than that. I get a thrill!"

Bob Woolf was like a little kid when it came to wanting to hang out and be around the sports athletes and celebrities he represented. But it was more than being a "jock sniffer," as he was cruelly called by some. He was genuinely interested in his clients as a people and how they were doing. There was only one Bob Woolf. After his passing, I was fortunate to be represented by two outstanding members of his firm, former Stanford and New England Patriots receiver Randy Vataha and attorney/agent Gregg Clifton. When Bob's widow Anne sold the agency, Bob Woolf's name and legacy were passed on to the new group of owners, but for my money the heart and soul of its founder simply could not be replaced. When I mentioned my thoughts of leaving the firm to former BC and NFL stand-out **Doug Flutie**, another Woolf client, good-natured Doug laughed and said, "You're not leaving. You're like me, you'll be here forever!" It was a difficult decision, but I did leave the firm after being represented by them for twelve years.

Well, I suppose now is as a good time as any to share my story about the time I felt slighted by Bob Woolf. It all came down to them not returning my phone calls fast enough, at least for my way of thinking. I needed legal advice regarding a potentially ugly situation at the station and no one called me back. I decided to call Bob about "the slight." While speaking with him, I mentioned that I didn't expect him or others in his office to jump through hoops every time I called, but that I appreciated a call back at some point. I also mentioned that I understood where I came in the pecking order and knew his "big buck boys" (referring to the big-name celebrities his firm represented) received preferential treatment. At that point, he stopped me and reassured me that was not the case.

He also invited me to stop by the office later that morning when I got off the air.

When I walked in to his palatial offices in the Prudential tower building, Bob Woolf greeted me with his usual warm handshake and a big smile. He also motioned me to step behind the receptionist desk. "Joe, come over here," he said, "I want to show you something." It was the call log listing the clients and others who had called his office that day. Also listed was the time of each call. There must have been a hundred names, and his office had only been open for business that day for a few hours! Pointing to the long list of names, Bob asked me to look at it. As I glanced over the list, I immediately recognized some names, like those of Larry King and former Celtics stars Larry Bird and John Havlicek. When I came to my name, I stopped. Interestingly, it appears I had called the office just before one of my all-time favorite NFL players, Joe Montana. That's when Bob spoke up. "I return ALL calls in the order in which they come in to this office. If your name is before Joe Montana or any other 'big buck boys' as you refer to them, you get the call first. It makes NO difference to me. In fact, I called you earlier today before getting back to the other Joe." Convincingly, but gently, Bob made his point. The "bucks" may not be pleased to read this, but they received no preferential callbacks over me or any of his clients, whatever their income. Was my face red!

Bob did mention that sometimes an urgency notation next to a specific client's name obviously warranted that person an immediate call back. He did admit that the day before had been an extremely busy day in the office, with many fires to put out and it may have been the reason I didn't receive an immediate call back. However, he emphasized that as a matter of practice, calls were returned in the order they were received. Bob didn't chastise me in any way, but made it quite clear in no uncertain terms what was procedural practice for him and his office. I got the message and felt deeply humiliated that I had taken up so much his time, simply because I felt slighted.

As we walked down the hall to his office, Bob said something to me that I'll always remember. "Because, you feel we have slighted you and this office has not given you the service expected, here's what I'd like to do for you, Joe. I am going to negotiate your next contract with the station [which was up for renewal] at no fee." Having been humbled enough by the call-in sheet experience, I told him it wasn't necessary. I appreciated his generous offer but that I was not looking for a free ride with his firm. "Nonsense," he replied, smiling that trademark Bob Woolf smile, "I want to make sure you will always feel comfortable with this office and with me."

Lesson learned: don't pre-judge others before knowing the facts.

For the record, my contract at the station was renewed for another three years and as promised Bob Woolf waived his usual fee. I'll always be grateful to "Mister Woolf" in so many ways, and the inscription he wrote in his book *Behind*

Closed Doors means so much to me: "To Joe, Best wishes and warmest regards to a superstar talent and human being and friend. Bob Woolf Aug. 27, 1987."

Do you need an attorney/agent-attorney: Gregg Clifton.

Until August of 2010, Gregg Clifton was VP, Sr. Counsel – Team Sports, Scottsdale, Arizona. Gregg was one of the attorney/agents who represented me during the latter part of my years on Boston radio. At the time he was associated with Bob Woolf Associates. Today, Gregg is still based in Phoenix as an attorney with the law firm of Jackson Lewis.

I specifically asked him questions directed to the career of "future radio stars" but his invaluable input is important for every "talent" interested in procuring the services of an attorney/agent. Here is an exact transcript of the author's questions and Gregg Clifton's replies:

> **JM:** Do you feel it is in the best interest of a future radio star seeking a career as a radio talent to be represented by an agent? Why? Is it more important for talent to have an attorney, an agent, or someone who is both? Why?
>
> **GC:** I think anyone pursuing a career as a radio personality should seek the counsel of an experienced attorney/agent from the inception of their career. An experienced attorney/agent can provide immediate knowledge and guidance to help the burgeoning talent avoid many pitfalls that personalities frequently experience at the beginnings of their careers. Specifically, an experienced attorney/agent can assist young talent with production of a quality demo tape. He can also help the young talent identify potential employment opportunities that the talent may be unaware of on his own. The relationships that experienced representation can provide are potential door-opening opportunities.
>
> **JM:** What type of relationship do you foresee as important in handling a successful partnership between attorney/agent and client?
>
> **GC:** A successful partnership between an attorney/agent and client *must* be based on a close relationship between the attorney/agent and the client. The basic foundation of the relationship must be *trust*. The attorney/agent must earn the trust of his client as he guides his client through the many twists and turns that are associated with a career in radio. The radio personality must know that his attorney/agent will be there to support him whether his career is at the top of the charts or when he suffers an unexpected downturn. A second critical component in a successful relationship is *honesty*. Once an attorney/agent is hired by the radio personality, he must guarantee his client nothing but truth and sincerity in his day-to-day representation.

An attorney/agent must present his client with truthful feedback regarding his performance, input from management, as well as needed data. While such a concept may appear obvious, it is often a difficult one for both parties to embrace. Many inexperienced attorney/agents are often fearful of providing straight and direct answers to their clients. They would rather sugar coat the truth for fear that their clients will either be unable or unwilling to hear any negative feedback regarding their radio career.

"Always be in tune with yourself and let your perceptions guide you."

As my attorney/agent, **Gregg Clifton** always had my best interests at heart. In 1995, when I underwent emergency lung surgery in Boston and the station decided not to renew my contract, many so-called friends abandoned us, but not Gregg. He fought for and obtained every dollar that was rightfully ours according to the terms of my contract. More importantly, I was out of work for a year convalescing, and during that time, Gregg Clifton stood by us and took time to visit us at our home.

He didn't have to, because it was unclear if I would even be able to return to the air, let alone continue to need the services of an agent. Talk about a stand-up guy. Thanks be to God, I did recover and returned to the air in no small part thanks to Gregg Clifton's support. We will always be indebted to him for his friendship and support during one of the darkest periods in our lives and in my career.

If you are looking for an agent who goes beyond the call of duty, I hope you will be as fortunate as me and find someone like Gregg Clifton to represent you. I'd urge you to contact Gregg, but it's my understanding that these days he is strictly into lawyering and no longer represents talent.

Randy Vataha was another agent at Bob Woolf Associates who represented me. Randy was another best of the best agents. He always displayed a friendly demeanor and easy-going style. Randy tried to look at the positive side of every situation, even when I was busy painting a doom and gloom portrait. He gave me plenty of solid advice, but one thing that stands out in my mind, especially for those of you trying to decide whether to use the services of an agent, is this: "In contract negotiations, both sides (management and talent) have to walk away feeling good about the deal. If one side feels low-balled or unhappy, it will usually surface somewhere down the road. You don't want that to happen!"

I've often thought agents and attorneys are not paid nearly enough for all the moaning, groaning, bitching, and complaining they have to put up with from their insecure, emotional, high-strung clients, yours truly included! I lucked out! Randy Vatha and Gregg Clifton were more than agents, they were our friends. I could turn to them whenever I felt things were slipping out of control at the radio station. My wife Kimmie and I enjoyed their company. When I needed them they were always there, even taking my calls at weird hours. I publicly thank them for being so patient and understanding whenever I reached out and cried, help!

Seattle morning drive guy **Bob Rivers** has always used an attorney. "It's a way to remove myself from the face-to-face part of the negotiating process," he explains. "If you talk to management yourself you are at a disadvantage. Your boss is likely and unable to make financial decisions without going up the corporate ladder. You, on the other hand, as talent are the emotional decision maker." Rivers never felt he needed an agent until around ten years ago. "The stakes started to get higher and negotiations became more complicated," he says. "Fortunately, I met a very good agent, Paul Anderson. We were friends and he was practicing law in Seattle. Since then, he has become one of the most successful and best in the industry."

Rivers, who had been on the air in Seattle for twenty-one years until leaving the air in early 2010, has this advice for radio newbies: "Early on in a talent's career be realistic and do what you can afford. As you make a bit more, always hire an attorney to look at a contract before you sign. As you make a bit more, hire an attorney to do your talking for you. Once you can afford the commission, call Paul Anderson," he suggests, "or another reputable media agent. You should still make all the decisions, but you'll have experienced counsel and someone who can represent you."

When does a "new" air-talent need an agent?

Bob Rivers feels this way: "One thing to remember - agents do not create your value, you do. Until you have leverage, an agent will likely just sit there and take a commission. When you know you are indispensable that's the time to hire the best advocate you can find. Some people think if they sign with an agent that person will find them work. In my experience," Rivers continues, "the agent can certainly help with the buzz, but if I haven't created the demand, he's not going to be able to either."

Author's note: as an air-talent, it's your life and income we're talking about! You are a radio pro and you deserve to be represented by the best legal pro available. This includes an attorney who understands contract law, particularly broadcast law! Based on my 41 years on the air, I had no less than nine people represent me at various times, four of whom were in the same firm. I feel that during your earliest and formative years on the radio, an agent is a question mark. However, a knowledgeable contract attorney who specializes in broadcast law is a *necessity!*

Once your radio career is established and you have a track record, including solid ratings to support it, a well-known agent/attorney can open an otherwise closed door for you. Besides, a good agent who is a good listener can do wonders for your career *and* your ego.

Radio talent needs to be kept grounded! Whether it's a supportive attorney/agent, a loving spouse, or a caring friend, as talent you need someone in your life to help you through the rough times. As popular air personality **Casey Kasem** says, "Keep your feet on the ground while reaching for the stars." These supportive individuals may not always tell you what you want to hear, but they will tell you what you NEED to hear. Keep an open mind to what they have to say.

Everyone loves a winner and the scenario is no different in radio.
As talent, you will notice more people will smile and chat with you in the hallways of your station when you're number one. It's just the way it seems to be! They will seem interested in your family, your animals, and everything else about you and your life. You'll also be invited to more free lunches and dinners, and you'll find yourself on the receiving end of a slew of concert tickets or baseball box seats. Don't be seduced by all the materialistic garbage into thinking these gestures are because these people want to be your friends. Some may be good-intentioned, but sad to say, more often than not that's not the case. Go ahead and grab all the loot you can before these shallow folks scoot, but try to keep in mind that it's not necessarily *you* they are paying homage to but your high ratings! Now, I can hear some of you saying, what a lousy attitude. No, what I'm trying to do is to prevent your feelings from being smashed to smithereens when your numbers drop and these same seemingly caring people turn their backs on you! When your ratings plummet, you may notice a totally different attitude from them. It's a sad but true commentary about the real radio world. When your ratings drop, you may get dropped, too! Just be thankful it's only concert tickets and free lunches that suddenly stop coming your way, and not your paycheck. Too often good talent gets shown the door when ratings take a tumble.

The tumultuous world of radio ratings.
Radio ratings both good and bad can create some strange bedfellows! It's not that you won't develop close friends at your radio station - on the contrary! I am only trying to prepare your fragile ego for a time when your numbers may drop. It happens to everyone, no matter how hard you work or how good you are, and those same folks who were little chatty Cathys when you were king of the hill and number one may now look the other way when you walk by. No one prepared me for that unsettling moment in radio. It's a killer. I don't care if you have thick skin like Jumbo the elephant, it will still hurt when your so-called friends at the station project their new uncaring attitude towards you. Rejection is a bitter pill for anyone to swallow, but to the fragile ego of most air-talent, it's cyanide.

When and if you find yourself in this uncomfortable situation in the tumultuous rise and fall world of radio ratings, above all do your best to keep smiling and keep doing your job! Try to keep in mind, it's not you personally that your radio station friends are snubbing; it's your low ratings.

"A real radio pro knows that when you get the numbers and win the battle of the radio ratings, you're an old pro. When you lose, you're an old washed-up man!"

The ratings - good or bad, first and foremost, are the radio stations report card.

However, as the station's air-talent, *you* are the person on the firing line and therefore bound to take the most hits for low ratings. You can scream bloody blue murder that you were just following the format and orders from the program director, but believe me, unless the GM is your golfing pal, it ain't gonna help. As air-talent, the reality is you live and die with your numbers, whether you feel the low numbers are justified or not. It's just the way it is!

No one took time to explain all this to me when I was a radio newbie. As a result, my trusting nature that those in charge will take responsibility for their actions and game plans landed me in a world of hurt at times. Perhaps you're a little savvier when it comes to the ratings game than I was when I first started out in the biz. If so, I'm happy for you! You're way ahead of the game. Your feelings may be spared when the same person who gave you a slap on the back for doing a great job suddenly and without any apparent provocation gives you the cold shoulder. Many times, more often than I care to admit, I would leave the station wondering what I had done to offend a certain person. In reality it had nothing to do with me personally, but was all about the ratings! It's the same old story. When you're winning, everyone loves you.

Rejection in radio is hard to handle.

Rejection for whatever reason is not a pleasant thing to endure. Over the years I've seen too many of my radio buds break down over being carelessly rejected by co-workers, especially management, folks who they mistakenly thought were their friends. Many will tell you that you have to toughen up and grow thick skin to be in radio. They're right, but in reality, if you are a mensch like me and trust people, then you'll find it hard to do. In his 1987 book, *My Life in Rock n' Roll Radio*, **Cousin Brucie Morrow**, one of America's legendary radio pros, talks about radio ratings and his decision to leave WABC. "After thirteen successful years, WABC wanted to tie my compensation to the ratings, while across the street, WNBC and I had already sewn up our deal. The only thing I had to say to management and the PD **Rick Sklar** was 'good-bye!' I had gotten the message that turned me away from my beloved WABC," laments Morrow, "that you're only as good as your ratings."

This is the other side of radio that can be so difficult to deal with - rejection, but it is one of the sad realties and the nature of the beast. It shouldn't make you jumpy and grumpy, nor should you mistrust everyone who throws an olive branch your way. The point is that in radio, you're not always judged on how great you sound or how nice a person you are - at least not when it comes to radio ratings. It's your numbers that matter most. You need to know it, and now you do!

Author's note: When it came to ratings, I remember getting physically ill in anticipation of the day ratings came out. If we had a down book, I was a basket case trying to figure out what I did wrong. Talk about beating myself up. It got me nothing other than a sleepless night, so don't you do it. I tried really hard never to get too high or too low when ratings came out! There are so many factors involved in the numbers game, many totally out of talent's control. You need to give yourself a break. Don't ignore them completely, but don't get too caught up in them either. By the time the ratings come out for the previous month or quarter, you should be focusing on what you're doing today and tomorrow on the radio! Those numbers only reflect what you did in the past and not what you're putting out today, which should be better than what you did yesterday! I'm not saying talent and management shouldn't look at the numbers - it's important to do so. If there is a downward trend, it probably means something needs fixing, so fix it by making the necessary adjustments; just don't over think the numbers.

Remember, it's all right to look at the ratings, just don't stare at them! The worst thing talent and or management can do is knee-jerk react to a bad ratings book. And a message to all talent, both future, and present: don't ever change your air style because of one down book! Look in the mirror and make any necessary adjustments, but by all means, stay the course!

Contracts and ratings - radio pro lesson.

When you are having your contract written, and specifically with regard to your bonus structure, make sure you have a complete and full understanding of what your station's target demo is and who they and you are trying to reach. What good is having a $50,000 bonus for coming in at #1 with males if your station is geared towards females? It makes absolutely no sense, but you'd be surprised how often contracts and bonus situations are written with totally unrealistic goals for the talent. Sure, it sounds good when you tell your spouse, "Honey, if we come in at #1 on the morning show, I'll make an extra fifty-grand! Call the pool people; we'll be splashing around before you know it!" File it under "great but unrealistic expectations." Unless your bonus numbers are in sync with your station's target demo, it ain't gonna happen, folks. Ratings numbers can be manipulated and deceiving!

We gullible, trusting show folk sometimes can be taken in big time by the smooth rhetoric of a station negotiator, be it manager or attorney. Be careful!

Why contracts can be misleading.

Even the best-written contracts which specifically state you will receive a bonus for hitting the target audience can be misleading. How? Simply by the language written in your contract. Unless you are an attorney specializing in broadcast law,[2] there's no way you can decipher the legal jargon put in many contracts. Trust me; even one word can change the entire meaning of a sentence. This is just one important reason why an agent/lawyer can be of much-needed help to air-talent in sifting through the legal language of a broadcast contract.

For example, let's say you have what appears to be a great bonus set up of $30,000 if you hit #1 in the audience demo of women listeners 18+. It looks super on paper, except for one important thing: your station's true target demo is men 18+. I'm not saying you won't score a direct hit and ace women and men 18+ and take home a bundle of cash. I'm rooting for it to happen for you, but the safest and surest way to insure you hit your ratings numbers - and remember, there are no guarantees when it comes to ratings - is to have a *solid, realistic, and attainable* bonus structure. When it comes to your bonus situation, don't be swayed by the flash and numbers that look good on paper. In reality, they may be impossible to attain because of the station's primary target audience.

Why as air-talent you need an attorney/agent to represent your best interests.

Most radio GMs I worked for were tough negotiators when it came to contracts, but one in particular was the toughest of the lot! One afternoon over lunch, my boss handed me pen and paper and said, "Write down what you think you're worth if you come in first, second or third in the ratings." Not wanting to appear too greedy, I wrote down forty grand for first, thirty for second, and twenty for third.[3] I believed I was worth more, but given the sales revenue on our morning show and what the market was paying talent, I figured I was in the ballpark. Without batting an eye, he said, "You're worth it!" He took the pen and wrote down the numbers on the contract we had been working on, trying to hammer out a mutually agreeable deal. When I asked to look at the contract to see what he had written, he said, "No problem, I'll have legal in New York look it over, type it up, shoot it back and you and I will meet for another nice lunch next week and get it done! Deal?" I hesitated but it sounded like a sure thing, so I said, "Fine, why not." A week later, the contract came back and once again, the GM and I met for lunch to sign the deal.

My boss opened the contract to the page where we both had to sign and date it. "There ya go, Joe, everything you want is in there, my friend. A three-year, no-cut deal, extra vacation time you requested, man, did I have to fight hard on that one," he tossed in as an aside.[4] " Your bonus structure. It's all there, now just sign and date it. I've already done so. Just sign on the line next to mine and we've got ourselves a deal, son!" I thanked him but when I asked to look it over before signing, he threw me a defiant look. "Don't you trust me?" he asked. "Joey," as he leaned across the table, his nose practically touching mine, "if we don't have trust, we've got nothing." I smiled, leaned back in my chair and said, "I trust you, boss. Corporate is a different story. I've been burned before by legal eagles representing the best interests of the radio station, which is their job. Let's just say they don't necessarily have *my* best interests in mind. I'd like to look it over, please." The GM hedged and hemmed but finally pushed the document to my side of the table. As I recall it was about twenty pages and had lots of things in it that I couldn't do, and if I did, could be fired for without compensation, that really caught my eye.

I quickly thumbed through the pages, sensing my boss's growing impatience. Several things looked okay. My base salary was what we agreed to, but other things were difficult for me to comprehend because of legal double talk. You know, "the party of the first if in accordance with the party of the second, blah, blah." Silently I thought, there's no way I'm signing this thing without having an attorney look it over first! Finally, I flipped to the page with the bonus structure. The numbers were almost impossible to find since they were buried beneath and under legal jargon. I managed to decipher one clause under demographics. It read something like this, "Wherein the party known as talent is able to reach a rating of first place in the station target demo, such talent will be compensated with a bonus of forty-thousand dollars." However, nowhere was the station target demo mentioned. A big ole red flag went up. The way radio stations change hands and formats without notice, leaving the target demo blank with a big bonus number attached had the potential for a major first-class problem down radio road. My other concern was I really didn't understand most of the legal language.

Radio Pro lesson: Always have an attorney check the wording in your contract before signing it!

I asked my boss if my attorney could look it over. The exasperated expression on his face told me all I needed to know. He wasn't crazy about the idea but agreed, and quickly added, "Just know one thing, this is the final copy and corporate [ahh corporate, that mystical radio haven that almost every radio GM refers to when it's time to bail their own butt out from oncoming disaster!], corporate," he repeated, "wants this contract done as soon as possible and without any further revisions."[5] Wonderful, I thought, but I'm a big believer in what's meant to be is meant to be. There was no way I was signing any contract without a lawyer reading it and advising me. Incidentally, I advise you to do the same. Never sign any contract without having an attorney read it first! In my many years of signing radio station contracts I came to learn, in some cases the hard way, that it's not that lawyers who represent radio stations, networks, etc. want to purposely mislead talent, but if they can insert language in their favor, you bet your boots they will do their best to pull it off.

Eventually, we got the deal done, thanks to my attorney. He removed any legal language that could possibly be misconstrued and spell potential disaster for me, and, believe me, there was plenty of room in the contract for some big trouble. Words that may look good on paper aren't necessarily in your best interest. If you're not represented by an agent, then for your own wellbeing and peace of mind, at least have a contract attorney, preferably one who specializes in broadcast law, look at the language of your contract before you sign it. A few dollars spent in advance may save you thousands in the future.

Notes:
1. CCD is Confraternity Classes of Christian Doctrine for Catholic school students.
2. Always have a lawyer, preferably one who is well-versed in broadcast law, look over your contract.
3. I did my homework and discovered the station had a great track record of coming in second or third in the ratings, so rather than ask for more for second or third place, I'd ask for a "reasonable" sum, figuring I could easily maintain second or third. With four rating periods yearly, if I hit second place twice and third twice that would be a nice yearly bonus of $100,000. My goal was to be #1, but knowing how the ratings game works, I didn't want to be greedy. During one ratings period in Boston, I lost a $30,000 bonus by one-tenth of a ratings point, when I dropped from first to second place in our demographic. Always do your homework and find out as much as you can about the radio station, particularly its financial situation, in advance of contract negotiations.
4. Three-year deals with outs by the station are not necessarily *three-year solid-no cut deals.* Talent, beware!
5. Rush to sign is usually a ploy by management to "scare you" into thinking if you don't sign this deal right now, the offer will go away. Don't worry. They wouldn't be negotiating with you in the first place if they didn't want you. It's in the station's best interest to hurry you along to sign, to prevent you from finding something you don't like in the wording of the contract. Keep in mind the words of agent Randy Vataha during contract negotiations: both sides need to be happy, and that includes **you!**

Bob Woolf, well known and respected sports and celebrity attorney.

CHAPTER 19

Some Things to Know About a Career in Radio as an On-Air Pro

"The deejays were hired on their ability to be entertainers"
– Chuck Blore, KFWB PD

THIS CHAPTER IS DESIGNED as a catch-all of radio information. As you can imagine, there are many topics to cover when it involves a career in radio. Here are just a few things you need to know about a career as a radio personality and are outlined in this chapter.

- The importance of radio internships
- How to handle your job interview
- Radio pros are found in cities and towns of all sizes and not just in major markets
- Weekend warriors & the importance of part-timers in radio; 10 commandments for weekend air-talent
- Don't burn the candle at both ends
- The role of a radio producer
- The importance of a solid working relationship between air-talent and sales staff
- How to do quality production
- Age discrimination and how it can affect you
- Always keep the keys to the radio station on you
- You know you're an aging radio pro, when…
- 10 Commandments for real radio pros

The importance of internships.

If your college or university offers an internship program at one of the radio stations in your town, grab it! College radio is a great learning ground, but there is no better way to learn about commercial radio and how it functions than by interning at a "real" radio station. While in morning drive at WROR (later MIX-98.5) Boston, we were most fortunate to have several college students intern on our show. Alice Pearce and Amy Doyle were two outstanding examples of interns who excelled in their positions. They learned the radio business quickly and upon graduating obtained full-time positions at the station.

Alice Pearce highly recommends internships for college students who are seriously interested in a radio career. "My junior year at Boston College I got an internship at WROR and I worked hard, learning everything I could and doing everything I could. The excitement of being a twenty-year-old college student and having the chance to work at a major market radio station was fabulous. Getting to be such an active, involved part of Joe Martelle's oldies show and making a whole round of new friends that weren't college friends proved to be a great support system for my first several years as a young, single, professional living and working in radio in Boston." She continues, saying, "I couldn't have been such an active and involved part of *Saturday Night "Live" at the Oldies* if it weren't for Joe. Not every major market radio personality would have had the lack of ego to let a kid get some of the spotlight like he did. And how about the 'new radio friends' that would be such a great support system? Joe was right up there."[1]

Former XM Satellite Radio's Music Director of '50s on 5 host **Matt "The Cat" Baldassarri** advises all future radio wannabes to do something he didn't do in college: get an internship. "I just didn't have time," explains Matt. "I also felt they wouldn't benefit me since I was already on the air in Boston. However, if I had internship connections I might have been better prepared for the my current career dry spell.[2] I've seen how friends of mine have benefited from internships and I also saw interns at XM Radio go on to full-time positions."

If you are in high school and there is a radio station in your town, find out who the PD or manager is and call them. Express your interest in radio and in a polite way, plead, beg, and even promise to empty the wastebaskets at the station if they will allow you to hang out and observe up close the internal workings of radio. Nothing beats the first-hand experience of learning from and watching a pro at work.

How to handle your job interview.[3] How to dress.

It almost goes without saying you should show up for your interview looking well-groomed and not like you've been camping out for the last few nights on the sofa in your frat or sorority house. Neat and clean is still the rule. Dress professionally. Even though you are applying for an on-air position,

Some Things to Know About a Career in Radio as an On-Air Pro • 583

where casual clothing is usually permitted, dress more business-like for your interview.

Contrary to what you may have heard, how you dress still says lots about you. As a former management person, I always noticed how the person dressed when I interviewed them. It gave me great insight of not only what the person thought about themselves, but also how they viewed me as a potential boss.

Show up on time.

Show up at least fifteen minutes early. Leave early. You never know what traffic jams or delays you may encounter. You don't want to take a chance on being late for your interview! If you arrive 45 minutes early, sit and wait in your car until it's time for your appointment. First impressions are important!

Don't forget your resume.

Don't forget to bring your resume. Three pages are usually sufficient. Your educational background is important, but so is any experience you have had in radio. List anything and everything you have accomplished that pertains to radio and highlights your interest in an on-air career. Keep your personal info to the basics. It is important that a prospective employer learn of your interests. It will tell them much about your character. For example, mentioning that you were in scouting is good; providing a complete list of your merit badges is not necessarily good. Now, if scouting happens to catch the person's eye and he or she brings it up, by all means talk your personal achievements. Bring a pad of paper and pen along to write things down so you can later check facts on what was discussed. Don't trust your memory, especially when you are nervous combined with the excitement of the interview.

Learn everything you can about the radio station or broadcast company in advance.

Read up on the radio station before the interview. Learn who the management team is and as much about the staff as humanly possible. Most station websites have a homepage that lists management, programming, promotion, and air-staff personalities. As painful as it may be, take time to read talent's personal bios online. Make the names on that list your new best friends. Go the extra mile and familiarize yourself with what the station is all about. What they do in the community? What promotions are they are currently running?, and so on. Know all about the station format and then learn some more! What is the format of the station where you are applying? What type of music is featured? Hopefully, you've already decided this is the format for you, or you wouldn't be applying at the station in the first place! Find every bit of info you can dig up on the place. You need to show up armed to the gills with enough information to make the interviewer want to hire you on the spot!

How to approach the actual interview.

It is important to approach the interview in a confident, friendly manner, by smiling, sitting up straight and looking your interviewer in the eye. It's not necessary to stare the interviewer down, but it is important to look at them to show your interest in what they are saying. Even if you are shaking in your boots and your heart is pounding at 200 beats a minute, it is important to project an air of confidence. This is particularly important when applying for a position as an on-air personality. Let the real you come through, but not in an arrogant or egoistical way. Small talk is important, just don't become too cutesy or ask too many personal questions. *Do ask questions* about the station and the opening and what is expected if you should you get hired. Always follow the lead of the person conducting the interview when responding to questions.

Use proper grammar.

Remember that you are applying for an on-air position. Communicate with complete thoughts and sentences. Save the "yeahs," "you know what," "say what," and "huhs?" for talkin' with your pals.

> *"Keep smiling ... a smile is just a window to let folks know that your heart is at home"* - *Wolfman Jack.*

Be professional during the interview.

You need to answer the questions, but not go on and on. Don't allow the employer's casual approach or easygoing manner to stop you from being professional. He or she may be trying to put you at ease, or it may be a ploy to see how you respond. Since you don't know the motive behind the behavior it is best to maintain a professional attitude, including sitting up straight and being businesslike. Try not to invade the interviewer's space by leaning too far forward, or with wild hand and arm movements. If the person conducting the interview takes on a more personal tone and urges you relax a little more, great, then you can adjust and go with the flow. But at the beginning, be a pro! Keep your answers brief and to the point. Keep in mind the old sales axiom, "Don't go beyond the sale."

Some other points to remember during your interview:

- Don't chew gum
- Listen carefully to every question before running off at the mouth.
- Do not interrupt the interviewer, no matter how eager you may be about answering a question.

Some Things to Know About a Career in Radio as an On-Air Pro • 585

- Turn your cell phone off beforehand, so it doesn't ring during the interview. It will send a signal of a lack of respect for the interviewer and may cost you the job.

Before the interview is over, make sure you know what the next step will be with your prospective employer - do they have more candidates to interview, when will they make a decision, will they call you, or are you expected to check back with them? It is most important that you get the straight scoop before leaving. Always offer a firm handshake and sincerely thank the person for their time. After you have left the building, immediately go over your notes while they are fresh in your mind. Call your agent, attorney, or recruiter to update them on how you feel the interview went. If you feel the interview went well that's all that matters and you should be pleased. Walk away with a feeling of self-satisfaction and use the experience to gain confidence for your next interview.

The lost art of the thank you letter.
Don't forget to send a thank you letter. Keep it brief, but reiterate your desire to work at their station. If you receive word that another candidate has been chosen for the position, send another note thanking the interviewer for their time. Let them know that if another on-air position opens, you would be most interested in being considered. It is so important to keep up your contacts in radio.

In the '80s, I was passed over for an on-air position at legendary WSB Atlanta. I kept in touch with the PM [Program Manager] and a few years later they approached me about an opening on their air-staff. It never came to fruition because when I was contacted, I was already firmly entrenched in morning drive at WROR Boston. You will find it gratifying to be contacted and considered for an opening at a radio station which may have passed you over once before in your career. I did.

It is important to make yourself stand out from all the other qualified job applicants. One colleague told me that when he was auditioning for an on-air position in radio, he sent an audition tape and resume in a wastebasket with a note on the outside that read, "I am looking forward to an interview with you. I hope you won't find it necessary to deep-six my work, but just in case, I've saved you the trouble." He put the whole thing in a box and mailed it to the program director. Later, during the interview, the PD told him he laughed so hard at the novel approach that he had to listen to the tape. He didn't have the heart to leave it in the wastebasket! He got the job. Creativeness will get you as far as you want to go. Do what is necessary to get the eye and ear of your potential employer.

Always bring a recent air-check or recording of your air-work.

Have a recent tape of your work. It is no excuse to say you don't have a radio job, so how could you possibly have a tape? There are all sorts of ways to record yourself, including your computer. All you need is a mic and a CD. Colleges and even many high schools have student-run closed-circuit stations; if you're not a member of their air staff, why not? If you are really interested in an on-air radio career, you should be on the station!! If not, ask or even beg them to let you use their studio for an hour or so to put together an audition tape. If all else fails, bite the bullet and cough up a few bucks to book an hour of recording time at a local recording studio. There are recording studios located in even the smallest towns. The cost should not be a consideration - not if you really want to make an audition tape and are sincerely interested in being on the air. You need to keep asking yourself, "How badly do I want radio?" Never show up at station for an interview without a sampling of your voice work. Your prospective employer wants to hear how you sound to see if you fill the bill and fit the needs of their radio station.

Since 1984, consultant **Walter Sabo** has been president of Sabo Media, a New York-based programming and management company. Some of his prestigious clients include Infinity, Greater Media, and Clear Channel Communications. Sabo has also worked with numerous radio stars, including Cousin Brucie Morrow, Casey Kasem, and Howard Stern. When listening to an audition tape for the first time, Sabo says he listens for three things. "The first is an intelligence in the voice. Not intellectualism. The voice is being controlled by a brain that is in charge. The person is aware of what they are saying and how to sell it. Their words sound original and their ideas are original. Secondly, I listen for an understanding of the science of radio. Radio performers know how listeners listen. They are proud and clever about how they incorporate the name of the station and other basic elements in to their show. Thirdly, and most importantly, I listen to hear if talent is having a good time. Is the person on the radio being a personality who would engage you in a restaurant, or in your home? Obviously," Sabo adds, "the people who meet these criteria are on a short list."

Radio pros are found in cities and towns of all sizes and not just in major markets.

Radio pros can be found everywhere. As show prep entrepreneur **Dan O'Day** points out on his website, danoday.com, "It's not the size of the market that matters, it's the relationship you have with your listeners. And small market radio listeners are no different than large market listeners."

Be realistic about where you are in your on-air radio career. It's okay to be in the 200th radio market if you're happy and having fun! There are many things that go into having a successful radio career other than a big paycheck! Sometimes being in a top-ten market isn't always the answer for every air-talent. Playing in the majors means more pressure, which translates to more scrutiny about what you say and do on the radio. It just makes more sense that you will have MORE ears and eyes watching your every move in New York or LA than you will in a Butte or Bangor, and I'm not simply referring to your total number of listeners. The larger the market and the bigger the radio station, the more suits will be listening and watching your every move. The saying, "Big brother is watching" definitely pertains to corporate radio in America these days, which means more stress in your life.

Texas Radio Hall of Fame member **Barry Kaye** says, "I was told once in the beginning of my career about working up the ladder to a bigger market that all you've done is gone on to a bigger toilet. I learned," he adds, "there's just as much stress in Beeville, Texas, as there was in Hollywood." There is a lot of truth to the statement, "A big fish in a little pond!" My longtime friend and former co-worker Dean Rogers made the decision a long time ago to stay and play in our hometown of Portland, Maine. I have no doubt that Dino could be on any station in any market in America. It was his call to stay put in Maine. His comments are coming up shortly.

Ryan Cote was someone who showed me he had passion for radio back in the mid-'60s. At the time, I was the morning guy and PD at WIDE in Biddeford, Maine, and Ryan was a student at St. Louis High School. I gave him a Saturday morning show and he proved to be the pro that I knew he was. Today, some forty years later, talented Ryan has worked in radio markets of all sizes, small, medium and major. Just like our mutual friend Dean Rogers, Ryan made the choice to be on the radio in Maine.

For the past fourteen years, Ryan Cote has been the account development manager and 3-7pm personality at WABK in the capital city of Augusta, Arbitron market #272. The station has been #1 for more than five years in a row and has consistently been top-rated for about a fifteen-year period.

Ryan Cote puts it all in perspective when it comes to working in radio markets of different sizes. "There is NO difference in working in major and medium markets, not if you want to be remembered, and not if you are a real pro! I loved being in a Big City; there are more perks and you can make a great living," but adds, "I love smaller markets where you can make a great life! In the major market I worked at," he says, "everyone got enough out of their contract to buy a house with a little land, 20 miles out of town, and commuted 50 minutes. In the market I live in, everyone's got a home 20 miles out of town with waterfront land and commutes 18 minutes. With mergers and downsizing, ratings and revenues are proportionate everywhere!" Ryan Cote has been on the radio for 35 years and proposes this scenario to talent everywhere, both newbie and senior pros: "What do you need? Could you be more important to that listener whether they put you on your very own special pre-set in Seattle or Salina? As yourself this question, what do you need?"

Since Ryan mentioned Salina, Kansas, that city is about 115 miles down I-70 from Topeka, which is radio market #194. That's where **Rose Diehl** has been a familiar voice to Topeka-area listeners for twenty-seven years! Rose held down the mid-day spot on KMAJ since 1982 and has been the station's program director since 1998. The Popular personality feels lucky to be working in a market smaller than the majors because, as she puts it, "You are a significant part of the listener's life.... I have never worked in a large market," she says, "but I assume it is more difficult to make that connection."

In the late '70s, warm n' fuzzy-sounding **Dean Rogers** worked with me in Portland, Maine, at AM-970- WCSH. A consummate radio pro, Dean landed his first radio job in 1969 and has been caressing the airwaves at numerous Maine radio stations ever since, including Portland stations WGAN-AM, WMTW-FM, WJAB-AM, and WYNZ. Until December 2008, Dino, as he is known to his loyal listeners, was host of the morning show on the Mt. Washington, NH, station WHOM-FM. Rogers believes that being a radio pro is the same no matter where you are, "I've been in the business almost forty years, and the only difference between a small market radio station and a large market station that I can tell is the size of the audience. No matter where you are, you still have to do your very best, period! No matter where you work the pressure is still the same, just at different intensity levels."

Willy Tyler is the morning host and PD at KWMY-Classic Hits-My 92.5 in Billings Montana, the #260 Arbitron radio market in the country. Willy thinks the difference between working in a smaller market as opposed to the majors comes down to having to work with what you've got. "A lot of smaller markets don't see a lot of corporate money trickle down," he says. "There are some major market guys who would tell you, Willy, there is no difference when it comes to where the big boys play every day. They don't see lots of money trickle their way either." He makes an excellent point that "It's harder in a smaller market than in a larger one to get the labels' attention for product giveaways and new music." That has been an on-going problem faced by small and medium market stations for many years. It's long overdue for the music labels to wake up and realize that there is a moving radio audience in towns and cities across the country, and not just in major markets!

The bottom line is that you should always do your best on the air! A mic is a mic and EVERY listener is important, whether you're on a superstation like WBZ Boston, or a smaller stick out in the 'burbs somewhere. When you're on the air, always give it your best shot. You never know who just might be listening.

Author's note: Case in point, during the summer of 1970, I was doing a weekend show on WGAN-AM 560 in Portland, Maine. The 5,000-watt station was and still is the city's heritage radio station. Today, GAN's format is talk, but back then it was middle-of-the-road music-based with heavy personality.

At the time, WLW Cincinnati's program director was Clif Hunter. He and his wife just happened to be vacationing in the Pine Tree State and he happened to be scanning the dial in his rental car, coming across GAN when I was on the air. Apparently, he liked what he heard and hired me to do the all-night show on WLW, one of America's legendary radio stations. Funny thing is, I had absolutely no illusions of grandeur about moving on to a larger radio market. I'm not so sure I qualified as a big fish in a small pond, but I do know this - I was quite happy being on the radio in my hometown and having the privilege of being on a great radio station like WGAN.

Radio lesson: Always do your best, no matter where or what station you're on, regardless of the market size. First and most importantly, do your best for your own self-pride, but also because *you never know* who is listening!

Weekend warriors and the importance of part-timers in radio.

How many times have I heard a PD make this comment? "If I just had one more reliable part-timer, I wouldn't have to worry about how our weekends sound." A good part-timer is more than worth their weight in gold. Longtime Portland, Maine, school teacher Dave Jackson had a second career as a weekender at WCSH-AM-970 Radio in Portland. Dave possessed two qualities which made him nearly irreplaceable as a permanent weekend radio fixture. He was good, and he was dependable!

Many present-day radio pros began their radio careers as weekend jocks at some small station somewhere out in the boonies! The key in radio is getting your foot in the door. Don't be choosy when you're first starting out. If the only shift available is part-time on the weekends, don't hesitate to grab it!

Give thanks that you're finally on the radio! Give it all you have, too. Make those four, five, or six hours you're on the radio on the weekend sound the very best you can! If need be, pretend you are on in AM-Drive on the #1 rated radio station in the country!

Richie Norris was born and raised in Schenectady, New York. His "real" job is working the emergency road service and member service departments of AAA, but since he was nine years old, Richie knew he wanted to be on the radio. "When I was sixteen and still in high school, my dream became a reality and I got my first job as a board-op Sunday mornings for the ethnic programming on 3WD (WWWD) in Schenectady, NY." Not too long after, he began doing weekend overnights at the station. Today, and of his own volition, the veteran radio pro prefers working part-time in radio. However, Richie always makes himself available to cover holidays and vacations. His weekend time spent on the air is lengthy, totaling twelve hours at Magic 100.9 in Albany, New York. On Saturday nights he hosts *Sock Hop Saturday Night* from 7 'til midnight. He then shoots home for a few hours' rest and is back on the radio for a marathon seven-hour shift on Sundays from noon-7pm.

When asked if he minds the long hours, Norris smiles and says, "I'm very happy with my weekend shifts and doing what I love to do - being on the radio, having fun, playing music, and entertaining the listeners!"

Norris passes this advice along to future radio wannabes: "From my own experience and looking back at when I started in radio, sure, the hours may not always be the greatest, and that very first part-time air-shift could possibly be weekend overnights, or maybe an early Sunday morning air-shift, but regardless of the time slot, it's giving YOU the opportunity to develop your skills as an on-air personality. Remember, whether it's 2am Saturday morning, or 2pm Saturday afternoon, someone is always listening." One of the most important qualities a weekend air-talent can possess, in addition to a decent voice and knowing how to turn on the mic, is dependability. Norris gets gold stars for all of the above. During his 26-year radio career, has he ever missed a shift or showed up late? "No, I've never missed an air-shift or been late. I always make it a point to get to the radio station early enough to prepare to go on the air." Solid advice for every air personality. He is the kind of talent PDs everywhere wish they had in their house.

Burning the candle at both ends and trying to serve two masters is not necessarily a good idea.

The early '60s was an eclectic time to be on the radio, with tremendous variety in programming. I'm one of the lucky guys who got to experience it at WIDE-Biddeford, ME.[4] At the time, as a radio newbie, I handled the 6pm until midnight (sign-off) shift. It was a long day, which began hours earlier with my second job in television - more on that coming up. My air-shift covered a wide variety of programming. After a news block at six, the *French Hour* was on at seven with host Don Roy. At eight, rock n' roll by request on *Teen Time* until eleven. Five minutes of world and national news at 11pm from the Yankee Network, followed by five minutes of local news, weather and sports, and then back to music, which changed dramatically from rock to easy listening on *Cozy Corner* until the station signed off at midnight. *Cozy Corner* was designed to help people unwind and prepare to end their day with relaxing music. Little did I know that one night it would lull me off to sleep, as well!

We played mostly piano and instrumental artists on *Cozy Corner*. It didn't take me long to discover that WIDE's music library was limited. Night after night, I found myself playing the same Roger Williams, Frank Chacksfield, and Mantovani albums. Something had to be done before the repetition drove our listeners, and me, bonkers.

One night, bored from listening to the same music over and over from the same six or seven albums, I was listening in cue (off the air) to the Network. That's when I made an exciting discovery. Following the Network news feed at eleven until the half hour at 11:30, they were playing 15 or 20 minutes of uninterrupted beautiful music. The *same type of music* we featured on *Cozy Corner*, only with a greater variety! After monitoring the 11:10 until midnight segment for a few more nights, I happily learned this music was featured right after the eleven o'clock network news feed until 11:30 without commercial interruption. On the half-hour, the network feed station WNAC (today WRKO) aired five minutes of Boston news and commercials, then went back to more uninterrupted segued "beautiful music" until midnight. And best of all, the program's host, Bill Marlowe, only opened and closed each segment with no further talking between record cuts! *Wow! What a find!* I thought this could actually be the answer of more beautiful music with less repetition on WIDE Radio!

I wisely monitored the program for a few additional nights to listen to what they were playing in order to make sure it fit our program, and also to insure no commercials were airing between 11:10 and 11:30 and any time up until midnight. Sure enough, music from *Studio X* on WNAC Boston was exactly the format of our *Cozy Corner*, except they had more variety. The very next night I sprung into action! After my local newscast at ten minutes past the hour, I played a three-minute album cut and listened in cue to WNAC. As soon as the mellifluous voice of Bill Marlowe intoned, "And now more music, beautiful music, from Studio X" and played his first cut, I segued from my album cut and brought up the network's music. It sounded great and until around 11:29, *new* beautiful music was heard on WIDE, thanks to WNAC-Boston. At 11:30, I played another cut or two while they aired five minutes of Boston news and a commercial or two. I usually rejoined them for more music around 11:37 pm and I'd stay with them and their beautiful music until approximately 11:55, when I would play our pre-recorded station sign off. Talk about something working slicker than you know what! Man, was I pleased with myself. My feeling of total satisfaction was short-lived. One night, it all came crashing down around me!

At the time, to make ends meet, I was doing double duty by working two jobs at opposite ends of the day. My $55 weekly radio salary was hardly paying the freight, so I took a second job working mornings at WMTW-TV, Channel 8. My TV hours were 8am until noon, five days a week. My hours at the radio station, 5pm-midnight, got me home around 12:30am. To be on time at the TV station, my alarm went off at 6:00am. It was a harrowing 40-minute drive over Route 26 from our home in Portland to the studios in Poland Spring. I had to be on time because I ran camera on a live show, *Teddy Bear Playhouse*, at 8:00am. It was a grueling schedule. In no time at all, it was beginning to affect me. By the time my day was winding down in radio around eleven at night, I was pretty beat!

One night, it all caught up with me. After struggling to stay awake through my 11:05 newscast and successfully making the segue to join the network for my "pirated" beautiful music, I had about had it. I made the mistake of tilting the comfy chair back and putting my feet up on the edge of the counter top by the control board console. Totally wiped out and exhausted, I remember thinking, "Okay, I'll only do it for a few minutes." The beautiful music from *Studio X* seduced me into a deep, deep slumber.

The next thing I remember is suddenly waking up and looking at the studio clock. It was around 11:45. I had been sound asleep for over half an hour! The beautiful music was still playing on our air, but I also noticed the red light blinking on and off on our telephone hotline, which meant the boss was calling and it wasn't to wish me a safe drive home.

I picked up the phone and the resonant voice of the station's owner and manager, J. Alan Jasper, calmly asked, "Is everything okay? Are you all right?" "Yes sir," was my feeble reply, my voice trembling, "Why do you ask?" "Well," he went on, "to begin with, I've been letting this phone ring for the past 15 minutes. I was just about to hang up and call the police when you answered!" Oh God, I thought to myself, I'm dead meat! This was my second full-time air-shift in radio, after being fired from my first job for changing the music format at night, and now this! "I was enjoying the music so much on Cozy Corner," Alan continued, "and even remarked to my wife, Barbie, gee, Joe is playing such a wonderful selection tonight. But, then," he paused slightly, "the voice of Bill Marlowe came on and said, music from *Studio X* will continue after a brief pause for the news from our WNAC studios. That's when I first thought something was dreadfully wrong and began calling the station trying to reach you!" My boss said he found it interesting to listen to Boston area news, but added, "When it was followed by a Lincoln fruit juice commercial and I knew they didn't buy advertising time on our station, I really began to wonder if something had happened to you and my radio station!" Shaking like a leaf with a sick feeling in the pit of my tummy and believing I was about to be fired from my second full-time job in radio, I blurted out what I had done. Thankfully, it didn't happen.

After listening to my explanation of what I had endeavored to do to enhance the music on Cozy Corner, rattled off in a machine-gun like delivery, Alan laughed. After saying he was happy I was safe and nothing was wrong with his station, he actually complimented me on my ingenuity. He also strongly suggested that I try to get more rest and to decide whether I really wanted to work in radio or television. His message came through loud and clear, but in a kind way. Oh, yeah, there was one other thing. He said before hanging up, "Tomorrow see Jeannine [the station's office manager] and tell her I told you to take $50 dollars out of petty cash and go buy some more easy-listening albums."

Lesson learned: you may be able to serve two masters, but not very well.

Top Ten Commandments for weekend Rock Jocks by Mark Summers.

Mark Summers was a popular morning drive radio voice in Florida, first, at alternative "Buzz" in West Palm Beach, later at Rock 105 in Jacksonville.

The Chicago native and Winona State grad knows the importance of weekend radio warriors to the success and sound of a station. He wrote his list of *The 10 Commandments of a Weekend Rock Jock.* It is based on his experience as a rock jock. It is primarily directed at radio newcomers, but I feel his list contains excellent advice and is a good refresher course for radio pros already on the air. I appreciate Mark's time and input, and I respect his opinion. I find myself in agreement with most things on his list. There are a few points it would be fun to debate with him, but isn't that true of most everything in life? Mark's list is food for thought, whatever format you find yourself working in. Take what you feel applies to your situation and think about the rest! Here is his list of commandments for a weekend jock on a rock station, printed with his permission.

Thou shall cherish my air shifts. Why? They can and will be taken away tomorrow if you don't.

Thou shall be a professional. Pros check their ego and attitude at the studio door, and strive to make *every break* their very best! Pros make it in this business, half assess don't. Pros cherish every opportunity to be on the air and use that time to hone their skills to become better broadcasters.

Thou shall be prepared. Every time you open that mic, you better know what you're going to say, how you're going to say it, and why you're even saying it in the first place. Rambling on like an un-prepared idiot is NOT being a pro. If you're not preparing every break, you're not being a professional. This means you're not cherishing the opportunity you're getting and you will probably lose your shifts. Show prep does not mean showing up a half-hour before your show and distracting the person who is on the radio before you. Stay out of the studio until you're on! Being prepared means you know what's going on in the world and at the radio station as well as what's going on with promotions, upcoming concerts, the morning show, sports, and news. Being prepared to go on the radio means you put together a planner before the show of how and when you're going to incorporate all that information into your show. Being prepared also limits you to one thought per break. Don't talk about more than one thing at a time. Don't go from a winner call into a bit about artist information. Listeners are doing things while listening to you and are distracted easily.

Thou shall be brief: If you talk for more than 30 seconds in one break than you have not prepared for that break. There is nothing that can't be said effectively and creatively in less than thirty seconds. [5]

Take note: Radio Pros prepare their breaks by meticulously handcrafting them to be either relatable, topical, timely, informative, or entertaining, usually in less than 25 seconds. Write your breaks out, beginning to end!

Then rewrite them to make them better, funnier, or more concise. Jay Leno, the President, and the local news people all have scripts so that they can sound like pros.

Thou shall always sell the station first: A pro knows and respects that the real star is the radio station and the music, not you. Your job is to sell the music, cross promote what is going on at the station, and to get people excited about the station. You are here for the station, and not vice-versa. In other words, do not come in thinking you can do whatever you want. You have a job to do in selling the station first. Every time you say the call letters, they should be said with pride and enthusiasm.

Thou shall know & respect thy limits and boundaries: As a weekender, you are not a wacky morning guy, a comedian, a talk show host, a political analyst, or a news guy. You are a DJ on a rock station! If you are using your shift to be anything but a great rock DJ, then you are not being a pro. Quit cross-talk babble. It sounds like horrible college radio. You are not allowed to use sound effects, ever!

Thou shall play the music only on the log: You are NOT the music director, nor do you understand the decision-making process behind choosing songs that are played by this station, therefore you do NOT ever veer from the log or drop songs that you just don't want to hear.

Thou shall respect the phones: Take requests, answer questions, get your winner and get the hell back to business. A pro knows he should be working on the next break and not gabbing with some 15 year-old for 15 minutes. Also, when it comes to airing calls, air only the best. If someone sounds stupid, or the quality of the connection sucks, don't air it. Just congratulate them and move on!

Thou art thy best and worst critic: You should be air-checking every show and then listening for ways to improve. Force yourself to come up with ways to make a boring break come to life. Ask yourself, how else could I have said that? Did I deliver that break briefly and effectively, and if not, what could I have done?

Thou will have fun: A pro can do all the above and still make it all sound fun! It does not take years of experience to get to that level, but if you have the drive, determination, and ambition to be a pro, someday you will continue to be given the opportunity to be one. If not, you will probably lose that opportunity and be asked to leave. It's time to separate the men from the boys, and the up-and-coming pros from the slackers and the boneheads. Which are you? (Prepared by Mark Summers.)

The role of a radio producer.

Radio producers and show hosts are responsible for planning and developing the show for the air. The producer takes the show from the planning stages, gathering information for the show host, news and entertainment that is geared towards the station's key audience, scheduling guests and pulling it all together, to air as a complete package on the radio. Quite often a producer is also responsible for operating the control board for the show host. In my case, like many other talent, I preferred running my own control board. Running the board carries the additional responsibilities of inserting commercials, sound bites, sound effects, and music at the appropriate points and keeping the show on time. On rare occasions, the producer may also serve as a call screener, but it is strongly advised that someone other than the producer do this job for a couple of very good reasons. First, a good call screener needs to devote all their time and energy to insure that quality calls reach the show host to go on the air. Secondly, there is no more hectic or chaotic scene than a morning drive show or popular talk program. A producer has his or her hands full coordinating everything. Distractions like answering the phone must be kept to a minimum, or a show will crash and burn! Thirdly, the producer needs to pay strict attention to what is going out on the air at all times. It means having one eye and listening ear on the program host and the other eye on the studio clock with an ear on the call screener. Distractions while doing live radio manifest themselves unexpectedly. You don't need a producer on the phone with a caller while the host is trying to get their attention!

Linda Smith produced *The Joe and Andy Family* on WROR Boston from the late '80s through the early '90s. She also did double duty in the producer's chair by working alongside me weekday mornings and again on Saturday nights on *Saturday Night "Live" at the Oldies*. Her incisive attention to detail gives you an excellent inside look in to the real working world of a radio producer. "The attraction, intrigue, and adrenaline rush that comes from producing a major market radio program, or any program for that matter, is that the actions and ability of the producer have a direct effect on the on-air product. The ability to control the chaos and grasp the pulse of the day inside the studio, inside the building, and in the community that surrounds us was always the key. Yes, it was chaos. Any live program is, but it was controlled and that was an element that also enhanced the on-air presentation."

Linda describes in detail what she believes was the most challenging component of her job as producer: "It was identifying each talent's idiosyncrasies. Our most-recognized air-talent wouldn't tolerate anyone other than the producer approaching him from behind while he was on the air. The producer needs to learn the comfort zone of the show host. You also need to know that each talent considers the role, importance, and activities of the producer differently. The most important consideration," says Smith, "is to understand that any negative interaction, interruption, organizational or technical blunder could result in a less than ideal on-air presentation. The talent's responsibility is to entertain the listener within the parameters of the format using all available tools (those may vary depending on the day part at the station)."

Smith believes the producer's job is to ensure that the talent can focus on performance and be confident that all support aspects of the program are overseen and that there are no snafus. "The producer is clearly a supporting role for talent, but that can take on many dimensions. In addition to the organizational and technical functions (writing copy, writing scripts, writing interviews, organizing hourly spots and log adherence, music playlist adherence, running the control board for some talent, screening calls, editing tape, scheduling guests, and general show prep), the producer is also a buffer of sorts for talent. There is a reason why the on-air studios are located at the end of the building," chuckles Smith, "the furthest away from business operations and the sales staff. Sales folks have a tendency to want to talk to talent while a show is in progress or directly after, about a new client, a live commercial read, a remote from the local dump, you get the idea!

"The radio sales staff feels that since they generate revenue they should be granted an audience whenever it behooves them. Wrong," says Linda with a sly smile. "The producer can and should deflect that kind of activity, especially during particularly inconvenient times for the talent. It can be done," she says, "and relations can be maintained when it's done properly! A good producer manages the real-time elements of the show so that the talent can relax and not obsess about program details. The difficulty and the beauty of the role," she adds, "is that one show is not a template for the next. Each day is entirely different from the previous one, so although experience, continuity and even temperament certainly matter, one cannot use the previous day as a barometer for today." Linda Smith concludes her excellent dissertation on her all-too-familiar role as a radio producer by sharing these thoughts: "There is great satisfaction in playing such an important role and affecting such influence. You cannot prepare enough, but you must always keep in mind that the prep is never enough so that you don't get thrown by the inevitable unexpected!"

Radio sales are tough.

One of the toughest, and in many ways, most thankless jobs I ever had in radio was in sales! Before sharing my story about my brief sojourn into the world of radio sales, please allow me say this right up front. I have nothing but the utmost respect for those in radio sales. For over forty years, I watched my broadcast brothers and sisters slugging it out in the trenches on a daily basis, doing their best to convince advertisers why they should spend their dollars on our radio station. Even though there are many clients who are kind and professional to deal with, there are others who can be demeaning, skuzzy, and downright mean! These tougher-than-tough advertisers come complete with a smoother-than-smooth veneer finish and a cold-blooded attitude that rivals that of the most vicious vermin! Come to think of it, I've known a few radio sales folks who could easily fit that description as well! Thankfully, most radio sales people I worked with during my lengthy broadcast career have been decent, hard-working radio pros. However, I often wondered what motivated these nice folks to enter the shark-infested waters of radio sales. Why do they subject themselves to the vile behavior and degrading comments from some of these demons of the deep? What is it that drives sales people? Is it the thrill of the chase and finally closing a deal, or is it something else?

Is it because radio sales is like a chess game and battle of wits between sales personnel and the advertiser, to see who can out-maneuver the other and ultimately win the match? Can't you just see the winner thrusting their arms high in the air and proudly belting out, "We Are the Champions!" [6] I've learned from talking with radio sales experts, it's all this and more! To get the inside scoop, I turned to my longtime friend and former senior radio account executive, **Steve Feldman**. In the early '80s, as radio pups in the business, Steve and I worked for RKO General, Boston. He was in sales and I was the new kid on the air. We were friends first, but also co-workers who knew the importance of what we, as individuals, brought to the table. It's a mutual respect and friendship that has matured and been maintained for the past thirty years.

Steve likens radio sales to a tennis match. "The words exchanged between the sales rep and the client are like tennis balls. A potential advertiser says no to your proposal, so you hit the ball back by asking, why not?" Feldman must know what he's talking about. He has been a survivor and a success in broadcast sales for thirty-five years. We'll delve deeper into his theory later, to learn more about his love for the sales game he describes as a tennis match! We'll also probe the mind of another Steve. Radio sales pro Steve Gillinsky shares his insight about never taking no for an answer in the sales game. But first, another slice of my own radio life and my sojourn into radio sales.

In the mid-'70s, I was on the air at WIDE-FM in Biddeford, just a snowball's throw from Portland, down the southbound lane of the Maine Turnpike. To supplement my meager earnings as the station's morning guy, I was gently coerced into giving radio sales a shot.

Radio sales can be a tough racket.

The station manager, who also doubled as general sales manager and chief sports play-by-play guy, said it would be a piece of cake. He didn't tell me that too much cake can be bad for the digestive system, while on the other hand without enough cake one can starve in sales. He also neglected to tell me my sales list would be the yellow pages of the local phone directory! My baptism in radio sales would be all cold-calls, no active station account list to follow up on to ease into selling. Talk about starting from scratch! Honestly, I didn't have a clue as to what I was doing, or what I'd be up against out on the street. There is something very special about working in the safe confines of a radio station control room. There, it's just you, the mic, and the listener. Out on the street, trying to sell air-time is a totally different animal. To repeat a well-used phrase, it can be a jungle out there, and it was! With a wife and young daughter at the time and in need of extra income, coupled with my attitude of always looking for a new challenge, I thought, why not?

It's truly ironic how radio talent, so adept at being great on-air sales people, can fail so miserably in trying to sell radio air time. Yes, I know all about the difficulty of trying to sell an intangible. With radio, you're selling *air*! It's not like you're selling someone a beautiful portrait of the Mona Lisa, or for that matter even a great looking reproduction. It's right there, for all to see! Some things do pretty well selling themselves and the sales person is merely the conduit to get the cash! Not so with radio sales. Radio sales are a heck of a lot harder! You *must* convince an advertiser why they should spend their money on your station. Having been there, tried it, and failed, here's my advice for air-talent looking to try part-time radio sales as a way of increasing their financial gain.[7] First and most importantly, make sure you have the blessings of your sales manager as you prepare to enter their world! Believe me, you will need their help and guiding hands in ways you never even dreamed about! Secondly, give serious thought to the long hours outside your air shift that will be involved in selling. Keep in mind, you will be making sales calls at times convenient to the advertiser, which may or may not mesh with your schedule.

In morning drive, as was my situation, it meant I hit the bricks when my three- or four-hour air-shift ended at 10:00am. Most of my clients (the few I managed to grab and hold on to) wanted to see me after they had lunch, which usually meant 3:00 or 4:00pm. That's fine for a nine-to-fiver, but for a morning drive person who has already been up for about twelve hours, it can be an absolute killer. Believe me, my brief exposure to radio sales was when I got used to taking frequent naps, anytime, anywhere, any place. Sometimes even sitting on a comfortable sofa in an outer office while waiting to be summoned in to talk turkey with a potential advertiser! If you decide to give radio sales a shot, you'll find yourself doing the same thing. Grabbing a few extra *zzzz's*, whenever and wherever you can!

Another important thing to remember before you dash off into the sphere of radio sales is that many radio stations, both large and small, cannot afford the luxury of employing a full-time copywriter, so another one of your duties will probably involve writing the advertising copy. Most likely you will also find yourself producing and recording it! More time spent on your part-time sales position! There are successful radio personalities who can double as very successful sales reps; I just wasn't one of them. At first glance, it appears to make total sense. Why not have the popular air-talent actually go out and meet and try and sell the advertiser? By being on the radio the talent already has a leg up by being known, and in most cases loved, by the client. So in theory, it looks like a match made in radio sales heaven. However, putting it into play is an entirely different matter!

"Radio sales is a tough game," says sales pro, **Steve Feldman.** "Sales of any kind, but especially radio, are not for the thin-skinned. You need to be tough. You also need to be knowledgeable about your station and your competition, both radio and other media. The biggest hurdle to overcome when first starting out in radio sales is handling rejection and being able to overcome objections. It's amazing how these simple words can shake up a person's whole attitude and state of mind," he says, shaking his head.

The veteran account executive goes on to explain why you should never take no as a final answer, at least not in radio sales. "No one likes to hear the word no, especially if they were hoping to hear yes! Keep in mind, when clients say no, they often want more information, or need to be better convinced that your radio station is right for them. It's up to you to prove to them why they should advertise on your station. That's why a sales rep can't take no at face value and run away, thinking they lost the order because of something personal. That's simply not the case! As I mentioned earlier, sales is like a tennis match. The words exchanged are the balls. If someone says no to your sales proposal, hit the ball right back to them and ask, why not or what makes them say no."

In all the years that Steve has been selling advertising, at this writing a total of 35 years, he laughingly admits he's heard all the objections. "I've heard 'em all and there really aren't that many of them. It's funny, the clients change and the markets may change, but human nature is the same. A sales person must first and foremost ask for the order. If you get a no, ask why. Hear the objection, and it's important to know how to handle and answer the objections." Steve is emphatic about being prepared *before* you call on the client. "You'll probably hear another objection, so answer it! Like I said, radio sales is a tennis match. Wear the client out to the point where you have a great sales success story to share about your station and what you can offer the client…so any NO you hear, you can easily turn into a YES!" Steve explains how he personally handles rejection: "I don't call it rejection. I prefer to call it a battle of wits; wearing down the client, answering his or her objections in polite fashion, so saying no is really no longer an option on their part and is no longer valid."

Prospecting for clients and NOT taking no in radio sales.

Steve Feldman ^{also} believes in prospecting![8] "It's important to prospect your clients before you make the call. Making appointments in advance with the right clients to sell them on your station is most important. If you believe your station is right for a potential client, and you have research and also have dealt with other similar clients, all with success, then it makes it even more difficult for a new advertiser to say no. You know your station is right for them to begin with," says Feldman, "or you would not be wasting their time. Show them a list of clients similar to what they sell who are already profiting by using your station. Many competing sales personnel will resort to lying about what you and your station can supposedly deliver, so it's up to you to set the record straight. Knowing your competition is very important," adds Steve. "The client you are trying to sell may give you an excuse by saying the other station is cheaper, or they will reach more listeners, or they'll be able to do such and such, and so on and so forth. By knowing your competition, you may detect a little white lie told by a competing sales person to get an order and consequently the client bought it and the other station got the order. By setting the record straight, you can win back an order!" Steve readily admits that with a few clients, they simply won't budge. "You can lead a horse to water, show it to him, sprinkle a few drops on his tongue, do everything but drink it for him, but there are those who still will not sip from the cup. No matter what you say or show them, or how much you wear them down, they just won't budge or buy!"

Parking Lot Assessment.

When a client won't buy, it's time to go into what Steve Feldman calls his parking lot assessment. "When I'm walking away from my client, after not getting an order, as I walk through the parking lot to my car, I run a checklist off in my mind, as to what I could have said that I didn't, or what I could have showed the person that I didn't, or what I could have offered that I didn't. If by the time I get to my car, and before I start it, I can honestly say I did everything possible, then I start my car and move ahead to start all over again with a new potential client. I also ask myself what I have learned from this sales process that will help me get the next one."

Radio pro **Steve Gilinsky** started on the air in 1979, but moved into radio sales in 1985. Today, thanks to voice-tracking, he's still on the air and still selling, but now is co-owner of Magic 101.7 in Binghamton, New York. Steve has an almost cavalier attitude about radio sales, especially about a client who says no to you. He recalls one such incident with an advertiser, "I remember being rejected nine times by a client, and I still pursued it! Hey, you have nothing to lose. They can't kill you, at least I hope not," he laughs. "On the tenth time, I got the order. They told me that because I didn't give up, there must be something going good about my product, which was the station." Gilinsky urges all future radio sales wannabes who wish to be successful to never give up. "Keep going after them. Come up with ideas that suit the client. Don't go in to see them with something you use for everyone else. Make that potential advertiser feel special. Talk about them and their product. Make them feel they are the most important person in the world at that very moment."

Why talent usually fails in the sales game.

Personally speaking, and from a talent's perspective, I believe most of us are abysmal failures in sales because we are too emotional! The emotional part of our make-up, which makes us so good on the air, can be detrimental to us off the radio, especially in sales. For openers, radio talent simply cannot handle rejection. As you just read, in radio sales, rejection and the word "no" are commonplace. Radio talent loves to be loved. Sales people are seldom loved by their clients. They may be respected, and if they make their clients' cash registers ring, there's a certain fondness, but I wouldn't call it love. Put it this way: a sales person always has his or her hand out looking for the order. In order to get the order, that means money needs to be paid to the sales person for the advertising by the client. No business person readily likes to part with their hard-earned cash, especially for advertising, when they've just come off the worst sales month in the history of their company. This is why radio sales can be tough. It takes a strong person to be able to get the advertiser to part with his cash when revenues are down and the economic conditions are less than favorable. Quite often, clients look at a sales rep as someone who simply wants to take their hard earned moola! A seasoned sales pro is quite aware of these feelings before entering the lion's den and doesn't expect to be greeted with hugs and kisses every time, unlike air-talent, who are looked up to and often revered by the client.

Let's face it, most talent needs, wants, and almost expects constant stroking and adulation! We love it and any radio personality who tells you differently is not dealing with reality, let alone a full deck. This is why air-talent should be friends with sales and should be encouraged to accompany sales reps on client calls. It's great for the client *and* the air-talent and usually is one big love fest, which makes it easier for the sales rep to ask for the order! In many instances, having talent present can be the difference in getting the order or not.

Point to be made to all air-talent: make client calls! It's an extension of your duties as an on-air sales person to help your off-air sales personnel bring revenues into the station. Joint talent and sales rep client calls can be a win/win for the station.

Radio sales is tough, but so is being on the radio! Both sides should work together.

It's important that each station staff member knows and appreciates what the other is up against. During my many years in radio, and having sat on both sides of the aisle, as talent and in sales, I can honestly say without hesitation or reservation, and as silly as it may sound, most stations do not encourage or allow the two forces to mix. It's commonplace to hear talent refer to sales people as sleaze. On the other hand, sales staffers often refer to talent as being prima donnas and station cash cows! Therefore, bringing both parties together should be of primary importance at any station! It's a no-brainer! Both forces working together can increase revenue while at the same time building a solid station team with mutual respect for each other's abilities. Air-talent and sales staff members should be joined at the hip! It's one of the dumbest moves I've seen in commercial broadcasting, to not encourage both to work together! Sales is the business end of the wacky world of radio, and the crazy, on-air end of the business is responsible for ratings. The ratings, in turn, can and will determine how much revenue the station can project and generate; the better the ratings, the better the rates, leading to higher revenue. Each one needs the other!

Let talent be talent and leave the selling to a sales pro.

In my opinion, it would be better if on-air folks remained air-talent and left the actual off-air selling to the radio account executives! Where talent can become a huge asset to sales, as mentioned, is accompanying them on client calls. Advertisers love to meet the person behind the voice they are paying to read their commercials. Keep it in mind! My wife Kim, who also dabbled in sales for a while, believes good sales personnel come equipped at birth with an extra sales gene! If that's true, then without question some of us in the talent pool came down the birthing tube without one!

How to do quality radio production and what sales needs to know.

Radio production people are there to help and assist you, but don't always expect them to do your job, which includes getting copious copy notes together and getting them back to the station and produced in plenty of time to go on the air! You'd be surprised how many sales folks rush in at the eleventh hour, festooned with scattered notes and expecting to have a full-fledged commercial produced quickly, complete with music provided by the Mormon Tabernacle Choir and the Boston Pops. Sound silly? Perhaps, but I can't overemphasize how many sales people, both newbie and seasoned pro, will run into the radio station late on a Friday afternoon screaming *HELP!*

One of the best production pros in radio, until he retired in early 2009, was my longtime friend **Bob Spicer**. Spice and I worked together at the original WROR- Boston. Later, he moved across town to do outstanding production work for Greater Media. I can't tell you how often Bobby would be nearly out of his mind when late on a Friday afternoon a sales staffer would race into his studio breathless and in a panic, pleading for help! The salesman, loaded to the max with copy notes but without a clue as to a central theme for the advertiser, would expect the production director to pull it all together before the schedule began on the radio that afternoon! More often than not, Spice would bail the sales person's butt out of the fire.

Bob Spicer has these tips for radio wannabes and seasoned pros, who have forgotten how to do quality production. "Keep it simple; humor works. Try not to start every piece of commercial copy with a question. It's too easy to start by asking a question. It's overused! Coming up with concepts is the hardest thing to do," he adds. "Sometimes the copy writes itself, sometimes the copy comes naturally from the product or service itself, sometimes you have to invent or really dig for the premise or unique selling point. USP, the marketing geeks call it." Spice says he found that the best ground for fertile ideas is the street. "Just wandering around sometimes will jog the creative banks. Remember the story of how the creative pukes at an agency came up with the Volkswagen line, 'drivers wanted'? Some creative dude who was working on the account on the creative side was driving along behind a cab and the cab company was looking to hire taxi drivers for the company, so they put a sign on the back of the cab that read drivers wanted. The rest is advertising history," he laughs.

Spicer, the creative commercial genius of Boston radio for well over thirty years, believes that production people should fight for their concepts. "Challenge the sales puke, oops, excuse me, the account executive, to sell YOU the concept you created like you were the client. That's really all that's necessary. Your job ends when they pick up the phone, log onto the website or walk in the store!"

Radio pro sales lesson: last-minute sales orders for *unexpected* copy change are expected and pretty much the norm. No one likes it or appreciates it happening right before the close of business at 5:00pm, especially on a Friday afternoon, but it happens. It's one of the realities of commercial radio, and the *immediacy* of radio is one of the positives of why radio advertising is so effective. Get it done and get it on the air, *right now!* However, blatant and willful last-minute sales BS because as the sales person you never got around to doing your job and didn't allow enough time to pull it all together, is inexcusable and totally unprofessional. It's also the fastest way to lose the respect of the production staff. Try pulling that little stunt more than once or twice and don't be surprised to lose your head, along with their respect and cooperation. A certain amount of leeway and growing room is allowed for radio newbies, but when last-minute sales copy issues become an ongoing occurrence…look out!

Age discrimination and how it can affect you in radio.

There are laws to protect against age discrimination, yet they are so often violated. If not publicly, at least privately, especially with regard to hiring and firing radio and TV personalities. The problem lies in trying to prove it.

Many personalities who are fired or laid off are forced to remain quiet because a generous severance package is offered to the employee if they promise, in writing, not to badmouth the station or company, including management. This translates to being nothing more than hush money. In other words, be nice and quiet and don't say anything bad about us and will give you a big chunk of change! When you have mouths to feed and a mortgage to pay, who can refuse such an offer? Of course, companies are extremely careful the way they spell out such things and verbalize it in such a way that it's not a violation of any law. Let's be upfront here, folks, to get the money and benefits, you have to sign a document that specifically states you will not say anything negative about the company that just terminated you. Obviously, that would include any thought or talk of a possible age problem. Sign on the dotted line, keep your mouth shut, and take the money and run! I know first-hand from what I say. Right or wrong, I've signed a few of these papers during my own radio career.

Some talent remain silent for fear of reprisals of not being hired by another station, which also serves as motivation not to raise the age discrimination flag. Wouldn't you love to know how many cases are settled out of court and how much money is spent to avoid potential age discrimination suits? I would! Many radio and TV personalities also shy away from talking about this volatile subject because of personal pride and ego. The mere thought of such a thing happening to them because of their age and a little gray around the temples makes them feel old and no longer productive. For obvious reasons, they don't want to go there. They'd rather move on down the road with their pride still intact and try to land another air position somewhere else. Radio is such an incestuous business that words, both good and bad about a personality, travel fast and can find their way to the ears of a prospective employer.

So what is the answer to ending age discrimination? Personally, I think every employer, not just in radio but in every business, should have to swear under oath that age was not a consideration in hiring or firing an employee. Radical, you say? You may feel differently when your hair begins turning gray and you no longer wish to color it. Or you develop a few wrinkles, or need a few days off from developing bursitis in your wrist from typing company documents every day for the past twenty years! Yes, you may find yourself thinking differently about age discrimination when you know in your heart you are more than qualified for your job, but suddenly find yourself passed over, laid off, given early retirement, or fired! Perhaps then, age discrimination and how blatantly the law is violated every day may hit a little closer to home!

Right about now, you may be shaking your head and asking yourself why the topic of age discrimination is included in a how-to book about being a radio pro, which is primarily directed at those of you just starting out on an on-air career. A good question, and one which requires one simple answer:

so you may prepare today for what you may expect down your own radio road one day! You too may one day find yourself on the receiving end of some form of age discrimination, so don't say you weren't warned!

I guess one final and important reason for including the subject of age discrimination in this book is so you future radio stars will show some empathy for senior radio pros who have given so much of themselves to a profession that in many ways gives so little in return except, as the late comedian and radio pro Fred Allen said so succinctly, "a one-way ticket to oblivion."

The one constant in radio is change! Always keep your antenna up!

As stated elsewhere in this book, the one constant in radio is change! There are changes in management, format, or in ownership. One day you're the happiest pig in the poke, riding the hog highway to success and feeling quite good about yourself. The next day, bam! Look out! Your blissful world is suddenly shattered by something unexpected and totally out of your control! It helps to be aware of what's going on at the station, so keep your eyes and ears open and your antenna up!

Sometimes, change is inevitable for an air-talent. Maybe you've learned all you can in your present position, or at least that's the way you feel, and you decide it's time to move up or down the dial. Perhaps it's a desire to move up from a night shift to the more coveted and lucrative morning drive slot. If that's the case, keep one thing in mind. Usually, the person holding down the morning show at your station is doing quite well and is not about to move aside just because you feel you're ready! It probably will mean a move for you to another station. It could be a move in your present town, or to another city or state!

Quite often, changes with talent are made by management with no apparent or logical reason. It's change, for the sake of change! Suddenly, a station is sold. In walks a new GM, armed with his own PD. They decide they want their own air staff! You're gone, history, under the bus! No reflection on you, they say! You've done a good job for the station for the past seventy-five years and to show their gratitude and appreciation, you're presented with a ten-dollar gift certificate for you and your wife to have a burger on them at Mickey D's. Oh yeah, one more thing - you've got twenty minutes to clean out your desk and turn in your keys with the receptionist on your way out! The words, "Nothing personal" echoes in your ears as you slowly leave the building and walk away from a job you love.

You may as well get used to it right now. The one constant in radio is change! Change along with a new challenge can be downright scary! But, change can also make you stronger. It can give you more discipline and focus. Inspirational speaker Ralph Marsden says "You'll run faster when you're chasing after something, or when there's something chasing you. You'll discover that you can do it, and you'll discover how great it feels to give change your very best."

Don't let change or a new challenge beat you up and take you down. Instead, allow it to push you forward.

TOP 20 WAYS YOU KNOW YOU'RE AN AGING RADIO PRO, WHEN…

- You were first hired by a GM who actually worked in radio before becoming GM.
- Engineers could actually fix things without sending them back to the manufacturer or tossing them away!
- You actually know the difference between good reel-to-reel tape and cheap reel-to-reel tape.
- You know what a splicing block is and know how to use it.
- You worked for just one radio station and actually could name the guy who owned it.
- Radio stations actually had enough on-air-talent to field their own softball team.
- You always had a screwdriver in the studio, so you could take a screwed-up cart apart in seconds and repair it.
- You could smoke in the control room and you, the staff, and listeners thought it was cool.
- You could actually smoke in the control room and nobody cared.
- You would fight with your news guy over air-time. After all, what's more important, your one-liner joke or the EBS alert?
- You actually knew what an EBS alert stood for.
- You remember and know what a CONELRAD alert was all about.
- You used Magnecorders, Ampex 601's, McKenzie repeaters and Spotmasters.
- You knew how to change the teletype ribbon in the AP and UPI machines and lived with the purple ink on your hands for days.
- You remember when music promotion men actually brought new 45s and albums to the station for you to listen to and hoped you would actually play them on the air!
- You have hundreds of photos of yourself with famous folks who wouldn't know you today if you bit 'em on the butt.
- You actually remember *Name That Tune*, *Stop the Music*, *Martin Block*, and *Alan Freed*.
- You ran a contest and nobody called, so you made up a name and gave the tickets to your family.
- People who ride with you in your car yell, "Why do you have the radio turned up so loud?"
- You remember the days when people actually thought radio was important!

Some Things to Know About a Career in Radio as an On-Air Pro • 607

TEN COMMANDMENTS to apply to your life and career as a real on-air radio pro!

1. Remember, silence can be a virtue. Sometimes the best reply is to say nothing, especially when dealing with management.
2. Learn your station's format, so you know how to break it properly.
3. Open yourself to change (it's the one constant in radio), but don't ever let go of your values and allow radio to change you!
4. When you lose in the ratings war, don't lose the lesson.
5. In disagreements with your PD, GM, other talent, or anyone, only deal with the present situation. Don't bring up the past; it only confuses the issue at hand.
6. Go easy on yourself and with others.
7. Share your knowledge. It's a way to achieve immortality.
8. Judge your success by what you had to give up to get it.
9. Remember, not getting what you want can sometimes be a big ole blessing.
10. Always try and follow the 3 R's: Respect for others, Respect for yourself and Responsibility for your own actions.

Always carry the keys to the station on your person, just in case you lock yourself out!

In the 1960s, **Berni Henri** was a weekender at WIDE in Biddeford, Maine, where I was PD. He was a great kid, always laughing and fun to be around. Bernie was also very bright, or at least so I thought. He learned a valuable lesson about always keeping the keys to the station on your person while at work. One summery Saturday afternoon, I was enjoying our backyard in Saco, listening to the Red Sox on WIDE. It was a beautiful day made even better, because our Sox were winning! The board operator on the game was our pal, Bernie. When they broke for a station break along the Red Sox line, I was surprised to hear flagship station WHDH's call letters, not ours. Damn it, I thought, Bernie must be out of the studio again and didn't hear them call for a break! Tying to be charitable, I figured perhaps he had gastric problems and was in the restroom. Oh well, one ten-second missed station break isn't going to ruin my day. It happens. I'm sure he had a good reason. I'd call him after his shift and find out what happened. I laid back in my recliner and continued enjoying the game.

At the end of the inning, we had a local commercial insert. I noticed we didn't breakaway to play our spot. Instead, it was a Boston advertiser. Now, I began sweating profusely and wondered what the devil was going on! I raced in the house and dialed the hotline at the station. This was before cell phones. It rang and rang! No one answered. I hung up the phone and was about to head for the station when my phone rang. On the other end was a frantic Bernie.

Immediately, I knew all was not well in Mudville! "Joe, will you tell this moron that I really work at the station," he pleaded. "Where are you? What's going on," I asked, "and who is the moron?" "He's the desk sergeant at the Biddeford police station, I've been arrested!" "Police station," I yelled! "What happened?" Evidently, always-hungry Bernie, thinking that with a full inning of baseball on the radio he had more than ample time to zip downstairs to grab a hot dog from the vendor, parked out in front. Young Bernard, being a speedster, thought he could pull it off and make it back upstairs to the studio before the inning was even half-over. After all, the lad was hungry. It was a pretty good plan, except for a couple of minor problems. First of all, no one is supposed to ever leave the control room unattended! When it's your shift you stay until relieved. Secondly, the door to the station automatically locks if you close it! It was the type of lock that has a little button to slide over to keep it in the locked or unlocked position. This time the button was in lock. As Bernie raced out, and heard the door slam shut behind him, he knew he was in trouble! He had left the keys on the console in the studio.

Always a quick-thinking kind of guy, he figured, no problem. He'd grab a couple of hot dogs, go around to the side alley of the building, and climb up the fire escape and in the window. Our studios were on the 2nd floor and the window off the fire escape was always unlocked. In the summer it was usually wide open to catch a breath of air, since the building's air conditioner was always on the fritz. Sounds doable, right? Yes, except for one thing young Bernard didn't take into account - the Biddeford police cruiser coming around the corner just as he was halfway up the fire escape. At gunpoint, Bernie was told to climb back down and keep his hands high in the air, which he wisely did. I guess because he was casually dressed in a sweatshirt and jeans and was young-looking, the officer didn't believe his story that he actually worked at the radio station, locked himself out, and was trying to get back in by scaling the fire escape. He was arrested. I forgot to ask him if he shared his hot dogs with the arresting officer on the drive to the police station. During this time, since no one was at the controls, Boston commercials and station breaks with WHDH call letters were airing on WIDE! I finally convinced the desk sergeant to release Bernie and drove to the radio station. Police headquarters was several blocks from the station but speedster Bernie beat me. He was sitting on the sidewalk out in front when I pulled up. The expression of a hurt puppy was written all over his face. It was not the time to berate him. There would be plenty of time for that later, but now it was time to get him back in the studio and at the controls! The downstairs door was always unlocked, except at night. We ran up the stairs and I unlocked the door to the offices and Bernie raced in. By now, we had missed an hour of commercials, which meant lost revenue.

Radio lesson learned: Always keep the station keys on your person, and bring a bag lunch!

Notes:
1. **Author's note:** I am most flattered and appreciative of Alice's kind comments. They were totally unexpected and unsolicited.
2. In the spring of 2009, Matt was one of the casualties of the merger between Sirius & XM.
3. There are many websites where you can learn more about how to conduct yourself during a job interview.
4. When I first joined WIDE in 1963, I was hired as the night announcer. In '64, I became program director.
5. **Authors Note:** obviously Mark's comments refer to a music-intense format where personality is kept to a minimum and emphasis is on the music. He is also speaking from his own radio experience in working a Hot AC format where brevity is emphasized. Some formats, even music-based, like AC, oldies, country and others, particularly in morning drive, require more personality with more set-up time than 30 seconds. Needless to say, this commandment does not apply to formats like talk, news, sports, etc. However, it is important to keep in mind that being concise in what you say is important in all radio formats!
6. "We Are the Champions" by Queen on the Elektra label got as high as #4 on Nov. 26, 1977. Source: *Billboard*.
7. It's not unusual for air-talent, especially in smaller markets, to do double-duty by handling a few accounts to earn a commission and make extra money. Many are quite good at sales. It was not my bag and I was most comfortable being on the air.
8. In 2009, Steve Feldman left radio to join the sales force at Comcast. He had been a senior account executive with Clear Channel Radio in Palm Beach, Florida, representing Classy 92.1-FM-WRLX and NewsRadio 1290- WJNO, both top-rated stations in South Florida.

Rose Diehl, PD and air talent, Topeka, Kansas.

Willy Tyler, morning-drive air talent and PD Billings, Montana.

Richie Norris, weekend air-talent, Albany, New York.

Linda Smith, former radio producer Boston WROR-FM 98.5.

Steve Feldman, veteran radio sales expert, Boston and So. Florida.

Steve Gilinsky, air talent and co-owner Magic 101.7 Binghamton, NY.

Bob Spicer, retired radio production ace, Boston.

CHAPTER 20
Who Inspired the Radio Pros Who Contributed to This Book

"He was a legend. There was no other disc jockey in the United States like him"

– Radio Pro, Sam Riddle on B. Mitchell Reed

In their own words, fifty of America's radio pros speak out on who inspired them to enter radio. Here are their memories of who they listened to while growing up, and who got them *hooked* on radio!

Mike Addams has been on the air since June 1965 and except for a couple of years on radio in Atlanta and Tampa in '83 and '84 has been on the air in Boston since Labor Day, 1973. He and I worked together at the original WROR-98.5 Boston back in the early '80s. Warm, personable Mike has been hosting his top-rated *Morning Magic* program on Magic 106.7 - Boston for years. Mike grew up in Daytona Beach, Florida, in the days of the transistor radio. "It now seems like an eternity ago, and it was," says Mike with a smile. "It was such a big deal to have a relatively small little device that was so portable you could ride your bike, deliver the afternoon newspapers, and listen to the World Series all at the same time! And, yes, there were World Series games played in daylight. And of course," he adds, "there was music to listen to. In those golden days of radio there was not a lot of rock n' roll on Daytona radio, but the radio was still a good companion. And, if you were in a car on the world's most famous beach at night, you could hear other radio stations from Jacksonville and Miami as their signals bounced up and down the coastline."

Addams says the importance of radio in his life all changed in the summer of 1963. "That's when the family vacation was a long drive to New

Jersey and a trip into New York City to visit relatives. That was my first taste of what BIG TIME New York City radio, WABC, and Cousin Brucie were all about![1] He just sounded bigger than life," recalls Mike, "and more exciting than anything I'd ever heard before. There was so much energy, and all the artists sounded like they were his friends. Imagine that! I kind of knew right then that I wanted to be a part of that world of excitement."

Mike remembers that as the vacation wound up and the trip back to Daytona began, he didn't want his dad to touch that dial. "I wanted to listen to WABC for as long as I could, as long as there was some sort of signal through all that static. Obviously, ABC faded away after a few hundred miles as we headed south, but my dad thought we might be able to hear WABC on the beach at night. I couldn't wait to find out if that was possible. Well, guess what? On a good clear night you could hear 77- WABC! Joe, this is kind of a corny story, but those faraway radio signals were always an inspiration to me.[2] I really wanted to be a part of that wonderful world of show biz that was inside my radio."

Malcolm Alter has been reporting Boston traffic since the '80s, when he first reported the comings and goings on infamous Route-128 and other troublesome spots on our Joe n' Andy morning show. An Emerson College grad, Alter grew up in the Boston area listening to Jess Cain, Norm Nathan, and Bill Marlowe. "I was not necessarily of my own generation as far as my musical tastes. I preferred a more adult or grown-up sound, big bands, etc., which eventually evolved into an appreciation and then a real passion for jazz. I did get to hear Arnie "Woo Woo" Ginsburg and the WMEX (AM) Good Guys when I was with my friends. I also loved listening to Jess Cain's morning show on WHDH which was very entertaining. I think not only did he influence me, but a few generations of people working in radio."

Dick Bartley is the creator, host, and producer of *The Classic Countdown* and *Rock & Roll's Greatest Hits*. In 2002, he was named one of America's Top-25 most influential syndicated radio personalities by *Radio Ink* magazine. Dick also hosted *American Gold* and *Rock & Roll's Greatest Hits* for the ABC Radio Network from 1991 until 2009. Dick grew up in Syracuse, New York, until age twelve, when he moved to Lynchburg, Virginia. "Both towns had excellent local Top-40 radio, WNDR and WOLF in Syracuse and WLLL and WWOD in Lynchburg. In addition to local stations, like so many other radio fans growing up in the '60s, I listened religiously to a number of 50,000-watt out-of-town signals, WABC, WLS, WBZ, WCFL, WOWO, and quite a few others. These were my primary radio inspirations. Later, I was a big fan of the work of Casey Kasem, Bob Kingsley, Wolfman Jack, and others."

Gary Berkowitz is the foremost broadcast authority when it comes to consulting AC (Adult Contemporary radio) stations. "Get ready," says Berko, "because there were many who served as an inspiration and prompted me to go into radio. So, let's start with the first radio station that allowed me to hang out, WGBB in Freeport, New York. PD Bob Lawrence, Buddy Carr (Tom Bigby), Mike Sullivan, Al Case, and all the guys there. They were all very kind and patient with the thirteen year-old kid from Oceanside. From WABC, it was Herb Oscar Anderson, Ron Lundy, Dan Ingram, Cousin Brucie, Charlie Greer, Bob-A-Loo, and, of course, the legendary, most incredible one of all, Harry Harrison. To this day, Harry and I are friends. From WMCA, it was Good Guys Joe O'Brien, Jack Spector, Danny Dan, and Gary Stevens. From spending my summers in Albany, New York, it was WPTR (which was my fave) and WTRY; both really had major influences on me. From famous 1540-PTR it was JW Wagner, Roy Reynolds (wow, was he good!), Boom Boom Branigan, and the many night jocks that went through that place, especially Chris "Topher" Randall (one of his jingles went, 'with Randall on the radio everything swings!'). At WTRY, it was Lee Gray and Jay Clark, who years later was my PD at WPRO in Providence. And everyone at Emerson College, Boston. I made many friends there that are still my friends today. Emerson was a great learning lab!"

Don Bleu is another true-blue radio pro who is the dean of the San Francisco Bay area morning radio scene. Don is now in his 27th year of waking up Bay Area listeners. "Growing up, I listened to WLS-Chicago and KOMA in Oklahoma City. Shadoe Stevens," Bleu says, "was my fraternity brother at the University of North Dakota. He was working at the radio station and I was working at Kinney's Shoes. It was a no-brainer for me, shoes or radio! Shadoe was my inspiration and invitation into radio. First, I started doing weekends so Shadoe could go to all the frat parties. Then I moved to Fargo in June 1968 and worked the summer there. I had to decide whether or not to stay and go to school or take a radio job in Minnesota at KDWB. I took the job at KDWB and was there for ten years, until 1978. Since that time, I was named to the Minnesota Radio Hall of Fame. In 1978, my family and I moved to Los Angeles where I did mornings on KHJ, but soon was replaced by Rick Dees. I was moved to middays and then out the door, buh-bye! Next stop," recalls Bleu, "I headed north to the Bay Area and KYUU and a new format, Adult Contemporary radio. I did afternoons for about six weeks, then moved to mornings, which I did for ten years. KYUU went away and became X100. I went bye-bye again and moved to K101 in 1990 and have been here ever since. K-101 became Star 101.3 in 2001."

Bruce Bradley was one of the most popular air-personalities *ever* on WBZ Boston from 1960-68. "I worked for nine raggedy-ass radio stations from July 2, 1951, three days after I graduated from high school, until May 1960," exclaims Bruce, "when I got my first good job at WKAL in Rome, New York. My boss was Chuck King, who I thought was a jerk (he wasn't). He hired me to do morning drive at 75 cents an hour. I wasn't worth it. He later became president of the Mutual Broadcasting System. When we met again years later in New York, each of us was surprised at how well the other had done!" Juicy Brucie, as he was affectionately known to his legions of loyal listeners, including your friendly author, listened to Dee Finch and Gene Klavan, the morning guys on WNEW. "You've got to have balls to think you can hold the attention of thousands of people for hours at a time and make them come back tomorrow. Klavan and Finch possessed that special radio ingredient needed, testosterone. Working with an on-air partner is as delicate a balance as a marriage, except with less sex and more money," says Bradley. "Klavan and Finch were excellent, and usually when half a team departs, the remaining person sinks like a rock! Not so in Gene's case - he got stronger, because he had to! That's a real radio pro. He worked solo for a long time, and basically did a morning zoo all by himself. When I was fourteen, I listened to the best New York had to offer, WNEW-1130 AM. I didn't say, 'I could do that,' I said, 'I'm better than they are already,' and that's what I mean about balls."

Stacey Cohen has been actively involved in the radio biz for the past twenty-five years. She began as an on-air-talent at KNIX Radio in Phoenix. Stacey was one of the first women in the country to co-host a morning show with another female while at KOMP in Las Vegas. Today, her voice is heard on Los Angeles radio. She also has her own agency, Cohen Creative in Redondo Beach. "I grew up in Columbus, Ohio," says Stacey, "listening to Spook Beckman on WCOL-AM. My neighbor across the street was Don Smith who did mornings on WBNS-AM. I used to go over to the Smith's house and play with their kids. They were Catholic and there were plenty of kids to play with. It seems like they were always having parties on weekends and I remember the kids would say, my dad is having people over from work again (typical of radio people, always partying!). When I was about twelve years old, I would take the bus downtown every Saturday to tour WCOL. They gave free station tours and it was the same every week, but I went because it always seemed so exciting to me! I was really good at prank phone calls and I used to buy Halloween sound effects albums and my friends and I would call boys and do crazy things over the phone with sound effects. When I finally got on the air, it just always seemed natural for me to play on the phones."

Joe Cortese has showcased his talents for the past twenty-eight years at three of Boston's more popular radio stations, the original WROR, WBMX and in 2001, he moved to WODS as APD and imaging director. Joe also hosts *Back to the '80s* on Friday nights. "Growing up in Westchester County, New York, it was WABC," says Joe. "Harry Harrison took us to school and Dan Ingram was there on the way home. I loved radio for the music and couldn't wait until Tuesday afternoon when the new *Music Power* survey came out by 3:30 p.m. It was Dan Ingram that I listened to the most with only AM radio in my first car, and without question, he was the biggest influence on me."

Tom Cuddy went from PD at WPRO and PRO-FM, Providence in 1987 to VP of Programming at the ABC Radio Networks in NYC. In 1990, he joined WPLJ. "When I was growing up in Newton, Massachusetts, in the late '60s, while in grammar school, I listened to WRKO and WBZ as often as possible. However, it was during a fifth-grade school tour of WBZ that I saw midday personality Dave Maynard in action and I was hooked! I said to myself that's what I want to do and I never changed my mind."

Captain Dan has been on the radio since 1971 and in morning drive at KKLI in Colorado Springs since July 1999. "When I was a kid (which some would say lasted well into my mid-30s), there were so many great broadcasters in the Twin Cities of Minneapolis-St. Paul, which is where I grew up. Charlie Boone and Roger Erickson were the morning team on 830 WCCO, 'Your Good Neighbor to the Northwest.' They were often schlocky, but always connected, informative and entertaining. They were the first thing I heard as a kid each morning when my parents' alarm clock went off. I was maybe ten when the Minnesota Twins moved to Minneapolis and WCCO carried the games which featured the broadcast team of Ray Scott (Ray had a delivery as smooth as warm butter), Herb Carnell, who shared play-by-play duties and was equally gifted, and Hallsey Hall, the old salt who had all the great baseball stories. He always sounded like he was chomping on a fat cigar and half in the bag! For the longest time, listening to them call a game was for me the real sound of summer in the Twin Cities.

"As my teen years progressed, says Capt'n Dan, "I became interested in my music (mid-to-late '60s). The guy I never missed was the 6-10am jock, Rob Sherwood on 63 KDWB. Rob had the BEST jingles, although for the longest time, we thought they sang 'Roger Wood' instead of 'Rob Sherwood.' He had incredible energy, put tons of calls on the air, and had a special way of walking the ramps to songs and the commercials as well. As I became older another KDWB personality caught my attention, the True Don Bleu . What a master! He could do more over a 15-second song ramp than any guy in the business. Don was always entertaining, energetic, and had a commanding presence. While on my honeymoon in San Francisco in 1984, I heard Don doing mornings on KYUU. I stole a contest I heard him do on that trip and I still use a variation of it today."

Jeff Davis was with WLS-AM from1974 until 1988 and today is still the voice of that great Chicago heritage station. "As a kid growing up in rural North Carolina, I listened to WKIX in Raleigh. I worked in the tobacco fields on my grandfather's farm and saved enough money to buy a little red two transistor radio that was made in Hong Kong. When I went to bed, I would plug the little earplug in and listen under the covers so my parents wouldn't bust me for staying up late. I'd DX [long-distance listening] stations like WLS, WCFL Chicago and WABC New York. On some nights I pulled in KAAY in Little Rock. I listened to KAAY's Clyde Clifford and his *Beaker Street* show. I was too young and too conservative to smoke pot but if ever a radio show was made for it, *Beaker Street* was the ticket. In college in Richmond at Virginia Commonwealth University, I joined the campus radio station WJRB and made fast friends with Bob Summers (real name John Valentine) and Bob Lewis (real name Norman Freedlander). They were my role models. Norm gave me lots of tips and pulled no punches when it came to criticism, but was quick to give me a compliment when it was deserved. Norm gave me some of the best advice and guidance I've ever gotten. It's unlikely I would have gotten into radio if it had not been for them."

Dale Dorman has been a favorite Boston-air personality for over thirty years, primarily at Kiss and Oldies-103. Dale says radio is all he ever wanted to do. "When I was six and asked my mom about the man in the radio, she told me he was miles away, taking into a microphone. I thought," smiles Dale," that's the coolest thing. I still feel the same way. As a youngster, I listened to Dick Biondi on WLS and Joey Reynolds on WKBW."

Rod Fritz has been a familiar radio news voice in Boston for well over thirty years. As a Navy brat, Rod grew up all over the country, from Pennsylvania to New York, Illinois, and California. "I used to sit in my bedroom at night when I was between twelve and fifteen and listen to any AM radio station that would come in," he says. "I always listened to Dick Biondi on WLS. Clark Weber was there, too, and Dick Summer on WBZ-Boston (the station Rod is now on). It was in 1962, while listening to Dick Biondi and his antics that really got me hooked on radio. I dreamed of the day I could be a radio disc jockey just like him, never realizing," Rod laughs, "that I would end up as a newscaster."

Bill Gardner has been a radio personality for over forty years. He has been on mic all over the United States, including San Diego, Dallas, San Francisco, Las Vegas, Chicago, Phoenix and in Philly at legendary rocker, WIBG. "I had the good fortune of growing up in Philadelphia's northern suburbs, so Philadelphia and New York radio stations were part of each day. Philadelphia's WIBG-AM with great talent like Joe Niagara, Hy Lit, "Humble" Harvey Miller and George Gilbert all made a mark on me. I remember," adds Gardner, "being impressed with how Jean Shepherd and Long John Neble on WOR New York could talk non-stop for an hour and ALL of it was interesting."

John Gehron has been in radio programming and management for many years. He has been GM of the following great radio stations: WLS Chicago, WRKO, WEEI and Oldies-103, all in Boston, and he has been Senior VP at CBS. Most recently he was GM of *Harpo Radio*, Oprah's channel on satellite radio. Today (2011), Gehron is involved in Internet radio. "Growing up, I loved listening to distant cities at night, because of the AM sky waves. I knew all about Chicago, Buffalo and New York before having visited because of radio. I was fortunate to hear radio at its personality peak, from Alan Freed at WINS and WABC personalities like Harry Harrison, Ron Lundy, Dan Ingram, Cousin Brucie, and Charlie Greer. Other stations I pulled in were WIBG, WFIL, WCFL, and WKBW, where I first heard Dick Biondi and Joey

Reynolds." Gehron points out with pride that later in his career, he got to work at WLS with Larry Lujack and other Chicago radio legends like Steve Dahl, Gary Meier, Bob Sirott, John Landecker, Don and Roma, and many more. "I also worked with Jerry Williams at RKO-Boston, WFIL and Jay Cook, Don Rose, George Michael and Long John Wade. Howard Stern used to send me tapes," says smiling John Gehron, "but I was having enough trouble with ABC radio management over Steve Dahl's show, and I wasn't ready to add more fire to the situation."

Steve Gilinsky (air name Steve Jay) is co-owner and VP/GM of MAGIC 101.7-WLTB in Binghamton, New York. His first radio job was in 1977 at WGRC in Spring Valley, NY. "I really caught the radio bug in December 1970," says Steve. "I was nine years old and listening to WABC's *Top 100 of 1970*. I fell in love with the music and listening to the personalities. After that, I listened so much that even while watching TV, I would have an ear piece in my ear so I wouldn't miss one word of the personalities. Harry Harrison, Ron Lundy, Dan Ingram were big favorites of mine. They were the inspiration to get me in the business. There were others; Chuck Leonard, later George Michael, Johnny Donovan, Steve O'Brien, and I really liked Bob Cruz."

Mike Haile has been working full time in radio since 1970 and for the past thirty years has been handling mornings in Champaign, Illinois, at WHMS. He is also assistant general manager. Mike says it was the legendary "Morning Mayor" of New York City radio, Harry Harrison, who served as his inspiration. "Harry was my main influence as I developed my talents as a morning personality. Harry Harrison is the best on-air radio sales person, period! His friendly delivery always kept the format moving, sold sponsors products with ease, and he loved the music he was playing. Harry was the best guy ever at connecting one-on-one with his listeners, especially during his CBS-FM years, when he was constantly dropping listener names on the air all the time. Something else which influenced me greatly as a future radio personality about Harry was how proud a family man he was and is. He always mentioned his wife, pretty Patti[3], and in doing so easily connected with every member of his audience."

Mark Hannon is GM of the Boston CBS radio stations. "I am a born and bred Bostonian and have been fortunate to spend my entire radio career in my hometown. Growing up," says Mark, "I was always glued to the radio and was most influenced by great air-talents like Jess Cain, Dale Dorman, Charles Laquidara, Dave Maynard, Matt Siegel, Joe & Andy, and Loren & Wally."

Les Howard Jacoby has been in radio since 1966, primarily in Florida as an air-talent and programmer. Les was my program director in 1999 at Sunny 104.3 in West Palm Beach. "When I was growing up," Les recalls, "radio was in the golden years of personality-based Top-40. As a native New Yorker, I was blessed to be able to listen to the industry's best during my formative years.

My list of favorites includes Alan Freed, Murray the K on WINS; WMCA's Good Guy Gary Stevens and, of course, WABC's Cousin Brucie Morrow. But, if I could identify the one personality who inspired me the most during my impressionable years, it's legendary Dan Ingram. I wanted to be just like Dan."

M.G. "Machine Gun" Kelly began his radio career in 1970 at KTEN in Ada, Oklahoma, while still a junior in high school. A year later, M.G. was on the air at KOMA in Oklahoma City, followed by a move to KSTP-Minneapolis. The gunner is a true radio pro who was on the air at several LA radio stations, including KHJ, KOST 103 and KIIS FM. "The station I listened to was WLS-Chicago, John Landecker, Gary Gears and Fred Winston. I also admired the Real Don Steele on KHJ. Interestingly, 25 years after hearing him, I developed a national show for Don called *Live from the 60s*."

Scott Mackay is a thirty-plus-year radio veteran who started his radio life in 1979 in Keene, NH. Scott says that at just six years old, he begged his mom for the microphone and speaker from the Sears wish catalog. It was there that his one-man show began, singing all his favorite songs to the best audience a mirror could offer. Since his auspicious beginnings in radio, Scott has worked on the air in Boston, Chicago, and other markets. Scott grew up in New Hampshire right near the Vermont border. "I used to listen to WTSA in Brattleboro, Vermont, and the DJ was Dan Taylor. I found out he was a Jaycee in my town and I started going to the station with him on Saturday mornings at 4am. I was just eleven years old. From then on I was hooked. Some of my other early influences were Sandy Beach at WKBW-Buffalo, Sonny-Jo White, Jo Jo Cookin' Kincaid, and Dale Dorman on KISS-108 Boston, and F-105 was alive with Mighty Mike Osborne and Pete Falconi."

Sam Malone has been a popular Houston wake-up voice on MIX-96.5 for the past 18 years. He says radio money adviser Bruce Williams inspired him. "He would come on while I was in the car going to work. It was so refreshing to hear an intelligent announcer at 4am. Plus, he never talked down to callers. It didn't matter how bad things were in their financial world, he kept his cool and put them on the right track for a better future. I learned a heck of a lot about rental property investments."

Wink Martindale is a well-known radio personality and host of 19 television game shows, including the popular favorite *Tic-Tac-Dough*.[4] Wink got his start in radio in his hometown of Jackson, Tennessee, making $25 a week on WPLI-AM. "From the time I was five or six years old, I was addicted to radio. I listened to all the shows, from *Burns and Allen* to *Mr. District Attorney* to *Your Hit Parade* and the *Grand Ole Opry*. My earliest regular listening was to the *Breakfast Club* with Don McNeill out of Chicago, and all the soaps in the afternoon that my dear mom listened to,[5] shows like *When a Girl Marries*, *Stella Dallas*, and *The Romance of Helen Trent*. In the evening, as a kid, I would literally plant the radio in my ear. My mom would make me turn off the radio and go to bed. But when I went to bed, I would listen on my crystal radio, my first radio, to Jack, Doc and Reggie and *I Love a Mystery*. That's how I went to sleep. As far as inspirations," he says, "I would have to include some of the best personalities and air salesmen ever at the top of the list; Art Linkletter and Arthur Godfrey. [6]

In game shows, Bill Cullen was the best!"

Dan Mason is CEO of CBS Radio. A native of Louisville, he is a graduate of Eastern Kentucky University. Dan began his radio career in 1975 at WZGC-FM in Atlanta. In 1977, he moved to WPGC-FM in Washington, DC, where he was program director. In 1979, at age 27, he was named VP/GM of KTSA/KTFM in San Antonio. "I was lucky to grow up in Louisville, Kentucky, when WAKY and WKLO battled it out. As a kid, I listened to Terril Metheny (Kevin's dad) and I won every contest they had! I can also remember Johnny Randolph buying me orange juice when I was fourteen and talking about radio. Was I ever lucky."

Mark McCray, known to his loyal listeners as Mark "McCrazy," was the talented morning show guy on X-102.3. He was also the station PD.

When growing up in the Chicago area, Mark listened to a variety of radio personalities. "Doug Banks and Tom Joyner on WGCI were definite influences. I also listened to Robert Murphy on WKQX (Q 101) and other personalities. But, two people I thank for inspiring me and served as wonderful mentors were the late Michael Spears and WGN Production Director Todd Manley. I was in college at Southern Illinois University and came home for the summer to get more experience during an internship.[7] I already had about three years' experience at WCIL FM (Top-40) in Carbondale when I took the internship in Chicago at WPNT-FM (AC). After about two weeks in the building, I played my tape for Michael Spears. He decided right then and there to put me on the air! I was only nineteen and enjoyed the experience and learned a lot from Michael and Todd, who was the station production director. I did weekends and swing and still have the tapes. Later, I worked with Michael Spears at KRLD-AM, News-Talk Dallas. Michael and Todd were wonderful mentors and served as a great inspiration for me."

Kelly Monson is one of Salt Lake City's veteran radio personalities, with 30 years of broadcasting experience. Kelly began his career at KUER (Univ. of Utah) while a student in Communications. He quickly got his first paying radio job for $4.25 an hour, working an all-night shift and weekends. Kelly has been on the air at Salt Lake stations KSFI, KRSP, KLZX, KUMT, and KBZN. He was born in Provo and moved to Salt Lake when he was fourteen. "Here in Salt Lake City, the cool station in the '60s," Kelly says, "was KCPX-AM - great Top-40 music. Lynn Lehman was one of my favorites. My older brother was a music nut and even worked in radio for a short time. He took me to the studio one night to sit in on his show and I was hooked." Kelly remembers being as young as thirteen and telling his friends that he was going to make radio his career. "I would stay awake at night with a small earpiece plugged into the radio and listen to the big AM stations from around the country and just imagine myself providing that much enjoyment to that many people - pure heaven!"

Melanie Morgan is the former morning host at KSFO in San Francisco. She has been addicted to gambling and was the subject of the TV movie *High Stakes: The Melanie Morgan Story*. In 2006, she told the *San Francisco Chronicle* she "had not placed a bet in thirteen years and has served as president of the California Council on Problem Gambling." Today, she is Chair of Move America Forward, a non-profit advocacy and military support group. Born in Kansas City, Missouri, Melanie Morgan says her munchkin years were spent in Kansas City. "It was the 1960s and I came from six generations of rabble-rousers, political activists, and malcontents, as well as a few drunks and pirates," she laughs.

"Some of my earliest memories of radio," says Melanie, "are attached to the legendary Johnny Dolan at WHB radio. He regularly hosted the Battle of the Bands at local schools. Dolan deejayed the first mixer I ever attended as a gawky, shy twelve-year-old. My favorite show on WHB was *Chickenman*, a spoof of comic book heroes conceived by the enormously talented, now gazillionaire Dick Orkin of WCFL Radio in Chicago. I can still chant the show open," laughs Melanie, "Bawk, Bawk, Bawk...Chickeman to the rescue! He's EVERYWHERE!

"As I matured into a gawky, shy fifteen-year-old," continues Morgan, "I switched over to WLS Radio in Chicago. I couldn't wait to hear the late Yvonne Daniels, whose smoky voice and fast chatter entranced me as she dominated the late-night airwaves across many parts of the country.[8] Daniels' overnight newsman at WLS was a polyester-clad, horn-rimmed, deep-voiced radio announcer by the name of Jack Swanson. Swanson later went on to become one of America's legendary radio program directors at KGO in San Francisco...and my future husband."

Harry Nelson has been a popular radio jock on both coasts, KFRC San Francisco and WRKO Boston. He was also my program director at the Original WROR -98.5 Boston in the '80s and again when the call letters were resurrected and reassigned to FM 105 in the late 1990s. Today, Harry is VP of Promotions for Ride Records with his associates Dave Sholin and David Shaw, along with country singing star, Steve Azar.

While growing up in Hattiesburg, Mississippi, a young Harry listened to a 5,000-watt daytime country station, WBKH 950AM. "The station was just a few blocks from my home and I would drop by on my way home from school and sit in the outer studio and watch the jocks through the glass and dream that I would one day be one of them. I was twelve years old at the time. I would spend a couple of hours in this little outer studio every weekday afternoon and all afternoon on Saturday and Sunday. After pestering them for a couple of years, I made my way into the main studio and was able to see the control console up close and actually meet the announcers. Ross Priebe, who worked weekends, was the first jock that I became friends with at WBKH. He would allow me to sit in the main studio with him on weekends. The station was Country, Monday thru Friday, and Top-40 on the weekends. I loved that," smiles Nelson.

WBKH in Hattiesburg finally gave Nelson his own show. "They gave me a weekend show when I was sixteen. I worked on Sunday mornings and I could talk between the recorded and sometimes live gospel music. When the live groups would come in, they had to pay for their time on the air. It was $18 per half-hour. I would collect their money in a cigar box and give it to the general manager on Monday morning. A year or so later, I met a man named Tommy Glenn. He became the PD at WBKH. Tommy was blind and had to overcome a lot to be the great radio personality that he was. Tommy not only inspired me, but took me under his wing and became my mentor. I mean, the man really taught me the basics of radio. He taught me so well that a year later, I was offered a job across town at the Top-40 station WXXX (Triple-X)."

Norm N. Nite is another true radio legend who is on Sirius Satellite Channel-5 Saturday and Sunday from 3-6:00pm on *LIVE at the Rock N' Roll Hall of Fame and Museum!* Norm says that while growing up he was influenced to be a radio personality by listening to Alan Freed, Bill Randle, and Pete "Mad Daddy" Myers. As far as which of the three inspired him the most, Norm credits the late Bill Randle. "He was the consummate pro who started many careers like Johnnie Ray, Elvis, the Everly Brothers and many, many more. He was the most intelligent and knowledgeable personality I ever heard on the air. He was also a PhD who taught college, was an attorney, and did dozens of other things besides being in radio."

Jack Oliver first started in radio in 1968. He has been PD at KEYN Wichita, Kansas, for the past eight years and before that was PD at KKRD for twenty-four years. The Wichita Hall of Fame veteran was born in Wynnewood, Oklahoma. "When I was growing up, I listened to WKY in Oklahoma City and KOMA. The first jocks I remember listening to," says Jack, "were Ronnie Kay in Oklahoma City and a guy in Kansas, Lee Nichols. I also heard Dick Biondi in syndication on a skip. I loved listening to radio. Some other guys in Wichita were Don B. Williams, Skinny Johnny Mitchell, Charlie Tuna, Uncle Harvey, and E. Alvis Davis. But the personalities who really helped influence me were Gene Rump, Barry Casey, and Bobbie Lawrence. I thought radio would be a great way to work my way through college. Actually, radio slowed down my college effort - it took me 12 years but I did graduate and I also have my master's degree."

Cary Pahigian is President and GM of Saga Communications/Portland Maine Radio Group. "I grew up with Boston radio. The names that influenced me were Ned Martin, the former voice of the Red Sox, Harry Nelson (Top-40 on WRKO), Jerry Williams on WBZ with talk, and Bruce Bradley and Dave Maynard, who were both very entertaining music personalities. They were all different and unique, but so interesting and compelling in their own way."

Judi Paparelli is a radio pro who has hosted talk shows around the country. A media pioneer, Judi developed Traffic Watch, a traffic reporting system broadcast jointly by WBZ-TV and KISS-108 Boston. Judi is currently writing a book on the American workplace. Born in Yonkers, New York, and raised on Long Island, her introduction to the wonders of radio came via legendary New York City stations. "For me," Judi says, "inspiration struck early and his name was Harry Harrison. As young as I was, listening to Harry Harrison when he was a WMCA Good Guy, I knew I was listening to something great! He was uplifting, enthusiastic and classy. Harry was, to me, the ultimate radio pro and I have him to thank for my love of radio. When he moved to WABC Radio, I followed, and started every morning by listening to him. The way he handled the 'ins and outs' of his show made a strong impression on me. He flowed so smoothly and rhythmically from one show element to the next. He was full of personality, but never, it seemed to me, spoke just for the sake of hearing his own voice. He always seemed smart, real, and sincere. Throughout my entire radio career, I remembered what I learned while listening to Harry Harrison. He was ALWAYS a pro, and he always sounded as if he loved and respected radio. He made this fan believe that if you LOVE radio, and consistently strive to be great on-air, your listeners will hear 'the real you.'"

Nancy Quill is the longtime midday personality on Boston's Magic-106-FM. She says she was "inspired by the styles of Boston radio personalities like the crew at WRKO, Dave Maynard at WBZ, and Ron Robin at WVBF. In the '60s and '70s there were few women on Boston's airwaves, that is until WCOZ debuted in the '70s. I heard two women on that station that have inspired me to this day," beams Nancy, "Leslie Palmeter and Lisa Karlin. They were the coolest, most conversational, greatest female voices I ever heard on radio. After listening to them, I knew that's how I wanted to sound."

Phil Redo is a native of Manhattan, and was an air personality before entering radio management. "I was enormously influenced by three radio people," says Phil, who was my colleague at WROR-Boston in the early 1980s. "First, there was Jean Shepherd, who I heard every night on WOR in NYC. He was a brilliant storyteller who made me think about radio in a very different way from either music or the typical breakfast show. Shepherd created 'night people,' who were all different ages. As a twelve- or thirteen-year-old, Shepherd provided a bond with my father, who also enjoyed his storytelling and philosophical take on modern life - and we were 30 years apart in age! There were kids at school who listened. We all shared the secret of Shep. Next was John Gambling. He influenced me because he sounded so normal. Not a DJ so much, but as a guy who happened to be talking from right next to your toaster. He would march us around the breakfast table every morning as my mom got me ready for school. It was an early memory from the late '50s to early 1960s that left an indelible mark on what radio could do. And finally, Imus in the Morning.

"The I-Man," as Phil continues, "arrived in NYC at WNBC when I was a junior in high school. I was so taken by his style, irreverence, and cool that I made up a story about working for the school paper just so I could get to meet him, to interview him. I did end up submitting the story to my school paper and they ran it complete with a picture taken by a buddy who was part of the scam. I still have the picture. (See photo at end of this chapter.) Me and my long hair, standing with a little notebook right beside the I-Man who was sitting at the controls. What a thrill! I've since told him about it. The others eventually shaped me and informed me, but Don Imus inspired me to get in myself! I never wanted to wear a tie to work, because of him. What happened!?"

Bob Rivers is a radio pro of more than twenty years. He got his start in Connecticut where he was heard on WAVZ, WNHC, WCDQ, WELI, WCCC, WWCO, and WLIS. With no more stations left to conquer in Connecticut, Bob moved to neighboring Massachusetts, Rhode Island, and New Hampshire. A PD stint in Claremont, New Hampshire, cured Bob of any further desire to be in management. "I worked at twenty stations in about six years," he says. "I wanted to make every mistake possible in this business." After being with WAAF in Worcester, Massachusetts, Bob began writing song parodies called *Twisted Tunes*. His *Twisted Christmas* has sold over 1.6 million units. Who inspired a young Mr. Rivers? We'll let him tell you as he shares a slice of his radio life.

"I was very young, probably around seven or eight, and my mom took me to the grand opening of a WT Grants Store in Branford, Connecticut. As we entered the front door with the excited throng all pushing and shoving their way to the value counters (remember when a department store opening was a real thrill?), there in front of my eyes sat a live radio remote board, complete with two turntables, a microphone, and a big, bulky cart machine. Behind the desk was DJ Bob Morgan of WNHC Radio New Haven. He was probably one of many Bob Morgans, not the famous Robert W. Morgan of K-EARTH fame. I was mesmerized. I never even went into the store! I watched records being cued up, the DJ talking, the jingles being played in the cart machines, all while holding my transistor radio to my head. Those Drake jingles still ring in my ears today: 'MORE MYOOOOO-ZICCC, DOUBLE YOU EN AYCHE SEEE!' It was the most exciting thing I had ever seen in my life, and I peppered the poor guy with questions: how does the music get from that turntable to my transistor radio? Why do the speakers go off when you talk? Does chain-smoking like that make your voice real deep? He mentioned something about chain smoking and whiskey in large amounts, and I knew he was only half kidding.

"Some years later," Rivers continues, "when I was a freshman in high school, I joined a Junior Achievement Club that met at that radio station and produced a weekly radio show that ran on Sunday mornings. Bob Morgan was one of the advisors and so was a young Alan Colmes. The thing I remember about Alan Colmes is that he was hitting on my girlfriend. Lydia was her name, and she was a beautiful blonde Russian bombshell who loved radio. Right then I realized that being on the radio could help you date a little out of your league."

Rivers' influences to enter radio were many. "I was and am a radio addict," he says. "Perhaps the greatest storyteller in old time radio was a guy named Jean Shepherd.[9] He was on WOR New York for many years. When I was growing up in Connecticut I would listen to him on Boy Scout camping trips, huddled around a battery-operated transistor radio. Once my high-school station got off the ground, I wrote him a letter requesting an interview. He responded, and off I went on the train to the Big Apple. To this day, I listen to his shows on iPod. You can too, just do a Google search. It wouldn't be fair not to mention Howard Stern. Even though I have steered away from being a shock jock, I owe him a lot for demonstrating that you really can be intimate on the radio and say things everybody is thinking that they either won't or don't know how to put into words."

Dave Robbins is the former VP/GM of CBS Radio-Chicago. "I may be different, but I knew from about age twelve where my life was headed. At age fourteen, I built an FM pirate radio station in my parents' basement. My school friends and I broadcast for miles around our house, had regular shifts and went 24 hours on weekends. Everyone thought it was a great idea except the FCC. When I wasn't working on the air in the basement in those days, I was listening to WLS, and always knew one day I would be working in Chicago radio."

Dave Ryan has been the morning drive guy at KDWB-Minneapolis for over fifteen years and is consistently top-rated! Growing up in Colorado Springs, Dave remembers the radio always being on in his house. "I can still picture it sitting on the kitchen counter. Mom and Dad listening to country music and the full-service station; news, weather, sports and so on. It was our family's main source for news and music, and I was always impressed with the DJs. The idea of a job that let you sit and play records and chat and be 'semi-famous' sounded awesome to me. In high school I used to listen to a nighttime talk show host out of Denver named Alan Berg. He was amazing! Funny, sarcastic, smart, and was actually rude to his callers in a funny way. For him to have the power to get me to turn the TV off at night and listen to him instead was pretty impressive. This same guy eventually got gunned to death in 1984 for something he said on the radio. Let that be a lesson for all of us on the air!"

Tom Shannon is another legendary radio personality who was a mainstay on WKBW, Buffalo and CKLW-Detroit-Windsor for years. Growing up in Buffalo and like other youngsters who lived in the Great Northeast, Shannon had a choice of listening to those big 50,000-watt stations from all over the country and across the border in Canada. He puts it this way, "I had a lot of ear candy to check out in my youthful days. Some of the names and stations were WSM Nashville with Ralph Emery doing the all-night show and talking with people from the country field. It was great radio. There were folks like John Richbourg or John R. as he was known on the air, and Hoss Allan from WLAC, also from Nashville. They were two white men playing and sounding as soulful as the Rhythm and Blues they were playing." Tom Shannon's own air style was undoubtedly influenced by listening to these popular radio personalities from across America, but two that he dug the most were on the radio right in his own hometown of Buffalo! "The local (Buffalo-area) radio people who really inspired me," says Shannon, "were George 'Hound Dog' Lorenz, who was another white man playing R&B and a very smooth and talented DJ named Frank Ward."

"Joe, Frank Ward, to me, was the perfect DJ image. His on-air style was smooth. He did not have any gimmick, just a wonderful way of weaving his conversation with the music or his subject matter. His off-air persona was fabulous, too. He was 6'3" and had dark wavy hair with a facial scar that added to the image. I remember quite vividly," says Shannon. "Frank would drive down Genesee Street, the main road in Buffalo, right past my street in a big black Buick convertible with the top down, and I'm telling you as a young guy, it knocked me out! At the time, Frank was working all-night at WKBW on a program called *Spotlight Serenade*. He later worked for WWOL, also in Buffalo, using the air name Guy King as many after him would also do, "including Dick Purtan who I worked with at WXYZ in Detroit and I understand also comments for your book, Joe.[10] I suspect Frank Ward and George 'Hound Dog' Lorenz not only inspired me," he adds, "but a lot of other would-be radio people in the '50s and '60s. Much later in my career," adds Shannon, "I would get to know both men very well and we even worked together."

Matt Siegel has been the host of *KISS-108's* AM-Drive show since 1981.[11] "When I was a kid growing up in New York, my favorite air-personality was Dan Ingram on WABC. He was the sharpest Top-40 jock I ever heard," says Matty. "To this day, he remains the wittiest ever. When I was in college, I preferred the so-called 'underground' FM sound. My favorite at that time was Jonathan Schwartz on WNEW-FM. His style was, of course, quite different from top forty, with longer music sets followed by long rambling commentary from the jocks. Schwartz, who later did a Sinatra-only show in New York, was brilliant! However, the person who inspired me to try radio was an English teacher in high school who saw me host my senior talent show, of all things. It was the first time I ever worked with a mic and I guess I sounded pretty good."

Mollie Simpkins' radio career began in 1991 as an intern at Metro Traffic in Miami. We had lots of fun working together in morning drive at Sunny-104.3 in West Palm Beach, from 2002 until 2004, under her air-name Kristy Kramer.

Growing up outside Chicago, Mollie's love of radio began in the '70s, listening to such greats as Larry Lujack on WLS (AM) and the late Wally Phillips on WGN. "How I loved Uncle Lar's *Animal Stories,*" she laughs. "It didn't matter if Larry wasn't on; my transistor was always tuned to AM 890, WLS! However, there were times I didn't have much of a choice. You see, in our home we had an intercom system. Yes, we were groovy! Anyway, sometimes, I would forget to turn the volume down on the unit in my room. Imagine my horror when I would be rudely awakened by Wally Phillips! WALLY PHILLIPS, talk radio, feh, that's for old people. Heh, I sure get it now!!"

Frank Kingston Smith is another radio icon.[12] In 1979, we worked together at the original WROR Boston. Frank began his radio journey in 1964 while a student at Penn State, on WMAJ-State College, PA. Big Frank, as he is known, also worked on the air in Philly, Providence, New York City, and Boston. "I got interested in radio as a little kid. I had started playing guitar at the age of six. Les Paul and Tex Ritter were my heroes. My original intent was to become a singing cowboy. Since there wasn't much call for singing cowboys in Philadelphia, I figured I'd become a rock n' roll guitarist. While spending summers in Ocean City, New Jersey, I used to bike downtown to a music store where WOND Pleasantville originated a midday show from the front window. Johnny Struckles was on the air at the remote broadcast." As Smith recalls, "He fascinated me. How did he think of all those cool things to say? And, slip cuing records? I cue-burned some of my folks' favorite albums trying to learn how to do that!![13]

"In Philly," Smith continues, "I became a fan of Georgie Woods deliverin' the goods on WDAS, Philadelphia's original urban or soul station. I was maybe fourteen years old when Georgie invited me into the studio with him. The jock who followed him on the air was Lee Wiles, who was blind. He would feel the grooves on a disc with the side of his thumb, then slip cue by feel. Damn! How cool is that? I also listened to Phil Sheridan on WFIL and to WIBG with Harvey Miller, Bill Wright, Joe Niagara, Hy Lit, and Don L. Brink, legends of Philly radio.[14] Rock n' roll was king. I wanted to do that! It took me three and a half years at Penn State before I got my first radio job. Within two years, I was on WFIL helping make radio history in '66 as one of the original Super-Six!"

Rick Snyder, my longtime friend, has been in broadcasting most of his adult life and without giving away any "age-old" secrets, that's a very long time! Rick grew up in Syracuse, New York, and says, "I was able to listen to out-of-town stations on our old Zenith console radio. What an adventure to be able to dial around and hear voices from New York City, Boston, Detroit, St. Louis, Philadelphia, Buffalo, and Toronto! Since I was a teen in the '50s, Rock and Roll was in its infancy and every day was an adventure in music as new artists and new sounds hit the airwaves. My first radio idol was Denny Bracken on WOLF. He was probably in his late 20s at the time; really smooth on the air with a friendly voice and he delivered his show with enthusiasm and believability. I met Denny when I rode my bike to the station and was invited to spend some time in the studio. He was a nice guy. He had an engineer who did all the work, cuing records and tapes - it was 1957, long before carts and computers. I remember thinking these words: this is the job for me."

Rick Snyder's inspiration to get into radio came from a girl he dated while in high school. "She was in love with all the DJs," he laughs, "especially Dusty Rhodes. When she and I went out, we spent hours listening to out-of-town stations on the car radio. We both loved the music and the jocks and she encouraged me to pursue my ambition." Rick's high-school sweetheart may have inspired him about radio and a few other things while they were parked in his car listening to the radio, but it was an air personality named Peter C. Cavanaugh who really helped motivate him towards a career in radio.

"Peter was a great early Top-40 jock," remembers Rick. "One night in the spring of 1959, he was missing from his show. The substitute jock said Pete was off that night because he was graduating from high school!! What, I thought! We were the same age and I had been listening to him for a couple of years. The next night, I visited Pete at WFBL. We became fast friends and remain in touch to this day. Pete was instrumental in helping me get my career started and moving forward in radio."

Greg Strassell is VP of programming for CBS Boston. His first radio job was at fifteen in his hometown at WTCJ, Tell City, Indiana, a locally-owned radio station by the Brewer family. "They gave me a pre-puberty shot on-air," he laughs, "but really stressed the less I talked and the more I segued, the better I sounded." Greg grew up hearing local voices in his Indiana hometown on a 1,000-watt AM station and then heard the AM voices from the bigger markets "Local talent," he recalls, included Dave Strycker (Strassell's first PD), who did morning drive. Sports was big there and I thought a guy named Mike Younce was one of the best play-by-play announcers ever. A friendship developed with Joe Bell, who did middays and we remain good friends. The voices I tuned in were from Top-40 voices of the Midwest and mid-south; John Landecker and Fred Winston at WLS, Big Ron O'Brien and Larry Lujack at CFL-Chicago, and the entire staffs of WAKY Louisville and WGBF Evansville in the mid-'70s.

"As far as my biggest inspiration" says Strassell, "it was probably Jim Wood. He programmed WGBF Evansville and it was a smokin' radio station. A 'worst to first' kind of story, mind-blowing radio, and branding of a Top-40 station that was way ahead of its time. Seeing a PD instantly build a great product like that inspired me the most to be a PD."

Paula Street has been on Oldies 103.3-Boston for over 20 years. Her smooth delivery and fun personality make her "must" listening. A Texan by birth, Paula grew up spending her summers in Colorado learning to trout fish with her dad and grandfather.

Paula says her summer vacations were much like the movie *A River Runs Through It* with the trout fishing competition that lasts a lifetime, except her brothers aren't as cute as Brad Pitt. "The radio station I fell in love with was KVIL FM in Dallas-Fort Worth with Ron Chapman in the morning.[15] It was great music and a fantastic air staff that I grew to think of as a family. I knew from being a listener that if anything important was going on in town, in politics, in weather, on TV, anything, I would find out about it on KVIL. Ron Chapman once said, 'If you entertain people, they will stay tuned in and if you entertain them for free, they will line up around the block to get in.' I find that statement to be true then and now. Ron Chapman was surrounded by characters like Suzie Humprey who drove the KVIL-O-Van and had been Laurie who flew the KVIL-O-Copter for morning traffic. KVIL was not only #1 with the best music, but they were KING of radio contests," as Paula explains. "One time, KVIL gave away a new car, every year, for the rest of your life. Can you imagine? Ron Chapman was big on call-letter branding, so they had bumper stickers that read, 'KVIL LOVES YOU.' Everyone put them on their cars and registered their plate number for the contest. The morning of the grand prize drawing, Ron announced a woman's name and gave her fifteen minutes to call back in and win. The woman called back and told Ron that she had crashed her car the week before and it was in a junkyard about to be crushed-bumper sticker and all! Ron called up the KVIL-O-Copter (all of this on the air) and had him fly to a school near the woman's house and pick her up. They flew the lady to another parking lot near the junkyard, where Suzie Humprey in the KVIL-O-Van picked her up (all on the air) and drove her to the junkyard to find her car and verify the bumper sticker. They got to the junkyard and found her car uncrushed (thank God) and she won a new car, every year, for the rest of her life! Now, that's great radio. After growing up with KVIL and being inspired by Ron Chapman, the standard of great radio in my world has changed forever."

Dick Summer is another master on mic. He played the radio roulette wheel well, from New Haven to Indianapolis to St. Louis to Cincinnati, back to Indy, before landing in Boston in 1963. That's when I first got hooked on his night-light show. For five years, until 1968, Summer, complete with his Venus Flytraps, spread his own *all-night-magic* on WBZ-Boston, long before the word magic became synonymous as a radio format with stations around the country. Dick grew up in New York and his station was WNEW-AM. "There probably never was, and I doubt there ever will be, another radio station with that kind of air-talent. Gene Klavan and Dee Finch in morning drive, Martin Block, Ted Brown, William B. Williams, Al "Jazzbeaux" Collins, and Art Ford. They were all world class, class, and New York sass, but the terminator was William B. Williams. His voice could tickle your sense of humor, play a symphony on your heart strings, teach you an unforgettable lesson, or throw an arm around your shoulder. There will never be another William B. Williams."

Melissa Sweeton has been rockin' the Nashville air-waves in one form or another for over twenty-three years. She grew up in Lebanon, TN, and asks, "Did ya know that Greg and Duane Allman went to school in Lebanon at Castle Heights Military Academy? They used to get in trouble all the time for climbing out on the dorm roof at night and playing their guitars." Growing up in the Nashville area, she says, "I listened to John R. and Hoss Allen on 1510AM WLAC, Grant Turner and Ralph Emery on 650AM WSM and Carl P. Mayfield on 103 WKDA-FM. Others who deserve mention: Scott Shannon, Smokey Rivers, Coyote McCloud, Rus Spooner, and Gerry House. They all inspired me and I think those folks warrant Icon status as far as the Nashville radio market goes. My favorite female jock was Chatty Patty Murray. She was very inspiring to me. Patty was one of the first female jocks to rock Nashville. She was so talented, funny, and personable, and what a set of pipes on her. She moved to the Miami market after several successful years at WKDA/WKDF. Unfortunately, Patty was taken from us in an auto accident. Ironically, the accident occurred when she was vacationing in the Destin, Florida, area. I had just returned from there after helping to sign on Destin's first FM signal."

Alpha Trivette has been in radio for over twenty years, working in markets of all sizes, including AM-Drive in Atlanta at B98.5. "Growing up in Ladysmith, Virginia, I'd wake up each morning to Alden Aroe on WRVA in Richmond," he says. "He's a radio legend and his full-service morning show was king of the airwaves. Often at night, I would pick up a strong signal from WKBW Buffalo, New York, with Rod Roddy. I could also pick up WOWO in Fort Wayne, Indiana, and WLS out of Chicago. After college, I moved to Louisville for a PR job and there I listened to Gary Burbank on WHAS. That's when I began to think he must have a fun job!"

Dick Tufeld is an announcer-narrator extraordinaire. He has also been an actor and voiceover performer from the early 1950s through today. I first heard Dick's exciting narration as the announcer on ABC Radio's popular fifties sci-fi program *Space Patrol*. His exciting narration of the latest high adventure in the wild, vast reaches of space with Buzz Corey, commander-in-chief of the space patrol, had us kids practically chewing the sleeves off our pjs. Although known to many for his work on radio's *Space Patrol*, Dick Tufeld is probably best remembered as the voice of the robot on the TV series *Lost in Space*. He also did voice work for the animated TV series *The Fantastic Four* and the *Lost in Space* feature film. Dick's voice is also familiar to many as the narrator on TV's *Voyage to the Bottom of the Sea* and *Time Tunnel* and as the announcer on Disney TV shows, including the 1957-59 series *Zorro*.

Tufeld was born on December 26, 1926, and grew up in Pasadena, California. Around ten or eleven is when he became an avid and fascinated radio listener. "I listened to all the programs; *The Lone Ranger, Jack Armstrong-the All-American Boy, Little Orphan Annie, Vic and Sade, Superman, Orson*

Welles' Mercury Theater, Arch Obler's Lights Out, Lux Radio Theater, Jack Benny, Fred Allen. It was almost an obsession with me," he recalls. "I listened to all these programs and many more, especially to the gifted actors and actresses, the announcers with their amazing voices, the work of the sound effects artists. I was completely immersed in the magic that was radio."

Dick remembers how, as his twelve birthday approached, his mother asked what he would like to do for his birthday. "At that time, KNX, the local CBS station in Los Angeles was promoting a tour of their radio facility and my instant response was, I'd like to take that tour! And so I did. I saw the CBS station and that did it! I was totally hooked and decided at age twelve that I wanted to be a radio announcer. I worked towards that goal for the rest of my life. It never came easy," adds Dick. "Trying to get it right took me several decades.

"Around 1941 and 1942, a couple of radio stations opened in Pasadena, KPAS and KWKW, and guess who, at the age of fifteen hung around those stations. I was flat-out lucky," says Tufeld. "I was able to capitalize on a difficult, terrible domestic situation: America was in the midst of World War II. So many men were in the service that it was hard for radio to find male voices. And in those days, there was no such thing as a female announcer. It was unheard of then! Oh yes, gender discrimination was in full flower. KWKW had a program director named Ted Robertson. He was a great guy and he allowed me to hang around and observe. He listened to me try to be an announcer, made some valuable suggestions and because he couldn't find another male voice when he needed one, offered me a part-time job, twenty hours a week, announcing at KWKW!! I was sixteen, still with another year of high school. I thought I had died and gone to heaven. So, that's how I got my start in radio back in 1942. I was blessed. I was able to have a successful career doing the thing I was passionate about and loved doing. I leave you with something I really believe to be true: no matter how gifted you are, how smart, how physically attractive, how creative, or how skilled, you'd better be LUCKY too. That's always played a part of an often frustrating work equation. So, good luck to all of you. Stick with it. You will get there!"

Ed Walsh began his career in broadcast journalism at Boston's WRKO, where he became news director.[16] He has also been in various news management positions in Phoenix and New York City. Ed grew up in Natick and Wellesley listening to WMEX and WRKO, where he and I worked together. Ed's other favorite Boston station was WBZ, where until his retirement in 2010, he co-anchored the morning news. "When I was a sophomore at Wellesley High, WBZ's Bruce Bradley did a record hop and rather than ask him for a song," says Walsh, "I asked if I could visit BZ and watch him do his show.[17] He was most gracious, and invited me in to see how a first-class air-talent did his job. My dad drove me and waited in the parking lot. I was hooked! My other inspirations," remembers Ed, "were Gary LaPierre, who I followed on BZ forty-four years after he started, Jerry Williams, whom I heard late-night on WMEX (Boston) and with whom I worked at RKO, Cousin Bruce Morrow of WABC in New York, and Joey Reynolds of WKBW Buffalo."

In the sometimes mysterious circle of life, Cousin Brucie and Ed Walsh became friends and Joey Reynolds did the all-night show before Ed's morning show when both worked at WOR New York.

Mark Williams is a nationally-known talk show host who has worked various radio markets from Boston to California.[18] Today, he does freelance air work from his home studio in California, located at the base of the Sierra Foothills. Mark and I first worked together in the 80s at RKO-ROR Boston.

Williams grew up in Attleboro, Massachusetts, and apparently from all accounts, the town is still standing! He left in his teens in 1977 and never looked back. While growing up, he admits to being a radio geek. "I listened, especially at night, to every signal I could pull in. Regular stops were the Providence stations WPRO, WEAN, and WJAR, Boston radio stations WBZ, WHDH and WEEI. My default station," Williams adds, "was WPRO. 63-WPRO, the station that reaches the beaches! How's that for a positioning liner that works," he laughs. "That one dates to some time in the 1960s or earlier because WPRO was the only station in the Providence market to blanket all of Narragansett Bay beach areas. From Memorial Day through Labor Day, time checks on the station were classic! First the sfx: 'Bing bong,' then the liner: 'it's ___o'clock, time to turn so you won't burn, from 63-WPRO, the station that reaches the beaches!' Salty Brine[19] was morning king on the radio at PRO, Charlie Jeffords held down mid-morning and PRO had a series of afternoon guys, evenings with mumbling Joe Thomas and late nights by Andy the Big Ange Jackson. WPRO was quite the station."

Mark didn't stop with New England radio stations. "Oh, no. If it had a powerful signal like WLW, WOR, WKBW, or WOWO in Ft. Wayne, Indiana, Williams was in tuned and turned on! As far as who served as an inspiration for Mark Williams to enter radio, he says, "There are a couple of answers to the question. When I was four years old, my old man took me on a tour of the factory he worked in. While I'm sure it was his idea to just show me how hard it was to come by money, what he did demonstrate to me was working for it was not the way to get money. At the same time," Williams continues, "I was a habitual viewer of *Captain Bob, Rex Trailer's Boomtown, Major Mudd,* and *Bozo the Clown* with longtime Channel 5 Boston personality Frank Avruch. To me, those guys had COOL JOBS. Our neighbor, Walter 'Wally' Cryan was a newsman on WARA in Attleboro, MA. I was only four but our neighbor went to work in the dashboard of my old man's '49 bullet-nose Ford where he shared space apparently with Wayne Newton and "Red Roses for a Blue Lady." I had no concept, but it wasn't a factory and radio sounded to be as much fun as the guys on TV looked to be having."

Notes:
1. Cousin Brucie kindly wrote one of the introductions for this book.
2. **Author's note:** Not corny at all, Mike. It's a dream shared by so many other radio wannabes back in the '50s and '60s, who just like you and me loved listening to those BIG CITY faraway AM radio stations, hoping one day to be part of that exciting on-air radio scene.
3. My friend Harry Harrison's beloved wife Patti died of liver cancer on May 20, 2003, almost two months to the day following his farewell program after 23 years on the air at WCBS-FM. The program was broadcast live from the Radio-TV Museum in NYC.
4. Wink Martindale also comments in Chapter 2.
5. Don McNeil is profiled in Chapter 1.
6. Pioneer radio legends Art Linkletter and Arthur Godfrey are both profiled in Chapter 1.
7. The value of a radio internship is covered in Chapter 19.
8. Read more about Yvonne Daniels in Chapter 13.
9. Jean Parker Shepherd was born on July 26, 1921. He is best-known to modern audiences for the film *A Christmas Story*, which he narrated and co-wrote. It is based on his semi-autobiographical stories of growing-up in Hammond, Indiana. Shep, as he was called, was a radio-TV personality who began his radio career in 1948 in Cincinnati at WSAI and later at WLW. Twenty-one years of his radio career were in a late night time-slot on WOR-New York, sharing stories and reading poetry. Several collections of Shepherd's brilliant radio work are available on CD from RadioSpirits.com. He passed away of natural causes at his Sanibel, Florida, home on October 16, 1999.
10. Dick Purtan comments in Chapter 14 and also is included in the Afterword to this book.
11. *Matty in the Morning* is the highest-rated show and the leading FM morning show in Boston. According to Arbitron ratings, Matty has consistently ranked #1 with women 18 to 49 for the past twenty years.
12. In 1993, he and his wife Linda moved to Scottsdale, Arizona, and today operate Showline Promotional Products.
13. Cue-burn is caused from rotating a record (usually a 45 rpm or an album cut) back and forth by hand to set it up (or cue) to the first few notes of the song. The rotating motion causes the grooves on-the-record to wear out and instead of music you get noise.
14. Don Brink had to change his first name to Scotty while working in LA radio. He comments in Chapter 14.
15. Dallas morning drive talent Ron Chapman offers his advice on how to break into radio and how to be a success in Chapters 3 and 4.
16. Ed Walsh comments on the state of radio news today and how one should prepare for a radio journalism career in Chapter 16.

17. Bruce Bradley was one of New England's most popular air-personalities in the '60s. His candid comments on what it takes to be a successful on-air personality can be found in Chapter 4.
18. Mark Williams comments in detail about how to develop your style for radio in Chapter 2 and also on talk radio in Chapter 16.
19. The late radio pro Salty Brine is the father of Boston radio personality Wally Brine.

Mike Addams and author, both Radio Pro's worked together at WROR-Boston in the 80's.

Dick Bartley, nationally syndicated oldies radio pro.

Don Bleu. legendary morning-drive San Francisco radio personality.

Kelly Monson, long-time morning-drive air talent in Salt Lake City.

Norm N. Nite, the oldies show host broadcast from the Rock N' Roll Hall of Fame in Cleveland on X-M Sirius Satellite.

Phil Redo with Don Imus (I Man).

Who Inspired the Radio Pros Who Contributed to This Book • 635

So. Florida air talent, Mollie Simpkins.

Rick Snyder, Albany, NY and Portland ME radio pro, also in radio sales on air from Revere Beach MA bandstand during 10th Anniv of author's show, Sat. Nite Live at the Oldies (1989).

Melissa Sweeton, popular Nashville radio personality, now VO talent.

Dick Tufeld, announcer on radio's *Space Patrol*, voice of robot on TV's *Lost in Space*.

CHAPTER 21
Radio's Future

"FM Radio will overtake AM by 1975"
— Harvard Univ. study in 1961 (guess they were right)

Radio's earliest beginnings.
Radio today is sometimes lost in a high-tech world, complete with Internet and satellite transmissions. Radio was the first modern mass medium for communication and gave birth to a generation of listeners who became enthralled with radio's ability to inform and entertain. Few radio listeners today under age forty know that at one time, radio was once the theatrical theater of the mind, bursting with top comedy and dramatic shows. During its formative years, the '20s through the '40s, known as radio's golden age, radio's outstanding cast of entertainers captured the minds, hearts and imaginations of America's listeners from coast to coast and most cities and towns in between.

"By his genius distant lands converse and men sail unafraid unto the deep"
— Epitath on the memorial tablet of the grave of Canadian radio pioneer Reginald Fessenden (1866- 1932)

To look at radio's future, one must first take a step back into radio's past. Radio's roots can be traced all the way back to the mid-1700s and inquisitive men like Benjamin Franklin, who experimented with electrical charges from lightning as early as 1752. There were many other men like Franklin, who pondered the possibilities of using electricity as a means of communication.

Radio is with us today because of early on experimentation in the field of electricity and magnetism by creative men like Joseph Henry, an American, who in 1843 successfully magnetized needles with electrically-charged wires located about 220 feet away. During the same era, Michael Faraday also conducted similar experiments in England. Around 1892, Sir William Crookes made a prediction that sending and receiving equipment could be built that would make communication through the air a reality. A huge advancement in this area was accomplished a short time later, when a brilliant German scientist, Heinrich Hertz, proved that electric waves could be sent out around an oscillating circuit. His *Hertzian waves* became the talk of scientific circles. During many lab experiments, scientists, referring to the earth's atmosphere as ether, led many to believe that Hertz was right and telegraphy could be made through space by using these waves. The Italians got into the radio act in 1895, when Guglielmo Marconi developed wireless telegraphy. But it was two Americans, Professor Reginald A. Fessenden of the University of Pittsburgh and a Yale graduate, Lee De Forest, who discovered methods that helped create radio as we know it today.

Fessenden believed the human voice and music could be reproduced, which until then could not be achieved by wireless transmitters. He did manage to develop a detector, which was a miniature light bulb with a fine filament that was capable of reproducing voice. However, it was never put into commercial use. Fessenden's discovery did open the door for De Forest, who in 1903 began experimenting with radio detectors like the one Fessenden developed. A few years later, De Forest invented the three-element electron tube, known as the *Audion,* which became an important device in modern radio by making it possible to actually broadcast voice and music. During the nineteenth century, hundreds of men studied electricity with each adding something new. Much credit for the invention of radio must be given to those early pioneers who paved the way for development of radio broadcasting. Men like Marconi, Fessenden, and De Forest were the catalysts, but it was Dr. Frank Conrad, assistant chief engineer at Westinghouse Electric, who in 1916 began broadcasting music from his garage in Pittsburgh suburb of Wilkinsburg, Pennsylvania.[1]

Conrad was using his wireless amateur station (8XK) and is credited as the man who really got radio started. Conrad chatted away on the air and played music, so it's safe to say he was one of America's first on-air radio pros. Many broadcast historians actually credit Conrad as being the father of radio broadcasting. His transmitter-powered station was the forerunner of present day KDKA-Pittsburgh. A newspaper story about Conrad's broadcasts caused so much interest that executives at Westinghouse decided to build a *real* radio station.

It took four years for the Westinghouse station to receive a license to broadcast. The license for their station, KDKA, was officially issued on October 27, 1920, but the radio station did not begin broadcasting until a week later, because they had to wait until the certificate of license was officially posted at their station.[2] Finally, on November 2, 1920, officially licensed to go on the air, KDKA-broadcast the Cox/Harding Presidential election returns. The election returns became the first radio programming to reach an audience of any measurable size. About one-thousand listeners were estimated to be totally captivated by this amazing, newfangled gadget called radio, which through some sort of incredible magic could actually transmit voices through the air.

Westinghouse Electric and Manufacturing Company of Pittsburgh had a great philosophy about radio. Build more radio stations and more folks would buy their radios. In 1921, the company began producing the first radio home receivers. The cost was around $60, not including headphones or a loud speaker. To sell even more of their radios, Westinghouse established several other radio stations.

In addition to KDKA-Pittsburgh, the company built KYW in Chicago and also WJZ in Newark, New Jersey. Later, Westinghouse built WBZ Boston with a repeater station, WBZA, about a hundred miles west of Boston in Springfield, Massachusetts. During this same time, the American Telephone and Telegraph Company financed and built WEAF in New York City. The phone company had been keeping a watchful eye on the development and growth of radio and Ma Bell, as the company became known, wanted in on the action. AT&T put lots of money into new techniques of broadcasting and was one of the leaders in setting up commercial sponsorship. The company led the way in developing programs and personalities on radio and selling blocks of air-time. WEAF sold ten-minute blocks of programming for $100 each.

The first regularly-scheduled broadcasts occurred on WJZ, which was granted a license for regular broadcasts in 1921. WJZ became a birthing place for some of broadcasting's first radio pros.[3] Many are profiled in Chapter One of this book, including comedian Ed Wynn.[4] The Dean of radio announcers Milton J. Cross was hired by WJZ in August 1922. He was gifted with an excellent speaking voice and soon became one of the most familiar voices on radio. For years, Cross announced the Saturday afternoon Metropolitan Opera broadcasts.

By May of 1922, there were 314 radio stations on the air without any type of regulation, since this was many years before the Federal Communications Commission was established. Stations had been operating like loose cannons and without any controls. The situation became so critical that President Warren Harding instructed Secretary of Commerce Herbert Hoover to hold a meeting of broadcasters and manufactures. Around this same time, *Variety* magazine greeted readers with a front-page headline stating "Radio Sweeping Country One-Million Sets in Use!"

Author's Note: For the serious-minded student who wishes to read further about the progression of radio, good information may be found in the pages *A Pictorial History of Radio* by Irving Settle. You will find much about radio's founding fathers going back to the eighteenth and nineteenth centuries, during its earliest development stages. Men like Baron Schilling, who in 1820 produced a telegraphic instrument. Long Island, New York, resident Harrison Grey Dyar, who in 1826 operated a telegraph line. Albany, New York, teacher Joseph Henry, who developed an electromagnetic telegraph. These men were followed by many other creative geniuses, like Englishmen Sir Charles Wheatstone and Sir William Cooke. Samuel Morse, an American professor at New York University, proved in 1835 that signals could be transmitted over wire. Inventor Thomas Edison took out a patent as early as 1872 on a wireless system, and around the same time, 1865, English inventor Sir W. H. Preece experimented with wireless telegraphy. On June 2, 1875, Alexander Graham Bell transmitted the first complete sentence over wire.

The **first** radio conference was held in Washington, DC. At the meeting, Secretary Hoover proclaimed that America was on the threshold of a new means of widespread communication which would have a profound effect on the listening public. Talk about a prophetic statement! That first radio conference established a need for a federal legal authority to control all transmitting stations except amateur and experimental. Another thought-provoking component which came out of radio's very first conference was that radio communication was considered a public utility and should be regulated by the Federal government to operate in the public interest. Given today's present state of affairs with radio, one can't help but wonder what happened to the notion that stations need to operate in the public interest.

In 1927, President Coolidge appointed the Federal Radio Commission, which Congress passed to control broadcasting. In 1934, the Federal Radio Commission became the Federal Communications Commission (FCC), and was originally established to clean up some of radio's programming, which included the quack doctors and psychologists who were hitting the airwaves in increasing numbers. The FCC officially began operations on July 11, 1934. It was comprised of seven commissioners who were appointed by the President and subject to confirmation by the Senate. It was and is the FCC's responsibility to regulate and control by law the activities of America's radio and television stations. In other words, the FCC is supposedly the watch dog for listeners to ensure that the operators or licensees of America's radio stations do in fact operate in the public interest.

In the late '40s and early '50s, radio was predicted to die at the hands of TV!

1950 signaled the coming of television and supposedly signaled the death of radio! Veteran Boston broadcaster **Don Latulippe** is a 2009 inductee in the Massachusetts Broadcasters Hall of Fame. Don has been on the air an incredible seventy-two years, ever since he debuted on radio at age 7 in 1937 as a singer on the *Laco Shampoo Hour* on WHDH Radio in Boston. Forty-two years later, when I was a brand-new weekender at WROR-98.5-Boston, it was Don who broke me in and showed me how to operate the control board. During the past three-quarters of a century, he has seen many changes in broadcasting. If anyone is qualified to venture a guess as to radio's future, it is Don!

"Back in 1948," he recalls, "when I was eighteen, television came to the Boston area. Everyone thought at the time that television would overcome radio and eventually put radio out of business. Such was not the case then and it is not the case now. Today's technology," adds Latulippe, "is giving more and more people radio jobs. There will always be AM and FM radio. AM stations will be devoted to one subject, like sports, talk and news. Those formats are also showing up on FM, too."

As far as a tip to future broadcasters, both young and old, Don strongly suggests learning how to use computers. "As they get older, most people are afraid of computers. Don't be, and don't be afraid to ask questions. Remember that you are constantly learning in the operation of a computer." The eighty-one-year-old Latulippe, who still works in radio and cable TV on a part-time basis, smiles and says, "Radio is a great life. I have been so fortunate and loved every moment."

Well-known critic John Crosby, writing in *Life* magazine, listed radio's seven deadly sins that led to its decline. They included selling its soul to advertising agencies, sticking to a few formulas, news relegated to five minutes on the hour, taking false satisfaction from counting heads and assuming they were contented heads, and radio's failure to develop new talent and ideas. Crosby's comments were made over sixty years ago in 1948, but they easily could have been written today. Given today's radio climate of downsizing, layoffs, and multiple ownership by big corporations with a bean counter mentality with little attempt to develop new talent and to program fresh ideas, is it any wonder radio is in trouble. Radio is far from dead, but once again, it's time for change. Radio needs to wake up from its coma and be ***alive*** again! Some fifty years later, the doomsayers are once again predicting the death of radio. It ain't gonna happen, folks! Just like in 1950, when television took over as the new kid on the entertainment block, the face of radio had to change to survive and it did just that.

It's time again for radio to change if it is to survive. In the '50s, music, news, and talk programming became the flavor-favorite formats for radio. Back then, competition from television for entertainment forced radio to focus on what TV didn't have, at least not in the '50s: mobility! Radio developed more on-the-spot news coverage and did frequent remote broadcasts, often from the stores of sponsors. Helicopters covered traffic and accidents scene. Radio focused more on "away from home listeners" and people commuting in their cars. The DJ became the local hometown personality and built up a loyal listener base. Nationally known disc jockeys like Alan Freed and programming minds like Todd Storz, Gordon McLendon, Bill Drake, and others helped popularize rock n' roll on radio with the birth of the Top-40 music format.[5, 6]

The 1950s also saw an increase in classical music stations, usually on FM and in stereo. Today, thanks to high definition, multiplexing, satellite radio and the internet, FM stereo, which was the embodiment of quality sound and preferred listening just forty years ago, is deemed old today - passé and antiquated! Today, just like yesterday, radio continues to face inevitable change. Contrary to the many detractors who predicted doomsday in the past and do so today, I believe they are wrong about radio's future. I believe radio will survive and will be around in some shape or form for many years and decades to come. In the words of one of radio's true creative geniuses, Norman Corwin, when asked in the late 1970s about radio's future, replied, "If it is to truly exist it must be worthy of its existence."[7] Corwin believed back then, as I do today, that radio is still very much alive but needs to be resuscitated with fresh new ideas! Radio may be in some sort of comatose state due to many of today's bottom line operators, but radio lies ready and willing to be vitally revived by today's creative forces. A whole new generation of creative radio people, like radio's forefathers Norman Corwin, Pat Weaver, Todd Storz, and others can infuse and instill new life into radio.

Radio is a survivor.

Radio has weathered three major wars and survived many other skirmishes. It has undergone many metamorphoses, from a full-service schedule of comedy, quiz, dramatic and news programming to the onslaught of more music and the Top-40 format and today's widely-accepted talk and news stations. Radio has also undergone many technological changes, too; from crystal sets to transistors, from AM to FM, and from satellite to digital.

Radio is a survivor, just like the Great Depression of yesteryear and today's economic downswing, radio will weather today's storms as well. It will outlive the present-day problems of a nation which finds itself at war and with diminishing sources of energy, a down housing market, and a sagging economy. It wasn't too many years ago that inflation soared under Jimmy Carter and radio survived!

Radio will survive, if it goes back to placing the emphasis on personality and creative programmers, instead of stock holders and bottom-line bean counters!

Radio will survive if it deemphasizes how many stations a huge megacompany can own in a single city and goes back to placing emphasis on what made radio great - the competitive spirit of stations going head-to-head against each other to win the coveted ratings war.

Louisiana radio personality **Shawn Dion** has a slightly different take on radio's future: "I don't do radio, I do audio," says the Shreveport morning personality, who has worked some of the biggest radio towns in the country, including Boston, New York City, Chicago, Detroit, Atlanta, and Philly. Dion left the radio big leagues due to family health issues. "Whatever form radio comes in, there will be entertainers to do it. As long as there is a car, we will have audio. Whether it comes in the form of HD or satellite or the Internet, people like listening to interesting people. Why is YouTube so popular?" asks Dion. "Because there are creative things happening there."

"Right now," says Dion, "radio is switching from Arbitron diaries to the people meter. Early research shows that people seem to listen to the music stations more than the stations with a lot of talk. That's because for years radio told them in our on-air positioning statements that a lot of talking on the air was bad! (Ex: "W*** gets back to the music faster," etc.) The listener didn't know it was bad to hear talk on radio until we told them. So, finally, they believe us. Because of this, a lot of great disc personalities/disc jockeys are not on the air anymore."

Dion poses an interesting scenario: "What will happen when all the radio stations are just playing music? They will need something to separate themselves from the other stations and the DJ/personality will be brought back. They will have to be the most entertaining personalities on radio to separate themselves from the rest of the pack. I think that is the cycle for radio." Now, as far as competition from satellite radio, Dion believes terrestrial radio will go back to stations being owned by one person or a small company again. "Radio makes money," he asserts, "it just doesn't make Wall Street money, which is impossible to do unless you are firing people every fall to increase the bottom line, or you become 'RADIO ENRON.'" The Louisiana radio pro believes strongly that radio stations can make a five-percent profit consistently, making a point that for a small company that wouldn't be bad. Shawn Dion reminds us that radio is free. "As radio folks, we need to harp on that point. One in four people in Louisiana don't have car insurance—I can't imagine them paying for radio!"

Bob Scherago was a radio engineer at WTIC Hartford from 1963 until 1977. Later, from '78 through 2006, he worked for the Voice of America. Today, Bob is retired and loving it. During his 43 years as a broadcast engineer, he witnessed many changes in radio, particularly in audio. Here are his comments on the changes he has seen over the years and what he sees in radio's future: "Digital audio and audio editing is a big change. I can't tell you how many hours I spent with a razor blade and splicing tape editing concerts, speeches, and regular radio shows. Now, digital audio editors can do it all and much better in no time flat. I have a less-than-$100 program on my home computer that can edit and equalize with accuracy I never achieved with tape and I was pretty good at it. Any of my colleagues will attest to that." Bob Scherago believes that using a computer to store music, commercials, and other audio to play back is a great innovation for radio's future. "I came from a time when audio cartridges were the newest, state-of-the-art playback equipment," he reflects. "They were so poor in the beginning, when the tape was graphite-lubricated, and I remember the graphite would get on the heads of the cartridge player and if they weren't cleaned often the cartridge cue tone (signals when it stops) would be missed and the cart would play forever."

As for radio's future, the former radio engineer says that with satellite transmission and syndication with centralized weather, traffic, and news, local stations don't even have to be manned. "Of course," Scherago adds, "stations in every market will sound the same, too!"

For you future radio stars wondering if there will be a "home" for you as a radio personality, let alone if radio will be around, *AllAccess* talk radio editor **Perry Simon** dishes this thought your way:

"Most people still listen to radio despite having many other options, from Pandora and Last.fm to iPods and cell phones. It's easy to be a jukebox, but it's hard to project personality and companionship. The host is the difference. Locally," he says, "syndicated or voice-tracked, the host is the primary differentiation between a pure jukebox and radio. A great host," Simon adds, "whether it be talk host or music jock, makes a huge difference. Strive to be a great air personality and radio pro."

Radio *will* survive *if* it once again it places emphasis on local talent, along with an emphasis on local content, supported by national sources for news, information, and entertainment. Network programming during radio's golden age, from the 1920s through the early '50s, was intended to provide various forms of programming to the local radio station. It was intended to be a service and NEVER to diminish the value and importance of programming a station at the local level.

How deregulation has affected radio.

There was a time when broadcasters were required to air a certain amount of local programming in order to have their station license renewed. It was also a time when there was a greater variety of local programming, including local news and talk, community service shows, and local sporting events.

There's no question that at station license renewal time, which everyone in radio management dreaded, there was a mountain of paperwork and many interviews had to be conducted with local community leaders. It had to be done, and in triplicate, if a station license was to be renewed. Yes, it was work, but it not only gave the owners and operators of the license an opportunity to see what it was airing for local programming, it gave the FCC an opportunity to see if the station was in fact operating in the public interest. Even though it was lots of work to complete the license application, there was a certain amount of pride in receiving news that the station license had been renewed and the FCC deemed the station had been operating in the public interest and serving the needs of the community! Whatever happened to the personal pride of operating a radio station in the interest and necessities of serving the needs of the public? When did radio stations stop serving the listeners within its primary coverage area? Isn't that why frequencies were distributed and issued by the FCC in the first place, to ensure each community had its own radio station or stations?

When and how did the good broadcasting code of ethics get lost along the way? Those radio station owners who look toward the greed which has manifested itself on Wall Street should look in the mirror. There are more than enough greedy owners and operators in broadcasting who care little about the needs of a station's listening area and look only at how much money they can squeeze out of each kilowatt. Somehow, somewhere, along the line local radio programming has been dropped into one huge melting pot to be boiled away and forgotten. Radio has managed to shoot itself squarely between the eyes. One problem commercial radio has brought upon itself is de-emphasizing local talent in exchange for national personalities. It's the author's opinion that too much emphasis has been placed on nationally-syndicated programs and not enough on local product. Syndicated talk personalities do a superb job presenting their views on national and world subjects and should be applauded for their efforts, but just as important are local radio personalities, who focus and comment on what's happening in their own backyard, or at least they should be.

When will station owners and managers wake up and realize there's no way a national talk show can ever replace the need for local input? Sure, the tastes and interests of Americans are the same on Main Street as they are on Wall Street, but informed Americans need more than just a view of national and global news. They need to know what's going on in their own towns and cities and what's brewing within their own local governments. Local radio should be a leading source for providing that vital information. I think we can all agree that informed Americans make a stronger and better America.

FCC deregulation has hurt local radio programming, particularly radio news.

Deregulation by the FCC has hurt local radio programming, particularly news and public affairs. Radio as a critical source and disseminator of news and information, both on a worldwide and local level, is critical if Americans are going to be able to form and make intelligent decisions based on facts and not fiction, rumors, or hearsay. A strong media, and that includes viable, productive radio stations providing strong national, world, and yes, LOCAL, news is not only an important source of information but is necessary if America is to grow as a well-balanced nation of free-thinking and well-informed citizens. With the ever-decreasing amount of local news staffs at radio stations around the country and less and less news content for listeners to hear, it's no big surprise that radio has lost some of its appeal and listening numbers are down. And for you bean counters, who only focus on radio's bottom line, just remember that when ratings disappear, so will the station's financial income.

If radio is to survive in the future, it needs to get back to being local.
   Local radio is needed to show and tell the populace what decisions local politicians are making and whether or not it's in their best interest. Radio can provide the all-important window to what's going on behind the closed doors of City Hall. An informed public makes for a strong union. Radio can provide this important local ingredient. It did so in the past and can do so today and in the future. All it takes is for radio station owners and operators to acknowledge their responsibility and radio's importance as a conduit of local news to its listeners. It's impossible and unrealistic to think that a nationally syndicated talk show or news network can or should provide much needed local news content. Not that national talk shows claim or attempt to undertake such an impossible task. They don't. Network syndicated talk and news programming is just the tip of the iceberg for the total news and information package that radio can and should provide. Well-informed Americans need a variety of sources for news, radio is just one, along with television, and newspapers and magazines for more for in-depth news analysis. There is also an ever-increasing flow of news and info available on the Internet. These outlets are important to help balance opinion and to keep the public informed as to what is happening, around the country and the world, but also in their own neighborhoods and backyards.

The need for more local radio personalities in radio's future.
   Today, radio listeners have precious few local air personalities to listen to and call their friends.
   What seems to have been overlooked by many radio programmers who insist on carrying more syndicated personalities on their air is that local radio personalities live in the same towns and cities as their listeners. Their kids go to school together! When there's a wedding, a bar mitzvah, or any other event, it's usually the local radio personality who is invited. Why? Because local radio personalities are viewed as a close friend and in some cases, even as a trusted member of the listener's immediate family. **Rose Diehl** is a radio personality in Kansas. She understands the major role she plays in her community. "I feel lucky to work on the air in a small-medium market, where you are a significant part of the listener's life. I can't tell you how many births,

graduations, weddings, and sadly, funerals I have attended. I feel so privileged to have continued to be a part of my friends' and listeners' lives." Rose was a popular midday personality on Magic in Topeka, Kansas, for 27 years, and like so many radio personalities across America understands the significance that radio plays on a local community-wide level. Radio pros like Rose Diehl who work in local radio across our country and continually give back to their communities in so many special ways deserve much praise and thanks.

For the reasons stated and others, it's virtually impossible for nationally-syndicated radio personalities like **Delilah**, **John Tesh**, and others to have the same impact on a local level the way a home-grown air-talent can have. The excitement of a nationally-known personality cutting the ribbon at the new supermarket or mall opening will certainly cause a certain amount of flash and draw a crowd, but it's not long-lasting. Compare the fee of bringing in a big-name celebrity to the cost of your local talent. In the long run, you'll get just as much bang for your buck by having the local personality handle the event. That same local radio pro will continue to shop locally after the grand opening and will talk about your place of business and employees on their show on a daily basis. It's impossible for a syndicated personality to provide that much local attention. In my opinion, and based on working in all size radio markets for over forty years, more local personality involvement is necessary for radio to survive. Of course, the ideal scenario is to have both national and local talent at the station event.

Incidentally, there is an important procedure to follow in handling a radio promotion and to insure you have a successful event. It is as follows: you need to talk about the event on the air before it happens, during the event, and you have to follow up afterwards. No way can a syndicated show and talent accomplish it for the local radio station. Well, you could, if you wanted to put them up for a month and pay them more than you'll probably make on the actual promotion. You need local personalities to do it, and do it effectively! So, for those of you in charge of America's radio stations, please remember: local talent can be MOST beneficial in making YOUR numbers and bottom line look good!

The need for more local radio personalities in radio's future.
Consultant Walter Sabo agrees that radio's future is with talent.

Internationally-known broadcast consultant **Walter Sabo** has always supported air-talent. I know this is true from first-hand experience. Walter was our station consultant at WROR -Boston and says "The single most important ingredient in radio's future is the celebration of on-air-talent on the part of management. Listeners listen to talent. They come to remotes to meet talent; they go to stores that sell services sold by air-talent. There is no business without great talent and there is no great talent without supportive, passionate management." Sabo points out that Canadian broadcasters understand the importance of great talent. "Ninety percent of the radio stations in Canada are run by former program directors. Most of the radio stations in the world are run by former program directors. In 2006 and '07, radio outside the United States had boom years. Radio in the US had bad years."

Thirty-year Buffalo radio pro **Joe Chille** lays the blame for today's radio's problems directly at the feet of broadcasters. "I think we are our own worst enemy. We believed that satellite, iPods, and Internet radio was the end of radio. We need to challenge ourselves. Stop being "cookie cutter." Chille also fires a salvo at music-intense radio. "We cannot be a jukebox and win! We are not all Howard Stern, nor are we Delilah," he emphasizes, "but we each have our own personality; find the niche! Radio today needs program directors who are willing to take a chance on a talent that may be walking to the beat of a different drummer." As operations manager for Buffalo's Regent Broadcast Group, in addition to handling morning drive at WJYE, Joe Chille strongly believes that "it's better to have to reel a jock in than to try to create a personality for them."

Radio's future is bright, says Chicago radio pro Jefferson Davis.

With the influx of satellite radio, the Internet, and more syndication, there's less and less local programming. **Jefferson Davis,** voiceover talent and longtime voice of WLS Chicago, shares his opinion. "I think the idea that local radio is going the way of the white wolf is overstated. In the recent past, Clear Channel decided to sell over three hundred of their stations. Many of those stations will end up in the hands of smaller companies that will bring back some of that local flavor. Technology, which has been one of our best tools, can be also become a pariah when it comes to efficiency that decreases the work force. In smaller markets, it's still possible to work part-time in non-air jobs. That's a great way to see what happens at a radio station and the dynamics of how the departments interact. College radio is still a vibrant force. Broadcast schools are often a waste of time, in my opinion. Internet radio is emerging, but it is unlikely that much money could be made from it due to the saturation of so many of them. If you want to do it just for fun, you certainly can. Satellite radio will never reach everyone because of the investment in equipment, certain technical restrictions, and, of course having to pay to hear it. Commercial terrestrial radio is free and evolving. HD Radio will take a few years to get some traction but it's early in the game and studies have shown that it is getting more publicity than FM did in its infancy."

Davis is very positive about the future of radio. "News and talk radio can't effectively be done via satellite for every market even though they carry the largest portion of syndicated and network programming. There are also some new delivery systems that will revolutionize the way people get free over-the-air commercial broadcasts. The future really is bright for those who learn as much as they can about emerging technologies. One of the things many broadcasters in generations that preceded mine lament is that there are no more giant AM powerhouse music stations that young talent can listen to and learn from. They say you can't DX a station a thousand miles away in a big city to listen to personalities that can be role models. That is a disconnect for some generations because there are even better, higher-quality ways to hear stations all over the world. It's called the Internet and most markets of all sizes are streaming more audio than Niagara's falls are spilling water." Jeff Davis strongly believes that "there is no gloom and doom in broadcasting, only change. It's difficult for people who resist it and impossible to succeed unless you embrace it."

Where will this new crop of radio entertainers learn how to do personality radio?

WBZ Radio personality **Jordan Rich**, who keeps the kilocycles humming with great talk and interesting guests every weekend, believes tomorrow's radio stars will be "talkers rather than spinners. Personality has always been radio's strength," says Jordan, "with talk formats providing fertile ground for aspiring talent." He points to in-car listening as a huge advantage for radio. "One of radio's greatest assets is still in-car listening, and until someone invents a car that can drive itself, radio will always be the first choice as a companion, entertainer and supplier of information. The new media is a great place to start. Internet talk shows are popping up everywhere, and getting air-time on the web is more doable every day." Jordan Rich, my friend and one-time Boston radio competitor, believes college radio is an excellent place to develop your air style and personality. "There are still some excellent broadcast courses and schools out there," emphasizes the Curry College grad.[8] "Many colleges have on-campus radio stations, TV facilities, and internship programs that allow students to work hands-on, which is the only way to get experience."

America's radio pros offer their opinions on radio's future! Terrestrial vs. satellite and more!

Alan Burns, who has been one of America's leading radio consultants for over twenty years, has a message for all radio people, both newbie and seasoned pros: "We're going to have to stop thinking of ourselves as radio and instead become content creators and marketers. When we think of radio, we are thinking 'distribution channel' instead of what we produce for distribution." Burns feels that satellite radio isn't going to be a major competitor, but wireless broadband will be. "It opens up new opportunities, such as video and interactivity, to expand what we do. But it also opens us up to massive amounts of new competition. Radio competition," says Alan Burns, "used to be restricted by the number of licenses in a given market.

Now, though, everybody and I mean everybody who wants to create content has a distribution channel."

Tom Baker, Radio GM: "I think you will see more of the large radio groups selling off some of their smaller-market stations and creating opportunities, and those opportunities will take us back to what made radio successful in the first place. I see a return to local, community-oriented radio. There is so much voice-tracking and syndicated shows companies are using to reduce costs that I believe there is an opening for developing good local programming with live talent. The initial costs will be tough but in the long run it will be a winner. Serve your community and the community will support you."

Dick Bartley, air-talent and oldies expert: "I feel there will always be a need for terrestrial radio. Nothing can take the place of committed, professional, on-the-spot local news, information, and programming."

Peter Casey, director of news & programming, WBZ-Boston: "With satellite radio, iPods, and other platforms, there will be a need for localism and I think it will materialize in the next four to eight years on local radio. Some of the smaller-market stations will settle into the hands of broadcasters who can make a go of it with dozens of stations in their portfolio and not hundreds."

Joe Chille, morning drive talent on WJYE Buffalo for the past thirty years: "I know you've probably heard it over and over, but as terrestrial radio moves into the future, make sure your station sounds local. It's something that satellite, internet radio, and iPod can't give you, and that's local content."

Steve Feldman, former Boston/South Florida radio advertising executive: "What satellite radio can't do that local radio can is program to the local listeners with news, sports, finance, traffic, weather, and gossip. People still like to have a tie-in to their community and it's important to know what their neighbor next door is up to as well as what's happening in Iraq. In order for terrestrial radio to compete in the marketplace with satellite, and to get the financing it needs to do so, it needs to continue selling its programming. The only way advertisers will pay for commercials to keep terrestrial radio going is if they know a certain number of people are still listening to their commercials, and the only way terrestrial radio can continue getting this revenue is to think, be, and do local radio! People still want a point of reference or a city they can relate to and identify with."

John Forsythe, former Albuquerque morning drive pro, now on the air in Orlando: "While some have feared satellite radio, to me it has felt like job security. The lack of penetration by satellite has helped me realize that what I and so many other personalities do can't be replaced. If you're just local, you could be dead. But, if you're local and entertaining, you have a bond with your listeners that's hard to break. There is lots of talent on satellite and they will do well, just as a great syndicated show can do well. The rest is just filler, just like hundreds of channels on your cable or Dish TV."

Steve Gilinsky, air-talent-owner of Magic 101.7-Binghamton, NY: "I believe that commercial radio will always have a place and be the dominant force in the marketplace amongst satellite, iPods, etc. For the demographics we look at, adults 35 to 54 and older, traditional radio will be it. I believe we need to worry about the younger listeners as they have and will stray to iPods, satellite, etc. We in commercial radio need to do a better job at what we do best. Consolidation has hurt us and we need to get back to the basics to preserve the radio business."

Mark Hannon, SVP/Mkt. Mgr. CBS-Boston: "This is cliché, but competition is good and it should challenge everyone to become better at what they do. Radio has some compelling and new competition from satellite radio, iPods, and Internet to name a few. To compete, radio must win by providing the most compelling content and by leveraging its localism and immediate connection to the marketplace where it operates. This creates a great opportunity for emerging talent, because what will differentiate radio from the rest is creating destination programming that features new personalities that listeners care about. New radio talent must know how to deliver their content in a fast-paced and relatable way that cuts through in today's advanced technology, user-generated, 'I-want-it-now' society."

Tim Johnson, Intranet director, Clear Channel Houston: "Actually, I see more opportunity in radio today than when I got into the business in the late '70s and early '80s. A friend, Sandy Patyk, started hosting a '80s music stream in the '90s with artist interviews that helped her fine-tune her skills. She would chase down artists and attend concerts with a tape recorder for backstage interviews. It wasn't long until she was hosting nationally syndicated reports from *Live Aid*. I know of another station that has a part-time host just for their HD stations. He walks in, records a full day of drops, and now has a strong demo of his air-work to pitch to radio stations. If you're striking, with a good voice and the gift of gab, all you need is a street-level marketing trick that creates an event everywhere you go. Learn magic, front a band, build a local following. Right now, there aren't enough personalities at stations to handle all the requests for personal appearances. The right idea that draws a crowd could generate you tens of thousands of dollars in appearance fees, while making you a well-known personality. After all, what does Paris Hilton really do but draw a crowd?

Dan Mason, Pres/CEO- CBS Radio, says he "considers it a privilege to have worked in radio for four decades, and believes that no other medium can compete with radio's ability to create local content. We've got all of the experience in that area…over eighty years worth."

Judi Paparelli, radio talent: "New technology, in my opinion, provides new opportunities for radio, from enhancement of sound and delivery to creation of altogether new on-air positions and direction. It seems to me that a whole new batch of innovative minds will be able to break into the business by landing these new positions. Radio, I believe, will thrive no matter what the technology. It will simply find new ways to remain relevant."

Phil Redo, radio GM: "Talent is the key. Great talent providing information and entertainment in a unique way. And there are so many other technologies that may very well provide these new voices and new talent—the Internet and podcasting are both hugely popular and pretty affordable. In many cases they are created by very talented folks who actually have something to say and to share. Satellite is allowing specific genres a space that had previously been shut down. The folks hosting these shows are often new to the medium but bring with then knowledge and passion and honesty about what they want to share with others, which is the key to good radio! And finally, HD Radio may eventually be a big chance to expand our offerings. We're doing it now on the web, only it tends to be a simulcast of our main channels. This will change."

Bob Rivers, Seattle morning talent, says he read that "in 1970, The NAB would not let you join if you were an FM station. Why? FM was not considered big enough for radio yet! Everybody knows that radio is about listening in the car, and that broadband will make every show available globally, yet few broadcasters are actually planning for it. When we finally figure out that we're not in the transmitter and tower business anymore, the same passion that was required to succeed in the '70s will once again be rewarded. Think out of the box," advises Rivers. "Google has a bigger sales staff in Seattle than any radio station. That should tell you something."

Dave Robbins, VP/GM-CBS: "Radio is free wireless audio and will always maintain a competitive advantage, regardless of delivery method. There is no such thing as terrestrial radio. Radio is not simply terrestrial and satellite. There is RADIO and there is PAY RADIO! Listeners of the future will not know the platform from which it originates, because it will be digital and available and that is what is important to the listener. I see radio (free wireless audio) as much more capable, broad, and wide-reaching than is described by a word like terrestrial. Radio is just now entering perhaps the most exciting growth phase it has seen in over 50 years, and how great is it that we are able to participate in the future of our great medium?"

Peter Smyth, Pres./CEO Greater Media: "I believe that we're seeing the flaws in the recent love affair between Wall Street and satellite. I also believe that its importance has been greatly exaggerated. But, both satellite and Internet broadcasting are either board-based (national in scope) or ultra-niche, like podcasts about botany. Neither of these two technologies will ever contain the hometown orientation and flavor that local radio does so well. We thrive not as a national medium, but as a local one. We make our impact felt and our revenue in our backyards. It's the impact of a dedicated local station in cities like New Orleans that sets us apart. No one was turning to the Internet or satellite when the water started rising! What local radio has to do better is to tell its unique story. Broadcasters are developing Internet extensions of their brands to interact with listeners in new ways, but the core of our link to our listeners is our local focus and intimate friendship with our listeners."

Nancy Widmann, broadcast management/consultant: "My heart will always be with radio. This wonderful medium gave me a terrific career, including being the first woman President at CBS, Inc., and I will be forever grateful. I am concerned about the current state of the economy and how radio will survive the onslaught of 'new media,' but people have been predicting its demise for years and it is still as vibrant as ever."

Debbie Enblom Wolvos is a successful thirty-year news and entertainment reporter on both radio and television in Minneapolis and Boston. As to radio's future, Debbie says she read somewhere that the average amount of time spent reading the news on-line was just seven minutes per day. "This tells me," she continues, "there's still great value in getting news from radio and other sources. It may be that radio has become sort of a dinosaur," Wolvos laughs, "but, then again, dinosaurs walked the earth for millions of years!"

"Don't be afraid of change, to change is to mature and to mature is to go on recreating yourself over and over again. Without change life would be boring. The same is true about changes in radio."

They say challenges and change build character. If that's true, then it explains why I'm one heck of a character! Seriously, throughout your radio career changes will challenge you over and over again. The key is to work through them and not give up. You must know when to move on if you find yourself in a difficult situation. Take it from someone who has been there; if you feel as an air personality you are capable of offering more than you are being allowed to do, then you must bite the bullet and move on. Your best barometer of what's right for you is your gut. If it feels right, do it! If you have any doubts, don't!

Change can be a challenge, a big challenge. It can also be downright scary!

Not many of us enjoy change. Change is important and should be perceived as an opportunity and not as a threat. However, change is not always easy, even if you hope and pray for it. As the old saying goes, be careful what you wish for, it just may come true! When change happens, it can leave us melancholy for what we leave behind is a part of ourselves. So, it's not easy to make a change, and an important part of us dies before we can move on. Radio didn't die when television came on the scene in the late '40s, because it changed. It took the steps required to survive. It wasn't easy saying goodbye to old friends like comedies and dramas, but those types of programs abandoned radio for television, so radio was left to reinvent itself and it did so with music and DJ-personality-based shows. Now, it's time for commercial radio to change again, if it is to survive!

I believe many of today's problems in radio have been created by those in charge! Station managers and programmers have put radio in a box and a very small box at that! Call me old school, but to me radio has always meant one thing, *variety!* Do you think for a minute radio would have made it through its golden age if it programmed 24 hours of the same type of programming!? How long do you think it would have taken the listening public to scream enough is enough, and demand more variety? What makes today's programmers believe 24/7 music stations or any sameness of format, perhaps with the exception of news, talk, and sports, because those constantly change, is the answer for radio's survival? Wake up, radio programmers; music alone is not where it's at. Today, if you want music, buy an iPod.

If, you're not performing to your full potential, then you're cheating yourself. As discussed in chapter-5, the one constant in radio is change. Change can be good, especially for the radio pro.

To be a creative force on the radio, you must be allowed the freedom to "do your own thing." Your unique personality is what you have to market and sell. It is your personal calling card which you bring to the table every time you go on the radio! Don't ever lose sight of that! It is MOST important! Don't get swept up in the trappings of your surroundings and being comfortable. If you're not satisfied creatively in what you are doing on your show, your situation can become a real drag! Even the best facilities at the best radio station in town, with top pay and benefits, can feel like a prison if you're unable to be you on the air! Your career as an air radio personality thrives on variety and change. If you're stuck in a rut, relegated to introducing the same 100 songs over and over again, day in and day out with no other creative outlet, you will soon find yourself overflowing with depression and acute anxiety. If you find yourself constantly at odds with the PD over creative differences and battling for change on your show and not getting anywhere, well, as difficult as it may be both financially and personally, you need to do yourself and everyone else a favor and move on!

We've moved away from the main topic of this chapter, radio's future, but I thought it important to discuss something that will more than likely will be part of your future in radio, change. There will be times when for many different reasons, some totally out of your control, change will take place in radio and affect your personal situation. It may be impossible to change your present circumstances, but you still have the power to change the way you look at your situation and the way you feel! Your radio career is a mirror that reflects back to you on what you think, what you expect, how you feel, and what you do. The way to improve the reflection is to improve on what's being reflected.

From moment to moment the radio world is constantly changing. Therefore, it is imperative to keep yourself grounded as to what is really important in your life. Stay connected to your values and don't compromise on what and who you are all about both on and off the radio. Don't ever forget that you, and you alone, have the power to choose and make decisions on which direction your radio career will take you! You can also make the decision to change the course of your radio career at any time. Personally, I did it on more than one occasion. Some were great moves, others not so hot. I do believe being in motion is good. Standing water becomes stagnant and non-moving parts can rust away.

Another point to keep in mind, regardless of who is in control of the radio station where you work, is that you have the power and control to make your next move. The person you feel like being is the person you will become! The life you feel like living is the life you will more than likely find yourself living. This is also true of your career as a radio personality, so be careful which life you choose to live. Feel positive about your life and the direction of your career and you will slowly begin to see your life and direction follow that feeling. It may seem silly or impossible to feel good about life and your radio career when things appear to be going down the tubes, but in actuality, feeling good is one thing you can do whenever you choose to do so! So, decide right now to feel good and be positive about your life and on-air career! Put your feelings to positive use and you will help yourself to a more positive life which will be reflected in your on-air presentation and your career as a radio pro.

Okay, thanks for allowing me to digress about change. It is so important and you need to know that change will knock on your door, usually when you least expect it. Now, back to the future of radio.

An important message to radio programmers and general managers! It's time to wake up!

Today, there are many different entertainment sources available for the consumer. Don't lose sight that radio is just one of them. Why give your listeners the opportunity to sample other forms of radio, namely the internet and satellite, by offering them the same old type of programming? Let the creative juices flow again on radio! And here's a little wake-up call for you FM programmers: it's time to begin focusing on program content other than music! Case in point: my brother-in-law, Les, has over 17,000 songs on his iPod. That's right, over 17,000 on a tiny device capable of fitting in his shirt pocket, and which delivers an incredible sound! And, think about it! *Seventeen-thousand* of his all-time *favorite* songs. How does that compare with your station playlist these days, with only 150 or maybe 200 songs at the most in daily rotation? Scary thought, isn't it? Today, music lovers, like Les, can program all their favorite songs on a tiny device and can listen to them at will. They no longer need to depend on radio for the music they enjoy and want to hear. It's time for station operators and PDs to wake up and get with the program! You need to change your way of thinking and programming. AM radio has found its niche with talk, news, and sports. FM broadcasters, on the other hand, continue to program music-based formats the same way they have for the past thirty years! It's time for change. Heed the wake up call, radio programmers. Give the listeners something new and creative. A good start would be to bring to FM what radio does best: live, local personalities who have something to say. As legendary radio pro Dick Summer says, "Take the person out of personality and you're not left with much on the radio."

After the cuts, downsizing and job layoffs, what then for radio?

Bill Figenshu is the President/CEO of FigMedia1 LLC. Formed in July 2005, FigMedia1 is the first and only company created to take advantage of the emerging trends in broadcasting. In 2008, Bill wrote an open letter, *After the Cuts*, to Joel Denver, President/Publisher of AllAccess.com. His suggestions on what's in store for radio's future got broadcasting tongues wagging and were right on target.

In 2010, *Radio Pro* asked Bill Figenshu if radio had made any inroads to fixing the problems he outlined in his *After the Cuts*. In other words, were downsizing and layoffs over?

"No, not yet," he replied. "However, as you can see, many radio station operators are trying to get their financial houses in order first. This year (2010) will be the year many refinance and set their companies on their courses for the future. What will they find? If you want to make money in radio, you are going to have to do it the old-fashioned way. Broadcasters will actually have to program, market, and sell advertising to a changing world that has more choices than ever before. Owners/operators of major broadcast companies will not recoup their investment by selling stations for more than they paid for them. The days of radio station arbitrage are over."

Figenshu goes on to say, "Pandora, iTunes, satellite radio, social networks, PPM and the myriad of entertainment choices at home and in the car, coupled with the declining revenue base that radio operators have enjoyed will forever, be burned into budgets for years to come. By the third quarter of 2009, radio broadcasters realized the business is fundamentally changing and it is not going to be the way it was ever again. The banks that financed the deals (station and group sales) of this decade have come to grips with the lower valuations and will/have to adjust accordingly to go forward."

What does the future hold for radio? Bill Figenshu stresses the following: "Successful owners now understand the new rules of the road. The cuts are just about over. There is nothing left to cut. Unique, creative content MUST become a higher priority. The days of consumers finding a radio station's programming at one place on the dial will be replaced with broad content distribution on-air, online, video, and mobile. Advertisers," he continues," will demand a broad platform of services and accountability from radio broadcasters. We can no longer simply run hastily cut and poorly produced audio spots and expect to grow revenue. Fig believes broadcasters will not retire on stock options, bonus structures or station sales. The next decade in radio will require hard, creative work and vision.

Let's go," emphasizes Bill Figenshu. "The future is now and we are already a few years behind!"[9]

Author's note: Today, much of radio's programming has become little more than an endless treadmill of music on the FM side, with talk and news and sports relegated to AM. However, even in its present distorted state of affairs, radio still has the edge over television as the choice most people prefer as their favorite type of media.

As far as radio's future is concerned, no one really seems to know where radio is headed. I do know this: radio has a long, great heritage. From the first broadcast on Christmas Eve, 1906, when Reginald Fessenden played his violin, sang a song, and read a Bible verse into a wireless telephone of his own invention, to today's digital transmissions, radio has indeed come a long way, but the principal which has made radio so popular for over 100 years remains the same: communicating on a one-on-one basis. As is so often stated in this book, today's broadcasters need to build on radio's glorious past with new creative programming.

"Radio is far from dead and has yet to take its last breath." Those were the words from one of America's finest radio communicators, the late David Brudnoy. His nightly Boston-based talk show aired on WBZ Radio for years and was a favorite with talk listeners. Shortly before his passing David issued this challenge to tomorrow's radio stars: "Radio is eagerly waiting for the next generation of creative personalities to inject new life into it again."

Radio is far from being obsolete or dead! According to a new poll released in June 2011, listening to radio makes people happier and gives them higher energy levels than watching TV or browsing the internet. Over 1000 adults were polled for the study, called, "Media and the Mood of the Nation." They were asked to record what media they were consuming and to rate their mood and energy levels while doing so. Radio came out on top, beating both TV and online, recording a 100% lift in happiness and 300% boost to their energy levels when listening to the radio versus not consuming any type of media at all.[10] The results showed that radio stimulates positive brain engagement levels.

In a 2011 interview with the *Los Angeles Times*, veteran broadcast executive Bob Pittman said, "The perception out there is that radio is somehow in trouble. The reality is that we [radio] have the same percentage of the population listening to radio today, 93%, as we did in 1970, when it was 92%. Radio listening is not declining."

One big advantage terrestrial radio has over other forms of entertainment like satellite and the internet is that it's **free**! It's **live**, and hopefully in the future we will read or hear about a re-emergence of more local programming with local talent. Syndication is fine for filling holes in your programming schedule and giving you a big city sound of professionalism if that's your thing, but it ain't the total answer for radio to survive. More creativity would be a good place to begin.

Radio is moving forward and has already moved in a new direction with more news, talk, and sports programming. Don't give up on radio, especially those of you looking to make it your chosen career as an on-air personality. Just like your family cat, radio has at least nine lives and will be purring away for many years to come! And a direct message to you future radio stars: as an air-talent, you need to hold on to what's good about you and your show and let go of the rest and move on. Remember, in the final analysis the ups and downs of your radio career will balance themselves out. Never quit and give up on yourself. Within you lies the strength to fulfill your dreams of being a success on the radio. One final thought, today radio reaches more than 90% of the population of the United States, so there's room for you if you have the passion and desire to be on the air.

"With the technology available today, everyone can have a home studio to hone their skills and produce programs, features, segments, music shows, etc. Don't wait for a station to have an opening for you. Create some compelling program they can't live without." Peter Casey-WBZ Boston.

Notes:
1. Read more about Dr. Conrad in Chapter 1.
2. Many sources credit KDKA as being the first commercially-licensed radio station in the nation, but it's worth noting that De Forest and Fessenden were doing experimental broadcasts before KDKA went on the air in 1920.
3. In 1923, WJZ moved from Newark to New York City.
4. Ed Wynn is profiled in Chapter 1.
5. Alan Freed, who is credited with giving birth to the phrase "Rock and Roll," was one of America's first disc jockeys.
6. Todd Storz and the others mentioned, and the birth of Top-40 radio are covered in detail in Chapter 17.
7. Norman Corwin was a writer-producer-director on radio who joined CBS in 1938 and remained with the network for many years. His writing for radio broke new ground in radio drama. His post-radio writing

accomplishments include the screenplay for *Lust for Life*, which won him an Academy Award nomination. The impresario died in 2011, at the age of 101.

8. Two of the best colleges in Boston for future radio pros to attend are Curry College and Emerson. Curry College is a small liberal arts college specializing in one-on-one communication. Located on 135 beautiful acres in the Boston suburb of Milton, MA, the school was founded in 1879 as "a school of expression." Now in its 75th year, few colleges can boast having such a long positive reputation of educating and training professional broadcasters as Curry. The college has an excellent communications department and many of its graduates have enjoyed successful broadcasting careers, including the one-time voice of the Boston Red Sox, the late Ken Coleman. Many other Curry graduates commented for this book, including Roger Allen, Bob MacNeil, and Jordan Rich. MacNeil, the former News Bureau Chief for Metro in Boston is senior lecturer at Curry. He also provides one of the introductions for this book. The college is proud of its more than two thousand full-time students. For those of you wishing for more information about the communications department at Curry College, log on to Curry.edu. Emerson College is one of the premier colleges in the US for the study of communications and the arts. Founded in 1880 by Charles Wesley Emerson as a "school of oratory," today Emerson boasts an excellent faculty with top-of-the-line facilities. My longtime friend Jack Casey is manager of Emerson's FM station, WERS-88.9, which was voted the #1 college radio station by the *Princeton Review* and *the Associated Press*. Located in the heart of Boston, its downtown location makes it a little easier to get around and to intern at a Boston station. Emerson is known for having produced many distinguished grads who went on to successful careers in radio, television and film. Some Emerson grads who commented for this book include Malcolm Alter, Matt Baldassarri, Gary Berkowitz, Steve Feldman, and Pam Triolo. Your friendly author also attended the broadcast division at Emerson. You can contact the college at Emerson.edu

9. Keep in mind that Bill Figenshu wrote this letter to AllAccess in Nov. 2008.

10. The study did not include how people felt when reading newspapers or magazines.

660 • *Radio Pro: How To Be A Professional Radio Personality*

Shawn Dion, Shreveport radio personality, one-time producer Boston radio.

Phil Redo, Leslie Seiler (author's one-time oldies show producer) and Tony Bristol (Providence, RI) air talent at WPRO.

Peter Smyth, Pres. CEO Greater Media and author (on-air at Prudential Center) WROR 107 Boston.

Bill Figenshu, creative agency broadcaster, former air-talent and radio manager.

AFTERWORD

For forty-one years, I was privileged to do something I loved, talking and hanging out with my friends every morning on the radio! I was one of the lucky ones to grow up and actually live out my boyhood dream of being a radio personality. Life has been good to me. I was extremely fortunate to meet my sweet wife Kimmie in November 1989. Was it love at first sight? No, not really. Well, at least not at first. Please allow me to explain. You see, we met on the phone! She was a phone guest on our Joe n' Andy morning show. Her heartfelt comments, regarding her broken marriage moved me so much that I sent her a dozen roses and thanked her for being on our show and for having such an upbeat, positive attitude. Later that day, she called to thank me and we chatted for an hour. The next day we chatted for several more hours, which led to daily phone calls, every night for the next month. All of this happening without having any idea what the other looked like. We finally decided it probably would be a good idea if we met. Kimmie was somewhat apprehensive. Even though we had come to know each other through our many hours on the phone, we still hadn't met! I managed to convince her to fly into Boston one weekend from her home in New Jersey. I had reserved a suite at the Boston Harbor hotel and reassured her [on the phone] it was all hers for the weekend with absolutely no strings attached. If, for any reason she was uncomfortable, she could stay or leave with no questions asked.

As the weekend approached, we both grew increasingly more hesitant about the whole idea. In fact, we called each other a couple of times to cancel, suggesting that perhaps it wasn't a good move, after all. Depending on who opted out at the time, the other was convinced to carry on with the date by the other. Neither of us had been involved with a blind date quite like this one before. My mind was racing with thoughts of "what if she doesn't like the way

I look?" I think we were both afraid, now that we had become friends on the phone, one or the other would be turned off by the way the other looked. We didn't want to ruin what had become a great phone friendship.

I reassured myself, saying, "hey, pinhead, don't be a shallow Hal. Have dinner with your new friend, a pleasant "in person" conversation and move on." Foolishly, I was still paranoid that she wouldn't like the way I looked. In hindsight, as if this wonderful woman I had come to know on the phone could ever be that shallow to allow appearance to be a factor in a friendship. However, back then, my insecurity raced on. Before heading for the hotel, I had taken a shopping bag, drew a face on it and made two holes for my eyes . It was my security blanket. Before knocking at her hotel door, I placed the bag over my head. When Kimmie opened the door, she laughed and said, "well, you look pretty good from the waist down, now take that silly looking bag off your head."

Believe me, I had NO problem with how she looked! Talk about a vision of loveliness. I can still feel my heart fluttering to this day. She was a dream come true. It was definitely love at first sight, at least from my point of view, and sky rockets in flight!

No one can ever say, I fell in love with her FIRST because of how beautiful she looks. Based on our lengthy phone conversations, I had already fallen for her warmth and personality, and now to see her beauty in person was truly something to behold. Talk about gorgeous. Kimmie was then and is now a vision of loveliness, both inside and out.

It was a long courtship. She lived in New Jersey and I was in Boston. Long distance relationships are difficult and since we both had been down the marital aisle before, we decided to take it slow and easy. Like other couples, we experienced a few bumps along the road, but thanks to our love for each other things worked out. We were married on March 3rd 1995. There isn't a day that goes by that I don't give thanks to God, for the gift of having Kimmie in my life. Her caring, loving nature is very special. I am a lucky guy!

Even though, my wife and I have faced several serious health issues along the way, we feel so blessed. Besides, who at some point in their lives hasn't had to deal with some adversity? You hang in and do your best to go with the flow. My radio friend Dick Purtan, who is regarded as Michigan's most respected and recognized air personality, says, "Trouble and diseases eventually fall at everyone's doorstep."[1] Sadly, Dick speaks from first-hand experience. The popular Detroit morning drive personality has lived with prostate cancer for fifteen years and his wife Gail has battled ovarian cancer for over a dozen years. In both instances, Dick and Gail Purtan sacrificed their privacy in exchange for informing the public about their health issues and in doing so have raised awareness about the importance of early detection through cancer screenings. Their life experiences are important for all to take note of.

"When trouble troubles you, it's not an easy thing to deal with, especially when you're faced with doing a daily upbeat radio show, but you need to carry on and perform," says Purtan, a member of the Radio Hall of Fame who has also won *Billboard's* Major Market Air Personality of the Year honors twice. Dick graciously agreed to share his feelings on how to make it through difficult times and continue to do good radio, when and if adversity strikes you: "It's not an easy thing to continue doing your radio show with the same drive and determination that you had before, but you have to do it. One way is to share your personal situation with your audience, if you feel it's appropriate for both you and your listeners. It makes the people listening view you as a regular guy who they can identify with. If you choose not to that's all right, as long as you can keep it bottled up inside and still continue to do a top-notch show. One way or another," Purtan adds, "it's not easy but at least for the hours you're on the air, you simply MUST keep your eye on the ball. In other words, the show must go on." Straight-from-the-heart advice from Detroit radio pro Dick Purtan, who in February 2010 announced that after 50 years on the air, he was retiring from doing his daily morning drive radio show.

After the loss of my voice and my wife's diagnosis with melanoma it was decision time. What would we do next with our lives? My wife was born in Colorado, and years ago we had purchased 60 acres from her stepfather, so it was sort of a no-brainer. We had no job in Florida and her family was in Colorado, so we packed up our belongings, including all my radio junk, and, along with our two kitties and two dogs, headed west for the Rocky Mountain State!

In December, 2004, Kimmie found an older Victorian home for us to rent in the town of Palisade. The town is located on Colorado's western slope in a beautiful peach tree- and vineyard-covered valley at the bottom of the canyon, which leads to the Grand Mesa. At the top of the canyon is the town of Mesa. It's where we own land and decided to build our home. Construction began in the spring of 2005 and we moved in New Years Eve of the same year. The movers didn't exactly share our excitement about "move-in day," since they were working on New Year's Eve. Even with the extra tip money we tossed their way, they weren't thrilled with their mission. Who could blame them? As for Kimmie and me and our critters, we were ecstatic. We all huddled around our new fireplace and with a light snow falling outside, gave thanks to the Lord for allowing us to be together as a family, healthy and happy in our warm, new home high in the mountains of Colorado. Gathered outside was a herd of about a dozen deer. They peered in at us through one of our picture windows, almost as if to say, "Welcome humans…now feed us." On the other side of our home, heading down the mountainside and moving across our lower pasture, we could make out the forms of at least a hundred elk foraging on what grass they could find under the freshly fallen snow.

> *"I would like my radio career of over forty years to be measured not by the pain and hardship I've experienced and endured, but by my will to keep coming back and moving forward, setting new goals, working hard, and seeking excellence in trying to achieve them."*
> – Joe Martelle, 9/23/06

At that moment, the fun but often chaotic and sometimes stress-filled life of a radio pro seemed to exist far away on another planet in another galaxy. Here in the mountains of Colorado's western slope, we feel protected from all that is wrong with the world. Here, life is good, really good! Like many of you, my wife Kimmie and I are survivors. We have so much to be thankful for, supportive family and friends, and animals we love that love us back, including a year-round resident mama deer and her son, who allow us to live on their land. It doesn't get much better than that, my friend.

For those of you who have kindly inquired as to how we're doing, I'm pleased to say we're doing fine! We're happy and extremely grateful for all that we have and we wish all good things for you. May the good Lord continue to watch over and bless you!

Take care!

Joey & Kimmie Martelle
Mesa, Colorado
July, 2011

Author and wife, Kimmie, with some of their critters.

Author on their ranch in Colorado with Buffy the buffalo.

Kimmie and Joey relaxing at home.

Dick and Gail Purtan.

INDEX

A

Aaroe, Alden, 629
A Beautiful Morning, The Rascals, 307
Abbott & Costello, 362-63
Abdul, Paula, *photo,* 209
Academy Award
Abrams, Lee, 549
Abramson, Herb
AC (Adult Contemporary radio format), xxiv, 74, 314-15, 350, 395, 539, 542, 612
A Civil Action, 136
Adam Ant, 128
Addams, Mike, 197, 551, 611-12, *photos,* 564, 633
Adventures of Helen & Mary, 331
Affairs of Ann Scotland, the , 332
After the cuts - Bill Figenshu, 656
AFTRA (American Federation of Television & Radio Artists), 474
AFRTS (Armed Forces Radio & Television Service), 334, 401, 467, 496
Age Discrimination, 604
A Girl Like You - The Young Rascals, 307
Ain't Too Proud to Beg - Temptations, 305
Air-checks and critique sessions, 266, 270
Air Edition of the Chicago Sun Times w/ Mike Wallace, 470
Alabama, 553
Alan Burns, Associates, 373-74
Alan, Lee, 551
Alarm Clock Club with Ray Mercier, 554
Alaska, 9
Albany, New York, 613, 640
Albany NY Radio Personalities and stations 550

Albuquerque, New Mexico, 650
Alexandria, VA, 458
Ali, Muhammad, 187, 498
Alka-Seltzer, 27
AllAcess.com, 73, 117-18, 509, 644, 656
Allen E. Allen, 554, *photos,* 563
Allen, Bill "Hoss," aka William Trousdale Allen III, 553, 625, 629
Allen, Fred, aka John F. Sullivan, 18-20, 102, 334, 630, *photo,* 37
Allen H. Neuharth Award, 498
Allen, Mel, 4, 518-19, *photo,* 531
Allen, Rocky, 261
Allen, Steve, 4, 21
Allen's Alley, 19, 102
Allman Brothers, Greg and Duane, 629
All News 1010 WINS NYC, 482
Alter, Malcolm, 86, 108, 612
AM Radio, 7, 364, 473, 499, 548, 616, 641, 649, 656-57
Amato, John, 565
Ambassador Hotel, 466
Ambrose, Marty, *photo,* 115
America (American), 8-9, 126, 315, 332, 337, 453, 456, 465, 468, 472, 490-91, 494, 496, 499, 516, 537, 622, 625, 630, 637-38, 645-47, 649
America Votes the #1 Songs, 56
American Bandstand, 56, 59
American Broadcasting Company (ABC), 3, 15, 17-19, 25, 28-30, 166-67, 201, 328, 332, 345, 465, 467-69, 492-93, 503, 519, 530, 612, 614, 617, 629
ABC-FM stations, 118, 260

667

ABC News, 313, 461, 482
ABC-TV, 5, 12, 56-57, 427, 466, 523-24, 526
AFL (American Football League), 523
American Forum of the Air with Theodore Granik, 492
American Gold & Rock & Rolls Greatest Hits w/Dick Bartley, 612
AHL (American Hockey League), 527
American Idol, 113, 140, 374, 377
American Newspaper Publishing Association, 454
American Radio Systems, 373
American Sportscasters on line by Lou Schwartz, 527
American Sportsman, 524
American Telephone, 639
American Top-40, 543
American Women in Radio & Television, 324
America's Town Meeting of the Air with George V. Denny, Jr., 492
Ames, Mary Ellis, 493
Amidon, Kim, 381-82
Amish Furniture, 380
Amos n' Andy, Freeman Gosden (Amos) & Charles Correll (Andy), 11-12, 130-31, *photo*, 38
Amos n' Andy Music Hall, 12, 130
Ampex Corp., 28
And I love you - The Beatles, 308
Anderson, Bob, 84, 554, *photo*, 278
Anderson, David, 461
Anderson, Ernie, 551
Anderson, Herb Oscar, 547, 553, 613
Anderson, Paul, 572
Andrews, Andy, 555
Angelo, Mike, 434
Ansbro, George, 5
Anthony, Dean, 546-47
Apache Proverb, 149
AP (Associated Press), 52, 201, 425, 428, 455, 464, 479
ARB (Arbitron), 262, 316, 403, 430, 459, 505, 539, 588, 643
Arch Bishop Bernard Law, 361, 432-34
Arch Bishop of Detroit, 489
Arch Bishop of St. Louis, 432
Archie Andrews, 330
Arch Obler's Lights Out, 630
Arlin, Harold, 516

Arlington Memorial - Washington DC, 454
Armstrong, Bob, 554
Armstrong, Jackson, 553
Arnold, Bob, xxix
Arthur Godfrey's Talent Scouts, 15
Ashley, Jean, 62, 109
Ask Eleanor Nash, 493
Assignment to Berlin - Harry W. Flannery, 461
A Tale of Two Cities - Charles Dickens, 523
A Taste of Ashes - Bill Stern, 519
AT& T'S Network Service, 454
Atlanta, 343, 503, 643
Atlanta Braves, 521
Atlanta GA Radio Personalities and stations 550-51, 629
Atlantic Records, 550
Atlantic (Ocean) Seaboard, 537, 546
Atom Smasher, 318
At the Hop - Danny and the Jr's, 59
Attleboro, MA, 631
Atwood, Jack, xv
Auburn Cemetery, Cambridge, MA, 524
Audio Advancements for radio news coverage, 471
  Audio cartridge, 471-72, 644
  Audio editing, 643
  Collins tape cartridge machine, 472
  Gates ST-101, 471-72
  Mackenzie repeater, 471
  Spotmasters, 472
Audion, 3-element electron tube, 638
Aunt Jenny, 331
Australia, 55, 312
Author's sisters, JoAn and Rosie, xv, 99
Autry, Gene, 9-10, 23-24, *photo*, 38
Autry, Jackie, 24
Avco Broadcasting, 245, 257
Avruch, Frank, 631
Azar, Steve, 260, 620

B
Baby Boomers, 288, 546
Baby I'm Yours - Barbara Lewis, 308
Baby Snooks Show, 329
Back in the saddle again - Gene Autry, 9
Back to the 80s with Joe Cortese, 614
Badger, Bob, 543
Baer, Ed, 546-47
Bailey, Bill, 352, 552

Bailey, Dave, *photo, 278*
Bailey, Dennis Jon, 551
Bailey, Jack, 4
Bailey, Michael, 138
Baker, Gene, 123-24
Baker, Tom, 281, 291, 359, 650, *photo, 296*
Baldassarri, Matt the Cat, 51, 79, 582, *photo, 92*
Ball, Lucille, 333, 379
Balance, Bill, 496
Balou, Dudley "Bud," 61
Baltimore Orioles, 186
Banjo Bowden story, the, 229
Bankhead, Tallulah, 333-34
Banks, Doug, 265, 619
Banks, Joan, 331
Barber, "Red" Walter Lanier, 256, 518-19, 529
Barker, Bob, 4
Barrett, Johnny, 551
Barry, Jack, 4
Barte, Belle, 493
Barton, Frances Lee, 493
Bartley, Dick, 612, 650, *photo, 633*
Battle of the Bands, 620
Battle of the Century, 516
Battle of the Sexes, 25, 289
Beachboys, 392, 550
Beach, Sandy, 543, 551, 618
Beaker Street Show, 615
Bearor, Wayne "B," *photo, 278*
Beasley, Irene, 330
Beatles, 6, 187, 198, 306
Beatty, Morgan, 462, 495
Beaufort SC Naval Hospital, 98
Beautiful Music from Studio X with Vill Marlowe, 591-92
Beck, Glenn, 74, 378-79, 392, 494, 508
Becker, Bob, 492
Becker, Sandy, 4
Beckman, "Spook" Frederick, 614
Beebe, Allen, *photo, 209*
Beemer, Brace, 12
Beeville, TX, 104, 587
Behind Closed Doors - Bob Woolf, 569-70, *photo, 579*
Believe Me - Royal Teens, 308
Bell, Alexander Graham, 640
Bell, Art, 499
Bell, Joe, 627
Bell, Upton, 496

Bell South Building, WPB, FL, 265
Belmont high school (LA), 31
Belushi, John, 363
Benaderet, Bea, 331
Ben Bernie's Orchestra, 333
Benchmarks & Fixed bits, 385-86
Bennett, Bill, 491
Bennett, Buzz, 177, 185, 554
Bennett, Constance, 333
Bennett, William J., 230
Benny, Jack, aka Benjamin Kubelsky, 10, 20-21, 629, *photo, 37*
Benzaquin, Paul, 509
Berg, Alan, 624
Berg, Gertrude, aka Gertrude Edelstein, 329
Bergen, Edgar, 10, 30, 31
Berger, Steve, 311
Bergeron, Tom, 56-58, 500, *photo, 71*
Berkley School of Music, 421
Berkowitz, Gary, 41, 74, 135, 147, 233, 237-38, 260, 265, 301, 318, 359, 545, 612, *photos, 91, 144, 278*
Berkowitz, Roger, 511
Berle, Milton, 10
Berlin, Irving, 326
Berlin, Paul, 552
Berns, Don, 39
Bernstein, Sumner, 565
Berra, "Yogi" Lawrence Peter, 528
Berry, "Chuck," aka Charles Edward Anderson, 6, 547
Bessie V. Hicks School of Broadcasting, 59
Bethany College, Bethany, WVA, 6
Betty and Bob, 332
Betty Crocker, 330, 492
Betty Ford Center, 252
Biddeford Maine Police, 608
Biddeford/Saco Journal, 454
Big Apple, 548, 553, 624
Big Beat Show with Alan Freed, 547
Big Show with Tallulah Bankhead, 333-34
Billboard Magazine, 113, 177, 556
Billboard Air Personality Award, 104, 663
Billboard Book of #1 Hits - Fred Bronson, 174
Billboard Book of Top-40 Hits - Joel Whitburn, 306, 309
Billboard Convention - 1972, Los Angeles, 308
Billboard's Major Market Air Talent Award- Dick Purtan, 663

Billboard's Music Survey charts, 59, 306, 369
Biondi, Dick, 49, 96, 219-21, 480, 551, 616, 621, *photo, 231*
Bird, Larry, 125, 567-69
Bishop Neumann High, So. Philly, 59
Blackberry, 403
Black Radio Hall of Fame, 335
Blackstone cigars, 25
Blair, Frank, 495
Blair, Tony, 498
Blake, Karen, 342
Blake, Mary, 222, 479-80, 483, *photos, 232, 486*
Blanchard, Dickie Doo, 550
Blavat, Jerry, *the Geator with the Heator*, 553
Bleu, Don, 398, 554, 613, 615, *photo, 634*
Blind Date, 332
Block, Martin, 4, 7, 24-25, 553, 628, *photo, 37*
Blondie, 128
Bloomfield Hills, MI, 489
Blore, Chuck, 75, 581
Blue Angel - Roy Orbison, 367, 407
Blueberry Hill - and Blue Monday - Fats Antoine Domino, 305
Blue Velvet - Bobby "Stanley Robert Vinton," 306
Bob and Ray, Bob Brackett Elliott & Ray Walter Goulding, 29, 495, 551, *photo, 38*
Bob & Ray show character voices and spoofs, 29-30
Boggs, Wade, 436
Bohannon, Jim, 499
Boliska, Al, 349
Bonaduce, Danny, 316
Bonzo and Cheeta, 542
Boogieman aka Scott Carpenter on CHUM-AM 1050, Toronto, Canada, 60
Boone, Charlie, 615
Boortz, Neal, 499
Boss Radio, 401
Boston, MA, xxx, 102, 111, 202, 211, 238, 243, 259, 261, 281, 285, 324, 342-43, 358, 368, 378, 421, 423-24, 429, 433, 437, 475, 480, 482- 83, 490, 496, 499, 501, 540, 542, 547, 565-66, 603, 612, 618, 626, 628, 631, 640, 643, 650, 653, 657, 662
 Archdiocese, 432
 Beacon Hill, 360

Bostonian Hotel (now the Millenium), 361, 428, 436
Charles River, 18, 367
Combat Zone, 365
Government Center, 128
Huntington Ave., 128
Logan Airport, 432-33
Mystic River - Tobin Bridge, 356, 367
Newbury St., 167
Prudential Tower, 128
Public Garden, 360
Quincy Market, 29
Storrow Drive, 356
Women's City Club, 360
Boston Bruins, 435, 527
Boston Catholic Community, 433
Boston Celtics,125, 526, 567, 569
Boston Children's Hospital, 386
Boston College, 80, 467, 568, 582
Boston Globe, 140, 366, 423, 526
Boston Harbor Hotel, 428, 435
Boston Herald, 140, 435, 661
Boston Long Wharf Mariott, 428
Boston Pops, 602
Boston Public Library, 18
Boston Red Sox, 125, 368, 427, 436-37, 508, 522-23, 525, 607, 621
 Fenway Park, 368, 437, 523-24, 526
 Hall of Fame, 522-23-24
Boston Sheraton Hotel, 361, 422, 524
Boston Radio Personalities and stations, 249, 292, 358, 366, 550-51, 603, 621-22, 649
Boston TV, Ch. 5, 427
Bowdoin College, 566
Boyles, Chuck, 553
Boy Scouts, 98, 165, 181, 624
Bozo, the Clown, 631
Bracken, Denny, 555, 626-27
Bradley, Bruce, 47-48, 86, 93-94, 551, 613-14, 622, 630, *photo, 115*
Brainard, Bertha, xxiii, 9, 324-25, *photo, 347*
Brando, Marlon, 498
Branigan, "Boom Boom" aka Joseph Motto, 543, 550, 613
Brant Rock, MA, 537
Braun, Bob, *photo, 276*
Breakfast Club, the with Don McNeill, 3, 15, 618
Breakfast with Binnie & Mike, (Binnie Barnes & Mike Frankovitch) 25-

26, 333
Breakfast with Paula, 494
Breckinridge, Mary Marvin, 331-32
Brennan, Bobby, 553
Brennan, "Dusty Discs," Dan, 552-53
Br'er Rabbit, 177
Brewer, Jim and Family, 627
Brice, Fanny, aka Fania Borach, 329
Bridges, Barbara, 119, 227, 260, 398, *photo,* 277
Brine, "Salty" Walter, Jr., 631
Brine, Wally, 633 (see footnote 19), *photo,* 278
Brink & Belzer, 402
Brink, Don L."Scotty," 401-02, 626, *photo, 413*
Brinker, Bob, 500
Brinkley, David, 155, 469-70, *photo, 483*
Bristol, Tony, *photo, 660*
Brite, Larry, 551
BBC (British Broadcasting Corp.), 557
Brittain, Ross, 122-123, 148, *photo, 143*
Broadcast Century, the - Michael C. Keith, 467
Broadcast Rites & Sites - Joe Castiglione, 525
Broadcasting Broadway, 9
Broadcasting Magazine, 177
Broadway, 334, 516
Broadway program, 325
Brockton High School, 476
Broderson, Dick, *photo, 278*
Bronson, Fred, 56, 174
Brooklyn Dodgers, 518-19, 521
Brooklyn - Paramount Theaters, NYC, 547
Brown, Charlie, 543, 554, *photo, 563*
Brown, Himan, 7
Brown, Jeff, 344
Brown, Jim, NFL, Hall of Fame running back, 522
Brown, Ted, 546, 628
Brown Univ. 74, 424
Brudnoy, David, 202, 491, 657
Bruni, Vinnie, xv
Bryan, William Wright, 461
Bryant, "Bear" Paul, 376
B-12 list for talk show hosts, 488
Bubba the Love Sponge, aka Todd Alan Clem, 168
Buick, 625
Buffalo, 616, 624-26, 631

Buffalo NY Radio Personalities and stations, 373, 551
Buffalo Sabres, 435
Bullpen, 264
Bump, Jeffrey, 477
Bump, Roger Allan, ix, 476-79, *photo, xiii*
Burbank, Gary, 551, 629
Burdette, Winston M., 460
Burke, Solomon, 550
Burkhart- Abrams, 549
Burks, Spider, 554
Burning up the Air - Alan Tolz & Steve Elman, 501
Burns and Allen - George Burns, aka Nathan Birnbaum, Gracie Allen, 22, 618, photo, 37
Burns, Alan, 649
Burns, Bob, 19
Burns, George, 20
Burns, Scott, 551
Burris "BQ" Robert, 554
Bush, Barbara, 498
Bush, George H.W. U.S. Pres., 469
Butler, Vida Jane, aka Janie Joplin, 334
Butte (MT) or Bangor (ME), 587

C

Cable, 311, 355, 641
Cable radio, 309
Cain, Jess, ix, x, xi, 48, 165-66, 349, 373, 508, 551, 612, 617, 618, *photo, xiii*
California, 480, 616, 631
   Culver City, 471
   Newport Beach, 178
   Redondo Beach, 109, 340
   San Jose, 537
   Santa Barbara, 281
   Sierra foothills, 631
California Angels, 368
California Council on Problem Gambling, 620
California Pacific Inter Expo, 194
Cal State Long Beach, 61
Calling All Sports, 496
Call To Music, 333
Cambridge, MA, 18, 524
Camus, 336
Canada, 246, 337, 416, 511, 517, 625, 648
   Windsor, Ontario, 552
Canadian radio broadcasters, 637, 648
   CFCF - Montreal, 471

CHUM-1050AM, Toronto, Canada, 549
CHUM Story - Allen Farrell, 349
CJFX-580AM, Antigonish, NS, Canada, after 60 years of service went off-the air in June 2003. Today, CJFX-FM operates as X-FM on 98.9. xxix
CKEY-590AM, Toronto, Canada, 405
CKLW-AM800, Detroit/Windsor, Ontario Canada, 552, 624
Cannon, Freddy "Boom Boom," *photo,* 564
Cantor, Eddie, 10, 27, 88, 131, 333-34, 362, *photo,* 35
Can You Top This, 42-43
Canobie Lake Park, 367
Capital bylines with Patty Cavin, 494
Capt'n Bob Cottle, 631
Capt'n Dan, KKLI-FM, Colorado Springs, 351, 400-01, 615, *photo,* 413
Capt. John Smith of Jamestown, VA, 178
Capitol Theater, NYC, 9
Caray, Chip, Dutchie and Skip, 521
Caray, Harry, aka Harry Christopher Carabina, xxiii, 521, 529
Carbondale, ILL, 619
Card, Dex, 554, *photo,* 563
Cardinal Bernard Law, former Arch-Bishop of Boston, 361, 425, 432-34, *photo,* 447
Carey, Drew, *photo,* 210
Caribbean, 246, 416
Carlin, George, 161
Carlin, Phillips, 518
Carlton, Fran, 331
Carnell, Herb, 615
Carney, Jack, 554
Caron, Bob, aka Jon E. Dee, 554
Carpentier, Georges, 516
Carr, Buddy, aka Tom Bigby, 613
Carr, M.L., 567
Carroll, Bill, 168
Carson, Johnny, 4, 42, 192-93, 200
Carson, Kit, (radio pro), 553
Carter, Amy, 424-25, newspaper article, 443
Carter, Boake, 458
Carter, Jimmy, U.S. Pres. & wife, Rosalyn, 424-25, 642, *photo,* 444
Carter, Ken, 108.
Carton, Craig, 168
Case, Al, 613
Case of Sports - WJAS Pittsburgh, 520

Casey, Barry, 621
Casey, Jack, 52, 85, 146, *photo,* 70
Casey, Peter, xi, 156, 260, 291, 512, 650, 658, *photo,* xiv
Casey, Sean, aka Roy Gilmore, 59, 65, 104, 542, 551, *photo,* 71
Cash, Johnny, 549
Casper, the Friendly Ghost, 331
Cassano Pizza King, 248
Cassidy, David, 203-04
Cassidy, Henry, 461
Castiglione, Joe, xxiii, 125, 522, 524, *photo,* 532
Castle Heights Military Academy, 629
Castro, Fidel, 200
Catholic education, 190, 565
Catholic, 366, 614
Cavanaugh, Pete, 555, 627
Cavett, Dick, viii, 4, 12, 202
Caywood, Betty, 528
Central City, 332
Cerf, Bennett, 294
Chacksfield, Frank, 590
Challenge of the Yukon, 2
Chamber Music Society of Lower Basin St., 333
Champagne Lady, the, 511
Champaign, ILL, 617
Chandler, Robin, 333
Change: It can be a challenge, 128, 653
Channel 6 - WCSH-TV, xv, 87, 310
Channel 7 - Boston, 128, 189
Channel 8 - WMTW-TV, xv, 91
Chaplin, W.W., 461
Chapman, Ron, 77, 113, 351, 393, 551, 628, *photo,* 92
Chapman University, 507
Charlie & Harrigan, 551, several morning-drive radio teams used these names. Credi for being the first goes to Ron Chapman at KLIF-Dallas. Irving Harrigan. Jack Woods was the original Charlie, followed by Dan (McCurdy) Patrick.
Charlie Tuna, 621
Charles, Kevin, aka Kevin Minatrea, 122, *photo,* 115
Charles, Nick, 61
Charles, Ray, 550
Charleston, 343

Charlotte, 383
Charm Kitchen, the, 493
Chart Productions, Inc.-Jordan Rich, 508
Chase, Chevy, 363
Chase Manhattan, 256
Chase & Sanborn Hour, the, 10
Chase's Calendar of Events, 173-74
Chastain, Jane, 527
Check It Out - Tavares, 305
Cheech & Chong, 423
Chesterfield Supper Club, the, 24, 29
Cheverus High School, Prin. Rev. William Campbell, SJ, xxix, 6, 40, 98-99, 105
Chevy Blazer, 356
Chevy Showroom, the, 333
Cheyenne, WY, 523-24
Chicago, 110, 192, 285, 394, 415, 419, 467, 470, 593, 615-20, 624, 626-627-28
  Grant Park, 327
  Michigan Ave., 467
  Stagg Field, 517
  Chicago Bears, 528
  Chicago Cubs, 517-18, 521
  Chicago Daily News, 324
  Chicago Maroons, 517
Chicago Radio Personalities and stations, 292, 371, 506, 551, 617, 624
  Chicago Theater, 220
  Chicago Tribune, 455-56
  Chicago White Sox, 517, 521-22, 528
  Chicago's Wrigley Field, 518
Childhood Leukemia, 429
Chickenman, 620
Childhood Leukemia, 429
Children's Christmas Fund, 135, 324, *photo,* 532
Childs world with Helen Parkhurst, 493
Chille, Joe, 373, 648, 650, *photo,* 412
CHR (Contemporary Hit Radio format), 50, 374, 390
Chris Charles, "Chuck" the Magic Christian, 61
Christie, Phil, 421
Christmas, 43, 359, 429, 472
Christmas carol, 300-01
Christmas Eve, 537, 657
Chrysler, 524
Churchill, Sir Winston, 98
Cincinnati, Ohio, xxx, 219, 245, 249, 256, 494, 565, 628
Cincinnati baseball, 518
Cincinnati Bengals, 530
Cincinnati Ohio Radio Personalities and stations, 292, 371, 551
Cincinnati Reds, 522
Circus, 374
Citadel Broadcasting, 118, 202, 260, 317, 345
Cities Service Concerts, 327
Clark, Buddy, 543
Clark, Dick, 4, 56, 59, 308, *photo,* 70
Clark, Jay, 550, 613
Clarksville, VA, 523
Classic Countdown, 612
Clear Channel, 102, 345, 418, 475, 503, 586, 651
Cleveland, Ohio, 493, 548, 586
  Cleveland Browns, 522
  Cleveland Indians, 525
Cleveland Ohio Radio Personalities and stations, 551
Clifford, Clyde, 615
Cliff Towers Hotel-Dallas, 555
Clifton, Gregg, 566, 568, 570-71
Cline, Patsy, 135
Clinton, Bill, William Jefferson, US Pres., 303
Clooney, Rosemary, 224, 333
  Clooney Sisters, Rosemary & Betty, 256
Clovis, New Mexico, 549
CMA (Country Music Association), 317
CNN (Cable News Network), 454, 460, 467, 473, 498-99
Coasters, the, 550
Coca-Cola, 31
Cochran, Eddie, 225
Coffey, Joe, xv
Coffey, Lissa, 187
Cohen Creative, 614
Cohen, Stacey, 109, 340-41, 394-95, 614, *photo, 116*
Cole, Nat King, 538
Coleman, Casey, 522
Coleman, Ken, xxiii, 508, 522, 525
Coleman Research, John Coleman, 312
Colgate Comedy Hour (NBC-TV), 362
Colgate Sports Newsreel with Bill Stern, 519
Colgate Univ., 524
College of Radio Engineering, 328
College radio, 318, 582, 586, 648

Collingwood, Charles, 460
Collins, Al Jazzbeau, 543, 628
Collins, Reid, 463
Collins, Ted, 326
Collinsworth, Chris, 530
Collyer, Bud aka Clayton Johnson Heermance, Jr, 4
Colmes, Alan, 494, 624
Colorado, 105, 213, 355, 627, 663
   Colo. Springs, 400, 624
   Cripple Creek, 457
   Grand Mesa, 663
   Hayden, 496
   Palisade, 663
   Rockies, 213
   Rocky Mtn. State, 663
   Western Slope, 664
CBS Columbia Broadcasting System, 11-15, 18, 20, 22-23, 25, 27-28, 30-31, 58, 102, 112, 119, 123, 130, 194, 200, 218, 224, 233, 263, 265, 282, 292, 326-34, 341, 345, 373, 454-60, 462-64, 468-70, 473, 489, 492-93, 518, 524, 527-28, 530, 543, 547,
   616-17, 619, 624, 627, 630, 651-53
   CBS London News Bureau, 459
   CBS Radio, World News Roundup, 463
   CBS Radio, World Tonight, 463
   CBS-TV, 22, 191, 424
   CBS-TV Newsbreak, 462
   CBS-TV *Sixty Minutes*, 4,169, 470
   CBS-TV *Survivor*, 374
   CBS War correspondents, WWII, 461
Columbia College, 342
Columbus, Christopher, 96
Columbus, Ohio, 614
Comedy Clubs, 318-19
Command Performance, 334
Como, Perry, 24, 224
Concord, MA, 439
Cone, David, 528
Congress St/ Portland, ME., 310
Conigliaro Brothers, Billy, Richie & Tony, 368
Conigliaro, Sal & Teresa, 368-69
Conigliaro, Tony, 368-70, *photo, 412*
Conn, Billy, 519
Connecticut, 313, 380, 492, 546, 624
Connecticut School of Broadcasting, 219
Conniff, Ray, 224

Connolly, Bobby, xvi
Conrad, Dr. Frank, 5, 538, 638, *photo, 35*
Considine, Bob, 460
Consultants, radio, 299
Contact, 495
Contemporary Black Biography, 335
Continental Bakers, 330
Contracts and Ratings, 575-78
Cook, Jay, 617
Cook, Joe, 553
Cooke, Sir William, 640
Coolidge, Calvin, U.S. Pres, 454, 640
Cornet, Doug, 553
Cortese, Joe, 104, 135, 614, *photo, 144*
Cosmic Dawn, 55
Corwin, Norman, 642
Costas, Bob, 186
Costco, 380
Costigan, Mary, 328
Cote, Ryan "Rick," 40, 47, 587-88, *photo(s), 69*
Coughlin, Rev. Fr. Charles Edward, xxiii, 489, *photo, 512*
Country radio format, 621
Courtney, Alan, 494
Couture, Faust, 224
Coviello, Tony, 428, *photo, 446*
Cowan, Tommy, 517
Cox Broadcasting, 100
Cox - Harding election results, 639
Cox, James, 454
Cozy Corner, 153, 228, 590-92
Cracker Jacks, 439
Crane, Ruth, 492
Critter Corner, photo, 409
Crocker, Frankie, 547
Croft, Mary-Jane, 331
Cronkite, Walter, aka Walter Wilcox, 462, 469, *photo, 484*
Crookes, Sir William, 636
Crosby, Bing, aka Harry Lillis, 27-29, *photo, 38*
Crosby, John, 641
Crosley, Powell, Jr., 245, 416
Cross, Milton, 639
Crouse, Barbara, 242
Cryan, "Wally" Walter, 631
Cruz, Bob, 617
Cruze, Linda, 343, *photos 115, 209, 210*
Crystals the, 550, 590
Cuba, 433

Cuddy, Tom, former PM, WPLJ-NYC, (not to be confused with long-time WBZ, Boston sportscaster, Tom Cuddy), 118, 260-61, 614, *photo, 143*
Culkin, Monsignor Francis, 434
Cullen, "Bill" William Lawrence, 4, 495, 553, 619
Culver City, 471
Cumberland County Civic Center, 170
CUME, 304
Cummings, Adelaide Hawley, 330
Cumulus Broadcasting, 345
Cup of Joe, 194, 356
Curry College, vii, ix, 476, 649
Curt Gowdy State Park, 524
Cushman Bakery, xxx
Cusick, Fred, 527

D

Dad for a Day, 437, newspaper article/photo, 451
Dahl, Steve, 551, 617
Dale Carnegie, 196
Dallas, 62, 85, 194, 555-56, 616
Dallas Cowboys, 524
Dallas Radio Personalities and stations 551
Daly, John Charles, 4, 462
Dana Farber Cancer Ctr (the Jimmy Fund) Boston, 429
Dancing with the Stars, 57, 500
Daniel, Dandy Dan, 546, 613
Daniels, Yvonne, xxiii, 110, 337, 551, 620
Dark, Johnny, 546, 553
Dary, Alan, 421, 551
Davies, Gwen, 331
Davis, Anne B., 100, 157
Davis, Don, 546
Davis, E. Alvis, 621
Davis, Elmer, 458, 461
Davis, Jeff, 58-59, 96, 615, 648-49, *photo, 115*
Dawn of Correction - The Spokesmen, 59
Day, Doris, aka Doris Mary Ann Kappelhoff, 256, 543
Day sheet, how to prepare one, 172
Dayton Ohio, 248, 332
Daytona Beach, FL, 611-12
Dean, "Dizzy" Jay Hanna, 530
Deane Jr. College, 78
Death and Dying, see *Child's World,* 493

De Camp, Rosemary, 331
December 7, 1941, Pearl Harbor, Hawaii, 462
Dee, Stephen, 175-76
Deering High School, Portland, ME, 87
Dees, Rick, 613
De Forest, Lee, 11, 323, 453, 537-38, 638
De Francesco aka Frankie Dee, 525, *photo, 533*
De Leath, Vaughn, *the original radio girl,* xxiii, 11, 325, *photo, 347*
Delilah, aka Delilah Luke, 332, 621, 647-48
Deline, Jim, 555
Dell, Bob, 555
Delray Beach, FL, 430
DeMartini, Marilyn, 242
Democratic Convention. 1924, Madison Sq. Garden NYC, 454
Demographics, 221, 559
Dempsey, Jack, 516
Denver, 78, 656
Denver boot, 424
Denver Broncos, 258
Denver, Joel, 73, 117, 656, *photo, 91*
Denver Radio Personalities and stations 551
De Suze, Carl, 48, 421, 551
Desimone, Joe aka Johnny Dollar, 309-10, 554
Detroit, 334-35, 550, 555, 557, 626, 643
Detroit Radio Personalities and stations 550-52, 663
Detroit Tigers, 530
Devil or Angel - Bobby Vee aka Robert Velline, 306
Dewar, Duncan, 84
De Young, Laurie, 49, 104, 316, 351, 393, 396
Diamond, Bob, 551
Dibiase, Dick, xvi
Dick & Dee Dee (Dick Gosling and Dee Dee Sperling), 305
Dickens, Charles, 522
Dick Summer's Good Night pod cast, 540
Diddley, Bo, 547
Diehl, Rose, 588, 646, *photo, 609*
DiGiovanni, Charlie, 511
Digital audio, 642-43
DiMillo's Restaurant, 237
Dion, (DiMucci) and the Belmonts, 225
Dion, Shawn, 643, *photo, 660*

Dish, 650
Disneyland, 239, 374
Disney TV Shows, 629
DisneyWorld, 265
D-J, disk (disc) jockey, dee-jay, 24, 105, 130, 337, 364, 367, 383, 427, 451, 509, 537-38, 541-42, 549, 552, 554, 556-57, 594, 616, 618, 622-25, 627, 641, 643, 654
Doc's Tavern, Augusta, ME, 224-26
Dr. Laura & Dr. Drew, 251
Dolan, Johnny aka Johnny Dollar, 552, 620
Domino, "Fats" Antoine, 225, 305
Dom Perignon, 424
Donahue, Phil, 4
Donahue, Tom "Big Daddy," 555
Donovan, Dan, 553, *photo*, 564
Donovan, Johnny, 617
Don Wade and Roma, 617
Dorman, Dale, 48, 211, 358, 616-18, *photo*, 231
Dory, Ray, 551
Dorothy Kilgallen & Dick Kollmar, 26, *photo*, 37
Doubleday, Deacon Robert, aka Elliot Apodnoz, 555
Dougherty, Chuck, 553
Douglas, Donna, 333
Douglas, Mike, xxiii, 4, 192, 194, 200
Dowd, Ken, 551
Dowe, Ken, 177
Downey, "Doc" Sean Morton, 552-53
Downs, Hugh, 4, 495
Downtown Joe, 381
Doyle, Amy, 81-82, 251, 582, *photo*, 232
Dozier, Lamont, 550
Dragnet, 31, 45
Dragonette, Jessica Valentia, 327
Drake, Bill, 313, 401, 551, 556-57, 642
Drake radio format, the, 557
Drake, Galen, 4, 53-54
Drake jingles, 623
Drees, Jack, 520
Drew, Paul, 550
Drier, Alex, 460
Drifters, the, 550
DuFresne, Don, 566
Dunaway, Chuck "Baby," 551
Dunkin Donuts, 354, 356, 426
Dunn, Dick, 472, 554
Dunn, Jay, 551, 554
Dunn, Shelly, 117, 138, 384
Dunphy, Don, 518-19
Durante, Jimmy, 334, 362
Dyar, Harrison Grey, 640
Dylan, Bob, 549

E

Early Risers Club with Chuck Sanford, 553
Eastern Kentucky Univ., 619
Easy Aces, 331-32
Edell, Dean, Dr., 500
Edgar Bergen and Charlie McCarthy Show, 30, *photo*, 37
Edison, Thomas, 640
Edmond, Oklahoma, 402
Ed Sullivan Show, 362
Edward R. Murrow Award, 187, 482
Edward Scissorhands, 166
Edwards, Bob, 474-75
Edwards, Douglas, 331, 462-63, *photo*, 484
Edwards, Ralph, 4
Edwards, Tommy, 110
Einstein, 374
Eisenhower Medical Center, 521
Ellerbee, Linda, *photo*, 210
Elliott, Winn, 4
Ellis, Grace, 493
Elstner, Anne, aka Stella Dallas on radio, 330
Elvis Presley, 128, 225, 306, 549, 621
Elvis' contract with RCA, 550
Elway, John, 258
Emerson College, xv, xxx, 52, 74, 78-79, 85, 101, 139, 146, 157, 318, 361, 373, 396, 399, 502-03, 612-13
Emerson,. Ralph Waldo, 87, 269, 280
Emery, Ralph, 553, 625, 629
Emily Post, 493
Emmis, 345
Emmy Awards, 57, 459, 469, 498, 524
Emory University, 469
Emrick, Mike, 527
England, 638
Enquirer, the, 113
Entercom, 345
ET (Entertainment Tonight), 435
Erick, Elspeth, 331
Erickson, Louise, 331
Erickson, Roger, 615
Ertegun, Ahmet and Nesuhi, 550
ESPN, 437, 543
Ethiopia, 456

Index • 677

Eubanks, Bob, 4, 165, 552
Europe, 334, 547
Eve of Destruction, Barry McGuire, 59
Everly Brothers, Don & Phil, 621
Experimental radio station, 8XK, 5

F
Fairness Doctrine, 473-74
Faith is a Song, autobiography of Jessica Dragonette, 327
Faith Percy, 224
Falconi, Pete, 64, 78, 618
Fantastic Four, TV Series, 629
Farber, Barry, 494, 509
Farrell, Reed, 554
Father Franc and Mother Goose story, 151-52
Faye, Alice, 10-11
Fayetteville, 262
Fear Factor, 374
Featherstone, Charlie, 555
FCC (Federal Communications Commission), 153, 160-61, 263, 309, 324, 473-75, 478, 490, 548, 624, 639, 644-45
FCC deregulation and radio, xxiii, 644-45
Federal Government, 537
Federal Radio Commission, 324, 640
Feldman, Steve, 597, 599-600, 650, *photo*, 610
Feller, Sherm, 526
Felton, Verna, 331
Feminine Forum, 496
Fenno, Ralph, 554
Ferrari, 430
Ferree, John, 552
Ferrell, Will, 42
Ferry Field, 518
Fessenden, Reginald, 537, 637-38, 657
Fey, Tina, 42
Fibber McGee and Molly - Jim and Marian Jordan, 23, 495, 503, *photo*, 37
Fidler, Jimmy, 464
Fields, W.C., 30
50/50 Club, the, 326, 494
5th Beatle, the, 548
Figenshu, Bill, 656-57, *photo*, 660
Fighting priest, the, 489
Filene's, 365
Finley, Charlie, 112
Fireside Chats (FDR) U.S. Pres. Franklin Delano Roosevelt, 459
Fire Chief Show for Texaco, 10
First Amendment and freedom of speech, 160
First Impressions Creative Services - Pam Triolo, 397
Fisher, Eddie, *photo*, 209
Fisk, "Pudge" Carlton, 524
Fishkin, Ken, 566
Fitzgeralds, the, Ed and Pegeen, 26
Five basic rules for success in AM-Drive, 377
560 Revue with Arnie Kuvent, 554
Fixaris, Dick, 237, 554, *photos*, 278, 563
Fixaris, Frank, 150, 554, *photo*, 563
Flaherty, Pat, 517
Flannery, Harry W., 461
Fleishmann Yeast Hour, the, 10
Flexall, 46
Florida, 262-63, 553, 566, 617, 663
  Daytona Beach, 611-12
  Destin, 629
  Ft. Lauderdale, 196
Florida cont:
  Gainsville-Ocala, 262
  Miami, 625, 629
  Myrtle Beach, 262
  Orlando, 292, 650
  Tampa-St. Pete, 262
  West Palm Beach, xxx, 45, 100, 146, 170, 204, 219, 242, 262, 264, 397, 429, 437, 566
Flutie, Doug, 568
Flynn, Ray, 433, *photo*, 447
FM Radio, 7, 315, 364, 473, 499, 548-49, 641-42, 648, 652, 655-57
Forbes, Earl, *photo*, 115
Forbes Field, 516
Ford, Art, 543, 628
Ford, 49, (bullet-nose), 631
Ford C. Frick Award, 524
Ford, Gerald, U.S. Pres., 461
Ford, Joe, 63, 104, 126, 552, *photo*, 72
Ford, John, 5
Format, basic execution, 559
Forsythe, John, 119, 182, 650, *photo*, 143
Fort Devens, MA, 367
Ft. Lee, NJ, 308
Fort Wayne, IN, 629
Founding fathers of Rock, 549
Four Seasons, the, 225, 428

Four Tops, the, 550
Fowle, Farnsworth, 460
Fowler, Jolly Rolly, 555
Foxborough, MA, 435
Fox News Channel, 76, 190, 222, 379, 454, 473, 491, 507
Fox, Sonny, 4
Foxx, Brian DeGeus, 51, 358, *photo, 409*
Foxx, Red, aka John Elroy Sanford, 160
Foy, Fred, vii, viii, 2, 5, 12, *photo, xiv*
Fractured Fairy Tales, Sherman, 226
Franc, Rev. Fr. Mark Franck, 151-152
France, 437, 439, 456
Francis, Arlene, aka Arline Francis Kazanjian, xxiii, 4, 332, *photo, 37*
Francis, Connie, 224
Frank, Barney, 247
Frank Crumit and Julia Sanderson, 25
Frankie Lyman and the Teenagers, 547
Franklin, Aretha, 250, 550
Franklin, Benjamin, 637
Franklin, Joe, 24
Frattare, Lanny, 521
Frawley, John, 344
Fred Allen Show, the, 19, 331, 334, 630
Frederick, Pauline, 323
Freed, Alan "Moondog," 1, 547-48, 553, 605, 616, 618, 621, 641, *photo, 562*
Freeman, Florence, 331
French Hour, the with Don Roy, 590
Freund, Jeff, 138
Fritz, Rod, 359, 480-81, 483, 616, *photo, 456*
Frost, David, 88, 111
Fujimoto, Joyce, 423
Fuller, Bob, 554, *photos, 563*
Fuller, Ken, 552
Furnod, Bob, 460
Future of Radio, 637

G
Gable, Clark, 559
Galati, Dr. Joe, 195-96, *photo, 207*
Galena, Illinois, 18
Gallagher, Mike, 491
Gallant, Norm, xv, 226
Galvin, Paul, 126
Gambling, John, 492, 533, 622
Gangbusters, 331
Garagiola, Joe, 186, 495, 524

Garde, Betty, 331
Gardner, Bill, 221, 351, 379, 616, *photo, 412*
Gardner, Gayle, 529
Garland, Judy, 334
Garland, Ken, 553
Garland, Les, 550
Garroway, Dave, 4, 495
Gears, Gary, 618
GE Home Circle with Grace Ellis, 493
Gehron, John, 110, 279, 285, 291, 293, 311, 403, 506, 616-18, *photo, 297*
Gene and Glenn (Gene Carroll & Glenn Rowell), 8, 23
Gene Autry's horse, Champion, 24
Gene Autry's Melody Ranch, 23
General Electric, 22, 29
General Mills (Foods), 330, 492
Genesee St. Buffalo, NY, 625
George Foster Peabody Awards, 498
George, Phyllis, former Miss America, 528
Georgia, 553
Gerberdine, Joan E., 344
Gere, Richard, 360
German broadcasters, 312
Gerson, Betty Lou, 331
Get Ready - Temptations, 305
Giants, New York and San Francisco, 519, 530
Gibb, Andy, 170
Gibbons, Floyd, 456-57, *photo, 484*
Gilbert, George, 616
Gilinsky, Steve, aka Steve Jay, 78, 600, 617, *photo, 610*
Gillette, 519
Gilman, Bob, 566
Gimbel's, 464
Ginsburg, Arnie "Woo Woo," 48, 551, 612, *photo, 564*
Gipper, 235
Glasscock, Duane, 388
Glasier, Bruce, 264
Glenn, Christopher, 463
Glenn, Tommy, 621
Glick, Larry, 51, 57, 118-19, 511-12, 551, *photo, pg. 515*
God, (reference to) 17, 65, 97, 100, 155, 213-14, 335, 438
God Bless America - Irving Berlin, 10, 326
Godfrey, Arthur, xxiii, 4, 12-15, 17-18, 126, 203, 328, 330, 619, *photo, 35*
Goldbergs, 325, 329, 331

Golden Age, Radio's, 1, 4-5, 12, 25, 127, 131, 155, 392
Golden Great 98.5 -WROR Boston, 60, 74, 121, 479
Golden Voice of the Golden Age of Radio, 324
Golden West Broadcasters, 24
Gone with the Wind, Rhett Butler & Scarlet O'Hara, 559-60
Good Guys, WMCA-570AM, NYC, 65, 546-47, 552, *photo, 562*
Good Lovin' - Young Rascals, 305, 307, 314
Good Vibrations - Beachboys, 550
Google, 4, 166, 179, 624, 652
Gordy, Berry Jr., 550
Gore, Al, 202
Gowdy, Cheryl, 523
Gowdy, Curt, xxiii, 4, 522-23, *photo, 532*
Grabman, Sandy, xvi
Graf Zeppelin, 457
Graham, Rev. Billy, 498
Graham, Sheila, 4, 329, 464, 493
Grahm, Jr. College, ix
Grandma got run over by a reindeer, Elmo & Patsy, written by Randy Brooks, 300
Grand Ole Opry, 618
GOP- Grand Old Party, Republican Convention, June 1924, 454, 461
Grand Slam with Irene Beasley on CBS, 330
Grange, "Red" Harold Edward, 520
Granik, Theodore, 492
Grant, Bob, 494
Gray, Barry, 494, 546
Gray, Dick, 553
Gray, Lee, aka Royce Lee Darling, 550, 613
Greaseman, aka Doug Tracht, 60
Great Balls of Fire - Jerry Lee Lewis, 225
Great Depression, the, 7, 8, 11, 455-56, 642
Greater Media, 132, 281, 345, 586, 602, 652
Green River, WY, 523
Greenville, VA, 326
Greer, Charlie, 547, 613, 616
Gregg, Virginia, 331
Griffin, Merv, 4, 200, 368
Grizzard, Herman, 553
Groovin' - Young Rascals, 307
Growing up in the 50s with Portland ME radio, photo, 563
Guedel, John, 21, 194
Guiney, Bob, 433

Gumbel, Bryant, 435-36
Gunderson, Roy "The Bellboy," 551

H

Hackett, Ted, 551, 555
Hahn, Helen, 9, *photo, 35*
Haile, Mike, 69, 283, 617, *photo, 71*
Hall, Claude, 556
Hall, Hallsey, 615
Hall, Monte, 4
Halper, Donna, xxiii, 53, 156, 337-38, 394-95, *photo, 163*
Hamden, CT, 524
Hamilton, Bob "Ham," 174, 177-179,
Hamilton, George, IV, 369
Hamilton, Jack, 368
Hamilton Music Store, 5
Hancock, Hunter, 552
Handel on the Law, 500
Hannity, Sean, 74, 191, 505, 507-08
Hannon, Mark, 282, 617, 651, *photo, 296*
Happiness Boys, the - Billy Jones & Ernie Hare, 8, *photo, 35*
Happiness Exchange, the, 495
Happy Homemaker on KMBC, 493
Harden and Weaver - Willard Scott & Ed Walker, 555
Harding, Warren, U.S. Pres. 454, 639
Harkness, Richard, 460
Harlem, New York, 329, 464
Harold Parker State Forest, 437
Harpo Radio Productions, 291, 616
Harriott, Jim, 546
Harris, Dean, 555
Harris Estelle, *photo, 210*
Harris, Radie, 493
Harrison, Harry, xi, 61, 65, 122, 158, 351, 357, 543, 546-47, 553, 613-14, 616-17, 622 , *photo, 409*
Harrison, Patty, 357, 617
Harrison, Michael, 491
Harry Potter, 439
Harry, Simeone Chorale, 83
Hart, Mary, *photo, 210*
Hartman, David, 4
Hartman, Harry, 518
Harvard College, 506
Harvard Medical Building, 3 Fenway Plaza, 128
Harvard University, 432, 637
Harvard Law School, 520

Harvey, Paul, aka Paul Harvey Aurandt, 168, 460, 466
　Harvey, "Angel," aka Lynne Cooper, 466
Harwell, Ernie, 530
Hasbrouck Heights, New Jersey, 18
Hauptmann, Bruno, 462
Havlicek, John, 569
Hawaii, 424, 427
Hawaii Radio Personalities and stations, 552
Hawaiian Telephone Co., 423
Hawkins, Dale, 220
Hawn, "Goldie" Jean, 439
Hawthorne, Jim, 552
Hay, Jean Ruth, 331, *photo, 347*
Hayden, CO, 496
Hayes, Bruce, 556
Haymes, Dick, 543
HD, 643, 648, 651-52
Hear It Now, 459
Hearns, Thomas, 519
Heater, Gabriel, 462, *photo, 484*
Heaven Must Be Missing An Angel - Tavares, 305
Hello Mary Lou - Rick Nelson, aka Eric Hilliard Nelson, 306
Hemingway, Ernest, 522
Henaberry, Bob, 52
Hendrix, Jimi, 336
Henley, Don, *photo, 209*
Henri, Bernie, 607-08
Henry, Bill, 461
Henry, Joseph, 637, 640
Herb Jepko's Nitecap Show, 496
Hercules (the movie), 421
Herlihy, Ed, 155, 334
Herman, Woody, 494
Herrold, Charles Doc, 537
Herrold College of the Wireless, 328
Herrold, Sybil, 328
Hertz, Heinrich (Hertzion Waves), 638
Hesburgh, Rev. Fr Ted, 375
Heston, Charlton, 140
Hewitt, Foster, 517
Hewitt, Hugh, 499, 505-07
Heywood, Bill, 553
Hi Ladies, 192
Hicks, George, 461
Hider, Ed, 551, *photo, 564*
High Bridge, NY, 537
High School Billboard, 47

High Stakes - The Melanie Morgan Story, 620
Higby Mary-Jane, the queen of daytime serials, 330, *photo, 347*
Hilltop House, 330
Hilton, Paris, 651
Hindenburg, 458
Hobbins, Barry, 565
Hoberman, Ben, 495
Hodges, Russ, 519
Hoffman, Howard, 555
Hoffman, Lynn, *photo, 232*
Hogan, Rev. Fr. Jerry, *photo-xxxiii*
Holiwski, Frank, S.Sgt. USMC ret., Drill Instructor, xvi, 98
Holland, Brian and Eddie, 550
Holland, "Doc" Leonard, 518
Holly, "Buddy," aka Charles Hardin Holley, 225, 549
Hollywood, 105, 421
Hollywood Walk of Fame, 23
Holt, Jim, 551
Holy Bible, 139, 336, 537, 657
Holy Cross College, 483
Holy Grail, 247
Holy Rosary, 151-52
Holy See, the, 489
Home Makers Club with Ida Bailey Allen, 492
Home with Arlene Francis on NBC-TV, 332
Honk Kong, 615
Honolulu City Morgue, 423
Honolulu Hawaii Radio Personalities and stations, 552
Hooper, C.E. ratings, 28, 75, 459
Hooters, 171
Hoover Herbert, US Pres., 489, 639-40
Hope, Bob, aka Leslie Townes, 26-28, 170-71, 334, 362, *photo, 38*
Hopper, Hedda, 329, 464, 493
Hot AC, 314
Hot Hits - Mike Joseph, 550
Hottelet, Richard C. (Curt), 461
Hour of Smiles, 19
House, Gerry, 629
House Party with Art Linkletter, 22, 194,
House Sitters, Steve Martin & Goldie Hawn, 439
Houston, *xxx*, 242-43, 249, 261, 343, 352, 418, 429, 437, 469, 555-56, 618, 651

Index • 681

Houston Astros, 215, 521
Houston NFL franchise, Oilers, Texans, 426
Houston Radio Personalities and stations 552
How Can I Be Sure - Young Rascals, 307
Howard Johnson's, 520
Howard, Specs, 83
Huckabee, Mike, 17
Hudson, "Emperor" Bob, 552
Hughes, Charles Evan, 453
Hughes, Nina, 242
Hull, Warren, 4
Humility Prayer, xiii
Hummert, Anne & Frank, 332
Humphreys, Suzie, 628
Hunter, Ben, 496
Hunter, Clif, 237, 246
Huntley-Brinkley Report, the, (Chet Huntley & David Brinkley), 469-70
Hurst, Wilson, 553
Husing, Ted, 457-58, 518-19
Hyland, Robert, 495

I

Ian, Janis, 549
I Do, I Do, again, 437, *photo,* 452
Igo, Chuck, 48, 390-91, *photo,* 69
I'll be right back - Mike Douglas, 193
Illinois, 480
I'll Walk Alone, 333
I Love A Mystery, 619
I Love Lucy, 379
I'm In Love Again - Fats Antoine Domino, 305
I'm Walkin' - Fats Antoine Domino, 305
Imus, Don (I-Man), 39, 94, 102, 106, 355, 364, 388, 553, 623, *photo,* 634
Incan Flute Temple, 326
Indianapolis, 628
Indianapolis Speedway Net., 494
Infinity Broadcasting, 586
Ingram, Dan, 364, 547, 553, 613-14, 616-18, 625
Ingraham, Laura, 39, 74, 494
Inside Radio/ M Street, 344
IRS (Internal Revenue), 436
Internet, 131, 174, 179-80, 291, 311, 502, 616, 643, 648, 651, 653, 655, 657-658
Invisible Stars, A Social History Women In American Broadcasting - Donna

Halper, 394
Ipod, 62, 131, 397, 403, 624, 644, 648, 651, 654-55
Irene Wicker, the Singing Lady, 329
Irwin, Jim aka Peter Martin, 554
It Only Takes A Minute Girl - Tavares, 305
It's A Miracle - Barry Manilow, 78
It's What's between the music that counts, 545
I-Tunes, 656
I've Been Lonely Too Long - Young Rascals, 307
Izod, 434

J

Jack Armstrong, the All-American Boy, Wheaties, 1, 415, 543, 629
Jack Benny Program, the, 19, 630
Jack Daniels, 360
Jackson, Andy "Big Ange" aka John Manzi, 631
Jackson, Dave, 589
Jackson (TN) High School, 50
Jackson, Lewis, 570
Jackson, Michael, 306, 435, promotional piece, 449
Jacksonville FL Radio Personalities and stations 552, 611
Jacobs, Ron, 313, 315, 552
Jacoby, Les Howard, 77, 197, 262, 617, *photos,* 207, 277
James, Dennis, 4
Jasper, J. Alan, xv, 149, 156, 228, 592
Jasper White's Restaurant (Boston), 424
Jay, Phil, aka Frank Coxe, 552
Jed the Fish (KROQ), aka Jed Gould III, 263
Jeffers, Herb, 499
Jeffers, Carl, 499
Jeffords, Charlie, 631
Jeffrey, J.J., 551, 554, *photo,* 563
Jello, 20
Jepko, Herb, xxiii, 496-98
Jergens lotion, 465
Jesuits, 6, 98, 432
Jesus, 97
Joe and Andy Family, the, vii, 43, 80, 121, 125, 128, 167, 189, 339, 350, 359, 361, 363-64, 370, 385-86, 422, 424, 426-27, 429, 435-36, 490-91, 500, 595, 612, 617, 661, *photos,* 409-10, 444, 447, newspaper

articles, 441-46, 448-451
Joe and Andy coffee mug, 435-36, photo's, 69,
Joe and Andy C-Note Orchestra & G-string band, 421
Joe and Andy Family, *photos, 447, moms, 452*
Joe and Andy 5:30 Club, 363
Joe and Andy, the Head Brothers, 363-64
Joe and Andy head to Rome...New York? 448
Johns, George, 318, 393
Johnson, Bea, aka Joanne Taylor KMBC, Kansas City, 330, 493
Johnson, Dick, 554, *photo-563*
Johnson, Harry, 527
Johnson, Richard "Rick B'wanna Johnny,"554
Johnson, Tim, 102, 242, 418-19, 651
John the mailman aka John Muscillo, *photo, 209*
Joint Communication - John Parikhal, 312
Jolson, Al, 28, *photo, 38*
Jonathan living Seagull - Richard Bach, 66
Jones, Candy, 495, 498
Jones, Davy, *photo, 209*
Jones, Mary, 494
Jones, Quincy, 118
Jones Radio Network, 394
Jones, Ted, 555
Joplin, Janie aka Vida Jane Butler, 334
Jordan Marsh, 365
Jordan, Michael, 94-95, 498
Josefberg, Milt, 21
Joseph, Mike, 550
Josephs, Lou, aka Lou Joe BuczynskI, 318-19, 542
Joshua from the Bible, 97
Joy Boys, Willard Scott and Ed Walker, 555
Joyce, Bob, xv
Joyner, Tom, 39, 103, 265, 619
Judeo-Christian principals, 17
Junior Achievement, 624
Jupiter Hospital, FL, 100
Just Plain Bill, 332
Justice, Larry, 542
Justin, Dan, 61

K
Kalmer, Ned, 461

Kaltenborn, H. (Hans) V., 457-58, *photo, 484*
Kamm, Herbert, 56
Kansas, 646
  Salina, 588
  Topeka, 588, 647
Kansas City, MO, 371, 460, 546, 620
Kansas City Athletics, 528
Kansas City Radio Personalities and stations 552
Kards for Kids, St. Jude'- Ranch for children, 429, *photo, 446*
Karlin, Lisa, 622
Karr, Buddy aka Tom Bigby,
Karr, Paula, 494
Kasem, Casey, 165, 168, 382, 573, 586, 612, *photo, 413*
Kate Smith Speaks, 326
Kaufman, Murray the "K," 547-49, 618
Kay, Ronnie, 553, 621
Kaye, Barry, 104-05, 552, 587, *photo, 116*
Kaye, Jefferson, 543, 551
Kay Kyser's Kollege of Musical Knowledge, 192
Kellogg Company, 329
Kelly, Jockey Joe, aka Joe Rateau, 551, *photo, 276*
Kelly, Joe, 251, 392, *photo, 564*
Kelly, MG, 53, 553, 618, *photo, 70*
Kelly, Skip, 84, 228
Kelly, Shotgun Tom, 554
Kelly, Steve, 551
Kennedy, Bob, 495
Kennedy, Jacqueline, 200
Kennedy, Jayne, 528
Kennedy, Tom, 4, 48, 551
Kent, Don, 509
Kerrigan, Nancy, *photo, 442*
Kerry, John Sen., 426
Kerwin, Tim, 361
Keyes, Don, 556
Khan, Julie, 340
Kids Say The Darnest Things - Art Linkletter, 22, 194
Kincaid, "Cookin" Jo-Jo, 618
King, Ben E., *photo, 209*
King, Billie Jean, 141
King, Chuck, 613
King, Jean, xxiii, 332
King, Larry, aka Lawrence Harvey Zeiger, xxiii, 4, 185-86, 467, 498-99, 569,

photo, 513
King of Queens, 182
King of Rock and Roll, 548
King, Steve, 109-11, 342, 551, *photo, 116*
Kingsley, Bob, 612
Kingsley, Myra, 493
Kingston, Steve, 52
Kinney's shoes, 613
Kirby, Durwood, 73
Kitchell, Alma, 324
Kitchen Party with Frances Lee Barton, 493
Klahr, Dave, 344
Klaven & Finch, Gene Klaven and Dee Finch, 553, 614, 628
Klestine, Fred, 551
Knapp, Chuck, 553, *photo, 564*
Knight, Russ, "the Weird Beard," 551
Knox, Ken, 556
Komando, Kim, 500
Koplowitz, Zoe, 114
Korean War, the, 496
Kraft, Bob, 125
Kraft Music Hall (Kraft Foods), 28, 155
Kravis Center, the, 204
Krispy Kreme, 354, 405
Kroeger, Gerry, Prof, 101-02, 139-40
Kruh, David, 364-67, *photo, 410*
Kuvent, Arnie, 242, 554

L

Labarbara, Jim, Cincinnati's Music Professor, 83, 109, 117, 551, *photo, 276*
Labine, Claire and Matt, 427
Labunski, Steve, 546
Lacey, Bob, 52, 104, *photo, 70*
Laco Shampoo Hour, 640
Ladd, Jim, 552
Ladysmith, VA, 629
Lakehurst, NJ, 457
Lamour, Dorothy, 27
Landecker, "Records" John, 617-18, 627
Landry, Ron, 551-52
Lange, Jim, 4
La Pierre, Gary, 186, 481-83, 630, *photo, 486*
Laporte, Leo, 500
Laquidara, Charles, 51, 388, 390, 617
Laramie, WY, 524
Larrabee, Seth, 554
Larsen, Don, 528

LaSalle College, 59
LaSorda, Tommy, 112
Lassie, photo, 210
Last Contest, the, KCBQ, San Diego, 438, 554
Last.fm, 644
Last Supper, the - Leonardo da Vinci, 138
Last Train From Berlin - Howard K. Smith, 460
Las Vegas, 61
Latulippe, Don, 349, 640-41, *photo, 486*
Lauper, Cyndi, *photo, 209*
LaVallee, Doug, 86, 295, 553, *photo, 92*
Lawlor, Ritchie, 1
Law Men vs. Real Law Men Softball Game, 429, 434, *photo, 447*
Lawrence, Bob (Bobbie), 613, 621
Lawrence, Gary, 344
Lawrence, Lucky, 553
Layne, Zella, 492
Leave it to the Girls, 333
Leavitt, "Gunny" Frank, USMC ret., xvi
Lebanon, TN, 629
Lee, Brenda, 224
Legal Seafoods, 511
Lehman, Lynn, 619
Leiber (Jerry) and Stoller (Mike), 550
Leigh, Vivien, 559
Lemke, William, 489
Leominster, MA, 396
Leno, Jay, 42, 124, 167, 374, 594, *photo, 208*
Leonard, Chuck, aka Charles Wesley, 617
Leonard, Dandy Dan, 555
Leonard, Harvey, 359
Leonard, Howie, 554, *photo, 563*
Leonard, Roy, 551
Leonard, Sugar Ray, 519
Leone, Jill, 566
Leslie, Kim, 398
L'Espalier's Restaurant, 436
Lester, Mickey, 405
LeSueur, Larry, Laurence Edward, 461
Let The Four Winds Blow - Fats Antoine Domino, 305
Let's Pretend, 331
Let's Talk it over, 324
Letter, the, Perry Simon's, 509
Letterman, David, 191, 204
Levasseur, Dave, xv
Levin, Mark, 499
Lewis, Abby, 331

Lewis, Bob-A-Loo, 613
Lewis, Bob, aka Norman Freelander, 616
Lewis, Fulton, Jr., 460
Lewis, Hal "Aku Aku," 55
Lewis, Jerry, 362
Lewis, Jerry Lee, 549
Lewis, Robert Q., 4
Lewis, Sinclair, 458
Lexington, KY, 58, 379
Leykis, Tom, 496
Liebert, Jerry and Mike Stoller, 550
Lifeboat - Alfred Hitchcock, 334
Life Magazine, 50, 641
Light, Joe, 553
Limbaugh, Rush, 57, 74, 76, 271, 488, 494, 499, 505-06, 508
Lincoln Jr. High School Band, Portland, ME, 86
Lindberg, 'Lucky" Charles, 456
Lindlahr, Victor, 492
Linkletter, Art, xxiii, 4, 21-22, 194, 619, photo, 37
Lipton Tea & Soup, 18, 328
Lit, Hy, 553, 616, 626
Little Foxes, the, 334
Little Orphan Annie, 332, 415, 629
Little, Patsy, 496
Little Richard, aka Richard Wayne Penniman, 6
Little Rock Arkansas, 462
Little Walter Devenne, 51
Live Aid, 651
Live 5, WLOB, Portland, ME, 554, photo, 563
Lloyds of London, 556
Lobell, Bob, 496
Local heroes: Baseball on Capital Region Diamond, 528
Lodge, John, 400
London, England, 437, 439
London, Joan, 4
Lone Ranger, the, viii, 2-3, 5, 10, 12, 503, 629
Lonesome Gal with Jean King, 332
Longfellow, 336
Long Island, 546, 549, 640
Loomis, Mary Texanna, 328
Looney Laws & Silly Statutes, 174
Loren & Wally, Loren Owens and Wally Brine, 617
Lorenz, George "Hound Dog,"551, 625

Lorenzo Jones, 332
Lorrain, Jimmy, xvi
Los Angeles, 5, 313, 340, 352, 379, 394, 496, 613
    Los Angeles Dodgers, (and Brooklyn), 112, 521
    Los Angeles Lakers, 113
Los Angeles Radio Personalities and stations 505, 548, 550, 552, 614, 630
Los Angels Times, 657
Lost 45s, 306
Lost in Space, 629
Louis, Joe, 519
Louisiana, 643
Louisville, Kentucky, 619, 629
Love Me Do - Beatles, 138
Love, "Baby" Walt, 550
Lowe, Jim, 543
Lowell Thomas and the News, 457
Lowe's New York, Broadway, 516
Luddy, Barbara, 331
Lujack, Larry, 353, 551, 617, 626-27
Lum n' Abner - Chester Lauck and Norris Goff *Jotem down store*, 11
Lund, Jon, 243
Lundy, Ron, 357, 364, 547, 613, 616-17
Lux Radio Theater, 334, 630
Lynnfield (MA) High School, 399
Lyons, Ruth aka Ruth Reeves, xxiii, 325-26, 494
Lynch, Bill, 463
Lynch, Sheri, 52
Lynchburg, VA, 612

M
Ma Bell, 639
Ma Perkins - Virginia Payne, 3, 256, 330, 503, photo, 347
MacAleney, Bob, 361, photo, 297
MacDonald, Margaret, aka Betty Moore, 493
Mack, Jay, aka James MacIsaac, 551
Mack, Jim, 554
Mack, Nila, 331
Mack, Ted, 4
MacKay, Scott, 78, 618, photo, 442
MacKenzie, Ken and Simone, 553, photo, 563
MacKenzie, Murdo, 28
MacNeil, Bob, vii, ix, x, *photos, xiv*, 486
Maddow, Rachel, 506

Madera, Johnny, 59
Madonna, 306
Magnum P.I.. 422-24
Maguire, Cindy, 82-83, 267
Maher, Jay, 554, *photo, 563*
Mail Call, 334
Maine, xxx, 29, 125, 228, 359, 496, 565
    Augusta, xxx, 40, 47, 226
    Bangor/Ellsworth, 61
    Biddeford, 40, 47, 52
    Brunswick, 566
    Bucksport, 61
    Old Orchard, 19
    Pine Tree State, 589
    Poland Spring, 591
    York Beach, viii
Maine Assoc. of Broadcasters, 317
Maine Line, 496
Maine Mariners, 527
Maine Turnpike, 48, 597
MLB, Major League Baseball, 77, 438, 516, 518-21, 523, 528-30
    All Star Game, 519, 523
    Hall of Fame, 524, 530
    Mon. Night Baseball, 521, 523
    Saturday Game of the Week, 523
    World Series, 517, 519, 522, 524, 611
Major Mudd, 631
Make Believe Ballroom, 7, 24
Malone, Sam, 618
Manhattan, 256, 548, 622
Manhattan College, 519
Manhattan Gazette, 331
Manilla, Guy, 496
Manley, Todd, 265, 619
Mann, Terry, 555
Manson, Charlotte, 331
Mantovani, 590
Mara, Ben, 399, *photo, 413*
Mara, Julee, aka, "Jewels," 399-400, *photo, 413*
Marantz recorder, 396
Marathon Oil, 248
March, Hal, 4
March of Time, 458
Marconi Award, 378
Marconi, Guglielmo, 638
Marine Corps Boot Camp, Parris Island, SC, xxix, 98, 107, 129
Marine Corps, USMC, Marine, xxix, 6, 107, 129, 159, 223, 359, 366, 387, 435, 456, 522
Marine Corps League, 456
Marlin Broadcasting, 500
Marlowe, Bill, 551, 591-92, 612
Marquette, Univ., 17
Marriott Long Wharf, Boston, 428
Marsden, Ralph, 605
Marshall, Gary, *photo, 210*
Marshfield, MA, 435
Martelle family members, *photos, xvi, xxxi, xxxii, xxxiii*
Martelle, Jenny, aka Joan, 99, *photo, xxxi, 452*
Martelle, Joe, vii, ix, 47, 51, 80, 167, 264, 349, 364-67, 386, 397, 582, 661-64, *photo's, xiv, xxxiii, xxxiv, 92, 115-16, 163, 207, 209-10, 231-32, 276, 278, 297, 410-11, 442, 446, 451, 532-33, 564, 610, 633, 635, 660, 664-66*
Martelle, Kimmie, xvi, 3, 99, 100-01, 157, 196, 214-15, 375, 436-37, 571, 602, 661-64, *photos, 664, 666*
Martelle, Marty, 23, *photo, xxxi*
Martin & Lewis, 362-63
Martin, Bob "Startin.", 247, *photo, 276*
Martin, Dave, 512, 550
Martin, Dean, 362
Martin, George, 6
Martin, Halloween, 394
Martin, Harry, 83
Martin, Howie, 149
Martin, Ned, 508, 522-24, 621
Martindale, Wink (Winston), 50, 552, 618-19, *photo, 70*
Maryland, 185
Mary Noble Backstage Wife, 332
Mason, Dan, 292-93, 619, 651, *photo, 297*
Massachusetts (Mass), 623
    Boxford, 356
    Brighton, 432
    Brookline, 332, 470
    Foxborough, 435
    Marshfield, 435
    Nahant, 368, 509
    Natick, 630
    Newton, 614
    Plymouth, 522
    Quincy, 522, 529
    Reading, viii
    Waltham, 528

Wellesley, 630
Mass Broadcasters Hall of Fame, 58, 349, 526
Mass Radio Stations, 318
Masters Golf Tournament, 520
Masters, John aka John Burgomaster, 48
Masucci, Dr. Peter, 386
Mathews, Pat, 554
Matinee Frolic, (WPOR-AM 1490-Portland, Me), 554
Matoin, "Mike" Gene aka Mike Gray, 65, 149, 467, *photo, 163*
Maxwell House Coffee, 329, 331
Mayberry RFD, 161
Mayfield, Carl P., 629
Maynard, Dave, 48, 118, 421, 551, 615, 617, 622
Mc Aleney, Bob, 361, *photo, 297*
Mc Bride, Mary Margaret, aka Martha Dean, xxiii, 4, 327-28, 492, *photo, 347*
Mc Cain, John, 191
Mc Call, Frank (Francis), 461
Mc Cambridge, Mercedes, 331
Mc Carthy, J.P., 551
Mc Cartney, C.C., 50, *photo, 116*
Mc Cartney, Paul, 6, 196-99, *photo, 207*
Mc Cay, Jim, 526
Mc Cloud, "Coyote" William, 629
Mc Coy, Joe, 282
Mc Cray, Mark, 85, 264-65, 357-58, 619, *photo, 277*
Mc Dermott, Jack, 554
Mc Donald, Walt, 344
Mc Donalds, aka Mickey D's, 238, 319, 437, 605
Mc Donough, Eddie, xv
Mc Elhone, Eloise, 333
Mc Fadden, Bernard, 492
Mc Gorrill, Chris, aka Chris Mack, 263-64, *photo, 277*
Mc Kee, Bob, 551
Mc Kenney, Clif, xvi
Mc Kenzie, Ed, 557, *photo, 38*
Mc Lane, Drayton, Jr., 215
Mc Lendon, Gordon, 75, 373, 555-56, 642
Mc Mahon, Ed, 495
Mc Mahon, Pat, 553
Mc Mahon, Vince, 54
Mc Millan, Joe, 61, 111, *photo, 72*
Mc Nair, Bob, 426
Mc Namee, Graham, 10, 456, 518-19,

photo, 35
Mc Neeley, Marty, 551
Mc Neil, Marty, 396
Mc Neill, Don, 3-4, 12, 15-18, 618, *photo, 35*
Mc Nellis, Maggie, 493
Mc Pherson, Aimee Semple, 324
Medved, Michael, 491, 499
Meet the WBZ Disc Jockeys, 421
Meet The Press, 47, 54, 201, 332-33, 493
Meier, Gary, 551, 617
Melendrez, Sonny, 552
Melrose, Edythe Fern, 493
Melvin X. Melvin, 48
Memorial Day thru Labor Day, 631
Memphis, 262, 335, 549
Memphis Radio Personalities and stations 550, 552
Menefee, Dave, xvi
Men in my little girls life, the - Mike Douglas, 193
Menino, Tommy, Boston Mayor, *photos, 210, 486*
Mercier, Ray, 554
Mercury Research - Mark Ramsey, 312
Mercury Theater of the Air with Orson Welles, 331
Merman, Ethel, 334
Merriman, Randy, 4
Merry Christmas, 300
Meserand, Edythe, 324
Metcalf, Fred, xv
Metheny, Terril, 619
Methodist Hospital - Houston, 196
Metro Networks & Shadow Traffic, vii, 293, 344, 397, 482, 625
Metropolitan Opera, 325, 639
Metropolitan Stadium, Minn., 528
MTA - Metropolitan Transit Authority, the "T," 365
Meyer, Ruth, 546
Miami, 494, 629
Miami Radio Personalities and stations 552-53
Michael, George, 617
Michaels, Al, 526
Michigan, 308, 662
Michigan Association of Broadcasters Hall of Fame, 147
Midwest Broadcasting School, 110
Mike and Mike on ESPN, Mike Greenwell

& Mike Golic, 543
Mikes Don't Bite by Helen Sioussat, 327
Milberg, David, 242
Millan, Cesar, 250
Miller, Dennis, 499
Miller, Howard, 551
Miller, Humble Harvey, 59. 616, 626
Miller, Mel, 134, *photo, 564*
Miller, Paul, 553
Miller, Stephanie, 394
Mills Brothers, 256
Mills, Heather, 198-99
Mills, Marjorie, 324
Miner, Jan, aka Madge, *the Palmolive girl*, 330- 31, *photo, 347*
Minetta, Ellen, aka Fanny Barbour on NBC's *One Man's Family*, 330
Minneapolis, MN, 215, 415
Minneapolis Radio Hall of Fame, 613
Minneapolis Radio Personalities and stations 553
Minnesota, 653
Minnesota Twins, 615
Minnesota Vikings, 528
Minot, ND accident story and radio, 475
Mr. District Attorney, 618
Mr. Keen, 332
Miskind, Barry, 329
Mississippi flood, 462
Mister D.A., 618
Mister Lonely - Bobby Vinton, 306
Mitchell, Bob, 59
Mitchell, Skinny Johnny, 621
MIW, Nassau Media Partners (Alliance for Women in Media article), 344
Mock, Jack, 552
Moes, Andy, 43-45, 127-28, 256, 339, 350, 355, 359-66, 386, 393, 423-26, 432, 435, 490-91, *photos, 231, 278, 297, photo of Andy's mom, Flo, and the author's mom, 452*
Mona Lisa, 598
Money Talks with Bob Brinker, 500
Monitor (NBC), 23, 30, 494-95, 540
Monroe, Marilyn, 200
Monsignor Francis Culkin, 434
Monson, Kelly, 619, *photo, 634*
Montana, Joe, 569
Montgomery Alabama Radio Personalities and stations 553
Montillo, Sam, 356

Montreal Expos, 528
Moody, Bill J., 553
Moore, "Gary" aka Thomas Garrison Morfit, III, 4
Moore, Harv, 555
Moore, Joe, 62
Moore Judge John Bassett, 200
Moorehead, Agnes, 331
Moore paints, 493
More Than A Woman - Tavares, 305
Morgan, Bob, 623-24
Morgan, Claudia, 331
Morgan, Edward P., 460
Morgan, Henry, 495
Morgan, Joe & Dorothy, 436-37, newspaper story, 450
Morgan, Louise, 551
Morgan, Melanie, 108, 202, 342, 460-61, 620, *photo, 346*
Morgan, Robert W., 63, 105-06, 552, 623
Mormon Tabernacle Choir, 602
Morning Mouth, the, 372
Morning Music Hall with J.P. McCarthy, 551
Morning Show survival kit, 355
Morning Skoop, the, 174-75
Morning Zoo, the, Z-100, NYC, 122
Morris, Jeannie, 527
Morrison, Herb, 457-58
Morrow, Bill, 28
Morrow, Cousin Brucie, vii, viii, ix, 7, 168, 313, 543, 547, 586, 610, 612-13, 616, 618, 631, *photos, xiv, 209*
Morse, Samuel, 640
Mortimer Snerd and Effie Klinker, 30-31
Morton, Ross "Mad Man," 555
Moses from the Bible, 97, 140
Most, Johnny, 526
Mother Teresa, 194
Motorola, 126
Motown, 550
Move America Forward, 342, 460, 620
Mowers, Bob, Spinners Sanctum, 554
M Street Publications, 344
MTV, MTV2, MTVU, 81
Mudd, Roger, 460
Mueller, Merrill, 461
Muller, Mathew Erich "Mancow," 371
Muncie, IN., 520
Muni, Scott, 549
Murdock, Carolyn, 359

Murdock, Charlie, 247
Murphy, Rev. Fr. Bernard, SJ, xv, 98, *photo, xxxii*
Murphy, Bob, 526, 530
Murphy, Eddie, 5, 42
Murphy, John, 257
Murphy, Robert, 265, 619
Murphy, Tom, 554
Murray, "Chatty" Patty, 629
Murrow, Edward R., x, 4, 200, 331-32, 453, 459-60, *photo, 484*
Museum of Radio-TV Broadcasting, 5
Musicitis, disease of, 544-45
Music from Studio X with Bill Marlowe, 591-92
Music of your Life, 50
Music Man - Meredith Wilson, 334
Music radio, see chapter 17, formats, 537
MBS (Mutual Broadcasting System), 30, 333, 458, 465, 473, 492-93, 497-98, 519-20, 530, 613
Mutual Street Arena, 517
MVP Awards, 193
Myers, Pete "Mad Daddy," 551, 621
My Girl - Temptations, 305
My Life in Rock n' Roll Radio, Cousin Bruce Morrow, 574
Myopia Polo Match for the March of Dimes, 429
My Space, 503
My Way - Frank Sinatra, 106

N

Nardone, Susan, *photo, 486*
Narragansett Bay beaches, 631
Narz, Jack, 4
Nashville, 178
Nashville Radio Personalities and stations, 394, 553, 629
Nathan, Mark, 302
Nathan, Norm, 108, 509, 551, 612
NAB (National Association of Broadcasters), 317, 338, 471, 652
NBA (National Basketball Association), 94-95, 520, 528-30, 567
NBC (National Broadcasting Company), 13, 19-22, 27-28, 30, 102, 130-31, 155, 167, 201, 243, 315, 324-25, 327-29, 332-34, 454, 458, 462, 469, 473, 492-95, 518-19, 549
  Laugh In, 551

News of the Day Roundup, 462
NIS - NBC Radio's News Information Service, 243, 473
Red and Blue Networks, 8, 11, 454, 464-65, 493
Sports, 523-24, 530
Talk Net, 201
Today Show, 427, 435
WWII NBC News Correspondents, 461
National Car Rental Center - Sunrise, FL, 196
NFL, National Football League, 180, 258, 381, 426, 520, 529-30, 568-69
  Mon. Night Football, 529
  Pro football Hall of Fame, 524
NHL, National Hockey League, 435, 517, 527, 529
NHL Pronunciation Guide, 527
NPR (National Public Radio), 395, 473
National Radio Hall of Fame, 147
National Sportswriters & Sportscasters Hall of Fame, 524
Nationwide Communications, 311, 313
Neal, Hal, 557
Neaverth, Dan, 543, 551
Nebel, Long John, xxiii, 494-95, 498, 616
Nebraska, 55
Negron, Chuck, *photo, 209*
Nellie Revell Show, the, 493
Nelson, Art, 556
Nelson, Gene, 554-55
Nelson, Harry, 259, 550-51, 620-21
Nelson, Howard, 509
Nelson, Jay, 551
Nelson, Lindsey, xxiii, 520, 530
Nelson, Rick, 225, 306-07
Nettleton, Jim, 553
Network, 311
Nevada Broadcasters Hall of Fame, 75-76
Never On Sunday, composer, Manos Hadjidakis, 497
New Bedford, MA, 305
New England, 111, 181, 367, 437, 522
New England Patriots, 480, 568
New England Tech, 78
New Hampshire, 228, 623
  Bedford, 500
  Claremont, 623
  Exeter, 228
  Keene, 78, 618
New Hanover (NH) High School, 469

Index • 689

New Haven, CT, 628
New Jersey, 302, 313, 325, 492, 546, 550, 612, 661-62
   Ft. Lee, 308
   Norwood, 357
   Ocean City, 626
   Pleasantville, 626
New Jersey Devils, 527
New Orleans, 305, 310, 653
News-Gazette, Inc., 283
NewsMax.com, 491
News Radio, 453
Newton, Graham, audio restoration service, 471-72
Newton-Wellesley Hospital, 99, 499
New Years Day, 518
New Years Eve, 663
New York American Newspaper, 453
New York City, 5, 18, 122, 177, 187, 256, 302, 313, 318, 323, 326-27, 332, 334-36, 351, 357, 427, 453-54, 457, 460, 463, 480, 482, 492, 494-96, 519, 540, 546-48, 610, 613-14, 616, 625-26, 628, 630, 643
New York City Radio Personalities and stations, 261, 301, 538, 543, 546-48, 550, 553, 617, 622
New York Post, 466
New York Daily Mirror, 464, 466
New York Film Critics Award, 334
New York Football Giants, 520
New York Giants, 517-18
New York George Washington Bridge, 357
New York Madison Sq. Garden, 328, 454
New York Marathon, 114
New York Mayor, Robert Wagner, *photo,* 37
New York Mets, 530
New York Post, 466
New York State Broadcasters Hall of Fame, xi
New York Statue of Liberty, 324
New York Stock Exchange, 77
New York Telephone Co., 459
New York Times, 325, 423, 466
New York Univ., 640
New York Yankees Stadium, 125, 328, 517-19, 528
New Yorkers, 494
Neyland, Robert R., 520
Niagara Falls, 649
Niagara, Joe, "the Rockin' Bird," 59, 553, 616, 626
Nichols, Lee, 621
Nightbird's final fling - Kathleen Warnock, 335
Night Owls, 246, 416
Night Prowl Show, 52. 79
Night Watch with Dan Reed, 471
Nights in White Satin - Moody Blues, 336
9-11, 204
Nitecap Radio Network (Nitecaps), 497
Nite, Norm N, 551, 621, *photo,* 634
Nobles, Gene, 553
Nolan, Jeanette, 331
Nomads without gonads, 239
Noory, George, 500
Norris, Richie, 589-90, *photo,* 609
Northeast Airlines "Yellow Bird," 228
North Carolina, 615
North Dakota, 489
Northeastern Univ. 53, 156
Norton, Mike, 554
Norwood, NJ, 357
Not Just A Sound, the Story of WLW Radio - Dick Perry, 256, 416
Notre Dame football, 520
Noveline, Nancy, 242
Now You're Talking, 505

O

Oakland A's, 112, 521
O'Brien, Joe, 546-47, 613
O'Brien, "Big" Ron, 627
O'Brien, Steve, 617
Ocean, Bobby (KCBQ), 550, 554
Ocean, Bobby "Ray," *photo,* 278
Ocean City, New Jersey, 626
Oceanside, NY, 74, 613
O'Connor, Paula, 119, 261, 292, 488
O'Day, Dan, 586
O'Day, DJ, 555
O'Day, Pat, 554
O'Donnell, Rosie, 384
Office of War Info, 458
Ogden Examiner, 497
Oh, God, starring George Burns, 22
Ohlone College, Fremont, CA, 125
Ohmart, Ben, xvi
Oh Wow! Songs, 307, 314
Okinawa, Japan, 62
Oklahoma, 8, 158
Oklahoma City, 75

Oklahoma City Radio Personalities and stations 553
Old Folk at Home, Stephen Foster, 11
Old Orchard Beach, ME, 19
Old Time Radio, 503
Old Time Radio Digest, 4
Oliver, Jack, 63, 76, 621, *photo, 91*
Olympics, 524, 526
Omaha, NE, 527, 556-57
One constant in radio is change, 654
One Man's Family, 330
O'Neal, Jimmy, 553
O'Neil, Bill, *photo, 278*
O'Neill, Jimmy, aka JFPO, 551, *photo, 276*
Ontario Canada, 471
Open the Door Richard - Jack McVea, Frank Clarke, 554
Opie & Anthony (Gregg Hughes & Anthony Cumia), 161, 318, 496
Orbison, Roy, 549
O'Reilly, Bill, xxiii, 188-90, 247
O'Reilly Factor, the, 188
Oreo's, 370
Orkin, Dick, aka Chickenman, 620
Orson Welles Mercury Theater, 629-30
Osborne, Mighty Mike, 618
Oscar Nominations, 344
Osgood, Charles, aka Charles Osgood Wood III, 117, 463-64
O'Shea, Michael, 177
Osmond, Donnie, 101
Our Gal Sunday with Vivian Smolen, 330, 332
Ovaltine, 415
Owens, Gary, 551
Oxford Univ., 98
Ozmon, Lorna, 238, 261, 268, 293, 316-18, 396, 423, 425, 436
Ozmon Media. 316-17

P

Paar, Jack, 4, 200, 202
Pahigian, Cary, 48, 114, 212, 235, 264, 292-93, 621, *photo, 231*
Paley, William S., x, 454
Palin, Sarah, 191
Pallan, Art, 553
Palmer, Jim, *photo, 532*
Palmer, John, 435-36
Palmer, Pattie, 242
Palmiter, Lesley, 622

Palmolive, 331
Palm Springs, 548
Palmolive Beauty Box, 327
Pandora, 644, 656
Paparelli, Judi, 105, 193, 199, 343, 622, 651, *photo, 207*
Paris, France, 334, 456
Paris, Missouri, 327
Paris, Ontario Canada, 333
Parker House, 435
Parks, Bert, 4
Parsons, Louella, 329, 464, 493
Partridge Family, the, 203
Pasadena, CA, 629-30
Patyk, Sandy, 651
Paul Harvey Drive, 468
Paul Harvey News & Comment, 187, 467, 482
Paul Harvey, the Rest of the Story, 467
Paul Harvey, You Said It, 466
Paul, Les, 549, 626
Pauley, Jane, 4
Paul Whiteman Presents, 333
Payne, Virginia, *aka Ma Perkins,* 330, *photo, 347*
Payola, 24
Pay radio, 652
Peabody Award, 469
Pearce, Al, 11
Pearce, Alice, 80-82, 582, *photo, 92*
Pearl Harbor, 170
Pearl, Jack, 19
Pearl Jam, 135
Pearson, Drew, 462
Pelletier, Jerry "JD," 58
Penner, Joe, 19
Penn State, 626
Pennsylvania, 616
People Are Funny, 21, 194
People Got To Be Free - Rascals, 307
People Magazine, 113
PPM (People Meter), 550, 656
Peoria, 262
Perkins, Carl, 549
Perry, Paul, 65, 77, 106, 168
Person to Person, 200, 459
Peter from the Bible, 97
Peter Pan peanut butter, 470
Peterson, Curt, 325
Pettengill, Todd, 261
Petty, Norman, 549

Index • 691

PGA Golf, 520, 530
Phazyme, 46
Philadelphia, 308, 458, 496, 616, 626, 643
Philadelphia Flyers, 326, 527
Philadelphia girls Catholic high school, 327
Philadelphia Phillies, 516
Philadelphia Radio Personalities and stations 553, 626
Philbin, Regis, 50
Philco radio, 152, 154
Philco Radio Time, 28
Phillies record label, 550
Phillips, Sam, 334, 549-50
Phillips, Wally, 352-53, 551, 626
Phoenix, 468, 482, 496, 570, 616, 630
Phoenix College, 496
Phoenix Radio Personalities and stations 553
Pickett, Wilson, 550
Pictorial History of Radio, A - Irving Settle, 639
Piel Brothers, Bert & Harry, 30
Pike's Peak, 401
Pio, Nonna Ma & Pa, 97
Pioneer radio pros, 8
Pioneer radio sportscasters, 517
Pitman, Linwood, xv
Pitt, Brad, 628
Pittman, Bob, 657
Pittsburgh, 520, 538
Pittsburgh Pirates, 516, 520-21
Pittsburgh Radio Personalities and stations, 309, 553, 639
Pittsburgh Steelers, 524
Please Don't Ask About Barbara - Bobby Vee, 306
Plugola, aka Payola, 24
Plymouth Rock, 537
Podcasts, 507
Pogue, Pogo aka Morgan White, 551
Points for PD and Talent, 272, 274, 283-84
Polo Grounds, NY, Braves VS Giants, 459, 518
P-1's (Preferred listeners), 304, 307, 315, 389
Poor Little Fool - Ricky Nelson, 306
Portland, ME, 16, 48, 111, 170, 212, 235, 242, 245-46, 259, 264, 292, 310, 358, 496, 527, 565, 587
Portland ME Radio Personalities and stations 553-54

Portland, OR, Marathon, 281
Post, Wiley, 9
Powers, Don, 45
Powers, Jimmy, 520
Prayer, 16
Preece, Sir W.H., 640
Prescott, Norm, 421
Presidential Medal of Freedom, 469
Pretty Woman - Roy Orbison, 314
Priebe, Ross, 621
Prince, aka Rogers Nelson, 498
Prince, "Bob" Robert Ferris, xxiii, 520-21
Princeton Review, 52
Princeton Univ. 517
Printer's Ink, 328
Pritchard, Florence, 333
Pro Bowlers Tour, 520
Procter & Gamble (Axiom), 15
Propeller One-Way Night Coach - John Travolta, 136
Provo, Utah, 619
Pryor, Richard, 5
Public Radio PD's Assoc., 317
Pupule, Aku, 552
Purdue Univ., 520
Purtan, Dick and Gail, 147, 221, 316, 358, 382, 552, 625, 662-63, *photo, 163, 666*
Purtan, Gail, 662, *photo, 666*
Purther, Jim, 344
Putman, Johnnie, 109-10, 342-43, *photo, 116*
Pvt. Ryan tour, 437, 439
Pyne, Joe, 4, 495

Q

Q Factor, 429
Quaker Oats cereal, 415-16
Quaker Oats early birds program, 8
Quaker Puffed Wheat & Rice Big Inch Land Contest, 415-16, *photo, 441*
Quasimodo, 372
Queen City of Cincinnati, Ohio, 518, 551
Quill, Barbara, 51, *photo, 486*
Quill, Joe, 51
Quill, Nancy, 51, 85, 132, 343, 622, *photo, 144*
Quillin, Ted, 75-76, *photo, 91*
Quinn, Sunny, So Florida radio pro/VO talent and wife of renowned drummer for Grand Funk Railroad, Don Brewer, 218-19

Quintal, Charlie, *photo montage A, Oldies show,* 411
Quivers, Robin, 379

R
RAB (Radio Advertising Bureau), 338
Radio City Music Hall, 9
Radio equipment *photo montage,* 485
Radio Formats, news, talk, sports and music, xxiv, 453-561
Radio City Music Hall, 9
Radio Hall of Fame, 30, 211, 337, 464, 466, 519, 548, 663
Radio Homemakers Club, 492
Radio Ink Magazine, 373, 612
Radio is a Survivor, 642, 646
Radio News, the evolution of, 472
Radio Premium Offer - Quaker Puffed Wheat & Rice
R& R, Radio & Records, 303, 351, 353
Radio Report, 178
Radio Spirits, 4
Radio Star, Radio Superstar - Bob Hamilton's, 174, 178
Radio Stars Magazine, 329

Radio Station call letters beginning with the letter "K"

KAAY-1090AM, little Rock, ARK, 615
KABC-790AM, LA, 495, 555
KABL-960AM, 92.1-FM, San Francisco, 61
KADY-1460AM & **KADI-96.5-FM** (the KADY TWINS), St. Louis, 554
KATT-1340AM, 100.5FM, Oklahoma City, 138, 384
KATZ-1600AM, St. Louis, 554
KBKH-950AM, Hattiesburg, MS, 620-21
KBZN-97.9-FM, Salt Lake City, 619
KCBQ-1170AM, San Diego, *The Last Contest,* 438, 554
KCBS-740AM, San Francisco, 560
KCMO-710AM, 103.7FM, Kansas City, MO, 463, 552
KCPX-1490AM, Salt Lake City, 619
KCTC-KGNR-1320AM, (originally KCRA), Sacramento, CA, 87
KDKA-1020AM, (originally 8XK in 1920), Pittsburgh, 516-17, 538, 553, 638-39

KDWB-63AM,101.3-FM, Minn.,105, 168, 215, 217, 351, 378, 613, 615, 624, 638
KELP-1590AM, El Paso, TX, 75
KEPO-690AM, El Paso, TX, today KHEY, 75
KEYN-103.7-FM, Wichita, KS, 63, 76, 621
KFAX-1100AM, San Francisco, 473
KFI-640AM, Los Angeles, 61, 75, 496
KFMB-760AM, 100.7, San Diego, 496, 552
KFOG-104.5-FM, San Francisco, 549
KFOX-1280AM, Los Angeles, 75
KFRC-1550AM, (today KZDG), San Francisco, 259, 350, 557, 620
KFSG-96.3-FM, Los Angeles, (today KXOL), 324
KFWB-980AM, LA, 75, 496, 552, 581
KFXY-pioneer station in Flagstaff, AZ in 1925, later station moved to Yuma, AZ, 328
KFYI-550AM, Phoenix, 482, 553
KGB-101.5-FM, 1360AM, San Diego, now 1360 is XTRA Sports, 21, 117, 138, 194, 384, 554, 557
KGBS-1020AM (today KTNQ) Los Angeles, 496, 552
KGMB-590AM (now KSSK) Honolulu, 552
KGO-810AM, San Francisco, 620
KGO-TV, Ch. 7, San Francisco, 342
KGU-760AM, Honolulu, 87
KHJ-930AM, LA, 53, 177, 313, 315, 401-02, 517, 552, 557, 613, 618
KHMX-MIX 96.5-FM, Houston, 618
KHOW-630AM, Denver, 402
KHVH-830AM, Honolulu, 552
KIIS-102.7-FM, Los Angeles, 618
KILT-610AM, 100.3-FM, Houston, 50, 177
KIMN-950AM, (today **KRWZ**), Denver, 50, 480, 551
KIOI-Star 101.3-FM, San Francisco, 398
KITS-105.3-FM, San Francisco, 550
KJR-950AM, Seattle, 554
KKDA-K-104-FM, Dallas, 103
KKLI-106.3-FM , CO. Springs, 351, 401, 615
KKRD-107.3-FM, Wichita, KS, 76, 621
KLDE-94.5-FM, Houston, 63, 99-100, 102, 104-05, 122, 195, 238, 343, 426, 545, 552

Index • 693

KLIF-570AM, Dallas, 476, 555-57, 628
KLUV-98.7-FM, Dallas, (KROW in the late 50s), 63, 77, 351
KLZX-95.9-FM, Salt Lake City, 619
KMAJ-107.7-FM, Topeka, KS, 588
KMBC-980AM, Kansas City, today KMBZ, 330, 493
KMET-94.7-FM, (today KTWV 'The Wave"), Los Angeles, 552
KMOX-1120AM, St. Louis, 432, 495, 554
KMPC-710AM, LA (today @ 1540AM), 352, 493, 552
KMPX-106.9-FM, San Francisco, 555
KNIX-1580AM, 102.5FM, Phoenix, 109, 395, 614
KNUZ-1230AM, Houston, 552
KNX-1070AM, Hollywood, 331, 473, 630
KOB-770AM, 93.3-FM, Albuquerque, today KKOB, 119, 182
KOGO-600AM, 95.7-FM, San Diego, 395
KOHL-89.3-FM, Ohlone College, Fremont, CA, 125
KOMA-1520AM, 92.5-FM, Oklahoma City, 53, 466, 553, 613, 618, 621
KOMP-92.3-FM, Las Vegas, 109, 395, 614
KOOL-94.5-FM, Phoenix, 221, 351, 379
KORK-920AM, Las Vegas (now KBAD), 75
KOST-103.5-FM, LA, 61, 351, 381, 618
KOWH-660AM (now KCRO), Omaha, 556-57
KOY-1230AM, Phoenix, 553
KPAS-1100AM, Pasadena, CA, 630
KPOI-1380AM, Honolulu, 552
KPOP-1110AM, Los Angeles, 552
KPRC-950AM, Houston, 195
KQV-1410AM, Pittsburgh, 553
KRBE-1070AM, 104.1-FM, Houston, 50
KRIZ-1230AM (now KFLR), Phoenix, 553
KRLA-1110AM, (originally KPAS) Pasadena, CA, 61, 75, 552, 630
KRLD-1080AM, Dallas, 619
KRQX-1590AM, Dallas, 63
KRSP-103.5-FM, Salt Lake City, 619
KRTH-K-EARTH 101-FM, Los Angeles, 552, 623
KRUX-1360AM, Phoenix, 553
KSFI-100.3-FM, Salt Lake City, (orig. KSL-FM), 51, 358, 619
KSFO-560AM, San Francisco, 202, 342, 620

KSL-1160AM, Salt Lake City, 496
KSTL-690AM, St. Louis, 554
KSTN-1420AM, 107.3-FM, Stockton, CA, 557
KSTP-1500AM, Minneapolis, 53, 618
KTAR-620AM, 92.3-FM, Phoenix, 553
KTEN, Ada, Oklahoma, 618
KTLN-950AM, Denver, 551
KTSA-550AM, San Antonio, 55, 501, 619
KUDL-1660AM, 98.1-FM, Kansas City, 342
KUER-90.1-FM, (Univ. of Utah), 619
KUMT-105.7-FM, Salt Lake City, 619
KVIL-1150AM, 103.7-FM, Dallas, 77, 113, 351, 628
KVNA-600AM, 104.7-FM, Flagstaff, AZ, 496
KVOO-1170AM, 98.5-FM, 466
KVUU-99.9-FM, CO Springs, 400
KWK-1380AM, FM106,(later became KADI), St. Louis, 554
KWKW-1350AM, Pasadena, CA, 630
KWMY-92.5-FM, Billings, MT, 588
KWOW-1600AM, Pomona, CA, (today KWOW is in Waco, TX), 60
KXLW-1320AM (later became KADI), St. Louis, 554
KXOK-630AM, St. Louis, 61, 466, 554
KYA-1260AM, San Francisco, 554
KYNO-940AM, Fresno, 557
KYSN-1460AM, CO Springs, 401
KYUU-X100-FM, (now Star 101.3), San Francisco, 613, 615
KYW-1060AM, Chicago, Cleveland, today in Philly, 394, 473, 639
KZEW-98-FM, Dallas/Ft. Worth, 63
KZOK-102.5-FM, Seattle, 124, 185, 351
KZZP-104.7-FM, Phoenix, 215

Radio Station call letters beginning with the letter "W"

WAAF-FM-107.3, Worcester, MA, 623
WABC-77AM NYC, W-A- Beatle- C (formerly WJZ), ix, 65, 74, 122, 177, 301, 313, 318, 351, 357, 454, 499, 517, 538, 543, 546-48, 554, 574, 610, 612-18, 622, 631
WABK-FM-104.3, (formerly WKME-FM), Augusta, ME., 40, 587

WAGF-1320AM, Dothan, AL, 462
WAKE-1340AM, Atlanta, GA, 551
WAKY-790AM, Louisville, KY, 619, 627
WAPE-690AM, (today on FM 95.1, WAPE AM is WOKV), Jacksonville, FL, 552
WARA-1320AM, (now WARL), Attleboro, MA, 631
WARE-1250AM, Ware, MA, 310, 631
WAVZ-1300AM, New Haven, CT, 623
WBAA-920AM, 101.3-FM, West Lafayette, IND, 520
WBAM-740AM ,"The Big Bam" Montgomery, AL, 553
WBAY-AM (later WEAF, today WFAN), NYC, 9
WBBM-780AM, Chicago (simulcast Newsradio on **105.9**), 110, 473
WBBM-FM-96.3, "B-96," Chicago, 110, 550
WBCN-FM-104.1, Boston (today WBMX-Boston is on 104.1), 390
WBKH-950AM, Hattiesburg, MS, 620-21
WBMT-FM-88.3, Masconomet Regional High School station, Boxford, MA, 51
WBMX-MIX FM-98.5, Boston, (today WBZ-FM), 43, 78, 81, 135, 251, 263, 314
WBNS-1460AM, Columbus, Ohio, 614
WBT-1110AM, FM99.3, Charlotte, NC, 52
WBZ-1030AM, Boston, *"The Spirit of New England"* 47-48, 57, 86, 94, 118, 156, 186, 202-03, 222, 260, 291, 324, 395, 421, 473, 476, 479-83, 495, 508, 511-12, 526, 540, 551-52, 555, 588, 612, 615-16, 622, 628, 630-31, 639, 649-50, 657-58
WBZA-1030AM, Springfield, MA, operated from the Westinghouse Electric plant as a Satellite (or feeder station) to sister station, WBZ Boston, 639
WBZ-TV, Ch. 4, Boston, 622
WCAP-980AM, Lowell, MA, **Note:** another Lowell station is **WLLH-1400AM,** and **WLLH-FM-99.5,** later became WSSH-FM, Lowell, MA, 479
WCAU-1210AM, Philadelphia, 402
WCBS-880AM, NYC (formerly WABC and WJZ), 482, 553

WCBS-FM-101.1, NYC, 60, 65, 282, 341, 351, 357, 463, 617
WCCC-1290AM, West Hartford, CT, 623
WCCO-830AM, Minneapolis, 615
WCDQ-1230AM, Hamden, CT, 623
WCFL-1000AM, Chicago, 110, 402, 612, 615-16, 620**,** 627
WCGL-FM-98.5, Cleveland, 53
WCIL-1020AM, Carbondale, ILL, 619
WCOL-1230AM, Columbus, Ohio, 614
WCOU-1240AM, Lewiston, Maine, 224
WCOZ-FM-94.5, (today WJMN), Boston, 622
WCRV-AM 640, Washington, Township, NJ, 480
WCSH-970AM, Portland, ME (originally 940AM, today WZAN), 45, 87, 105, 243, 263-64, 473, 553, 566, 588-89
WDAF-610AM, Kansas City, (today simulcast on 106.5 WDAG-FM), 552
WDAS-1480AM, 105.3-FM - Philadelphia, 59, 626
WDIA-1070AM, Memphis, 334, 552
WEAF-660AM, NYC (later WRCA, WNBC, today WFAN), 10, 327, 454, 518
WEAN-790AM, (now WPRV) Providence, RI, 631
WEAT-Sunny-104.3 - West Palm Beach, FL (today 104.3 is WMSF, Sunny is on 107.9) 262, 397, 502, 523, 617, 625
WEEI-590AM (today WEEI is 850AM) Boston, 43, 291, 340, 359, 480, 509, 616, 631
WEEI-FM-93.7- Boston, formerly Star 93.7 & Mike 93.7, 399
Radio Station call letters beginning with the letter "W"(cont) 52
WEEX-1230AM, Easton/Allentown, PA, 480
WEIM-1280AM, Fitchburg, MA, Knight Quality station, 74
WELI-960AM, New Haven, CT, 623
WERS-FM-88.9, Emerson College, Boston, 52, 80, 85, 146, 318, 399
WFAN- 660AM, New York City, (formerly WNBC), 518

Index • 695

WFAU-1340AM, Augusta, ME, today FAU is on 1280AM, WMDR on 1340AM, 215, 224-25
WFBL-1390AM (once called,"Fire-14,"), Syracuse, 550, 555, 627
WFBR-1590AM, Baltimore (originally WEAR 1300AM), 13
WFGL-960AM, Fitchburg, MA, 318, 396,
WFIL-560AM, Philadelphia, 494, 553, 616-17, 626
WFIL-TV-Ch.6, Philadelphia, 59
WFMJ-TV-Youngstown, Ohio, 525
WFLA-970AM, Clearwater/Tampa, FL, 476
WFQX-FM-99.3, Strasburg, VA, 82
WFUN-790AM, Miami, 552
WFUV-FM-90.7, Fordham, Univ. 463
WFYV-Rock 105-FM, Jacksonville, FL, 592
WGAN-560AM, Portland, ME, 48, 61, 150, 237, 242, 496, 553-54, -588-89
WGBB-1240AM, Freeport, LI, NY, 613
WGBF-1280AM, Evansville, IN, 627
WGBS-710AM, (today WAQI), 494
WGCI-FM-107.5, Chicago, 103, 265, 619
WGN-720AM, Chicago, 11, 109, 111, 265, 329, 342, 455, 551, 619, 626
WGRC-1300AM, Spring Valley, NY, 617
WHAS-840AM, Louisville, KY, 629
WHB-710AM, Kansas City (today on 810AM), 60, 552, 620
WHEN-620AM, Syracuse, NY, 555
WHDH-850AM, Boston (now 850 is WEEI-AM), x, 29, 48, 60, 61, 65, 480, 551, 607-08, 612, 631, 640
WHEN-630AM, Syracuse, NY, 555
WHER-1430AM, Memphis, *(in 1955, billed as "All Girl " radio" air-staff),* 334, 352
WHET-1210AM, Troy, AL, 462
WHFS-Washington, DC, (several FM frequency changes over a 50 year period, including 102.3. Today, the call letters are in Tampa, FL), 549
WHMS-FM-97.5 & **WDWS 1400AM**, Champaign, ILL, 60, 283, 617
WHN-1050AM- NYC (formerly WMGM) today, WEPN, 30, 538
WHTT-FM-104., Buffalo, 50
WHTZ-Z100-FM, NYC, 374

WHYT-FM-96.3, Detroit, (originally Imlay City, Michigan), 476
WIAE-pioneer station in 1922 in Vinton, Iowa, and the first station to be owned & operated by a woman in 1922, 328
WIBG-990AM, aka "wibbage" Philadelphia (today WNTP), 59, 401, 616, 626
WIDE-1400AM, Biddeford, ME, 40, 47, 52, 65, 149-56, 228-29, 472, 496, 590-91, 597, 607-08
WINR-680AM, Binghamton, NY, 78
WINS-1010AM, NYC, 473, 519, 538, 546-48, 616, 618
WINZ-940AM, Miami, 494
WIOD-610AM, Miami, 498
WIP-610AM, Philadelphia, 553
WIRE-1430AM, (today WXNT), Indianapolis, 494
WIRK-FM-107.9, West Palm Beach, FL (today 103.1), 58
WIYY-98-FM Rock, Baltimore, 186, 223
WIZN-106.7-FM, Burlington, VT, 318
WJAB-1440AM, Westbrook/Portland, ME, 554, 588
WJAR- 920AM, (now WHJJ) Providence, 631
WJAS-1320AM, Pittsburgh, 520-21
WJBQ-FM-97.9, Portland, ME, 61
WJLB-FM-98, Detroit, 335
WJMK-FM-104.3, Chicago, 220
WJOB-1230AM, Hammond, IN, 110
WJPC-95AM-Mixx 106-FM, Chicago, 103
WJR-760AM, Detroit, 475-76, 489, 551
WJRB-820AM, Voice of Virginia Commonwealth Univ. 616
WJSV-1460AM, Washington, DC (WTOP), 14, 458
WJTO-730AM, Bath, ME, 264
WJW-850AM (Today WKNR) Cleveland, OH, 547-48, 551
WJXA-MIX-92.9-FM, Nashville, 119, 168, 227, 260, 398
WJYE-FM-96.1-FM, Buffalo, 373, 648, 650
WJZ-830AM, NYC, (now WJZ licensed to Baltimore) 9-11, 26, 323-25, 517, 639
WKAL-1450AM, Rome, NY, 613
WKBW-1520AM, (now WWKB), Buffalo, 47, 49, 211, 543, 551-52, 616, 618, 624-25, 629, 631

WKDA-FM-103, **WKDF-FM**, Nashville, 629
WKGN-1340AM, Knoxville, TN, 520
WKIO-FM-92.5, Champaign, ILL, 61
WKIX-1340AM, 850AM, Raleigh, NC, 615
WKLB-FM-102.5, Boston, 400
WKLI-FM-100.9, Albany, NY, 589
WKLO-1080AM, Louisville, KY, 619
WKMH-1310AM, Detroit, 551-52
WKMZ-FM-97.5, Martinsburg, VA, (today WAVE 105.3), 83
WKOX-1430AM, Framingham, MA, x, 318
WKQK-FM-94.1, (formerly 94.3), Memphis,
WKQX-Q87.7-FM, (moved from 101FM), Chicago, 265, 619
WKRC-550AM, Cincinnati, 325
WKRP-Cincinnati (TV series), 105
WKTU-FM-103.5, NYC, 301-02, 549
WKY-930AM, Oklahoma City**,** 462, 553, 621
WKYC-1100AM, **FM-105.7**, Cleveland, 83-84
WLAC-1510AM, Nashville, 220, 553, 625, 629
WLBC-1340AM, FM-104.1 (today WXFN), Muncie, IN, 520
WLIR-FM-92.7, FM-107.1, Long Island, NY, 549
WLIS-1420AM, Old Saybrook, CT, 623
WLKI-Magic FM-100.9, Albany, NY, 589
WLKZ-FM-104.9, Wolfboro, NH, 318
WLLH-1400AM, WLLH-FM-99.5, later became WSSH-FM, Lowell, MA
WLLL-930AM, Lynchburg, VA, 612
WLOB-1310AM, Portland, ME, 84, 170, 310, 554
WLS- 890AM, Chicago, 49, 58, 96, 177, 220, 402, 337, 419, 421, 480, 499, 551, 612-13,
 615-18, 620, 624, 626, 629, 648
WLS-FM-94.7, Chicago, 49, 58, 78, 96, 110, 219, 337, 457, 551
WLTB-FM-101.7, Binghamton, NY, 600, 617, 651
WLUP-FM-97.9, Chicago, 551
WLW-700AM, Cincinnati, *The Nations Station, Cradle of Stars, The Big 700, 83, 273,* 242, 245-49, 256, 325-26, 330, 333, 416, 494, 497, 499, 518, 551, 589, 631, *photo 276*

WLZW-FM-98.7, Utica, NY, 62
WMAJ-1450AM, Magic-99.5-FM, State College, PA, 626
WMAQ-670AM, Chicago, (originally WGU), 11, 324, 352, 517
WMAS-FM-94.7, Enfield, CT/Springfield, MA, (now WHLL), 318
WMBX-X-102.3-FM, West Palm Beach, FL., 619
WMCA-570AM, NYC (formerly WHN, now WEPN), 11, 65, 74, 494, 546-47, 552, 613, 618, 622
WMEX-1510AM, Boston"Wimmex" color radio-1-5-1-0 (formerly WITS, now WWZN) 48, 61, 494, 551, 612, 630-31
WMGM-1050AM (today WEPN) NYC, 546
WMJX-Magic 106.7-FM, Boston, 51-52, 61, 132, 197, 260, 343, 400, 611, 622
WMRO-Magic 1560AM, and **WAUR-FM** was WMRO-FM, Aurora, IL, 342
WMTW-FM-94.9, (now WHOM), Poland Spring/Portland, ME, 588
WNAC-680AM, Boston (today WRKO), 324, 551, 591-92
WNBC- 660AM, NYC (formerly WRCA, today WFAN), 402, 547, 549, 553, 574, 623
WNBP-1450AM, Newburyport, MA, 64
WNDR-1260AM, (today WSKO) Syracuse, NY, 555, 612
WNEW-1130AM, NYC, 7, 24, 94, 538, 543, 553, 614, 628
WNEW-FM-102.7, NYC, (was WHFI) 335-36, 625
WNHC-1340AM, New Haven, CT, 623
WNMB-900AM, North Myrtle Beach, SC, "Wonderful North Myrtle Beach," 220
WNOE-FM-101.1, New Orleans, 476
WNSX-FM-97.7, Winter Harbor, Ellsworth/Bangor, ME, 61
WNTS-1590AM, Indianapolis, 191
WNUA-FM-95.5, Chicago, 337
WNYW-NYC, shortwave radio broadcast from Scituate, MA, 318
WODS-Oldies 103, Boston, 61-63, 65, 80, 135, 341-42, 400, 614
WOGL-FM-98.1FM, Philadelphia, 122, 148

Index • 697

WOKV-690AM and FM-106.5, Jacksonville, FL, 476
WOLF-1490AM & FM-105.1, Syracuse "The Wolf Pack Party," 85, 555, 612, 626
WOLL-KOOLFM-105.5, WPB, FL, 84, 228
WOMC-FM-104.3FM, Detroit, 147, 475-76
WOND- 1400AM, Pleasantville, NJ, 626
WOOD-1300AM & FM-106.9, Grand Rapids, MI, 470
WOR-770AM, NYC, 26, 30, 66, 318, 324, 327-28, 332, 482, 492, 494-95, 498, 553, 616, 622, 624, 631
WOR-FM-98.7, NYC (today WEPN-FM), 60, 318, 401, 547, 549
WOVK-FM-98.7, Wheeling, WVA, 84
WOW-590AM, Omaha, 476
WOWO-1190AM, Ft. Wayne, IN, 612, 629, 631
WPBZ-The Buzz FM-103.1, (today, Now 103), West Palm Beach, 592
WPEN-950AM, Philadelphia, 480, 553
WPEP-1570AM, Taunton, MA (license turned in to FCC in Oct. 07), 76
WPEX-1490AM, Hampton, VA, 62
WPGC-1580AM, (today 95.5 is WPGC-FM), Washington, DC, 555, 619
WPIX-FM-101.9, NYC, (today WRXP), 336
WPIX-TV, Ch. 11, NYC, 528
WPLI-1490AM, Jackson, TN, 50, 618
WPLJ-FM-95.5, NYC (formerly WABC-FM), 60, 260, 614
WPLM-FM-99.1, Plymouth, MA, 65
WPLO-610AM, Atlanta, 551
WPNT-FM-100.3, (today WILV), Chicago, 265, 619
WPOC-FM-93.1, Baltimore, 49, 104, 351, 393, 396
WPOR-1490AM, Portland, ME (today WBAE), 496, 554
WPRO-FM-92- & 630AM, Providence, RI, 74, 260, 613-14, 631
WPTR-1540AM, Albany, NY, 543, 550, 613
WQAM-560AM, Miami, 494, 548, 552
WQBH-1400AM, Detroit, (call letters were tribute to Jean "The Queen" Steinberg, "
Queen back home" (today 1400AM is WDTK), 335
WQXR-FM-105.9, Newark, NJ/NYC, 461

WRC-980AM, Washington, DC (today 1260AM) 13
WRKO-680AM, Boston (WNAC), x, 48, 55, 61, 134, 136-137, 222, 259, 291-92, 364, 370, 402, 477, 479-80, 482, 495, 500, 557-58, 591, 597, 615-17, 620, 622, 630-31
WRLM-FM-93.3-FM, Taunton, MA, 51
WRLX-Classy FM-92.1,West Palm Beach, FL, 84
WROL-950AM, Boston (was WRYT and WORL), 108
WROR-98.5-FM, Boston ,(later, WBMX-MIX-98.5, today WBZ-FM is on 98.5, while **WBMX** has moved to 104.1, vii, ix, 40, 43, 59-60-61, 65, 80-82, 99, 104, 108, 128, 134-137, 167, 189, 197, 222, 237-38, 242, 251, 263, 265, 281, 316, 318, 358-59, 363-65, 367, 370, 392, 418, 422, 434-35, 464, 476, 479-80, 495, 500, 542, 558, 565-66, 582, 585, 595, 602, 611, 614, 620, 622, 626, 631, 641, 647
WROR-FM-105.7, Boston, formerly **WVBF-F-105FM,** 65, 77, 99, 168, 343, 620
WRVA-1140AM, Richmond, VA, 629
WSAI-1530AM, Cincinnati (former freq. 1360AM), 325, 476, 551
WSAR-1480AM-Fall River, Knight Quality station, 55, 74, 118
WSB-740AM, Atlanta, 383, 462, 585
WSDM-FM-92.7, Chicago, (now WLUP), 110
WSIX-FM-97.9, Nashville, 50
WSM-650AM, Nashville, 372, 625, 629
WSRO-650AM, Marlboro, MA, 78
WSUN-590AM, 97.1-FM, Tampa, (today WSUN is 620AM, St. Petersburg, FL), 480
WSYR-570AM, Syracuse, NY, 555
WSYR-TV, Ch. 9 (today WSTM-TV) Syracuse, NY, 525
WTCJ-1230AM, Tell City, IN., 627
WTIC-1080AM, Hartford, CT. 643
WTIC-FM-96.5, Hartford, 550
WTIX-690AM & 94.3-FM, New Orleans, 177
WTKK-FM-96.9, Boston, 222, 292, 302, 400
WTOP-1500AM, Washington, DC, 333

WTRY-980AM, (now WOFX), Troy/Albany, NY, 550, 613
WTRY-FM-102.7 (now WPYX), Troy/Albany, NY, 550
WTSA-1450AM, 96.7-FM, Brattleboro, VT., 618
WUBE-B105.1-FM, Cincinnati, Ohio, 554
WUUU-FM-102, Rome, NY, 434
WVBC-88.1-FM, Bethany College, Bethany, WV, 262
WVBF-F-105-FM-105.7, Boston, (today WROR-FM) 61, 318, 618, 622
WWCO-1240AM, Waterbury, CT, 623
WWDB-860AM, 96.5, Philadelphia, 500
WWJ-950AM, Detroit, (originally 8MK), 453
WWOD-1390AM, FM 100.1, Lynchburg, VA, 612
WWOL-FM-104.1, Buffalo, 625
WWRL-1600AM, NYC, 547
WWWD-1240AM, Schenectady, NY, 589
WWWQ-Q-100-FM, Atlanta, GA, 371
WXKS-KISS-108-FM, Boston, 85, 165, 378, 616, 618, 622, 625
WXLO-FM-104.5, Worcester, MA, 318
WXRK- K-Rock-92.3-FM, NYC, (today WNOW), 336
WXXX-1310AM, (now Triple X-95.5 licensed to Colchester, VT), Hattiesburg, MS, 621
WXYZ-1270AM, Detroit (now WXYT), 221, 462, 470, 493, 551, 557, 625
WYNZ-Oldies100.9-FM, So. Portland, ME. 48, 390, 588
WYOO-980AM, U100, St. Paul, MN (today 980AM is WAYL), 476
WYYY- Y94.5-FM, Syracuse, NY, 62
WZGC-Z93-FM, Atlanta, 476, 619
WZZP-Zip 106-FM, Cleveland, Ohio, (now WHLK), 52
Radio Superstar, 178
RTNDA (Radio-Television News Directors Association), x, 479
Radio Today Annual Report, 459
Radio-TV Mirror Magazine (later, TV-Radio Mirror), 14-15, 54, 56, 123, 126, 195, 203, 330, 470, 487, 538
Raised on the Radio, Gerald Nachman, 21
Raleigh, 262
Raleigh, Bob aka Rolle Ferreira (sometimes spelled Ferrar), 554-55
Raleigh-Durham Inter. Airport, 523
Ralphie & Karen's Morning Show, 399
Rambling with John Gambling (see Gambling., John)
Randle, Bill, 551, 621
Randall, Chris "Topher," 613
Randall, Eunice, 328
Randolph, Johnny, 619
Raphael, Sally Jesse, xxiii, 4, 187, 201-02, 315, 504, *photo,* 208
Ray, Johnny, 621
Rayburn, Gene, 4
Reagan, Nancy, 498
Reagan, Ronald, U.S. Pres., 187, 461,491
Real Duct Tape Stories, 174
Reasoner, Harry, 460
Red Cross, 325
Redo, Phil, 292-93, 622-23, 542, 622-23, 652, *photos, 278, 634, 660*
Red River Valley, (folk song), 23
Red Roses for a Blue Lady by Sid Tepper and Roy C. Bennett aka Roy Brodsky, 631
Reed, Dan, 471
Reed, B. Mitchell, 145, 546, 552, 611
Regan, Russ, 220
Regent Broadcast Group, 373, 648
Reilly, Leandra, 528
Remember What I told you to forget - Tavares, 305
Republican Convention, Cleveland 1924, 454, 460
Respect- Aretha Franklin, 250
Reveille with Beverly, 331
Revere, 421
Revere Beach (MA)Bandstand, 367
Rex Trailer's Boomtown, 631
Reynolds, Debbie, *photo, 210*
Reynolds, Frank, 166
Reynolds, Joey, 211, 551, 616, 631
Reynolds, Roy, 550, 613
RFD Channel, 355
Rhode Island, 158, 623
  Providence, 424, 501, 626, 631
  Woonsocket, 78
Rhodes, Dusty, 555, 627
R&B, Rhythm and Blues, 625
Rhythm Rockers, 367
Riccardi, Jack, 55, 501
Rice, Grantland, 517-18
Rice, Rosemary, 331

Index • 699

Rich, Charlie, 549
Rich, Jordan, 202, 476, 508-09, 649, *photo,* 208
Richards, Stan, 551
Richbourg, John R., 553, 625, 629
Richmond, VA, 629
Ricker, John, xv
Riddle, Sam, 552, 611
Ride Records, 620
Righteous Brothers, 550
Ripley's Believe it or not, 310
Rise of the Goldbergs, 329
Ritter, Anna-Marie, 168, 353, 394, 398-99, *photo,* 409
Ritter, Tex, 626
Ritz-Carlton Hotel, 437
River Forest, ILL, 468
River Runs Through It, A - Brad Pitt, 628
Rivers, Bob, 103, 124, 182-83, 185-86, 223, 351, 380-81, 572, 623-24, 652, *photo,* 207
Rivers, Smoky, 629
RKO-General - Boston, 76, 136, 464, 479, 495, 499-500, 542, 550-51, 557-58, 597, 617
Road of Life, 3, 470
Robbins, Dave, 112-13, 119, 123, 178, 292, 624
Robbins, Fred, 538. *photo, 561*
Roberge, Bill, xvi
Roberts, Art, 551
Roberts, Jim, aka Joe Noga, 542, *photo,* 278
Roberts, Lan, 554
Roberts, Ron, 555
Roberts, Stan, 551
Roberts, Tony, 520
Robertson, Ted, 630
Robin, Ron, 622
Robinson, Gene "Yours Truly," 555
Robinson "Smokey" William, 550
Rochester, NY, 519
Rock Around the Clock - Bill Haley & the Comets, 547
Rock It Radio, 75
Rock and Roll, 547-48, 626
Rock and Roll Greatest Hits, 612
Rock and Roll Hall of Fame, 53, 335, 548, 621
Rock and Roll Is Here To Stay, Danny & the Juniors, 59

Rock and Roll Reunion photo, 564
Rock Radio Scrapbook - Dale Patterson, provided some of the comments from radio pros at the beginning of chapters, including, pages 211 and 349
Rock, Roll and Remember, 56
Roddy, "Rod" (Robert Ray), 551, 629
Roe, Alden, 629
Rogers, Dean, 105, 587-88, *photo, 278*
Rogers, Neil, 168
Rogers, Will, 8-9, 128, *photo, 35*
Romance of Helen Trent, the, 330, 332, 618
Romani, Joseph, Rev. Fr, 98
Rome, Italy, 434
Rome, Lindy, 344, 394, 397, *photo, 116*
Rome, New York, 434
Ronettes, the, 550
Rook, John, 551
Roosevelt, Eleanor, 493
Roosevelt, Franklin Delano, U.S. Pres., 458-59, 462, 489
Roosevelt, Long Island, NY, 489
Roots of radio, 637
ROR Accu-traffic, 359
Rose Bowl, 517-18, 524
Rose, Charlie, 4, 202
Rose, Dr. Don, 350, 554, 617
Rosenfeld, Big Joe and *the Happiness Exchange,* 495
Roses Are Red - Bobby Vinton, 306
Rosko aka William Roscoe Mercer, 549
Ross Brittain Report, the, 122, 148
Rothafel, Roxy, 9
Roundtree, Martha, 332-33, 493
Rowswell, Rosey, 520
Royal Gelatin, 325
Rozelle, Pete, 524
Rudy Vallee Hour, the, 329
Rumble - Link Wray, 308
Rump, Gene aka Gene Edwards, 621
RuPaul, aka Andre Charles, 302
Russell, Andy, 543
Russett, Tim, 4, 201
Ryan, Dave, 105, 168, 215-16, 351, 378, 624, *photo, 232*
Ryan, Marty, NBC-TV *Today Show* producer, 436
Ryan's Hope, 427, newspaper article, 444

S

Sabo Media, 315-16, 586
Sabo, Water, Jr, 41, 167-68, 301, 315, 350, 355, 372, 426, 500, 586, 647, photo, 321
Sacco, Frannie, 421
Saco, Maine, 565
Saco tannery, 152, 229
Saga Communications, 114, 212, 235, 264, 292, 621
Sagamore Village, 1
St. Joseph's Catholic Church, Biddeford, ME, 151-52
St. Francis Xavier Univ. xxix
St. Jude's Ranch for children, 429
St. Louis, 434, 462, 521, 554, 626, 628
St. Louis Cardinals, 521-22
St. Louis High School, Biddeford ME, 47, 587
St. Louis Radio Personalities and stations 554
St. Patrick's Cathedral, 54
St. Paul, MN., 191
St. Peter's Basilica, 434
St. Peter's Catholic Church, Portland, ME, 98, 434
St. Valentine's Day, 327
Salem Radio Network, 505, 507
Salina, Kansas, 588
Salt Lake City, UT, 379
Sam and Henry, later, Amos n' Andy, 11
San Diego, 281, 341
San Diego Radio Personalities and stations 554
San Diego State University, 194-95
Sands, Jack, 566
Sands, Jim, 554, photo, 563
Sanford, "Chuck" Charles, 553
San Francisco, 194, 332, 368, 371, 394, 538, 613, 615-16
San Francisco Chronicle, 620
San Francisco Radio Personalities and stations, 550, 554
Santa Claus, 46, 300-01
Santos, Gil, 526
Sarandis, Ted, 359
Satellite Radio, 616, 642-43, 648, 650-53, 656, 658
Saturday Night Live - NBC -TV, 363
Saturday Nights Alright For Fighting - Elton John, 82

Saturday Nite "Live" at the Oldies, ix, 80, 121, 305, 308, 339, 364-65, 367-69, 386, 582,
newspaper article, 446, photo, oldies show montage, 411, 446
Saturday Nite "Live" at the Oldies, loyal listeners, 367
Saunders, Gus, 551
Saunders, Tommy, 85, 555
Savage, Michael, 499
Saving Pvt. Ryan Tour, 437, 439
Sawyer, "Bud," Wellington, photo, 278
Sawyer, Diane, 4
Schechter, Abe, 462
Schemaille, Mike, xvi
Schenectady, NY, 589
Schenkel, Chris, 520
Scherago, Bob, 643-44
Schilling, Baron, 640
Schlessinger, Dr. Laura, 500
Schreiber, Jeff, 566
Schuller, Dr. Robert, 112
Schuman, Bob, 475-76
Schwartz, Jonathan, 625
Scott, Jim, 219
Scott, Ray, 615
Scott, Willard, 435
Screen Guild Players, 334
Screen Director's Playhouse, 334
Scully, Vin, 4, 521, 529
Seacoast Kaleidoscope, 248, 496
Seacrest, Ryan, 39, 248
Sears Wish catalog, 618
Seattle, 652
Seattle Radio Personalities and stations 554, 572, 652
Seattle Seahawks, 381
See It Now, 459
Seeley, Norm, 553
Seiler, Leslie, photo, 660
Seinfeld, 374
Selleck, Tom, 422-24, newspaper articles, 442-43
Sergeant Pepper's Lonely Hearts Club Band, 198
Sergeant Preston of the Yukon, 1-2, 415
Sergio, Lisa "the golden voice of Rome," 461
Serling, Rod, 256
Sevareid, Eric, 460
Seven Powerful P's to perfection as a radio pro, see chapter 5, 117

Index • 701

Seven Swingin' Gentlemen, 75
Sevareid, Eric, 460
Seymour, Robin, 552
Shakespeare, William, 336
Shane, Mary, 528
Shannon, Bob, 553
Shannon, Scott, 39, 261, 629
Shannon, Tom, 49, 551-52, 624-25, *photo, 69*
Sharing You - Bobby Vee, 306
Shaw, Bob, 553, *photo, 92*
Shaw, Charles, 461
Shaw, David, 620
Shaw, George Bernard, 375
Shaw, Rick, 553
Shaw, Stan, 543
Shepherd, Ann, 331
Shepherd, Jean, 4, 495, 509, 616, 622, 624
Sheridan, Phil, 626
Sherwood, Don, 554
Sherwood, Lee, 352
Sherwood, Rob, 615
Shevenell, Surfer Joe, 554, *photo, 564*
Shire, Lydia, 360
Shirer, William L., 461, 463
Sholin, Dave, 550, 620
Shore, "Dinah" Frances Rose, 4, 333, 543
Shovan, Tom, xv, 543
Show Prep Services, 183-84
Shreveport, LA, 643
Shrine of the Little Flower, Royal Oak, MI, 489
Shubert, Cody, 553
Sidekicks, side-chicks and second bananas, 384
Siegel, Matt, aka Matty in the Morning, 85, 165, 378, 617, 625, *photo, 412*
Silen, Bert, 461-62
Simms, Ginny, 543
Simon, Perry Michael, 509-10, 644
Simpkins, Mollie aka Kristy Kramer, 293, 344, 625, *photo, 635*
Sinatra, Frank, 106, 135, 224, 336, 542
Since I Lost My Baby - Temptations, 305
Sioussat, Helen, 327
Sirius X-M Satellite, 51, 79, 105, 315, 397, 490, 621
Sirott, Bob, 119, 551, 617
Sisters of Charity, 327
Six C's to Success as an air personality, 377
Skelton, "Red" Richard Bernard, 11, 17, 170, 256, 388

Ski NH, 81
Skin of our teeth, the, 334
Sklar, Rick, ix, 74, 415, 547, 574
Sky King, 1, 470
Smith, Anna Nicole, 502
Smith, Bill, *photo, 486*
Smith, Don, 614
Smith, Frank Kingston, 60, 359, 418, 542, 626, *photo, 71*
Smith, Howard K (Kingsbury), 460-61
Smith, "Kate" Katherine Elizabeth, xxiii, 10-11, 323, 326, 492, *photos, 35, 347*
Smith, Ken, 105, 195, *photo, 207*
Smith, Linda, 121, 339-40, 432, 595-96, *photos, 411, 610*
Smithsonian, the, 31
Smolen, Vivian, aka *Veronica* on radio's *Archie Andrews* & *Laurel* on *Stella Dallas*, 330
Smyth, Peter, 279, 281, 359, 652, *photo, 296, 660*
Snyder, Rick, 84-85, 626-27, *photo, 635*
Snyder & Snyder (Rick & Mary-Jo), 84, 554
Snyder, Tom, 4
Sock Hop Saturday Night, 589
Sommers, April, 125, 394, 398, *photo, 143*
Sony TC-110 cassette tape recorder, 473
Sorkin, Dan, 554
Soundtrack of the 60's, 549
South Florida, 249, 264, 430, 496, 650
South Philly, 59
Southern Illinois Univ., 265, 619
Space Patrol, with Commander Buzz Corey, 629
Spears, Michael, 265, 619
Spector, Jack, 546-47, 613
Spector, Phil, 550
Speleotis, Charlie, 566
Spenser: for Hire, 424, 427, *photo, 231*, newspaper article, 445
Spicer, Bob, 602-03, *photo, 610*
Spirit of St. Louis, 456
Spivak, Lawrence, 332-33, 493
Spokesmen, the, 59
Spooner, Russ, 629
Sports radio, see chapter 16, radio formats, 516
Spotlight Serenade, 625
Sputnik, 508
Stafford, Jo, 24

Stanford University, 568
Stanley Cup Playoffs, 527
Starr, Bob, 525
Statler Hotel, Boston, 8
Steele, Alison, "the Nightbird," xxiii, 335-36
   Nightbird Flying - Jimi Hendrix, 336
   Nightbird's final fling, the - Kathleen Warnock, 335
Steele, Don "the Real," 106, 401, 552, 618
Steinbeck, John, 200
Steinberg, Martha "Jean the Queen,"xxiii, 323, 334-35, 552
Steinbrenner, George, 528
Stella Dallas, 330, 332, 618
Sterling, Jack, 528
Sterling, John, 528
Stern, Bill, 4, 518-19, 526, 624, *photo, 531*
Stern, Howard, xxiii, 19, 42, 66, 168, 248, 318, 361, 379, 394, 489-90, 496, 543, 586, 617, 624, 648
Steve Lawrence & Eydie Gorme, 336
Stevens, Gary, 546-47, 613, 618
Stevens, Jerry, 59
Stevens, Meg, 396
Stevens, Shadoe, 613
Stewart, Bill, 556
Stickle, Frank, 546
Stiller, Jerry, *photo, 210*
Stock Club, Sherman Billingsley's, 465
Stock Market Crash 1919, 456
Stockton, Dick, 125, 524, 526
Stop The Music, 19-20
Storz, Todd, 546, 556-57, 642
Straight Arrow, 1
Straley, Kevin, 501-02, *photo, 514*
Stranger on the Shore - Mr. Acker Bilk, 224
Strassell, Greg, 263, 314, 627, *photo, 442*
Strasser, Lee, 146
Strasser, Jared, *the All-American Sports Kid, photo, 532*
Street, Paula, 62, 65, 341-42, 627-28, *photo, 72*
Strube, Carl, 64
Struckles, Johnny, 626
Strycker, Dave, 627
Stuart, Bob, 542
Stuart, Streeter, 511
Stubborn Kind of Fellow - Marvin Gaye, 41
Sullivan, Gary, 500
Sullivan, Mike, 613

Summer, Dick, 480, 540-42, 551, 616, 628, 656, *photo, 562*
Summers, Bob aka John Valentine, 616
Summers, Mark, 592-95
Summerline, Dino, 552
Sun Label, the, 549
Sunny 104.3, West Palm Beach, FL, 45, 77, 146, 170, 173, 192, 265, 310, 344, 396-97, 523, 617, 625
Sunoco 3-Star Extra, the, 457
Sunshine Boys, the, 22
Superman, 214, 629
Super 6 on WFIL, 626
Super 8 Motel, 55
Supple, Dave, 551
Supremes, the, 128, 550
Suskind, David, 4, 202
Suzie Q. - Dale Hawkins, 220
Swanee River - Stephen Foster, 323
Swanson, Jack, 620
Swayze, John Cameron, 460, 495
Sweat and sacrifice equals success, 112
Sweeney, Frank, 554
Sweet, Marion, 331
Sweeton, Melissa, 629, *photo, 636*
Swift-Premium, 18
Swingin' radio England, pirate radio, 557
Swingin' Soiree, 548
Switzerland, 460
Syatt, Dick, 359, 370
Sylvia, Madame, 493
Syracuse, NY, 85, 612, 626
Syracuse Radio Personalities and stations 555
Syracuse, Russ, 551
Syracuse Univ., 525

T
Tacoma, WA, 29
Take Good Care of my Baby - Bobby Vee (Velline), 306
Talkers Magazine, 491
Talk Radio, 495, 500
Tavares, 305
Taylor, Dan, 618
Taylor, Jim, 551
Taylor, Mary Lee, 329, 493
Taylor, Tom, Editor, *Inside Radio,* 467
Team Sports, Scottsdale, AZ, 570
Ted Ruscitti Associates, 312
Teddy Bear Playhouse, 591, *photo, xxxiv*

Index • 703

Teehan, John, xvi
Teen Time, 153, 590
Teens, Topics and Tunes, 554
Telecom bill, 303
Tell City, IN, 263
Tell Me - Dick and Deedee, Dick Gosling & Deedee Sperling, 305
Temptations, the, 550
Ten Commandments starring Chalton Heston, 140
Ten Commandments of a radio pro, 607
Ten Commandments for a weekend jock, 593
10th Engr Co. USMCR, Portland, ME., 223
Terrestrial radio vs. Satellite, 649-650, 652-53
Tesh, John, 316, 647
Tex and Jinx, Tex McCrary and Jinx Falkenburg, 26, *photo,* 37
Texas Radio Hall of Fame, 63, 105, 126, 587
The Mountain's High - Dick & Deedee, 305
The Night Has A Thousand Eyes - Bobby Vee, 306
The Way You Do The Things You Do - Temptations, 305
Theater Guild of the Air, 334
There I've Said It Again - Bobby Vinton, 306
There Used To Be A Ballpark - Suzyn Waldman, 528
35 Tips on how to succeed in Morning-Drive, 404
This Is Nora Drake, 330
This Week with David Brinkley, 469
Thomas, Joe, 631
Thomas, Lowell, 457, 487, *photo, 484*
Thompson, Dorothy, 458
Three Queens from Brooklyn, 302
Three Rivers Stadium, 521
Three Stooges, 55
Tic, Tac, Dough, 50, 618
Tilton, Martha, 543
Time Magazine, 457
TSL - Time Spent Listening, 182, 304, 309, 314
Time Tunnel, 629
Timex, 460
Titusville, PA, 83
Tolster, George Thomas, 461
Tolucca Lake, CA, 170
Tolz, Alan, 500-01, *photo, 514*
Tom Mix Ralston Straight Shooters, 1, 415
Tonight Show with Jay Leno, 167

Toothacher, Mona, 226
Topeka, Kansas, 588
Top-20 ways to know you're an aging Radio Pro, 606
Top-40 Radio, 48, 110, 364, 472, 536, 538, 546, 548, 550-53, 555-57, 621, 627, 642
Top sportscaster, 524
Top-100 of 1970, 617
Toronto Canada, 626
Toronto Maple Leafs, 517
Toronto Mutual Street Arena, 517
Toronto Star, 517
Totten, Hal, 517
Town Hall Tonight, 19
Townsend, Dallas, 463
Tracey, Robert Charles "Bob" also Johny Ryder, 553
Traditional radio, 651
Travelin' Man - Rick Nelson, 306
Travolta, John, 135
Traynor, Tom, 461
Trendle, George W., 2, 10
Trent, Sybil, 331
Triangle Birdseed & Pet Shop, 13
Tribune, 549
Triolo, Pam, 394, 396-97m 502-03
Triple-A ball club, 438
Triple Crown, 520
Tripp, Peter, 546
Trivette, Alpha, 383, 629
Trombley, Skip, 356
Trout, Robert aka Robert Albert Blonheim, 458, 463, *photo, 484*
Tube Talk, 327
Tucker, 127
Tufeld, Dick, 629-30, *photo, 636*
Tulane Univ., 460
Tulsa OK, 466
Tuna, Charlie, 621
Tune in Tomorrow - Mary Jane Higby, 330
Turner, Grant, 629
Turtles, the, aka Mark Volman & Howard Kaylan, *photo, 209*
Tuskegee, AL, 103
Tuttle, Lurene, 331
TV Guide, 498
Twenty-Twenty (ABC), 169
Twilight Zone, 256
Twin Cities of Minneapolis/St. Paul, 553, 615
Two-Way Talk Radio, 494

Tyler, Willy, 588, *photo, 609*
Tyson, Edwin "Ty," 517

U
Uecker, Bob, 521
Uncle Harvey, 621
Uncle Lar's animal stories, (Larry Lujack), 626
Univ. of Mass, 479
Univ. of Michigan, 470
Univ. of Michigan Law School, 506
Univ. of No. Carolina, 469
Univ. of North Dakota, 613
Univ. of Pittsburgh, 638
Univ. of Texas - Arlington, 62
Univ. of Utah, 619
Untouchables, 466
UP - United Press, 455
UPI - United Press International, 201, 229, 463, 479
Urich, Heather, *photo*, 210
Urich, Robert, 137, 211, 424, 427, 434, *photos, 210, 231*
US (United States), 177, 337, 473, 494, 507, 516, 556, 616, 648, 658
USA Hockey, 526
USA Today, 113, 200, 436-37
U.S. Armed Forces, 342
U.S. Army, 469, 496
U.S. Customs, 433
U.S. Information Agency, 460
US Magazine, 113
U.S. Navy, 476, 537
USO, 170
U.S. President, 498
U.S. Supreme Court, 155
Utica, NY, 496

V
Valentines Day, 437, 521
Vallee, Rudy, 10, 11, 334, *photo, 35*
Vanderbilt University, 469
Van Dyke, Charlie, 105, *photo, 564*
Van Dyke, Dave, 178
Van, Gary, 555
Van Voorhis, Westbrook, 458
Variety, 639
Vataha, Randy, 565-66, 568, 571
Vatican, 434
Vax Computer, 178

Vee, Bobby Velline, 306
Vermont, 618
Verizon store, 430
Vic & Sade, 8, 11, 629
Viet Nam War, 14
View, the with Barbara Walters, 333, 374, 384
Vinton, Bobby, aka Stanley Robert Vinton, 306, *photo, 209*
Virginia Commonwealth Univ., 615
Visser, Leslie, 528-29
Voice of America, 643
Voice of Broadway with Dorothy Kilgallen, 493
Vola, Vicki, 331
Volkswagen, 603
Von Zell, Harry, 458
Voyage to the bottom of the sea, 629

W
Wade, Long John aka Carl Wehde, 553, 617
Wagner, J.W., 550, 613
Waite, Mike, *photo, 278*
Waitin' In School - Ricky Nelson, 307
Wake County, NC, 458
Waldman, Suzyn, 528
Waldo, Janet, 331
Wall, Lucille, 331
Wallace, Brad, 419-20
Wallace, Don, 553
Wallace, "Mike" Myron Leon, 4, 14, 201, 470
Wallengren, Mark, 351, 381-82, 505, *photo, 412*
Waller, Judith, xxiii, 324
Wall Street, 303, 307, 416, 643, 645, 652
Wall Street Journal, 416
Wally Phillips People Book, 352
Walmart, 319
Walpole High School marching band, 436
Walsh, Ed, 482-83, 630, *photo, 486*
Walters, Barbara, 4, 201, 460-61, 495
Wanted Dumb or Alive, 174
Ward, Frank, aka Guy King, 551, 625
Ward, Johnny, xv
Warfield, Harvey, 48
Warner, Albert, 461
Warwick, Dionne, 170
Washington, DC, 10, 328, 470, 640
Washington DC Radio Personalities and stations, 267, 555

Index • 705

Washington Merry-Go-Round, 462
Waukegan, 20
Wayne, PA, 522
We are the Champions - Queen, 597, 639
Weaver, Pat, 642
Weber, Clark, 616
Webb, Jack, xxiii, 31, *photo*, 38
Webb, Jane, 331
Weber & Fields, Joe Weber & Lew Fields, 8
Weekday Club - 930AM-KHJ, 123
Weinstein, Little Jeff, 554
Weiss, Bert, 371
Weiss, Fred, 557
Wells, Orson, 5, 630
Wellesley High School, 630
Wendy Warren and the News, 331
Westchester County, NY, 614
Western Maine Music Festival, Auburn, ME, 86
Western Union, 517
Westinghouse Electric, Corp., (later, Westinghouse Broadcasting), 5, 364, 454, 520, 538, 638-39
Westover, Jim, 509
Westwood One, 498, 503
Wexler, Jerry, 550
What's My Line, 462, 494
What's Your Dosha Baby - Lissa Coffey, 188
What's Your Idea with Imogene Walcott, 493
Wheaton, ILL, 62
Wheatstone, Sir Charles, 640
Wheeler, Bonnie, Sgt., USMC, 435
When a Girl Marries with Mary Jane Higby as Joan Davis, 330, 618
When The Moon Comes Over The Mountain - written by Howard Johnson, Harry M. Woods and Kate Smith, who sang the song as her theme on radio, 326
Where's Harry - Steve Stone, 521
Whitburn, Joel, 306, 309
White, Betty, 4
White, Dave, 59
White House, 510
White House correspondent (NBC's lst) 469
White, Jasper, 360
White, Joseph M., 10
White, Sonny Joe aka Joseph White, 618
Whiteman, Paul, 25
Whitmore, Ken, 553
Whitney, Bill, 463
Whitten, Will, 553
Whittinghill, Dick, 352, 552
Who Dunit - Tavares, 305
Whole Lotta Lovin' - Fats Antoine Domino, 305
Who Makes a Better Manager? 288
Who's Who in Radio & TV, 330
Why Don't They Understand - Tony Conigliaro, 369
Whyte, Bill, 372
Wichita Radio Hall of Fame, 63, 621
Wick, the, 497
Widmann, Nancy, 282, 341, 653, *photo, 297*
Wigglesworth, C. Truman aka Larry Light, 555
Wikipedia, 179
Wild Bill Cody Memorial, 55
Wiles, Lee, 626
Wilkinsburg, PA, 5, 638
Willett, "Cousin" Bob, xv
William Tell Overture - Rossini, 2
Williams, Andy, 256
Williams, Bruce, 500, 618
Williams, Cindy, *photo, 210*
Williams, Danny, 553
Williams, Don B., 621
Williams, Jerry, 134-35, 494-95, 500-01, 509, 617, 622, 631, *photo, 513*
Williams, Mark, 54, 76, 503, 631
Williams, Roger, 590
Williams, Ted (Hall of Fame slugger), 523
Williams, William B., 540, 543, 553, 628, *photo, 562*
Williamsport, PA, 401
Willie & Jojo (Willie Fisher & JoJo Turnbaugh, 401
Wilmington Morning Star, 469
Wilmington, NC, 469
Wilson, "Big," aka John Wilson, 553
Wilson, Bob, 527
Wilson, Brian, 550
Wilson, Jill, xxvii
Wilson, Meredith, 334
Wilson, Woodrow, U.S. President, 453
Winchell, Walter, 464-65, *photo, 484*
Winchester, Jody, *photo, 232*
Wingate, Chick, 50
Winona State, 593
Winston, Fred, 551, 618, 627
Winter Haven, FL, 125
Winter Olympics, 526

Winters, Jim, 554
Wireless age Magazine, 516
Wireless broadband, 649, 652
Wolf, Peter, 51
Wolf, Warner, 521
Wolfe, Miriam, 331
Wolfman Jack, aka Robert Smith, 106, 552, 584, 612
Wolvos, Debbie, 653
Women's Exchange, 324
Woods, Georgie, 626
Woods, Jim - WGBF, Evansville, IN, 627
Woods, Jim, 522
Woolf, Bob, 499, 567-71, *photo*, 579
World War I, 325, 456, 537
    Battle of Belleau Wood, 456
    Croix de Guerre with Palm, 456
World War II, 14, 25, 28, 102, 170, 200, 288, 326, 331, 333-34, 437, 458-63, 470-71, 630
    American Cemetery, Normandy, 437
    Battle of Britain, 459
    Battle of the Bulge, 463
    Berlin, 460
    Caen, 437
    China-Burma, 460
    D-Day, 437
    Europe, 331, 334, 460, 463
    Germany invaded Poland, 331
    Japanese Army, 456
    London, 200, 331, 334, 459-60
    Manila (NBC News), 461-62
    MacArthur, Gen. Douglas, 462
    Manchria, 456
    Munich crisis-1938, 457
    Mussolini's Italy, 461, 456
    Nazi Germany, 59-60, 331, 457, 459-60
    North Africa, 460, 463
    Pearl Harbor, Hawaii Dec. 7, 1941, 462
    Philippine POW Camp, 461
    Radio war correspondents, 459
Worthing, Craig, 150-55, 496, *photo*, 163
Wright, Bill, Sr., 59, 326
Wrigley, William (Wrigley's Doublemint Gum), 23
W.T. Grants Store, Branford, CT, 623
WWE, (World Wrestling), 54
Wynn, Ed, 10, 19, 639, *photo*, 35
Wynnewood, OK, 621
Wyxie Wonderland - Dick Osgood, 557

X

Xanax, 240
X-M Sirius Satellite Radio, ix, 62, 80, 304, 315, 501, 582
X-102.3, WPB, FL, 264, 357, 619
X-TRA - 690AM, LA, 473

Y

Yahoo, 166, 179
Yale University, 638
Yankee Network, x, 153, 551, 590
Yankee Stadium, 125, 328
Yastrzemski, Carl "Yaz," 568
Yellow Pages, 293
Yolanda, *photo*, 410
Yonkers, NY, 62
You Better Run - Young Rascals, 307
You Gotta Have Heart, 237
You know you're an aging radio pro when, 606
You Tube, 179, 421, 503, 530
You Were Mine - Fireflies, 308
Younce, Mike, 627
Young, Bill, 177
Young Emotions - Rick Nelson, 307
Young, Nick, 463
Young, Roland L., 456
Young Widder Brown, 5
Youngstown, OH, 525
Your Health First - Dr. Joe Galati, 195-96
Your Hit Parade, 542-43, 618
Your Voice and You, 156
Yukon King, 2
Yvette's Beauty Salon, 152

Z

Zagieboylo, Cindy, 435, newspaper story, 450
Zapoleon, Guy, 87, 301-04, 307, 309-15, *photo*, 321
Zellner, Jon, 62
Zenith console radio, 85, 626
Zimmerman, Marie, 328
Zito & Karen Blake's Morning Show (due format change at Oldies 103-Boston, Karen Blake left the station in July 2012), 400
Zorro, 629

www.ingramcontent.com/pod-product-compliance
Lightning Source LLC
Chambersburg PA
CBHW070836020526
44114CB00041B/1352